SOCIAL ISSUES, JUSTICE AND STATUS

OVERCOMING DOMESTIC VIOLENCE

CREATING A DIALOGUE AROUND VULNERABLE POPULATIONS

SOCIAL ISSUES, JUSTICE AND STATUS

Additional books in this series can be found on Nova's website
under the Series tab.

Additional e-books in this series can be found on Nova's website
under the e-book tab.

SOCIAL ISSUES, JUSTICE AND STATUS

OVERCOMING DOMESTIC VIOLENCE

CREATING A DIALOGUE AROUND VULNERABLE POPULATIONS

MYRA F. TAYLOR, PH.D.
JULIE ANN POOLEY, PH.D.
AND
ROBERT S. TAYLOR, PH.D.
EDITORS

publishers
New York

NOTICE TO THE READER

The Publisher has taken reasonable care in the preparation of this book, but makes no expressed or implied warranty of any kind and assumes no responsibility for any errors or omissions. No liability is assumed for incidental or consequential damages in connection with or arising out of information contained in this book. The Publisher shall not be liable for any special, consequential, or exemplary damages resulting, in whole or in part, from the readers' use of, or reliance upon, this material. Any parts of this book based on government reports are so indicated and copyright is claimed for those parts to the extent applicable to compilations of such works.

Independent verification should be sought for any data, advice or recommendations contained in this book. In addition, no responsibility is assumed by the publisher for any injury and/or damage to persons or property arising from any methods, products, instructions, ideas or otherwise contained in this publication.

This publication is designed to provide accurate and authoritative information with regard to the subject matter covered herein. It is sold with the clear understanding that the Publisher is not engaged in rendering legal or any other professional services. If legal or any other expert assistance is required, the services of a competent person should be sought. FROM A DECLARATION OF PARTICIPANTS JOINTLY ADOPTED BY A COMMITTEE OF THE AMERICAN BAR ASSOCIATION AND A COMMITTEE OF PUBLISHERS.

Additional color graphics may be available in the e-book version of this book.

Library of Congress Cataloging-in-Publication Data

Overcoming domestic violence : creating a dialogue round vulnerable populations / editors, Myra F. Taylor, Julie Ann Pooley and Robert S. Taylor.
    pages cm. -- (Social issues, justice and status)
 Includes index.
 ISBN: 978-1-63321-956-4 (hardcover)
 1. Family violence. 2. Intimate partner violence. 3. Marital violence. 4. Abused women. 5. Abused wives. 6. Victims of family violence. I. Taylor, Myra, 1962- II. Pooley, Julie Ann.
 HV6626.O94 2014
 362.82'926--dc23
                    2014034854

Published by Nova Science Publishers, Inc. † New York

CONTENTS

PREFACE

This book presents a range of interesting and diverse papers in order to demonstrate the importance and need for intervention programs that deal with the harmful effects that domestic violence causes to primary and secondary victims as well as to perpetrators. These papers reveal that the traditional within family home male-upon-female definitional understanding of domestic violence in the modern needs era to be broadened to include such experiences as dating violence, LGBT intimate partner violence and the childhood witnessing of domestic violence, to name but a few. Additionally, it is argued that intervention programs, given the scale of the domestic violence problem within society, need to be delivered in a non-gendered and non-stigmatizing manner to both the survivor and the perpetrator. For, regardless of the gender of the perpetrator, it is the act itself of committing violence that needs to be eradicated. Moreover, it is argued that this eradication will best be achieved through eliminating the destructive construct of blame which is embedded within society's understanding of domestic violence. The need to eliminate the harms blame is evident in the debilitating intergenerational transfer of the abused-abuser perpetrator label. For embedded in this label is the suggestion that a cycle of violence exists in which maltreated children (i.e., children who have experienced or witnessed abuse) are destined to grow up to be abusive perpetrators of domestic violence and/or child abuse. The editors contend that the way forward lies in changing this embedded notion and in altering the public's indifference or acceptance of domestic violence, educating the upcoming generation of youth on the unacceptability of fiduciary relationship violence and in creating resilient futures for both the primary and secondary survivors of domestic violence as well as for perpetrators.

The chapters are based on recent research conducted in different countries by researchers from multiple disciplines (e.g., medicine, social work, psychology, law, nursing, sexology, health sciences, education) situated in universities around the world (e.g., Australia, Canada, England, Lebanon, Scotland, Spain, and the United States of America). The book is comprised of seven separate sections that aim to provide diverse perspectives on the issue of domestic violence.

INTRODUCTION

In: Overcoming Domestic Violence   ISBN: 978-1-63321-956-4
Editors: Myra F. Taylor, Julie Ann Pooley et al.   © 2015 Nova Science Publishers, Inc.

Chapter 1

BROADENING THE DOMESTIC VIOLENCE DEBATE

Myra F. Taylor and Julie Ann Pooley

Edith Cowan University, Joondalup, Western Australia, Australia

INTRODUCTION

Domestic violence is without doubt one of society's most pressing issues. Within this book a range of interesting and diverse papers are presented all of which have as their central aim the broadening of the current domestic violence debate. To achieve this aim the papers are grouped into five sections.

SECTION ONE: DEFINING DOMESTIC VIOLENCE

In Section One, Chapter 1, readers are challenged to think beyond the traditional definition of domestic violence so as to include all people involved in a fiduciary relationship. A fiduciary relationship being one wherein one person within the relationship knows the other person's personal information, beliefs, frailties, and emotional fears and, then, breaks these intimate trusts by intentionally wounding the other person either psychologically or physically. In particular, Allan and Allan analyze the key role that trust plays within fiduciary relationships. They then examine the various forms (verbal, physical, sexual, financial, social, spiritual, and legal) which domestic violence can take. The readers are then provided with information on both the personal features and the environmental influences that can predispose some people to either be a perpetrator or a victim of domestic violence. Next the factors that contribute to victim vulnerability are described and the consequences that domestic violence can have on both the primary and secondary victims are detailed. Following on from there a brief account of the prevalence of domestic violence is provided. The sole chapter in this section reaches a conclusion that assistance needs to be provided to both the primary and secondary victims and perpetrators of domestic violence if a meaningful reduction is to occur in the occurrence of this vexing social issue.

SECTION TWO: DATING VIOLENCE

The second section is an exposition of a little considered aspect of domestic violence, namely, dating violence. In the first chapter in this section Ellis and McCarry analyze the prevention discourse as a means of addressing a range of social issues, but with particular reference to young people's experience of abuse and violence in dating relationships in the United Kingdom.

They argue that the current governmental focus on prevention is an attempt to discipline the future through identifying and predicting future occurrences of a present day social problem. Moreover, they claim that this approach is problematic because it does not explain or solve current manifestations of violence within the youth population. They recommend that a greater focus be placed on improving existing services while at the same supporting research. For instance, research into why some young people consider relationship violence to be an acceptable form of behaviour.

Carter-Snell in the second chapter in this section discusses the different types of dating violence (e.g., bullying, non-consensual sexting, harassment, stalking, physical and sexual violence) that mainstream secondary and post-secondary students commonly experience, as well as the risk factors for such violence. She contends that risk is a multilevel construct which occurs at an individual level (e.g., child abuse, child witnessing of parental violence, substance abuse, low education, early sexual activity), a family relationship level (e.g., older parents, low parental income, non-conforming parental norms, and parental power dynamic imbalance), at a community level (e.g., insufficient support and normalization of violence) and at a societal level (e.g., gender inequalities). Carter-Snell concludes by positing that given dating violence is a multilevel construct there is a need for greater multidisciplinary collaboration among professionals working in the field of youth violence.

In the third chapter of this section Blais, Hébert,and Gervais detail the prevalence of dating violence in sexual minority youth (SMY) (i.e., lesbian, gay, bisexual, transidentified, queer, and questioning [LGBTQ]).They contend that while SMY face the same dating violence risk factors as do youth in the general population, however, SMY also have the added vulnerabilities of internalized heterosexism, sexual identity concealment shame, outing threats, and a lack of older sexual-minority survivor role models. The chapter concludes by recommending that greater awareness needs to be raised within the sexual minority community of the manifestations of dating violence and, in addition, SMY need to be provided with greater LGBTQ support services.

SECTION THREE: THE FEMALE PERSPECTIVE ON DOMESTIC VIOLENCE

Section Three presents the prevailing feminist conceptualization of domestic violence that exists within society and the body of abuse literature, namely, that women are overwhelmingly the victims of domestic violence and men overwhelmingly are the perpetrators. Consequently, the common recommendation emanating out of Section Three's nine chapters is for governments to increase and improve the legal protections and practical resources made available to females exiting an abusive relationship.

The first chapter in this section opens with Henderson, Thurston, and Roy revealing the plight of immigrant women in Canada and the systemic harms (i.e., financial and housing insecurities) they experience when attempting to leave a domestic violence situation. This situation is made worse, the authors contend, by the women's social isolation, their uncertainty about what formal services are available to them, as well as the inadvertent policies and poorly delivered programs that are provided for them as they all add to the female victimization experience. The challenge the authors see for society is to improve the training and understanding of service providers (e.g., police, language educators, social welfare workers, settlement agents, clinicians and shelter staff) so that they can provide immigrant women with the information and intervention programs they need in a non-stigmatizing manner.

In the next chapter Sabri contends that domestic violence among South Asian women is a major social and public health concern given that the culture's understanding of domestic violence is rooted in socio-cultural factors such as patriarchal family structures, rigid gendeed norms, and the justification of domestic violence in instances where women are viewed as not confirming to expected gender norms. Using an ecological perspective, Sabri reviews the literature on risk and protective factors, as well as the outcomes of domestic violence among South Asian women. The focus of the chapter is on macro-level factors (e.g., cultural beliefs, traditional gender norms), exosystem-level factors (e.g. access to resources, community sanctions against domestic violence), micro-system factors (e.g., relationship conflict, alcohol problems) and individual-level factors (e.g., socio-demographic characteristics such as young age, low socio-economic status). The chapter concludes by identifying the barriers at the different ecological levels that affect South Asian women's responses to violence and, then, relates these barriers to their implications for practice and policy implementation.

Mahapatra and Schatz in the third chapter of this section provide an explanation of the domestic violence incident factors that are specific to the South Asian migrant community (i.e., migrants from India, Pakistan, & Bangladesh). In this regard, the chapter uses real life vignettes to illustrate the varied roles practitioners and domestic violence agency workers perform in providing formal assessments, resilience building programs, and informational services to migrant women separating from an abusive partner in the United States of America. The chapter concludes with the suggestion that as women are 'harbingers of change within the migrant South Asian community', they should be 'applauded' and acknowledged for their efforts to instigate change through ending their own experiences of domestic violence.

In the fourth chapter Schineanu and Earnest present an overview of the domestic violence situation within India. They detail the coping strategies (i.e., social support, spirituality and Eastern beliefs) used by Indian women experiencing domestic violence. Although, they conclude that spirituality in reality appears to be the only refuge for many Indian women. They suggest that changes in the prevalence rates of domestic violence in India will not occur until 'men take responsibility for their actions' and, until 'policy makers institute programs that engage men… to change their attitudes towards domestic violence and protect women'.

McInnes in the fifth chapter clearly articulates the reporting difficulties that women face when engaging with the systems and services that exist to help them exit an abusive relationship. She argues for the better integration of front-line government services as well as for an end to the requirements placed on Australian women to not only disclose the nature of the abuse they have experienced, but also to prove that violence was committed before they are deemed eligible for assistance.

The sixth chapter in this section petitions for a broader acceptance of the existence of interpersonal violence within the lesbian, gay, bisexual and transgender (LGBT) community within America's Deep South. Schroeder, Osby and Bruns claim that Southern homophobic attitudes are continuing to marginalize and stigmatize Southerners. Whereas, formerly they claim Southern discrimination was a facet of skin colour, now they suggest it exists in relation to a person's sexual orientation. In this regard, they use a case study of a lesbian who was subjected to sustained violence by her partner to highlight the types of institutionalized heterosexism she encountered when trying to end her violent relationship. The authors conclude by suggesting that a pressing need exists to not only end interpersonal LGBT violence discrimination within America's Southern states, but also to improve the emergency services available to same sex victims of violent fiduciary relationships.

The seventh chapter by Williams, Gavine and Carnochan asserts that domestic violence is a public health problem and that its burden is overwhelmingly shouldered by women and their children who witness violence in the family home. Drawing on the Cycle of Violence Hypothesis they add their support to its overarching contention, namely, that children who witness domestic violence are likely to grow up to be the next generation of abusers. Hence, the authors recommend that family processes need to be the primary focus of domestic violence primary prevention programs if an intergenerational cycle of violence is to be broken.

Usta and Singh in the eighth chapter of this section contend that although women traditionally have been less likely to orchestrate and perpetuate war, they continue to endure a high proportion of the psychological, physical and social harms experienced in times of war. In particular, they point to *structural* (e.g., patriarchy, gender inequalities, displacement, lawlessness, & poverty), *community* (e.g., altered gender ratio, changed societal norms, increased availability of weaponry), *relationship* (e.g., radical shift in gender role) and *individual* (e.g., perpetrator abuse of alcohol) factors which exacerbate the female experience of domestic violence during wartime. Hence, they claim that advocating for greater gender equality is the logical preventive measure to decrease female fiduciary relationship violence.

In the penultimate chapter in this section Ferrer-Pérez and Bosch-Fiol assert that violence and intimate partner violence are health problems of epidemic and global proportions. While recognizing that there is no single perpetrator or victim profile or individual/ family socio-demographic social indicators for domestic violence, they suggest that the inadequate social supports and economic protections that are available to females are the underlying reasons why women continue to struggle to exit domestic violence situations. They conclude by cautioning that while the effects of the austerity policies that many Western countries put in place to deal with the last economic crisis are not yet visible, in their estimation they are likely to further contribute to the invisiblization of the problems female victims of domestic violence face.

While acknowledging that the link between domestic violence and sport is at present correlational and, as such, further research needs to be completed to unequivocally prove the link, Williams and Neville in the last chapter of this section posit that the 'holy trinity' of sports, alcohol, and hegemonic masculinity are the underpinning factors that contribute to domestic violence. As such, they suggest sport has a pivotal role in combating domestic violence through engaging players and spectators *'in confronting and tackling the toxic practices that are often associated with hegemonic masculinity, in conjunction with female empowerment and the pursuit of gender equality'.*

SECTION FOUR: THE MALE PERSPECTIVE ON DOMESTIC VIOLENCE

Given that the domestic violence discourse up to now has been largely driven and dominated by the feminist perspective this section attempts to bring some gendered balance to the current understanding of domestic violence by providing a male perspective. In this regard, Section Four is comprised of five chapters. The first four chapters relate to a study which examined the adult repercussions of childhood experiences of maltreatment in males. The fifth and final chapter in this section by Wells, Turner, and Cooper suggests that the way to reduce the occurrence of domestic violence is to strengthen the fathering role.

The opening chapter of this section provides a definitional description of two components parts of the umbrella term 'child maltreatment', which encapsulates both the abuse and the witnessing aspects of domestic violence. In addition, prevalence figures, risk factors and gender differences are provided for both child abuse and child witnessing acts. Next, the authors provide a detailed description of the methodology used in the design, data collection and analysis of the study's findings. The chapter closes with a discussion of the difficulties associated with research which is reliant on its participants' reflected memories.

In the second chapter Taylor, Goddard and Pooley document adult males' recollections of their childhood experiences of child maltreatment, as well as their lives as young boys growing up in dysfunctional and abusive family environments. The chapter culminates by detailing the progressive adolescent realization that child abuse and interparental domestic violence are not acceptable societal norms. The authors conclude that although adolescents are able by weight of their increased physicality and independence to end their '*walking on ice*' maltreatment experiences, however, by this juncture in their development considerable damage has already often been done to their psyche.

In the third chapter of this section Taylor, Goddard, Pooley detail the repercussions that childhood experiences of maltreatment can have had on male victims' adult lives. The males' collective experiences are summarized in the chapter's core theme: '*Damaged lives*'. The chapter opens by describing how certain triggers can reignite adult males' childhood memories of being abused and/or of their witnessing of acts of domestic violence in the family home, which in turn lessens their adult sense of internal control. Moreover, how this loss of control allows their former childhood emotions of shame, guilt and anger to resurface and, in doing so, weaken their adult sense of self-worth. The study's males claim that these negative emotions contributed to their failed adult interpersonal relationships and their consequent disillusionment with life. The chapter closes with a discussion of the harm that society's widely held 'abused child – adult abuser' hypothesis has had on the males' adult lives.

In the fourth chapter in this section Goddard, Taylor, and Pooley reveal the pathway that the study's males took towards establishing a more fulfilled adult life. This pathway is encapsulated in the chapter's core theme: '*Endeavouring to move forward through engaging in the therapeutic process of psyche repair*'. The first step along this adult male journey was to create external strategies for dealing with the triggers that unleash their loss of internal control and negative thoughts. Indeed, it was through a process of establishing practical coping strategies that the men revealed they were first able to begin to configure a pathway forward. This pathway involved seeking professional therapeutic assistance for their underlying problems. This help-seeking process enabled them to create a resilience platform on which their damaged psyche could be repaired. Once this resilience platform was in place, then the adult male victims experienced a noticeable growth in their emotional intelligence. The chapter closes with a discussion on the need for therapeutic services for males and an increased societal understanding of the factors that precipitate incidents of domestic violence.

The final chapter in this male perspective section is contributed by Wells, Turner, and Cooper. They maintain that the entrenched gender dyad of 'female victim' and 'male perpetrator' in the domestic violence discourse undoubtedly influences the underlying philosophy and assumptions that guide the design of government policies, programs and community activities aimed at reducing the prevalence of domestic violence as well as limiting the systematic long-term, dismantling of the socio-cultural conditions which allow violence to exist. The authors contend that what is also needed is the promotion of a positive fatherhood social perspective, as well as a constructive strategy for engaging boys and men in current domestic violence prevention efforts. For, they maintain that it is only through broadening the current gendered conception of vulnerability to domestic violence that a societal shift will occur.

SECTION FIVE: CONCLUDING THOUGHTS

In the concluding chapter, Taylor and Pooley summarize the main message arising out of each of the chapters, present a series of interlinked strategies for reducing the occurrence of domestic violence, provide suggestions of what could be done to empower all individuals damaged by experiences of domestic violence, and, importantly, to help them devise resilient posttraumatic growth pathways forward in their lives. While, collectively and unequivocally all contributing scholars involved with this book are united in their condemnation of acts of domestic violence, the book's Editors are hopeful that this book will broaden the debate both around what acts constitute domestic violence and, as well generate a wider acceptance that it is the act of domestic violence that is intolerable and, as such, what is needed is a gender inclusive approach to solving this pressing societal issue.

We trust you will find this collection thought provoking.

SECTION ONE: DEFINING DOMESTIC VIOLENCE

In: Overcoming Domestic Violence
Editors: Myra F. Taylor, Julie Ann Pooley et al.

ISBN: 978-1-63321-956-4
© 2015 Nova Science Publishers, Inc.

Chapter 2

THE DEFINITION AND NATURE OF DOMESTIC VIOLENCE

Alfred Allan [*] *and Maria M. Allan*

Edith Cowan University, Joondalup, Western Australia, Australia

ABSTRACT

We define domestic violence broadly in this chapter to reflect the richness of the contributions of the other authors in this book but also to challenge readers, researchers, policymakers and clinicians to think beyond the traditional conceptualisation of the construct.

In the rest of the chapter we briefly analyse the key role trust plays in the dynamics of domestic violence before examining the different forms domestic violence can take, the personal characteristics that may predispose people to become perpetrators and/or victims and what factors make people vulnerable. After considering the consequences of domestic violence to primary and secondary victims and society we examine its prevalence.

Keywords: Domestic violence, definition, etiology, forms, interpersonal relationships

INTRODUCTION

Some of the authors in this book conceptualise domestic violence in a broad and non-traditional way thereby challenging readers, researchers, policymakers and clinicians to think beyond the normal conceptualisation of the construct. To match this approach we define domestic violence as an unwanted, deliberate and sustained pattern of culturally inappropriate behaviour by people that harms vulnerable others with whom they have a fiduciary relationship and which primarily occurs in their place of residence.

---

[*] Corresponding Author: Dr. Alfred Allan, School of Psychology & Social Science, Edith Cowan University, Joondalup, Australia, WA 6027. Tel: (08) 6304 5536. Email:a.allan@ecu.edu.au.

We exclude isolated incidents or unintentional harmful behaviour and behaviour by perpetrators who cannot form an intention, such as people suffering dementia or young children. Only unwanted behaviour can be classified as domestic violence because some people freely and voluntarily allow others they trust to do objectively painful or humiliating things to them, such as happens during masochistic activities.

We use the word fiduciary (from the Latin word ficucia, i.e., trust, Simpson, 1971, p. 247), which non-lawyers seldom use, advisably to emphasise that domestic violence takes place in relationships where people trust others because they are, or feel, dependent on them. Domestic violence therefore involves people betraying the trust of others they have relationships with, who cannot, or do not want to, defend themselves or terminate the relationships.

People find themselves in relationships based on trust either owing to their circumstances or their choice. They are engaged in *circumstantial fiduciary relationships* when they have limited or no autonomy such as babies, young children and older people whose cognitive, communication and physical disabilities make them reliant on others to survive. Virtually all other people's innate needs at various stages of their lives drive them to enter into *choice fiduciary relationships* with another. People's survival needs sometimes require them to seek refuge from danger by sheltering with somebody they feel they can trust, disabled people, for example, may employ carers, whilst others may work as domestic servants or enter into relationships with citizens from another country to obtain visas. Most people's desire to belong, for affection, and to feel loved and wanted motivates them (Baumeister & Leary, 1995) to enter into intimate relationships which may not necessarily be physically close as people can communicate with each other by writing and/or using technological means, such as the internet.

At least one person, but mostly both people, within fiduciary relationships will usually have access to intimate personal information of the other, such as their beliefs and frailties, emotions they feel, fears they have, their opinions about issues, and their finances. People in dependent relationships must rely on others to attend to their needs. Even relatively independent people may sometimes have to disclose information to gain assistance, such as people with disabilities who give carers the Personal Identification Number (PIN) numbers of their bank accounts because they cannot otherwise withdraw money. People build choice relationships by doing things together, deliberately sharing information and obtaining information by perceiving what the others say and do. Parties to fiduciary relationships therefore generally learn confidential and intimate information about one another leaving them vulnerable (from the Latin word vulnus which means wound, Merriam-Webster Online Dictionary, 2014), that is, capable of being physically or psychologically wounded and open to be exploited by people who abuse the knowledge and direct and indirect access they have to them.

FORMS OF DOMESTIC VIOLENCE

Strictly and objectively only behaviour considered as immoral in a *specific* culture can be classified as domestic violence. We will nevertheless use the typology of misconduct that many Western researchers (see, e.g., Fulu, Jewkes, Roselli, & Garcia-Moreno, 2013; Hegarty,

Hindmarsh, & Gilles, 2000) use because it is well established even though it could be criticised. We will discuss the different categories sequentially for clarity although they overlap to some degree and often occur concurrently.

Verbal Abuse

Verbal abuse, which must arguably be the most prevalent form of domestic violence, takes place when people use sound, including words, to degrade, demean, humiliate, or intimidate another person, or to overpower another person's will. Verbal abuse can take the form of ongoing taunting, yelling degrading remarks, name-calling, screaming, ranting, slurring and using crude or foul language and may be disguised as jokes. In contrast, people can also abuse others by deliberately refraining from communicating with them, for instance by not talking to them at all at home.

Physical Abuse

Physical abuse is the stereotypical, and most studied, form of domestic violence and involves violence, credible threats of violence, physical gestures or stares meant to threaten. Scholars consider threats to be credible if the behaviour is such that reasonable people perceiving it would in the circumstances consider it to be aimed at evoking feelings of fear for their personal well-being or safety.

Violent behaviour include biting, burning, choking, fire-setting, hitting, kicking, pinching, punching, pushing, stabbing, shaking, slapping, strangling and throwing objects or dangerous fluids such as acid at victims. Perpetrators may also deprive people of their liberty by, for instance, preventing them from leaving their homes, or conversely, depriving them of shelter by selling the family home or barring their access to it. They may fail to attend to the medical, nutritional and hygiene needs of people in their care, or do it in a way that causes physical discomfort such as feeding them in a way that they choke or bathing them in water that is physically uncomfortable. Alternatively they may force people to use legal or illegal drugs or give it to them covertly, such as by adding it to food or liquid they consume. Parents may also fabricate their children's medical histories leading to extensive, unnecessary and painful medical treatment that can involve invasive procedures and/or radical drug treatment that can cause disfigurement and even death.

Sexual Abuse

Sexual abuse can narrowly be defined as involving another in sexual behaviour by exploiting a position of trust or intimidating or overpowering them by physical violence, threats of violence, undue persuasion or stealth, such as by making them intoxicated or comatose.

Typically sexual abuse here ranges from anal and/or vaginal penetration by penis, finger or any other object, to inappropriate touching, masturbating or having oral sex with others, or forcing them to do this to perpetrators. Sexual abuse can, however, also be defined more broadly to cover all situations where people do something or expose others to sexually degrading, demeaning or humiliating behaviour without their consent or even awareness. This may happen when people expose others to pornography (e.g., a father who displays sexually explicit photographs) or sexual behaviour (e.g., disabled person who masturbates while being bathed by a carer). Or people may share visual recordings they made of their partners while they were naked, engaged in sexual acts or otherwise doing something sexually with one or more other people, without their partners' free and voluntary consent. Victims' sense of betrayal may be even higher if the recordings were made without their knowledge and consent. The increased availability of cheap technology that makes it possible for most people to capture, permanently store and easily communicate good quality digital visual images to huge audiences make this a form of abuse easy to perpetrate and with irreversible consequences for victims.

Psychological Abuse

Researchers and scholars traditionally identify *psychological abuse* as a distinct form of domestic violence even though most, if not all, forms of domestic violence involve a psychological dimension. Some use the term emotional abuse as a synonym for psychological abuse, but this ignores the interrelatedness of emotions and cognitions (O'Hagan, 1995). Parents who repeatedly shun young children's attempts to show them what they had done at kindergarten undermine their self-respect and sense of worth which could be described as emotional abuse. They could also, however, undermine their children's cognitive processes by dampening their pride in their achievements and causing them to develop the belief that it is wrong to be enthusiastic and proud about their achievements. Putting aside definitional issues, psychological abuse can take many forms. People may destabilise others' self-worth and dignity by privately humiliating or insulting them verbally or in writing, or by using gestures, images or symbols. If they do so in public they also injure their victims' public reputation. Those who constantly give negative or inconsistent feedback to others regarding their behaviour may cause them to believe they are incompetent and undermine their confidence to attempt new things. People may also try to intimidate others by slamming doors, driving dangerously, breaking their valued possessions or by threatening to harm their property, their kin or even pets.

Financial or Economic Abuse

Financial or economic abuse involves situations where perpetrators unreasonably deny people goods they require to participate in social life, or seize or control their income or assets. People may, for instance, prevent people from earning an independent income, take their earnings, or use money on non-essentials (e.g., buying alcohol or gambling) causing family members avoidable hardship. Carers may, for instance, without authority or under false pretences withdraw and steal money of those in their care, or use their pensions or grants for their personal use.

Social Abuse

Social abuse takes place when people socially isolate others by controlling their social activity, depriving them of their liberty, or deliberately creating unreasonable dependence. Perpetrators may, for instance, insist that their partners spend all their time with them, prohibit them from obtaining driver s' licences or driving family cars or prevent their partners' family and friends from visiting them. Another example would be parents who thwart their children's age appropriate autonomy needs.

Spiritual Abuse

Spiritual abuse can take three broad forms. First, people may impair others' spiritual life or well-being by depreciating their spiritual beliefs, deeds or worth and/or preventing them from performing spiritual rituals or causing them to violate their spiritual norms. A liberal Moslem husband may, for instance, prevent his wife from wearing a burka in public or shame or belittle her by ridiculing her religious practices in the company of children and/or friends. Conversely, spiritual abuse occurs when perpetrators use their actual, or sometimes fabricated extreme, unsubstantiated and self-serving, spiritual beliefs to manipulate and exploit other people. Perpetrators may cite from religious scriptures to justify their abusive behaviour or to persuade partners to forgive their abusive behaviour. In extreme cases perpetrators may involve or force family members, including children, to engage and/or witness ritual abuse that objectively may be frightening, such as sacrificing pets. Finally, people may control others by threatening, or taking steps, to have them expelled from religious groups they belong to by making actual or fictitious dogmatic complaints about their behaviour.

Legal and Administrative Abuse

Legal and administrative abuse takes place when people use, or threaten to use, legitimate legal and administrative resources to the detriment of others. This may take the form of falsely accusing them of sexually abusing or mistreating them or their children, or ironically, vexatiously using procedures that were introduced to combat and minimise domestic violence such as restraining orders (Tilbrook, Allan, & Dear, 2010). Similarly, former clients married to professional people who ignored a professional prohibition against such marriages may threaten to disclose this incriminating information causing the professionals to lose their right to practise.

PERPETRATORS AND VICTIMS

People from both genders can be perpetrators, or victims, or both of domestic violence. As people need some degree of psychological and physical maturation to engage in sustained behaviour with the intent to cause significant harm perpetrators' ages typically range from the teens to old age. People can, however, at any stage of their life become victims if they temporarily or permanently lack the psychological and physical characteristics required to fend for themselves.

Researchers have since the middle of the 20th century tried to explain the dynamics of domestic violence and why some people commit it, and/or are vulnerable to it. The limitations of the initial feminist and learning theories, that explained offending with reference to single factors, became apparent when social-cognitive psychologists such as Bandura and Walters (1959) demonstrated the complexity of such behaviour and others like Toch (1969) proposed that there may be different pathways to domestic violence. Researchers further found that both person and situational factors (Megargee, 1976) contribute to offending behaviour, and that some of the person factors may be *static* (i.e., historical and therefore not changeable), whilst others are *dynamic* and therefore can be changed (Kantor & Jasinski, 1998). Neuroscientists furthermore found that the complex decision making process largely takes place automatically and unconsciously (e.g., Reynolds, 2006). Psychologists such as Huesmann (1988) have therefore since the 1980s argued that offending behaviour such as domestic violence can only be explained by multi-factorial theories that take into account a range of biological, behavioural, cognitive, cultural, environmental, motivational and social factors of both perpetrators and victims.

Personal Features

People's genetic makeup is arguably the most important, but not necessarily conclusive, biological influence that predispose them to become perpetrators, or victims, or both of domestic violence. Monoamine oxidase A and serotonin transporter genes, for example, heighten the risk of aggression (see, e.g., McDermott, Tingley, Cowden, Frazzetto, & Johnson, 2009). Genes determine the gender of the foetus which is relevant because men are more likely to be physically violent than females. Genes also influence physical power and physically strong people are generally more confident their threats of physical violence will be taken seriously and cause more physical harm if they actually engage in violent behaviour. People's genetics also predispose them to develop mental illnesses, such as paranoid and delusion disorders and substance-related disorders which may influence how they behave in relationships. Genes further affect people's psychological features such as their dispositional traits. Some people have a genetic predisposition to be more susceptible to real or imaginary threats to their psyche or person and consequently may perceive their partners' behaviour to be hostile where most other people would not (Crick & Dodge, 1994).

The genetic makeup of individuals can, however, be modified and it starts in the womb because mothers' physical and mental health, experiences (e.g., poverty) and behaviour (e.g., substance use) influence the development of foetuses in uteri (Robinson, 2013). Mothers' use of alcohol may result in their children being born with *fetal alcohol syndrome* with symptoms such as problems with learning, impulse control, and managing emotions that may not only influence their development, but also their future relationships (for an overview see, e.g., Schneider, Moore, Kraemer, Roberts, & DeJesus, 2002). To use intellectual development as an illustration, children with fetal alcohol syndrome may as adults feel inadequate and inferior in their relationships with peers, and actually be treated as inferior by peers and, therefore, may be more prone to be abused, and find it difficult to deal constructively with relationship problems.

New born babies have a unique genetic makeup, innate moral intuitions (Haidt, 2001), physical and psychological features and needs that predispose their behaviour through their lives. These features may, however, evolve during the course of their lives. The most dramatic changes will take place in their early formative years because babies have an innate ability and craving to learn from their physical, social, and cultural environment (for an overview see, e.g., Patterson & Vakili, 2013). Babies and young children's physical (e.g., health and appearance) and psychological characteristics (e.g. temperaments or dispositions) influence how people interact with them. Colic babies, for example, tend to receive more attention from their parents, but they may also make parents feel inadequate and frustrated and therefore evoke harsh treatment from them at the time and this may even shape how their parents treat them in future.

The ability of infants and their primary caregivers to attend to, and actively match, each other's affect states influences babies' immediate and future development and functioning. First, babies deprived of optimal bonding with their primary caregivers experience a high degree of chronic stress that not only makes life unpleasant for them, but will affect their responses and ability to regulate stress in later life.

Second, babies' bonding with their primary caregivers influence their attachment, that is, their ability to form lasting psychological relationships with other people that involve an exchange of care, pleasure and security. Infants with secure attachment tend to have a desire to be near their attachment figures and become anxious in their absence. In the presence of their attachment figures they happily explore the immediate environment returning to them only for comfort and safety if they face threats. Babies with insecure attachment on the other hand may avoid, or be ambivalent or resistant towards their caregivers or confused and disorganised in their presence. Children with insecure attachments tend to have problems socialising with peers, behave inappropriately in class where they tend to be aggressive and disruptive, and find it difficult to develop secure relationships as young adults and adults if their attachment styles have not changed.

Environmental Influences

Babies and young children interact with, and observe the interactions of, others in their environment, such as siblings, extended family members, people who provide services to the family, and later peers and authority figures such as teachers. Their experiences interacting with these people and observing how they interact with each other provide them with a wealth of information. They, for instance, acquire knowledge about the explicit and implicit norms of their culture regarding matters such as the equality of people (e.g., servants are inferior), the acceptance of authority (do not question the decisions and behaviour of people in authority), loyalty to kin (even if they do wrong), and the tolerance of aggressive behaviour.

Young children also copy the behaviour of these role models from an early stage and adjust their behaviour in response to the feedback they receive in the form of rewards and punishment. They use the feedback to develop an understanding regarding the acceptability of behaviour and the appropriateness of targets, such as that they can hit less powerful people such as small children and servants, but not those with power such as parents.

The explicit and implicit feedback children receive also influences their personalities. At a most basic level personality consists of a set of dispositional traits of which some are more prominent in specific people and will remain so over the course of their lives. People, however, constantly adapt these characteristics in response to their social environment by developing and modifying several cognitive structures that operate unconsciously. They develop *attitudes* about themselves, people, events, situations and issues, such as that they can generally rely on people close to them or cannot trust them; or that people should be punished harshly if they do not follow rules; or that you protect vulnerable people irrespective of their behaviour. They develop *beliefs* about the world and what the outcomes will be if they act in a certain manner. People who believe they cannot control events and outcomes develop a sense of helplessness (Seligman, 1975; Wortman & Brehm, 1975) which can cause depression but may also lead them to accept unpleasant situations without trying to do something about them. They further develop *values*, that is, views about what are generally desirable behaviours or outcomes which they then use to guide their selection of behaviour and evaluation events (Schwartz & Bilsky, 1987). Some children may therefore develop pro-social values (it is wrong to harm other people) whilst other may develop anti-social values (it is acceptable to take money from those who have more than they need).

Young people therefore have scripts about relationships with parents, siblings, children, peers, romantic partners and other people. They further construct life scripts in the form of selective and simplified reconstructions of their past and usually idealised visions of the future that influence their behaviour, mental health and relationships. People constantly revise their life scripts in response to their circumstance and some may therefore develop visions of themselves as determined and resourceful people who get what they want in all settings and by any means. Others conceptualise themselves as people who cannot function well on their own and who need to rely on strong people. Some see themselves as good at outwitting other people, feel competent that they can defraud others and feel proud if they succeed and angry at themselves if they fail. Circumstances that influence people can be proximal, such as their interaction with peers, or distal in the form of socio-historical events. Researchers examining the dynamics of male-perpetrated domestic violence on females amongst Aboriginal people in Australia, for example, found that their participants believed that Aboriginal males feel disempowered by the impact colonisation has had on them (Blagg, 2000).

These cognitive constructs mostly operate rapidly and unconsciously. Judgments people think that they have made consciously and rationally are often post hoc rationalisations. People's decisions and behaviour are therefore often instinctive and when they realise the social unacceptability of what they did they will often justify their behaviour by using palliative comparisons such as "I only slap her and never use a weapon" or euphemistic labelling such as "I just borrowed the money because she is dying and has no use for it".

People's environments and experiences further influence their physical and/or mental health. Physical disorders during childhood may affect people's psychological development and make them more demanding in relationships. Physical disorders may also force people to rely on others for care to some degree or they may suffer chronic pain and discomfort which may lead them to feel frustrated and act aggressively (Berkowitz & Harmon-Jones, 2004). People due to their social circumstances (war and/or civil conflict), employment (emergency workers), life style (e.g., substance abuse) or misfortune (trauma or brain injuries) can develop disorders often associated with impulsive, unpredictable and/or aggressive behaviour.

People may also because of their genetics, biological limitations or environmental influences fail to develop skills which are essential in any relationship, such as the ability to cope with stressful situations and assertiveness. Those who are alexithymic (i.e., poor at interpreting emotional experiences and situations and to respond appropriately) could find it difficult to identify and communicate their emotions to partners in relationships.

People who intentionally and effectively cause harm to others may therefore be predisposed by their unique genetic, physical and psychological characteristics and developmental history to perpetrate domestic violence. Many of them will adhere to the moral and legal norms of their culture and desist, except perhaps if something impairs their reasoning, judgment and ability to restrain their behaviour, such as substance abuse. Those who become perpetrators, however, share the common feature that they do so against people they perceive to be vulnerable.

VULNERABLE PEOPLE

Perpetrators usually offend against vulnerable people they have an existing relationship with. Sometimes they may groom people they perceive to be potentially vulnerable by deliberately cultivating relationships and establishing emotional connections with them after befriending them directly or indirectly through people they trust, such as their parents or carers. Men may, for instance, deliberately cultivate relationships and move in with single mothers in order to have access to young children who they can abuse.

People's vulnerability stems from the complex interaction of their physical and psychological characteristics and contextual circumstances such as their culture, society and situation. We will, however, discuss them separately for the sake of clarity.

Physical Characteristics

People normally think of vulnerability in physical terms because the consequences of physical, cognitive, perceptual and communication impairment can be observed. These forms of impairment also explain the high incidence of domestic violence perpetrated against children, females and older people. People's physical abilities may not, however, be decisive. A frail female house owner may verbally and physically abuse her physically stronger domestic servant who works on a temporary working visa, needs her income to support her ailing mother and does not want to risk losing her job by complaining because she will then be deported.

Psychological Characteristics

Similarly, people's beliefs that they must be loyal and protective of kin may lead them to ignore or underestimate the severity of abuse. People's personalities, altruistic inclinations, fear of rejection, desire to be accepted and loved, or a combination of these can make them vulnerable. People who feel psychologically threatened may deny reality, for example some males do not define their experiences as abuse because to do so would challenge their masculine identity and lead to gender-role conflict (O'Brian, Hunt, & Hart, 2005). People who fiduciary relationship experience shame or guilt may ignore or underestimate the abuse they suffer, for instance parents who fail to disclose abuse by their children because they feel ashamed of their children's behaviour or partly blame themselves for the situation. Some people may be vulnerable because they are emotionally dependent on perpetrators, feel helpless or lack effective coping skills. Lonely and shy people who lack social skills and support may engage in online romantic relationships where they may be financially abused by those they communicate with.

Males' culturally influenced perceptions about masculinity may discourage them from disclosing domestic violence irrespective of the gender of the perpetrators. Some people's high levels of anxiety may cause them to have unrealistic fears about what could happen if they act assertively and therefore make it difficult for them to cope effectively with abusive situations. Some people's fears could, however, be realistic. Illicit drug users or prostitutes are vulnerable because their criminal behaviour could be exposed if they make formal complaints. A young woman living at home may fear that her lesbian girlfriend will disclose their sexual relationship if she reports her abusive behaviour. Similarly refugees suffering abuse whilst sheltering from civil unrest and/or war may have good reason to fear that their situation will be worse if they leave the abuse setting.

Contextual Circumstances

People's social circumstances are therefore important, and even people in countries where there is no war or civil unrest may feel, or actually be, vulnerable in the absence of policies to monitor and protect potentially vulnerable people. Some cultures and societies, for instance, consider relationships such as those between romantic partners, parents and children and employers and domestic servants untouchable. They therefore create closed systems which contribute to domestic violence by discouraging external scrutiny. In patriarchal cultures and societies the interests of people such as females, children and servants may not be a priority, and those who dare complain about abuse may be accused of violating cultural and societal norms rather than be helped.

Other societies may have good intentions and policies, but lack the resources to effectively assist victims, or may be able to do so only in certain areas (e.g., metropolitan but not rural areas). Some people fear that the response to their reports of abuse will not be effective and may even place them or others in danger. In some countries the policy is to remove the male from the home where the alleged abuse takes place irrespective of who is identified as the abuser. A male victim may therefore not disclose abuse by his wife to avoid removal that will, at least temporarily, leave his small children in the care of his wife whose aggressive behaviour may be caused by a prefrontal brain injury. Other victims fear that owing to the nature of the abuse they will not be believed or taken seriously. Victims of verbal abuse may remain silent because of the invisibility of their harm, whilst people subject to social, spiritual or financial abuse may feel that authorities will consider their experiences trivial.

In some societies the existing policies may not protect all people, or may officially or unofficially not be applied consistently. Officials in some countries or regions may ignore, or give little attention to, complaints from people who come from lower social classes, specific language groups, or genders. In Tilbrook and her colleagues' (2010) study males reported that service providers and/or authorities disbelieved, minimised or ridiculed their reports of domestic violence. Ironically victims and those close to them believed that the anti-domestic violence public campaigns in some countries which depict males as perpetrators and females as victims make it difficult for the public and officials to comprehend that males may also be victims (Tilbrook et al., 2010).

Members of small relatively insular groups that form subcultures, such as indigenous, migrant, and lesbian, gay, bisexual and transgender groups, also feel unsupported because they often experience discrimination and feel marginalised when it comes to the provision of services that address their specific needs. They further feel they will be seen as disloyal if they disclose domestic violence taking place in their group because it could invite scrutiny and reflect negatively on members of the group. They therefore, often realistically, anticipate resistance and possible isolation from members of their group if they disclose the abuse, especially by prominent members of the group.

HARM

It makes intuitive sense that domestic violence leads to harm, but researchers find it difficult to determine the exact nature of some forms of abuse, such as verbal abuse (see, e.g., Inoue, Tsukano, Muraoka, Kaneko, & Okamura, 2006; Jay, 2009). There is, however, enough evidence that offending has a ripple effect that influences both those directly and indirectly involved.

Primary Victims

The exact nature and severity of the consequences for primary victims depend on a range of issues, but it is likely that all of them will experience *psychological harm* because all forms of domestic violence involve a betrayal of trust. Researchers have established that the level of trust predicts the severity of mental health outcomes for victims with those in high trust relationships presenting with more intense symptoms of depression, dissociation and post-traumatic stress disorder (Martin, Cromer, DePrince, & Freyd, 2013). Victims' developmental stage at the time of the abuse plays an important role. Children and adolescents who are betrayed in high trust relationships appear to be more distrustful in general and in relationships, and are at higher risk of revictimization during the rest of their lives (Gobin, 2012). Researchers further found an association between chronic child abuse and avoidant (Lyons-Ruth, Connell, Zoll, & Stahl, 1987) and disorganized attachment patterns (E. Carlson, 1998; V. Carlson, Cicchetti, Barnett, & Braunwald, 1987). Children with disorganized attachment patterns appear to perceive their mothers as more threatening than the rest of the environment and are more likely to be aggressive later than even those babies with avoidant or ambivalent attachment patterns. When children grow up their attachment styles furthermore influence their own parenting styles and therefore impact on how they treat their own infants. This suggests that the consequences of child abuse therefore may be carried on across generations (Fonagy, Steele, & Steele, 1991).

All forms of domestic violence, irrespective of the level of trust involved, may have *mental health consequences*. Most, if not all victims feel angry, anxious, ashamed and, sometimes, guilty because they partially blame themselves (Gobin, 2012). Victims of financial abuse may, for instance, experience high levels of shame and also guilt if as a result of their financial losses their kin suffer hardship. They may also have to endure the emotional stress of protracted litigation if they try to recover damages or prosecute perpetrators. Researchers looking at the association between domestic violence and severe mental health consequences have mostly focussed on the consequences of physical and sexual abuse (see, e.g., Vos et al., 2006). They have established that victims of these forms of abuse have a higher likelihood than those in a general population of suffering of anxiety related disorders (including post-traumatic stress disorder, depression, dissociative disorders, eating disorders, and substance-related disorders). They are also more likely to report self-harm attempts.

Physical and sexual abuse can also have *physical consequences* which can range from no visible external signs to death, with South African researchers, for example, reporting a mortality rate of 8.8 per 100,000 (Abrahams et al., 2009; Roman & Frantz, 2013). Even the invisible consequences of physical and sexual abuse can, however, be life-threatening. Female victims of domestic violence, particularly those of sexual abuse, have an increased risk of sexually transmitted disorders (World Health Organization, 2004). Adults and children may suffer a range of injuries such as bruises, burns, cuts and fractures and acquired brain injuries (Kwako et al., 2011; Merten, Osborne, Radkowski, & Leonidas, 1984; Valera & Berenbaum, 2003) which in the case of babies are often part of the so-called shaken baby syndrome.

Mostly victims suffer direct or indirect *financial consequences*. Access Economics (2004) estimated the financial cost borne by Australian victims of domestic violence, defined to include physical, sexual, emotional and social abuse and financial deprivation, in the 2002-2003 financial year as $A 4 billion. They placed a value of $A 3.5 billion on pain, suffering and premature mortality of victims. These researchers estimated the total cost to society as $A 8.1 billion. Direct financial expenses can include medical costs or the loss of cash (e.g., victims of financial abuse), and legal costs (e.g., victims of legal-administrative abuse). Indirect costs can include loss of earnings when victims cannot work because of their injuries or when they have to take time off to make complaints, attend court or go for medical treatment. Victims may therefore have to endure severe financial hardship for the rest of their lives.

Victims may also suffer significant *reputational consequences*, particularly those involved in financial, legal-administrative and sexual abuse. People's reputation can be ruined irreparably by, for instance, the publication of sexual images of them online and can do very little to remove or restrict access to such images.

Secondary Victims

Researchers have done little research on the impact of domestic partner abuse on secondary victims, but several have studied the mental health of the children of victims and/or perpetrators. Researchers such as Carlson (2000) and Kernic et al. (2003), for example, found that these children in comparison to those from homes where intimate partner abuse did not occur, have a higher likelihood of experiencing academic difficulties, adopting pro-violent attitudes and, as adults, involvement in abusive intimate relationships. Children whose parents were involved in abusive relationships were also more likely to present with anxiety, attachment, conduct, eating, mood, or substance-related disorders and to report suicide ideation and being harassed and bullied at school. Access Economics (2004) estimated the cost of domestic violence to the children of perpetrators and victims at $A 0.77 billion during the report period.

Family, friends and those close to the victim and/or the perpetrator may be involved in many ways including having to take time off work to support victims. Access Economics (2004) estimated the cost of domestic violence to significant others at $A 0.7 billion during the 2002-2003 financial year.

PREVALENCE

It is difficult to establish the prevalence of domestic violence at a global level because of a lack of research in some geographical areas and the general lack of research regarding some forms of abuse and exploring females as possible perpetrators. Scholars must further be cautious when interpreting and, especially, comparing the available data due to differences in approaches and definitions used by researchers.

Researchers furthermore often rely on relatively unreliable perpetrator and victim self-reports as their primary sources of information. Perpetrators may not be reliable sources of information because even those who admit their behaviour may under-report and minimize their behaviour if they realise that it may not be socially acceptable. Victims may be unreliable informants because characteristics that make them vulnerable to domestic abuse may also influence their reporting. Some may not realise they experience domestic violence because they lack the cognitive abilities to make sense of their experiences, others may psychologically deny the reality, or comprehend the situation but be unable to, or not have an opportunity, to communicate their experiences to researchers. Victims may also under-report their experiences because they fear that perpetrators will find out what they had said despite assurance of confidentiality, or their feelings of shame and embarrassment related to the stigma that is still attached to victimhood in some societies.

Prevalence researchers have mostly focussed on the physical abuse of females. In an attempt to improve the accuracy of the information they gather, they use a broad range of research tools, such as anonymous community surveys where they ask participants to report about behaviours they engage in or are exposed to, emergency room observations and the examination of court, morgue and police records. Researchers have also developed specialised measures to quantify domestic violence of which the Conflict Tactics Scales (Straus, 1979; Straus, Hamby, Boney-McCoy, & Sugarman, 1996) is arguably the best known.

An examination of the prevalence data, albeit overshadowed by research about the physical and sexual abuse of women, show that domestic violence occurs in all cultures, geographical areas, communities, age groups and irrespective of socio-economic status, educational status, or sexual orientation. Researchers using multiple sources of data estimated that globally 30% of women who have been in a relationship have experienced physical and/or sexual violence by their partner (World Health Organisation, 2013).

Even in regions such as the European Union researchers found that out of 42, 000 women they interviewed, 27% of the about 40,000 who reported that they had partners (past or present) affirmed that they had experienced partner violence (physical and/or sexual) at some stage since they were 15 years old (European Union Agency for Fundamental Rights [FRA], 2014). When researchers used a definition of domestic violence that included emotional and economic abuse the prevalence increased even more with research finding that 39% of male participants in Sri Lanka to 87% in Papua New Guinea reported that they engage in abusive behaviour (Fulu et al., 2013).

CONCLUSION

Given these prevalence data it will be difficult even for the most critical and conservative person to deny the seriousness of domestic violence as a global social problem that directly and indirectly impacts on many people and costs individuals and societies dearly. This complex problem has cultural and genetic roots that probably go back to the beginning of humankind and has since been maintained by events such as the trauma people experience in wars and civil conflict.

People may feel discouraged when faced with such an enormous and complex problem, but as the content of this chapter also shows there are many possible points of intervention, both at an individual and a societal level. There appears, however, to be a lack of research, policy, and interventions beyond what have traditionally been seen as domestic violence and the people usually seen as the primary and secondary victims and perpetrators thereof.

It would be a great concern if society ignores some primary and secondary victims' plights and perpetrators' needs because of a narrow definition of domestic violence. All victims of domestic violence as defined here face the contradiction that those they trust and depend on abuse them. Victims with the physical, psychological and material means face the painful decision whether to escape or fight back and in the case of the latter, how they can do it in the most constructive way for all involved. Those who lack the resources to escape or fight back often pay for it dearly materially, physically, and psychologically. All victims, irrespective of who they may be, therefore should be supported by society.

As demonstrated above the psychological trauma suffered by victims may in turn predispose them to perpetrate domestic violence. This paradox of victims who become perpetrators underlines the complexity of perpetrating behaviour and the difficulty of changing such behaviour. Society must help perpetrators to change, and to help them society must identify them and their needs. Societies cannot afford missing perpetrators because they use narrow definitions of domestic violence or refuse to recognise certain people as perpetrators as then neither perpetrator nor victim receives assistance.

All primary and secondary victims and perpetrators of domestic violence need all the assistance they can get from society. Such assistance should be at the individual and public level and should be aimed at preventing domestic violence, supporting those involved and providing remedies. Whilst the cost of assisting those involved may be high, failure to assist may be higher.

REFERENCES

Abrahams, N., Jewkes, R., Martin, L. J., Mathews, S., Vetten, L., & Lombard, C. (2009). Mortality of women from intimate partner violence in South Africa: a national epidemiological study. *Violence and Victims, 24*(4), 546-556.

Access Economics. (2004). The cost of domestic violence to the Australian economy. Retrieved 17 September, 2008, from www.fahcsia.gov.au/our-responsibilities/women/ publications-articles/reducing-violence/the-cost-of-domestic-violence-to-the-australian-economy>.

Bandura, A., & Walters, R. (1959). *Adolescent aggression.* New York: Ronald.

Baumeister, R. F., & Leary, M. R. (1995). The need to belong: Desire for interpersonal attachments as a fundamental human motivation. *Psychological Bulletin, 117*(3), 497-529.

Berkowitz, L., & Harmon-Jones, E. (2004). Toward an understanding of the determinants of anger. *Emotion, 4*(2), 107–130.

Blagg, H. (2000). *Crisis intervention in Aboriginal family violence: Strategies and models.* Perth: Crime Research Centre, University of Western Australia.

Carlson, B. E. (2000). Children exposed to intimate partner violence: Research findings and implications for intervention. *Trauma, Violence, and Abuse, 1*, 321- 342.

Carlson, E. (1998). A prospective longitudinal study of attachment disorganisation/ disorientation. *Child Development, 69*, 1129-1144.

Carlson, V., Cicchetti, D., Barnett, D., & Braunwald, K. (1987). Disorganized/disoriented attachment behaviors in maltreated infants. *Developmental Psychology, 25*, 525-531.

Crick, N. R., & Dodge, K. A. (1994). A review and reformulation of social information-processing mechanisms in children's social adjustment. *Psychological Bulletin, 115*(1), 74-101.

Fonagy, P., Steele, H., & Steele, M. (1991). Maternal representation of attachment during pregnancy predict the organization of infant-mother attachment at one year of age. *Child Development, 62*, 891- 905.

Fulu, E., Jewkes, R., Roselli, T., & Garcia-Moreno, C. (2013). Prevalence of and factors associated with male perpetration of intimate partner violence: findings from the UN Multi-country Cross-sectional Study on Men and Violence in Asia and the Pacific. *The Lancet Global Health, 1*(4), e187-e207.

Gobin, R. L. (2012). *Trauma, trust, and betrayal awareness.* (Doctor of Philosophy), University of Oregon.

Haidt, J. (2001). The emotional dog and its rational tail: A social intuitional approach to moral judgment *Psychological Review, 108*(4), 814-834.

Hegarty, K., Hindmarsh, E. D., & Gilles, M. T. (2000). Domestic violence in Australia: Definition, prevalence and nature of presentation in clinical practice. *Medical Journal of Australia, 173*, 363-367.

Huesmann, L. R. (1988). An information-processing model for the development of aggression *Aggressive Behaviour, 14*, 13-24.

Inoue, M., Tsukano, K., Muraoka, M., Kaneko, F., & Okamura, H. (2006). Psychological impact of verbal abuse and violence by patients on nurses working in psychiatric departments. *Psychiatry and Clinical Neurosciences, 60*(1), 29-36.

Jay, T. (2009). Do offensic words harm people? *Psychology, Public Policy, and Law, 15*(2), 81-101.

Kantor, G. K., & Jasinski, J. L. (1998). Dynamics and risk factors in partner violence. In J. J. L & W. L. M (Eds.), *Partner violence: a comprehensive review of 20 years of researc* (pp. 1-43). Thousand Oaks (CA): Sage.

Kernic, M. A., Wolf, M. E., Holt, V. L., McKnight, B., Huebner, C. E., & Rivara, F. P. (2003). Behavioral problems among children whose mothers are abused by an intimate partner. *Child Abuse and Negligence, 27*(11), 1231-1246.

Kwako, L. E., Glass, N., Campbell, J., Melvin, K. C., Barr, T., & Gill, J. M. (2011). Traumatic brain injury in intimate partner violence: A critical review of outcomes and mechanisms. *Trauma, Violence, and Abuse, 12*(3), 115-126.

Lyons-Ruth, K., Connell, D. B., Zoll, D., & Stahl, J. (1987). Infants at social risk: Relationship among infant maltreatment, maternal behavior, and infant attachment behavior. *Development Psychology, 23*, 223-232.

Martin, C., Cromer, L., DePrince, A. P., & Freyd, J. J. (2013). The role of cumulative trauma, betrayal, and appraisals in understanding trauma symptomatology. *Psychological Trauma: Theory, Research, Practice, and Policy, 5*(2), 110–118.

McDermott, R., Tingley, D., Cowden, J., Frazzetto, G., & Johnson, D. D. P. (2009). Monoamine oxidase A gene (MAOA) predicts behavioral aggression following provocation. *Proceedings of the National Academy of Sciences, 106*, 2118–2123.

Megargee, E. J. (1976). The prediction of dangerous behavior. *Criminal Justice and Behavior, 3*, 3-22.

Merriam-Webster Online Dictionary. (2014). Retrieved 2 February from http://www.merriam-webster.com/word/word.php?date=Apr-14-2010.

Merten, D. F., Osborne, D. R. S., Radkowski, M. A., & Leonidas, J. C. (1984). Craniocerebral trauma in the child abuse syndrome: radiological observations. *Pediatric Radiology, 14*(5), 272-277.

O'Brian, R., Hunt, K., & Hart, G. (2005). Its caveman stuff but that is to a certain extent how guys still operate: men's accounts of masculinity and help seeking. *Social Science and Medicine, 61*, 503-516.

O'Hagan, K. P. (1995). Emotional and psychological abuse: Problems of definition *Child Abuse & Neglect, 19*(4), 449-461.

Patterson, J., & Vakili, S. (2013). Relationships, Environment, and the Brain: How Emerging Research is Changing What We Know about the Impact of Families on Human Development. *Family Process, 10* 1-11.

Reynolds, S. J. (2006). A neurocognitive model of the ethical decision-making process: Impliciations for study and practice. *Journal of Applied Psychology, 91*(4), 737-748.

Robinson, M. (2013). How the first nine months shape the rest of our lives. *Australian Psychologist, 48*(4), 293-245.

Roman, N. V., & Frantz, J. M. (2013). The prevalence of intimate partner violence in the family: A systematic review of the implications for adolescents in Africa. *Family Practitioner, 30*, 256-265.

Schneider, M. L., Moore, C. F., Kraemer, G. W., Roberts, A. D., & DeJesus, O. T. (2002). The impact of prenatal stress, fetal alcohol exposure, or both on development: perspectives from a primate model. *Psychoneuroendocrinology, 27*(1-2), 285-298.

Schwartz, S. H., & Bilsky, W. (1987). Toward a psychological structure of human values. *Journal of Personality and Social Psychology, 53*(3), 550-562.

Seligman, M. E. P. (1975). *Learned optimism* New York: Knof.

Simpson, D. P. (1971). *Cassell's New Latin-English Dictionary* (5th ed.). London, UK: Cassell.

Straus, M. A. (1979). Measuring intra family conflict and violence: The Conflict Tactics Scale. *Journal of Marriage and the Family, 41*, 75-88.

Straus, M. A., Hamby, S. L., Boney-McCoy, S., & Sugarman, D. B. (1996). The Revised Conflict Tactics Scales (CTS2): Development and preliminary psychometric data. *Journal of Family Issues, 17*(3), 283-316.

Tilbrook, E., Allan, A., & Dear, G. (2010). Intimate partner abuse of men. from www.ecu.edu.au or www.man.org.au.

Toch, H. (1969). *Violent men*. Harmondsworth: Penguin.

Valera, E. M., & Berenbaum, H. (2003). Brain injury in battered women. *Journal of Consulting and Clinical Psychology, 71*, 797-804.

Vos, T., Astbury, J., Piers, L. S., Magnus, A., Heenan, M., Stanely, L., . . . Webster, K. (2006). Measuring the impact of intimate partner violence on the health of women in Victoria, Australia. *Bulleting of the World Health Organization, 84*(9), 739-744.

World Health Organisation. (2013*). Global and regional estimates of violence against womenPrevalence and health effects of intimate partner violence and non-partner sexual violence.* Retrieved 6 March, 2014, from http://apps.who.int/iris/bitstream/10665/85239/1/9789241564625_eng.pdf.

World Health Organization. (2004). *Violence against women and HIV/AIDS: critical intersections—intimate partner violence and HIV/AIDS.* http://www.who.int/hac/techguidance/pht/InfoBulletinIntimatePartnerViolenceFinal.pdf).

Wortman, C., & Brehm, J. C. (1975). Responses to uncontrollable outcomes: An integration of reactance theory and the learned helplessness model. In L. Berkowitz (Ed.), *Advances in Experimental Social Psychology* (Vol. 8, pp. 278-336). San Diego CA: Academic Press.

BIOGRAPHICAL INFORMATION

Dr. Alfred Allan is qualified in law and psychology and is endorsed both as a clinical and forensic psychologist in Australia. The current focus of his practice, teaching and research is on mental health and professional law, ethics, policy and practice; corrective interchanges and violent offending. He is currently Professor of Psychology and acting Director of the Social Justice Research Centre at Edith Cowan University in Perth, Western Australia.

Dr. Maria Allan is qualified in psychology and lectures at Edith Cowan University in Perth, Western Australia. The current focus of her teaching and research is on psychometric assessment; corrective interchanges; and violent offending.

Section Two: Dating Violence

In: Overcoming Domestic Violence
Editors: Myra F. Taylor, Julie Ann Pooley et al.

ISBN: 978-1-63321-956-4
© 2015 Nova Science Publishers, Inc.

Chapter 3

THE PREVENTION PARADIGM AND YOUNG PEOPLE'S ABUSIVE INTIMATE RELATIONSHIPS

Jane Ellis[*] *and Melanie McCarry*
University of Central Lancashire, UK

Stop calling me resilient. Because every time you say, "Oh, they're resilient," that
means you can do something else to me. I am not resilient
Tracie L. Washington, Louisiana Justice Institute [poster tacked onto tree in street]

ABSTRACT

This chapter will consider prevention models in relation to abuse and violence in young people's intimate relationships in the UK context. It will critically analyse the prevention discourse and the way this is a key strategy for addressing a range of social issues.

It is argued that prevention was so enthusiastically advanced by the New Labour government, through a plethora of research, policy and legislation, that it has an almost uncontested dominance in contemporary UK social policy. It could even be argued that current politics and policy are driven by 'preventionism', which is defined as 'the belief that social problems can be prevented rather than resolved' In this chapter, the prevention discourse is problematised in relation to the role it plays in the consideration of abuse and violence in young people's intimate relationships.

Keywords: Prevention, young people, abuse, relationships

[*] Corresponding Author: Dr. Jane Ellis, Senior Research Fellow, School of Social Work, Harrington Building, Room 226, University of Central Lancashire, Preston, Lancashire, PR1 2HE, UK. Tel: 01772 895128. Email:jellis2@uclan.ac.uk.

INTRODUCTION

This chapter considers what has come to be known as 'the prevention paradigm' (France & Utting, 2005; France, 2008) and explores how it relates to violence[1] in young people's intimate relationships[2]. Prevention is widely deployed in the UK as a key strategy for addressing a range of social issues with a particular focus on children and young people [CYP](Allen, 2011; Chief Secretary to the Treasury [CST], 2003; Department for Children Schools and Families [DCSF], 2010; HM Government, 2008; Parton, 2006; Sutton et al., 2004;). Indeed prevention was so enthusiastically advanced by the New Labour government[3], through a plethora of research, policy, and legislation that it appears to have an almost uncontested dominance in contemporary social policy and its legacy continues. It underpins the current Coalition government policies in relation to children and families, but is now more often referred to as 'early intervention' (Allen, 2011). It could be argued that current politics and children and young people's policies are driven by 'preventionism,' which Billis (1981) defines as 'the belief that social problems can be prevented rather than resolved' (p.375). In the UK, whilst there is an ever-increasing amount of literature promoting prevention/early intervention in work with CYP and a taken-for-grantedness about it as a practice there is an emerging critique particularly in relation to youth justice (Case, 2007; Case & Haines, 2010; France et al., 2010). In the area of violence against women and girls the prevention paradigm is under-theorized and the underlying discourses remain uninterrogated (Ellis, 2014, in press). This chapter considers the relevance of this prevention paradigm in relation to violence in young people's intimate relationships. It is argued that the prevention paradigm disregards the voluminous evidence that the most effective model to conceptualise interpersonal violence is through a model which recognises gendered structural inequalities and advantages rather than the arguably often individualising framework of prevention.

VIOLENCE IN YOUNG PEOPLE'S INTIMATE RELATIONSHIPS

It remains a normative experience for young people to experience an intimate relationship in adolescence and UNICEF (2007) data indicates that 40 per cent of young people in the UK are having sexual intercourse by age 15 (compared to 15-28% for other European countries). These early experiences are profoundly significant for young people (Allen, 2003; Chung, 2005; 2007; Holland et al., 1998; Sears et al., 2006). However, little is known about the dynamics, patterns or impact of behaviour within these relationships and particularly what characteristics lead to abuse or violence. Data from the US suggests that about one third of high school students have had experiences with 'dating violence' (Foshee, 1996; Foshee et al., 2013; Hamby et al., 2012; Jezl et al., 1996; Malik et al., 1997; Molidor & Tolman, 1998) and that this has a negative impact on young people, and specifically young women's, physical and psychological well-being (Hickman et al., 2004; Sears et al., 2006; Silverman et al., 2001). It is also suggested that emotional abuse may be the most prevalent form of abuse

---

[1] Violence is used here to mean sexual, emotional, verbal, psychological and financial as well as physical abuse.
[2] The authors' preference is for 'young people's intimate relationships' but recognise that the term teen dating violence is more popular in the United States of America [USA]; it refers to the same phenomenon (please see Barter et al., 2009 for fuller discussion of terminology).
[3] The UK administration 1997 to 2010.

in young people's relationships, have the most serious impact and be a precursor to other forms of violence (Barter et al., 2009; Gallaty & Zimmer-Gembeck, 2008; Murphy & Smith, 2009; Stark, 2007). Thus, a developing body of evidence suggests that control, violence and abuse feature in young people's intimate relationships (Banyard et al., 2006; Barter et al., 2009; Foshee, 1996; Hickman et al., 2004) but there is little understanding about why this occurs, in what contexts, and what factors differentiate these relationships from those which are positive for young people.

The issue of violence in young people's own intimate relationships is a relatively new field of inquiry and much of the UK scholarship has developed out of work on domestic abuse in adult relationships. In UK the severity and frequency of abuse and violence in adult relationships are inextricably linked to gender, with more men protagonists and more women victims (Home Office, 2011). McCarry's research (Barter et al., 2009) with young people supports the need for a gendered analysis as the data illustrates that young women experience more types of violence, more frequently, and with more negative impacts. This research was the first study across England, Wales and Scotland to investigate violence in young people's intimate relationships. Findings indicated that of the sample of over 1,300 young people, three quarters of girls and half the boys experienced emotional violence, one quarter of girls and 18 per cent of boys experienced physical violence, and one third of girls and 16 per cent of boys experienced sexual violence (Barter et al., 2009). These data are commensurate with research in the US and Australia for example (DeGue et al, 2013; Foshee et al., 2013; Hamby et al., 2012). As a consequence of the UK findings the then New Labour government implemented strategies such as a social marketing campaign targeted at young people, which the current government has also endorsed (Home Office, 2014). One other outcome has been efforts to extend primary prevention work in schools on young people's relationships (see for example, End Violence Against Women [EVAW], 2012) where previously such work existed in relation to domestic abuse in adult relationships (Ellis, 2004). Additionally, in 2013, the government definition of domestic abuse was expanded to explicitly incorporate 16 and 17 year olds (Home Office, 2013). These are positive developments in recognising the seriousness of the problem for young people; however it is a worrying step with potential to criminalise young people for their conduct.[4]

PREVENTION IN SOCIAL POLICY

Explicit use of the term 'prevention' has a relatively long history in certain disciplines and professions. It appeared in the late nineteenth and early twentieth centuries in criminology, medicine, and in public and mental health. It has also been employed in voluntary sector work with children since this time, as in the title of the National Society for the Prevention of Cruelty to Children (NSPCC). As statutory social work emerged, prevention became a key aspect of the services it offered with, as Hardiker et al. (1991) suggest, the Children Act 1948 marked the beginning of the contemporary debate about prevention. The term has thus circulated in discourses of justice and welfare whilst education

---

[4] A further concern relates to adult and young women's propensity to overstate the extent of their violence and particularly defensive violence, such as protecting themselves or their children from an abuser, which leads to them being identified as perpetrators and embroils them in the criminal justice system.

has been harnessed as a strategy for prevention in health (Petersen, 1996; Stone, 1989), child abuse (Bagley et al., 1996; Barron & Topping, 2010), crime (Home Office, 2004), family support, where it manifests itself mostly as parenting programmes (Home Office, 1997; Home Office, 1998) and in relation to domestic abuse (De Grace & Clarke, 2012; Wolfe & Jaffe, 2001).

Whilst prevention is frequently used in criminology, health, and childcare social work, explicit definitions are less often proffered in the literature. As the term itself suggest, prevention entails some sort of action and as Freeman (1992) suggests, it incorporates the idea of prediction: x is undertaken in order that y will not happen. This implies that not only are the causes and causal relationship of a 'problem' known, but also that they can be acted on in some way to reduce or remove them. There is also a temporal aspect where the event or outcome to be stopped, hindered or avoided is imminent: it is not in the present, but always at some point in the future. In this respect, prevention can be regarded as precautionary or pre-emptive. Additionally, there is a moral connotation where the event or outcome to be prevented is constructed as a 'problem', as undesirable in some way and therefore action can be justified. Finally, prevention is implicitly associated with social change; it has been deployed by the Left as a means of social reform and by the Right as a way of reducing welfare expenditure and state intervention (Billis, 1981). It is evident that there is a lack of conceptual clarity, partly as a result of prevention being deployed to describe both policy and practice. Consequently, different academic disciplines and professions developed distinct models and practices for preventive work with CYP. Recently however, two models have come to dominate across the social policy spectrum and it is these to which we now turn. Before doing so we want to make clear that in engaging in a critique of prevention it is not our intention to undermine the project of attempting to end violence in young people's intimate relationships. There is little discursive space to argue against prevention since its intentions appear both benign and compelling, and there is a consensus that it 'is a good thing' (Freeman, 1992, p.47). More we hope to illuminate the context in which prevention has developed in order to inform reflective and reflexive policy and practice so that adults might better engage with young people in this endeavour.

MODELS OF PREVENTION

Public Health Model

Despite difficulties in defining prevention, a commonly accepted framework for conceptualizing it in relation to violence and its prevention is the tripartite model drawn from public health. This model has three divisions termed primary, secondary and tertiary which principally describe decisions about the timing of a prevention activity, judged according to the stage of 'problem' development rather than specific intended outcome(s), target group or activity. Primary prevention refers to the stage prior to the onset of the 'problem' with the intention of stopping the problem from happening at all. This is usually targeted at whole populations, through universal services, although specific individuals or groups who are considered particularly 'vulnerable' are also targeted. So, for example, school-based interventions which target young people's intimate relationships that are delivered to all young people in the whole population or specific year groups falls into this category. Secondary prevention refers to the stage when a 'problem' has become evident and action is deemed necessary to stop it getting worse or recurring. This might take the form of targeted services with identified populations deemed 'at risk' and may take place in groups. In the UK there are a number of new projects in this area including CRUSH which target young people 'at risk' of perpetration or victimisation with a focus on violence in young people own intimate relationships (West Mercia Women's Aid, 2014). Young people are referred to the project and whilst some of the work is conducted in schools most is not (Thiara & Ellis, 2013).Where a problem has become intractable or is multi-faceted, prevention at a tertiary level would be undertaken in order to reduce harm. Such activity is likely to involve specialist services who would work with individuals or families.

Primary prevention in schools which aims to foster discussion of respectful or healthy relationships and thus reduce or end abuse in young people's intimate relationships serves a purpose in confronting and putting the issue on a public platform. However, measuring the success of such interventions is challenging, as discussed later in the chapter. Primary prevention models of this type often operate on the belief that attitudes predict behaviour whereby influencing attitude will lead to changes in behaviour. However, this view is challenged by a number of authors and McCarry's work with young people in schools found that even though prevailing attitudes towards physical violence was of universal condemnation, when the use of violence was discussed in relation to men and women in intimate relationships there was less certainty about what was un/acceptable (McCarry, 2004). Further, a possible unintended outcome is that those who receive the intervention but are then victimised by their intimate partners may feel in some way responsible or culpable in their victimisation as they have been 'educated' to know better. This is a particular concern in respect of abuse and violence in young people's intimate relationships as a tactic of many abusers is to convince the victim that they are to blame for their victimisation (Chung, 2005, 2007; Stark, 2007).

The Prevention Science Model

In response to the deficits in the tripartite model, prevention science, or the risk and protective factor model, has been developed. In essence, this is a model for the prevention of crime, which has attained a dominant position not only in the UK, but in other Western countries including the USA, Australia and the Netherlands, as the solution to the 'youth problem' (France, 2004). Prevention science is a model of social crime prevention and, as such, it focuses on people, those who do or who might commit crime, and the social conditions that give rise to criminality, rather than on the management or design of the environment. Social crime prevention, as Sutton states, 'embraces almost any program that can claim to affect the pattern of behaviour, values and the self-discipline of groups seen as having the potential to offend' (1994, p.10). The approach is thus seen as particularly relevant to CYP and is instigated through a broad range of social policies and services including housing, family, youth work, employment, and education (Graham, 1990). Given the potential breadth of activity within social crime prevention, Tonry and Farrington (1995) suggest a sub-division into 'developmental prevention' and 'community prevention'. Developmental prevention 'seeks to prevent the development of criminal potential within individuals' (Gilling, 1997, p.6) whilst community prevention, using situational and social approaches, aims to prevent crime through changing the social conditions in communities. While prevention science is a form of developmental crime prevention, community prevention, in the form of community safety partnerships, also promote strategies to address domestic violence.

Prevention science has a focus on preventing 'adolescent problem behaviours' (Hawkins et al., 1992), particularly youth crime. It draws on a theory of delinquent development (Farrington & West, 1993) and the social development model of behaviour (Catalano & Hawkins, 1996) and has been extensively developed in the USA, principally by Hawkins and Catalano (see for example, Catalano et al., 2004; Hawkins, 1999) and in the UK by Farrington (see for example 1994, 1999) and Utting et al., 2001; see also Sutton et al., 2004). Rooted in developmental and social psychology, particularly social learning theory (Bandura, 1977, 1986) and in Hirschi's criminological social control (bond) theory (1969), it hypothesizes that a range of future 'problem' behaviours, variously and interchangeably labelled 'crime', 'anti-social behaviour' [ASB], 'delinquency', 'drug (ab)use' and 'violence', can be predicted from a set of risk factors. Once identified, these risk factors can be diminished through a range of interventions, mostly cognitive-behavioural in approach (Pitts, 2003), in order to prevent the 'onset, escalation, [and] maintenance' and promote the 'de-escalation, and cessation or desistance' from the 'problem' behaviours (Catalano & Hawkins, 1996, p.150). Interventions are referred to as 'protective' or 'pro-social' factors and these are 'those internal and external forces which help children resist or ameliorate risk' (Fraser, 1997, p.3). Principal amongst protective factors is the family: 'a stable and supportive family can protect young people … balancing some of the risks they face and helping them to achieve their potential and make a successful transition to adulthood' (Social Exclusion Unit, 2000, p. 97). However this approach legitimises the controversial intergenerational transmission of violence thesis (see Tschann et al., 2009) which posits that if children growing up in a home where abuse and violence are deployed for conflict management purposes then they will subsequently model their own behaviour on this. This model is problematic on many grounds. Firstly, it is inherently deterministic suggesting that boys who see fathers/father figures using violence will adopt this form of behaviour against their partners, and girls who see their mothers abused will gravitate towards abusive intimate partners. Clearly, CYP are affected by the behaviours of their caregivers, but whether a child adopts or rejects that behaviour is contested. Secondly, it is overly essentialising suggesting that girls implement the behaviours of their mothers and boys of their fathers. Thirdly, it implies that domestic abuse is a product of poor conflict management rather than the systematic control and terror by one partner (usually male) of the other (usually female) (Johnson, 1995; Stark 2007).

Risk factors have been identified through longitudinal and small sample experimental studies and the Cambridge Study in Delinquent Development, longitudinal research led by West (1969) and then Farrington, is the most often cited work[5]. Whilst an extensive list of risk factors has been put forward, relatively few protective factors are identified. Risk factors covering genetic, biological, psychological and social factors are grouped into 'domains' of

---

[5] The Cambridge Study documented offending and antisocial behaviour, from age 8 to age 46, of a cohort of 411 south London men born in 1953-54. It studied the intergenerational transmission and desistance of offending and ASB in relation to family background throughout the life course. The latter stages focussed on whether crime, ASB and mental health can be predicted by behavioural measures earlier in life (see West & Farrington, 1973, 1977).

family, school, individual and community but appear in various combinations. The aim of work based on this model is to reduce the risk factors that are considered to 'have a significant impact on an individual's adjustment at later points of his [sic] development' (Tremblay & Craig, 1997, p.34) and to increase protective factors. Intervention/prevention activity is preceded by a process of risk assessment where individuals are 'measured' against risk factors in order to ascertain the level of risk they are deemed to face or, more contentiously, pose in relation to particular outcomes. No single risk factor is regarded as predictive; it is clusters of factors that are significant and the more risk factors 'there were in young people's lives, the greater the risk of them committing offences' (McCarthy et al., 2004, p.15). It is therefore proposed that risk factors are best tackled together, leading to the development of, at best, a comprehensive community initiative (CCIs)[6], or multi-agency working and joined-up or 'holistic' services. In relation to intimate partner violence, there is a substantial evidence base which illustrates that domestic abuse perpetrators come from a range of backgrounds cutting across economic, geographical, class, ethnicity, socio-cultural divides and there is no direct causal relationship with alcohol use, stress, unemployment or any other external factor; clearly these factors may exacerbate difficult home circumstances and can have an aggravating effect, but they are not causal.

Thus, there is no neat typology with which to categorise and aggregate risk factors in order to identify a potential perpetrator. The risk factors are less well understood in relation to young people's relationships where some of the aggravating factors in adult relationships may not be present such as financial dependency/stress or issues relating to cohabitation.

Prevention science has been whole-heartedly adopted as a framework for work with CYP and their families in England. Initially it was utilised solely in relation to 'youth crime' but also through integrated 'welfare' initiatives such as *Sure Start* and the Children's Fund and more recently in early intervention strategies.

Prevention science was adopted in relation to all services for CYP and their families in Every Child Matters (ECM)[7]. Whilst the Coalition government no longer refers to ECM it has not formally been rescinded and practitioners still use it as a framework for their work. The primacy of prevention science was apparent in ECM in a number of ways, but principally shown through a list of risk and protective factors following the claim that: 'We have a good idea of what factors shape children's life chances. Research tells us that the risk of experiencing negative outcomes is concentrated in children with certain characteristics and experiences' (CST, 2003, p.17). The early intervention strategies of the current government are explicitly based on it (Allen, 2011).

---

[6] CCIs aim to 'foster a fundamental transformation of poor neighborhoods and the circumstances of individuals who live there. The change they seek is comprehensive, that is, inclusive of all sectors of the neighborhood ... and focused on ... strengthening the capacity of neighborhood residents, associations, and institutions' (Kubisch, 1996: not numbered). An example in the UK is Communities That Care (1997).

[7] Every Child Matters was a government initiative introduced in 2003 and was a precursor to the Children Act 2004. Its main aims were for every child to meet five outcomes: Be Healthy, Stay Safe, Enjoy and Achieve, Make a Positive Contribution, Achieve Economic Well-being.

RISK, PREVENTION AND THE REGULATION OF CHILDREN AND YOUNG PEOPLE

The appeal of prevention science is compelling: 'the paradigm is easy to understand and to communicate [it] avoids difficult questions about which risk factors have causal effects' (Farrington, 2000, p.7). It is a grand theory since its proponents claim that 'by seeking to predict and understand both prosocial and antisocial behaviour [it] attempts to identify general processes of human behaviour' (Catalano & Hawkins, 1996, p.150). Its appeal and credibility may also relate to its 'scientific' basis which, in the demand for evidence-based policy and practice, seemingly provides answers or solutions, for policy-makers and practitioners alike, to what are regarded as intractable social problems.

Risk in prevention science is used in a particularized form, where it is 'largely treated as a taken-for-granted objective phenomenon' (Lupton, 1999, p.2). This is not the existential uncertainty of Beck's risk society (1992) but is deployed in the pseudo-scientific epidemiological form where populations are screened for risk factors which are used to pre-detect potential 'pathological' outcomes (Castel, 1991; Dean, 1999). Risk factors are abstract categories drawn from statistical correlations which 'dissolve the notion of the subject or a concrete individual and put in its place a combinatory of factors' (Castel, 1991, p.281). The list of risk factors is so extensive that it is almost unlimited and, as Bessant et al. (2003) argue, it varies from 'indicators of specific disadvantage such as gender ... to indicators that appear common to all [CYP]' (p.33). In fact, some characteristics form risk factors themselves: for example, being female is seen as a protective factor while being male is a risk factor for involvement in anti-social behaviour or crime (YJB, 2005). Not only is this a highly unsophisticated understanding and analysis of gender, it also simplifies complex social issues to one factor and reproduces dominant discourses of gender and crime. In addition, gender can never be predictive for a particular individual as witnessed, for example, by the way a significant number of girls use physical violence in their intimate relationships (Barter et al., 2009).

Demographic information gathered about individuals is aggregated to establish norms against which individuals are then compared and conduct is normalized, simultaneously homogenizing and individualizing. Individuals are categorized and assigned to a specific 'risk group', not on the basis of their past actions or any actual danger they might pose, but through a systematic assessment of their characteristics against abstract factors, and of the incidence of particular outcomes in a population. Prevention focuses on the probability of some undesirable outcome occurring and on the deduction and pre-detection of individuals who are 'at risk' in order to 'anticipate all the possible forms of irruption of danger' (Castel, 1991, p.288).

Deeply embedded in developmentalism, prevention science not only essentializes childhood and powerfully normalizes CYP (Burman, 1994), it positions them without agency and as malleable and suggestible since they imitate 'behaviour' modelled by adults. Additionally, life transitions are seen as problematic because they can produce negative outcomes (Durlak, 1995). Concern over transitions is illustrated in ECM where two appear to be of particular concern: that from childhood to adulthood, and at age 11 when 'a critical transition is from primary to secondary school and the onset of puberty' (CST, 2003, p.20). The former demonstrates children as 'becomings', the latter elides a socially constructed administrative transition (albeit legitimated by developmental psychology) with puberty which has been constructed as a problematic life stage. This has led to some commentators arguing that adolescence has now been construed as a risk factor in itself thereby problematising all CYP. In relation to this, many young people start having intimate relationships at this age and thus having an intimate partner can *a priori* be labelled as a risk factor.

Prevention science is highly deterministic since relationships between characteristics, events, or circumstances in early life are seen as precursors to criminality so that 'what happens to a small child sets in stone the pattern of his or her future life' (Waiton, 2001, p.35)[8]. 'Problems' might also be seen as 'emerging' at younger and younger ages because certain conduct is read as indicative of some future problem that must be 'nipped in the bud' (Dennis, 1997). The adoption at a policy level of prevention science as the basis for all services to CYP and their families means that it is now an approach directed towards the delivery of universal as well as targeted and specialist services. Consequently, a model theorized and utilised for 'problem' CYP, who represent a very small proportion of the population, now encompasses all CYP. It could be argued that within this discourse not only are all CYP problematized, but that childhood per se (re-)emerges as problematic. Adopting this model to underpin all services for CYP effectively means that the risk of criminality has come to the fore, and that other services, agencies and agendas have been co-opted into preventing crime; Gilling & Barton (1997) refer to this as the criminalization of social policy.

The prevalence of risk has meant that safety has become of paramount concern: Safer Schools, Safer Routes to School, health and safety, community safety, personal safety, Superhighway Safety, safeguarding and child safety orders are all high on the agenda. Consequently, every aspect of CYP's lives are deemed to be of concern with no child impervious to the dangers which are seen as potentially awaiting them or which they are seen as potentially posing to others and society. CYP are 'at risk': from themselves through teenage pregnancy, precocious sexuality, truancy, obesity, underachievement, or illicit drug use; from adults who are 'paedophiles', absent or violent fathers, inadequate teachers unable to impose discipline, or single mothers; from the media through advertising, video games, or the Internet; and from each other through peer violence or street crime. Prevention science, in deploying a broad set of abstract risk factors, effectively positions all CYP at risk in some way on a risk continuum. Children and young people are either at high or low risk but never at no risk (Dean, 1999), and they are always positioned as deficient.

In response, a plethora of legislation, policies, programmes and practices intended to ameliorate these problems have been introduced by governments seemingly committed to increasing children's well-being and opportunities. CYP are subjected to a range of programmes, intensive 'rehabilitation', or punitive measures; their access to unsupervised time, which is predominantly viewed as 'children having nothing to do', is used to explain working class children's involvement in criminality or ASB, justifying the use of curfews or the corralling of CYP into supervised adult-approved spaces (Furedi, 1997). However, the impact of changed policies and practices is often antithetical to their intended and stated purposes and contributes to the increased surveillance and regulation of CYP (Waiton, 2001). The aim here is not to minimise or obscure the harsh and harmful realities of many children's lives and instead the contention is that CYP themselves are less often asked about their

---

[8] See discussion above in relation to intergenerational transmission of violence theory.

concerns or the possible solutions, and instead are positioned as 'the problem'. CYP have an understanding of this, as one young person, involved in the National Youth Agency's [NYA] consultation on the implementation of Children's Rights, illustrated with the comment, 'I'm a person, not a problem' (NYA, 2002).

While epidemiological risk underpins the preventative agenda of current CYP's policies, it circulates and intersects with other forms of risk. Socialized or collective risk management is, according to Ewald (1991), a characteristic of actuarial or insurance risk where risk is spread across the population. Risk in the actuarial sense is calculable; it is not danger or peril. Risks are knowable through the statistical regularity of events where the probability of a risk happening can be calculated so, unlike epidemiological risk, its ethos is restorative or compensatory rather than preventive (Dean, 1999). However, within neo-liberal regimes, underscored as they are by individualism and the market, risk management has been privatized and the responsibility for managing risk is handed back to the individual. O'Malley (1992, 1996) refers to this individualized risk management as new prudentialism; each person is responsible for their own actions and is viewed as a self-determining subject able to gather information and make rational - prudent - choices. Risk is then 'associated with the injunction to make one's life into an enterprise and for the individual to become an entrepreneur of him or herself' (Dean, 1999, p.134). Life is a project, of investment in the self as capital, and we are required to 'skill' ourselves to operate in a market economy and conduct life in a 'healthy' way as a subject 'capable of exercising a regulated freedom and caring for themselves as free subjects' (Rose, 1993, p.288). The idea of the responsible and entrepreneurial self has implications for the governing of CYP through education and schooling.

Given the liberal tradition of education as a process of self-improvement, it is unsurprising that education has been harnessed as prevention; the idea that learning contributes to the development of rationality means the possession of knowledge is regarded as equipping individuals to make the 'right' choices and conduct their lives prudently - to avoid or minimise risks through changing attitudes or 'inner states' (O'Malley, 1992, p.267) - and CYP are exhorted to invest in themselves and engage in their own transformation. Since this positions them as informed and active, prevention becomes the responsibility of the individual. Any failure to protect oneself from 'risks' effectively leads to blaming the victim (O'Malley, 1992) which, in respect of abuse and violence in young people's intimate relationships can lead to the double victimisation of young women and girls. In general, CYPs ability to protect themselves is seen as a measure of their competence and failure to manage risks becomes a failure of the self (Cruickshank, 1996). This is evident in the discourses on violence in young people's intimate relationships where young women are implicitly or even explicitly blamed for picking a bad partner and making poor choices in their relationships rather than focusing on the wider structural inequalities that perpetuate gender roles supportive of ideologies of male dominance.

Some commentators, such as Hogan and Murphey (2000) reiterate the comment above about the legitimacy of the relationship between activities labelled 'prevention' and outcomes for CYP: '[we] are well aware of the difficulties in establishing convincing cause-and-effect relations where ... these arguments rest on evidence that is, admittedly, circumstantial' (p.1). Nonetheless, they subsequently present twenty-three pages of 'evidence' to support an argument for prevention. Establishing the effectiveness of prevention activity is, however, no straightforward matter. Bloom (1981) once referred to the process of evaluating prevention as the 'impossible science'. His argument, and that of others (Albee, 1998; Billis, 1981;

Freeman, 1999), is that, since the aim of prevention is to stop something happening and since success is measured by its absence, there is no certain way of knowing if the something might have happened irrespective of the prevention activity. For example, if at the end of an intervention with young people in school only 10 per cent of students report abuse and violence in their intimate relationships does this prove success of the intervention or simply that the other 90 per cent were never going to perpetrate or be victimised in their intimate relationships. Put simply, if the something does not happen does that mean the prevention activity worked or that the prediction was wrong. Thus, we might question if the omission of abuse and violence in young people's intimate relationships is a positive outcome of prevention or an error in the identification of prevalence.

CONCLUSION

This chapter has examined the discursive field of prevention and established that, whilst it is conceptually confused and can be deployed in a number of ways, it now dominates social policy in relation to work with CYP. The idea that prevention is a 'good thing' obscures the social and political ends which it serves in governing and regulating the conduct of CYP through the intersection of particular discourses of risk with those of childhood. Prevention is arguably an attempt to discipline the future; to bring the future into the present through identifying and predicting rather than explaining or solving social problems, threats, or undesirable conduct. Conceivably, strategies or activities to 'prevent' put change into the future, since they are not about addressing the present needs of CYP but about avoiding predicted outcomes. However, as Billis (1981) argues, better and/or more services are desirable in themselves to help improve CYP's lives now. Nowhere is this more relevant than in relation to abuse in young people's intimate relationships where instead of undertaking work to prevent future domestic abuse in adult relationships, work should be undertaken to support CYP now, challenging the use of any abusive conduct and to better understand why some young people believe that this is either acceptable or without alternative.

REFERENCES

Albee, G. (1998). The politics of primary prevention. *The Journal of Primary Prevention, 19*(2), 117-127.

Allen, L. (2003). Power talk: young people negotiating (hetero)sex. *Women's Studies International Forum. 26*(3), 235-244.

Allen, G. (2011). *Early Intervention: The Next Steps*. London: The Stationery Office.

Bagley, C., Thurston, W. & Tutty, L. (1996). *Understanding and Preventing Child Sexual Abuse. Critical Summaries of 500 Key studies. Volume 1 Children: Assessment, Social Work and Clinical Issues, and Prevention Education.* Aldershot: Arena/Ashgate Publishing.

Bandura, A. (1977). *Social Learning Theory*. Englewood Cliffs, NJ: Prentice Hall.

Bandura, A. (1986). *Social Foundations of Thoughts and Actions: a Social Cognitive Theory.* Englewood, NJ: Prentice Hall.

Banyard, V.L., Cross, C. &Modecki, K.L. (2006). Interpersonal Violence in Adolescence. *Journal of Interpersonal Violence, 21*(10),1314-1332.

Barron I. & Topping K. (2010). School-based Abuse Prevention: Effect on Disclosures *Journal of Family Violence, 25*, 651–659.

Barter, C., McCarry, M., Berridge, D. & Evans, K. (2009). *Partner exploitation and violence in teenage intimate relationships.* University of Bristol and NSPCC.

Beck, U. (1992). *The Risk Society: Towards a New Modernity*. London: Sage.

Bessant, J., Hil, R., & Watts, R. (2003).*"Discovering Risk. Social Research and Policy Making*, New York: Peter Lang Publishing.

Billis, D. (1981). At risk of prevention. *Journal of Policy Studies, 10(3),* 367-379.

Bloom, M. (1981). *Primary Prevention: The Possible Science*. Englewood Cliffs, NJ: Prentice Hall.

Burman, E. (1994). *Deconstructing Developmental Psychology*. London: Routledge.

Case, S. (2007). Questioning the 'Evidence' of Risk that Underpins Evidence-led Youth Justice Interventions. *Youth Justice, 7,* 91-105.

Case, S. & K. Haines (2010). Risky business? The risk in risk factor research. *Criminal Justice Matters, 80,* 20-22.

Castel, R. (1991). From dangerousness to risk. In Burchell, G., Gordon, C. and Miller, P. (Eds.) *The Foucault Effect. Studies in Governmentality.* Chicago: The University of Chicago Press.

Catalano, R., Berglund, L., Ryan, J., Lonczak, H. & Hawkins, D. (2004). Positive Youth Development in the United States: research findings on evaluations of PYD programs. In Peterson C. (Ed.). *Positive Development: Realizing the Potential of Youth*, Thousand Oaks, Ca: Sage.

Catalano, R. & Hawkins, D. (1996). The social development model: a theory of antisocial behavior. In Hawkins, D. (Ed). *Delinquency and Crime. Current Theories.* Cambridge: Cambridge University Press.

Chief Secretary to the Treasury (2003). *Every Child Matters*. London: The Stationery Office.

Chung, D. (2005). Violence, control, romance and gender equality: Young women and heterosexual relationships. *Women's Studies International Forum, 28*(6), 445-455.

Chung, D. (2007). Making Meaning of Relationships: Young Women's Experiences and Understandings of Dating Violence. *Violence Against Women, 13*(12), 1274-1295.

Cruickshank, B. (1996). Revolutions within: self-government and self-esteem. In A. Barry, T. Osborne, & N. Rose (Eds.). *Foucault and Political Reason*, London: Routledge.

Communities that Care (UK) (1997). *Communities that Care: A New Kind of Prevention Programme*. London: CtC.

Dean, M. (1999). *Governmentality. Power and Rule in Modern Society*. London: Sage.

De Grace, A. & Clarke, A. (2012). Promising Practices in the Prevention of Intimate Partner Violence Among Adolescents. *Violence and Victims, 27*(6), 849-859.

DeGue, S., Massetti, G.M., Holt, M.K., Tharp, A.T., Valle, L.A., Matjasko, J.L., & Lippy, J. (2013). Identifying Links Between Sexual Violence and Youth Violence Perpetration: New Opportunities for Sexual Violence Prevention. *Psychology of Violence, 3*(2), 140–156.

Dennis, N. (1997). *Zero Tolerance: Policing a Free State*. London: Institute of Economic Affairs.

Department for Children School and Families (2010). *Early intervention: Securing good outcomes for all children and young people*. London: DCSF.

Durlak, J. (1995). *School-Based Prevention Programs for Children and Adolescents*. Thousand Oaks, CA: Sage.

Ellis, J. (2004). *Preventing Violence Against Women and Girls. A study of Educational Programmes for Children and Young People*. London: Womankind Worldwide.

Ellis, J. (2014 in press). Preventing VAWG through education: dilemmas and challenges. In Ellis, J. and Thiara, R.K. (Eds.) *Preventing violence against women and girls. Educational work with children and young people*. Bristol: Policy Press.

End Violence Against Women (EVAW) (2012). *Schools Safe 4 Girls Campaign*. Available http://www.endviolenceagainstwomen.org.uk/schools-safe-4-girls[Accessed12.2.14].

Ewald, F. (1991).Insurance and risk. In G., Burchell, C., Gordon, &P. Miller (Eds.). *The Foucault Effect. Studies in Governmentality*. Chicago: Chicago University Press.

Farrington, D. (1994). Early developmental prevention of juvenile delinquency. *Criminal Behaviour and Mental Health, 4*, 209-227.

Farrington, D. (1999). Delinquency prevention using family-based interventions. *Children and Society, 13*, 287-303.

Farrington, D.P. (2000). Explaining and Preventing Crime: The globalization of knowledge. The American Society of Criminology 1999 Presidential Address. *Criminology 38(1)*, 1–24.

Farrington, D.P. (2003). Developmental and life-course criminology: key theoretical and empirical issues: the 2002 Sutherland Award address. *Criminology 41(2)*, 221-225.

Farrington, D. & West, D. (1993). Criminal, penal and life histories of chronic offenders: risk and protective factors and early identification. *Criminal Behaviour and Mental Health, 3*, 492-523.

Foshee, V. A. (1996). Gender differences in adolescent dating abuse prevalence, types and injuries'. *Health Education Research, 11*, 275-286.

Foshee, V. A., Benefield, T. S. McNaughton H. L. Reyes, S. T. Ennett, R. Faris, & Chang, L. (2013). The Peer Context and the Development of the Perpetration of Adolescent Dating Violence. *Journal of Youth Adolescence, 42*, 471-486.

France, A. (2004). Talking Across Paradigms: Debating risk and protection in late modern society. *An International Symposium at Pennsylvania State University*, USA.

France, A. (2008). Risk factor analysis and the youth question. *Journal of Youth Studies, 11*, 1-15.

France, A. & D. Utting (2005). The Paradigm of 'Risk and Protection-Focused Prevention and its Impact on Services for Children and Families. *Children & Society, 19*, 77-90.

France, A., Freiberg, K. and R. Homel (2010). Beyond Risk Factors: Towards a Holistic Prevention Paradigm for Children and Young People. *British Journal of Social Work, 40*, 1192-1210.

Fraser, M. (1997). *Risk and Resilience in Childhood: An Ecological Perspective*, Washington DC: NASW Press.

Freeman, R. (1992). The idea of prevention: a critical review. In Scott, S., Williams G., Platt, S. and Thomas, H. (Eds.). *Private Risks and Public Dangers*, Aldershot: Avebury.

Freeman, R. (1999). Recursive politics: prevention, modernity and social systems. *Children and Society, 9*, 232-241.

Furedi, F. (1997). *Culture of Fear: Risk Taking and the Morality of Low Expectation*. London: Cassell.

Gallaty, K., & Zimmer-Gembeck, M.J. (2008). The Daily Social and Emotional Worlds of Adolescents Who Are Psychologically Maltreated by their Romantic Partners. *Journal of Youth Adolescenc*e, *37*, 310-323.

Gilling, D. (1997). *Crime Prevention. Theory, Policy and Politics*. London: UCL Press.

Gilling, D. & Barton, A. (1997). Crime prevention and community safety: a new home for social policy. *Critical Social Policy, 17*(3), 63-83.

Graham, J. (1990). *Crime Prevention Strategies in Europe and North America*. Helsinki: HEUNI.

Hamby, S., Finkelhor, D., & Turner, H. (2012).Teen Dating Violence: Co-Occurrence With Other Victimizations in the National Survey of Children's Exposure to Violence (NatSCEV). *Psychology of Violence, 2*(2), 111–124.

Hardiker, P., Exton, K., & Barker, M. (1991). *Policies and Practices in Preventive Child Care*. Aldershot: Avebury.

Hawkins, D. (1999). Preventing crime and violence through Communities that Care. *European Journal on Criminal Policy and Research, 7*, 443-458.

Hawkins, J. D., Catalano, R.F.& Miller, J.Y. (1992). Risk and protective factors for alcohol and other drug problems in adolescence and early adulthood: Implications for substance abuse prevention. *Psychological Bulletin, 112*(1), 64-105.

Hickman, L., Jaycox, L. & Aronoff, J. (2004).Dating violence among adolescents; Prevalence, gender distribution and prevention program effectiveness. *Trauma, Violence and Abuse*. 5(2), 123-142.

Hirschi, T. (1969). *Causes of Delinquency*. Berkeley: University of California Press.

HM Government (2008). *Youth Crime Action Plan*. London: Home Office, Ministry of Justice, Cabinet Office and DCSF.

Hogan, C. and Murphey, D. (2000). *Toward an "Economic of Prevention": Illustrations from Vermont's Experience*. Available http://www.financeproject.org/vermont.htm 06.12.04.

Holland, J., Ramazanoglu, C., Sharpe, S. & Thompson, R. (1998). *The Male in the Head*. London, Tufnell Press.

Home Office (1997). *No More Excuses: A New Approach to Tackling Youth Crime in England and Wales*. London: HMSO.

Home Office (1998). *Supporting Families: A Consultation Document*. London: Home Office.

Home Office (2004). *The Role of Education in Enhancing Life Chances and Preventing Offending*. London: The Stationery Office.

Home Office (2011). *Call to End Violence Against Women and Girls: Action Plan*. London: HM Government.

Home Office (2013). *Ending Violence Against Women and Girls in the UK*. London: HM Government.

Home Office (2014). *Ending violence against women and girls in the UK*. London: HM Government.

Jezl, D., Molidor, C. & White, T. (1996). Physical, sexual and psychological abuse in high school dating relationships: Prevalence rates and self-esteem issues. *Child and Adolescent Social Work Journal,13*, 69-88.

Johnson, M.P. (1995). Patriarchal Terrorism and Common Couple Violence: Two Forms of Violence against Women. *Journal of Marriage and Family*, *57*(2), 283-294.

Kubisch, A. (1996). *Comprehensive Community Initiatives: Lessons in Neighborhood Transformation*. New Jersey: National Housing Institute. Available http://www.nhi.org/online/issues/85/compcominit.html 12.03.05.

Lupton, D. (1999). *Risk*. London: Routledge.

Malik, S., Sorenson, S.B. & Aneshensel, C.S. (1997). Community and dating violence among adolescents: Perpetration and victimization. *Journal of Adolescent Health, 21*(5),291-302.

McCarry, M. (2004). *The Connection Between Masculinity and Domestic Violence: What Young People Think*. University of Bristol: Unpublished PhD Thesis.

McCarthy, P., Laing, K. & Walker, J. (2004). *Offenders of the Future? Assessing the Risk of Children and Young People Becoming Involved in Criminal or Antisocial Behaviour*. London: DfES/HMSO.

Molidor, C. & Tolman, R.M. (1998). Gender and Contextual Factors in Adolescent Dating Violence. *Violence Against Women, 4*(2), 180-194.

Murphy, K.A. & Smith, D.I. (2009). Adolescent Girls' Responses to Warning Signs of Abuse in Romantic Relationships. Implications for Youth-Targeted Relationship Violence Prevention. *Journal of Interpersonal Violence, 25*(4),626-647.

National Youth Agency (2002) *Righting Wrongs: Taking Action to Implement the UN Convention on the Rights of the Child*. Briefing Paper 6, Leicester: National Youth Agency.

O'Malley, P. (1992). Risk, power and crime prevention. *Economy and Society, 21*(3), 252-275.

O'Malley, P. (1996). Risk and responsibility. In Barry, A., Osborne, T. and Rose, N. (Eds.). *Foucault and Political Reason: Liberalism, Neo-liberalism and Rationalities of Government*. London: UCL.

Parton, N. (2006). *Safeguarding Childhood: Early Intervention and Surveillance in Late Modern Society*. Basingstoke: Palgrave Macmillan.

Petersen A. (1996). Risk and the regulated self: the discourse of health promotion and the politics of uncertainty. *Australian and New Zealand Journal of Sociology, 32*(1), 44-57.

Pitts, J. (2003). *The New Politics of Youth Crime: Discipline or Solidarity?* Lyme Regis: Russell House Publishing.

Rose, N. (1993). Government, authority and expertise in advanced liberalism. *Economy and Society, 22*(3), 283-299.

Sears, H., Byers, S., Whelan, J., Saint-Pierre G. & the Dating Violence Research Team (2006). "If it hurts you, then it is not a joke" Adolescents' ideas and experiences of abusive behaviour in dating relationships. *Journal of Interpersonal Violence, 21*(9),1191-1207.

Silverman, J. G., Raj, A., Mucci, L. A., & Hathaway, J. E. (2001). Dating violence against adolescent girls and associated substance use, unhealthy weight control, sexual risk behaviour, pregnancy, and suicidality. *Journal of the American Medical Association, 286*(5), 572-579.

Social Exclusion Unit (2000). *National Strategy for Neighbourhood Renewal: Report of Policy Action Team 12: Young People*. London: SEU.

Stark, E. (2007). *Coercive control: how men entrap women in personal life*. Oxford: Oxford University Press.

Stone, D. (1989). Upside down prevention. *Health Service Journal, 99,* 890-891.

Sutton, A. (1994). Crime Prevention: Promise or Threat? *Australian & New Zealand Journal of Criminology, 27*, 15-20.

Sutton, C., Utting, D., & Farrington, D. (eds) (2004). *Support from the Start. Working with Young Children and their Families to Reduce the Risks of Crime and Anti-social Behaviour.* Research Report 524, London: DfES.

Thiara, R.K. & Ellis, J. (2013). *Centralising Young People: An Evaluation of the CRUSH Programme*, University of Worcester, Worcester.

Tonry, M. & Farrington, D. (1995). Strategic approaches to crime prevention. In M. Tonry, & D. Farrington (Eds.). *Building a Safer Society: Strategic Approaches to Crime Prevention.* London: Chicago University Press.

Tschann, J.M., Pasch, L.A., Flores, E., Marin, B.V.O., Baisch E.M., & Wibbelsman C.J. (2009). Nonviolent Aspects of Interparental Conflict and Dating Violence Among Adolescents. *Journal of Family Issues, 30,* 295-319.

Tremblay, R. & Craig, W. (1997). Developmental juvenile delinquency prevention. *European Journal on Criminal Policy and Research, 5*(2), 33-50.

UNICEF (2007). *Child Poverty and Perspective: An Overview of Child Wellbeing in Rich Countries.* UNICEF: Florence.

Utting, D., Rose, W. & Pugh, G. (2001). *Better Results for Children and Families. Involving Communities in Planning Services Based on Outcomes.* London: National Council of Voluntary Child Care Organisations.

Waiton, S. (2001). *Scared of the Kids? Curfews, Crime and the Regulation of Young People.* Sheffield: Sheffield Hallam University Press.

West, D.J. (1969). Present Conduct and Future Delinquency. London: Heinemann.

West, D. & Farrington, D. (1973). *Who Becomes Delinquent?* London: Heinemann.

West, D. & Farrington, D. (1977). *The Delinquent Way of Life.* London: Heinemann.

West Mercia Women's Aid (2014) *The CRUSH Project* Available online: http:www.westmerciawomensaid.org/crush [Accessed 12.2.14].

Wolfe, D. & Jaffe, P. (2001). Prevention of domestic violence: emerging initiatives. In S. Graham-Bermann, & J. Edelson (Eds.). *Domestic Violence in the Lives of Children. The Future of Research, Intervention and Social Policy*, Washington, DC: American Psychological Association.

Youth Justice Board (2005). *Role of Risk and Protective Factors.* London: Youth Justice Board.

Biographical Information

Dr. Jane Ellis is Senior Lecturer in Social Policy at Anglia Ruskin University and Senior Research Fellow at the University of Central Lancashire where she is involved in the PEACH Project, a scoping review of evidence on preventive interventions in domestic abuse for children and young people in the general population. Previously she has conducted research and consultancy on prevention work in schools for voluntary organisations and government, and was a member of the DCSF/DfE Advisory Group on Violence Against Women and Girls. She has a number of publications on violence prevention. Before undertaking her PhD she worked with children, young people and their families in formal and non-formal educational settings, as a teacher and community education worker.

Dr. Melanie McCarry is a Guild Senior Research Fellow in the Connect Centre for International Research on Interpersonal Violence and Harm, University of Central Lancashire, UK. Melanie is advancing theoretical frameworks on abuse and violence in young people's relationships and developing ethical models for working with children and young people. She recently conducted the first UK national study on violence and exploitation in young people's relationships, which made a significant impact in critical understanding and government policy. Recent research includes children affected by domestic violence; violence against women in rural areas; forced marriage and domestic violence in same sex relationships.

In: Overcoming Domestic Violence   ISBN: 978-1-63321-956-4
Editors: Myra F. Taylor, Julie Ann Pooley et al.   © 2015 Nova Science Publishers, Inc.

Chapter 4

YOUTH DATING VIOLENCE: A SILENT EPIDEMIC

*Catherine J. Carter-Snell**

Mount Royal University, Calgary Alberta, Canada

ABSTRACT

Teenagers and young adults are extremely vulnerable to dating violence and suffer significant consequences. Despite this, dating violence among youth is often not included in discussions on domestic violence. As many as a third of elementary and high school students and at least half of postsecondary students have been victims. These data are most likely a conservative estimate, especially in the instance of sexual assault. The majority of sexual assaults occur between recent acquaintances in a form of dating situation yet these are often not counted as dating violence. Adolescents and young adults who experience dating violence develop high rates of adverse mental health consequences such as anxiety, academic dropout, substance abuse, posttraumatic stress disorder, and depression. Physical effects include injury, homicide and suicide as well as long term chronic health issues.

In this chapter we discuss the types of dating violence that teenagers and young adults may experience. Technology and developmental issues increase the vulnerability of youth to certain types of dating violence such as sexual bullying, sexting, and cyberbullying. Risk factors have been identified for both victimization and perpetration of various types of YDV such as adverse childhood experiences, age, gender, and sexual orientation. There is overlap between the risks for victimization and risks of perpetrating the violence. An understanding of these risk factors provides a framework for prevention. Prevention and health promotion are discussed using a social-ecological model. Recommendations are also made for interventions and promotion of resilience when dating violence has already occurred.

---

* Corresponding Author: Dr. Catherine Carter-Snell, RN PhD SANE-A ENC-C, Nursing Education Scholar/ Associate Professor, School of Nursing and Midwifery, Mount Royal University, 4825 Mount Royal Gate SW, Calgary, Alberta, Canada, T3E 6K6. Tel: (403) 440-6679. Email:ccartersnell@mtroyal.ca.

INTRODUCTION

Dating violence among adolescents and young adults is extremely common and associated with significant consequences, yet it is not often included in national data, research or violence initiatives related to domestic violence. Domestic violence is typically assumed to involve adults in established relationships who are, or have been, cohabiting and thus excludes dating violence among youth. Some attempts have been made to broaden the definitions of domestic violence by using terms such as "intimate partner violence" or "relationship violence". Even these terms, however, still exclude adolescents and those involved in shorter term or more casual relationships such as first dates or casual relationships.

For these reasons we fail to recognize the extent of dating violence among adolescents and young adults, and cannot therefore appreciate the impact of the violence on their health and futures. Youth dating violence (YDV) is a silent epidemic that is creating life changing and far too often fatal consequences for youth. We must recognize YDV as an issue affecting the health and futures of our youth and work to prevent it. Effective violence prevention requires an understanding of dating violence and its consequences, using a social-ecological approach to explore the risk factors and determine related prevention strategies (World Health Organization, 2010).

TYPES OF DATING VIOLENCE

Dating violence in this chapter is defined as any emotional, physical or sexual violence directed at someone in a relationship at any phase (beginning, current or former). This may be an early relationship, such as recently having met, or an established relationship. Casual sexual relationships are sometimes not included in definitions of dating or violence but do involve intimacy and may involve one or more forms of violence. Common phrases for these casual relationships include "one night stands", "friends with benefits", "booty calls" or "hooking up".

Adolescent and young adults experience the same three types of domestic violence as older adults (Table 1), including psychological, physical and sexual forms of violence (Breiding, Chen, & Black, 2014). Sexual violence frequently co-occurs with other forms of violence among college-aged victims (Thompson, 2014).

Table 1. Types of Dating Violence

Type	Definition
Psychological	Actions or communications that threaten or affect self-worth (e.g. name calling, embarrassing, isolating from friends or family, bullying, stalking, threaten victim or induce fear)
Physical	Non-sexual violent acts (e.g. punched, hit, slapped, shoved, kicked)
Sexual	Non-consensual sexual activities including coercion or threats to obtain sexual contact

Adolescents and young adults are also vulnerable to methods of YDV that may result in more than one type of dating violence (e.g. psychological and sexual). These methods tend to involve use of technology and social media. Youth may have limited maturity and decision making skills, and are often more susceptible to peer pressure than at other ages. This combination makes youth vulnerable to dating violence methods such as sexual bullying, sexting, cyberbullying and online dating.

"Sexual bullying" refers to bullying behaviour that involves sexual harassment (Fredland, 2008). It includes use of sexually related verbal, written or physical forms of violence. Sexual bullying can be either psychological or sexual abuse and is inflicted by partners or peers. Verbal sexual bullying is comments related to someone's sexuality or sexual attributes, such as derogatory remarks, spreading rumours, passing on jokes, or name-calling (e.g. "slut"). Graffiti or sharing of messages and photographs with peers are examples of documented sexual bullying. Physical forms of sexual bullying include touching or grabbing breasts or genitals, grabbing clothing to expose parts or make the person uncomfortable (e.g. "wedgies"), making sexual advances, or being forced to engage in sex acts.

Cyberbullying involves the use of digital media to send harassing or threatening messages to victims or distribution of embarrassing information or photographs to others to humiliate the victim (Wigderson & Lynch, 2013).It may include sexual bullying. Cyberbullying can also be used by a peer, partner or ex-partner for purposes of retaliation, embarrassment, threats, monitoring communications or even stalking. Those who bully are more likely to eventually perpetrate physical dating violence (Foshee et al., 2014). The impact of cyberbullying on emotional and physical health has been recognized (Wigderson & Lynch, 2013), but may even be greater than for direct abuse. One can walk away from direct abuse but the abuse remains on digital media and continues to be spread, re-exposing the victim further. Cyberbullying in dating violence is more strongly related to depression and delinquency symptoms in teens than any other form of dating violence (Zweig, Lachman, Yahner, & Dank, 2013). Online dating sites pose additional risks for dating violence and cyberbullying. Teens, particularly females, tend to place risky information online which in turn places them at risk for sexual predators as well as for cyberbullying (Pujazon-Zazik, Manasse, & Orrell-Valente, 2012). Although there is limited data on the consequences of online dating for youth, online dating in older adults has been linked to greater risks of financial exploitation, threats and physical harm than traditional relationships(VandeWeerd et al., 2014).

"Sexting" is the transmission of sexually explicit words or images through technology such as smartphones and the Internet. Approximately 10% of adolescents have sent sexts, increasing to 53% among those over 18 (Klettke, Hallford, & Mellor, 2014). Although both males and females may send sexts, females often send them in response to pressure from the males (Korenis & Billick, 2014). The main risk with sexting is that the message is the likelihood that it will be sent to others outside the relationship. At least one in five teens who received sexts indicated that they would pass them on to at least one other person (Steeves, 2014). Circulation of sexts to others has been linked to a number of suicides by the teen depicted in the sext (Crimmins & Seigfried-Spellar, 2014). Involvement in sexting has also been linked to high risk dating behaviours such as being sexually active, having unprotected intercourse, web-chatting with strangers on the Internet, higher drug and alcohol use, developing a sexually transmitted infection, and viewing pornography (Crimmins & Seigfried-Spellar, 2014; Klettke et al., 2014). Governments are struggling with how to manage the issue of sexting. Criminal charges are possible for distribution of child pornography if the circulated sext involves a victim under the age of majority. The distribution may also result in other charges such as harassment or bullying in instances where the sexting can be related to the victim's self-harm or suicide.

EXTENT OF DATING VIOLENCE

Determining exact rates of dating violence is difficult, as rates vary according to the inclusion criteria used (Hamby & Turner, 2013). Generally, incidence estimates range from 15 to 80%. On average, a third of all adolescents and young adults have experienced one or more dating violence incidents (Haynie et al., 2013). A third of the 2013 youth population data (Population Reference Bureau, 2013) would mean that 21 million youth in North America and 587 million youth worldwide have likely been victims of dating violence.

Exposure to some types of YDV varies by gender according to some studies. Male teens were more likely to experience physical dating violence than females (Hamby & Turner, 2013) with females perpetrating the violence. Females were more likely to experience higher rates of emotional/psychological and sexual violence and incidents inducing fear (Hamby & Turner, 2013).

The extent of YDV in very young teens and age at which dating begins is also significant. More than half of Canadian youth have had their first dating relationship by age 12 and the majority by age 15 (Mahoney, 2013). Male university students described their first episodes of dating violence as occurring before age 15, while females experienced controlling behaviors between 13 and 15 years and sexual pressure between age 16 and 17 (Bonomi et al., 2012). Female victims of sexual assault revealed having experienced prior dating violence (Breiding et al., 2014). The first incident of YDV occurred between 11 and 17 years of age for 22% of victims, and between 18 and 24 years for 47% of girls. This finding emphasizes not only the risks of re-victimization after dating violence but the increasing risks of YDV with age. This increase is reflected in police reports which reveal a spike in relationship-related violence among 15 year olds which peaks at approximately age 30 and then begins to decline by age 40 to 50 (Mahoney, 2013).

A third of girls and a quarter of boys in sixth grade with partners reported initiating physical dating violence such as punching or slapping (Simon, Miller, Gorman-Smith, Orpinas, & Sullivan, 2010). More than half of students said it was acceptable for girls to hit boys if they were mad or jealous, and a quarter believed it was acceptable for boys to hit girlfriends. Longitudinal data show that the trajectories for violence increase from grade six to grade twelve for at least 25% of students (Orpinas, Hsieh, Song, Holland, & Nahapetyan, 2013). Dating violence, therefore, affects a vast number of adolescents and young adults. It starts at very early ages and the rates increase with age. The extent and impact of YDV is even more overwhelming when the consequences of dating violence are considered.

CONSEQUENCES OF DATING VIOLENCE

Consequences of YDV are examined using the World Health Organization's social-ecological model (Krug, Dahlberg, Mercy, Zwi, & Lozano, 2002; World Health Organization, 2010). This model includes an exploration of four key areas of influence which can be used to explore impact, risk and prevention: the individual, relationship or family, community, and society.

INDIVIDUAL CONSEQUENCES

Physical injuries can occur as a result of dating violence, although most often these injuries are considered "minor" and do not require hospitalization. Typical injuries include scratches or bruises and muscle strains. Approximately half of victims (male and female) reporting to police sustained injuries but only 1 to 2% had serious injuries (Mahoney, 2013). Homicides as a result of dating violence are less common in the adolescent and young adult population, although risk increases with age (Sinha, 2012).

The emotional and mental health effects on victims of dating violence, however, are extensive and may be severe and long term (Fiorillo, Papa, & Follette, 2013). Dating violence has been linked to substance use, depression, poor academic performance, posttraumatic stress disorder, self-cutting behaviour, weight problems and high risk sexual behaviour. Multiple levels of fear have been described by adolescent female victims of YDV (Burton, Halpern-Felsher, Rehm, Rankin, & Humphreys, 2013). These included fear for themselves related to injury or loss and a state of "fearful expectation" or being on "high alert" for subsequent episodes of violence. There was also fear of losing relationships with family, peers or social standing if the abuse was discovered. An added stressor was "managing" the situation to make the other partner happy to hopefully reduce conflict.

Suicide is one of the leading causes of death among teens and young adults in many countries. There are significant links between YDV and both suicidal ideation (Chiodo, Wolfe, Crooks, Hughes, & Jaffe, 2009) and completed suicides (Crimmins & Seigfried-Spellar, 2014; Holmes & Sher, 2013).Approximately half of adolescents with suicidal ideation reported having experienced physical dating violence, either as victims or perpetrators (Nahapetyan, Orpinas, Song, & Holland, 2014).

The long term effects of dating violence on physical and mental health are also profound. The experiences may well affect their normal psychosocial development and health and alter their life course. The Adverse Childhood Experiences (ACE) studies have demonstrated a well-established link between children or adolescents who experience violence and later development of chronic health conditions such as cancer, heart disease, inflammatory conditions and premature mortality (Larkin, Shields, & Anda, 2012).

RELATIONSHIPS

Dating violence has an intergenerational impact, potentially affecting both current and future relationships. Children or adolescents who have been victims of abuse, including YDV, are at higher risk of becoming either future victims of abuse or in some cases even perpetrators (Manchikanti Gómez, 2011). This continued victimization has also been called a "legacy of abuse" (Martsolf & Draucker, 2008). The experience of YDV can therefore become a risk factor for dating violence re-victimization in future relationships (Holmes & Sher, 2013).

COMMUNITY AND SOCIETAL IMPACT

The community and society are impacted by YDV through increased utilization of healthcare and social agencies, decreased education and decreased work productivity, as well as through the intergenerational transmission of the violence. Across Canada the 2009 government costs for intimate partner violence, including dating violence, were estimated at 7.4 billion dollars for the year (Zhang, Hoddenbaugh, McDonald, & Scrim, 2012). The majority of the expenses were for health care costs and shelters. Costs for sexual assault services were an additional 1.9 billion dollars per year (McInturff, 2013). The costs associated with YDV specific to adolescents and young adults have not been estimated but can be anticipated to be high given the vulnerability of youth, volume of violence, and demonstrated effects of violence on health.

Dating violence raises issues at a societal level in terms of human rights awareness and legislation, policies related to abuse or which support gender inequity, and funding for preventative and interventional programs. Although there is only limited legislation related to domestic violence we are seeing an increased recognition by governments that more needs to be done to reduce domestic violence and child abuse. There is a serious gap in legislation related to dating violence as it relates to adolescents and young adults and little societal incentive to prevent it.

RISKS FACTORS FOR DATING VIOLENCE

There is considerable overlap between risk factors for becoming a perpetrator of YDV and a victim (Kaukinen, 2014). This is in contrast to the finding with adults that mutual conflict among adults was relatively uncommon (Johnson & Leone, 2005). Johnson and Leone's (2005) typology of domestic violence perpetration is shown in Table 2.

Table 2. Johnson's (2005) Typologies of Domestic Violence

Type	Description
Situational Violence	Violence occurs only with crisis, control not used in between
Intimate Terrorism	Use of control and intimidation throughout relationship
Violent Resistance	Violence is in response to or retaliation for partner's violence
Mutual Conflict	Both partners use control and violent tactics

College students demonstrated the same typologies but had some key differences (Straus & Gozjolko, 2014). Females were more likely to be the sole perpetrators of situational violence while men were more often victims. Despite this, female victims were more likely to be injured. Intimate terrorism was not often used but when it occurred it most often involved mutual violence by partners.

INDIVIDUAL

Key individual risk factors include adverse childhood experiences, mental health, attitudes, and age. An individual's experience with violence in childhood poses a risk for further victimization as an adolescent or adult. Childhood physical abuse is linked to increased risk of dating violence in both adolescents (Pattishall, Cruz, & Spector, 2011)and college students (Fiorillo et al., 2013). Adverse childhood experiences such as childhood abuse, including witnessing parental domestic violence, are associated with an increased risk of subsequent perpetration and victimization of YDV (Foshee et al., 2014).

Mental health issues such as substance abuse or depression and emotional regulation can increase risks of perpetration (Dardis, Dixon, Edwards, & Turchik, 2014). Alcohol and substance use predicted both same day physical, emotional or sexual coercion perpetration and victimization for a group of college males but did not for females (Borofsky, Kellerman, Baucom, Oliver, & Margolin, 2013). Lack of sleep was found as a risk factor for college women's aggression toward their partners, but was thought to be linked to difficulties regulating emotions when fatigued (Keller, Blincoe, Gilbert, Haak, & DeWall, 2014).

Attitudes of entitlement and gender inequity increase risks for perpetration of both physical violence and sexual violence (Dardis et al., 2014).These attitudes are also seen with the "undetected rapist", who select women and increase their vulnerability with drugs or alcohol, and then believe they are entitled to the sex regardless of whether the woman is willing (Lisak & Miller, 2002).

Age and lack of experience also pose a risk for victimization. Adolescents are usually less experienced in dating relationships, and may not have well-developed skills or understanding of healthy relationships and communication. At the same time adolescents and young adults are increasingly independent from adult supervision and exposed to situations where alcohol, drugs, or other risk factors may be present along with members of the opposite sex. Lack of experience may contribute to failure to recognize certain behaviours as violent or feelings that may indicate they are in an abusive relationship or an inability to respond to coercion. There are increasing concerns about the ability of adolescents to fully understand the implications of consent to sexual activity and wide differences in age of consent for sex across countries. Some countries have limits for adolescents restricting the age gap between sexual partners. Relationships in which there is a larger age gap between the victim and perpetrator involve greater odds of early sexual activity and unwanted sexual behaviours (Oudekerk, Guarnera, & Reppucci, 2014).

Youth tend to only recognize physical acts as violence. The majority of teens in one study reported they did not feel abused, and yet 15.2% reported feeling afraid in their relationship and 27% felt trapped (Ayala et al., 2014). Lack of recognition of other forms of abuse poses a risk for psychological harm, and a potential failure to recognize escalation of violence or the risks of homicide in a relationship. Having a partner or ex-partner constantly nearby, following them or monitoring their communications may be misconstrued as love rather than controlling and/or stalking behaviour. Stalking is a form of psychological violence which is significantly associated with risk of death to females, also known as femicide (Campbell, Webster, & Glass, 2009).

A number of other risk factors have been explored including socioeconomic status, education, gender and sexual preferences. Lower socioeconomic status and education have been noted as risks for perpetration (Foshee et al., 2011). Caution is required, however, in interpreting these indicators.

It has been noted that domestic and dating violence are associated with loss of work, school dropouts and that victims of YDV may have witnessed domestic violence or experienced abuse. Gender differences have been found in motivations for physical violence among college students (Kelley, Edwards, Dardis, & Gidycz, 2014). Men were more likely to become violent if they were jealous or concerned the relationship is about to be ended, while women became violent as a means to stop emotional abuse or in retaliation for being hurt emotionally. Sexual minority groups such as lesbians, gays or transgendered youth experience twice as much physical dating violence and sexual coercion as heterosexual youth and other forms of abuse are also somewhat higher (Dank, Lachman, Zweig, & Yahner, 2014).

RELATIONSHIP AND FAMILY

The attitudes and behaviours of peers and family have an influence on risk or resilience to YDV. Perpetration of YDV is more likely for males and females if family or peers have low expectations of relationships or if peers are involved in violent activities themselves (Dardis et al., 2014).

Males are more likely to perpetrate YDV if they perceive their peers as having attitudes that support or accept violence (Hertzog & Rowley, 2014). Peer social control has a stronger influence on reducing violence with males than females however, while family conflict and school deviance were likely to increase violence risk (Foshee et al., 2011).

There is increasing pressure to find a partner as individuals get older. This comes from peers, family, communities and society. Failure to find intimacy is thought to result in loneliness and isolation. A group of Canadian university students reported "settling" for a less than ideal mate due to fear of potentially being alone (Spielmann et al., 2013). This type of partner selection may place the person at even greater risk for dating violence through a tendency to overlook warning signs or to take action. Youth described a need to belong and a fear of isolation from family and peers if they disclosed abuse (Burton et al., 2013). These feelings may further limit their disclosure of a violent relationship and willingness to remain in the relationship. This may be particularly true if they were raised with low expectations from relationships and how they should be treated. Those with low expectations are more likely to be victimized as well as to be perpetrators (Loeb, Deardorff, & Lahiff, 2014).

COMMUNITY AND SOCIETY

Societal norms can increase risk for YDV. Sexual assault is more likely to occur in a society that emphasizes the importance of sexual prowess while requiring females to be chaste, a community where heavy drinking occurs, and where there are peers who normalize the use of coercion to obtain sex (Littleton, 2014). The community and society may also perpetuate violence through supporting activities, behaviour or messaging that includes violence or gender inequity. The result is normalization of violence and reduced likelihood of reaction or action.

Violence is often normalized through various forms of media which may contribute to adolescent and young adults' failure to recognize violence. Relationships that include coercion, force, intimidation or violence have been portrayed as romantic or acceptable (Friedlander, Connolly, Pepler, & Craig, 2013). Media depicting violence in relationships replaces our understanding of healthy relationships and provides the messages that it is all right to use violence to solve problems in a relationship. For example, the book "Fifty Shades of Grey" portrays controlling and intimidating behaviours and responses by the female character typical of victims of dating violence such as fear and managing their behavior (Bonomi, Altenburger, & Walton, 2013). Despite this it is one of the top best-selling books and the dating violence is unacknowledged. Advertising portrays abused women, music videos show a woman throwing a man over the balcony and video games promote violent acts. Use of aggressive media over time is linked to increased risks for perpetrating dating violence (Friedlander et al., 2013). Adolescents and young adults may not have experience in communicating about sexual preferences or boundaries and may be unable to safely negotiate potentially violent activities. Furthermore, if they have experienced prior abuse they may be further traumatized or unable to respond.

The interaction of these risk factors or levels of influence combine to create unique risks for each individual. They may also provide additive risk or resilience. For instance, the combination of family, community and peer high expectations for positive relationships is more protective against YDV than any single component (Loeb et al., 2014). This highlights the importance of the social-ecological model of violence prevention aimed at multiple levels of risk and influence to prevent violence.

PREVENTION

Prevention of dating violence is essential given the number of adolescents and young adults affected and the magnitude of the consequences they may sustain. Prevention may save lives, prevent long term health problems, and reduce the strain on services. There may also be substantial cost savings. Although cost-benefit data are not available for this population there are some data for adult domestic violence that can provide an idea of the impact of prevention. Domestic violence prevention for only one province in Canada is estimated to generate a net cost-benefit of 54 million dollars in a single year, providing a savings of six dollars for every one dollar spent on prevention (Wells, Boodt, & Emery, 2012).

PRIMARY PREVENTION

Primary prevention in public health means reducing the number of new cases of violence. These activities may focus on changing individual behaviour, altering peer attitudes and family relationships, and working with communities and social programs to reduce risks. The benefits for prevention programs are greatest with the youngest children. Children aged five to nine who received higher quality violence prevention programs had lower levels of both violence perpetration as well as victimization than those receiving programs later in adolescence (Finkelhor, Vanderminden, Turner, Shattuck, & Hamby, 2014).

There are a number of primary prevention programs being developed in an attempt to address the risk factors identified and promote resiliency to the effects of violence. The focus is typically on promoting healthy relationships, changing attitudes and norms related to violence, and recognizing early signs of unhealthy relationships. These skills are important to reduce multiple forms of violence, therefore potentially reducing violence across the lifespan. Prevention programs should include both males and females. This is important, given that dating violence is often mutually initiated (Littleton, 2014), and that males may also be victims. Additionally, male involvement provides messages from peers that do not support violence, communicates more positive norms and builds awareness that both genders play a role.

There has been limited research on the effectiveness of programs in reducing dating violence or risk factors, and variability in measures of effectiveness. Examples of evaluated programs for adolescents include Safe Dates (Sylaska & Walters, 2014) and Making Waves (Cameron et al., 2007). Benefits have included improved awareness of healthy relationships, improved awareness of dating violence and its causes, less acceptance of dating violence, improved communication skills, reduced gender stereotyping and greater awareness of community resources. Programs for college students are now emerging as well. One example is the Stepping Up program (Warthe, Kostouros, Carter-Snell, & Tutty, 2013), adapted from Making Waves to the needs of post-secondary students. Stepping Up has been found to result in increased knowledge and behaviours that promote healthy relationships in undergraduate populations, knowledge of community resources and increased intent to intervene as a bystander intervention.

Many programs focus on change at the individual or relationship level. Examples included victim resistance, bystander intervention or changing perpetrator behaviour. There is a risk with victim focused programs that it may be perceived as victim blaming but at the same time it is important for victims to recognize unhealthy behaviour and risks. Bystander programs focus on increasing the likelihood that people will step in or help the person access resources. While only half of college students surveyed would report victimization or perpetration, more than 80% said they would attempt to intervene if they observed dating violence (Branch, Richards, & Dretsch, 2013). It is also important to discuss ways in which to intervene so the bystander is not placed at more risk (Warthe et al., 2013). Perpetrator programs have had some limited success. An example is the SaFER teen's education program trialed in Emergency with aggressive teens who have a history of alcohol use (Heady & Huntley, 2013). Teens in Emergency were studied if they had both a history of aggression as well as alcohol use. Those who committed moderate levels of violence showed a reduction in violence, although there was limited change in those who committed severe levels of violence. Perpetrator programs also need to incorporate coping skills and ways to decrease dating violence accepting attitudes. Women were found to benefit more from programs incorporating emotion regulation and communication skills, while men needed assistance deconstructing patriarchal values (Shorey, Seavey, Quinn, & Cornelius, 2013).

The community needs to be actively involved in prevention. Schools, sports programs, community centres and other agencies working with adolescents and younger children need to have an awareness of YDV, the risk factors and resources. A multidisciplinary approach is helpful to provide messages about self-esteem, healthy relationships, communications and what to do if they experience violence. Although programs such as these increase awareness about violence and reporting, they do not yet seem to reduce the actual number of YDV episodes (Harvey, Carcia-Moreno, & Butchart, 2007).Change is also needed among the staff and people working with students. They may hold attitudes that support gender inequity, or support practices that pose risks for violence or inequity. An example is freshmen activities on campus that support a rape culture such as chants and hazing activities. Failure of university staff to respond to or limit these activities sends a message of acceptance. Researchers and educators need to work with these populations to challenge their assumptions and support change (Kaukinen, 2014).

Social prevention programs have largely used advocacy campaigns and implementation of laws to deter perpetrators (Harvey et al., 2007). An example is the types of cyberbullying legislation being implemented in many countries. Other important measures are those aimed at reducing gender inequality, changing norms related to violence and improving access to social supports. There is very little information about the effectiveness of such programs however and a need for research and monitoring in this area.

SECONDARY PREVENTION

Secondary prevention is aimed at identifying the violence early and providing effective interventions. Examples of strategies include universal screening, increasing awareness of dangers and safety planning, accessing resources, and provision of positive support.

Universal screening for violence is one strategy for identification. This may be done in multiple settings such as public health clinics, the school health office or in campus services. We have seen that there is an overlap between child abuse and dating violence, and dating violence with later violence. Many health centres have screening in place for women of childbearing years and for children, but very also screen males and teens. Asking about violence at multiple times in multiple places increases the likelihood that abuse will be noted. The outcome of YDV is often substance abuse, depression or other forms of acting out behaviour. An awareness of this link may help professionals delve deeper into what is happening with youth and link them with appropriate resources. There is increasing recognition that collaborative prevention programs need to be developed for multiple types of violence due to the overlap of risk and protective factors (Foshee et al., 2011). Thus prevention programs could be effective at reducing more than one type of violence, such as peer bullying and dating violence. More research is required to identify risk and protective factors in this younger population and the context of the dynamics involved for adolescents and college students (Kaukinen, 2014).

Interventions to reduce violence or its consequences for the adolescents must include information on signs of dating violence, especially given that they may not recognize their fear or controlling behaviours as a sign that they are in an abusive relationship. They also need to know how to assess danger in the relationship and safety planning (Campbell et al., 2009). Safety planning is perhaps a little more complicated than for adults, since it is difficult to relocate the adolescent. The perpetrator will know where they are living (usually with their parents) and may continue to encounter them at school. Professionals can assist with access to protection orders if required and putting mechanisms in place for communication and safety as well as educating peers and victims about where to obtain help.

The victims may need counseling to deal with their abuse, as well as to manage their traumatic symptoms. Victims of YDV tend to disclose more often to peers than to formal service providers (Fry et al., 2014). Peers therefore need information about how to support friends and access assistance. Professionals such as educators and school nurses are often used as resources for peers. These professionals may provide direct support or be able to empower youth peers to provide appropriate referral and support. Easily accessible forms of information are being developed such as smartphone applications outlining signs of abuse and where to obtain help.

There are unique reporting considerations in some instances with adolescent victims of YDV. If there is sexual activity, even consensual, but the victim is under the legal age for consent to sex it may be necessary to report to police. Police may also request forensic evidence collection and a physical examination although victims have the right to refuse these. Professionals need to be aware of their local legislation for reporting, how to obtain health services for victims of dating violence including sexual assault and how to support victims in the interim. Many communities are forming multidisciplinary advisory groups to keep each other informed of resources and to develop common strategies. Members may include teachers, counselors, pastors, coaches, health professionals and emergency service workers.

There are some factors about individuals that improve victims' resilience or ability to recover. People show higher resiliency if there is a sense of autonomy, self-efficacy, and self-esteem, which are related to having expectancies (Loeb et al., 2014). Helping the victim regain control and choice is therefore important. Support from peers and the community aids in recovery and resilience to the consequences of dating violence. Youth may disclose either victimization or perpetration. A negative response to disclosure such as blaming or making them feel guilty is likely to increase distress and risks of trauma symptoms (Edwards, Dardis, Sylaska, & Gidycz, 2014). Telling victims what to do (e.g. to leave) or taking control from them in other ways can also increase their distress (Edwards et al., 2014). Victims who receive positive reactions and support from peers after the first episode are significantly less likely to perpetrate physical and emotional dating violence, and less emotional victimization (Richards, Branch, & Ray, 2014).

Prevention programs, either primary or secondary, are mainly focused on changing attitudes and increasing recognition about YDV. Having multiple points of prevention and intervention, use of interdisciplinary collaboration, and acting at multiple levels of influence (individual, relationship, community, society) is the most effective way to prevent violence (Carnochan, Butchart, Feucht, Mikton, & Shepherd, 2010).

CONCLUSION

Dating violence affects approximately a third of our youth and their risk of dating violence increases with age. The consequences of dating violence are extensive and potentially life changing. Dating violence is often not captured in traditional definitions of domestic or intimate partner violence and yet this is a particularly vulnerable population. It is recognized that dating violence is often perpetrated by both partners and that there are a number of individual, peer, community and social influences on their risk of perpetration. Prevention programs need to reach youth at an early age and incorporate multiple strategies and multiple professionals.

More information is required on factors increasing effectiveness of prevention programs specific to dating violence and across various forms of violence. Collaborative approaches to prevention are important given the significant interactions between dating violence and child abuse, bullying and witnessing domestic violence. The association between adverse childhood experiences and dating violence highlights the need to link child abuse and dating violence programs. The social ecological model has been used as a framework to examine dating violence but also emphasizes the importance of multifaceted and multidisciplinary collaboration among professionals. It is through this collaboration and generation of evidence based strategies that we may be able to impact this silent epidemic affecting our youth and improve the health of future generations.

REFERENCES

Ayala, M. D. C., Molleda, C. B., Rodríguez-Franco, L., Galaz, M. F., Ramiro-Sánchez, T., & Díaz, F. J. R. (2014). Unperceived dating violence among Mexican students. *International Journal of Clinical Health & Psychology, 14*(1), 39-47.

Bonomi, A. E., Altenburger, L. E., & Walton, N. L. (2013). 'Double crap!' abuse and harmed identity in fifty shades of grey. *Journal of Women's Health (15409996), 22*(9), 733-744.

Bonomi, A. E., Anderson, M. L., Nemeth, J., Bartle-Haring, S., Buettner, C., & Schipper, D. (2012). Dating violence victimization across the teen years: Abuse frequency, number of abusive partners, and age at first occurrence. *BMC Public Health, 12*(1), 637-646.

Borofsky, L. A., Kellerman, I., Baucom, B., Oliver, P. H., & Margolin, G. (2013). Community violence exposure and adolescents' school engagement and academic achievement over time. *Psychology of Violence, 3*(4), 381-395.

Branch, K. A., Richards, T. N., & Dretsch, E. C. (2013). An exploratory analysis of college students' response and reporting behavior regarding intimate partner violence victimization and perpetration among their friends. *Journal of Interpersonal Violence, 28*(18), 3386-3399.

Breiding, M. J., Chen, J., & Black, M. C. (2014). *Intimate partner violence in the united states-2010.* Atlanta, GA: National Center for Injury Prevention and Control, Centers for Disease Control and Prevention.

Burton, C. W., Halpern-Felsher, B., Rehm, R. S., Rankin, S., & Humphreys, J. C. (2013). 'It was pretty scary': The theme of fear in young adult women's descriptions of a history of adolescent dating abuse. *Issues in Mental Health Nursing, 34*(11), 803-813.

Cameron, C. A., Byers, S., Miller, S. A., McKay, S. L., St.Pierre, M., & Glenn, S. (2007). *Violence prevention in New Brunswick.*. Fredericton: Status of Women Canada.

Campbell, J., Webster, D. W., & Glass, N. (2009). The danger assessment: Validation of a lethality risk assessment instrument for intimate partner femicide. *Journal of Interpersonal Violence, 24*(4), 653-74.

Carnochan, J., Butchart, A., Feucht, T., Mikton, C., & Shepherd, J. (2010). *Violence prevention: An invitation to intersectoral action.* World Health Organization.

Chiodo, D., Wolfe, D. A., Crooks, C., Hughes, R., & Jaffe, P. (2009). Impact of sexual harassment victimization by peers on subsequent adolescent victimization and adjustment: A longitudinal study. *Journal of Adolescent Health, 45*(3), 246-252.

Crimmins, D. M., & Seigfried-Spellar, K. (2014). Peer attachment, sexual experiences, and risky online behaviors as predictors of sexting behaviors among undergraduate students. *Computers in Human Behavior, 32*, 268-275.

Dank, M., Lachman, P., Zweig, J. M., & Yahner, J. (2014). Dating violence experiences of lesbian, gay, bisexual, and transgender youth. *Journal of Youth and Adolescence, 43*(5), 846-857.

Dardis, C. M., Dixon, K. J., Edwards, K. M., & Turchik, J. A. (2014). An examination of the factors related to dating violence perpetration among young men and women and associated theoretical explanations: A review of the literature. *Trauma, Violence & Abuse, January 13 (electronic).*

Edwards, K. M., Dardis, C. M., Sylaska, K. M., & Gidycz, C. A. (2014). Informal social reactions to college women's disclosure of intimate partner violence: Associations with psychological and relational variables. *Journal of Interpersonal Violence, May 8 (electronic).*

Finkelhor, D., Vanderminden, J., Turner, H., Shattuck, A., & Hamby, S. (2014). Youth exposure to violence prevention programs in a national sample. *Child Abuse & Neglect, 38(4), 677-686.*

Fiorillo, D., Papa, A., & Follette, V., M. (2013). The relationship between child physical abuse and victimization in dating relationships: The role of experiential avoidance. *Psychological Trauma: Theory, Research, Practice & Policy, 5*(6), 562-569.

Foshee, V. A., McNaughton Reyes, H. L., Vivolo-Kantor, A., Basile, K. C., Chang, L., Faris, R., & Ennett, S. T. (2014). Bullying as a longitudinal predictor of adolescent dating violence. *The Journal of Adolescent Health: Official Publication of the Society for Adolescent Medicine, Apr 23 (electronic).*

Foshee, V. A., Reyes, H. L. M., Ennett, S. T., Suchindran, C., Mathias, J. P., Karriker-Jaffe, K., Bauman, K.E, &Benefield, T. S. (2011). Risk and protective factors distinguishing profiles of adolescent peer and dating violence perpetration. *The Journal of Adolescent Health : Official Publication of the Society for Adolescent Medicine, 48*, 344-350.

Fredland, N. M. (2008). Sexual bullying: Addressing the gap between bullying and dating violence. *Advances in Nursing Science, 31*(2), 95-105.

Friedlander, L. J., Connolly, J. A., Pepler, D. J., & Craig, W. M. (2013). Extensiveness and persistence of aggressive media exposure as longitudinal risk factors for teen dating violence. *Psychology of Violence, 3*(4), 310-322.

Fry, D. A., Messinger, A. M., Rickert, V. I., O'Connor, M.K., Palmetto, N., Lessel, H., & Davidson, L. L. (2014). Adolescent relationship violence: Help-seeking and help-giving behaviors among peers. *Journal of Urban Health: Bulletin of the New York Academy of Medicine, 91*(2), 320-334.

Hamby, S., & Turner, H. (2013). Measuring teen dating violence in males and females: Insights from the national survey of children's exposure to violence. *Psychology of Violence, 3*(4), 323-339.

Harvey, A., Carcia-Moreno, C., & Butchart, A. (2007). *Primary prevention of intimate-partner violence and sexual violence: Background paper for WHO expert meeting may 2-3, 2007*. (). Geneva: World Health Organization.

Haynie, D. L., Farhat, T., Brooks-Russell, A., Wang, J., Barbieri, B., & Iannotti, R. J. (2013). Dating violence perpetration and victimization among U.S. adolescents: Prevalence, patterns, and associations with health complaints and substance use. *The Journal of Adolescent Health: Official Publication of the Society for Adolescent Medicine, 53*(2), 194-201.

Heady, C., & Huntley, M. (2013). Brief ED intervention may reduce teen dating violence. *Journal of Pediatric Nursing, 28*(6), 609-610.

Hertzog, J. L., & Rowley, R. L. (2014). My beliefs of my peers' beliefs: Exploring the gendered nature of social norms in adolescent romantic relationships. *Journal of Interpersonal Violence, 29*(2), 348-368.

Holmes, K., & Sher, L. (2013). Dating violence and suicidal behavior in adolescents. *International Journal of Adolescent Medicine & Health, 25*(3), 257-261.

Johnson, M. P., & Leone, J. M. (2005). The differential effects of intimate terrorism and situational couple violence: Findings from the national violence against women survey. *Journal of Family Issues, 26*(3), 322-349.

Kaukinen, C. (2014). Dating violence among college students: The risk and protective factors. *Trauma, Violence & Abuse, Feb 4 (electronic)*.

Keller, P. S., Blincoe, S., Gilbert, L. R., Haak, E. A., & DeWall, C. N. (2014). Sleep deprivation and dating aggression perpetration in female college students: The moderating roles of trait aggression, victimization by partner, and alcohol use. *Journal of Aggression, Maltreatment & Trauma, 23*(4), 351-368.

Kelley, E. L., Edwards, K. M., Dardis, C. M., & Gidycz, C. A. (2014). Motives for physical dating violence among college students: A gendered analysis. *Psychology of Violence,*

Klettke, B., Hallford, D. J., & Mellor, D. J. (2014). Sexting prevalence and correlates: A systematic literature review. *Clinical Psychology Review, 34*(1), 44-53.

Korenis, P., & Billick, S. B. (2014). Forensic implications: Adolescent sexting and cyberbullying. *The Psychiatric Quarterly, 85*(1), 97-101.

Krug, E. G., Dahlberg, L. L., Mercy, J. A., Zwi, A. B., & Lozano, R. (2002). *World report on violence and health*. Geneva, Switzerland: World Health Organization.

Larkin, H., Shields, J. J., & Anda, R. F. (2012). The health and social consequences of adverse childhood experiences (ACE) across the lifespan: An introduction to prevention and intervention in the community. *Journal of Prevention & Intervention in the Community, 40*(4), 263-270.

Lisak, D., & Miller, P. M. (2002). Repeat rape and multiple offending among undetected rapists. *Violence & Victims, 17*(1), 73-84.

Littleton, H. (2014). Interpersonal violence on college campuses: Understanding risk factors and working to find solutions. *Trauma, Violence & Abuse, Jan 30 (electronic)*.

Loeb, A., Deardorff, J., & Lahiff, M. (2014). High expectations across multiple domains, peer norms and physical dating violence among California adolescents. *Journal of Interpersonal Violence, Feb 10 (electronic).*

Mahoney, T. H. (2013). *Police-reported dating violence-2008.* Retrieved May 17, 2014, from http://www.statcan.gc.ca/pub/85-002-x/2010002/article/11242-eng.htm

Manchikanti Gómez, A. (2011). Testing the cycle of violence hypothesis: Child abuse and adolescent dating violence as predictors of intimate partner violence in young adulthood. *Youth & Society, 43*(1), 171-192.

Martsolf, D. S., & Draucker, C. B. (2008). The legacy of childhood sexual abuse and family adversity. *Journal of Nursing Scholarship, 40*(4), 333-340.

McInturff, K. (2013). Preventing violence a good investment. *Herizons, 27*(2), 11-12.

Nahapetyan, L., Orpinas, P., Song, X., & Holland, K. (2014). Longitudinal association of suicidal ideation and physical dating violence among high school students. *Journal of Youth & Adolescence, 43*(4), 629-640.

Orpinas, P., Hsieh, H., Song, X., Holland, K., & Nahapetyan, L. (2013). Trajectories of physical dating violence from middle to high school: Association with relationship quality and acceptability of aggression. *Journal of Youth & Adolescence, 42*(4), 551-565.

Oudekerk, B. A., Guarnera, L. A., & Reppucci, N. D. (2014). Older opposite-sex romantic partners, sexual risk, and victimization in adolescence. *Child Abuse & Neglect Apr 11 (electronic).*

Pattishall, A., E., Cruz, M., & Spector, N., D. (2011). Intimate partner violence, mental health disorders, and sexually transmitted infections: Important screening opportunities for pediatric healthcare providers. *Current Opinion in Pediatrics, 23*(6), 674-683.

Population Reference Bureau. (2013). *The world's youth: 2013 data sheet.* Washington, DC: Population Reference Bureau.

Pujazon-Zazik, M., Manasse, S. M., & Orrell-Valente, J. (2012). Adolescents' self-presentation on a teen dating web site: A risk-content analysis. *The Journal of Adolescent Health: Official Publication of the Society for Adolescent Medicine, 50*(5), 517-520.

Richards, T. N., Branch, K. A., & Ray, K. (2014). The impact of parental and peer social support on dating violence perpetration and victimization among female adolescents: A longitudinal study. *Violence & Victims, 29*(2), 317-331.

Shorey, R. C., Seavey, A. E., Quinn, E., & Cornelius, T. L. (2013). Partner-specific anger management as a mediator of the relation between mindfulness and female perpetrated dating violence. *Psychology of Violence, 4*(1), 51-64.

Simon, T. R., Miller, S., Gorman-Smith, D., Orpinas, P., & Sullivan, T. (2010). Physical dating violence norms and behavior among sixth-grade students from four U.S. sites. *Journal of Early Adolescence, 30*(3), 395-409.

Sinha, M. (2012). *Family violence in canada: A statistical profile, 2010.* (No. 85-002-X). Ottawa, ON: Statistics Canada.

Steeves, V. (2014). *Sexuality and romantic relationships in the digital age.* (). Ottawa, ON: MediaSmarts.

Straus, M., & Gozjolko, K. (2014). 'Intimate terrorism' and gender differences in injury of dating partners by male and female university students. *Journal of Family Violence, 29*(1), 51-65.

Sylaska, K., & Walters, A. (2014). Testing the extent of the gender trap: College students' perceptions of and reactions to intimate partner violence. *Sex Roles, 70*(3), 134-145.

Thompson, M. P. (2014). Risk and protective factors for sexual aggression and dating violence: Common themes and future directions. *Trauma, Violence & Abuse,* Retrieved from
http://search.ebscohost.com/login.aspx?direct=true&AuthType=ip,url,cookie,uid&db=cmedm&AN=24472793&site=ehost-live

VandeWeerd, C., Corvin, J., Coulter, M., Perkins, E., Telford, R., Yalcin, A., & Yegidis, B. (2014). A preliminary investigation of risks for adverse outcomes of relationship seeking on social network sites (SNS): A descriptive study of women over 50 seeking relationships on MySpace in hillsborough county, florida. *Journal of Women & Aging, 26*(2), 127-145.

Warthe, D. G., Kostouros, P., Carter-Snell, C., & Tutty, L. M. (2013). Stepping up: A peer-to-peer dating violence prevention project on a postsecondary campus. *International Journal of Child, Youth and Family Studies, 4*(1), 100-118.

Wells, L., Boodt, C., & Emery, H. (2012). Preventing domestic violence in alberta: A cost savings perspective. *The School of Public Policy, 5*(17), Aug 10, 2012.

Wigderson, S., & Lynch, M. (2013). Cyber- and traditional peer victimization: Unique relationships with adolescent well-being. *Psychology of Violence, 3*(4), 297-309.

World Health Organization. (2010). *Preventing intimate partner and sexual violence against women: Taking action and generating evidence.* Geneva: World Health Organization.

Zhang, T., Hoddenbaugh, J., McDonald, S., & Scrim, K. (2012). *An estimation of the economic impact of spousal violence in canada, 2009.* (No. rr12-07-e). Ottawa, ON: Department of Justice Canada.

Zweig, J. M., Lachman, P., Yahner, J., & Dank, M. (2013). Correlates of cyber dating abuse among teens. *Journal of Youth and Adolescence. Nov 7 (electronic).*

BIOGRAPHICAL INFORMATION

Dr. Catherine Carter-Snell is a faculty member with the School of Nursing and Midwifery at Mount Royal University in Canada. She is certified as a sexual assault nurse examiner and Emergency nurse with years of clinical practice working with victims of trauma in Emergency and Intensive Care. She frequently provides expert court testimony related to sexual violence. Dr. Carter-Snell has been teaching online post-baccalaureate courses to professionals who work with victims of violence since 1998. Her research focus is on prevention of violence and early effective intervention to limit the consequences of violence. Particular interests include improvement of sexual assault services for men and women especially in rural areas, implementation and evaluation of dating violence prevention programs for university students, injury identification and mental health consequences of violence.

In: Overcoming Domestic Violence
Editors: Myra F. Taylor, Julie Ann Pooley et al.

ISBN: 978-1-63321-956-4
© 2015 Nova Science Publishers, Inc.

Chapter 5

DATING VIOLENCE AMONG SEXUAL-MINORITY YOUTH (SMY) IN THE WESTERN WORLD

Martin Blais, Martine Hébert, Jesse Gervais and Félix-Antoine Bergeron*

Université du Québec à Montréal, Canada

ABSTRACT

While several studies have documented the prevalence of dating violence in the adolescent population, data remain scarce on sexual-minority youth (SMY). The most studied forms of dating violence are psychological/emotional, physical and sexual. Overall, dating violence estimates among SMY range from 8% to 89% for victimization and from 4% to 59% for perpetration. Psychological and emotional are the most prevalent forms of dating violence. Threats of outing by partners, a form of dating violence unique to SMY but rarely assessed, vary from 4% to 29%. SMY face the same risk factor as youth from the general population regarding dating violence vulnerability. However, heterosexism and minority stress contribute to increase SMY vulnerability to dating violence through internalized heterosexism and shame, sexual identity concealment, lack of external support and isolation within the relationship, reluctance to seek help because of fear of exposure, and reduced exposure to sexual-minority survivor role models. Dating violence prevention among SMY must take into account both general and SMY-specific risk factors. Providing tools to SMY to recognize and disclose dating violence, targeting specific protective and risk factors such as heterosexism and minority stress, increasing the capacities of sexual-minority communities, training domestic violence resources staff to sexual-minority specific issues are promising avenues for improving dating violence intervention among SMY.

Keywords: Dating violence, sexual-minority youth, heterosexism, internalized heterosexism, minority stress

---

* Corresponding author: Dr. Martin Blais, Department of sexology, Université du Québec à Montréal, Montreal, Canada, H3C 3P8, Tel: 1 (514) 987-3000 poste 4031, Email: blais.martin@uqam.ca.

INTRODUCTION

Rates of victimization in the context of intimate relationships are high among the general youth population (Foshee & McNaughton Reyes, 2012) and dating violence is now recognized as a significant public health concern (Baker, Buick, Kim, Moniz, & Nava, 2012; Blosnich & Bossarte, 2009; Carvalho, Lewis, Derlega, Winstead, & Viggiano, 2011; Welles, Corbin, Rich, Reed, & Raj, 2011). Data remain scarce, however, on dating violence among sexual-minority youth (SMY), such as lesbian, gay, bisexual, transidentified, queer and questioning (LGBTQ) youths. The invisibility or trivialization of intimate partner violence (IPV) and dating violence in sexual-minority communities may be fueled by factors such as general cultural taboos regarding IPV (Krug, Mercy, Dahlberg, & Zwi, 2002) and same-sex relationships (Banks & Fedewa, 2012; Woodford, Luke, Grogan-Kaylor, Fredriksen-Goldsen, & Gutierrez, 2012), and by gender stereotypes such as "girls don't hit other girls" or "only men are violent" (Hassouneh & Glass, 2008; Ristock, 2003). Moreover, well-accepted models suggesting that power differential is based on gender differences alone result in the belief that only females can be victims and only males can be perpetrators (Brown, 2008; Kaschak, 2001). As such, individuals involved in IPV are "double closeted", as they are "entombed in both the same-gender identity and in their personal pain of abuse" (McClennen, 2005, p. 150).

This chapter pursues three main goals. First, we describe the Western scholarly literature regarding the prevalence of dating violence among sexual-minority youth (SMY). Second, we review the main risk factors for victimization and perpetration of dating violence among teenagers, and describe risk factors specific to sexual minorities. Third, we discuss issues and recommendations for dating violence prevention for SMY. We conclude by reviewing the major pitfalls in dating violence research among SMY, and make recommendations for future investigations.

PREVALENCE OF DATING VIOLENCE

Disclosure of interpersonal violence such as dating violence is a complex process and youth may be reluctant to talk about such experiences to their peers, parents or teachers (Close, 2005; Sylaska & Edwards, 2014). Several studies have documented, however, the prevalence of dating violence in the general population of adolescents and scholarly data converge in attesting that a significant proportion of teenagers experience violence in the context of their early romantic relationships. Representative studies among the general adolescent population estimate that about a third of the students experienced some form of victimization in a romantic relationship over a 12 or 18-month period (Halpern, Oslak, Young, Martin, & Kupper, 2001; Traoré, Riberdy, & Pica, 2012). In recent Canadian data, girls reported higher rates of psychological (27%) and sexual (15%) dating victimization compared to boys (respectively 17% and 5%), while boys were slightly more likely to experience physical dating victimization (13%) compared to girls (11%; Traoré et al., 2012). The NEXT Generation Health Study conducted in 2009-2010 revealed that boys and girls reported different rates of psychological and physical violence over a 12-month period: 40% of girls reported victimization and perpetration, while 27% of boys disclosed victimization and 19% reported perpetration (Haynie et al., 2013).

Data on SMY suggest that they experience higher rates of dating violence compared to heterosexual teenagers. Probabilistic school-based surveys from the United States of America (USA) showed that 8% to 40% of SMY experienced physical dating victimization over a 12-month period (Kann et al., 2011). Self-identified SMY were more likely to experience physical dating violence victimization compared to heterosexual youths, with few differences found among homosexual, bisexual and questioning youths. When taking into account partners' gender, SMY reporting partners from both genders were particularly at risk for physical dating violence.

Among SMY aged 12 to 21 years in same-sex relationships from the National Longitudinal Study of Adolescent Health, Halpern, Young, Waller, Martin, & Kupper (2004) estimated the rate of psychological dating violence at 21% and the rate of physical violence at 11% over an 18-month period. SMY females were more likely to report at least one form of dating violence compared to SMY males. Contrariwise, Martin-Storey (2014) found that SMY males were more likely to suffer from dating violence than SMY females when sexual orientation was assessed by sexual partners' gender. When sexual orientation was measured based on self-identification, bisexual females reported higher rates of dating violence than bisexual males while the opposite was true for questioning youths.

Dank, Lachman, Zweig, and Yahner (2014) assessed rates of various forms of dating violence victimization among self-identified heterosexual and SMY aged 12 to 19 years old. As in other studies, they found much higher rates of dating violence among SMY compared to heterosexual youth: psychological dating violence (59% in SMY vs. 46% in heterosexuals), physical dating violence (43% vs. 29%), and sexual dating violence (23% vs. 12%). SMY also reported higher perpetration rates of psychological dating violence (37% vs. 25%), physical dating violence (33% vs. 20%), and sexual dating violence (4% vs. 2%) compared to heterosexual youth, although the difference was not statistically significant for the latter.

Transidentified individuals have generally been neglected when studying dating violence. Dank et al. (2014) found higher rates of dating violence victimization among transidentified youths, with about 10% experiencing physical dating violence, and about 60% reporting psychological and/or sexual dating violence. Similarly, they reported higher rates of perpetration for physical (59%) and sexual (18%), but not psychological (29%), dating violence.

Threatening the partner with telling others about their sexual minority status (i.e. "outing" the partner) is an important and unique form of dating violence among sexual minorities (Duke & Davidson, 2009), although rarely taken into account. In a community sample, Freedner, Freed, Yang, and Austin (2002) found high rates of the threat of outing among self-identified bisexual youth (Males = 29%, Females = 13%) compared to self-identified homosexual youth (Males = 7%, Females = 4%).

RISK FACTORS ASSOCIATED WITH DATING VIOLENCE

In the last decade, several studies have documented risk factors associated with dating violence among adolescents as well as factors that are specific and unique to sexual minorities.

General Risk Factors for Dating Violence

Studies exploring possible risk factors associated with dating violence have assessed socio-demographics, individual (personal and interpersonal), environmental (family, peer group, community) and contextual factors related to the relationship itself (for a review, see Vézina & Hébert, 2007). The risk factors most strongly associated with dating violence for both boys and girls include childhood behavior problems, family conflict, parental violence, witnessing interparental violence, dropping out of school, a history of child sexual abuse, having peers who experience dating violence, deviant peer affiliation and other forms of violence and victimization such as physical intimidation by peers, relational aggression by peers, Internet harassment (both sexual and non-sexual), sexual harassment and bias-motivated attack (Banyard, Arnold, & Smith, 2000; DiLillo, Giuffre, Tremblay, & Peterson, 2001; Foshee & McNaughton Reyes, 2012; Hamby, Finkelhor, & Turner, 2012; Hébert, Lavoie, Vitaro, McDuff, & Tremblay, 2008; Wekerle et al., 2009).

Studies show that SMY are more vulnerable to most of these risk factors. Meta-analyses have found that SMY were more likely to report sexual abuse and parental abuse (Friedman et al., 2011) and substance use (Marshal et al., 2008). Retrospective studies conducted with adult samples suggest that sexual minorities are also more likely to report witnessing inter-parental violence (Andersen & Blosnich, 2013; Roberts, Austin, Corliss, Vandermorris, & Koenen, 2010). SMY also exhibit greater school difficulties, such as missing school because of fear (Friedman et al., 2011), unexcused absences and a lower sense of school belongingness (Robinson & Espelage, 2011), a lower intention to pursue any post-secondary education (Kosciw, Greytak, Diaz, & Bartkiewicz, 2010) and, among male SMY, lower grades and higher course failure (Pearson, Muller, & Wilkinson, 2007).

SMY-Specific Risk Factors for Dating Violence

Homonegativity is widespread globally and in several countries same-sex relationships are still illegal. Even in those parts of the world where homosexuality has been decriminalized, such as most of the Western world, same-sex relationships and gay marriages are still unrecognized under the law or heatedly debated (Kelley, 2001; Stulhofer & Rimac, 2009). This social and cultural environment characterized by heterosexism and homonegativity must be taken into account when considering the experiences of sexual minorities (Balsam & Szymanski, 2005).

Heterosexism is "an ideological system that denies, denigrates, and stigmatizes any non-heterosexual form of behavior, identity, relationship, or community […] manifested both in societal customs and institutions […] and in individual attitudes and behaviors" (Herek, 1990, pp. 316–317). Heterosexism manifests itself at the cultural level through political, legal and religious systems that condemn same-sex sexual behavior and oppose legal recognition of same-sex couples or parents. Homophobia initially described an irrational fear, intolerance and hatred of homosexuality (Weinberg, 1972) or any negative feelings or thoughts about homosexuals or homosexuality (Bell, 1989). Today, both homophobia and homonegativity broadly describe prejudice and stigmatization based on nonconformity to cultural expectations regarding gender identity or sexual orientation, encompassing specific forms of gender and sexuality oppression such as biphobia, lesbophobia, transphobia, transqueerphobia, etc. (conceptual and measurement issues are discussed in Herek, Kimmel, Amaro, & Melton, 1991; Herek, 1990; O'Donohue & Caselles, 1993).

Heterosexism and homonegativity impact both mainstream communities and LGBTQ communities. In mainstream communities, heterosexism and homonegativity may incur social tolerance, or apathy toward the challenges faced by the LGBTQ communities (Duke & Davidson, 2009), such as a higher vulnerability to victimization, the legal recognition of same-sex relationships or same-sex IPV. They send the message that non-heterosexual relationships are unwelcome, undervalued or illegitimate, contributing to their stigmatization and marginalization (Barrett & St. Pierre, 2013). In the social and cultural context of heterosexism and homophobia, sexual and gender nonconforming individuals experience minority stress, a chronic form of stress aroused by difficult social experiences such as stigmatization targeting their minority status (Meyer, 1995, 2003). While people who object to homosexuality on religious or cultural grounds may be unaware of the inadvertent detrimental effects that their views can have on sexual-minority individuals, these views still contribute to legitimate homophobic prejudices and behaviors.

Not only may SMY suffer from the same forms of victimization as the general youth population, but they also experience specific prejudice based on sexual orientation (Blais et al., 2013; Chamberland, Richard, & Bernier, 2013; Katz-Wise & Hyde, 2012). This includes exclusion, rejection, humiliation, damage to reputation, cyberbullying, physical violence, sexual harassment and coercion, threats or coercion to do things against their will, and vandalism of personal goods. Such heterosexism and homophobia increase the level of stress in sexual-minority individuals that affects their relationships.

Although data on dating violence among SMY remain scarce, both theoretical perspectives and empirical findings on sexual-minority adults contribute to the identification of 5 main mechanisms through which heterosexism increases the vulnerability of SMY to dating violence: (1) internalized heterosexism and shame, (2) sexual identity concealment, (3) lack of support and isolation within the relationship, (4) reluctance to seek help and (5) reduced exposure to sexual-minority survivor role models.

Internalized heterosexism and shame: Heterosexism and homonegativity convey negative messages toward non-exclusive heterosexuality, same-sex relationships and sexual minority lifestyles. The process of internalizing these negative messages and the resulting self-loathing of sexual-minority people related to being a sexual minority person (Szymanski, Kashubeck-West, & Meyer, 2008) is called "internalized homophobia", "internalized homonegativity" or "internalized heterosexism" (for a historical overview, see Szymanski et al., 2008). Internalized heterosexism increases the likelihood of both IPV victimization and perpetration (Balsam & Szymanski, 2005; Carvalho et al., 2011; Edwards & Sylaska, 2013; Stephenson, Rentsch, Salazar, & Sullivan, 2011). As internalized heterosexism is associated with lower self-esteem (Blais, Gervais, & Hébert, 2014), isolation and shame about sexuality (Gillum & DiFulvio, 2012), it may lead SMY to believe that they are somehow defective and deserve to be abused (Balsam & Szymanski, 2005). From the perpetrator's perspective, IPV may be an attempt to deal with the internal conflict related to sexual minority status through externalization (Mendoza, 2011). As Allen and Leventhal (1999, p. 78) argued, sexual-minority dating violence perpetrators "have at their disposal the weapons of their own and their partner's internalized oppression to help erase their partner's sense of pride".

Internalized heterosexism is also associated with factors that have been linked to IPV and dating violence. Examples of potential mediators in this relationship are substance use and abuse (Klostermann, Kelley, Milletich, & Mignone, 2011; Lewis, Milletich, Kelley, & Woody, 2012), psychological distress (Szymanski, Chung, & Balsam, 2001; Szymanski & Chung, 2002), relationship satisfaction (Balsam & Szymanski, 2005) and stress (Otis, 2006). In Balsam and Szymanski's (2005) study, relationship satisfaction fully mediated the impact of internalized homophobia on IPV in women's same-sex relationships. Individuals with higher internalized heterosexism experience more distress, discord on sexual-minority specific issues with their partner or substances to cope with stress, all of which can lead to IPV. As they also report lower levels of social support and connection to the LGBT community (Herek, Cogan, Gillis, & Glunt, 1997; McGregor et al., 2001; Szymanski et al., 2001), they are also deprived from a protective factor against dating violence (Wright, 2012).

Sexual identity concealment: Knowing that one's identity is devalued and potentially exposed to hostile talk and attitudes leads to a fear of being outed and stigmatized (Quinn & Chaudoir, 2009). Accordingly, the degree of SMY outness or concealment about their sexuality can have multiple impacts on dating violence vulnerability. The stress of staying closeted can negatively affect the quality of same-sex relationships and exacerbate other relationship problems such as IPV (Balsam & Szymanski, 2005; Ossana, 2000). Carvalho et al. (2011) suggested that individuals with higher stigma consciousness are more likely to be involved in a violent relationship and to keep the abuse silent. The abuser may also threaten to disclose their closeted partner's sexual orientation to others, including family members and friends (Duke & Davidson, 2009). Peers may play a crucial supportive role during adolescence and the more there is at stake for closeted SMY (for instance, fear of losing peer support), the more likely they can be to tolerate abuse from their partner. As sexual identity integration and acceptance is a developmental process that takes time, the younger the SMY, the more vulnerable they can be to internalized heterosexism and sexual identity concealment.

Edwards and Sylaska (2013) also found that sexual identity concealment was significantly and positively related to physical perpetration of same-sex partner violence. Some studies, however, did not reveal a significant relationship between outness and IPV among sexual-minority adults (Balsam & Szymanski, 2005; Carvalho et al., 2011). Balsam and Szymanski (2005) suggested that a discrepancy between, or discord over partners' level of outness may be the crucial element influencing the relationship rather than outness itself.

Lack of support and isolation within the relationship: Same-sex couples often lack cultural or external validation and support for their relationship (Clarke, Burgoyne, & Burns, 2013; Connolly, 2004). This might result from hiding their relationship, internalized heterosexism –which impairs the ability to make significant connections with other sexual-minority individuals (Balsam, 2001), or from not receiving social affirmations that they should stay together (Duke & Davidson, 2009). Thus, sexual minorities often depend on their partners for information on the LGBTQ culture (Ristock, 2003) and have to rely on their partner as their sole source for support and validation (West, 2002).

As West (2002) observed, while a sense of fusion may serve as a buffer against adverse experiences outside the relationship, it may impair the sense of independence within the relationship and transform disagreements into threats of rejection. For example, in Gillum and DiFulvio's (2012) study, participants in same-sex relationships stated that when the "assumed connection" was not present, tension may arise and lead to violence. For the victims, dependence on their perpetrators can make it more difficult to leave the abusive relationship. For the perpetrators, isolation within the relationship can create a situation of heightened emotional intensity and conflict that may lead to episodes of dating violence.

Reluctance to seek help: Reluctance to seek help is often reported among victims of abusive relationships. The ability to seek help is sustained or impaired by individual, interpersonal and sociocultural factors (Liang, Goodman, Tummala-Narra, & Weintraub, 2005). Specific factors have been identified as crucial among sexual minorities. At the individual level, internalized heterosexism, sexual identity concealment, and stigma anticipation can fuel the fear of being exposed (Balsam & Szymanski, 2005) and not taken seriously (Gillum & DiFulvio, 2012).

At the interpersonal level, anticipated or experienced homophobic revictimisation by service providers and law authorities and the fear of being outed, either by the partner as retaliation or by the service providers as a consequence of seeking help, may prevent SMY from seeking services and support (Duke & Davidson, 2009; Gillum & DiFulvio, 2012). For SMY, reporting dating violence to authorities can result in having to disclose their same-sex relationship to their parents (Gillum & DiFulvio, 2012).

In close-knit communities, community members often know one another and couples often share the same friends (Duke & Davidson, 2009). This proximity can pose several obstacles to seeking help, including relationship breakups threatening the circle of friends, the difficulty for survivors to convince their friends that a mutual friend or member of their own community is abusive and the insistence of friends that there must be visible indications of abuse (e.g., bruises; (Duke & Davidson, 2009). For example, Hassouneh and Glass (2008) reported how describing female intimate violence as a "cat fight" reflects the view that women's violence is less serious and dangerous than men's, resulting in friends witnessing violence without taking it seriously.

At the cultural level, agencies, programs and laws have been described as inadequate in addressing sexual-minority specific issues. Surveying professionals affiliated with domestic violence prevention and/or intervention networks in Los Angeles (USA), Ford, Slavin, Hilton, and Holt (2013) noted low levels of staff training on sexual-minority IPV, failure to assess clients' sexual orientation or gender identity at intake, and agency/program policies or practices inattentive to LGBTQ-specific needs. Guadalupe-Diaz and Yglesias (2013) found that while LGB residents of Central Florida (USA) have legal protection under domestic violence law, their survey participants described the law to be non-inclusive, heterosexist or unresponsive to same-gender domestic violence.

Reduced exposure to sexual-minority survivor role models: Despite the increasing visibility of sexual-minority issues and same-sex relationships in the public sphere (Adam, 2003; Chamie & Mirkin, 2011; Fassin, 2001; Liebler, Schwartz, & Harper, 2009), this coverage has done little to challenge hegemonic heteronormative definitions of marriage (Liebler et al., 2009). Living in a heterosexist environment can pressure sexual minorities to maintain a positive image of same-sex relationships for the prospect of future acceptance into society (West, 2002). This can fuel denial of domestic violence by community members, activists, perpetrators and victims to protect the community image (Duke & Davidson, 2009; West, 2002). In this context, sexual-minority survivor role models are still mostly invisible. Balsam and Szymanski (2005) suggested that the reduced visibility of same-sex relationships and exposure to role models may create a sense that victimized partners lack other options, making the victim more likely to tolerate abuse from their partner.

ISSUES AND RECOMMENDATIONS FOR DATING VIOLENCE PREVENTION FOR SMY

Victimization in the context of romantic relationships has been linked to several pervasive consequences on mental, physical as well as sexual health in youth. Examples of such outcomes are post-traumatic stress and dissociation symptoms, depression, anxiety, suicidal thoughts, poorer educational achievements and unprotected sexual activities (Ackard, Eisenberg, & Neumark-Sztainer, 2007; Banyard & Cross, 2008; Brown et al., 2009; Howard, Debnam, Wang, & Gilchrist, 2012), among SMY (Gillum & DiFulvio, 2014; Hipwell et al., 2013). The high prevalence of dating violence and its negative outcomes have motivated the implementation of several prevention initiatives. The following section provides a brief overview of dating violence prevention programs designed for the general youth population and highlights the SMY-specific issues to be considered.

DATING VIOLENCE PREVENTION PROGRAMS FOR YOUTH

Prevention programs are often described as either based on a universal approach or a selective approach. Universal prevention programs are mostly conducted in school settings and aim to change attitudes and reduce myths related to dating violence (Vézina & Hébert, 2007). A recent meta-analysis of 38 studies selected from strict methodological criteria shows no convincing evidence that the programs reduce dating violence or that they improve the attitudes, behaviors, and skills of the participants (Fellmeth, Heffernan, Nurse, Habibula, & Sethi, 2013). The results only showed a slight increase in participants' knowledge concerning dating violence and relationships. Still, promising programs share characteristics such as an ecosystemic framework, the involvement of several actors (parents, other significant adults, schools, and community organizations), practitioner training, a longer duration of the curriculum and a variety of strategies (poster contests, theatrical plays), including activities aimed at parents. Such programs are associated with changes in behaviors, dating violence norms, gender-role norms, and awareness of community services (Foshee et al., 2004).

Issues for the Prevention of Dating Violence among SMY

Dating violence prevention initiatives designed for SMY must also include the following features: a) raising awareness, b) targeting LGBTQ-specific protective and risk factors, c) building community capacities, d) making available LGBTQ-specific resources and services, and e) promoting inclusivity and sensitivity among domestic violence resource staff.

Raising awareness: The sexual-minority community needs to be specifically targeted for prevention efforts regarding IPV, given that they may not recognize dating violence as an issue that concerns or relates to them and consequently may not recognize the signs of violence in their relationship (Kulkin, Williams, Borne, de la Bretonne, & Laurendine, 2007). Furthermore, it is important to dispel harmful stereotypes in same-sex relationships, define healthy relationships and raise awareness about the warning signs of IPV, particularly among those who are new to same-sex relationships (Bornstein, Fawcett, Sullivan, Senturia, & Shiu-

Thornton, 2006; Ristock, 2003). Publishing articles about same-sex IPV in bulletins, newsletters or community web sites can contribute to these goals (Turell, Herrmann, Hollander, & Galletly, 2012).

Targeting LGBTQ-specific protective and risk factors: SMY should be supported in identifying and recognizing the negative impact of heterosexism on their life and in becoming empowered to fight the heterosexist culture and the negative stereotypes about sexual minorities (Szymanski, 2005). Interventions should aim at developing a sense of personal and social power and promote egalitarian relationships (Szymanski, 2005) as well as building skills to handle conflicts and to seek help (Cornelius & Resseguie, 2007). Professionals should support SMY in their coming out process, help them identify the potential gains and costs of disclosing their sexual orientation, and work with family members to accept and support LGBT youth (Crisp & McCave, 2007).

Building community capacities: To increase the community response to sexual-minority dating violence, it is necessary to change norms regarding conflict management and the use of violence among same-sex partners, build capacities within LGBTQ communities and reinforce collaborative ties with external domestic violence resources (Bornstein et al., 2006; Kulkin et al., 2007; Todahl, Linville, Bustin, Wheeler, & Gau, 2009; Turell et al., 2012). Strategies such as facilitating connection to, and responsibility for, each other's neighbors (Todahl et al., 2009) or visiting community leaders to discuss IPV incidents (Turell et al., 2012) can help build what Todahl et al. (2009) called "cooperative protection" among community members. Community leaders need to be proactive in implementing such initiatives.

Making available LGBTQ-specific resources and services: In the design of prevention material and media approaches, using representations and pictures of same-sex couples, posting LGBTQ friendly symbols (such as the rainbow flag), and relying on non-heterosexual or gender neutral vocabulary is recommended (Duke & Davidson, 2009; Todahl et al., 2009). Organizations should also increase the availability and accessibility of LGBT-specific services, such as 24-hour hotlines, legal advocacy, counseling, shelters and safe housing for LGBT people, etc. (Bornstein et al., 2006; Duke & Davidson, 2009; Ford et al., 2013).

Promoting inclusivity and sensitivity among domestic violence resource staff: Inclusivity and sensitivity may promote the disclosure of victimization by SYM (Kulkin et al., 2007). Practitioners must learn to create a safe space for survivors of same-sex dating violence and for SMY in various stages of the coming out process, being careful not to re-victimize or reinforce the stigma they already experience (Crisp & McCave, 2007; Duke & Davidson, 2009). To achieve this goal, training programs should aim at developing a comprehensive understanding of the barriers and tools unique to the LGBT communities (Duke & Davidson, 2009; Todahl et al., 2009). Inclusivity and sensitivity should be promoted by using non-heterosexist language (e.g., partner instead of boyfriend/girlfriend; Duke & Davidson, 2009) and avoiding dichotomies such as "us and them", "victim (women)/perpetrator (men)" or "passive/active" (Duke & Davidson, 2009; Ristock, 2003; Todahl et al., 2009). To achieve such goals, resources must be developed and professionals from all types of agencies on LGBT dating violence must be trained (Ford et al., 2013).

CONCLUSION

Violence within SMY romantic relationships is an important issue. Overall, dating violence among SMY ranges from 8% to 89% for victimization and from 4% to 59% for perpetration, psychological/emotional being the most reported form and the sexual form being the least prevalent. Threats of outing by partners, a form of dating violence unique to SMY but rarely assessed, vary from 4% to 29%. While SMY face the same risk factor as youth from the general population regarding dating violence, heterosexism and minority stress contribute to increase their vulnerability through internalized heterosexism and shame, sexual identity concealment, lack of external support and isolation within the relationship, reluctance to seek help, and reduced exposure to sexual-minority survivor role models. Promising avenues for improving dating violence prevention and intervention among SMY have been identified, such as providing tools to SMY to recognize and disclose dating violence, targeting LGBTQ-specific protective and risk factors such as heterosexism, building the skills of sexual-minority communities, making available sexual-minority-specific resources and services, and promoting inclusivity and sensitivity among domestic violence resource staff.

While empirical reports provide relevant information as to the specific challenges experienced by SMY youth, existing studies present shortcomings. Issues related to sampling and representation need to be considered, as several studies rely on small or non-probabilistic samples, precluding the possibility of exploring the specificities among SMY. Some sexual-minority groups, such as bisexual youth and those questioning their sexual orientation or gender identity, are particularly understudied, yet potentially facing increased vulnerability to dating violence because of the specific stressors they face (e.g. biphobia, transphobia). Providing a more comprehensive account of the diversity of experiences among SMY through larger, probabilistic samples will support designing better intervention and prevention initiatives for SMY subgroups.

Several measurement issues were also identified, some precluding cross-study comparisons. First, sexual orientation assessment varies considerably across studies. Some studies consider partners' gender, while others pinpoint self-identification or sexual attraction. Second, studies exploring dating violence derive prevalence estimates from different definitions, measures and time frame (e.g. 12 or 18 months). Third, in most studies, threats of outing, the sole form of dating violence specific to SMY, are not assessed. Finally, the potential impacts of social stigma and prejudice on victimization reporting and denial need to be assessed.

While scholarly reports have begun to ascertain the issues confronting SMY in romantic relationships and possible victimization, clearly future investigation is needed to better understand dating violence in SMY. Hopefully, the next decade will see a clear research agenda unfold and the design and implementation of intervention and prevention services that can adequately address the needs of SMY.

ACKNOWLEDGMENT

This work was supported by Canadian Institutes of Health Research (www.cihr-irsc.gc.ca) grant FRN: 103944.

REFERENCES

Ackard, D. M., Eisenberg, M. E. & Neumark-Sztainer, D. (2007). Long-term impact of adolescent dating violence on the behavioral and psychological health of male and female youth. *The Journal of Pediatrics*, *151*(5), 476–481. doi:10.1016/j.jpeds.2007.04.034.

Adam, B. D. (2003). The Defense of Marriage Act and American exceptionalism: The "gay marriage" panic in the United States. *Journal of the History of Sexuality*, *12(2)*, 259–276.

Allen, C. & Leventhal, B. (1999). History, culture, and identity: What makes GLBT battering different. In B. Leventhal & S. Lundy (Eds.), *Same-sex domestic violence: Strategies for change* (73–81). Thousand Oaks: Sage Publications.

Andersen, J. P. & Blosnich, J. (2013). Disparities in adverse childhood experiences among sexual minority and heterosexual adults: results from a multi-state probability-based sample. *PloS One*, *8*(1), e54691. doi:10.1371/journal.pone.0054691

Baker, N. L., Buick, J. D., Kim, S. R., Moniz, S. & Nava, K. L. (2012). Lessons from Examining Same-Sex Intimate Partner Violence. *Sex Roles*, *69*(3-4), 182–192. doi:10.1007/s11199-012-0218-3.

Balsam, K. F. (2001). Nowhere to Hide. *Women & Therapy*, *23*(3), 25–37. doi:10.1300/J015v23n03_03.

Balsam, K. F. & Szymanski, D. M. (2005). Relationship Quality and Domestic Violence in Women's Same-Sex Relationships: the Role of Minority Stress. *Psychology of Women Quarterly*, *29*(3), 258–269. doi:10.1111/j.1471-6402.2005.00220.x

Banks, J. R. & Fedewa, A. L. (2012). Counselors' Attitudes Toward Domestic Violence in Same-Sex Versus Opposite-Sex Relationships. *Journal of Multicultural Counseling and Development*, *40*(4), 194–205. doi:10.1002/j.2161-1912.2012.00017.x

Banyard, V. L., Arnold, S. & Smith, J. (2000). Childhood Sexual Abuse and Dating Experiences of Undergraduate Women. *Child Maltreatment*, *5*(1), 39–48. doi:10.1177/1077559500005001005

Banyard, V. L. & Cross, C. (2008). Consequences of teen dating violence: understanding intervening variables in ecological context. *Violence against Women*, *14*(9), 998–1013. doi:10.1177/1077801208322058

Barrett, B. J. & St. Pierre, M. (2013). Intimate Partner Violence Reported by Lesbian-, Gay-, and Bisexual-Identified Individuals Living in Canada: An Exploration of Within-Group Variations. *Journal of Gay & Lesbian Social Services*, *25*(1), 1–23. doi:10.1080/10538720.2013.751887

Bell, N. K. (1989). AIDS and women: remaining ethical issues. *AIDS Education and Prevention: Official Publication of the International Society for AIDS Education*, *1*(1), 22–30.

Blais, M., Gervais, J., Boucher, K., Hébert, M., Lavoie, F. & Équipe de recherche PAJ. (2013). Prevalence of victimization based on sexual minority status in youth among youths in the province of Quebec (Canada). *The International Journal of Victimology*, *11*(2), 1-13.

Blais, M., Gervais, J. & Hébert, M. (2014). Internalized homophobia as a partial mediator between homophobic bullying and self-esteem among youths of sexual minorities in Quebec (Canada). *Ciência & Saúde Coletiva*, *19*(3), 727–735.

Blosnich, J. & Bossarte, R. M. (2009). Comparisons of intimate partner violence among partners in same-sex and opposite-sex relationships in the United States. *American Journal of Public Health*, *99*(12), 2182–2184. doi:10.2105/AJPH.2008.139535

Bornstein, D. R., Fawcett, J., Sullivan, M., Senturia, K. D. & Shiu-Thornton, S. (2006). Understanding the experiences of lesbian, bisexual and trans survivors of domestic violence: A qualitative study. *Journal of Homosexuality*, *51*(1), 159–181. doi:10.1300/J082v51n01_08

Brown, A., Cosgrave, E., Killackey, E., Purcell, R., Buckby, J. & Yung, A. R. (2009). The longitudinal association of adolescent dating violence with psychiatric disorders and functioning. *Journal of Interpersonal Violence*, *24*(12), 1964–1979. doi:10.1177/0886260508327700

Brown, C. (2008). Gender-Role Implications on Same-Sex Intimate Partner Abuse. Journal of *Family Violence*, *23*(6), 457–462. doi:10.1007/s10896-008-9172-9

Carvalho, A. F., Lewis, R. J., Derlega, V. J., Winstead, B. a. & Viggiano, C. (2011). Internalized Sexual Minority Stressors and Same-Sex Intimate Partner Violence. *Journal of Family Violence*, *26*(7), 501–509. doi:10.1007/s10896-011-9384-2

Chamberland, L., Richard, G. & Bernier, M. (2013). Les violences homophobes et leurs impacts sur la persévérance scolaire des adolescents au Québec. *Recherches & Éducations*, *8*(June), 99–114.

Chamie, J. & Mirkin, B. (2011). Same-Sex Marriage: A New Social Phenomenon. *Population and Development Review*, *37*(3), 529–551. doi:10.1111/j.1728-4457.2011.00433.x

Clarke, V., Burgoyne, C. & Burns, M. (2013). Unscripted and Improvised: Public and Private Celebrations of Same-Sex Relationships. *Journal of GLBT Family Studies*, *9*(4), 393–418. doi:10.1080/1550428X.2013.808494

Close, S. M. (2005). Dating violence prevention in middle school and high school youth. *Journal of Child and Adolescent Psychiatric Nursing : Official Publication of the Association of Child and Adolescent Psychiatric Nurses, Inc*, *18*(1), 2–9. doi:10.1111/j.1744-6171.2005.00003.x

Connolly, C. M. (2004). Clinical Issues with Same-Sex Couples. *Journal of Couple & Relationship Therapy*, *3*(2-3), 3–12. doi:10.1300/J398v03n02_02

Cornelius, T. L. & Resseguie, N. (2007). Primary and secondary prevention programs for dating violence: *A review of the literature. Aggression and Violent Behavior*, *12*(3), 364–375. doi:10.1016/j.avb.2006.09.006

Crisp, C. & McCave, E. L. (2007). Gay Affirmative Practice: A Model for Social Work Practice with Gay, Lesbian, and Bisexual Youth. *Child and Adolescent Social Work Journal*, *24*(4), 403–421. doi:10.1007/s10560-007-0091-z

Dank, M., Lachman, P., Zweig, J. M. & Yahner, J. (2014). Dating violence experiences of lesbian, gay, bisexual, and transgender youth. *Journal of Youth and Adolescence*, *43*(5), 846–857. doi:10.1007/s10964-013-9975-8

DiLillo, D., Giuffre, D., Tremblay, G. C. & Peterson, L. (2001). A Closer Look at the Nature of Intimate Partner Violence Reported by Women With a History of Child Sexual Abuse. *Journal of Interpersonal Violence*, *16*(2), 116–132. doi:10.1177/088626001016002002

Duke, A. & Davidson, M. M. (2009). Same-Sex Intimate Partner Violence: Lesbian, Gay, and Bisexual Affirmative Outreach and Advocacy. *Journal of Aggression, Maltreatment & Trauma*, *18*(8), 795–816. doi:10.1080/10926770903291787

Edwards, K. M. & Sylaska, K. M. (2013). The Perpetration of Intimate Partner Violence among LGBTQ College Youth: The Role of Minority Stress. *Journal of Youth and Adolescence*, *42*(11), 1721–1731. doi:10.1007/s10964-012-9880-6

Fassin, E. (2001). Same Sex, Different Politics: "Gay Marriage" Debates in France and the United States. *Public Culture*, *13*(2), 215–232. doi:10.1215/08992363-13-2-215

Fellmeth, G. L. T., Heffernan, C., Nurse, J., Habibula, S. & Sethi, D. (2013). Educational and skills-based interventions for preventing relationship and dating violence in adolescents and young adults. *The Cochrane Database of Systematic Reviews*, *6*, CD004534. doi:10.1002/14651858.CD004534.pub3

Ford, C. L., Slavin, T., Hilton, K. L. & Holt, S. L. (2013). Intimate partner violence prevention services and resources in los angeles: issues, needs, and challenges for assisting lesbian, gay, bisexual, and transgender clients. *Health Promotion Practice*, *14*(6), 841–849. doi:10.1177/1524839912467645

Foshee, V. A., Bauman, K. E., Ennett, S. T., Linder, G. F., Benefield, T. & Suchindran, C. (2004). Assessing the long-term effects of the Safe Dates program and a booster in preventing and reducing adolescent dating violence victimization and perpetration. *American Journal of Public Health*, *94*(4), 619–624.

Foshee, V. A. & McNaughton Reyes, H. L. (2012). Dating Abuse: Prevalence, Consequences, and Predictors. In R. J. R. Levesque (Ed.), *Encyclopedia of Adolescence* (602–615). New York, NY: Springer US. doi:10.1007/978-1-4419-1695-2_51

Freedner, N., Freed, L. L. H., Yang, Y. W. & Austin, S. B. (2002). Dating violence among gay, lesbian, and bisexual adolescents: Results from a community survey. *Journal of Adolescent Health*, *31*(6), 469–474.

Friedman, M. S., Marshal, M. P., Guadamuz, T. E., Wei, C., Wong, C. F., Saewyc, E. M. & Stall, R. D. (2011). A meta-analysis of disparities in childhood sexual abuse, parental physical abuse, and peer victimization among sexual minority and sexual nonminority individuals. American *Journal of Public Health*, *101*(8), 1481–1494. doi:10.2105/AJPH.2009.190009

Gillum, T. L. & DiFulvio, G. (2012). "There's so much at stake": sexual minority youth discuss dating violence. *Violence against Women*, *18*(7), 725–745. doi:10.1177/1077801212455164

Gillum, T. L. & DiFulvio, G. (2014). Examining Dating Violence and Its Mental Health Consequences Among Sexual Minority Youth. In D. Peterson & V. R. Panfil (Eds.), *Handbook of LGBT Communities, Crime, and Justice* (431–448). New York, NY: Springer New York. doi:10.1007/978-1-4614-9188-0

Guadalupe-Diaz, X. L. & Yglesias, J. (2013). "Who's Protected?" Exploring Perceptions of Domestic Violence Law by Lesbians, Gays, and Bisexuals. *Journal of Gay & Lesbian Social Services*, *25*(4), 465–485. doi:10.1080/10538720.2013.806881

Halpern, C. T., Oslak, S. G., Young, M. L., Martin, S. L. & Kupper, L. L. (2001). Partner Violence Among Adolescents in Opposite-Sex Romantic Relationships: Findings From the National Longitudinal Study of Adolescent Health. *American Journal of Public Health*, *91*(10), 1679–1685. doi:10.2105/AJPH.91.10.1679

Halpern, C. T., Young, M. L., Waller, M. W., Martin, S. L. & Kupper, L. L. (2004). Prevalence of partner violence in same-sex romantic and sexual relationships in a national sample of adolescents. *The Journal of Adolescent Health : Official Publication of the Society for Adolescent Medicine*, *35*(2), 124–31. doi:10.1016/j.jadohealth. 2003.09.003

Hamby, S., Finkelhor, D. & Turner, H. (2012). Teen dating violence: Co-occurrence with other victimizations in the National Survey of Children's Exposure to Violence (NatSCEV). *Psychology of Violence*, *2*(2), 111–124. doi:10.1037/a0027191

Hassouneh, D. & Glass, N. (2008). The influence of gender role stereotyping on women's experiences of female same-sex intimate partner violence. *Violence against Women*, *14*(3), 310–325. doi:10.1177/1077801207313734

Haynie, D. L., Farhat, T., Brooks-Russell, A., Wang, J., Barbieri, B. & Iannotti, R. J. (2013). Dating violence perpetration and victimization among U.S. adolescents: prevalence, patterns, and associations with health complaints and substance use. *The Journal of Adolescent Health : Official Publication of the Society for Adolescent Medicine*, *53*(2), 194–201. doi:10.1016/j.jadohealth.2013.02.008

Hébert, M., Lavoie, F., Vitaro, F., McDuff, P. & Tremblay, R. E. (2008). Association of child sexual abuse and dating victimization with mental health disorder in a sample of adolescent girls. *Journal of Traumatic Stress*, *21*(2), 181–189. doi:10.1002/jts.20314

Herek, G. M. (1990). The Context of Anti-Gay Violence: Notes on Cultural and Psychological Heterosexism. *Journal of Interpersonal Violence*, *5*(3), 316–333. doi:10.1177/088626090005003006

Herek, G. M., Cogan, J., Gillis, J. R. & Glunt, E. (1997). Correlates of internalized homophobia in a community sample of lesbians and gay men. *Journal of the Gay and Lesbian Medical Association*, *1*(2), 17–25.

Herek, G. M., Kimmel, D., Amaro, H. & Melton, G. (1991). Avoiding heterosexist bias in psychological research. *The American Psychologist*, *46*(9), 957–63.

Hipwell, A. E., Stepp, S. D., Keenan, K., Allen, A., Hoffmann, A., Rottingen, L. & McAloon, R. (2013). Examining links between sexual risk behaviors and dating violence involvement as a function of sexual orientation. *Journal of Pediatric and Adolescent Gynecology*, *26*(4), 212–218. doi:10.1016/j.jpag.2013.03.002

Howard, D. E., Debnam, K. J., Wang, M. Q. & Gilchrist, B. (2012). 10-year trends in physical dating violence victimization among U.S. adolescent males. *International Quarterly of Community Health Education*, *32*(4), 283–305. doi:10.2190/IQ.32.4.c

Kann, L., Olsen, E. O. O., McManus, T., Kinchen, S., Chyen, D., Harris, W. A. & Wechsler, H. (2011). Sexual Identity, Sex of Sexual Contacts, and Health-Risk Behaviors among Students in Grades 9-12--Youth Risk Behavior Surveillance, Selected Sites, United States. *Morbidity and Mortality Weekly Report*, *60*(7), 1–133.

Kaschak, E. (2001). Intimate Betrayal. Women & Therapy, 23(3), 1–5. doi:10.1300/ J015v23n03_01

Katz-Wise, S. L. & Hyde, J. S. (2012). Victimization experiences of lesbian, gay, and bisexual individuals: a meta-analysis. *Journal of Sex Research*, *49*(2-3), 142–167. doi:10.1080/00224499.2011.637247

Kelley, J. (2001). Attitudes towards Homosexuality in 29 Nations. *Australian Social Monitor*, *4*(1), 15–22.

Klostermann, K., Kelley, M. L., Milletich, R. J. & Mignone, T. (2011). Alcoholism and partner aggression among gay and lesbian couples. *Aggression and Violent Behavior*, *16*(2), 115–119. doi:10.1016/j.avb.2011.01.002

Kosciw, J. G., Greytak, E. A., Diaz, E. M. & Bartkiewicz, M. J. (2010). *The 2009 National School Climate Survey. The Experiences of Lesbian, Gay, Bisexual and Transgender Youth in Our Nation's Schools.* New York, NY: Gay, Lesbian and Straight Education Network.

Krug, E. G., Mercy, J. A., Dahlberg, L. L. & Zwi, A. B. (2002). The world report on violence and health. *Lancet, 360*(9339), 1083–1088. doi:10.1016/S0140-6736(02)11133-0

Kulkin, H. S., Williams, J., Borne, H. F., de la Bretonne, D. & Laurendine, J. (2007). A review of research on violence in same-gender couples: a resource for clinicians. *Journal of Homosexuality, 53*(4), 71–87. doi:10.1080/00918360802210185

Lewis, R. J., Milletich, R. J., Kelley, M. L. & Woody, A. (2012). Minority stress, substance use, and intimate partner violence among sexual minority women. *Aggression and Violent Behavior, 17*(3), 247–256. doi:10.1016/j.avb.2012.02.004

Liang, B., Goodman, L., Tummala-Narra, P. & Weintraub, S. (2005). A theoretical framework for understanding help-seeking processes among survivors of intimate partner violence. *American Journal of Community Psychology, 36*(1-2), 71–84. doi:10.1007/s10464-005-6233-6.

Liebler, C. M., Schwartz, J. & Harper, T. (2009). Queer Tales of Morality: The Press, Same-Sex Marriage, and Hegemonic Framing. *Journal of Communication, 59*(4), 653–675. doi:10.1111/j.1460-2466.2009.01451.x

Marshal, M. P., Friedman, M. S., Stall, R. D., King, K. M., Miles, J., Gold, M. a, … Morse, J. Q. (2008). Sexual orientation and adolescent substance use: a meta-analysis and methodological review. *Addiction (Abingdon, England), 103*(4), 546–556. doi:10.1111/j.1360-0443.2008.02149.x

Martin-Storey, A. (2014). Prevalence of Dating Violence Among Sexual Minority Youth: Variation Across Gender, Sexual Minority Identity and Gender of Sexual Partners. *Journal of Youth and Adolescence.* doi:10.1007/s10964-013-0089-0

McClennen, J. C. (2005). Domestic violence between same-gender partners: recent findings and future research. *Journal of Interpersonal Violence, 20*(2), 149–154. doi:10.1177/0886260504268762

McGregor, B. a., Carver, C. S., Antoni, M. H., Weiss, S., Yount, S. E. & Ironson, G. (2001). Distress and Internalized Homophobia Among Lesbian Women Treated for Early Stage Breast Cancer. *Psychology of Women Quarterly, 25*(1), 1–9. doi:10.1111/1471-6402.00001

Mendoza, J. (2011). The Impact of Minority Stress on Gay Male Partner Abuse. In J. Ristock (Ed.), *Intimate Partner Violence in LGBTQ Lives.* Florence, KY, USA: Routledge.

Meyer, I. H. (1995). Minority stress and mental health in gay men. *Journal of Health and Social Behavior, 36*(1), 38–56.

Meyer, I. H. (2003). Prejudice, social stress, and mental health in lesbian, gay, and bisexual populations: conceptual issues and research evidence. *Psychological Bulletin, 129*(5), 674–697. doi:10.1037/0033-2909.129.5.674

O'Donohue, W. & Caselles, C. E. (1993). Homophobia: Conceptual, definitional, and value issues. *Journal of Psychopathology and Behavioral Assessment, 15*(3), 177–195. doi:10.1007/BF01371377

Ossana, S. M. (2000). Relationship and couples counseling. In R. M. Perez, K. A. DeBord, & K. J. Bieschke (Eds.), *Handbook of counseling and psychotherapy with lesbian, gay, and bisexual clients* (275–302). Washington, DC: American Psychological Association.

Otis, M. D. (2006). Stress and relationship quality in same-sex couples. *Journal of Social and Personal Relationships*, *23*(1), 81–99. doi:10.1177/0265407506060179

Pearson, J., Muller, C. & Wilkinson, L. (2007). Adolescent Same-Sex Attraction and Academic Outcomes: The Role of School Attachment and Engagement. *Social Problems*, *54*(4), 523–542. doi:10.1525/sp.2007.54.4.523

Quinn, D. M. & Chaudoir, S. R. (2009). Living with a concealable stigmatized identity: the impact of anticipated stigma, centrality, salience, and cultural stigma on psychological distress and health. *Journal of Personality and Social Psychology*, *97*(4), 634–651. doi:10.1037/a0015815

Ristock, J. L. (2003). Exploring dynamics of abusive lesbian relationships: preliminary analysis of a multisite, qualitative study. *American Journal of Community Psychology*, *31*(3-4), 329–341.

Roberts, A. L., Austin, S. B., Corliss, H. L., Vandermorris, A. K. & Koenen, K. C. (2010). Pervasive trauma exposure among US sexual orientation minority adults and risk of posttraumatic stress disorder. *American Journal of Public Health*, *100*(12), 2433–41. doi:10.2105/AJPH.2009.168971

Robinson, J. P. & Espelage, D. L. (2011). Inequities in Educational and Psychological Outcomes Between LGBTQ and Straight Students in Middle and High School. *Educational Researcher*, *40*(7), 315–330. doi:10.3102/0013189X11422112

Stephenson, R., Rentsch, C., Salazar, L. F. & Sullivan, P. (2011). Dyadic characteristics and intimate partner violence among men who have sex with men. *Western Journal of Emergency Medicine*, *12*(3), 324–332.

Stulhofer, A. & Rimac, I. (2009). Determinants of homonegativity in Europe. *Journal of Sex Research*, *46*(1), 24–32. doi:10.1080/00224490802398373

Sylaska, K. M. & Edwards, K. M. (2014). Disclosure of intimate partner violence to informal social support network members: a review of the literature. *Trauma, Violence & Abuse*, *15*(1), 3–21. doi:10.1177/1524838013496335

Szymanski, D. M. (2005). A Feminist Approach to Working With Internalized Heterosexism in Lesbians. *Journal of College Counseling*, *8*(1), 74–85. doi:10.1002/j.2161-1882.2005.tb00074.x

Szymanski, D. M. & Chung, Y. B. (2002). Internalized Homophobia in Lesbians. *Journal of Lesbian Studies*, *7*(1), 115–125. doi:10.1300/J155v07n01_08

Szymanski, D. M., Chung, Y. B. & Balsam, K. F. (2001). Psychosocial correlates of internalized homophobia in lesbians. *Measurement and Evaluation in Counseling & Development*, *34*(1), 27–38.

Szymanski, D. M., Kashubeck-West, S. & Meyer, J. (2008). Internalized Heterosexism: A Historical and Theoretical Overview. *The Counseling Psychologist*, *36*(4), 510–524. doi:10.1177/0011000007309488

Todahl, J. L., Linville, D., Bustin, A., Wheeler, J. & Gau, J. (2009). Sexual assault support services and community systems: understanding critical issues and needs in the LGBTQ community. *Violence against Women*, *15*(8), 952–76. doi:10.1177/1077801209335494

Traoré, I., Riberdy, H. & Pica, L. A. (2012). Violence et problèmes de comportement. In *L'Enquête québécoise sur la santé des jeunes du secondaire 2010-2011, tome 2. Le visage des jeunes d'aujourd'hui : leur santé mentale et leur adaptation sociale*. (81–110). Quebec: Institut de la statistique du Québec.

Turell, S., Herrmann, M., Hollander, G. & Galletly, C. (2012). Lesbian, Gay, Bisexual, and Transgender Communities' Readiness for Intimate Partner Violence Prevention. *Journal of Gay & Lesbian Social Services*, *24*(3), 289–310. doi:10.1080/10538720.2012.697797

Vézina, J. & Hébert, M. (2007). Risk factors for victimization in romantic relationships of young women: a review of empirical studies and implications for prevention. *Trauma, Violence & Abuse*, *8*(1), 33–66. doi:10.1177/1524838006297029

Weinberg, G. (1972). *Society and the healthy homosexual.* New York, NY: St. Martin's.

Wekerle, C., Leung, E., Wall, A.-M., MacMillan, H., Boyle, M., Trocme, N. & Waechter, R. (2009). The contribution of childhood emotional abuse to teen dating violence among child protective services-involved youth. *Child Abuse & Neglect*, *33*(1), 45–58. doi:10.1016/j.chiabu.2008.12.006

Welles, S. L., Corbin, T. J., Rich, J. a, Reed, E. & Raj, A. (2011). Intimate partner violence among men having sex with men, women, or both: early-life sexual and physical abuse as antecedents. *Journal of Community Health*, *36*(3), 477–85. doi:10.1007/s10900-010-9331-9

West, C. M. (2002). Lesbian Intimate Partner Violence. *Journal of Lesbian Studies*, *6*(1), 121–127. doi:10.1300/J155v06n01_11

Woodford, M. R., Luke, K. P., Grogan-Kaylor, A., Fredriksen-Goldsen, K. I. & Gutierrez, L. (2012). Social Work Faculty Support for Same-Sex Marriage: A Cross-national Study of U.S. and Anglophone Canadian MSW Teaching Faculty. *Social Work Research*, *36*(4), 301–312. doi:10.1093/swr/svs033

Wright, E. M. (2012). The Relationship Between Social Support and Intimate Partner Violence in Neighborhood Context. *Crime & Delinquency.* doi:10.1177/0011128712466 890.

SECTION THREE: THE FEMALE PERSPECTIVE ON DOMESTIC VIOLENCE

In: Overcoming Domestic Violence
Editors: Myra F. Taylor, Julie Ann Pooley et al.

ISBN: 978-1-63321-956-4
© 2015 Nova Science Publishers, Inc.

Chapter 6

SYSTEMIC VIOLENCE AND IMMIGRANT WOMEN HAVING ESCAPED DOMESTIC ABUSE: MEANINGFULLY REDUCING STRUCTURAL BARRIERS TO LEAVING INTIMATE PARTNER AND FAMILIAL VIOLENCE

Rita Isabel Henderson*, Wilfreda E. Thurston and Amrita Roy
University of Calgary, Calgary, Canada

ABSTRACT

For immigrant women in Canada who endure domestic violence, structural violence is commonly normalized in the forms of poverty, racism, and patriarchy, increasing risk for further harm, such as housing insecurity. This chapter focuses attention on signs of systemic harm that emerge in the words of a group of 37 immigrant women living in three Canadian cities who participated in longitudinal interviews about their experiences of leaving domestic violence. In particular, it focuses on forms of harm impeding the effectiveness of assistance extended to this population by, among others, police, language educators, social welfare workers, settlement agents, clinicians, and shelter staff. Attention to structural violence offers several advantages beyond policy-level relevance, including analytical innovation and the possibility of integrating complex dynamics into the design and evaluation of effective health promoting interventions.

INTRODUCTION

To what extent do systems designed to help victims of domestic violence transition out of unsafe homes potentially undermine efforts by immigrant women to escape abuse? This

---

* Corresponding author: Dr. Rita Isabel Henderson, Postdoctoral Research Fellow, Voices against Violence Project, Community Health Sciences, Cumming School of Medicine, University of Calgary, Calgary, Canada, Tel: (403)210-9874, Email: rihender@ucalgary.ca.

question frames the discussion here of the pressing need for policy and services to account for the realities facing immigrant women experiencing intimate partner and other forms of familial violence. Lack of social networks, uncertain control over immigration status, and weak language skills within a host society are known barriers to fleeing domestic violence among this population. Nevertheless, without situating an understanding of such barriers within larger social and institutional contexts, the actions taken may be less effective than predicted. This chapter highlights forms of structural violence specific to social service systems that may, contrary to intentions, compound the effects of intimate partner violence within the domestic sphere. In so doing, it furthers a call made elsewhere; namely, that addressing the health of immigrant women depends on moving beyond individual and micro-level variables to accounting for interpersonal and institutional dynamics at the meso- and macro-scales (Thurston et al., 2013; Thurston & Vissandjée, 2005). In particular, through the voices of immigrant women who have sought pathways out of domestic violence, points are identified at which services may heighten risk for women and children from vulnerable communities to remain in or return to abusive homes.

For researchers, engaging a structural violence analytical framework offers the possibility of overcoming conventional dichotomies of victims and perpetrators, or violent and non-violent actors (James et al., 2003), instead revealing how norms of subjugation are routinely enacted, challenged, and also habitually perpetuated. Structural violence refers to social, systemic, and historical sources of domination as root causes of interpersonal harm. Sociologist Johan Galtung (1969) coined the term more than 35 years ago to signal processes by which certain groups monopolize resources, thus penalizing those who lack these, in turn perpetuating inequalities in systematic ways. Structural and social determinants of wellbeing have been of growing concern in recent decades (see Berman et al., 2000; CSDH, 2008; Galabuzi, 2009; Gough et al., 2005; Veenstra, 2011). This is largely because attention to broader social contexts offers a framework for improving health outcomes through the examination of inadvertent ways in which policies and programs often contribute to the added victimization of marginalized groups, if only by minimizing the particularity of experiences or reinforcing exclusion through neglect. In this light, conceptualizing structural violence summons a broader scope of analysis than conventional literature on violence, as it discourages analysis and solutions invested uniquely in individual causes and consequences. While the harm produced by structural violence often has physical costs for those who experience it, structural violence is so embedded in social systems (i.e., bureaucracies, networks, hierarchies), that it is frequently experienced as subtle, indirect, and even permissible (see Scheper-Hughes 2004). The gendered nature of structural violence is clear in much research (Vissandjée et al., 2007).

For immigrant women who endure intimate partner violence, structural violence is commonly normalized in the forms of poverty, racism, and patriarchy; it is thus experienced in heightened risk for further harm, such as housing insecurity. Attention to structural violence therefore offers a number of advantages beyond policy-level relevance, including analytical innovation and the possibility of involving complex dynamics in the design and evaluation of effective health promoting interventions. As structural violence is commonly manifested in cultural expression (Galtung, 1990) —that is, in beliefs, values, ideologies, and language itself— it is particularly ripe for narrative analysis. This makes a narrative approach especially appropriate for research among those who endure structural violence, such as immigrant women seeking to escape abuse in the home. Throughout this chapter, attention is drawn to signs of systemic harm that emerge in the words of such women, focusing in particular on harm that impedes the effectiveness of assistance extended to this population.

A MULTI-SITED LONGITUDINAL PERSPECTIVE ON HOMELESSNESS RISK

This chapter is based on a longitudinal mixed methods study of housing (in)security among 37 immigrant women in three Canadian cities (Calgary, Alberta; Winnipeg, Manitoba; and Halifax, Nova Scotia). The study was approved by the University of Calgary's Conjoint Health Research Ethics Board. The participants were women who had sought assistance through the study's community partner agencies in the three cities to escape from personal experiences of domestic violence; women were eligible to participate if they had been born outside of Canada and moved to establish residence in the country, as well as had left their abusive relationships at least 21 days prior to recruitment. This timeline reflected a window beyond which the agency contacts indicated that their clients were less likely, and therefore less vulnerable, to return to abusive homes. A detailed safety and retention protocol was followed to protect both participants and interviewers. Furthermore, by collaborating with support agencies, participants had a consistent point of contact for services throughout the project's six month duration. Participants engaged in qualitative, open-ended interviews of one to two hours in length at three-month intervals, for a total of three interviews each; 32 of the original recruits participated in all three, 5 women declined follow-up due to reasons such as disinterest or work and school schedules. The interviews addressed participants' awareness of and access to services, especially those related to housing and health. All four interviewers were female migrants to Canada and each participant had a single interviewer throughout.

Other data gathered for the original project included qualitative, open-ended interviews with a total of twenty-six service providers including front-line workers and mid-level managers from immigrant settlement agencies, domestic violence shelters, housing or homelessness organizations, and assistance centres for employment, health, and legal counsel. These one-time interviews focused on existing programs and policies that affect immigrant women experiencing a combination of domestic violence and housing insecurity. Quantitative data from a Calgary-area shelter, the Brenda Strafford Centre, were also analyzed. That data included abuse history, information about children of clients (number and ages), employment status, education, income sources, and service needs. The data were gathered in such a way as to compare the profiles of immigrant women with those of Canadian-born women (non-Aboriginal[1] and Aboriginal) who used the shelter in the decade preceding the study.

Analysis examined both systemic and individual factors prompting homelessness and recourse to service providers. Individual and social levels of explanation were brought together by taking a pathways approach to deciphering factors leading into and out of homelessness during the six months of the study. This allowed development of a model for program and policy planning relevant in diverse service contexts (see Thurston et al. 2013). The data highlights indicators of both increased and decreased risk of homelessness, as well

---

[1] In Canada, the term Aboriginal refers broadly to Indigenous peoples of diverse backgrounds, encompassing First Nation, Métis, and Inuit populations.

as the most effective contexts for assisting this population exit domestic violence and housing insecurity.

Profile of Participants

About two thirds (65%) of participants were located in Calgary, with another quarter (27%) in Winnipeg and a smaller proportion (8%) in Halifax. More than half (53%) were between 30 and 39 years of age, and about 85% had at least one child. In all, the women originated from 26 different countries and 60% had been in Canada for 5 or more years. Nearly half of the participants (49%) held Canadian citizenship at the time of their first interview, and more than half (52%) had earned a post-secondary certificate or degree. Despite this relatively high level of education, a low proportion reported being employed (38%).

The three cities were demographically diverse, but presented as having similar domestic violence systems with similar access barriers for immigrant women. Some differences between the regions nevertheless impacted available solutions; for instance, while wait times for subsidized housing were long in all three sites, Calgary's private rental market proved especially expensive for the participants. Furthermore, compared to Halifax, the prairie cities of Calgary and Winnipeg also had larger immigrant communities. In Halifax, available services for immigrant women were limited and recruitment proved difficult due to women's concerns around confidentiality in light of the small size of ethno-cultural networks.

Operationalizing Domestic Violence and Homelessness

The study began with a focus on women because those who seek assistance for dealing with domestic violence are predominantly women (Federal-Provincial-Territorial Ministers Responsible for the Status of Women, 2002). Domestic violence includes forms of physical, emotional, social, and financial abuse that undermine the safety, health, and wellbeing of those who endure it, particularly in the home.

Definitions of "homelessness" are problematic for the ways in which they may shape data collected and potentially obscure variations within and between vulnerable populations (Braun et al., 2003). For the purposes of this chapter, homelessness is defined as the lack of permanent residence to which one may return at choice (City of Calgary, 2002). This includes the hidden homeless, such as temporary living situations with family and friends, as well as staying in emergency or second stage shelters or in other forms of impermanent housing. While most of the women in this study eventually moved from shelters to stable housing, stability did not necessarily mean security. The broader notion of housing insecurity refers to housing situations that the women themselves considered inadequate or impermanent due to high cost or low quality. Therefore, while participants often secured longer-term residence, that is, homes to which they could return to at their choice, many nevertheless expressed a desire to move again. Reasons included lack of safety from their abuser(s), unsafe neighbourhoods, inaccessible basic services, difficult access to transportation, distance from work or schools, social or physical isolation, and factors affecting the healthy development of their children. Importantly, the immigrant women in this study defined housing security as having housing that is permanent, affordable and safe.

Collaborative Analysis

For the original analysis, qualitative software QSR N6© was used to facilitate the sharing of analysis among a team of researchers located across Canada. Five iterative phases structured data analysis: "(a) describing, (b) organizing, (c) connecting, (d) corroborating or legitimating, and (e) representing the account" (Miller & Crabtree, 1999: 130). Preliminary analysis of interviews was completed by the research coordinator and coordinators in each site, together with the support of additional team members. The whole team then reviewed concepts and themes from the data. Once key themes were determined, summaries of results were provided to several of the immigrant women interviewed, particularly with three who were available for knowledge exchange activities. These emphatically agreed that the findings matched their personal experiences. In Calgary, key informants on policy were engaged in reviewing and commenting on the report in a workshop. By triangulating data sources and researchers, as well as validating findings with participants and establishing congruence across the three sites, the fidelity of the results was assured (Creswell, 1998; Morse & Richards, 2002).

For this chapter, a secondary analysis included an extended lexical search of transcripts of the interviews with the immigrant women. Queries targeted negative and ambivalent comments about points of intervention (i.e., courts, shelters, social assistance offices, schools, employment agencies) and professional service providers. The goal was to generate a deeper understanding of the nature of negative and ambivalent statements, rather than to quantify these. The resulting interview segments were then reviewed to include only responses where the participants spoke about personal experiences rather than speculative or hypothetical information.

What follows is a summary of the pathways approach developed from this study to understand the interplay between domestic violence and homelessness at distinct points from migration through to settlement in Canada. The subsequent section then turns to the voices of the immigrant women to explore their uncertainties, hesitations, and even distrust of certain service providers. The participants' cautions are interpreted as a point of departure for developing a more nuanced understanding of client experiences and whether existing systems are perceived by clientele to achieve what service providers claim, and also whether and how systems potentially undermine their own stated objectives. Gaps in the women's knowledge of services do not necessarily point to a lack of services, but could be an indicator of systemic problems and areas for the improvement of service delivery.

PATHWAYS OUT OF HOMELESSNESS

In Canada, abused immigrant and refugee women endure several challenges not faced by their Canadian-born counterparts. Language barriers and lack of culturally competent services may impede access to shelters or drop-in facilities (Shirwadkar, 2004; Tutty et al., 2003;

Supporting Communities Partnership Initiative, 2003). Barriers known to arise within familial and cultural communities, such as severe financial restrictions and controlled mobility (Crandall et al., 2005; Shirwadkar, 2004; Calgary Coalition on Domestic violence & Calgary Immigrant women's Association, 1998), have also been identified as means by which abusers perpetuate vulnerability (Bhuyan et al., 2005). Furthermore, abusers may use immigration status as a mechanism of control, as sponsored women may be kept from leaving violent relationships by threats of reversing their residency or citizenship applications. Similarly, abusers exploit lack of legal awareness about personal rights by threatening the loss of child custody (Ibid). Lastly, fear of racism and of deportation of a person upon whom she and her children depend, both financially and socially, may prevent her from accessing criminal justice services (Salcido & Adelman, 2004; Burman & Chantler, 2005). Therefore, while immigrant and Canadian-born women who are abused face similar barriers to independent living, migration presents additional challenges affecting pathways into and out of homelessness.

The pathways approach enabled us to identify a series of phases marked by where the woman was in her migration experience at the time of recruitment, as well as her experiences of domestic violence, her attempts to leave it, and her ability to find secure housing. While some women only experienced domestic violence upon moving to Canada, for others it was already part of their lives prior to arrival in the country. Regardless, the women did not always know that domestic violence was recognized in Canada as including social, psychological, spiritual, and economic abuse. Nor were many participants previously aware that networks for services and aid exist for victims and perpetrators, regardless, at least in principle, of one's immigration status (Thurston et al., 2013). Stories about the participants' discovery of services reveal circumstances that are more likely to bring an immigrant woman into contact with service providers. For example:

> *I found [the shelter] through my friend, she told me there is [an education] program here that is for the ladies, for domestic violence… but I didn't talk to my husband before coming, 'cause I'm taking this [other] program, so he doesn't care, I just say I'm going to study and I come here [instead, to see the program]. Then I found out about domestic violence, they taught us where to seek help when you have some problem about your partner. One lady… she's teaching about what you will do, they give us so many information about immigration, about welfare, when you get help. Don't be afraid about get some help about many, many things, and about Women's Advocacy. They taught us about where to go for resources, and where you have to run when you get some problem and need to hide. I want to escape from my partner, but three times he hits me [before I came here].* (Participant, Winnipeg, 1st interview)

While each woman encounters the services she needs through her own networks and efforts to seek help, the previous comment highlights the broad value of educational outreach initiatives at distinct points, as a means of engaging with vulnerable women early in their search for supports.

Figure 1 represents the framework developed for envisioning pathways that the women followed towards increased housing security. For purposes of clarity, stages are portrayed as chronological and distinct, though lived experiences certainly varied between the women.

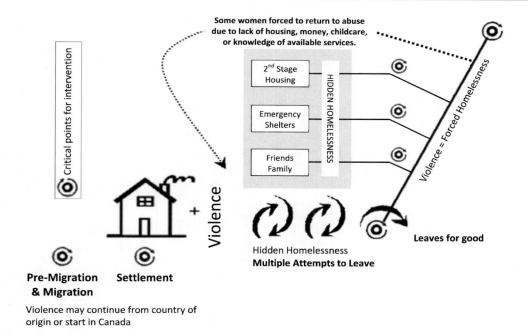

Figure 1. Pathways into and out of homelessness.

Homelessness may be prevented at many points along the various pathways out of domestic violence (Thurston et al., 2013), though the testimonies in this study emphasize the need for greater awareness among service providers of the longer trajectory of clients. After all, key indicators for risk (e.g., immigration status) are not necessarily modifiable or appropriate for prevention-focused interventions. Therefore, homelessness prevention among this population requires programs and policies tailored and evaluated according to the realities of immigrant women (Thurston & Potvin, 2003). Figure 2 illustrates how factors affecting the situation for immigrant women stem from both social and built environments, coinciding with a range of individual and systemic factors also affecting non-immigrant women.

As systemic factors are of interest here, elements in the lower portion of the diagram are particularly relevant, such as available, safe, and affordable housing, language barriers, social assistance rates, culturally competent services, and resources for children.

One especially troubling area, in which systemic factors undermined attempts to leave a dangerous situation, arose among women whose immigration was sponsored by their spouses. In Canada, sponsors can be retroactively held financially responsible for services provided as state-funded social assistance (Burman & Chantler, 2005), a situation that, for the women in this study, augmented reasons to fear later retribution from an abusive spouse.

> At that time when my husband started to threaten my life and I had to go into hiding, I wasn't able to get social services because he was sponsor. Even I called Immigration. I told them that he threatened to kill me, that he had a contract out to kill me and my children... They said "we don't have anything to do with this. You need his sponsor[ship]. If you need some support, he has to help you." So that was very difficult for me to understand. I felt neglected, not supported... Society didn't help me. (Participant, Calgary, 3rd interview)

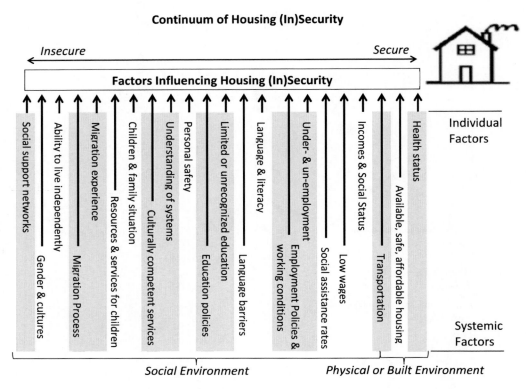

Figure 2. Individual to systemic continuum of factors influencing housing (in)security.[2]

Despite serious concerns for her safety and the safety of her children, this woman was not able to be connected with protective services by the highest authority on immigration in the country, Citizenship and Immigration Canada. This suggests either that no mechanism was in place to facilitate such a connection, or that an existing mechanism was not sufficiently effective. Being a sponsored newcomer also restricted certain housing agencies from even assisting this class of immigrant women, as sponsors technically remain responsible for the living costs of their dependents. For example, in the words of one service provider:

> If you are sponsored and you flee a domestic violence situation, forget normal living. Just to say a domestic violence situation, you are not eligible to get into [City] Housing. So [the agency] says that if you are sponsored, you cannot get into [their program], period. It doesn't matter whether there's a domestic violence situation or not. So that's a very insecure place for a woman who is fleeing domestic violence who doesn't have much money, who doesn't speak English, who has no employable skills, you know, I mean where does she go? (Service Provider, Calgary)

In 2012, the federal government introduced a regulation to 'crack-down' on immigration fraud in the sponsorship category. An additional condition affecting all newly sponsored spouses was established in order to qualify for permanent residency. In order to qualify for permanent resident status and avoid loss of immigration status, the sponsored spouse must

---

[2] Previously published in Thurston at al. 2013.

now cohabitate with their sponsor in a conjugal relationship for at least two years upon arriving in Canada (Douglas et al., 2012). No coordinated protections have been introduced to minimize the risk this poses for women experiencing domestic violence. Some domestic violence shelters nevertheless extend emergency aid to sponsored women, though knowledge about places for unconditional access to assistance appears limited among both shelter clientele and staff. As one service provider explained to us, available services exist, but someone has to fulfill the role of connecting women to them, to make sure that potential clients *"have all the information, even when there's a language barrier."* The scenario highlights the importance of inter-agency communication and collaboration in order to ensure that relevant information is reliably provided to women, regardless of where assistance is sought. Even so, whether that assistance is sufficient to safely transition out of domestic violence invites critical reflection.

Arguably, denial of services is experienced not only by women sponsored by their spouses, but also by undocumented migrants. Such women experiencing domestic violence are even more vulnerable than many of the women in this study. As the testimonies in this chapter reveal, immigrant women are regularly turned away from services several times before securing the support sought. Without documentation with which to insist on assistance, those with illegal status in Canada (e.g., denied asylum-seekers and others having overstayed their visas) are in a poor position to demand their rights. In recent years, the 'No One Is Illegal' movement for global citizenship has contributed to the development of grassroots activism pushing some municipal leaders to render services accessible to all persons, including undocumented migrants. Since 2013, two Canadian cities—Hamilton and Toronto—have passed motions to become Sanctuary Cities; that is, they are committed to promoting safe communities by removing fear among vulnerable populations of being turned away from services, or worse, of being revealed to immigration authorities and potentially detained or deported (Keyng, 2013; Nursall, 2014). However, in spite of motions by municipal politicians and the important work of advocacy groups, systemic factors may nevertheless continue to deny access to those in greatest need.

The means by which factors denying access to services work to impede pathways out of domestic violence and homelessness are diverse. For instance, when the woman quoted above approached the immigration authority, she was informed that it was her responsibility alone to enforce her spouse's financial responsibilities towards her and her children, a burden that would effectively translate into both a heightened risk of additional abuse by him and denied assistance in leaving a violent home. Of particular concern is that this woman was unaware that due to the death threats that she was receiving, she was within her rights to petition police involvement and protection. In spite of the death threats, which alone should be cause for involving the police, she was not made aware of resources within her city that could ensure her wellbeing. Her story demonstrates how the federal government's 'crackdown' on immigration fraud in the spousal sponsorship category risks increasing the vulnerability of abused women, by rendering it more difficult for this population to seek aid from formal service providers. This example illustrates ineffective service delivery when both immigration authorities and housing agencies convey to abused women that, due to one's immigration status, a woman must resolve her domestic violence situation without recourse to community resources. Meanwhile, service gaps emerge in the new regulation's weak grounding in research evidence; protections from the unintended harms of the expectation that sponsored spouses cohabit with a potential abuser for an extended period of time in order to retain immigration status, are incorporated into neither policy, nor practice.

SYSTEMIC VIOLENCE: POLICY GAPS, SERVICE DELIVERY AND UNINTENDED HARM

From neglect in appropriately transmitting critical information about available resources, to the lack of safeguards against inadvertent harm from social policies, to the expectation of frontline workers that the needs of clients neatly correspond to what is on offer from discrete agencies — structural violence appears so commonplace that its prevalence would seem a daunting task to overcome. However, much as the pathways framework highlights patterns of interaction with service providers, the voices of abused immigrant women expose avoidable patterns of fear, disappointment, and frustration. By identifying the unintended harm perpetuated by ineffective service delivery and by gaps in policy and programming, distinct sites of action for interventions intended to diminish systemic violence are proposed.

Violation of Trust

One recurrent theme among those women from migrant backgrounds, who sought help from multiple services over extended periods of time before finally leaving domestic violence, was lack of trust. They expressed discomfort with divulging abuse to male service providers. One woman, whose injuries from a beating sustained at the hands of her husband brought her to an emergency room, responded with silence to a male doctor who indicated to her that he recognized the true cause of her wounds. Unconvinced that he could or would help her leave the hospital safe from her abuser, she did not disclose. For another woman, when a man answered the phone at a shelter, she refrained from elaborating on the magnitude of her situation. Only when she had nowhere else to turn for a place to sleep, did she request to speak with a female staff member.

> *When I called the first time, a man answered, so I didn't tell the whole thing that happened, because I was afraid of him. I was afraid, you know… And then my girlfriend took us in and then I couldn't sleep at her home, so at 6:00 in the morning, I woke up and I called the shelter again, and I talked to a man this time and then asked to talk to a female counsellor.* (Participant, Calgary, 1st interview)

Trust was also something that service providers could earn and lose, as some women felt that promises of safety and improved wellbeing were impermanent within the shelter system.

> *How I got into the shelter was their promise to me that I would be safe. And after 3 weeks' time, we had to leave and I have to go downtown, to the Y. We told them "that's not safe, you know, you got me into here, you took me here, to keep me safe, and now you are kind of throw — sending me out on the street again." So it was kind of a difficult situation.* (Participant, Calgary, 3rd interview)

For this woman, shelters created only a temporary physical safety, where the social and emotional safety of permanent escape was transitory. Her words questioned the extent to which her departure from an abusive partner put her on a path to increased autonomy, or whether it had merely replaced dependence on her husband with reliance on the decisions of shelter staff who did not have the ability to effectively guarantee her safety. For such women, it was not that services were poor, per se, but rather that they were lacking in social and emotional capital to ensure effective service delivery. Women reported feeling vulnerable due to the limited housing, transportation, and employment options available; however, they still emphasized the importance of seeking the support of service providers in escaping domestic violence. For instance, when asked what advice they would offer others facing similar experiences of domestic violence, time and again these women highlighted the importance of insisting on help from service providers.

> *If [a woman] feels not safe, they have to call the police. If they think the police doesn't work anyway, they have to call again, to call again, to call again the police anyway. It was hard for me to call the first time the police. I feel very, "oh no, why I have to call the police? Maybe people will know my situation." I was a little disappointed, but anyway, the last time I call, the police help me very well, and yes, it's a start, starting open the doors.* (Participant, Winnipeg, 3rd interview)

While this advice to expect support from service providers portrays a system that, to a great extent, helped many of these women escape violence in their homes, the message to not lose hope or confidence in service providers is nevertheless cautionary. Participants emphasized that while services can be beneficial, and even life-saving and crucial to exiting abuse, responsibility ultimately seems to fall on the targets of abuse to know how to communicate their eligibility for help to the police and others, while also overcoming fear and barriers to speaking with strangers about abuse.

The implication is that protective services appear to be successfully accessed by only the most enterprising clientele. This challenges us to reimagine how service planning and delivery function. For one, solutions to the burden of having to repeatedly insist on gaining access to support are situated in multiple realms. On a practical level, for instance, offering women who call crisis lines and who approach other first points of contact with service providers (e.g., nurses, doctors, police, shelter staff) the opportunity to immediately speak with a culturally competent female may help establish trust. However, cultural competence, which is the ability to have a standard interaction with all clients regardless of background (Oelke et al., 2013), does not address the problem that women must be their own advocates. In this case, they must be persistent and protective of themselves and their children while waiting for a positive response, which is intended to be the "standard interaction." Thus, cultural competency commands critical understanding of individualist norms within Canadian society, such as the tendency to pathologize the struggles of more marginalized groups as lack of assertiveness, over-timidity, or fear of authority. It also requires sensitivity and recognition of varied understandings of what constitutes need and eligibility for service.

The Violence of Inaction

Organizations dedicated to legal assistance with immigration regulations often neglected the needs for support experienced by abused immigrant women. Such situations indicate lack of informed and coordinated efforts to ensure that women learn in a timely fashion of available resources, regardless of which type of service is first approached (e.g., legal, medical, welfare).

> *I went to the Immigration Association for legal advice, which was no help for they told me the same, you know. "There is nothing you can do about it. You can go out and try to make a living cleaning houses or whatever, to just get out of the situation," was the only suggestion.* (Participant, Calgary, 3rd interview)

The presumption that an abused woman could merely work her way to autonomy through gainful employment is problematic; it fails to consider the burden of childcare commitments and other barriers, as well as the issue of safety from the abuser. It also overlooks the threat of engagement in sex-trade work or other illicit activities that are often the options put forward or most available to marginalized women. Furthermore, the scenario reveals a common view of how women in general are expected to deal with domestic violence; that is, individually and with whatever resources (e.g., education, social networks) they do or do not have at their disposal. When service providers do not adequately assess the reality in which their clientele live, then the potential for added harm is amplified. However, some service providers were well aware of the challenges facing immigrant and other women; these professionals indicated that inaction did not reflect incompetency so much as disillusionment in a prevailing system that did not address inequities:

> *I contacted [City's] Legal Aid, and that was not a very good experience because the lawyer that I had, he got very discouraged that at the end he just didn't get anything from the father of my child, who is my sponsor and who is the one responsible to support and to pay for me. [My lawyer] got afraid from the private lawyer of my husband at that time... He started with very much energy doing this and the case, writing all about [it]... and this and that, and "you're going to have your own place." He just at the end, nothing happened... Because he got scared of the private lawyer that my husband has.* (Participant, Calgary, 1st interview)

While the consequences of inaction on the part of service providers were often not linked to specific future harms experienced by women, the potential harm of failing to assist the women emerges in the frequency with which participants first learned about shelters from police officers called in to crisis situations. In other words, while prevention and outreach initiatives engaged some women in services, a larger number of the study participants only discovered adequate services after domestic violence had escalated to the point of entering the justice system. Importantly, that system is only designed to provide immediate relief if criminal assault has occurred or to make referrals to other services. One method to addressing the above would be improved coordination between agencies that regularly come into contact with immigrant women.

Harmful Policy and Program Gaps

The absence of adequate policies and programs was observed across professional sectors, including in language education, welfare assistance, medical support, and the limits of the law in detaining accused abusers. Often, the unintended harm from services was compounded for the women; for instance, in the months after leaving, several women described enduring chronic exhaustion and headaches, relating these to overwhelming stress from inflexible work, school, and childcare schedules. While counselling support was available, it was generally during school or work hours. Meanwhile, the hassle of getting to a service provider at an inconvenient hour sometimes outweighed the potential benefits of receiving support.

> *I find myself very confident to be in front of group and explain myself like what I know in my field... The problem I feel a lot of struggle with English, even though I am taking the English course in college. I find it very no helpingful, in the way I need right now... This week I went to Winnipeg on Tuesday and I went to hospital Wednesday, but I decided don't go [to class] on Tuesday and Friday, because my kids was going to be everyday all week with somebody else, in the morning to 7:00 or 8:00 o'clock in the evening.* (Participant, Winnipeg, 2nd interview)

Another issue is the limitation of services and creation of categories of vulnerability. In the following example, "benchmarking" refers to a standardized system for the evaluation of English language learning in Canada. In the end, the participant accessed relevant learning tools through her own initiative, as access to educational opportunities through social workers was limited to low-level English and computational training.

> *If you don't know the ABCs or you totally don't know how to speak English, then it is helpful, like they will tell you for the ESL classes or little bit starting up for a computer class... but when you have a higher education, they don't know what to do... They have programs, but it's just the start-up programs... They send me for benchmarking and I did benchmarking myself and everything already. So they don't know what next, so they told me to go to Red River College, and then Red River College doesn't know anything, so I find out on myself and with little help from director about College of Nursing.* (Participant, Winnipeg, 1st interview)

Women with professional skills and education might seem to have an advantage, but in the context of domestic violence survival this might not always be true. Meanwhile, social assistance proved insufficient to cover basic costs of living.

> *I pay for the 2 kids' bus tickets, bus like $90 a month, to go to school. Welfare don't cover the bus fare, I have to pay $96 every month with the tax.* (Participant, Winnipeg, 2nd interview)

Praise of existing systems by women from marginalized communities does not necessarily mean that these are optimal. The narrative approach revealed this complexity, as mixed messages emerged; for example, one woman's expressed appreciation for the services on hand finds nuance in her emphasis that others should also be thankful, as she enacted in her final interview the role of a 'grateful immigrant'.

> *You have to be thankful for the benefits and everything, because in other countries you don't have nothing like no help forever.* (Participant, Calgary, 1st interview)

CONCLUSION

The voices of women escaping domestic violence highlight that both the experience and risk of homelessness are integrally gendered (DuMont et al. 2000; Novac et al. 1996), as are the housing and financial needs of abused women and the service provision they may access (Baker 2005). This reality is compounded among foreign-born women whose immigration status already puts them at increased risk for homelessness due to greater vulnerability to poverty, social and geographic isolation, discrimination in rental housing markets, and mental illness (Supporting Communities Partnership Initiative, 2003; Abraham, 2000; Baker et al., 2003; Thomas, 1995).

A cyclical nature of homelessness, complicated by both social isolation and uncertainty about formal services available (Donahue et al., 2003) was highlighted; however, this research also showed that neither experiences of migration (Meadows et al., 2001; Thurston & Verhoef, 2003; Ramaliu & Thurston, 2003; Graham & Thurston, 2005), nor of domestic violence are uniform (Thurston, 1998; Thurston et al., 1998). This challenges researchers and service providers to develop interventions adapted to the diversity of clientele. Diversity here refers not only to countries or cultures of origin, but also to adaptions to Canadian society, such as language skills, employment and educational status, geographic location and mobility within a city, reliable and flexible access to childcare, and support networks. The voices of abused immigrant women called for assistance in learning of their rights (see Crandall et al., 2005; Bui, 2003).

In order to facilitate the above, it is worth emphasizing the importance of increased cultural competency training and attention to language barriers among service providers (See Bhuyan et al., 2005; Bui, 2003; Shirwadkar, 2004; Latta & Goodman, 2005), but also that systematic attention to inequity is required.

This study suggests that intervention is needed at key moments of interaction that immigrant women already have with service providers; as such, the domestic violence sector is not only responsible for preventing violence. A well-connected, collaborative service-provision safety net to engage vulnerable women wherever they may turn for assistance is needed. Critical analysis of eligibility norms are needed in designing outreach. One key stage for educational intervention among immigrant women occurs shortly after they arrive in Canada, during a period of relatively heightened interaction with service providers. Transmission of critical information in a non-stigmatizing fashion not only normalizes help-seeking, but also highlights the progress that has been made in Canada in terms of services and attempts to prevent abuse. A structural violence framework broadens the conceptualization of violence experienced by abused women to include harm perpetuated by social structures outside of the home. In this fashion, a more nuanced understanding of the complexities at play in ending domestic violence becomes possible.

REFERENCES

Abraham, M. (2000). Isolation as a form of marital violence: The South Asian immigrant experience. *Journal of Social Distress and the Homeless*, 9(3), 221-236.

Baker, C. K., Cook, S. L. & Norris, F. H. (2003). Domestic violence and housing problems: a contextual analysis of women's help-seeking, received informal support, and formal system response. *Violence Against Women*, 9(7), 754-783.

Baker, H. (2005). Involving children and young people in research on domestic violence and housing. *Journal of Social Welfare and Family Law*, 27(3-4), 281-297.

Berman, H., McKenna, K., Traher, G. & MacQuarrie, B. (2000). Sexual Harassment: Everyday violence in the lives of girls and women. *Advances in Nursing Science*, 22(4), 32-46.

Bhuyan, R., Mell, M., Senturia, K., Sullivan, M. & Shiu-Thornton, S. (2005). "Women must endure according to their karma" Cambodian immigrant women talk about domestic violence. *Journal of Interpersonal Violence*, 20(8), 902-921.

Braun, T. & Black, J. (2003). *It Shouldn't Take an Inquest: A Review of the Literature Examining Links Between Domestic Violence and Homelessness*. Calgary: Violence Information & Education Centre.

Burman, E. & Chantler, K. (2005). Domestic violence and minoritisation: legal and policy barriers facing minoritized women leaving violent relationships. *International Journal of Law and Psychiatry*, 28, 59-74.

Calgary Coalition on Domestic violence & Calgary Immigrant women's Association. (1998). *Piece of Mind: Integration Needs of Abused Immigrant women*. Available: http://www3. telus. net/ccfv/peaceofmind. html.

City of Calgary. (2002). *The 2002 Count of Homeless Person*. Available: http://www. calgary. ca/docgallery/bu/cns/homelessness/2002_calgary_homeless_count.pdf

Crandall, M., Senturia, K., Sullivan, M. & Shiu-Thornton, S. (2005). "No way out" Russian-speaking women's experiences with domestic violence. *Journal of Interpersonal Violence*, 20(8), 941-958.

Creswell, J. W. (1998). *Qualitative Inquiry and Research Design: Choosing Among Five Traditions*. Thousand Oaks: Sage Publications.

CSDH (2008). Closing the gap in a generation: health equity through action on the social determinants of health. Final Report of the Commission on Social Determinants of Health. Geneva: WHO.

Douglas, D., Go, A., Blackstock, S. (2012). Canadian immigration changes force women to stay with sponsoring spouse for two years. *The Toronto Star*. Wednesday, December 5. Retrieved April 4, 2014: http://www. thestar.com/opinion/editorialopinion/2012/ 12/05/canadian_immigration_changes_force_women_to_stay_with_sponsoring_spouse_f or_two_years. html

DuMont, J. & Miller, K. L. (2000). Countless abused women: homeless and inadequately housed. *Canadian Women's Studies*, 20(3), 115

Federal-Provincial-Territorial Ministers Responsible for the Status of Women. (2002). *Assessing Violence Against Women*. Ottawa: Status of Women Canada.

Galabuzi, G. (2009). Social Exclusion. In D. Raphael (Ed.), *Social Determinants of Health*, pp. 235-266. Toronto: Canadian Scholars' Press Inc.

Galtung J. (1969). Violence, Peace, and Peace Research. *Journal of Peace Research*, 6(3), 167-191.

Galtung J. (1990). Cultural Violence. *Journal of Peace Research*, 27(3), 291-305.

Graham, J. M. & Thurston, W. E. (2005). Overcoming adversity: resilience & coping mechanisms developed by recent immigrant women living in the inner city of Calgary, Alberta. *Women's Health and Urban Life*, 4(1): 63-80.

Gough, P., Trocmé, N., Brown, I., Knoke, D. & Blackstock, C. (2005). Pathways to the Overrepresentation of Aboriginal Children in Care. CECW Information Sheet #23E. Toronto: University of Toronto. Retrieved from http://www. cecw-cepb.ca/publications/ 424.

James, S. E., Johnson, J., Raghaven, C., Lemos, T., Barakett, M. & Woolis, D. (2003). The violent matrix: A study of structural, interpersonal, and intrapersonal violence among a sample of poor women. *American Journal of Community Psychology*, 31(1/2), 129-141.

Keyng, N. (2013). Toronto Declared 'Sanctuary City' to Non-Status Migrants. *The Toronto Star*. February 21. Retrieved from http://www. thestar.com/news/gta/2013/02/21/ cisanctuarycity21. html

Meadows, L. M., Thurston, W. E. & Melton, C. (2001). Immigrant women's health. *Social Science & Medicine*, 52(9), 1451-1458.

Miller, W. & Crabtree, B. (1999). The dance of interpretation. In B. Crabtree & W. Miller (Eds.), *Doing Qualitative Research* (127-144). Thousand Oaks: Sage.

Morse, J. M. & Richards, L. (2002). *Readme First for a User's Guide to Qualitative Methods*. Thousand Oaks: Sage Publications.

Novac, S., Brown, J. & Bourbonnais, C. (1996). *No Room of Her Own: A Literature Review on Women and Homelessness*. Ottawa: Canadian Mortgage and Housing Corporation. Available: http://www. ginsler.com/documents/noroom. pdf

Nursall, K. (2014). Hamilton Declares Itself Sanctuary City. *The Toronto Star*. February 12. Retrieved from: http://www. thestar.com/news/gta/2014/02/12/hamilton_declares_itself _sanctuary_city_for_undocumented_immigrants. html

Oelke, N. D., Thurston, W. E., Arthur, N. (2013). Intersections between interprofessional practice, cultural competency and primary healthcare. *Journal of Interprofessional Care*, 27, 367-372.

Ramaliu, A. & Thurston, W. (2003). Identifying best practices of community participation in providing services to refugee survivors of torture: a case description. *Journal of Immigrant Health*, 5(4), 165-172.

Salcido, O. & Adelman, M. (2004). "He has me tied with the blessed and damned papers": Undocumented-immigrant battered women in Phoenix, Arizona. *Human Organization*, 63(2), 162-172.

Scheper-Hughes, N. (2004). Dangerous and endangered youth: Social Structures and determinants of violence. *Annals NY Academy of Science*, 1036, 13-46.

Shirwadkar, S. (2004). Canadian domestic violence policy and Indian immigrant women. *Violence Against Women*, 10(8), 860-879.

Supporting Communities Partnership Initiative. (2003). *Best Practices for Working with Homeless Immigrants and Refugees*. Toronto: Access Alliance Multicultural Community Health Centre. Available via the Virtual Library of the PCERII Metropolis website: http://pcerii. metropolis. net/frameset_e.html.

Thomas, T. N. (1995). Acculturative stress in the adjustment of immigrant families. *Journal of Social Distress and the Homeless*, *4*(2), 131-142.

Thurston, W. E. (1998). Health promotion from a feminist perspective: a framework for an effective health system response to woman abuse. *Resources for Feminist Research*, *26*(3/4), 175-202

Thurston, W. E., Cory, J. & Scott, C. M. (1998). Building a feminist theoretical framework for screening of wife-battering: key issues to be addressed. *Patient Education & Counselling*, *33*(3), 299-304.

Thurston, W. E. & Potvin, L. (2003). Evaluability assessment: a tool for incorporating evaluation in social change programmes. *Evaluation*, *9*, 453-469.

Thurston, W., Roy, A., Clow, B., Este, D., Gordey, T., Haworth-Brockman, M., McCoy, R., Saulnier, C. & Carruthers, L. (2013). Pathways Into and Out of Homelessness. *Journal of Immigrant & Refugee Studies*, *11*, 278-298.

Thurston, W. E. & Verhoef, M. J. (2003). Occupational injury among immigrants. *Journal of International Migration and Integration*, *4*(1), 105-124.

Thurston, W. & Vissandjée, B. (2005). An Ecological Model for Understanding Culture as a Determinant of Women's Health. *Critical Public Health*, September, *15*(3), 229-242.

Tutty, L. M., Thurston, W. E., Christensen, J. & Eisener, A. (2003). *Evaluation of the CDVC Domestic Violence Training and Protocol Project for Immigrant Serving Agencies.* Report for the Calgary Domestic Violence Committee. Calgary, AB: RESOLVE Alberta.

Veenstra, G. (2011). Race, Gender, Class, and Sexual Orientation: Intersecting Axes of Inequality and Self-Rated Health in Canada. *International Journal of Equity Health*, *10*(1), 3-14.

Vissandjée, B., Thurston, W. E., Apale, A. & Nahar, K. (2007). Women's health at the intersection of gender and the experience of migration. In M. Morrow, O. Hankivsky, & C. Varcoe (Eds.), *Women's Health in Canada: Critical Theory, Policy and Practice* (221-243). Toronto, ON: University of Toronto Press.

In: Overcoming Domestic Violence
Editors: Myra F. Taylor, Julie Ann Pooley et al.

ISBN: 978-1-63321-956-4
© 2015 Nova Science Publishers, Inc.

Chapter 7

DOMESTIC VIOLENCE AMONG SOUTH ASIAN WOMEN: AN ECOLOGICAL PERSPECTIVE

Bushra Sabri[*]

School of Nursing, Johns Hopkins University, Baltimore, MD, US

ABSTRACT

Domestic violence among South Asian women is a major social and public health concern. Although domestic violence is a problem in all communities, manifestations of domestic violence among South Asians is rooted in socio-cultural factors such as patriarchal family structures, rigid gender norms, and justification of domestic violence when women are viewed as not confirming to expected gender norms. Using an ecological perspective, this chapter reviews the literature on risk and protective factors and outcomes of domestic violence among South Asian women. The focus is on macro-level factors (e.g., cultural beliefs, traditional gender norms), exosystem-level factors (e.g. access to resources, community sanctions against domestic violence), micro-system factors (e.g., relationship conflict, alcohol problems) and individual-level factors (e.g., socio-demographic characteristics such as young age, low socio-economic status). The chapter identifies barriers at different ecological levels that affect responses to violence. An examination of factors at ecological levels is critically important for informing strategies and programs which eliminate risk and protect women from exposure to violence and its negative effects. Finally, the chapter discusses practice and policy implications.

INTRODUCTION

Domestic violence is a major criminal and public health problem. Domestic violence against women is defined as '*any act of gender-based violence that results in, or is likely to result in, physical, sexual or mental harm or suffering to women, including threats of such*

---

[*] Corresponding author: Dr. Bushra Sabri, Faculty Research Associate, School of Nursing, Johns Hopkins University, 816 N Washington Street, Baltimore, MD-21205, Tel (319) 331-3732, Email: bushrasabri@gmail.com.

acts, coercion or arbitrary deprivation of liberty, whether occurring in public or in private life' (World Health Organization (WHO), 2013). In a 2013 global review of available data, approximately 35% of women worldwide experienced physical and/or sexual violence by an intimate partner (WHO, 2013). Although all women are at risk for domestic violence, the risk is alarmingly high in women living in societies ignoring or condoning violence against women.

The problem of domestic violence is acute in South Asia (i.e., India, Pakistan, Nepal, Bangladesh, Sri Lanka and Bhutan; (Ahmad, Driver, McNally, & Steward, 2009). For instance, in India, the domestic violence prevalence estimates range from 6% in one state (i.e., Himachal Pradesh) to 59% in another (i.e., Bihar) (Charlette et al., 2012; Garcia-Moreno, Heise, Jansen, Ellsberg, & Watts, 2005) and has been associated with severe negative outcomes such as injuries to the head, strangulation injuries (Sabri, Renner, Stockman, Mittal & Decker, 2014) and deaths (Prasad, 1994). The perpetrators include both intimate partners and extended family members (Raj, Livramento, Santana, Gupta, & Silverman, 2006). Furthermore, the prevalence of domestic violence has been found to be notably high among South Asian women who belong to immigrant groups in other countries (Raj & Silverman, 2002).

South Asian women typically experience violence in the form of economic control, verbal abuse/degradation, forced domestic servitude, kidnapping, harassment due to the inability of a woman's family to make dowry payments at the time of marriage, rape, physical assault, acid throwing and honor killings (Niaz & Hassan, 2006; Raj et al., 2006). Other examples of violence against South Asian women include the control of children by in-laws or in-laws turning children against their mothers. Women who grow up in a domestic violence environment and marry early, early marriage can be a way of escaping their abusive childhood home environment. However, these marriages are often unsuitable as women's ability to exercise choice and consent before marriage is limited and, thus, may place them in another domestic violence environment (Gupta, 2008).

ECOLOGICAL MODEL OF VIOLENCE AGAINST WOMEN

Bronfenbrenner's (1977) ecological model of systems at multiple ecological levels provides a useful framework for understanding South Asian women's exposure to violence and its outcomes. The ecological framework is "the scientific study of the progressive mutual accommodation, throughout the life span, between a growing human organism and the changing immediate environments in which it resides, as this process is affected by relations obtaining within and between these immediate settings, as well as the larger social contexts, both formal and informal in which the settings are embedded" (Bronfrenbrenner, 1977; p. 514; Sabri, Hong, Campbell & Cho, 2013). The framework has been applied to understand exposure to violence and has been modified to suit the subject under study (e.g., children or adults) and the author's personal style (Brownridge, 2009). In intimate partner violence literature, the model attributes the development of violence to the interplay of characteristics at four levels: 1) macrosystem (societal); 2) exosystem (community); 3) microsystem (familial or other proximal social relationships); and 4) individual (Sadowski, Hunter, Bangdiwala, & Munoz, 2004). It highlights "the ways in which factors at the individual, interpersonal and systemic levels interact to influence the continuation and cessation of violence in relationships" (Goodman, Dutton, Vankos, & Weinfurt, 2005; p. 312-313). The ecological model facilitates a comprehensive public health approach that not only allows careful examination of multiple layered risk factors associated with becoming a victim, but also the norms, beliefs and social and economic systems that create the conditions for domestic violence to occur (Sadowski et al., 2004; WHO, 2010).

Researchers have used the Bronfrenbrenner's (1977) model in violence against women scholarship to inform research, prevention, and treatment (Campbell et al., 2009). It has been used to explain the underlying causes of violence against women (Heise, 1998), including risk factors for violence among immigrant women (Brownridge, 2009), and impact of violence (i.e., sexual assault) on women's recovery process, mental health, and well-being (Campbell et al., 2009; Neville & Heppner, 1999). Additionally, the model has been adapted by the WHO to develop multi-level models for the prevention of gender-based violence (Campbell et al., 2009; Krug, Mercy, Dahlberg, & Zwerg, 2002).

Violence against women cannot be attributed to a single factor. It is a multifaceted phenomenon resulting from the interaction between various characteristics of the individual and their environment (Heise, 1998; Krug, et al., 2002; Stith, Smith, Penn, Ward, & Tritt, 2004; Sabri et al., 2014) at macrosystem, exosystem, microsystem and individual levels (Heise, 1998; WHO, 2010; Sabri et al., 2014). The *macrosystem* involves general cultural values and beliefs that help to create a climate in which violence is encouraged. The examples include notion of masculinity linked to honor, rigid gender roles, sense of male entitlement over women, cultural ethos that condones violence as a means to settle interpersonal disputes, and the lack of responsiveness of the criminal justice system (Heise, 1998; Krug et al., 2002; Stith et al., 2004). Cultural values and beliefs that condone violence against women can a) promote violence in intimate partner relationships, b) lead women to blame themselves for the abuse while taking the responsibility away from the abuser, and c) inhibit help-seeking. Thus, in South Asia, culturally-specific risk factors (e.g., strict adherence to patriarchal values), and cultural constructions of women in society can promote violence against women (Pinnewala, 2009).

The *exosystem* context includes the byproducts of changes taking place in the larger social milieu (e.g., migration, disadvantaged neighborhoods). The exosystem factors may or may not directly affect women, but can influence their lives in the microsystem. For instance, factors such as resources for social support (Stith, et al, 2004) and social isolation can result in decrease or increase in the severity of domestic violence in a relationship. The exosystem level includes formal and informal institutions and social structures within the community and the state. (Pinnewala, 2009). The third level is the *microsystem* which includes characteristics of the immediate setting in which violence takes place. Factors in the microsystem such as traditional family structure, forced sex (Campbell et al., 2003; McFarlane et al., 2005), partner's threats of harm, jealousy and controlling behaviors (Dalal & Lindqvist, 2012; Pandey, Dutt, & Banerjee, 2009; Sabri et al., 2014) have been positively associated with domestic violence. In South Asia, the cultural meanings and constraints of how relationships work in the microsystem affects a woman's own resources the relationship, the ways of developing effective coping and recovery from abuse. Due to male control of resources within the family, recovery from violence is a slow and difficult process, which is dependent to a great extent on a woman's emotional and physical resources (Pinnewala, 2009). Finally, the fourth level is the *individual* level which includes women's developmental experiences or personality and influences their responses to microsystem and exosystem stressors. For instance, factors such as younger age (Campbell, Glass, Sharps, Laughon, & Bloom, 2007; Pratt, & Deosaransingh, 1997), low education (Ackerson, Kawachi, Barbeau, & Subramanian, 2008), history of experiencing or witnessing abuse in childhood (Davis & Briggs, 2000; Henning, Leitenberg, Coffey, Turner & Bennett, 1996) have been found to be positively associated with domestic violence.

The ecological model can be used to understand factors related to exposure to violence, the impact of domestic violence experiences on South Asian women's health and well-being and barriers to seeking or receiving help. In addition, the model can be used as a guide to assess the need for macrosystem-level, exosystem-level, microsystem-level and individual-level prevention and intervention programs for women in abusive relationships.

MACROSYSTEM FACTORS

The macrosystem, referred to as a cultural "blueprint" (Bronfrenbrenner, 1977), includes socio-cultural, and political contexts that influence women's exposure to violence. Patriarchal cultural values of the society, often mirrored in its legal structure, community attitudes and the broader social context, including the media, play a significant role in the acceptance and promotion of violence against women (Abraham, 1998; Niaz, 2003). Literature and films have endorsed images of women as long-suffering, patient, unquestioning women who fatalistically accept their abuse and do little to change it. Women are lauded for silently suffering from abuse but still staying home and not desisting from their expected roles as wives, mothers or daughters (Narula & Narula, 2012). Women who violate gendered family roles are viewed as those who need to be disciplined. In a review of 14 cultures by Counts and colleagues (1999), physical discipline of wives was tolerated and even considered necessary in most societies (Counts, Brown & Campbell, 1999; Niaz 2003). In some South Asian regions, women are considered a property, to be transferred from father to husband and finally to the son, which negates their independent status (Abraham, 1998). Practices of arranged marriages (i.e., grooms selected by families) contribute to South Asian women's disadvantaged and devalued position. Women are viewed as commodities in arranged marriage settings in which women's worth often depends on their material assets such as money or property they bring to the groom's family (Chaudhuri, Morash, & Yingling, 2014).

The South Asian cultural norm of joint family systems involve the woman leaving her home at marriage and residing in the home of her husband with his parents, siblings and other extended family members. The joint family norm may facilitate South Asian women's exposure to domestic violence by in-laws who hold patriarchal ideologies and entitlement to abuse. Failure to conform to culturally accepted behavioral norms, inability to do housework, ill-temper and disrespect shown to family members are considered justifiable reasons for abuse by in-laws (Chaudhuri et al., 2014). Other causes of violence include dowry-related hostilities, and assaults on women accused of being witches (Dhakal, 2008). A study among South Asian women, for example, found in-laws' support or incite of intimate partner violence against women, with some women even reporting direct physical abuse by their in-laws, even during pregnancy (Raj et al., 2006). Further, women who become widows are also vulnerable to violence by in-laws as women become part of a husband's family after marriage and typically continue to live with their in-laws even after marriage. Widows, perceived as unwanted burdens, report being blamed for their husbands' deaths and often considered the purveyors of ill-fortune. Such factors result in physical, verbal, sexual and economic abuse by the family members (United Nations Division for the Advancement of Women, 2001).

According to Niaz (2003), in South Asian societies, women experience violence due to: 1) the "macho" concept of masculinity and masculine traits of dominance, strength and aggression; where men show off their strength by being aggressive to women; 2) male chauvinism, according to which, women are perceived as inferior to men and thus deserving of less than equal treatment; 3) the concept of men's loss of control over women who are educated or economically independent and where men try to regain control by using violence against women; and 4) the concept of displacement of affect (i.e., suspension of economic progression) which can lead to frustration and aggression in society and requires an outlet. Thus, men's use of violence against their weak and dependent female partners serves to displace their aggression without putting themselves at personal risk (Niaz, 2003).

South Asian women suffer tremendous physical and psychological stress due to prevailing cultural norms and associated exposure to domestic violence. Religious injunctions, feudal traditions, tribal codes and discriminatory laws expose women to a lifetime of social and psychological disadvantage (Niaz & Hassan, 2006). In a review by Niaz and Hassan (2006), abused women in South Asian countries (i.e., India, Nepal and Bangladesh) were found to show a significantly greater number of mental health problems than men. This could be attributed to women's inferior status in the family, lack of control over the environment and lack of support from the criminal justice system, which considers it a domestic dispute (Niaz & Hassan, 2006). The cultural norms of dowry and family honor have been related to lethal outcomes of domestic violence. Dowry is a form of marriage payment, in which a bride brings property or money to her husband and his family at the time of marriage (Prasad, 1994). Many domestic violence-related homicides of women in South Asian families have been found to occur due to their inability to pay dowry. Due to the practice of dowry, many traditional families consider a girl child as a liability while a male child as an asset. The preference of a male child over a female child has resulted in other forms of violence against women such as sex-selection abortions and female infanticide and psychological/verbal abuse of women for giving birth to a female child (Sehgal, & Kour, 2012).

In addition, many South Asian women become victims of honor killings. Honor killings in South Asia are ancient practices in which "men kill female relatives in the name of family 'honor' for forced or suspected sexual activity outside marriage, even when they have been victims of rape" (Tripathi & Yadav, 2004; p. 64). Thus, traditional South Asian cultural norms that promote women's victimization create a difficult socio-cultural context which has a strong negative impact on women's ability to live healthy, safe or violence-free lives.

Religion plays an important role in South Asian cultural milieu. On the one hand, religion and spirituality can be an important source of support for South Asian abused women and part of their recovery process (Comas-Diaz & Greene, 2013). On the other hand, strict adherence to traditional religious beliefs which legitimize women's subordinate status to men may contribute to violence against women (Abraham, 1998). In South Asia, what goes on in the family is considered personal and secret (Niaz, 2003). Traditional cultural attitudes about men's rights and privileges in families, and women's adherence to such cultural beliefs place pressure on women to remain silent about their abusive situations and inhibit them from seeking help (Gage & Hutchinson 2006; Kamat et al., 2010).

South Asian immigrant women continue to be impacted by the traditional cultural norms of their countries of origin such as patriarchal beliefs, rigid gender roles, and myths about partner abuse (Ahmad et al., 2009; Yoshihama, M., Ramakrishnan, A., Hammock, A.C., & Khaliq, M., 2012). The two patriarchal concepts of 'izzat' (honor) and 'sharam' (shame) are used to control and silence women in abusive relationships. Both men and women are supposed to uphold family and community honor. Women, however, are most often held accountable. Women who leave the abusive relationship or disclose abuse face rejection by family and community members (Gupta, 2008). Despite high rates of abuse reported among South Asian immigrant women (e.g., 41%; Raj & Silverman, 2002), women infrequently seek help or disclose abuse.

EXOSYSTEM/COMMUNITY-LEVEL FACTORS

The exosystem includes both formal and informal social structures such as neighborhood, extended family, the state, and other social institutions (Pinnewala, 2009). The formal and informal social networks in the exosystem can help abused women with support, advice and means of leaving an abusive relationship and protect them from re-victimization (Brownridge, 2009). However, multiple risk factors in the exosystem place women at risk for domestic violence and serve as barriers to seeking help and associated negative consequences. For instance, social isolation has been found to be both a cause and consequence of violence against women (Heise, 1998), and a barrier to seeking help for South Asian women (Ahmad et al., 2009). Research on South Asian immigrant women in the USA shows that perpetrators of domestic violence isolate women by limiting their contact with family in the USA, in the country of origin as well as prohibiting friendships with people outside of the family domain (George & Rahangdale, 1999; Raj & Silverman, 2002). Loss of social networks and extended family system after immigration, and isolation by husband and in-laws served as barriers to help-seeking for abuse (Ahmed et al., 2009). Disclosure of domestic violence may seem dangerous to women due to the lack of power that they experience within family (Singh, 2006).

The quality of social support from informal networks (e.g., family and friends) is crucial for women's health and safety. Negative social reactions from the informal networks can have a stronger detrimental impact on abused women's mental health because of the expectations of sympathetic reactions from these people. Negative reactions may prevent women from further disclosures or help-seeking, which is associated with higher distress (Campbell et al., 2009). Contrary to this, the presence of positive support and reactions from social network in the exosystem can be protective against exposure to domestic violence and its negative effects (Mahapatra, 2012). Social support have been found to be an important factor in disclosing abuse and seeking help among immigrant South Asian women in the US (Yoshioka, Gilbert, El-Bassel, & Baig-Amin, 2003 cited in Mahapatra, 2012).

Women exposed to violence have extensive service needs that could facilitate recovery from abuse and provide a safe environment. Thus, availability, access and utilization of domestic violence, legal and healthcare resources may serve as protective factors for South

Asian women. Researchers, however, have found that South Asian women are less likely to seek help, and only seek help when they can no longer endure abuse, when abuse becomes life threatening or severe, or when their children are at risk (Decker et al., 2013; Naved, Azim, Bhuiya, & Persson, 2006; Panchanadeswaran, & Koverola, 2005; Sabri et al., 2014). Women's perception of domestic violence as common and acceptable has also been negatively associated with women's help-seeking (Sudha & Morrison, 2011). Other factors include lack of education and skills (Dalal, 2011; Kamat et al., 2010), responsibilities towards children and hope that circumstances would improve (Panchanadeswaran & Koverola, 2005).

South Asian women, who are immigrants, may not seek help due to factors such as lack of awareness of available domestic violence and legal services for abused women and lack of culturally or linguistically competent services (Raj & Silverman, 2002). Among women who seek help, unmet needs for care and safety, and insensitive treatment of practitioners can magnify feelings of powerlessness and result in negative outcomes (Campbell, Dworkin, & Cabral, 2009). Thus, practitioners must be trained in culturally and gender sensitive interventions with South Asian women who are facing or have faced abuse in their lives. There is a need for formal and informal support networks in the exosystem to increase knowledge, access and utilization of services among South Asian women. Further, efforts should focus on eliminating barriers to resource utilization among women in abusive relationships.

MICROSYSTEM FACTORS

The microsystem level for women includes people in their family relationships with whom they interact and assign subjective meanings to those interactions (Heise, 1998). Women's exposure to violence in interpersonal relationships within their microsystems (e.g., violence by an intimate partner), directly threaten their safety, health and well-being. For instance, in a community-based sample (n=218) of South Asian women (i.e., from India, Bangladesh and Nepal), exposure to domestic violence was found to be associated with poor physical health, injuries, depression, anxiety, and suicide ideation. Further, domestic violence-induced depression and anxiety affected women's sleep, appetite, energy and well-being (Hurwitz, Gupta, Liu, Silverman & Raj, 2006). Moreover, women's poor mental and physical health may interfere with their ability to seek help or disclose abuse and lead to re-victimization.

The microsystem factors that have been shown to increase risk for domestic violence include gender inequity in intimate partner relationships, partner's jealousy and controlling behavior, partner dominance in the family, partner control of family's wealth, and marital conflict (Heise, 1998). Further, violence perpetrated by family members of the women's partner has been linked with women's exposure to intimate partner's violence (Falb et al., 2013). Formerly married women (i.e., widows in South Asia) are perceived as unwanted burdens on families due to inadequate policies and procedures to address their needs. Therefore, they become frequent victims of violence and abuse by in-laws (Alexander & Regier, 2011; Coomaraswamy, 2005). In addition, lack of education and employment resources of women's partners in the microsystem may contribute to their likelihood of experiencing violence (Brownridge, 2009). All these factors have been found to play a role in the occurrence and maintenance of domestic violence in South Asian countries such as Sri Lanka (Pinnewala, 2009), Nepal (Alexander & Regier, 2011; Budhathoki, 2012; Lamichhane, Puri, Tamang, & Dulal, 2011;Ministry of Health and Population-Nepal, New Era & ICF International, 2012) and in India (Sabri et al., 2014). Further, families with multiple children are more likely to report domestic violence due to increased stressors within the family system (Martin et al., 1999). Other factors include women's higher educational attainment than the partner (Ahmad et al., 2009; Heise, 1998; Sabri et al., 2014). Additionally, studies in India have found a partner's alcohol use as a risk factor for severe physical domestic violence, domestic violence-related injuries (Sabri et al., 2014) and homicide of women (Vindhya, 2000). Being in a long term relationship has been related to the likelihood of experiencing domestic violence (Brown & Bulanda, 2005; Sabri et al., 2014). In a study of 751 women living in slums in Calcutta, India, Pandey, Dutt and Banerjee (2009) found that a long duration of marriage was associated with a greater likelihood of reporting domestic violence. Women who remain in abusive relationships for long periods of time are more likely to experience domestic violence that escalates over time.

South Asian women who are immigrants face both culturally-specific forms of abuse (e.g., abuse due to culturally based gender roles) as well as immigration related abuse (e.g., threat of deportation) by their intimate partners. For instance, immigrant women's acculturation and moving out of traditional gender-based norms promote men's desire to control them by the use of violence. In addition, women with less protected immigration status also face domestic violence by their partners who use fear of deportation and economic abuse to control them (Raj & Silverman, 2002).

INDIVIDUAL-LEVEL FACTORS

The individual-level factors that place South Asian women at risk for domestic violence and related negative health outcomes include socio-demographic variables such as low levels of education in male partners or an educational gap between spouses, where women have higher education than their spouses (Ackerson et al., 2008; Martin, Tsui, Maitra, & Marinshaw, 1999). Additionally, a woman's lack of education or low education can be a barrier for her to move out of an abusive relationship and become economically independent. Further, there is strong evidence that domestic violence is more common in families with low socio-economic status (Jeyseelan et al., 2007; Sabri et al., 2014) and unemployed men (Heise, 1998). The experience of living in poverty and associated stress such as hopelessness, frustration, and a sense of inadequacy in some men for failing to live up to their culturally defined role of provider, may result in domestic violence (Heise, 1998).

Some research shows that South Asian women may have fewer opportunities for paid employment due to low level of education/lack of job skills or traditional gender norms. This negatively impacts their mental health (Niaz & Hassan, 2006) and ability to break free from abuse. Other research shows that education and employment can increase the risk for domestic violence among South Asian women (Dalal, 2011, Kamat et al., 2010; Krishnan et al., 2010; Sabri et al., 2014). Forced unemployment whereby some partners forcibly stop women from gaining or continuing employment marginalize abused women and is a barrier to help-seeking (Pinnewala, 2009). Women's employment may serve as a protective factor if it is connected with education and awareness and modified cultural norms against gender roles (Dalal, 2011; Sabri et al., 2014)

Other individual-level risk factors for domestic violence are growing up in a violent home and women's overall health. Jeyaseelan et al. (2007), for example, found that Indian women who witnessed their fathers beat their mothers were at increased risk of violence victimization by their husbands. Women's poor mental health and poor overall health have been found to increase the risk for domestic violence (Jeyaseelan et al., 2004) and to have a negative impact on their ability to disclose abuse and seek help (Alaggia, Regehr, & Jenney, 2012). Factors at the individual level are further complicated by the culture-specific notions of extreme shame and guilt a woman is socialized to feel if she seeks help for domestic violence (Pinnewala, 2009).

IMPLICATIONS FOR POLICY AND PRACTICE

In South Asia, traditional cultural and religious beliefs and women's low status in society appear to drive abuse and mistreatment of women. Cultural practices such as dowry, female murders committed by family members in order to protect the family honor, restrictions on women's mobility, limited access to education and work clearly indicate the role of cultural and religious beliefs in enabling violence against women. An ecological framework provides a holistic view of the problem of domestic violence and can be used to identify risk and protective factors and outcomes of domestic violence for South Asian women in multiple contexts. In addition, the model can be used to identify different support systems at each level, the barriers to gaining access to each type, and whether the support systems were beneficial (Pinneswala, 2009). Given that religion plays an important role in the lives of South Asian women, health care experts and social service agencies may collaborate with religious and spiritual leaders at the community level to address domestic violence and develop prevention strategies (Lee & Hadeed, 2009). At the macro level, awareness/prevention education should address culture-specific patriarchal values, the construction of women as responsible for family integrity (Pinnewala, 2009), and barriers keeping women from seeking help. Policy initiatives must be put in place to support abused women at all levels, and to minimize their barriers to seeking help. There is need for programs that promote healthy relationships and improve access to employment, housing and educational opportunities for abused women.

Many South Asian women living in Western countries still adhere to traditional cultural expectations and are socialized to accept domestic violence. For South Asian women living in the Western world, policies must ensure culturally competent services for abused women considering factors such as cultural perceptions of violence, immigration status and language barriers. In South Asian countries, policies must be in place to address factors such as socio-cultural norms promoting violence, lack of awareness of women's problems and needs, and insensitivity of the criminal justice system. Policies must ensure that there is no justification for the use of violence in relationships and perpetrators are accountable. Overall, at the macro level, there is need for prevention and intervention policies that support abused women's opportunities to live violence-free lives.

At the exosystem (community) and microsystem (family) levels in South Asia, women's sources of support can include both formal and informal institutions. However, research on South Asia immigrant women in western countries and women living in South Asia illustrates few women share experiences of violence, and far fewer seek formal services (Decker et al., 2013; Lee & Hadeed, 2009; Naved et a;., 2006; Raj & Silverman, 2007). Those South Asian women who do disclose, tend to prefer informal support over formal support which is considered a constant source of help (Pinnwala, 2009).

Therefore, informal sources of support (i.e., community members), for both immigrant South Asian women and women living in South Asia, should be educated on domestic violence, culturally specific contributing factors, health consequences, the need for emotional support and tangible aid or other resources for domestic violence survivors in the community. Formal sources of support such as crisis intervention centers, law enforcement agencies, health care and social services can play a critical role in addressing abuse in South Asian families (Pinnewala, 2009). Thus, improvements must be made to the assessment and intervention of domestic violence in these settings in South Asia. Formal screening and safety assessments should examine both intimate partner and in-laws' abuse among South Asian women.

At the individual level, interventions may focus on dispelling myths about domestic violence, empowering abused women to seek help or escape abusive situations, promoting healthy coping and addressing their individual needs. Researchers and practitioners may continue to address factors in ecological contexts that place women at risk for violence victimization or promote factors that protect them from developing adverse outcomes. An ecological approach to understanding South Asian women's exposure to violence can be used as a tool to identify which aspects of women's contexts and functioning need attention for prevention as well as for alleviating harm.

CONCLUSION

This chapter has examined current literature on domestic violence among South Asian women. The review of literature highlights that women in South Asia are exposed to violence and its negative effects due to factors operating at multiple levels in their environment. The macrosystem level factors include patriarchal ideology, religious cultural beliefs, traditional gender norms and norms that justify use of violence against women when women are unable to conform to their gender role expectations. Among exosystem level factors, lack of social support from informal networks and inability to access domestic violence, legal and healthcare resources play a role in South Asian women's vulnerability to violence and its negative effects. The microsystem factors that serve as catalysts to women's exposure to violence include poor quality of intimate partner and extended family relationships, and lack of women's decision-making power in the family. The individual-level factors include education, employment, growing up in a violent home and mental health issues. Outcomes of domestic violence range from physical and mental health problems to injuries and even deaths of women. Women victimized in the family at the microsystem level and further victimized by socio-cultural forces at the macro and exosystem levels may face poorer outcomes such as mental health problems, low self-esteem and inability to seek help.

Evidence shows that women's exposure to more types of victimization (e.g., both domestic violence and property crime) can result in worse outcomes, for example, higher levels of distress and impairment in functioning (Linares, 2004). Thus, South Asian women exposed to violence need interventions across the macro, exo, micro and individual levels. Interventions should include public education campaigns about women's issues, creating awareness, addressing socio-cultural beliefs affecting women's lives and linking women to services. Further, efforts should focus on empowering survivors of violence and addressing their individual needs. There is need for programs that provide education, housing and employment opportunities for women to break free from abusive relationships. An ecological model can provide a more comprehensive examination and understanding of South Asian women's exposure to violence and areas of prevention and intervention for practitioners and policymakers. The framework can be utilized to identify modifiable factors at multiple ecological levels such as employment, education, the availability and accessibility of resources, women's willingness to seek help and change in socio-cultural norms that support violence against women.

REFERENCES

Abraham, M. (1998). Speaking the unspeakable: Marital violence against South Asian immigrant women in the United States. *Indian Journal of Gender Studies*, *5*(2), 215-241.

Ackerson, L. K., Kawachi, I., Barbeau, E. M. & Subramanian, S. V. (2008). Effects of individual and proximate educational context on intimate partner violence: A population-based study of women in India. *American Journal of Public Health*, *98*(3), 507-514.

Ahmad, F., Driver, N., McNally, M. J. & Stewart, D. E. (2009). Why doesn't she seek help for partner abuse?'' An exploratory study with South Asian immigrant women. *Social Science & Medicine*, *69*, 613-622.

Alaggia, R., Regehr, C. & Jenney, A. (2012). Risky business: An ecological analysis of intimate partner violence disclosure. *Research on Social Work Practice*, *22* (3), 301-312.

Alexander, E. & Regier, E. (2011). Speaking out on violence and social change: Transmedia storytelling with remotely situated women in Nepal and Canada. *Canadian Theatre Review*, *148*, 38-42.

Bronfenbrenner U. (1977). Toward an experimental ecology of human development. *American Psychologist*, *32*, 513–531.

Brown, S. L. & Bulanda, J. R. (2005). *Relationship violence in young adulthood: A comparison of daters, cohabitors, and marrieds*. Center for Family and Demographic Research working paper 06-06.

Brownridge, D. A., (2009). "Situating research on vulnerable populations within the family violence field" (4-14). In Violence Against Women-Vulnerable Populations: Routledge: New York and London.

Budhathoki, N., Dahal, M., Bhusal, S., Ojha, H., Pandey, S. & Basnet, S. (2012). Violence against women by their husband and postpartum depression. *J Nepal Health Res Counc*, *10*(22), 176-180.

Campbell, R., Dworkin, E. & Cabral, G. (2009). An ecological model of the impact of sexual assault on women's mental health. *Trauma, Violence & Abuse*, *10* (3), 225-246.

Campbell, J. C., Glass, N. E., Sharps. P. W., Laughon, K. & Bloom, T. (2007). Intimate partner homicide: Review and implications for research and policy. *Violence. Trauma, & Abuse, 8*(3), 246-269.

Campbell. J. C., Webster, D., Koziol-McLain, J., Block, C., Campbell, D., Curry, M. A… Laughon, K. (2003). Risk factors for femicide in abusive relationships: Results from a multisite case control study. *American Journal of Public Health, 93*(7), 1089-1097.

Charlette, S. L., Nongkynrih, B. & Gupta, S. K. (2012). Domestic violence in India: Need for public health action. *Indian Journal of Public Health, 56*(2), 140-145.

Chaudhuri, S., Morash, M. & Yingling, J. (2014). Marriage migration, patriarchal bargains and wife abuse: A study of South Asian women. *Violence against Women, 20* (2), 141-161,

Comas-Diaz, L. & Greene, B. (2013). *Psychological health of women of color: Intersections, challenges and opportunities.* ABC-CLIO: California.

Coomaraswamy, R. (2005). Human security and gender violence. *Economic and Political Weekly, 40*(44/45), 4729-4736.

Counts, D. A., Brown, J. K. & Campbell, J. C. (1999). *To have and hit: Cultural perspectives on wife beating.* University of Illinois Press: Illinois.

Decker, M., Nair, S., Saggurti, N., Sabri, B., Jethva, M., Raj, A., Donta, B. & Silverman, J. G. (2013). Violence-related coping, help-seeking and health care based intervention preferences among perinatal women in Mumbai, India. *Journal of Interpersonal Violence, 28*(9), 1924-1947.

Dalal, K. (2011). Does economic empowerment protect women from intimate partner violence? *Journal of Injuries and Violence Research, 3*(1), 35-44.

Dalal, K. & Lindqvist, K. (2012). A national study of the prevalence and correlates of domestic violence among women in India. *Asia-Pacific Journal of Public Health, 24*(2), 265-277.

Davis, J. & Briggs, E. (2000). *Witnessing Violence Fact Sheet.* Retrieved from http://www. musc. edu/vawprevention/research/witnessing.shtml

Dhakal, S. (2008). Nepalese women under the shadow of domestic violence. *The Lancet, 371*, 547-548.

Falb, K. L., Annan, J., Hossain, M., Topolska, M., Kpebo, D. & Jhumka, G. (2013). Recent abuse from in-laws and associations with adverse experiences during the crisis among rural Ivorian women: Extended families as part of the ecological model. *Global Public Health, 8* (7), 831-844.

Garcia-Moreno, C., Jansen, H. A. F. M., Ellsberg, M. Heise, L. & Watts, C. (2005). *WHO Multi-country study on women's health and domestic violence against women.* Retrieved from http://www. who. int/gender/violence/who_multicountry_study/en/

George, M. S. & Rahangdale, L. (1999). Domestic violence and South Asian women. *North Carolina Medical Journal, 60*, 157-159.

Gupta, A. (2008). Support for South Asian Women. *Community Care, 1735*, 22-23.

Heise, L. L. (1998). Violence against women: An integrated, ecological framework. *Violence against Women, 4*(3), 262-290.

Henning, K., Leitenberg, H., Coffey, P., Turner, T. & Bennett, R. T. (1996). Long-term psychological and social impact of witnessing physical conflict between parents. *Journal of Interpersonal Violence, 11*(1), 35-51.

Hurwitz, E. J., Gupta, J., Liu, R., Silverman, J. G. & Raj, A. (2006). Intimate partner violence associated with poor health outcomes in US South Asian women. *Journal of Immigrant Minority Health, 8*, 251-261.

Jeyaseelan, L., Kumar, S., Neelakantan, N., Peedicayil, A., Pillai, R. & Duvvury, N. (2007). Physical spousal violence against women in India: Some risk factors. *Journal of Biosocial Science, 39*(5), 657-670.

Kamat, U., Ferreira, A. M. A., Motghare, D., Kamat, N. & Pinto, N. (2010). A cross-sectional study of physical spousal violence against women in Goa. *Healthline, 1*(1), 34-40.

Krishnan, S., Rocca, C. H., Hubbard, A. E., Subbiah, K., Edmeades, J. & Padian, N. S. (2010). Do changes in spousal employment status lead to domestic violence? Insights from a prospective study in Bangalore, India. *Social Science & Medicine, 70*, 136-143.

Krug, E. G., Mercy, J. A., Dahlberg, L. L. & Zwi, A. B. (2002). The world report on violence and health. *Lancet, 360*(9339), 1083-1088.

Lamichhane, P., Puri, M., Tamang, J. & Dulal B. (2011). Women's status and violence against young married women in rural Nepal. *BMC Women's Health, 11*(19).

Lee, Y. S. & Hadeed, L. (2009). Intimate partner violence among Asian immigrant communities: Health/mental health consequences, help-seeking behaviors, and service utilization. *Trauma, Violence, & Abuse, 10*, 143-170.

Linares, L. O. (2004). Social connection to neighbors, multiple victimization, and current health among women residing in high crime neighborhoods. *Journal of Family Violence, 19* (6), 355-358.

Mahapatra, N. (2012). South Asian women in the U. S. and their experience of domestic violence. *Journal of Family Violence, 27*, 381-390.

Martin, S. L., Tsui, A. M., Maitra, K. & Marinshaw, R. (1999). Domestic violence in Northern India. *American Journal of Epidemiology, 150*(4), 417-426.

McFarlane, J., Malecha, A., Gist, J., Watson, K., Batten, E., Hall, I. & Smith, S. (2005). Intimate partner sexual assault against women and associated victim substance use, suicidality, and risk factors for femicide. *Issues in Mental Health Nursing, 26*, 953-967.

Ministry of Health and Population (MOHP) [Nepal], New Era, and ICF International Inc. (2012). *Nepal Demographic and Health Survey 2011*. Kathmandu, Nepal: Ministry of Health and Population, New ERA, and ICF International, Calverton, Maryland.

Narula, D. K. & Narula, A. (2012). Patriarchal societies and domestic violence: Need for empowering women. In Charak, P. & Mohan, C. (Eds). *Women and Development-Self, Society and Empowerment* (p. 169-183). New Delhi, India: Primus Books.

Naved, R. T., Azim, S., Bhuiya, A. & Persson, L. A. (2006). Physical violence by husbands: Magnitude, disclosure and help-seeking behavior of women in Bangladesh. *Social Science & Medicine, 62*, 2917-2929.

Niaz, U. (2003). Violence against women in South Asian countries. *Archives of Women's Mental Health, 6* (3), 173-184.

Niaz, U. & Hassan, S. (2006). Culture and mental health of women in South-east Asian. *World Psychiatry, 5* (2), 118-120.

Panchanadeswaran, S. & Koverola, C. (2005). The voices of battered women in India. *Violence against Women, 11*(6), 736-758.

Pandey, G. K., Dutt, D. & Banerjee, B. (2009). Partner and relationship factors in domestic violence: Perspectives of women from a slum in Calcutta, India. *Journal of Interpersonal Violence, 24*(7), 1175-1191.

Prasad, B. D. (1994). Dowry-related violence: A content analysis of news in selected newspapers. *Journal of Comparative Family Studies*, *XXV*(1), 71-89.

Pratt, C. & Deosaransingh, K. (1997). Gender differences in homicide in Contra Costa county, California: 1982-1993. *American Journal of Preventative Medicine*, *13*(6 Suppl), 19-24.

Pinnewala, P. (2009). Good women, martyrs, and survivors: A theoretical framework for South Asian women's responses to partner violence. *Violence against Women*, *15* (1), 81-105.

Raj, A., Livramento, K. N., Santana, M. C., Gupta, J. & Silverman, J. G. (2006). Victims of intimate partner violence more likely to report abuse from in-laws. *Violence against Women*, *12* (10), 936-949.

Raj, A. & Silverman, J. (2002). Violence against immigrant women. *Violence Against Women*, *8* (3), 367-398.

Raj, A. & Silverman, J. (2007). Domestic violence help-seeking behaviors of South Asian battered women residing in the United States. *International Review of Victimology*, *14*, 143-170.

Sabri, B., Hong, J. S., Campbell, J. C. & Cho, H. (2013). Understanding children and adolescents' victimizations at multiple levels: An ecological review of the literature. *Journal of Social Service Research*, *39* (3), 322-334.

Sabri, B., Renner, L. M., Stockman, J. K., Mittal, M. & Decker, M. R. (2014). Risk factors for severe intimate partner violence and violence-related injuries among women in India. *Women & Health*, *54*, 81-300.

Sadowski, L. S., Hunter, W. M., Bangdiwala, S. I. & Munoz, S. R. (2004). The world studies of abuse in the family environment (WorldSAFE): a model of a multi-national study of family violence. *Injury Control and Safety Promotion*, *11* (2), 81-90.

Sehgal, S. & Kour, N. Women's emancipation and selective abortion in India: A source of gender discrimination. In Charak, P. & Mohan, C. (Eds). *Women and Development-Self, Society and Empowerment* (p. 97-108). New Delhi, India: Primus Books.

Singh, A. A. (2006). *Resilience strategies of South Asian women who have survived child sexual abuse.* (Counseling and Psychological Services Dissertations), Georgia State University. (Paper 4). Retrieved from: http://digitalarchive. gsu. edu/cgi/viewcontent. cgi?article=1003&context=cps_diss

Stith, S. M., Smith, D. B., Penn, C. E., Ward, D. B. & Tritt, D. (2004). Intimate partner physical abuse perpetration and victimization risk factors- A meta-analytic review. *Aggression and Violent Behavior*, *10*, 65-98.

Sudha, S. & S. Morrison. (2011). Marital violence and women's reproductive health care in Uttar Pradesh, India. *Women's Health Issues*, *21*(3), 214-221.

Tripathi, A. & Yadav, S. (2004). For the sake of honour: But whose honour? "Honour crimes" against women. *Asian-Pacific Journal on Human Rights and the Law*, *2*, 63-78.

United Nations Division for the Advancement of Women. (2001). Widowhood: invisible women, secluded or excluded. *Women 2000*. Retrieved from: http://www. un. org/womenwatch/daw/public/wom_Dec%2001%20single%20pg. pdf

Vindhya, U. (2000). "Dowry deaths" in Andhra Pradesh, India. *Violence Against Women*, *6*(1), 1085-1108.

Yoshihama, M., Ramakrishnan, A., Hammock, A. C. & Khaliq, M. (2012). Intimate partner violence prevention program in an Asian immigrant community: Integrating theories, data, and community. *Violence against Women*, *18*, 763-783.

Yoshioka, M. R., Gilbert, L., El-Bassel, N. & Baig-Amin, M. (2003). Social support and disclosure of abuse: comparing South Asian, African American, and Hispanic battered women. *Journal of Family Violence*, *18* (3), 171-180.

World Health Organization (2013). *Violence against women: Intimate partner and sexual violence against women.* Retrieved March 10th 2014 from: http://www.who.int/mediacentre/factsheets/fs239/en/

World Health Organization/London School of Hygiene and Tropical Medicine (WHO; 2010). *Preventing intimate partner and sexual violence against women: taking action and generating evidence.* Geneva, World Health Organization. Retrieved from: http://www. who. int/violence_injury_prevention/publications/violence/9789241564007_eng. pdf

In: Overcoming Domestic Violence
Editors: Myra F. Taylor, Julie Ann Pooley et al.

ISBN: 978-1-63321-956-4
© 2015 Nova Science Publishers, Inc.

Chapter 8

DOMESTIC VIOLENCE: PREVALENCE AMONG SOUTH ASIAN MIGRANT WOMEN

Neely Mahapatra[1], and Mona C. S. Schatz[2]*

[1]Assistant Professor, Division of Social Work, University of Wyoming, WY, US
[2]Professor, Division of Social, University of Wyoming, WY, US

ABSTRACT

According to the 2010 United States Census, South Asians (mostly from India, Pakistan, and Bangladesh) are one of the prominent immigrant groups in the United States with individuals belonging to a range of socioeconomic tiers from wealthy businessmen, professionals, computer technocrats to college students, blue collar workers and undocumented workers. South Asian families are spread throughout the U.S. Studies report high rates of domestic violence against South Asian migrant women in the U.S. Using narrated experiences reported to the authors from practice and research endeavors, this chapter explains various factors specific to domestic violence among this group, factors such as cultural norms and behaviors, societal norms, and issues of legal status. This chapter illuminates the role of resiliency among South Asian women who experience domestic violence. Resilience and intertwined sociocultural factors aide South Asian migrant women to not only survive abuse but rebuild their lives. Finally, this chapter discusses the important role of practitioners and domestic violence agencies in understanding and providing services to this group including assessment, intervention, community networking and coalition building and general assistance. Using vignettes depicting domestic violence cases, this chapter also elucidates key factors in providing services for social workers and professional practitioners who work with migrant domestic violence victims.

Keywords: South Asian women, migrants, domestic violence, resiliency, practice

* Corresponding author: Neely Mahapatra, Assistant Professor, Division of Social Work, University of Wyoming, 1000 E. University Ave., Dept 3632, Laramie, WY 82071, Email: nmahapat@uwyo.edu, Ph: (307).766.6864 Fax: (307).766.6839.

INTRODUCTION

Najma, a 35-year old South Asian immigrant woman, moved to the United States in 2004. Currently separated from her abusive husband, she lives in a transitional home supported by a local community shelter. Recently, she was granted a temporary green card for permanent residency. Leaving her husband meant leaving her two children whom she misses. It has been a long arduous journey for her in a foreign land with no immediate family. In the past year, she has come to depend on strangers in the form of a counselor, a lawyer, and other survivors of domestic violence, who have now become her source of support whether it is financial, mental, or legal. She shares that she still loves her husband and often wonders why he did all those things to her. She says, "all I wanted was to be his wife and love him." Najma is one among many immigrant women who dreamt of starting a new life in America after her marriage. That life in her dreams has drastically changed and now she faces the harsh reality of being a victim of domestic violence and rebuilding her life from scratch.

Najma's story represents one of many unfolding stories that illustrate the convolutions of abusive marital relationships among migrant/immigrant[1] South Asian women. The associated complexities of family violence among this unique group of women will be addressed using a multidimensional lens rather than the more typical perspective of victimology. This chapter will highlight socio-cultural aspects of domestic violence among migrant/immigrant women, specifically South Asian immigrant women in the United States and other English-speaking Westernized countries (South Asian women are from countries that include India, Pakistan, Nepal, Bangladesh, Sri Lanka, Maldives, and Bhutan (Niaz, 2003; Raj & Silverman, 2002; Raj & Silverman, 2003; Rudrappa, 2004; Sheehan, Javier, & Thanjan, 2000).

Using six vignettes gleaned from these authors' practice and research, this chapter will address resiliency factors associated with South Asian women's zeal to overcome adversity and their experience of domestic violence. Women featured in these vignettes are those who have migrated to the U.S. with their husband who is either South Asian or an American citizen of South Asian origin. In four of these vignettes, women lived with their in-laws in the same household. Most of them were without immediate or extended family members in America. The experiences that are presented here were selected because they illustrate multiple dimensions of the problems faced by migrant women, women who share similar cultural paradigms. Finally, culturally relevant intervention approaches that improve the quality of professional work for South Asian migrant women will be discussed.

DOMESTIC VIOLENCE: PREVALENCE AMONG SOUTH ASIAN WOMEN

Domestic violence has been extensively studied among immigrant women groups in the United States (Menjívar & Salcido 2002), specifically examining women in heterosexual relationships. Between 41% and 60% of Asian American women experience abuse at some point during their lifetime as compared with about 25% to 30% of women in the U.S. population overall (Lee, 2013). Domestic violence is one of the most common forms of abuse

---

[1] Throughout this chapter, the terms migrant and immigrant are used interchangeably.

experienced by immigrant women (Erez, 2002). Several studies narrate some of the common experiences of domestic violence by immigrant women from various countries (Yoshioka, Gilbert, El-Bassel, & Baig-Amin, 2003; Kulwicki, Aswad, Carmona, & Ballout, 2010; Van Hightower, Gorton, & DeMoss, 2000; Muftic, & Bouffard, 2008; Crandall, Senturia, Sullivan, & Shiu-Thornton, 2005). These studies enlightened us about the various important experiences of immigrant women (e.g. Asian, Hispanic, Middle Eastern, and European), in the context of domestic violence.

SOCIOCULTURAL FACTORS AND STRESSORS

Scholars have focused on a wide variety of topics related to domestic violence among immigrant women including sociocultural factors, family stressors, and challenges that impede their position in a new country and thus leading to subordination of women, their help-seeking behaviors, impact of immigration laws and domestic policies on battered immigrant women, access to health care, and restoration of basic human rights and advocacy. Domestic violence though common is also a surreptitious occurrence in most patriarchal societies such as the South Asian society. Family structure and the traditional gender roles of men and women are an important factor contributing to inequality and violence against women (Tse, 2007).

DOMESTIC VIOLENCE STUDIES DESCRIBE COMPLEXITIES

In the case of the South Asian woman staying home full time or the mother working outside the home, subtleties can be different, but at the same time the woman is still held by gender roles ascribed by the "traditional" community. Unfortunately, women who do not fit these traditional roles – including those who are divorced, separated, single, or battered – have a challenging path in order to receive the much needed support and respect of family and community members.

Women in traditional patriarchal roles are often abused by not only their husband, but also by other family members (e.g., fathers, brothers, and in-laws). In many instances, a South Asian women, after marriage, moves in with the husband's family (patrilocal family arrangement) that could include the husband's father and mother, unmarried sister-in-law(s), unmarried brother-in-law(s), or a married brother-in-law living in the same house. In situations of marital conflicts and abuse from husbands, women are often pressured by immediate family members, extended family, in-laws, and sometimes friends coerce women to remain in the marriage and adopt a subservient role.

Raj, Livramento, Santana, Gupta and Silverman (2006) in their study of South Asian immigrant women (n=169) and abuse from in-laws found that there was a significant relationship between intimate partner violence or domestic violence and in-laws. Twenty-three percent of the women in the sample (n=169) reported abuse, and of that group, 5.9% reported abuse from their in-laws. Women experienced physical and emotional abuse, support of abuse by in-laws, and financial difficulties. The authors further explained that these women were isolated from their own family and under constant surveillance by their in-laws.

Expenditure decisions were made by in-laws (a mother or father-in-law), which greatly affected the wife's self-esteem. Additionally, the emotional and financial abuse was accentuated by verbal abuse. Women reported experiences of being demoralized by verbal humiliation by other family members, having to do excessive domestic chores, and having restricted access to food (Raj et al., 2006).

ACCULTURATION PLAYS A ROLE IN ADJUSTING TO DOMESTIC VIOLENCE

Acculturation is understood as the process of acquiring cultural behaviors in the dominant cultural (adopted from the external dominant environment) and retaining one's own cultural heritage and traditional behaviors, language, etc. Acculturation is viewed on a continuum, as every person chooses or adopts new cultural behaviors in their own way. This process of acculturation plays an important role in immigrant women's lives as adjustments are made to adapt to the mundane affairs in her home, traditions in line with one's personal culture, as well as adopting new experiences emerging from the behaviors, values, and rules of the adopted country.

Yoshioka et al. (2003) explain that women are expected to acculturate by their spouses and at the same time experience abuse for doing so. The rates of acculturation vary among different generations of immigrant women. The first generation South Asian women are keen on upholding the traditional South Asian values, while the second or later generation South Asian women, who are born and brought up in the United States, assimilate faster into the mainstream culture and are less likely to adhere to traditions and customs. They hold more egalitarian views about gender roles than their native-born counterparts (Dasgupta, 1998).

THE ROLE OF SOCIAL SUPPORT

A South Asian woman's immediate or primary support network may include immediate family members, extended family members, close friends, sometimes co-workers and others, depending on their physical location and social status (Streeter & Franklin, 1992). An outside support network may include neighbors and friends at work and other members in the community (Abraham, 2000). South Asian women are more likely to disclose abuse to their father or brother or their kin network compared to other ethnic groups such as African American or Hispanic women (Yoshioka et al., 2003). Sometimes, women in abusive circumstances just need someone to have a listening ear and that could be instrumental for their survival.

Yet, for many immigrant women, they leave behind an essential support network. Thus, as they begin the process of setting up the domiciliary (for example, taking care of everyday matters including cooking, grocery shopping, and cleaning and taking care of family and children), they have little time to socialize and create a support network. The more isolated and disconnected the migrant South Asian woman is, her ability to build a support system is limited.

LEGAL STATUS CHALLENGES

Many South Asian women enter the host country with an immigration legal status dependent on their spouse. Depending on the legal status of their husbands, women may not be legally allowed to work and the naturalization process could take longer than anticipated so situations as such create further subjugation of women. In some instances, a woman could be forbidden to have her own legal documents in her possession; therefore she is at the mercy of her potential abuser(s) (husband and/or in-laws). Deliberate delays in the immigration and legal processes also prohibit women from participation in the work force and enrollment in educational institutions. Women remain in these vulnerable conditions because returning home means facing humiliation (due to rejection by their husband) in their country of origin.

ECONOMIC FACTORS THAT PLAY A ROLE IN DECISIONS

Economic factors play a major role in a woman's decision to remain in an abusive relationship. In most cases, South Asian women are financially dependent on their spouse and may not have alternative support networks such as an extended family member who can provide financial support. Leaving husbands may not be an option for many, as divorce means being ostracized by one's own community and family that can provide support and employment (Alarcón, 2000). On the contrary, a woman's economic independence can aid her in the decision to leave an abusive relationship (Kameri, 2002).

THE ROLE OF RESILIENCY FOR MIGRANT SOUTH ASIAN WOMEN

Resiliency has been defined in the context of vulnerable populations such as female victims of child sexual abuse, female victims of intimate partner violence, and refugee populations, to name a few. Resiliency is frequently referred to as "springing back" similar to a rubber band, "stretching" primarily from a situation of lower state of mental or physical condition. Some have described resiliency as a process or a trajectory that begins with a distressing event but ends with a successful outcome (Kumpfer, 2002; Bonanno, Westphal, and Mancini, 2011). Others have used the person-in-environment framework, where they have explained that resiliency is not static, rather it is a constant interaction and exchange that takes place between one's own self and the outer world (Lenette, Brough, & Cox, 2013; Williams, & Mickelson, 2004).

Additionally, McClure, Chavez, Agars, Peacock, and Matosian (2008) in their sample of university woman who had experienced childhood sexual abuse have defined important components of resiliency as "level of well-being" which means "self-acceptance", "positive relations with others", and "environmental mastery" (p. 81). Further, Singh, Hays, Chung, and Watson (2010), in their phenomenological exploration of resilience strategies of South Asian immigrant women in the United States who survived child sexual abuse, address the importance of ethnic identity and resilience. They explain that it is important to consider the ethnic identity or resilience experiences of ethnic minority groups along with individual factors.

South Asian survivors of domestic violence seem to exhibit an amazing amount of tenacity and resiliency in situations of abuse. Most of these women have defied conventions of timidity and suppression to confront their abuser by utilizing a strategy or strategies to either persevere or separate themselves from the abuse and the abuser. There are various intertwined sociocultural factors that aide these women in adopting one or many of these strategies to survive the abuse. Some of the factors may include their own ethnic membership in the larger society that is their country of migration (Abraham, 2000, p. 152), their patriarchal belief systems, presence or absence of any immediate or primary support system, presence or absence of any other support system, having children (Abraham, 2000, p. 148) or no children, their immigration status, access to finances or their economic capability (Abraham, 2000, p.152), to name a few. Their demonstration of resiliency could be significant in their survival of abuse either before their separation from their abuser or abusers (if they were abused by multiple family members including in-laws) or after their separation from their abuser or abusers. When they are still in the relationship with the abuser, South Asian victims of intimate partner violence could display an array of behaviors that influences their decisions to either endure or take action to change the situation.

Examining Personal Traits and Social Behaviors

Through a series of vignettes based in both author's research and practice, this section will address some typical personal traits and sociocultural behaviors intersecting with and impacting women who experience domestic violence. With an examination of these women's experiences, we will be able to explore the role of the professional practitioner who might provide assistance to migrant women, comparable to these women.

Personal Traits

For many South Asian women, their personal traits help them to actively fight back and take control in both contemplation and rebuilding phases. Karuna's experiences give us a glimpse how one's personal traits become vital in finding a new path.

When Karuna married, in India, to someone who was a U.S. national and was also South Asian, she and her family were assured that her dependent spouse visa was in process and she would soon be joining her husband. For several months after her husband left India and returned to the U.S., she received no visa or information from her husband about when she would receive her visa. She phoned him on several occasions. Finally, her visa arrived and she joined her husband. They lived in the same house as his parents.

Shortly after she moved into her new home, her mother-in-law told her that her son, Karuna's husband, was in a "love" relationship with a local woman. Her mother-in-law guaranteed Karuna that his affair would end soon. Karuna needed to be patient. During this period Karuna did not share a bedroom with her husband, and instead slept in a separate room. Every day Karuna returned to her room, her only respite once her daily chores had been completed.

After eight months, her mother-in-law began talking to Karuna about divorce and tried to coerce her into filing for divorce. Her own family hoped things would change, so she could enjoy her married life. Her mother-in-law increased the pressure on Karuna insisting she file for divorce, convincing her that she would be better off. One day Karuna's mother-in-law came to her with divorce papers and asked her to sign them. Karuna refused. She knew that she would lose her immigration status if she signed these papers. She called law enforcement.

Karuna exhibited unwavering courage not only to endure mistreatment by her husband and in-laws, but her ability to be straight-forward and determined, gave her the strength to cope with a very deceptive experience. Unfortunately, she was aware that her family would feel the shame that comes when a marriage does not work. She knew exactly what it meant to suffer the shame of rejection. Abraham (2000) explains that, "South Asian culture tends to place men in a dominant position over women; women are frequently rejected and experience a loss of self-esteem, shame, and a sense of failure" (p.30). Importantly, however, Karuna was willing to ask for assistance from law enforcement officers who helped her. Her personal strength, persistence and strong spirit against injustice done to her and her family helped her change her situation by taking a bold step to seek outside help.

FAITH AND HOPE

Faith has proved to be instrumental in the lives of victims by providing the essential strength to face hardships (Faulkner, Mahapatra, Heffron, Nsonwu, & Busch-Armendariz, 2013). For some South Asian women, faith and their religious belief systems have played an important role since childhood. They have not only relied on faith for inner strength but also the motivation to heal and recover.

Sita, married for more than three decades, learned that her husband had found someone else. He wanted a divorce. During the many years of their marriage, she was often emotionally abused by her husband, but she always found that sharing sacred traditions with Indian friends and family softened these hard experiences. The two children were nearing adulthood but the divorce shocked them and they worried about their mom. Her health had been difficult and she was using her prayer and chanting to get her through the periods of pain she experienced daily. She said that her prayer was her salvation. She prayed her husband would find his love for her as well. Now, with no work experience outside her home, Sita became scared about her future. What would she do? How would she live?

Faith and hope helped Sita not just persevere through hard times, but also connected her with others in the Indian community, instilling a sense of hope for the future. The support sometimes came from immediate family members (either living nearby or in their country of origin), close friends, extended family members, counselors, and staff members at the shelter, or a priest or other community members. Sita was able to find the strength in herself, with support from friends and her children, to build a new life and heal from the deep depression she had experienced.

THE ROLE OF FAMILY HONOR

Nusrat Ameen, a staff member at a large South Asian organization in a Southern metropolitan city in the U.S. that provides services to women and children victims of violence, shares that girls in South Asian culture are taught to be perseverant from a very young age. In many households, there is a differential treatment that exists in the upbringing of girls and boys within the culture. They are expected to confirm to these social and cultural mandates. (N. Ameen, personal communication, March 20, 2014).

Family honor is given the utmost importance and women in the household the responsibility of upholding the family honor while withstanding all kinds of pain and suffering. South Asian women are constantly trained that maintaining family harmony and saving face is a high priority (Gill, 2004). Women are expected to forgive and therefore divorce is not an option. Leaving one's family is simply not an option and is often not permitted in South Asian communities (Nankani, 2000). The societal norms could be extremely oppressive for women, but the same culture could provide the tools to survive and could help make important decision regarding individual safety.

> Trishna had already left her abusive husband. She and her two children were living with a relative. She had recently lost her job and was experiencing increased verbal and physical abuse from her husband. In the past, things were not so good, but more recently, she was often taunted for not having a job and therefore "good for nothing". She was in two minds when she spoke to the counselor. She realized that her experience of abuse was harmful on her children. At the same time, she didn't want her children to not have a father figure in their lives. The counselor supported her decision to protect her children from the ill effects of abuse. With further help from the local South Asian agency, she managed to take control of her life and found a job to sustain her family.

SILENCE AND NON-ACTION

The duration of abuse vary in this group among South Asian migrant women. For some, many years pass before deciding to do something about the abusive life they endured. Nonetheless, this does not indicate that their silence or non-action corresponds to doubts about their resiliency. Most women used this time to reflect and review their situation. Lenette, Brough, and Cox (2012) based on their work with refugee women emphasize the everyday and mundane nature of resiliency where women tackle stress and strain. They explained that "resiliency was a process operating inter-subjectively in the social spaces connecting them [refugee women] to their environment" (p. 627).

HELP-SEEKING AS A PROCESS: FINDING THE COURAGE AND STRENGTH TO SEEK HELP FROM OUTSIDERS

The next several stories about migrant South Asian women, give us insight into the process of finding informal (immediate support network) and formal (outside) help.

The examples illustrate how challenging circumstances lead one to seek help from others and build new lives.

Sudha joined her husband (who was a naturalized U.S. citizen) in the U.S a year after their marriage. Within a month of being in U.S. with her husband, father-in-law and mother-in-law, she came to understand that she did not have any freedom, even inside the house. She was simply treated as a domestic servant. She cooked four times a day, cleaned, took orders from her in-laws, and fulfilled all duties of a good wife.

Her phone calls from India and to India to talk to her family were strictly supervised. She was not allowed to use the computer expect for very specific occasions. She was not allowed to go outside of the house on her own. She realized that she did not have any immediate support and had to utilize strategies that would help her to connect to someone outside.

She found her opportune moment when her husband took her out to meet some business associates. She shared some of her experiences with the wife of her husband's colleague. This woman was empathetic and listened to her story. She later helped Sudha with information about the local South Asian domestic violence shelter. Her South Asian friend also helped her find a distant relative of Sudha's who lived in the same city. A few months later, Sudha called the police because she believed she needed to move out of the house. She took refuge in a relative's house for few days and then with the help of the South Asian Women's Organization she started a new life.

In Sudha's case and many others, seeking help from outside sources in absence of kin was their first step to help themselves. Their help-seeking depended on several factors including who was providing the help, the person's membership in the South Asian community, the kind of help that they were seeking, accessibility of these sources, and most importantly, their reason to seek help, in terms of, their expectations from the whole process or their goals for finding help. These women exhibited determination and fortitude in changing their existing state of affairs and moving toward ending violence against them. In some cases, women's decision to access help failed initially and they had to rethink their approach in terms of their goals and who to approach next. In fact, it made them more aggressive in their ways to reach for help.

LEAVING AND FINDING MEANING

Many South Asian immigrant women survivors of abuse have shown great courage and resiliency in circumstances of abuse and have forged ahead by attaining significant goals in their lives. Some of the meaningful goals have included locating a stable job, taking care of their children, getting remarried, building a new family, and some have become strong advocates of violence against women. They have continued to dedicate their time to helping abused women in similar situations as they were in once.

Nasreen is another South Asian woman who had to leave her children because of the serious abuse she experienced. She sought help from the domestic violence shelter.

Nasreen now lives with her brother and his family. For more than 10 years, Nasreen was regularly physically and emotionally abused by her husband and her brother-in-law. One night the police arrived at their home due to a neighbor's call to the police. The police took Nasreen to a domestic violence shelter after she received emergency care at the hospital. After several weeks of help at the domestic violence shelter, she realized that she had to start fresh. She found full-time employment. She found an apartment so she could move out of the shelter.

Nasreen was so grateful for the help she received at the shelter that she now volunteers at the domestic violence shelter as a translator and participates in most of their outreach and advocacy programs. She talks to women in her community who are experiencing abuse. She says, "This is the least I can do to help those who are the most vulnerable".

ROLE OF PRACTITIONER AND THE DV AGENCY/ RELATED PROFESSIONALS

In our professional roles as social workers, psychologists, counselors, and human service workers, our intervention with South Asian women who experience domestic violence requires that we bring a basket of specialized and core practice skills as well as specialized knowledge and skills specific to the field of domestic violence. Critical in our initiation with any migrant woman who has been a victim of domestic violence is our professional belief that the person has strengths, and, they will find ways to move forward. Importantly, our practice stance promotes "no fault and no blame." For the person who has experienced physical, verbal or emotional abuse from someone who they cared about, the experience of recounting that experience and "making-meaning" of the experience is difficult. Thus, our professional work requires our non-judgment along with our willingness to listen to their pain and struggles. We will introduce a variety of skill areas that can be important in our work with this diverse population of women along with examples that illustrate the ideas presented.

THE ASSESSMENT PROCESS

Often, South Asian women who experience abuse will consider contacting a women's shelter program on the phone, as a first step in seeking help outside of their informal system. At times, the women may have received the phone number for the agency from a police officer or a neighbor. Initial calls are exploratory. The potential client wants to know who and what the agency can do for her. Thus, those professionals who respond to "intake" and "screening" calls have a special role for this potential client. In the initial phone contact, the professional worker wants to provide timely, valuable information that helps the person ascertain what kind of assistance is available. Often, agencies that serve South Asian migrant women indicate that the woman who comes to their agency may have called them for several months, even more than 12 months, before actually coming to the agency location. Thus, phone contacts might be a "life line" for some South Asian women who are too afraid to actually come to the organization.

FORMAL SOCIAL ASSESSMENT PROCEDURES

Many researchers and practice experts recognize the important of assessment procedures that include examining whether domestic violence exists as a matter of routine initial screening (Schacht, Dimidjian, George, & Berns, 2009). With a population that directs its services to programs that are specific to victims of domestic violence, the assessment may make arbitrary assumptions about the abuse experience. This should be avoided because our assessment process should be an experience of collecting information and synthesizing the information without preconceived ideas.

Several visits may be required when engaging in the in-person formal social assessment interview. The worker needs to begin by assessing how comfortable the woman is speaking in English, or is a language interpreter needed. Second, building a trusting professional relationship is vital. For example, a professional may ask about the women's legal status, and she may not be sure how much to disclose about this kind of question. Asking about the women's family members, where they are located, etc., may be complicated in the view of the woman, creating some fear about what the worker is really wanting her to disclose. When assessing a migrant South Asian woman, particularly in the initial assessment interview process, workers need to take more time in order to explain why they are asking the range of questions they are using, why these assessment questions are important.

In the assessment, the practitioner should listen carefully, asking those questions that continue to open up the discussion for the client. Additionally, many who are bilingual, often need time to "translate" the thoughts that they are hearing as well as the thoughts which they will share. Thus, longer periods of silence may exist because of the language conversion that is needed. Our assessment process should help the practitioner to identify range of areas that includes: 1) the strengths and capabilities of the client, 2) potential resources that can be utilized, 3) what types of attempts have been made by the client to try to resolve the issue at this point and time, 4) how safety is achieved, and 5) additional health inquiries, where appropriate.

Gaining a longer term perspective about the person being assessed, obtaining information that examines the family of origin is vital. Research has shown the value in examining family of origin because when a person experienced violence in their relationships in their early years, they are more likely to experience violence in their current relationships as adults, experiences both as victims of violence and as perpetrators of violence (Busby, Holman, & Walker, 2008).

A central question in the first assessment interview is evaluating the safety for the client. Will this person be able to return to their home? Are they concerned that they will be harmed physically, particularly, needing medical attention, possibly emergency medical assistance. Building a "safety plan" may be a potential "first step" that helps the client to consider what help she might need to remain safe (Najavits, 2002). Are there family members who would be able to help? Are there any neighbors who might be helpful, if called upon?

INTERVENTIONS: RESILIENCY BUILDING STRATEGIES

The intervention responses that may be needed when working with a South Asian migrant women require multi-level interventions. In the next several sections, individual counseling will be described, as well as other small-sized system responses, including the family(ies).

The initial intervention strategy for many South Asian migrant women is individual counseling. Individual counseling uncovers the person's internal strengths and then uses those strengths to facilitate the development of external avenues of communication and support. Such resilience building is critical for migrant women are unfamiliar with "asking" for services, or afraid that they will be turned away from the service because of their legal status. This fear has substance as some services, such as public assistance is not available for migrant women and children.

Many texts address unique counseling approaches with women who have experienced domestic violence (e.g., Lawson, 2013; Roberts, 2002). Central to these counseling texts are the tenents that direct the intervention and include (i) every experience is unique, there is no one domestic violence experience common to all victims; (ii) victims of domestic violence are often traumatized by their experience; (iii) victims of domestic violence relate their experiences of domestic violence in different ways and at different rates of disclosure; and (iv) opening the wounds of abusive experiences is not the goal of counseling, but rather, the goal is to help the victim heal. This healing process is achieved, through integrating their domestic violence experience into their existing life story instead of allowing the abuse to define the victim (Schatz & Rigg, 1996).

When considering the counseling process with migrant women, there are many ways to direct the counseling experience toward a strengths-based process, one that recognizes how resilience may serve as the "bounce back" process. Resilience can be understood using the metaphor of a trampoline. The person who is bouncing on the trampoline is locating their resilience each time they are thrust into the air—giving them the energy needed for future progress and change. Strengths may be located in the personal narrative—the 'stories" shared by the client.

Group therapeutic counseling is an intervention that may be very valuable for a woman seeking counseling who needs more help with emotional issues that can include emotional regulation and the ability to make decisions that are beneficial for emotional well-being. Two group approaches include therapeutic groups that are specific to members who have experienced domestic violence and support group approaches where the approach is a bit different. Therapeutic counseling approaches are directed by trained, credentialed professionals, often licensed (by government law or statute). Support groups are organized by others who have experienced domestic violence, but generally these groups promote personal sharing without the facilitation and leadership of a trained professional.

Moving to the use of a group therapy counseling intervention may be used if individual counseling has provided positive movement for the client, and, it is anticipated that a group experience may give the client a new therapy experience with multiple members. Group members share their experiences, and members may find validation for their own ideas and feelings which may not be accomplished through individual counseling. Additionally, group members can contribute "solutions," that may inform a group member about ways to change personal circumstances. The use of a support group that is formed to serve South Asian migrant women, specifically, could be a valuable intervention approach because the women may find "commonalities" because of their legal status and their unique cultural framework(s).

GENERAL ASSISTANCE INTERVENTION PROGRAMS

When migrant women consider making a change in their family status, leaving their husband and locating a new home for themselves and their children, they may need financial resources and other emergency services. Though many government programs exclude migrant people, this is not the case in all communities across the globe. Local municipalities may have cash assistance for emergency purpose to aid families who are broken apart due to persistent domestic violence. Additionally, churches provide vital emergency services including cash assistance and food banks in both urban and rural communities could also help these families in crises. In the next sections, some of the important needs of migrant women including South Asian women that need to be addressed are highlighted.

LEGAL NEEDS

Most migrant women who are considering a break up in their family have great difficulties due to their migrant status. These women believe that if they no longer live with their husband, they will be deported immediately, and returned to their country of origin. In the U.S., as an example, if a migrant woman has experienced domestic violence, she can request a visa on her own. This is written into U.S. law. The same may not be true in other countries so work must be done to understand the legal issues that will face migrant women who need to leave their spouse.

EMPLOYMENT NEEDS

Becoming economically self-sufficient is a goal for all families, thus, for the migrant woman who needs to establish a new family home, employment is a vital need. The initial assessment can be structured to learn about the educational and employment capabilities of the migrant woman, yet, as time with the woman continues, returning to this area is important. For some clients, employment training programs may be valuable including programs that provide "training" for specific jobs open in the community. A fork-lift job may require that the person enroll in a local college or technical school where this skill is taught.

EDUCATIONAL NEEDS

For some migrant women, language courses are an important service that is needed. When earlier, the migrant woman was solely in the home, she was not exposed to the language of the country where she is currently in residence. Importantly, language courses may be both conversational in nature as well as language courses that teach writing and literacy level competency.

Opportunities for higher educational learning, at the university or professional skill level should be considered for migrant women. Many migrant women come with educational degrees from their home country, thus, they have a high aptitude for professional careers.

ORGANIZATIONS SPECIFICALLY ADDRESSING THE NEEDS OF MIGRANT SOUTH ASIAN WOMEN

South Asian women's organizations provide services specifically to South Asian victims of violence including women and children are aggressively involved in outreach activities raising consciousness about adverse effects of domestic violence in South Asian communities (Merchant, 2000). These organizations are in the forefront of proving social justice advocacy to victims of violence. They provide a range of services including advocacy, counselling and culturally specific services besides having establishing help lines. As evident in some of the cases discussed above, South Asian women who have access to informal friend networks, South Asian community, or the larger society of the country of migration may have more opportunity to learn about the formal systems of help.

Due to the acculturative process, South Asian families make adjustments to assimilate into the mainstream environment by changing attitudes and adapting to newer set of values. South Asian families inculcate egalitarian belief systems that allow a sense of equality among all member of the family including sons and female members or daughters in the family. These adjustments have benefited the younger generation of South Asian women who are much more aware of the gender role stereotypes and situations at-risk for domestic violence.

In Mahapatra's study (2011) exploring factors influencing formal help-seeking behaviors of abused women of South Asian origin who lived in the United States, she found that there has been an increasing trend of South Asian women accessing formal sources of help including help due to a domestic violence situation. This trend appears to be the result of greater levels of acculturation among South Asian women and their knowledge about outside agencies, legal options in this country, and their access to information (Mahapatra, 2011).

COMMUNITY NETWORKING OPPORTUNITIES AND COALITION BUILDING STRATEGIES

Working with migrant women, particularly South Asian women, highlights the challenges and unique issues that may be embedded in serving this population. To help women who have unique cultural and legal experiences may require that practitioners work with a range of organizations and agencies in a community. South Asian women's organizations in many cities providing services to victims of violence have collaborated with similar agencies, mainstream domestic violence shelters, and the law enforcement to form coalitions so that they can help and benefit each other.

CONCLUSION

We began this chapter looking at Najma's life at a crossroads. Today, her crushed spirits have been restored and she is on the road to recovery and taking control of her life.

She is happy to start her first job (part-time) in a grocery store. For the very first time, it dawns on her that she will be doing this all by herself and it makes her quiver inside. Then immediately she thinks about her children and their faces the last time she saw them. She feels she has only won half the battle and has a long way to go. She has begun the process to gain partial or full custody of her children who still live with her ex-husband.

In this chapter, we presented a broad array of information about the intricacies that contribute to intimate partner violence, specifically among South Asian immigrant women with the help of their narratives. We also have described these women's resiliency and complex characters. We examined the important role for practitioners to use a range of service delivery approaches that bring successful outcomes. In the end, we can recognize that these women are harbingers of change in the migrant South Asian community, and therefore, it becomes important for the community to come together to applaud the positive changes made by these women and lend full support to end violence against South Asian women. Last, there is a role for educators as well, to provide educational curriculum that addresses intimate partner violence with greater awareness of the varied experiences of women of different cultural backgrounds.

REFERENCES

Abraham, M. (2000). *Speaking the unspeakable: Marital violence among South Asian immigrants in the United States.* New Brunswick, N. J. & London: Rutgers University Press.

Bonanno, G. A., Westphal, M. & Mancini, A. D. (2011). Resilience to loss and potential trauma. *Annual Review of Clinical Psychology, 1,* 1.1-1.25.

Busby, D. M., Homan, T. H. & Walker, E. (2008). Pathways to relationship aggression between adult partners. *Family Relations, 57*(1), 72-83.

Crandall, M., Senturia, K., Sullivan, M. & Shiu-Thornton, S. (2005). "No way out": Russian-speaking women's experiences with domestic violence. *Journal of Interpersonal Violence, 20*(8), 941–958.

Dasgupta, S. D. (1998). Gender roles and cultural continuity in the Asian Indian immigrant community in the *U.S. Sex Roles: A Journal of Research, 38*(11-12), 953-974.

Erez, E. (2002). Migration/immigration, domestic violence and the justice system. *International Journal of Comparative and Applied Criminal Justice, 26*(2), 277–299.

Faulkner, M., Mahapatra, N., Heffron, L. C., Nsonwu, M. B. & Busch-Armendariz, N. (2013). Moving past victimization and trauma toward restoration: Mother survivors of sex trafficking share their inspiration. *International Perspectives on Victimology, 7*(2), 46-55.

Gill, A. (2004). Voicing the silent fear: South Asian women's experiences of domestic violence. *The Howard Journal, 43*(5), 465-483.

Kameri, C. M. (2002). Designing policies that address the relationship between woman abuse and economic resources. *Journal of Sociology & Social Welfare, 29*(3), 109-124.

Kulwicki, A., Aswad, B., Carmona, T. & Ballout, S. (2010). Barriers in the utilization of domestic violence services among Arab immigrant women: Perceptions of professionals, service providers, and community leaders. *Journal of Family Violence, 25*(8), 727-735.

Kumpfer, K. L. (2002). Factors and processes contributing to resilience: The resilience framework. In M.D. Glantz & J.L. Johnson, *Resilience and Development: Positive Life Adaptations* (179-224). New York, NY: Kluwer Academic/Plenum Publishers.

Lawson, D. M. (2013). *Family violence: Explanations and evidence-based clinical practice.* Alexandria, VA: American Counseling Association.

Lee, M. (2013). Breaking barriers: Addressing structural obstacles to social service provision for Asian survivors of domestic violence. *Violence Against Women, 19*(11), 1350-1369.

Lenette, C., Brough, M. & Cox, L. (2013). Everyday resilience: Narratives of single refugee women with children. *Qualitative Social Work, 12*(5), 637-653.

Mahapatra, N. (2011). Using key informants to explore help-seeking among South Asian women who experience domestic violence in the United States. *Human Rights Global Focus Domestic Violence, 6*, 30-47.

McClure, F. H., Chavez, D. V., Agars, M. D., Peacock, M. J. & Matosian, A. (2008). Resilience in sexually abused women: Risk and protective factors. *Journal of Family Violence, 23*, 81-88.

Merchant, M. (2000). A comparative study of agencies assisting domestic violence victims: Does the South Asian community have special needs? *Journal of Social Distress and the Homeless, 9*(3), 249-259.

Muftic, L. R., and L. A. Bouffard. 2008. Bosnian women and intimate partner violence: Differences in experiences and attitudes for refugee and nonrefugee women. *Feminist Criminology, 3*(3), 173–190.

Najavits, L. (2002). *Seeking safety: A manualized treatment for PTSD and substance abuse.* New York, NY: The Guilford Press.

Nankani, S. (2000). *Breaking the silence: Domestic violence in the South Asian-American community.* Philadelphia, PA: Xlibris Corporation.

Niaz, U. (2003). Violence against women in South Asian countries. *Archives of Women's Mental Health, 6*(3), 173-184.

Raj, A. & Silverman, J. (2002). Intimate partner violence against South Asian women residing in greater Boston. *Journal of the American Medical Women's Association, 57*(2), 111-114.

Raj, A. & Silverman, J. G. (2003). Immigrant South Asian women at greater risk for injury from intimate partner violence. *American Journal of Public Health, 93*(3), 435-437.

Roberts, A. R. (2002). *Handbook of domestic violence intervention strategies: Policies, programs and legal remedies.* NY: Oxford University Press.

Rudrappa, S. (2004). Radical caring in an ethnic shelter: South Asian American women workers at Apna Ghar, Chicago. *Gender & Society, 18*(5), 588-609.

Schacht, R.L., Dimidjian, S., George, W. H. & Berns, S. B. (2009). Domestic violence assessment procedures among couple therapists. *Journal of Marital and Family Therapy, 35*(1), 47-59.

Schatz, M. S. & Rigg, G. A. (1996). *Understanding and addressing the trauma from abuse: A model of safety, reconnection and integration for the victim of abuse.* Education and Research Institute for Fostering Families, Colorado State University, funded under a grant from the Colorado Dept. of Human Services. (Also available from ERIC Clearinghouse on Counseling and Guidance (ERIC-CASS) CG028340. University of North Carolina at Greensboro, 1998).

Sheehan, H. E., Javier, R. A. & Thanjan, T. (2000). Introduction to the special issue on domestic violence and the South Asian community. *Journal of Social Distress and the Homeless, 9*(3), 167-171.

Singh, A. A., Hays, D.G., Chung, Y. B. & Watson, L. (2010). South Asian immigrant women who have survived child sexual abuse: Resilience and healing. *Violence Against Women, 16*(4), 444-458. doi: 10.1177/1077801210363976

Streeter, C. L. & Franklin, C. (1992). Defining and measuring social support: Guidelines for social work practitioners. *Research on Social Work Practice, 20*(1), 81-98.

Tse, S. (2007). Family violence in Asian communities, combining research and community development. *Social Policy Journal of New Zealand, 31*, 170-194.

Van Hightower, N. R., Gorton, J. & DeMoss, C. L. (2000). Predictive models of domestic violence and fear of intimate partners among migrant and seasonal farm worker women. *Journal of Family Violence, 15*(2), 137-154.

Williams, S. L. & Mickelson, K. D. (2004). The nexus of domestic violence and poverty: Resilience in women's anxiety. *Violence Against Women, 10*(3), 283-293.

Yoshioka, M. R., Gilbert, L., El-Bassel, N. & Baib-Amin, M. (2003). Social support and disclosure of abuse: Comparing South Asian, African American, and Hispanic battered women. *Journal of Family Violence, 18*(3), 171-180.

In: Overcoming Domestic Violence
Editors: Myra F. Taylor, Julie Ann Pooley et al.

ISBN: 978-1-63321-956-4
© 2015 Nova Science Publishers, Inc.

Chapter 9

COPING WITH DOMESTIC VIOLENCE IN INDIA: THE ROLE OF SPIRITUALITY AND SOCIAL SUPPORT

Andreia Schineanu[1,2] and Jaya Earnest[2]*
[1] School of Humanities & Social Science, Charles Sturt University,
Wagga Wagga, Australia
[2]Curtin University, Western Australia

ABSTRACT

Experiences of domestic violence in Indian women are a relatively common occurrence, with at least 30% of women abused by their intimate partner (husbands) on a regular basis. There is a large degree of overlap between emotional, physical and sexual violence with 1 in 10 women experiencing all three. Domestic violence is a major contributor to the mental, physical, sexual and reproductive ill health of women, with consequences extending to affect their overall health, the welfare of their children and even their economic standing. Common mental disorders such as depression and anxiety have a dose-response relationship with the severity and length of domestic violence experiences. Resilience and coping mechanisms have been found to confer protective benefits particularly on the mental health of women experiencing domestic violence. Coping strategies and behaviours have been studied extensively in Western literature and have been categorised into active and passive forms, with active coping associated with lower levels of psychological distress. In India, sociocultural factors and gender-role expectations drive Indian women into using predominantly passive coping modalities. In this chapter we provide an overview of the issue of domestic violence in India and the underlying social and cultural factors that contributes to it. We will also discuss coping strategies used by Indian women experiencing domestic violence, in particular the role of social support, spirituality and Eastern beliefs in building resilience against common mental disorders to allow women to continue living in an often unescapable and appalling situation.

Keywords: Domestic violence, India, coping, spirituality, social support

---

* Corresponding author: Dr. Andreia Schineanu, School of Humanities & Social Science, Charles Sturt University, Wagga Wagga, Australia, NSW 2650, Tel: 0404 523 926, Email: aschineanu@csu.edu.au.

INTRODUCTION

India is a patriarchal and patrilineal society where culture, customs and traditions play a vital role in legitimising, obscuring, and denying the existence of domestic violence (DV). The strong belief in family and marriage as a sacred institution permits violence within its boundaries to be regarded as a private affair, and is viewed as above public scrutiny. To understand DV, particularly in India, one must first understand the concepts of gender and gender inequality and how they act to affect women's health and well-being. Gender, a social and cultural construct that defines what it means to be male or female, encompasses elements such as gendered behaviours, values, expectations, roles and environments which are culturally dependent and can change over time and over a life course (McCloskey et al., 2005). For example what is expected of a young unmarried woman is different from what is expected from a married mother, and these expectations are different in different cultures. Gender also determines the social position and role of a person in society, and usually gives women less power and resources than men (Russo & Pirlott, 2006).

The prevailing attitudes and values that ascribe and define the social roles and behaviours associated with both genders are called gender norms. These are firmly entrenched in every culture's social structures and there is no country in the world where women are equal to men legally, socially and economically, not even in the most equalitarian societies in Scandinavia (Lopez-Claros & Zahidi, 2005). Gender norms are used to organise and maintain social relations and order at individual, community and institutional levels, and these norms are present at all levels of society, from household and family level to neighbourhoods, communities and wider society and are perpetuated by social customs and establishments that produce codes of conduct that maintain gender inequities (Keleher & Franklin, 2008).

All countries, but in particular developing countries like India, experience tensions related to the conflict between the changing roles of women in society with the traditional concepts of women's lives (Keleher & Franklin, 2008). The outcomes of these interactions are usually unequal, as the inequitable dynamics expose women and girls to risks such as violence, discrimination, denial of education, poverty, social and economic injustices, exploitation, restrictions on mobility and political activity. At the same time gender inequality reinforces male behaviours that affect women such as sexual violence and unsafe sexual practices, denial of women's rights and support for males to maintain control over their female partners (Keleher & Franklin, 2008). Gender inequality limits women's access to and control over resources, in economic opportunities, in power and political voice which in turn systematically empowers men to the detriment of women who become socially, economically and politically dominated. Whilst the mechanisms of action of gender based inequality are complex and varied they are to a large extent dictated by the cultural norms of a particular society that define the distinct roles, values and behaviours of women.

THE PLACE OF WOMEN IN INDIA

India's economic restructuring which began in the early 1990s, has undergone dramatic transformations since then with new avenues for prosperity and mobility (social and physical), and new technologies, media and services which have affected the lives of rural and urban Indians in many novel ways (Tenhunen, 2008). At the same time, the patterns of poverty and social exclusion along the lines of caste, class, region and gender continue to exist and thrive within the overall patterns of economic transformation. Gender inequality in India is rooted in centuries old religious texts, customs and social norms that class women as socially inferior to men; husbands 'own' their wives and have the right to dictate and dominate every part of her life, including disciplining her (Koenig et al., 2006).

The feminist movement in the 1970s and 1980s has brought the issue of DV to the forefront of Indian national discourse, and effected changes in legislation culminating in the Protection of Women from Domestic Violence Act in 2005. The state and national policies against DV are informed by international conventions and India is committed to the Beijing Platform for Action and a signatory to CEDAW (UN Committee on the Elimination of Discrimination Against Women (CEDAW), 1992). Most recently at the 58th Commission on the Status of Women (CSW58) in 2014 the Agreed Conclusions made explicit reference to eliminating all harmful customary practices, including child, early and forced marriage. Despite this, responses to DV in India are marked by the dichotomy between modernity and tradition. Institutions such as the police, the legal system and the health sector are underwritten by modern laws and policies yet are embedded in traditional structures of patriarchy that are influenced by society. These institutions are largely operated by individuals who rather than transform patriarchal structures through their actions tend to perpetuate them instead (Jacobsen, Kjosavik, & Nyborg, 2012).

It can be argued that the context of rapid socio-economic and cultural transformation that is occurring in India reinforces the modernity-tradition dichotomy in responses to DV and this is reflected in the minimal changes in norms and roles for Indian women (Parashar, 2008). Thus Indian society condones the use of violence against women in certain circumstances for example, wife's alleged sexual infidelity, neglect of household duties, disobedience of husband's dictates and disputes over dowry, and when DV occurs within certain boundaries of severity (Koenig et al., 2006).

DV in the martial home is also viewed as acceptable by many women, lending support to the theory of 'system justification' which states that subordinate groups tend to embrace ideologies promulgated by dominant groups that justify their own inferiority (Vindhya, 2007). However, long term trend analysis of attitudes of men and women to violence has shown a dramatic change for both groups between 1992 and 2007, with more men and women finding violence unacceptable (Simister & Mehta, 2010). Indian women are becoming more liberated as indicated by increasing trends in attitudes that do not justify violence from partners, but at the same time the incidence of DV has increased. There is evidence to suggest that some DV is a male response to the increasingly modern attitudes of Indian women and this increase in DV may be temporary, as India transitions to a modern society (Simister & Mehta, 2010).

At marriage, which is usually arranged by the parents in India, women leave their natal family and join their husband's family. This tradition has reinforced women's position as a burden, not valued enough to expend food, education and other resources on, as she will leave the natal family and move to her husband's family. Dowry, although illegal and banned by law, is still expected and given at marriage by the bride's family. In fact, dowry deaths, where women are murdered by their husbands and/or his family because of inadequate dowry has increasingly emerged as a worrying trend in recent decades, with thousands of women killed annually (Go et al., 2003).

For abused Indian women, leaving their husbands and/or pressing charges is not a viable option, and most women are aware that their identity is almost exclusively linked to their marital status, whilst a lack of social security means that there are few viable alternatives to the life of violence. While there is legislation in place to protect women against 'all types of violence' those responsible for upholding the law, the police, and the justice system are hampered by excessive bureaucracy and corruption (Schuler, Bates & Islam, 2008). Women are reluctant to press charges or imprison their husband because the husband can often bribe his way out of the charges, the process is expensive, and the women fear reprisals by his family or believe he will divorce them and take away the children (Cho, 2012).

The law is often biased against women when it comes to assets, for example, it does not protect a woman's right to the matrimonial home, while shelters, legal aid and other organizations that have the potential to help battered women are scarce in India. Besides, the victim is usually ignored or disowned by her relatives for bringing shame on the natal family and she has to cope with the immense stigma attached to being divorced or unmarried. This in turn causes the woman and her children to become social outcasts further ostracizing her and making her life even more difficult if not impossible (Subadra, 1999).

CONSEQUENCES OF DV

The effects of DV are well documented in the literature and include adverse consequences in the short and long term, on women's health, on the health system and on the community and economy. Short term effects such as injuries, bruises and broken bones are the most obvious, however the long term consequences of prolonged exposure to DV are also significant and include organ damage, unwanted pregnancies and adverse pregnancy outcomes, ongoing infections and systemic disorders and other chronic conditions such as hypertension, diabetes and asthma. DV also contributes to ill health by increasing the negative behaviour of the victims, such as smoking, excessive alcohol and drug use (self-medication).

Of importance in this chapter is the association between DV and Common Mental Disorders (CMD). Currently rates of CMD such as depression and anxiety in Indian women have been found to be around 30% but a proportion of the women suffering CMD are not victims of DV. Additionally, these values are all based on relatively small localised groups of women rather than population based prevalence studies, thus it is likely that these figures are under-reported however it is clear that DV has significant negative effects on the mental health of women (Nayak et al., 2010; Patel et al., 2006).

The magnitude and effect of DV on mental health is related to how women perceive the causes of DV and how these opinions influence their help-seeking and coping patterns as studies have shown that DV coping modalities are embedded in sociocultural context and influenced by the gender-role expectations from the community. Understanding these processes in an Indian context is even more important considering:

1. That India is currently the second most populous country in the world, with over 1.21 billion people (2011 Census of India), which means that more than a sixth of the world's women (600 million) live in India.

2.   The high rates of DV currently experienced by Indian women, estimated at between a third and three quarters equate to between 200 and 450 million women being victims of DV.

3.   The high rates of CMD that develop as a result of experiencing DV means that between 50 and 300 million Indian women could be suffering depression, anxiety and PTSD as a direct result of DV.

PREVALENCE OF DV IN INDIA

Determining the magnitude of DV in any community is a difficult task, mainly due to extensive under reporting because of shame and lack of recognition of the violence as a health issue. The majority of Indian women in a recent study admitted to experiencing DV but had not disclosed their abuse to anyone other than the interviewer and the main reason given was the shame associated with DV (Schineanu, 2013).

In India this is further complicated by system justification and normalisation of violence based on cultural and societal expectations; that is many women are not even aware that their experiences of DV are wrong or a violation of their rights. Research studies (Jejeebhoy, 1998; Schineanu, 2013; Subadra, 1999) found that women will respond negatively when asked if they experience DV, yet at the same time they will freely talk about being hit or threatened by their husbands, completely unaware that they are one and the same thing.

Despite these challenges, in the last decade there has been a significant increase in the number of research studies focusing on violence experienced by Indian women at the hands of their husbands and his family, see for example Babu & Babu, 2011; Heilman, 2010; Kaur & Garg, 2010; Krishnan et al., 2010. Common themes emerging from these studies are that violence against women is very prevalent even in pregnancy, the in-laws, particularly the mother-in-law, are often instigators or abusers as well, women have limited recourse and the violence has significant effects on the women's physical and mental health.

Between 30% - 75% of Indian women experience any DV in their lifetime with one in ten experiencing all three types, namely psychological, physical and sexual violence. DV rates are highest in the Muslim community (43%) followed by the Hindu community (39.7%), the Christian (33.6%) and the Sikh (25.3%) (Schineanu, 2013; Heilman, 2010). The most recent National Family Health Survey NFHS-3 which surveyed women in all the 29 states of India indicated an all India average prevalence of emotional violence of 14%, less severe physical violence such as slapping or hitting was 31%, severe physical violence such as punching or using a weapon was 10%, and sexual violence was 8% (Dalal & Lindqvist, 2010). However there were large differences between the states, for example in Himachal Pradesh the prevalence of all types of violence was 6.2% while in Bihar it was 59.9% (Heilman, 2010).

The main protecting mechanisms against the development of CMD in women experiencing DV are coping styles, social support and spirituality. In the next sections we provide an overview of the reactions to stressors in Eastern cultures, then discuss coping, social support and spirituality as they relate to maintenance of mental health when experiencing DV.

STRESS AND COPING: THE INDIAN PERSPECTIVE

Indian society is collectivist and operates on a vertical social structure with caste and hereditary hierarchies defining the order of the society. India has been shaped by thousand year old philosophies of life and religions that have provided stable social structures and values, and the association between religion and society is closely related. Thus the meaning and purpose of life and all its encompassing experiences are viewed quite differently compared to Western society. Life as posited by traditional Indian philosophies is a cycle of birth, life, death and reincarnation. The ultimate aim of this cycle is to attain *moksha* or liberation from the perpetual chain of reincarnation, and for this to occur a person must follow the interrelated concepts of (Laungani, 2002):

- *Dharma* – defined as 'correct conduct', not morally or ethically but in terms of keeping within the laws of nature, life and cultural existence;
- Detachment – meaning that one should not be too involved with the pursuit of positive or pleasurable experiences, nor get attached to material possessions or try to avoid negative experiences such as suffering;
- Impulse control – to obtain control over the body and the self by the use of practices such as fasting and abstinence;
- Belief in rebirth and *karma* – whereby the deeds of a person whether good or bad, accumulate and define their destiny in the next life and through the practices of dharma and detachment a person aims to bring the sum of these karma credits to zero;
- Transcendence – found in most religions, literally means to 'get out of something' and in this case means to get out of the rebirth cycle but its most common meaning is belief in something supernatural.

Within this Indian worldview of life, stress and coping are also conceptualised differently than in Western societies. In fact, in the languages of India there is no equivalent word for stress and the closest words that approximate the Western concept of stress are *klesha* and *dukha*. Taken from Indian indigenous philosophies on which Hinduism, Buddhism and Jainism are based; *klesha* refers to unavoidable experiences of life while *dukha* could be translated as sadness or unhappiness (Laungani, 2002). In Indian culture both *klesha* and *dukha* are considered an integral part of life and of being human (Shamasundar, 2008) and are not viewed with much concern.

By emphasizing the importance of *dharma* (way of life) and *karma* (destiny), the Indian belief system assigns low significance to outcomes, people are encouraged to relinquish control to a higher being and even outcomes that are controlled by individuals tend to be attributed to a higher being. Suffering is viewed as the outcome of misdeeds in previous lives (bad *karma*) and this attribution of the cause to factors beyond individual control provides relief from responsibility while at the same time accepting the suffering is a way to atone for past misdeeds and invoke good *karma* thus taking a step closer to liberation or *moksha* (Awasthi & Mishra, 2011). The implications of these beliefs in DV cases are around using causal attribution of violence to *karma* to enable psychological recovery in the victims.

COPING

Simply put, coping is any action that is taken to deal with a situation that is stressful or perceived to be stressful. Coping is a very individual and subjective process that is influenced by culture (Pargament, 1997) as well as constrained by it. Coping modalities have been categorised into two groups by a number of researchers:

1. Problem-focused vs. emotion-focused coping (Lazarus & Folkman, 1984) – where coping focuses on changing the problem so it becomes less stressful versus the use of emotional responses to cope with the stress caused by the problem.
2. Locus of control and responsibility (Rotter, 1966) – where control and responsibility for a stressor are attributed to either internal or external factors, and coping mechanisms follow accordingly.
3. Assimilative vs. accommodative coping (Brandtstädter, 1992) – where coping mechanisms try to restore the situation to pre-stressor state versus accepting the stressor as an unchangeable factor and coping consists of acceptance, priority setting, and cognitive restructuring.
4. Mastery vs. meaning coping (Taylor, 1983) – where coping involves attempts to control the stressor and modify it versus finding meaning in the stressor and its consequences.
5. Primary control vs. secondary control coping (Rothbaum, Weisz & Snyder, 1982) where primary control coping consist of attempts to change the stressful circumstances versus secondary control coping mechanisms that involve efforts to adjust to circumstances as they are.

The common denominator for each of these categories is that the first coping modality involves attempts by the individual to change the stressor in relation to themselves while in the other modality the individual attempts change within themselves in relation to the stressor. Coping is also time dependent, that is coping can occur before, during and after exposure to a stressor and is process oriented, where strategies and actions change with time, experience and the nature of the stressor and the processes are constantly assessed within the context of the stressful situation (Beehr & McGrath, 1996). Coping protects people from psychological harm related to stressful experiences, and this can occur by eliminating or minimizing the stressor, by mentally controlling or defining the meaning of the stressor in a way that is acceptable or attempting to control the stress reactions and consequences (Koenig, 2009).

COPING STRATEGIES IN WOMEN EXPERIENCING DV

Women who experience DV use a combination of help seeking and coping strategies to deal with the physical and/or mental health effects of violence and to help secure safety, and it is proposed that help seeking resources are related to women's coping styles. Goodman (2003) summarized these help seeking responses into:

- Informal networks (talking or staying with family, friends),
- Formal and legal networks (clergy, employers, domestic violence shelters, violence restraining orders),
- Safety planning (hiding money, improving safety),
- Resistance (fighting back, shouting, physical retaliation, leaving home), and
- Placating (keeping quiet and doing what is asked by the perpetrator).

For women in DV situations problem-focused coping strategies include action oriented practices to manage stress such as changing the environment, attempts to resolve the problem, modifying their own behaviour to lessen the stress or taking action to change the source of stress. By contrast, emotion-focused strategies aim to lessen the emotional distress arising from DV and consist of techniques that modify emotions in the victim rather than change the stressor or environment (Lazarus & Folkman, 1984). It is theorised that initiation of formal and informal help seeking and the type of help sought are influenced by the coping styles used by the victim of DV (Ambuel et al., 2011).

We believe that this Western model is to a large degree inappropriate or unfeasible in India due to:

- The different socio-cultural context which often sanctions violence, which promotes the dependence of women on men throughout life and which places women's rights and needs below that of men;
- The joint family structure whereby a woman marries into her husband's family and thus is unlikely to receive support from in-laws;
- The old traditions whereby upon marriage a woman ceases to be part of her natal family and belongs to her husband's family. She often lives apart and with limited, and in some instances no, contact with her natal family;
- The lack of legal and community agencies as well as legislative backing to provide support and resolution to abused women.

In a recent study on coping and DV, the overwhelming majority of Indian women used passive coping styles such as turning to prayer, distracting themselves from the event through sleeping, watching TV or keeping busy with household chores (Schineanu, 2013). Active coping styles such as seeking help through formal and informal networks were not even considered by the women in this study due to their social, financial and cultural situation. The variety of coping strategies engaged by Indian women and associated process occurs in stages where the woman progresses and regresses through stages repeatedly as she attempts to develop effective coping skills in response to violence (Cho, 2012; Patel et al., 2007).

Initially, women react to the violence by denial of the abuse or the extent of its consequences, and particularly in India, they may be unaware that violence constitutes a legitimate issue. Then women tend to engage in emotion regulation, seeking support from informal sources and avoidance strategies due to issues such as stigma attached to disclosure and a lack of resources or alternatives. Emotion-focused or avoidance coping and the use of religion are more frequently used in non-Western cultures particularly in those that emphasize group benefit over individual benefit and have strict hierarchical concepts (Shepard & Pence, 1999).

Seeking informal support from friends, family, and other community members to resolve the violence is also favoured over accessing formal supports such as pursuing the legal process. Active problem-solving through accessing external support systems, including crisis counselling tends to be a longer process particularly in places where external resources are minimal or difficult to access, and is thus one of the later stages of the coping process. In India and most other South Asian countries, the majority of women do not go beyond preparation to leave the abuser, and the few that do leave end up returning to the relationship due to societal pressure, economic dependence, inability to support their children, stigma, and lack of social support (Cho, 2012). Indian women recognise that any actions to address DV that take the issue outside the privacy of the home will only be carried out as a last resort, when all else has failed and when they have nothing to lose (Schineanu, 2013).

SOCIAL SUPPORT

Social support is defined as "resources provided by others" (Cohen & Syme, 1985), or as "coping assistance" (Thoits, 1983) and it is derived from the effects of loss of relationships (Stansfeld, 2005). Definitions of social support can include the structure of individual social life such as group memberships, and existence of family ties, as well as the roles they may serve such as emotional support. There is considerable evidence that social support has beneficial outcomes on both physical and mental health; and in relation to its benefits in lessening the effects of DV, may help to diminish shame and affirm the worth and value of the victim as well as plays a role in providing a sense of safety, (see for example Carlson at al., 2002; Madsen & Abell, 2010). Helpful or positive social support leads to health behaviours such as exercising, not smoking and eating right, as well as compliance with medical treatments. By contrast, unsupportive social relationships can increase risky health behaviours such as alcohol and other drug use.

In relation to DV, social support affects the link between violence and negative health outcomes by increasing individual perceptions of control and self-worth which then improve well-being and immunity to disease. Social support acts as a buffer by allowing the threat of the stressor to be reappraised through discussion with a supportive person and enabling the threat to be downgraded or avoided. In the form of practical help, social support may also moderate the impact of the stressor enabling the person to deal with the consequences of the situation in a more appropriate manner (Stansfeld, 2005).

Another important consideration in relation to the beneficial effects of social support is the existence and size of the social support network. Seeking social support is possible only for those that have a network of family and friends that they can access as and when needed. So before we can even analyse the effects of social support on mental health, we need to ensure that there is a social network through which women can seek support.

In one study, the social support network of the women surveyed was very small with less than 3 people (consisting of husband, mother and/or children) although for many women their social support network consisted of only one person, usually a child (Schineanu, 2013). Most often, the people in these social networks were family members that only provided practical help such as food preparation when the woman was sick, rather than emotional help, and very few women had a non-related individual (a friend) to call upon in times of need.

An interesting although not surprising finding was that women with membership in a *mahila mandal* (a local women's group) reported higher levels of social support and wellbeing. However less than 30% of the 907 women in Schineanu's (2013) study were members of the *mahila mandal*. These findings have grave implications for Indian women that experience DV as it means that another avenue through which they can seek support and protect their mental health is significantly limited.

SPIRITUALITY

Religion has played an important role in the life of people for thousands of years, with evidence of religious rituals dating as far back as the Palaeolithic period over 500,000 years ago. Koenig (2009) argues that the purpose of religion, and the reason why it has survived this long, is to enable people to cope and make sense of suffering, provide a perception of control over situations that are outside their control and understanding, and facilitate communal living and cooperation through promotion of social rules.

Spirituality is something people define for themselves, it is largely free of rules, and can be understood as the process of searching and experiencing what is perceived as sacred or divine. Most people define themselves to be both religious and spiritual, and there is a large degree of overlap between the two terms (Verma et al., 2006). In this chapter religiosity and spirituality are considered synonyms and used interchangeably unless otherwise specified.

Coping through the use of religion is very common across the world, particularly in times of great stress and Koenig (2009) explains why this is so:

> *"Religious beliefs provide a sense of meaning and purpose during difficult life circumstances that assist with psychological integration; they usually promote a positive world view that is optimistic and hopeful; they provide role models in sacred writings that facilitate acceptance of suffering; they give people a sense of indirect control over circumstances, reducing the need for personal control; and they offer a community of support, both human and divine, to help reduce isolation and loneliness."* p 285.

Religious coping in response to illness has been extensively studied particularly among patients with cancer, HIV and other life threatening illnesses (for a review see Sherman & Simonton, 2007). There are two types of religious coping, "positive religious coping" which provides comfort and reassurance and "negative religious coping" which consists of a sense of struggle or doubt. Interestingly, there have been mixed results for the effects of positive religious coping on health outcomes, but negative religious coping has constantly been associated with poorer health outcomes.

It is believed that religious beliefs and practices aid in coping with the stresses of life and are beneficial to mental health with the strongest and most consistent association found by comparing different degrees of religiousness or spirituality (from a non-religious to a deeply religious person) rather than between different religious denominations. The protective effects of religiousness are consistent even after controlling for age, gender and socio-economic status and are similar across different countries, religions, races and age. It also seems to be stronger for people under psychosocial stress so the more stressed one is the bigger the protective effects of religiousness (Koenig, 2009; Smith, McCullough, & Poll, 2003). It must be noted, however, that there are some for whom religious beliefs and practices emphasise neurotic predispositions, increase fears or guilt, and limit life rather than enhance it (Koenig, 2009).

One of the mechanisms of action for religiousness is thought to occur via the social support obtained through church attendance and participation in religious activities. However once again this opportunity seems to be closed to Indian women, as Eastern religions such as Hinduism, Buddhism and Jainism are practiced individually in homes or at temples, and there are no regular gatherings where women can seek social support (Schineanu, 2013).

For some Indian women who experience DV, their belief system allows them to attribute the violence to an external force, view the pain as only a temporary condition that does not affect their inner self and by putting up with it or accepting it, the women believe that it will have a positive outcome in their next life (Vos et al., 2009), and this can lessen the psychological distress caused by the ongoing violence (Tsey et al., 2007).

This sense of connection to a higher being allows women to maintain healthy mental functioning despite adverse life experiences, acts as a mental and emotional safe haven, assists in the process of meaning making, and builds resilience by creating a sense of hope (Bryant-Davis et al., 2011). In the case of Indian women, the belief that the violence is punishment for something that occurred in a past life is turned into a positive element by belief in *karma* which stipulates that hardships experienced in the current life will be rewarded in the next life. Despite this positive element, these women may relinquish control over their fate as they see it as something that they cannot change since their current situation is a result of behaviours in a previous life. As such they resign to their fate, and deal with the violence using avoidance and denial, which is a protective mechanism in the short term but it can be detrimental to mental health in the long term.

Abused Indian women's distress in relation to DV is also likely to increase with increasing awareness that DV should not be happening, that not every woman is a victim of DV, that there is legislation to protect them but it is not enforced and so on, yet they are still forced to 'put up with it'. Women stated that they had faith in God to guide them and help resolve the DV issue but at the same time they believed that a lifetime of suffering will result in harm to their mental and physical wellbeing (Schineanu, 2013). So in a sense although they professed to be hopeful of a resolution and of a life without DV, there was also recognition, even if only subconsciously, that in fact it was unlikely that they would ever escape DV and its consequences.

DISCUSSION

In South Asian cultures, patriarchy and associated factors tend to prevail and women are held responsible for the maintenance of the well-being of the family and its members even at a personal, emotional, and physical cost to themselves. Indian victims of DV are in a more difficult situation than their Western counterparts due to the combination of factors such as the importance of collective identity, the societal construct of women as sacrificing, dutiful partners, wives, and mothers, inadequate legislation and lack of external support systems to assist victims of DV.

For a more in-depth understanding of Indian women's help-seeking and coping strategies within the broader social context of cultural values and norms within gender and class, religious affiliation, and attitudes towards the use of violence, and how these affect their perceptions of violence is an issue needs to be examined. Pinnewala's work (2009) on the development of a new theoretical framework for South Asian women subjected to partner violence supports the view that women's help-seeking behaviours and coping mechanisms are determined by cultural factors and societal constructs of womanhood.

Interestingly, abused women of Indian and other South Asian origin that live in Western countries such as USA, Canada and Australia follow a similar coping pattern as women in India. However, the large majority extend these processes to include active coping such as making use of women's refuges, police and legal recourses and many leave the abusive husband permanently. This suggests that most women in India experiencing DV, do not progress beyond the initial passive coping stages because the social and cultural climate acts as a barrier to women escaping abusive situations.

The cultural and social context of India also prevents women from seeking social and emotional support through the use of shaming and blaming attitudes and the promotion of ideal womanhood which endures all kinds of injustices without retaliation or complaint. The evidence base supporting the beneficial effects of social support on depression and other common mental disorders in victims of DV is quite extensive. A consistent finding is that abused women who report low or negative social support are significantly more likely to be depressed than women who report high levels of social support (Carlson, et al., 2002; Raistrick et al., 2006).

The evidence from India, while not as extensive as that from Western countries also shows that the mental health status of women who report having good social support is better than women who report poor social support (Jeyaseelan et al., 2007; Kumar, et al., 2005). However, considering most Indian women's reluctance to discuss DV with anyone, it is questionable whether many Indian women would actually seek support from others in matters related to their experiences of DV. The perception of a measure of control over their future lives by enduring through the hardships of the current life may assist Indian women in dealing with DV, a situation that is out of their control. On the other hand, it is possible that some Indian women do not employ this 'positive' viewpoint on their situation and end up using 'negative religious coping' (Schineanu, 2013).

These coping modalities that espouse endurance of hardships are further exacerbated by the strong traditional views of Indian womanhood and in particular of mythological role models of femininity such as Sita, the wife of Rama (an incarnation of the Hindu god Vishnu), which all Hindu women are supposed to model. She is the personification of divine womanhood and is said to be patient, all-suffering, ever-faithful, and ever-pure wife, who despite the terrible injustice inflicted on her never retaliates.

The dissonance between what the ideal woman should be and the reality they live in can create mental issues for Indian women in the long term, particularly as they are mostly powerless to change their situation. The lack of options when it comes to leaving abusive relationships, the social and cultural structures that make seeking social support shameful and the cultural and social traditions that place family honour, happiness and existence entirely on the women's shoulders contribute to their emotional and mental strain.

CONCLUSION

In this chapter the issue of spirituality and social support in coping with DV in the Indian context was examined. DV is a widespread issue maintained by gender inequality and cultural and social structures and attitudes which justify and reinforce the use of violence against women, while simultaneously preventing them from escaping their situation. Indian women tend to use only emotional or passive coping mechanisms which are ineffective in preventing the development of DV associated CMD. The chapter also highlighted that for Indian women, particularly those who are largely confined to or do not work outside the family home or do not participate in women friendly community activities such as *mahila mandals*, the likelihood of having friends or a social support network is low.

As leaving the relationship or a marriage is not a valid option, Indian women need to engage in strategies that minimize the violence. They also need to develop resilience to cope with trauma by utilising their cognitive resources and the limited community resources and support systems. The use of spirituality appears to be the only available refuge for Indian women, yet even this may not provide the same benefits as Christian religious practices because of the individualistic nature of the practice and lack of regular group activities through which women could seek social support. Finally, no change is possible unless men take responsibility for their actions. Policy makers and programmes should consider health and community education strategies that would engage men in the process to change their attitudes towards domestic violence and protect women.

REFERENCES

Ambuel, B., Trent, K., Lenahan, P., Cronholm, P., Downing, D., Jelley, M., et al. (2011) *Competencies needed by health professionals for addressing exposure to violence and abuse in patient care*. Eden Prairie (MN): Academy on Violence and Abuse.

Awasthi, P. & Mishra, R. (2011). Illness, beliefs and coping strategies of diabetic women. *Psychological Studies*, *56*(2), 176-184.

Babu, G. & Babu, B. (2011). Dowry deaths: a neglected public health issue in India. *International Health*, *3*(1), 35-43.

Beehr, T. A. & McGrath, J. E. (1996). The methodology of research on coping: Conceptual, strategic, and operational-level issues. In Zeidner M & Endler NS (Eds.), *Handbook of coping: Theory, research, applications*, (65-82). New York: Wiley.

Brandtstädter, J. (1992). Personal control over development: Implications of self-efficacy. In R Schwarzer (Ed.), *Self-efficacy: Thought control of action*, (127-145). Washington, DC: Hemisphere.

Bryant-Davis, T., Ullman, S. E., Tsong, Y. & Gobin, R. (2011). Surviving the storm: The role of social support and religious coping in sexual assault recovery of African American women. *Violence against Women*, *17*(12), 1601-1618.

Carlson, B. E., McNutt, L., Choi, D. Y. & Rose, I. M. (2002). Intimate partner abuse and mental health: The role of social support and other protective factors. *Violence against Women*, *8*(6), 720-745.

CEDAW *General Recommendations* Nos. 19 and 20, adopted at the Eleventh Session, 1992 (contained in Document A/47/38) (1992).

Cho, H. (2012). Use of mental health Services among Asian and Latino victims of intimate partner violence. *Violence against Women, 18*(4), 404-419.

Cohen, S. & Syme, S. (Eds.). (1985). *Social Support and Health*. New York: Academic Press.

Go, V. F., Sethulakshmi, C. J., Bentley, M. E., Sivaram, S., Srikrishnan, A. K., Solomon, S. & Celentano, D. D. (2003). When HIV-Prevention messages and gender norms clash: The impact of domestic violence on women's HIV risk in slums of Chennai, India. *AIDS and Behavior, 7*(3), 263-272.

Heilman, B. (2010). *A lifecourse perspective of inimate partner violence in India: What picture does the NFHS-3 paint?* Master of Arts in Law and Diplomacy Masters, Tufts University, Medford/Sommerville.

Jacobsen, I., Kjosavik, D. & Nyborg, I. (2012). *The hidden violence against women: Challenges and obstacles in responses to domestic violence in Neoliberal Kerala, India*: Centre for International Climate and Environmental Research, Oslo.

Jejeebhoy, S. L. (1998). Wife-beating in rural India: A husband's right? *Economic and Political Weekly, 33*, 855 - 862.

Jeyaseelan, L., Kumar, S., Neelakantan, N., Peedicayil, A., Pillai, R. & Duvvury, N. (2007). Physical spousal violence against women in India: Some risk factors. *Journal of Biosocial Science, 39*(05), 657-670.

Kaur, R. & Garg, S. (2010). Domestic violence against women: A qualitative study in a rural community. *Asia-Pacific Journal of Public Health, 22*(2), 242-251.

Keleher, H. & Franklin, L. (2008). Changing gendered norms about women and girls at the level of household and community: A review of the evidence. *Global Public Health, 3*, 42-57.

Koenig, H. G. (2009). Research on religion, spirituality, and mental health: A Review. *Canadian Journal of Psychiatry, 54*(5), 283-291.

Koenig, M. A., Stephenson, R., Ahmed, S., Jejeebhoy, S. J. & Campbell, J. (2006). Individual and contextual determinants of domestic violence in North India. *American Journal of Public Health, 96*, 132 - 138.

Krishnan, S., Rocca, C. H., Hubbard, A. E., Subbiah, K., Edmeades, J. & Padian, N. S. (2010). Do changes in spousal employment status lead to domestic violence? Insights from a prospective study in Bangalore, India. *Social Science & Medicine, 70*(1), 136-143.

Kumar, S., Jeyaseelan, L., Suresh, S. & Ahuja, R. C. (2005). Domestic violence and its mental health correlates in Indian women. *British Journal of Psychiatry, 187*, 62-67.

Laungani, P. (2002). Stress, trauma, and coping strategies: Cross-cultural variations. *International Journal of Group Tensions, 31*(2), 127-154.

Lazarus, R. & Folkman, S. (1984). *Stress, appraisal, and coping*. New York: Springer.

Lopez-Claros, A. & Zahidi, S. (2005, December). *Women's empowerment: measuring the global gender gap*. Geneva Switzerland World Economic Forum 2005.

Madsen, M, & Abell, N. (2010). Trauma resilience scale: Validation of *Protective Factors Associated With Adaptation Following Violence. Research on Social Work Practice, 20*(2), 223-233.

McCloskey, L., Lichter, E., Ganz, M., Williams, C., Gerber, M., Sege, R. Herbert, B. (2005). Intimate partner violence and patient screening across medical specialties. *Academic Emergency Medicine, 12*(8), 712-722.

Nayak, M., Patel, V., Bond, J. C. & Greenfield, T. (2010). Partner alcohol use, violence and women's mental health: population-based survey in India. *British Journal of Psychiatry*, *196*(3), 192-199.

Parashar, A. (2008). Gender Inequality and Religious Personal Laws in India. *Brown Journal of World Affairs*, *14*(2), 103-112.

Pargament, K. (1997). *The Psychology of Religion and Coping: Theory, Research, Practice.* New York: Guilford Press.

Patel, V., Araya, R., Chatterjee, S., Chisholm, D., Cohen, A., De Silva, M... van Ommeren, M. (2007). Treatment and prevention of mental disorders in low-income and middle-income countries. *The Lancet*, *370*(9591), 991-1005.

Patel, V., Kirkwood, B. R., Pednekar, S., Weiss, H. & Mabey, D. (2006). Risk factors for common mental disorders in women - Population-based longitudinal study. *British Journal of Psychiatry*, *189*, 547-555.

Pinnewala, P. (2009). Good women, martyrs, and survivors: A theoretical framework for south asian women's responses to partner violence. *Violence against women*, *15*(1), 81-105.

Raistrick, D., Heather, N. & Godfrey, C. (2006). *Review of the effectiveness of treatment for alcohol problems* (212). London, UK: National Treatment Agency for Substance Misuse.

Rothbaum, F., Weisz, J. R. & Snyder, S. S. (1982). Changing the world and changing the self: A two-process model of perceived control. *Journal of Personality and Social Psychology*, *42*(1), 5-37.

Rotter, J. (1966). Generalized expectancies for internal versus external control of reinforcement. *Psychological Monographs*, *80*, 1-28.

Russo, N. F. & Pirlott, A. (2006). Gender-based violence. *Annals of the New York Academy of Sciences*, *1087*(1), 178-205.

Schineanu, A. (2013). *Intimate partner violence and common mental disorders in Indian women: Effects of autonomy, social support and spirituality.* PhD, Curtin University, Perth.

Schuler, S. R., Bates, L. M., & Islam, F. (2008). Women's rights, domestic violence, and recourse seeking in rural Bangladesh. *Violence against Women*, *14*(3), 326-345.

Shamasundar, C. (2008). Relevance of ancient Indian wisdom to modern mental health: A few examples. *Indian Journal of Psychiatry*, *50*(2), 138-143.

Shepard, M, & Pence, E (Eds.). (1999). *Coordinating Community Responses to Domestic Violence: Lessons From Duluth and Beyond.* Thousand Oaks, CA Sage Publications, Inc.

Simister, J. & Mehta, P. (2010). Gender-Based Violence in India: Long-Term Trends. *Journal of Interpersonal Violence*, *25*(9), 1594-1611.

Smith, T. B., McCullough, M. & Poll, J. (2003). Religiousness and Depression: Evidence for a main effect and the moderating influence of stressful life events. *Psychological Bulletin*, *129*(4), 614-636.

Stansfeld, S. (2005). Social support and social cohesion. In M Marmot & R Wilkinson (Eds.), *Social Determinants of Health* (2 ed., 32-79). Oxford: OUP Oxford.

Subadra. (1999). Violence against women: Wife battering in Chennai. *Economic and Political Weekly*, *34*(16/17), WS28-WS33.

Taylor, S. E. (1983). Adjustment to threatening events: A theory of cognitive adaptation. *American Psychologist*, *38*(11), 1161-1173.

Tenhunen, S. (2008), Mobile technology in the village: ICTs, culture, and social logistics in India. *Journal of the Royal Anthropological Institute*, *14*, 515–534.

Thoits, P. A. (1983). Dimensions of life events that influence psychological distress: An evaluation and synthesis of the literature. In HB Kaplan (Ed.), *Psychosocial Stress: Trends in Theory and Research*, (33-103). New York: Academic Press.

Tsey, K., Wilson, A., Haswell-Elkins, M., Whiteside, M., McCalman, J., Cadet-James, Y. & Wenitong, M. (2007). Empowerment-based research methods: a 10-year approach to enhancing Indigenous social and emotional wellbeing. *Australasian Psychiatry*, *15*(s1), S34-S38.

Verma, R., Pulerwitz, J., Mahendra, V., Khandekar, S., Barker, G., Fulpagare, P. & Singh, S. (2006). *Shifting support for inequitable gender norms among young Indian men to reduce HIV risk and partner violence Horizons Research Summary*. New Delhi: Population Council.

Vindhya, U. (2007). Quality of Women's Lives in India: Some Findings from Two Decades of Psychological Research on Gender. *Feminism & Psychology*, *17*(3), 337-356.

Vos, T., Barker, B., Begg, S., Stanley, L. & Lopez, A. (2009). Burden of disease and injury in Aboriginal and Torres Strait Islander Peoples: The Indigenous health gap. *International Journal of Epidemiology*, *38*(2), 470-477.

In: Overcoming Domestic Violence
Editors: Myra F. Taylor, Julie Ann Pooley et al.

ISBN: 978-1-63321-956-4
© 2015 Nova Science Publishers, Inc.

Chapter 10

A FEMINIST PERSPECTIVE: SYSTEM RESPONSES TO AUSTRALIAN MOTHERS EXITING AN ABUSIVE RELATIONSHIP

Elspeth McInnes[*]
University of South Australia, Australia

ABSTRACT

Displacement from home and family is a common outcome for victims of domestic and family violence, creating new risks and compounding existing vulnerabilities. These include exposure to physical and sexual assault, poverty, dependence on others – benign or otherwise, addictions and other psychological and physical legacies of abuse. Common strategies of abusers include isolating targets from supportive networks of family and friends, leaving them without support and often carrying stigmatizing labels generated by the perpetrator, and sometimes by service professionals if they end the relationship. The specific service frameworks which may interact with mothers and children leaving abusive relationships include family law and family relationship services, government and community based social welfare services, police, criminal courts, child protection, domestic violence services, homelessness and housing services, health services and drug and alcohol services. These services span state and federal jurisdictions and can have contradictory impacts on the lives of mothers and children leaving violent relationships. The complex interactions between service systems can create adverse outcomes for victims and inhibit help-seeking. This chapter focuses on the trajectories into homelessness and relationships to services for mothers of young children leaving violent relationships. Further to this, the ways in which services interact with victims is examined, as well as the ways in which services interact with each other to deliver outcomes to mothers and the children seeking their help.

Keywords: Domestic and family violence; parental separation; service integration

---

[*] Corresponding author: Dr. Elspeth McInnes, Senior Lecturer, School of Education, University of South Australia, Magill, Australia, SA 5072. Tel: (08) 8302 4042, Email: Elspeth.McInnes@unisa.edu.au.

INTRODUCTION

Domestic and family violence is a persistent social problem and the primary driver of both homelessness and homicide of women and children in Australia. The Australian National Plan to Reduce Violence against Women and Children (DSS, 2013) notes that around one third of Australian women have experienced physical violence and nearly one-in-five have experienced sexual violence since the age of 15. The most recent data from the Australian Bureau of Statistics (2013) identified that 1,267,200 Australian women had ever experienced violence from a previous partner since the age of 15, and a further 237,100 had experienced violence by a current partner since the age of 15. The Personal Safety Survey (ABS, 2006) identified that 59% of women who had experienced violence since aged 15 had children in their care. Richards (2011), notes that violent households were consistently found to be significantly more likely to have children than non-violent households, and these children were significantly more likely to be aged under five. Recent Victorian data identified a 40% increase in police callouts to family violence reports over the past two years. 'Victoria Police dealt with more than 60,000 family violence incidents in 2012-13 - including 29 murders, which account for a little less than half of all murders committed in the state' (Elder, 2014, p.2). The National Homicide Monitoring Program reported that 122 Australian women were killed by their partner in the two years from July 2008 to June 2010 (Chan & Payne, 2013).

Despite, or perhaps because of, the prevalence and severity of domestic and family violence against women and children, many victims remain unable to get effective help to achieve safety and recovery. Many victims who leave violent relationships become internally displaced refugees of the Australian suburbs and country towns. This chapter examines the difficulties faced by women and children affected by domestic and family violence in the context of interactions of systems with which they are engaged. The focus on women domestic violence victims and parental separation is not intended to imply that all parental separations are related to violence, or that women never commit violence. The focus reflects the social statistics which identify that women are more likely than men to be victims of family violence (ABS, 2013) and that ending the relationship is a strategy to stop the violence.

WOMEN'S CONTEXT AS CHILDREN'S PRIMARY CARERS

Key interconnected social contexts of women's experiences of domestic and family violence are their social roles as mothers and primary unpaid carers in the majority of couple and single parent families (ABS, 2003) and their unequal position in the labour market. Alongside their unpaid family care role, women spend less time in paid work, are paid less for the work they do and have less opportunity to work in higher paid secure jobs (Workplace Gender Equality Agency, 2013). The report by the Australian Human Rights Commission, "Investing in Care: Recognising and Valuing those who Care" (2013) confirms the economic plight of unpaid carers of children and dependent adults and that most carers are women. The report identifies the risks of long-term unpaid care provision as a pathway to lifelong poverty, as carers forgo earnings, savings and career development opportunities. Women's primary carer role as mothers increases their vulnerability in abusive relationships by limiting their access to income; having the additional responsibility and costs to support and care for their children, while struggling for their safety and survival (McInnes, 2004). In addition, mothers fear losing care of their children to either child protection services or the perpetrator if they are deemed unable to act protectively (Douglas & Walsh, 2009; Meyer, 2011).

Whilst there have been some improvements in state and federal Australian governments' responses to domestic and family violence in the past decade, there are numerous complex systemic issues for governments and their agencies which continue to contribute to women's experiences of lack of safety for themselves and their children. The complexity begins with the different state and territory laws against domestic and family violence applying across eight different jurisdictions with diverse definitions and provisions. These legal frameworks interact with the federal Family Law Act governing marriage and parental separation and divorce and the social security laws administering income support and family payments and the transfer of child support between separated parents. In state and territory jurisdictions the issues include police and criminal justice system practices, problems securing emergency housing, service responses which blame victims for their 'choice' of abusive relationships and mothers' difficulties with both child protection and family law systems in maintaining care of their children. Additional complexities arise when violence victimisation results in mothers' mental illness and/or addictions (Bromfield, Lamont, Parker & Horsfall, 2010). These women are often excluded from emergency housing services because of mental illness or addiction.

These systemic problems arise partly from a continuing retreat from feminist approaches to implementing service responses to domestic and family violence which aimed to avoid 'victim-blaming' and support mothers and children to recover in safety together (Hume, McInnes, Rendell & Green, 2011). Although feminist theory and practice has been central to the social recognition of violence against women and the development of service responses (McGregor & Hopkins, 1991), domestic violence and homelessness services have increasingly been transferred away from community based women's agencies to large corporate service providers with no gender analysis informing service delivery. Nichols (2013) identifies that feminist advocates for domestic violence victims emphasize survivor-defined practices focused on women's empowerment and encouraging women to make their own decisions. Feminist approaches to implementing service responses to domestic and family violence also recognized intersections with other forms of social oppression by class, ethnicity and sexual orientation and advocated for broad social changes to reduce women's social inequality. In contrast, non-feminist responses to domestic and family violence can easily replicate the power dynamic of exerting control over women's decision-making, individualizing her situation as a personal problem and subscribing to a gender–neutral approach to violence which fails to recognize the localised and wider contexts of women's social subordination. Hume et al. (2011) identify that a combination of neo-conservative politics, funding pressures, professionalization of staff, segmentation of services and the growth of large corporate service providers have together created a service environment without commitment to feminist theories and practices. A commitment to women's support and empowerment, which was central to the formation of advocacy against domestic and family violence, has transformed into an individualized "case-based" approach with an undertone of scepticism and victim-blaming. Such views are rendered rhetorically in the question "Why doesn't she leave?" with its attendant assumptions that victims can always control their situation and that leaving would stop the violence. In practice intimate partner homicide research shows that women are at greatest risk when they seek to end a relationship (Easteal, 1993). Limited income means they often also struggle to find accommodation (Salvation Army, 2013), while family law provisions mean they will likely to be forced to regularly place children in the 'care' of the offender (Kaye, Stubbs & Tolmie, 2003).

Women and children leaving violent domestic relationships form the largest group (25%) of homeless people in Australia seeking accommodation from homelessness services (Homelessness Australia, 2013). A recent report by the Salvation Army, currently the largest provider of homelessness services in Australia, identified that 53% of women accessing a service identified domestic and family violence as their main presenting issue (Salvation Army, 2013). Children accompanying their mothers leaving domestic violence accounted for two-thirds of child clients of homelessness services (MacDonald, 2007, as cited in Richards, 2011). According to Homelessness Australia data, one in every two people seeking emergency accommodation in Australia is turned away each night (Hume et al., 2013). Revealing domestic and family violence to government agencies can lead to victims' loss of housing, income and care of children.

REPORTING DOMESTIC AND FAMILY VIOLENCE TO POLICE

In Australia, police provide the 'front-line' response to domestic and family violence events reported by witnesses or participants. Women victims of domestic and family violence have become more willing to formally report domestic and family violence over the past two decades. Australian Bureau of Statistics surveys in 1996 and 2006 showed a significant increase in the proportion of women victims of domestic and family violence reporting violence to police during that period. In the Women's Safety Survey in 1996, only 19% of women who had been assaulted in the previous 12 months notified police. By the time of the Personal Safety Survey published in 2006, 36% of women victims had reported incidents of violence in the past 12 months to police. Those experiencing violence from a current partner were less likely to tell anyone compared to those who were separated from the perpetrator (ABS, 2006). In 2012 (ABS, 2013), one in four women with a current violent partner had told no-one, compared with only 7% of those with violent ex-partners. Of the women with previous violent partners, 62% had first told friends and family, 10 % had told police and 9.4% had told a health professional. Of the women with current violent partners, 48% had first told friends or family and 15% had told a health professional (ABS, 2013).

Although reporting family violence to police or other government agencies is necessary in order to get help, reporting also carries risks for victims. Victims' preferences to confide in friends and family reflect some of the uncertainties of system and professional reactions of blame, minimization or disbelief to women's disclosures of family violence (Breckenridge, 1999). Disclosing family or domestic violence to others is recognised as a difficult process for victims, potentially involving numerous responding services. Risks include retaliation from the perpetrator, being disbelieved or blamed for the violence against them, being required by child protection services to leave the relationship or lose care of their children (Humphreys, 2014). Meyer's (2011) study of mothers' considerations in reporting domestic and family violence noted the frequency of 'victim-blaming attitudes' from criminal justice and child protection services which lacked understanding of the dynamics of intimate partner violence.

She noted that victims found themselves 'trapped' between child protection system expectations that they end the relationship and "a reluctance" by judicial officers to include children on intervention orders (2011, p. 436). Birdsey and Snowball's (2013) New South Wales survey of victims attending domestic violence services found that 48 % did not report their most recent incident to police. The most common reasons were fear of retaliation by the perpetrator, shame, or a belief the incident was too trivial. Participants stated that the main barrier to reporting was that police either did not understand, or were not proactive in handling domestic violence (2013).

Victims' reports of lack of police action are corroborated by research. Research into family violence victims with protection orders identified problems of delays in orders being served and lack of police action in response to breaches of orders (Katzen, 2000). Research into family violence in Australia in 2009 found that 80% of a national sample of 267 respondents with protection orders reported the orders had been breached. Of these, police attended in only 72% of cases, and then proceeded to prosecution in just 36% of cases (Bagshaw et al., 2010).

To improve police responses to domestic and family violence, most Australian states have engaged in reforms to policing practices over the past decade. Holder's (2007) report into police action in response to domestic violence incidents in the ACT identified that a 'pro-arrest' stance and improved police training in domestic violence as a criminal act, had resulted in more consistent responses to victims of domestic and family violence. In contrast, an evaluation of Tasmania's 'Safe at Home' domestic and family violence strategy found that the pro-arrest stance had also increased 'dual arrests' of both victim and offender in incidents of domestic violence (Success Works, 2009b). Women's Legal Services NSW also noted an increase over five years to 2010 in the numbers of women victims of violence who were the subject of intervention orders against them (2014). Their research found that over two-thirds of women who had intervention orders sought against them, were in fact the primary victim and that fewer than two in five of such intervention order applications were eventually confirmed by a court:

> Many of the women defending AVOs in the study reported that when police had been called after a violent incident, they felt that their version of events had not been viewed as credible compared with the other party, due to the circumstances of their heightened stress and anxiety. Other women reported that they believed the other party had deliberately initiated AVO proceedings as a further mechanism of controlling their behavior, by giving them the ability to threaten them with reports to police in the future (Women's Legal Services NSW, 2014).

Braaf and Sneddon (2007) note that police pro-arrest policies are correlated with a rise in dual arrests and single arrests of women for domestic violence. They recommend the use of primary aggressor policies, risk assessment and tighter integration between police and prosecutors to minimise the incidence of dual arrests and the adverse consequences for victims of domestic and family violence. Such consequences include increasing victims' vulnerability due to loss of victim status and an increased reluctance to seek help from police (Braaf & Sneddon 2007, p. 5).

DOMESTIC AND FAMILY VIOLENCE SERVICES INTEGRATION FRAMEWORKS

State and territory government initiatives to improve police responses to domestic and family violence have been accompanied in some states by the implementation of integrated case management approaches to cases assessed as being high risk. At the same time, rationalization and competition processes have been transforming domestic and family violence services from feminist-informed specialist women's services into large generic social service agencies which do not recognize gendered power relationships as an important factor impacting on experiences of family violence, homelessness or mental illness (Hume et al., 2013). Instead of mental illness and/or addiction problems being recognized as consequences of coping with exposures to violence and abuse (Bromfield et al., 2010), victims can be blamed for failing to make protective choices (Hume et al., 2013; Meyer, 2011). Instead of holding the perpetrator accountable for the physical and emotional injuries, victims become the problem to be 'fixed'.

Whole-of-government integrated responses to domestic and family violence have been introduced in Australia over the past decade or so. Tasmania was one of the first Australian jurisdictions to introduce an integrated approach to domestic and family violence with its Safe at Home framework commencing in 2004. Integrated Case Coordination under Safe At Home involves "weekly meetings in each of the four police districts attended by all relevant government Safe At Home services including the Victim Safety Response Team, Police Prosecutions, Family Violence Counselling and Support Service, Court Support and Liaison Service, Child Protection and Special Needs Liaison Service. The meeting considers all new and 'active' family violence 'cases' in the district" (Success Works 2009b, p. 13). Bringing agencies together is intended to provide better understanding of the features of high risk cases and more coordinated responses to victims.

When agencies have different views of risk assessment and responses to domestic and family violence, victims face hurdles negotiating their needs with each relevant agency. For example, the Safe at Home evaluation identified that "Housing Tasmania did not always understand the need to provide secure accommodation for victims and children", and that Child Protection staff sometimes "blamed" victims of family violence for not providing adequate protection for their children (Success Works 2009b, p. 36). In an earlier report, the evaluator noted that housing services saw family and domestic violence victims as "using family violence as a way of getting ahead in the public housing waiting list" (Success Works 2009a, p. 45). Blaming the victim and constructing the victim as making false reports to gain advantage form part of a culture of social support for domestic violence in which women either "deserve" abuse or lie about abuse to serve some imagined purpose such as "revenge" or "advantage". A national survey of community attitudes to violence against women in 2009 identified that attitudes which "condone, justify or excuse" violence against women persist (VicHealth, 2010). Such responses underline the need for shared priorities and risk assessment processes in responses by state policies, agencies and programs to victims of domestic and family violence.

In 2007 South Australia also commenced an integrated response to domestic and family violence under its Family Safety Framework. The Framework involves a common risk assessment tool and information sharing at Family Safety Meetings between key stakeholders including police, child protection, health services, public housing, corrections, education and domestic violence. The evaluation of the Framework identified that whilst it was supporting better safety outcomes for victims, it was not improving the accountability of perpetrators, with the focus of intervention on victims (Marshall, Ziersch & Hudson, 2008). By focusing on victims, women victims become subject to assessments, interventions and requirements of multiple services, whilst the perpetrator is left without active surveillance or intervention. In 2011 the South Australian government extended police powers to enable them to issue on-the-spot intervention orders and introduced changes to sexual assault and domestic violence laws to improve prosecutions of these crimes (Office for Women, 2011).

As noted in the Tasmanian evaluation, the increasing integration between services responding to domestic and family violence has meant that child protection services become involved when children are present at domestic or family violence incidents attended by police. In most states of Australia, police attending a domestic violence event where children are present are required to notify state child protection services that children are being exposed to violence. This in turn can result in child protection officers advising victims to end the violent relationship or their children could be taken into care (Humphreys, 2011; Meyer, 2011). Child protection systems focus on mothers' actions to protect children from domestic violence (Higgins & Kaspiew, 2011), substantiating notifications as "emotional abuse" by mothers when children are found to have been exposed to family violence. Child protection data accordingly reflects "emotional abuse" as the most commonly substantiated type of child abuse in Australia, accounting for 36% of substantiated cases (AIHW 2013, p. 11). Bearing in mind that substantiation cannot occur unless a case is investigated, across Australia, police were the most common source of notifications (25%) which resulted in investigations (AIHW 2013).

Mothers who end their violent relationship to protect and maintain care of their children face daily difficulties gaining emergency accommodation, along with meeting their children's basic needs for food, a place to sleep, education and health care (McInnes, 2004). They have to manage the impacts of the violence and abuse on their own physical and mental health and cope with the consequences of children's exposures to direct and indirect violence and abuse. Such consequences vary with the ages of children, the age of onset of violence, its frequency and severity (Tomison, 2000). Many children have difficulties with anxiety, increased aggression or withdrawal as an outcome of abuse, further compounded by the loss of security of a home and their possessions (McInnes, 2004). Mothers reported their children did not want to be separated from them to attend school or child care because the children were fearful for their mother. The child protection system focus on 'saving' the child often means that the recovery of the mother-child bond is not prioritised.

Humphreys notes:

> Domestic violence is not only an attack on an individual woman it is also an attack on the relationship between mother and child. The research demonstrates that rebuilding mother-child relationships in the aftermath of domestic violence is critical to the recovery process for both mothers and children (2011, p. 6).

The strategies used by domestic and family violence perpetrators to destroy the mother-child relationship include preventing the mother from tending to her children, undermining, insulting, attacking and humiliating the mother in front of their children, (Humphreys, 2011), forcing the children to join in abusing their mother (Bancroft & Silverman, 2002), disrupting mothers' bonding with their children (Buchanan, 2008), telling the child their mother wanted him to abuse them or that she would not believe them or help them if they told her about the abuse (Morris, 2003). These perpetrator strategies, along with protocols of mandatory police reports to child protection when children are present at domestic violence incidents, mean that it is not uncommon for mothers to lose care of their children to the perpetrator through child protection action (Meyer, 2011). Higgins and Kaspiew (2011) note that child protection units focus on whether the mother is acting protectively. Child protection responses approach the child's context as one of maternal 'failure to protect' and can place children with the perpetrator on the grounds that 'he is only violent to the mother and has good discipline with children' (Families SA child protection worker, personal communication, August 18, 2013). The distress of victims, the impacts of the abuse on their ability to present themselves as competent parents and the characterisation of the mother by the perpetrator can persuade child protection workers that the children are better off with an in-control father who uses violence than an apparently incoherent mother.

The adverse impacts of abuse on victims' mental health have long been recognized by research (Golding, 1999; Herman, 1992; Itzin, 2006). Exposures to violence and abuse have a cumulative effect on the mental health of victims depending on the age of onset of violence and abuse, the frequency, duration and severity of the abuse (Afifi et al., 2009). Depression, suicidality, Post-traumatic Sstress Disorder, alcohol and drug abuse have all been linked to domestic and family violence victimization (Golding, 2009). Butterworth (2004) found that Australian lone mothers were significantly more likely than partnered mothers to experience mental illness and that exposures to physical and sexual violence were the best predictors of mental illness, ahead of family type or socio-economic status. When victims engage with services such as police, child protection and emergency housing, where traumatizing impacts are not understood, their self-presentation often undermines staff perceptions of their credibility and capacity. The traumatising and disabling impacts of the violence they have experienced easily become interpreted against them, for example as being a highly reactive, or affected by drugs or alcohol, choosing, provoking and deserving of violence against them. As Bromfield et al. (2010) note, victims of violence with mental illness or substance abuse issues can end up being referred to different services without any one service having a coherent knowledge of the family circumstances and needs.

FEDERAL GOVERNMENT SYSTEMS

Systemic service difficulties for victims of domestic and family violence continue into the federal sphere. State based integrated service approaches do not include federal agencies and services. The evaluation of Tasmania's Safe at Home system noted that the federal family law system did not align with the goals of the state system with regard to children's best interests:

> The State's laws and the Family Court offer two very different understandings of what is in the best interests of the child. State laws emphasize a child's rights to safety and the impact of accumulated harm and specifically seek to protect children who have experienced family violence in the understanding that, even if they are not directly

victims themselves, the trauma of living in a home where violence takes place is in itself potentially harmful. The Family Court, on the other hand, is required to understand that the best interests of the child are met by "ensuring that children have the benefit of both of their parents having a meaningful involvement in their lives…" (Section 7, Family Law Amendment (Shared Parental Responsibility) Act 2006) (Success Works, 2009b, p. 49-50).

The report goes on to describe the state and federal approaches to child safety as a "major disconnect" requiring "urgent rectification" (Success Works, 2009b, p. 50). In the federal sphere, victims of domestic and family violence engage with the income support and family payment systems through Centrelink, child support through the Department of Human Services and the family law system through family relationship services and the family law courts.

Mothers leaving violent relationships, and often their main source of income, usually have to secure government income support and comply with work participation requirements to remain eligible for support (McInnes, 2004). Parents are subject to workforce participation requirements once their youngest child turns six (DHS, 2014a). Victims of violence are eligible for Domestic Violence Exemptions from work participation requirements, but in practice, many victims miss out on these provisions because they have not known that they existed, or their assessment has focused on their health status instead of their exposures to domestic and family violence. Instead of a 16 week exemption from workforce participation requirements many are given much shorter exemptions with a requirement to seek medical treatment for conditions such as Post-traumatic Stress Disorder or depression and anxiety. The health consequences of victimization may be medically treated, but the wider context of domestic and family violence in relation to factors such as children's needs, legal proceedings and housing needs are not recognized in illness based exemptions.

Women who have left violent relationships may also be eligible for Crisis Payments (DHS, 2014c), but without prior knowledge of provisions to assist victims of violence, women cannot seek this support. As noted earlier, many victims are reluctant to discuss their experiences of domestic and family violence and do not know that failing to reveal their experiences at each Centrelink and employment agency staff encounter could result in them missing out on supports and assistance for victims of violence. On the other hand, revealing domestic or family violence could also result in them being assessed as 'vulnerable' and placed on Income Management (DHS, 2014b) which controls and restricts their expenditures.

After separation, family payments and child support paid by the non-resident parent are calculated against the amount of time each parent has with a child. Mothers with majority care of the children are required to apply for child support from the father to be eligible for more than the minimum family payment. Claiming child support can trigger violence from the paying parent and a short-term exemption from being required to seek child support is available to victims of domestic and family violence. Once again, mothers who do not disclose their experiences of domestic and family violence to either Centrelink or Child Support staff cannot access such exemptions.

Family payment and child support requirements push parents into making formal post-separation parenting arrangements which are used as the basis for calculation of family payments and child support. The federal family law system requires parents to attempt to reach agreements using family dispute resolution services before applying to the courts for resolution. Although there are exemptions from mediation available for victims of domestic and family violence, these depend on the assessment of the service provider. Victims of violence may still be expected to mediate with their violent ex-partner. Bagshaw et al. (2010) report that only one in ten research respondents who reported violence to a family dispute resolution service were exempted from using the service. They note that women were more likely than men not to disclose violence but were twice as likely to report that mediation proceeded, despite their disclosure. Women reported feeling that family law system professionals did not understand the complexities of domestic and family violence, including perpetrator tactics and the psychological impacts on victims. Women also reported feeling coerced by lawyers into parenting arrangements which they felt were unsafe for their child, whereas men did not report feeling pressured (Bagshaw et al., 2010). Protracted court proceedings have also been identified as a strategy for men who use violence to force their ex-partners to continually attend hearings and to bear the stress and expense of legal assistance (Kaye, Stubbs, & Tolmie, 2003).

Bagshaw et al. (2010) identified that many victims of domestic and family violence felt that they were disbelieved in the family law system. Just over one in four women victims and one in five male victims felt that they were believed and taken seriously when they disclosed violence against them. The research identified a range of consequences for victims arising from not being believed:

> …a consequent lack of assistance that ranged from their problem and themselves being ignored, to their being belittled and labelled as alienating or unfriendly parents, to being offered patently unsuitable proposals (with a sense of coercion about them), to actual further harm. The respondents felt they were fighting the services as well as the violent parent (Bagshaw et al., 2010, p.184).

Since July 2006, the Family Law Act Section [1975] 60 (B) 1 specifies that children's best interests are met by ensuring the child has meaningful involvement with both parents, is protected from abuse, receives proper and adequate parenting and that parents meet their responsibilities to their child's care, welfare and development. These provisions mean that the law presumes children to have a continuing relationship with both parents, including those with an established record of domestic and family violence or abuse. The future focused outlook of the family law system means that past violence or abuse is not recognized as indicative of current or future safety concerns, but a feature of the couple's defunct relationship (Rathus, 2007). An evaluation of the 2006 law reforms identified that domestic and family violence was pervasive in the population of separating parents, with 26% of mothers and 17% of fathers reporting physical injury before separation. Further, 17% of fathers and 21% of mothers reported having safety concerns as a result of ongoing contact with the other parent (Kaspiew et al., 2009).

In June 2012 the Family Law Act was amended to provide, amongst other things, that the right to safety should be privileged ahead of a meaningful involvement of a parent, if these principles were in conflict (Section 60CC 2A). A second wave survey of separated parents sampled before the change took effect identified that 20% of mothers and 14% of fathers were concerned for the safety of their child during contact with the other parent (De Maio, Kaspiew, Smart, Dunstan & Moore, 2012). The study found that 47% of parents with experiences of violence and safety concerns did not disclose these to the family law system.

Around half of those who did report their concerns about violence found that it made "no difference", with shared care arrangements being the most common outcome for this group (De Maio et al., 2012, p. E2-3). The impacts of the June 2012 family law changes on the system's responses to domestic and family violence and child abuse were under evaluation at the time of writing.

Although research identifies that disclosures of domestic and family violence in the family law system do not usually affect contact outcomes, mothers raising safety concerns about the children risked being accused of alienating the child from the other parent. In the study by Bagshaw et al., (2010, p. 81), mothers described judges' responses to them as "abusive" "scathing", "trivialising", "unsympathetic" or "unwilling". Mothers with safety concerns for their children, who consequently sought to limit the father's time with them, faced being variously labelled as "vengeful", "delusional" or "enmeshed" with their child and potentially deemed too dangerous to be the child's primary carer (McInnes, 2013). In 2009 the Family Court of Australia published statistics on decisions in children's matters from 2007 to 2008 which showed that mental illness was the reason for limiting child contact with mothers in 30% of limited contact cases, but in only 2% of cases limiting fathers' contact to less than 30% contact time (Family Court of Australia, 2009). A subsequent comparison of cases in which parental mental illness was the primary presenting issue and cases in which mothers' possible mental illness was used to explain her allegations of child abuse, found that mothers' "possible" mental illness was used to justify changes in residence, awarding primary care to the alleged offender (McInnes, 2013, p 88). Mothers' loss of residence of children to the father, after alleging child sexual abuse by the father, was the most commonly identified pattern of court order in such cases. This pattern has been persistently identified by researchers investigating family law responses to allegations of child sexual abuse (Foote, 2006; Hume, 1996; McInnes, 2013; Shea-Hart, 2006). Confirming such judicial attitudes, a retiring family court judge expressed his belief that mothers were increasingly inventing allegations of child sexual abuse to stop fathers seeing their children (Alexander, 2013). A difficulty with the judge's view is that such allegations normally result in mothers losing custody to the alleged perpetrator (McInnes, 2013) or the allegations make no difference to orders for regular contact or shared care with the alleged perpetrator (De Maio et al., 2012; Foote, 2006; Shea-Hart, 2006).

CONCLUSION

This chapter details some of the systemic problems across state and federal services and agencies responding to domestic and family violence which limit the efficacy of responses to the continuing high incidence of domestic and family violence in Australian homes. Initiatives which were conceived as ways of addressing domestic and family violence reduction and prevention have contributed to perverse effects in some cases which work against the safety and recovery of victims.

The implementation of police training in pro-arrest policies has increased the numbers of victims of family violence being arrested and taken to court for intervention orders. Requirements that police notify child protection services when they attend an incident of family violence where children are present, have resulted in a steady rise in victims being recorded as "emotionally abusing" their children (AIHW, 2013). Child protection interventions in domestic and family violence cases have led to a rise in the numbers of children being placed in the care of the perpetrator and women being blamed for the violence against them (Meyer, 2011). Child protection services threats to remove children unless the mother ends the relationship pressures victims to leave without access to housing, income or safety (Higgins & Kaspiew, 2011; Humphreys, 2011; Meyer, 2011). Provisions for support for victims of domestic and family violence can be seen by services as incentives for victims to falsely claim that they have been victimised (Success Works, 2009a). Mental illness and substance abuse problems arising from experiencing abuse are not commonly recognized by services staff as the results of traumatizing events and can be used to delegitimize mothers' capacity as parents. Such conditions can also result in them being excluded from services such as emergency housing and referred between services without an effective response to the trauma of exposure to domestic and family violence (Bromfield et al., 2010).

The integration of service responses brings together front-line state and territory agencies dealing with domestic and family violence as a way to achieve shared risk assessments and thresholds for action, however the focus is commonly on managing the victim's safety rather than the perpetrator's violence (Marshall et al., 2008). For example victims can be required to undergo therapy to address their 'choice' of violent relationships rather than a focus on the perpetrator's violence.

Once victims leave relationships they need to negotiate the complex income support, family payment and child support systems which require victims to have post-separation parenting arrangements. Access to supports and exemptions on the basis of being a victim of domestic and family violence relies on victims having knowledge of relevant payments and exemptions and disclosing their experiences to agency staff. Victims report being assessed by job search agencies on the basis of health problems arising from the violence rather being exempted from workforce participation requirements on the basis of being a victim of domestic violence. Those without presenting health problems can miss out on any domestic violence exemptions. Conversely, victims could also be classified as 'vulnerable' and subjected to Income Management, under which their access to income and expenditure was controlled.

Making parenting arrangements brings victims into contact with the family law system as they are unable to safely negotiate directly with their abusive ex-partner. The family law presumption of "shared parental responsibility" and "meaningful parental involvement" requires victims of domestic and family violence to make arrangements for the children to spend time with the perpetrator (Bagshaw et al., 2010, p. 73). Although victims can be exempted from compulsory mediation before applying to the court, many victims reported that they were forced to mediate with their abuser (Bagshaw et al., 2010). When victims entered the courts they found that past violence towards them was not deemed relevant in parenting decisions and they would face hostile scrutiny by the court if they raised allegations of child abuse (Rathus, 2007). Victims who persisted in the belief that the children were not safe and resisted court orders faced the prospect of losing care of the children to the perpetrator (McInnes, 2013).

Together these state and federal systemic hurdles reinforce Australian cultural attitudes which disbelieve, discount or blame and stigmatize victims of domestic and family violence. Victims are attributed motives of making false claims to secure support from services or supposed advantages or to take revenge on their ex-partner. They face being categorized as mad or bad with constant demands that they disclose and prove the violence against them in order to get help. Without a feminist orientation, with its commitment to women's empowerment and support and social advocacy for women's gender equity, services responding to domestic and family violence remain vulnerable to subversion into individualized woman-blaming; re-inscribing controlling power dynamics without fundamentally changing a pervasive cultural tolerance of violence against women.

REFERENCES

Afifi, T., MacMillan, H., Cox, B., Asmundson, G., Stein, M. & Sareen, J. (2009). Mental health correlates of intimate partner violence in marital relationships in a nationally representative sample of males and females. *Journal of Interpersonal Violence*, *24*, 1398-1417.

Alexander, H. (2013, July 6). False abuse claims are the new court weapon, retiring judge says. Sydney: *Sydney Morning Herald*.

Australian Bureau of Statistics. (1996). *Women's safety Australia.* Catalogue No. 4128.0. Canberra: AGPS.

Australian Bureau of Statistics. (2003). *Australian social trends.* Catalogue No. 4102.0. Canberra: AGPS.

Australian Bureau of Statistics. (2006). *Personal safety survey.* Catalogue No. 4906.0. Canberra: AGPS.

Australian Bureau of Statistics. (2013). *Personal safety.* Catalogue No. 49060DO006_2012. Canberra: Australian Bureau of Statistics.

Australian Human Rights Commission. (2013). *Investing in care: Recognising and valuing those who care.* Sydney: Australian Human Rights Commission.

Australian Institute of Health and Welfare. (2013). *Child protection Australia: 2011–12.* Child Welfare series No. 55. Catalogue No. Child Welfare Series 43. Canberra: Australian Institute of Health and Welfare.

Bagshaw, D., Brown, T., Wendt, S., Campbell, A., McInnes, E., Tinning, B., Batagol, B., Sifris, A., Tyson, D., Baker, J., & Fernandez Arias, P. (2010). *Family violence and family law in Australia: The experiences and views of children and adults from families who separated post-1995 and post-2006.* Canberra: Attorney-General's Department.

Bancroft, L. & Silverman J. (2002). *The batterer as parent: Addressing the impact of domestic violence on family dynamics.* London: Sage.

Birdsey, E. & Snowball, L. (2013). *Reporting to police: A survey of victims attending domestic violence services.* Issue paper No. 91. Crime and Justice Statistics Bureau Brief. Sydney: NSW Bureau of Crime Statistics and Research.

Braaf, R. & Sneddon, C. (2007). *Arresting practices: Exploring issues of dual arrest for domestic violence.* Stakeholder paper No. 3. Sydney: Australian Domestic & Family Violence Clearinghouse.

Breckenridge, J. (1999). Subjugation and silences: The role of the profession in silencing victims of sexual and domestic violence. In J. Breckenridge & L. Laing (Eds.). *Challenging silence: Innovative responses to sexual and domestic violence.* Sydney: Allen and Unwin.

Bromfield, L., Lamont, A., Parker, R. & Horsfall, B. (2010). *Issues for the safety & wellbeing of children in families with multiple &complex problems: The co-occurrence of domestic violence, parental substance misuse, and mental health problems*, National Child Protection Clearinghouse issue paper No. 33. Melbourne: Australian Institute of Family Studies.

Buchanan, F. (2008). *Mother and Infant Attachment Theory and Domestic Violence: Crossing the Divide*, Stakeholder paper no. 5. Sydney: Australian Domestic Violence Clearinghouse

Butterworth, P. (2004). Lone mothers' experience of physical and sexual violence: Association with psychiatric disorders. *British Journal of Psychiatry*, 184, 21-27.

Chan, A. & Payne, J. (2013). *Homicide in Australia 2008-00 to 2009-10*: National Homicide Monitoring Program Annual Report. Canberra: Australian Institute of Criminology.

De Maio, J., Kaspiew, R., Smart, D., Dunstan, J. & Moore, S., et al. (2013). *Survey of Recently Separated Parents a study of parents who separated prior to the implementation of the Family Law Amendment (Family Violence and Other Matters) Act 2011*. Canberra: Attorney-General's Department.

Department of Human Services. (2014a). *Flexible arrangements for parents and principal carers*. Canberra: Centrelink. Retrieved March 13, 2014 from: http://www.humanservices.gov.au/spw/customer/publications/resources/lw065/lw065-1211en.pdf

Department of Human Services. (2014b). *Income management*. Canberra: Centrelink. Retrieved March 13, 2014 from: http://www.humanservices.gov.au/customer/services/centrelink/income-management

Department of Human Services. (2014c). *Crisis payment*. Canberra: Centrelink. Retrieved March 12, 2014 from: http://www.humanservices.gov.au/customer/services/centrelink/crisis-payment.

Department of Social Services. (2013). *The national plan to reduce violence against women and children*. Retrieved February 19, 2014 from: http://www.dss.gov.au/our-responsibilities/women/programs-services/reducing-violence/the-national-plan-to-reduce-violence-against-women-and-their-children

Douglas, H. & Walsh, T. (2009). Mothers and the Child Protection System. *International Journal of Law, Policy and the Family, 23*,211-229.

Easteal, P. (1993). *Killing the beloved*. Canberra: Australian Institute of Criminology.

Elder, J. (2014, April 27). The brutal price of domestic violence. *The Age*. Melbourne: Fairfax Press.

Family Court of Australia. (2009). *Family court bulletin, Issue 4*. Melbourne: Family Court of Australia.

Foote, W. (2006). *Child sexual abuse allegations in the family court*. Sydney: Thesis Collection. Sydney: University of Sydney Faculty of Education and Social Work.

Golding, J. M. (1999). Intimate partner violence as a risk factor for mental disorders: A meta-analysis. *Journal of Family Violence*, 14, 99–132.

Herman J. (1992). *Trauma and recovery: The aftermath of violence - from domestic abuse to political terror*. New York, N.Y. USA: Basic Books.

Higgins, D. & Kaspiew, R. (2011). *Child protection and family law: Joining the dots*. National Child Protection Clearinghouse Issues Paper No. 34. Melbourne: Australian Institute of Family Studies.

Holder, R. (2007). *Police and domestic violence: An analysis of domestic violence incidents attended by police in the ACT and subsequent actions.* Research Paper No. 4. Sydney: Australian Domestic and Family Violence Clearinghouse.

Holt, S., Buckley, H. & Whelan, S. (2008). The impact of exposure to domestic violence on children and young people: A review of the literature. *Child Abuse and Neglect*, 32, 797–810.

Homelessness Australia. (2013). *Homelessness and women fact sheet.* Australian Capital Territory: Homelessness Australia. Retrieved February 27, 2014 from: http://homelessnessaustralia.org.au/images/publications/Fact_Sheets/Homelessness_and_Women.pdf

Hume, M. (1996). *Child sexual abuse allegations and the family court of South Australia.* Adelaide: Masters Thesis, University of South Australia.

Hume, M., McInnes, E., Rendell, K. & Green, B. (2013). How is a lack of feminist analysis within domestic violence and contemporary services contributing to a reproduction of women's and children's homelessness and continued risk of domestic violence victimisation? *Parity*, *26*, 24-26.

Hume, M., McInnes, E., Rendell, K. & Green, B. (2011). Women's services in the 21st Century: Where are we heading? *Australian Domestic & Family Violence Newsletter*, *46*, 3-4. Retreived February 20, 2014 from http://www.weaveinc.org.au/index.html

Humphreys, C. (2014). Children and family violence: Finding the right response. *Insight*, *9*, 40-42.

Humphreys, C. (2011). Rebuilding together: Strengthening the mother-child bond in the aftermath of violence. *Domestic Violence Resource Centre Victoria Quarterly*, *3*, 6-10.

Itzin C. (2006). *Tackling the health and mental health effects of domestic and sexual violence and abuse.* London: Home Office.

Kaye, M., Stubbs, J. & Tolmie, J. (2003). *Negotiatinc residence and contact arrangements against b of domestic violence.* Queensland: Families, Law and Social Policy Research Unit, Griffith University.

Kaspiew, R., Gray, M., Weston, R., Moloney, L., Hand, K., Qu, L. & the Family Law Evaluation Team. (2009). *Evaluation of the 2006 family law reforms.* Melbourne, Australian Institute of Family Studies.

Katzen, H. (2000). It's a family matter, not a police matter: The enforcement of protection orders. *Australian Journal of Family Law, 14*, 119-141.

Marshall, J., Ziersch, E. & Hudson, N. (2008). *Family safety framework: Final evaluation report.* Adelaide: Office of Crime and Statistics Research SA Department of Justice.

McGregor, H. & Hopkins, A. (1991). *Working for change: The movement against domestic violence.* Sydney: Allen and Unwin.

McInnes, E. (2004). The impact of violence on mothers and children's needs during and after parental separation. *Early Childhood Development and Care*, *174*, 357-368.

McInnes, E. (2013). Madness in family law: Mothers' mental health in the Australian Family Law System. *Psychiatry, Psychology and Law*, March 14 DOI:10.1080/13218719.2013.774688 http://dx.doi.org/10.1080/13218719.2013.774688

Meyer, S. (2011). 'Acting in the children's best interest?' Examining victims' responses to intimate partner violence. *Journal of Child and Family Studies*, *20*, 436-443.

Morris, A. (2003). The mother of the victim as potential supporter and protector: Considerations and challenges. *Child Sexual Abuse: Justice Response or Alternative Resolution Conference*. Adelaide: Australian Institute of Criminology, May 1-2.

Nichols, A. (2013). Meaning-making and domestic violence victim advocacy: An examination of feminist identities, ideologies and practices. *Feminist Criminology*, 8, 177-201.

Office for Women, (2011). *A right to safety: The next phase of the Women's Safety Strategy 2011-2022*. Adelaide: South Australia Office for Women.

Rathus, Z. (2007). Shifting the gaze: Will past violence be silenced by a further shift of the gaze to the future under the new family law system? *Australian Journal of Family Law*, *21*, 87-112.

Salvation Army. (2013). *Salvation Army Homelessness Report*. Sydney: Salvation Army.

Shea-Hart, A. (2006). *Children exposed to domestic violence: Whose 'best interests' in the family court?* Adelaide: Thesis Collection University of South Australia.

Success Works. (2009a). *Review of the integrated response to family violence: Interim report*. Hobart: Department of Justice, Tasmania.

Success Works. (2009b). *Review of the integrated response to family violence: Final report*. Hobart: Department of Justice, Tasmania.

Tomison, A. (2000). Exploring family violence: Links between child maltreatment and domestic violence. *Issues in Child Abuse Prevention,* No. 13. Winter, National Child Protection Clearinghouse, Melbourne: Australian Institute of Family Studies.

VicHealth. (2010). *National survey on community attitudes to violence against women 2009*. Melbourne: VicHealth.

Willis, M. (2011). *Non-disclosure of violence in Australian Indigenous communities*. Trends and Issues Paper No. 405. Canberra: Australian Institute of Criminology.

Women's Legal Services NSW. (2014). *Police should identify primary victim in domestic violence incidents*. Sydney: Women's Legal Services NSW.

Workplace Gender Equality Agency. (2013) *Graduate pay gap blowout: Females earn $5K less*. Retrieved March 15, 2014 from: https://www.wgea.gov.au/content/graduate-pay-gap-blowout-females-earn-5k-less

In: Overcoming Domestic Violence
Editors: Myra F. Taylor, Julie Ann Pooley et al.

ISBN: 978-1-63321-956-4
© 2015 Nova Science Publishers, Inc.

Chapter 11

MISSISSIPPI STILL BURNING: THE LGBT STRUGGLE FOR INTIMATE PARTNER VIOLENCE PROTECTION UNDER THE LAW – A CASE STUDY IN THE DEEP SOUTH

*Julie Schroeder[1], Olga Osby[1] and Diana Bruns[2]**
[1]Jackson State University, Mississippi, US
[2]Southeast Missouri State University, Cape Girardeau, MO, US

ABSTRACT

Experts in the United States estimate the incidence of domestic violence in lesbian, gay, bisexual and transgender (LGBT) relationships occur in parallel frequency and severity as found in heterosexual relationships. However, violence between same-sex couples continues to be underreported as a social problem in societies across the globe. This case study will provide the reader with unique insights into the struggles and stressors of one of the most marginalized members of the LGBT community in the South – that of an African American lesbian couple involved in intimate partner violence. LGBT individuals are faced with the reality of living in society where its institutions and organizations were built on the foundation of heterosexist ideology. Homophobia results in discrimination at all levels of society with many anti-gay legislative, organizational, and religious organizations openly advocate for continued marginalization of LGBT individuals. Institutionalized heterosexism results in devastating physical, psychological, and psychosocial consequences as LGBT victims of IPV navigate through an unfriendly legal and social service systems. Stigmas associated with seeking help and treatment, as well as prevention, intervention strategies and legal perspectives on domestic violence in LGBT populations are examined. Future directions for research, policy, and practice are described in efforts to address biases and discrimination involved in the detection, reporting and intervention of violence in LGBT relationships.

* Corresponding author: Professor Diana Bruns: dbruns@semo.edu.

INTRODUCTION

In 1988, a controversial film entitled "Mississippi Burning" was released that depicted the racist history of the State of Mississippi and the effort throughout the southern part of the United States (US) to deny civil rights and civil liberties to its African American citizens. 2014 marks the 50th Anniversary of Freedom Summer, the pivotal effort to reverse racism and racial discrimination that was based in Mississippi. Freedom Summer brought activists from around the country to stage protests, advocate for and demand equality and justice for African Americans. Ironically, while Mississippi has been celebrating the gains made in this State and throughout the US to combat and overcome racism over the past 50 years, Mississippi has again become ground zero for another civil rights and civil liberties movement for Lesbian, Gay, Bisexual and Transgendered (LGBT) People. The States' Legislature and Governor passed one of the most discriminatory laws in the US. The legislation known as Senate Bill 2681 and titled the "Mississippi Religious Freedom Restoration Act" will allow businesses to openly discriminate against members of the LGBT community, based on their religious beliefs. Mississippi, part of the cluster of southern states also known as the Bible-Belt, is politically conservative and has a history of oppressing individual rights and freedoms of minorities, women and now LGBT.

This chapter provides an overview of the nature of the oppression of the LGBT community in the Deep South. Additionally, a case study is presented that will give the reader unique insights into the struggles and stressors of one of the most marginalized members of the LGBT community in the South – that of African American lesbians involved in intimate partner violence (IPV).

While the LGBT community has been making strides in some states they continue to be denied rights in others. Same sex couples are often denied rights that heterosexual couples have long enjoyed including marriage, hospital visitation, insurance coverage, property inheritance, adoption, housing, and employment. As a result members of the LGBT community face discrimination and have been marginalized to the edges of society. This increases the likelihood of victimization, subjugation, and trauma that often goes undetected, unreported, or ignored to such an extent that concerned allies find it difficult to access information or data to bring these atrocities to the forefront of public discourse. For example, prior to 2010 the Department of Justice and the Centers for Disease Control did not provide data on LGBT IPV (Shwayder, 2013). The Department of Justice Violence Against Women Act did not include explicit protections for LGBT persons until the recent version passed in 2014 (DOJ, 2014). However, the Office on Violence Against Women FY 2015 budget submitted to Congress in March 2014 provides no specified funding to study IPV in the LGBT community (OVW, 2014). The Centers for Disease Control (2013) only recently published results of the 2010 the National Intimate Partner and Sexual Violence Survey (NISVS). Their key findings under the victimization by sexual orientation are the first of its kind, admitting, "Little is known about the national prevalence of intimate partner violence, sexual violence, and stalking among lesbian, gay, and bisexual women and men in the United States".

If you are a LGBT individual in America, where you live matters. While the same- sex marriage landscape continues to shift in rapid fashion, currently 12 states in the Northeastern region of the country have all passed legislation legalizing same sex marriage, opening the door to friendly policies on hospital visitation, adoption, and anti-discrimination employment laws. Four Midwestern, two Northwestern, and three Southwestern states have all recently legalized same sex marriage and the issue is moving swiftly through courts in nine other states (Botelho, 2014; Guardian, 2014). As noted earlier, one part of the U.S. remains untouched; the Deep South denies all rights to same sex couples. Mississippi, Alabama, Louisiana, Georgia, Florida, North Carolina, and South Carolina remain true to their Bible-Belt ideology where discrimination, poverty, and marginalization of LBGT individuals continues to thrive making it difficult to obtain an accurate picture of their lives.

This chapter uses the case study method to explore an African American lesbian's experience in a decade long same- sex relationship marred by IPV in the Deep South. The story of Sophia, and her partner and batterer Deborah sheds light into the complexities of being LGBT and enduring an IPV relationship in a deeply southern state. Sophia's perspective additionally illuminates the impact of homophobia and heterosexist ideology and policies on reporting and confronting IPV. The names of our couple were changed to protect their privacy.

LITERATURE REVIEW

Experts in the United States estimate incidence of domestic violence in LGBT relationships occur in parallel frequency and severity as in heterosexual relationships (Ard & Makadon, 2011; Center for American Progress, 2014; Lilith, 2001; Lundy, 1993; Serra, 2013). Gay and lesbian respondents to victim surveys, consider themselves to be a sexual minority, reporting IPV at rates equal to or higher than their heterosexual counterparts (Shwayder, 2013).

The National Coalition of Anti- Violence Programs (2012) focuses on measuring IPV in LGBT relationships, with data coming from 19 anti-violence programs in 20 states; only seven of which are Southern states. Reports of IPV increased by 29.6% between 2011 and 2012. Bisexual females have been found to be at greatest risk of IPV as 75% of them reported having been in a violent relationship. Nearly half (46%) of lesbian women and 43% of heterosexual women have been in violent relationships at some point. Bisexual men also reported the highest rates of IPV (47%) compared to their gay (40%) and straight (21%) counterparts.

Deaths

Twenty-one people died as a result of IPV in 2012. However, this represent a threefold increase from 2010 when there was only six reported homicides. Gay males were the victims in these homicides in nearly half the cases (47.6%). Over half of the victims were persons of color (52.4%) with African Americans representing 28.6% and 23.8% being Latino. In nearly a quarter (23.8%) of these cases neither race nor ethnicity were reported.

Survivors

While people of color represented 62.1%) of victims in 2012, and this number fell from 65.8% in 2011, NCAVP calls for increased focus on the intersection on age, race, social class, and immigration status.

Power and Control

Treatment professionals define domestic violence (DV) as a multidimensional concept rooted in power and control. Since the mid 1980s the Power and Control Wheel has been used in prevention programs to educate the general public and treatment providers, as well as advocates, victims, and perpetrators in the criminal justice system (DIAP, 2011). Same-sex IVP follows the same relationship dynamics described using the Cycle of Violence model (Peterman & Dixon, 2003) with tension building, and acute violence, followed by a period of calming (Burke & Owen, 2006).

The original Duluth Model identified heterosexual males as perpetrators of DV arguing that battering was a learned behavior reinforced by social and cultural norms institutionalized in patriarchal societies. Over time, the model has expanded to include same-sex couples suggesting that, "same-sex intimate relationships ha[ve] many of the same characteristics of battering in heterosexual relationships, but happens within the context of the larger societal oppression of same-sex couples" (DIAP, 2011).

While relationship dynamics share common features with heterosexual IPV, there are distinct differences faced by LGBT couples as a result of living in a heterosexist society. Additional tactics of abuse have been identified in LGBT relationships and persist due to discrimination and lack of protection under the law.

- Isolation through fear of the abuser 'outing' the victim, possibly resulting in job loss, eviction, and loss of children.
- Using children as pawns in relationships due to the lack of parental rights granted to same-sex partners.
- Using small communities, LGBT networks are often small and cannot offer safe spaces for victims.
- Threatening involvement with institutions historically unfriendly to LGBT individuals including police, medical and mental health facilities.
- Using the threat of transferring power to police and correctional institutions vis a vis alcohol and drug use as a result of LGBT persons being forced to socialize on the margins of society in bars and historically criminalized for alcohol and substance using behaviors. (Tucker, 2009).

CONSEQUENCES OF IPV IN SAME-SEX RELATIONSHIPS

Minority Stress

Minority stress is a result of living in a patriarchal society with its foundation in heterosexist ideology where attitudes, bias, and discrimination of people who identify themselves as being outside of the heterosexual ideal is not condoned. This provides justification for heterosexuals to practice discrimination, harassment, and mistreatment of anyone who lives outside this ideology. This has resulted in anti-gay policies and laws restricting the rights of members of the LGBT community, often criminalizing their lifestyle (Russell, Bohan, McCarrol, & Smith, 2011; Szymanski, & Balsam, 2011). Mississippi's Senate Bill 2681, The Mississippi Religious Freedom Restoration Act (2014) is a clear example of a Southern state's effort to impose their ideology on sexual norms and sexual preferences by instituting a law that aimed at targeted groups, particularly the LGBT community.

Institutionalized Discrimination

LGBT individuals are faced with the reality of living in society where public and private institutions and organizations were built on the foundation of heterosexist ideology. Homophobia results in discrimination in all levels of society with many anti-gay legislative, organizational, and religious organizations advocating for continued marginalization of LGBT individuals (Serra, 2013). While the federal government and many states are revisiting their laws, particularly same-sex marriage, many others continue to bring forth punitive statues. This is particularly acute in the Southern US, as a result, many victims fail to report incidences of IPV due to heterosexist policies that could lead to further victimization (Potocaniak, et al., 2003).

Physical and Psychological Abuse

Physical and psychological abuse creates a toxic mix of negative health outcomes resulting in poor physical health, and chronic mental illness, and increased risk for future injuries. Physical injuries often go untreated for a variety of reasons related to the power and control dynamic of IPV relationships and are exacerbated by additional minority stressors which result in decreased access to care (Ard & Makadon, 2011). As a result, victims are often left suffering permanent chronic pain and disability (Coker, Smith, & Fadden, 2005; Stevens, Korchmaros, & Miller; 2010; Wuest, et al, 2008; Wuest, et.at 2009). Coker, et al., (2005) found that women who reported being a victim of IPV were twice as likely to report a disability. Disabilities were most often associated with heart disease, back injury, chronic pain, arthritis, and respiratory problems.

Current research shows that there is a substantial relationship between minority stress, high rates of suicide, and substance use problems (Mereish, O'Cleirig, & Bradford, 2014). While a causal relationship has not been established, research suggests IPV increases the risk for mental health problems including depression, PTSD, and suicidal ideation (Golding, 1999). Indeed, only recently has LGBT IPV been identified as an important component of a growing effort to understand violent trauma. LGBT victims suffer the additive effects interpersonal trauma and sexual discrimination that result in "increased likelihood of suicidal and non-suicidal self-injury" (Brown, 2011, p. 1). Heterosexual discrimination is identified as a type of oppressive experience that does not fit the standard diagnostic criteria for PTSD. Although, heterosexist discrimination resulting from interactions where institutional bias results in physical and psychological trauma at the hands of law enforcement, or denial of treatment, or shelter has been found to be predictive of PTSD in lesbian victims. This interaction between ongoing IPV and these types of discrimination results in women being twice as likely to develop PTSD in their lifetimes (Szymanski, & Balsam, 2011). In addition, heterosexist discrimination occurring in the lives of lesbians (e.g., being passed over for employment advancement, becoming the victim of a crime based on their sexual orientation, or verbal harassment) has been empirically linked to depression, anxiety, global distress, suicidal ideation, and self- medication resulting in substance abuse. Substance abuse is also a precipitator of violence (Cruz &Peralta, 2001) with lesbian batterers exhibiting higher incidence of substance abuse than their non-battering counterparts, as well as higher levels of aggression and psychopathology including anti social, borderline, and paranoid behaviors. (Fortunata & Kohn, 2003; Friedman & Loue, 2007; Stevens, Korchmaros, & Miller 2010).

BARRIERS TO NEEDED SERVICES

Shelter Care

Safe housing is a vital resource for all victims of IPV. Neither emergency shelter nor transitional housing is funded to the level of need for those protected under the Violence against Women Act, (DOJ, 2014) which did not specifically include protections for LGBT victims until the current reauthorization. Haugen (2012) cites considerable funding cuts to these services in both the 2005 and 2011 reauthorizations of the Act.

The Violence Against Women Act of 2014 (DOJ, 2014) was authorized by the US Congress, but only after several years of political wrangling that resulted in budget cuts to a variety of programs and initiatives to assist victims of crime, survivors of DV and sexual violence. While the funding bill will assist DV programs and shelter services, the funding crises remains as the funding shortage will continue to decrease services including shelter care. Kim Gandy, the President and CEO of the National Network to End Domestic Violence (NNEDV) responded, "The ongoing funding crisis means that victims must be turned away when they are at their most vulnerable. While service providers work with each victim who comes to them to find safety, they cannot create shelter beds out of thin air, hire case managers on a promise, or build affordable housing with a magic wand. They need funding to provide help and refuge for victims" (NNDEV, 2014).

Historically, DV shelters have lacked tangible resources to meet the needs of victims and staff and volunteers have been trained to serve the needs of heterosexual females and, thus, can present a non-welcoming environment (Lundy, 1993; Zaligson, 2007). Consequently, LGBT IPV survivors are reluctant to seek support as a result. A lack of awareness of these barriers to care has resulted in lack of outreach to LGBT communities as well as fostering an impression that shelters are for straight women only.

It is not unusual for heterosexual shelter survivors to hold homophobic biases and racist attitudes, therefore, LGBT shelter victims often feel uncomfortable accessing shelter as they fear for their safety if their shelter mates learn they are gay. Straight shelter mates and shelter staff have expressed their discomfort with superficial issues like haircuts and clothing, and shown blatant disrespect resulting in LGBT victims fearing for their safety. Homophobia does not disappear just because two people share the same IPV experience, and as a result, gay clients often leave shelters and return home to their batterers (Merrill & Wolfe, 2000).

Finally, Zaligson (2007) found that the vast majority of DV shelters are for women only. Gay males are often refused emergency shelter based on heterosexist beliefs that men cannot be victims. Transgendered persons often face shelter refusal due to their gender versus their gender assignment. The lack of emergency shelter services for gay males often results in referrals to homeless shelters where they face myriad dangers from homophobic residents. A general lack of training about the needs of LGBT victims, regardless of their gender, results in shelter workers who lack cultural competence can re-traumatize a victim. It can only be estimated how many lesbians would seek informal shelter care, such as with a friend or family member, rather than be subjected to the added trauma of entering a shelter with heterosexual women, served by heterosexual women who would not understand the plight of a lesbian woman.

Ard and Makadon's (2011) research found very few LGBT- specific shelters. Zaligson, (2007) stresses the lack of institutionalized networks available for LGBT IPV victims despite prevalence of violence in these relationships. Shelter providers lack training, education, and policies about the care of LGBT IPV victims. To date, most shelter providers that participated in Zaligson's research have no policies in place to meet the needs of transgendered victims.

Legal Protection

Seeking protection from a violent partner begins with a call to the police. Historically, LGBT IPV victims have encountered unsympathetic law enforcement personnel. Some police officers still demonstrate heterosexist prejudice, lack understanding of same-sex relationships, and lack understanding of gender roles in same-sex relationships (Letellier, 1994; Talicska, 2012). If a case is carried forward following an arrest, victims can similarly face attorneys, judges, and juries who demonstrate negative biases in their behavior and decision-making.

Heterosexist attitudes are found at the highest levels of the legal system resulting in state-sanctioned discrimination upheld by state legislatures. LGBT individuals face discrimination and the right to legal protection making victims of IVP reluctant to seek legal remedies. Many states still maintain anti-sodomy laws resulting in victims of IPV admitting to breaking the law before being able to seek protection from a violent partner (Harvard Law Review, 2005; Talicska, 2012) or restraining orders (Serra, 2013).

Medical and Mental Health Treatment

LGBT victims of IVP are often met with minimal awareness or sensitivity of service providers responsible for screening, assessment, treatment, and referral. Research suggests untrained and unsympathetic counselors fail to understand the power and control dynamics in LGBT clients, minimize the abuse often resulting in blaming the victim. Often confusion around the roles in LGBT relationships, correctly identifying the aggressor, and focusing on the individual or couple as the source of the problem results in ignoring the larger context of discrimination and minority stress (Borstein, Fawcett, Sullivan, Senturia, and Shiu-Thornton, 2006; Murray, 2006; Ristock, 2003; Turell, 1999).

The DV community has historically referred to advocacy and awareness of battered women and is based in feminist theory and ideology. These theories do not adequately address IPV in same-sex relationships. As a result, most victim services are dedicated to women and batterer programs for men. This paradigm ignores gender-related power dynamics in same- sex relationships (Burke & Owen; 2006; Younglove et al., 2003). Turell, Herrmann, Hollander, & Galletly, (2014) sought to investigate the readiness of gay communities for organized prevention activities. They found that while members of these communities indicated that there is local concern about IPV they lack the motivation to do anything about it. This lack of motivation came from a variety of sources including community fatigue resulting from fighting for same-sex marriage legislation, living in gay-friendly urban areas where there is a feeling of being in the mainstream resulting in increased privilege, and IVP not being an issue for people they know (Turrell, Herman, Hollander, Galletly 2014). Clearly, there is still much to be done as illustrated in Sophia's story below.

SOPHIA'S STORY

Sophia is a 33 year old African American female survivor of an abusive same sex relationship her partner Deborah that lasted for 10 years. Despite the end of the relationship, Sophia continues to deal with debilitating emotional and physical wounds. Sophia has lived much of her life on the margins of society in the US. She is black, female, poor, physically disabled, and a lesbian. When Sophia was able to work, her employment history consisted of low-wage jobs in the fast food industry. She discussed the early stages of her difficult life, "I didn't have much of childhood. My Mom was a drug addict. I tried to take care of my sisters and brother."

Her relationship with Deborah was abusive from the beginning. Sophia stated that, "I worked 2-3 jobs and after I paid the bills, the left over went to her. It was not good because I was given an allowance. If I went over I was just out of luck." Deborah never maintained a job for very long, so it was Sophia who once again found herself responsible for taking care a household and having herself and her needs abused and neglected. "I made sure she had everything she wanted. I made sure that there was dinner on the table every night as soon as I got home. I did all her laundry, everything." Sophia stated that the abuse was both mental and physical. Deborah complained that she was too soft and that she needed to be "toughened up". About nine months into the relationship, the abuse turned physical. "The first time it got really bad, she was going to see another girl. I told her she might as well stay with that girl. She punched me in the face. Gave me a black eye. But she didn't leave and hook up with that other girl. She stayed at home. I didn't see my family for 3 weeks until my face healed."

Sophia recognized that "she would go through bad moods and she would want to go mess with another girl. She would want me to fight with her and the more I didn't the angrier she got. She would lock me in the bathroom or closet and hold the doorknob for hours." Deborah "cheated on me many times, we would argue and she would cuss at me. She used to lock me in the bathroom just to keep me from leaving. She pushed me out of a second story window onto a balcony one time. While expanding on this incident, Sophia recounted that, "the day she pushed me out the window she had cheated on me with another girl. I was upset and wanted to leave. She blocked the door. I asked her to let me go. She locked me in the bathroom for half a day. I got out of the bathroom and she got on top of me to keep me from leaving. I got away from her, but then she pushed me out the window onto the balcony.

Violence in their relationship continually escalated. "One day she got mad at me so she picked me up and slammed me down on the concrete. I couldn't feel my legs, feet, hands - they were numb. I went to the ER. They wanted to admit me after the x-rays. The doctor said, 'I can't believe you are sitting up. We can't believe it, your back is broken and you are sitting here talking to us.' They wanted to keep me in the hospital, but she made me go home."

Sophia was able to keep the abuse hidden from her family and friends for years. "We were together 4 years before anybody found out. She moved me almost two hours away from my family and my friends, that way they didn't see. She isolated me from every one." Because Sophia hid violence and/or evidence of the violence, she stated "my family loved her. She had them wrapped around her finger. She even told my grandma that I was the aggressor. She told my family that I was mean to her." It was Sophia's mother who first witnessed the violence in the relationship. "We were at my mom's house and she got mad. I was trying to get away from her. She was chasing me. My mom got between us as I was trying to leave but she reached over my mama's head and she hit me and fractured my jaw.

Despite witnessing this act of violence, Deborah had manipulated her way into Sophia's circle of family and friends. After the incident that resulted in Sophia's jaw being broken, she managed to leave Deborah. "We separated for 3 months. I moved to my own apartment. Mom had surgery and wanted to stay with me while she recovered. I said yes. When it was time for her to get out of the hospital my ex (Deborah) was the one who brought my mom to my place from the hospital. I couldn't believe it. She had been working on my family the whole time. She would call my sisters and brother and grandma and tell them that I was mean to her but she wanted me back. She had my family calling me begging me to take her back. Had all relatives on both sides telling me I needed to get back with her and forgive her. We had been together too long to throw it away. I let her stay. I felt hopeless."

Sophia's hopelessness turned to despair at least once. After Deborah reappear in her life, and with family seemingly siding with her about the nature of their relationship, Sophia attempts suicide. "I tried to kill myself. It happened when my mom was staying with us. I was working two jobs. I got home one day, and she jumped me because there was no food on the table. I ran into the bathroom to get away from her. My mom's pain pills were on the sink. I took all of the pills. I came out of the bathroom with the bottle in my hand. That's all I remember. When I woke up I had an IV in my foot. They had pumped my stomach. I was in the hospital for 4 days."

This particular incident of violence finally made family, friends and co-workers aware of the nature of the violence that Deborah was capable of and the seriousness of the domestic violence. "We (Deborah and Sophia) worked together at Sonic (fast food restaurant), I cooked, she delivered (food to the cars). She got mad at me one day at work and hit me in the face. Others tried to get her off of me. Cops were called but she left before they got there. The head manager was supportive and offered to help me. She told me she would find me a place to stay. My friend came and got me but my ex (Deborah) told me if I didn't come home she would kill me. That scared my friend so bad that she told me to go back home with her.

My friend came the next day to check on me. It was tax time and I went with her to work on her taxes. It took awhile to get it done. When my friend dropped me off back at home she (Deborah) told me I was gone too long. She hit me and tore my shirt right off of me. I was on the phone with my friend when I came in the door. She heard what was going on. I ran out the house. She was still there and I got in her car. She (Deborah) got in her car and she rammed my friend's car three times in her door. She got out of her car and snatched me by my hair and pulled out a hand full of hair then she started choking me. I was half in and half out of the car. My friend pulled me in the car and drove to the police station. They took pictures of me, and my friend pressed charges against her. After that she moved out and stayed gone for a while, for about 2 months. Her family got her and she hid out to avoid the cops. She tried to commit suicide. After that, our Moms got together and got us together to talk. She promised to stop and she did for a year. When she saw she was going too far she would leave.

Sophia tried to leave the relationship on at least 3 to 4 times before the final fight between them. "The last bout that ended the thing was when I came to pick her up from work. When I got there I saw her kissing her manager. I told her to just go with her manager. But she got in my car and drove away. She snatched the steering wheel saying she was gonna kill us both. She was swerving across all three lanes of traffic. I was fighting to keep the car on the road. I was able to stop the car. I had been on the phone with my mom. She heard all of it and met me at the exit. I ran to my mom who was dialing 911. She took off in the car. My arm hurt so bad the next day. I couldn't lift it. This last time, I was so scared and my mom finally realized how dangerous she was. She believed me then.

During her relationship with Deborah, Sophia had little informal support from family and even less formal support for counseling or police. According to Sophia, "the police were the worst. They never believed me. She manipulated them just like she did our families." One incident illustrates the lack of support from law enforcement. "One time we were fighting and I didn't know it then, but a neighbor called the police. I was able to escape from her. I ran outside and saw the cops driving toward me. They stopped and said, "You need to come here right now." They took me back to the apartment. They tried to arrest me! They told her to tell them what happened so they could arrest me. She began crying and sobbing at this point.

That happened 3 times. They didn't help me, eventually I didn't even want to bother to call them. (Deborah) acted like the victim and that she didn't want to press charges. She'd say, "We were just arguing. She didn't mean to hurt me." After the cops would leave she would say, "You'll never win." She also said that when my family took her side. It got so that my friend would say, "why do we bother taking you to the police? I do a better job protecting you than them!"

For women like Sophia, it was a slow process of seeking help and understanding from family about the nature of the violence in her same sex relations. "My family would say "it can't be that bad, she's a women like you are." And, it is an on-going process of getting law enforcement to take these cases seriously. "The police saw the extreme nature of the abuse toward the end and were looking for her after she rammed my friend's car and pulled my hair out, but they looked for her for the first week but never kept up with it. "

Sophia is still in the process of overcoming the scares of her physical and emotional abuse. The relationship ended in October, 2013. She is in the process of reflecting on her past and trying to move forward. "This is first time in my life that I am alone. I'm not used to being by myself - just me. I get lonely, and I miss her. I have to fight those moments. I call a friend, exercise. One thing I don't want to do is call her. After that last time I got so depressed I stopped eating. I lost 50 pounds. I'm just getting used to looking at myself. I used to be a size 22 and now I'm a 14. I do feel stronger though. My neighbors are very nice to me. I talk to them when I'm out walking. If I don't walk for a couple days they come and check on me. That feels really good.

However, the results of the physical and mental abuse suffered by Sophia at the hands of someone she loved will linger for some time. "I still have to deal with my legs, feet, hands, going numb. When the weather changes my jaw locks up. I'm getting used to not being fearful, getting used to being 'just me'. I'm also getting used to being alone and silence. No drama. I got a dog for protection and love. I'm starting to stop being scared to be in a closed room with someone. I still get panicky when someone is between me and the door. I have a lot of anxiety. I'll always love her, I was with her for 10 years, but I have to love myself."

DISCUSSION

Hill, Woodson, Ferguson & Parks (2012) identified the risk factors that previous research has found that speaks to the high risk of IPV among the LGBT community that includes: 1) poverty or low economic stratus, 2) insufficient access to educational and employment opportunities, 3) childhood victimization, 4) witnessing violence at home or in the community, 5) mental illness, 6) psychological disorders such as PTSD, anxiety and depression, and 7) substance abuse (Anderson, 2002; Carvalho, Lewis, Derlega, Winstead, & Viggiano, 2011; McKenry, Serovich, Mason & Mosack, 2006; Ploderl & Fartacek, 2007; Powell, 2008). The abuse and neglect of Sophia's basic needs in childhood, normalized in her life, became the norm in her relationship with her partner Deborah. Her mother's substance abuse forced Sophia into becoming aware of her surrounding at a very early stage of her development, and with this awareness, she became the caretaker of herself and her younger siblings. Her lack of educational attainment, and later locked into low-wage and low-skilled employment, secured her continued exposure to poverty and living in low-wealth minority communities overpopulated with drugs and crime (McDonald, 2012).

This dynamic may also explain Deborah's behavior and Sophia's acceptance of the high level of violent abuse. Research has recently began to assess the phenomena of female batterers and whether the level of violence toward their partners is as sever as their male counterparts. McDonald (2012) found that this level of psychological and physical abuse that exist in some lesbian relationships can be just as sever, and the most sever cases often stems from childhoods littered with years of abuse, neglect and violent episodes from which the abuse seems the normal way that love and caring for another is displayed.

Deborah's violent behavior is in keeping with research into lesbian batterers (Rohrbaugh, 2006). The idea of woman-on-woman violence is often overlooked, or ignored among African American women, even by close family members. Sophia's family, when they began to recognize the violence in their relationship, also dismissed the severity of the danger and degree of violence that one woman could do to another by asking how bad could it be since it was just two women fighting. But the degree of violence perpetuated by women like Deborah often stems from their improvised and harsh childhoods much like that of the partner they abuse. Colemen's (2003) study of the literature found that female batterers, like their male counterparts who batter their heterosexual and homosexual partners, "frequently feel powerless, have low-self esteem, tend to abuse alcohol and drugs, and are generally over dependent and jealous"(2003, p. 163). Violent lesbians like Deborah, coming from economically and socially oppressive backgrounds, mirror their male counterparts in feelings of powerless (Fortunata & Kohn, 2003). It has also been found that lesbian batterers have a fear of abandonment, have poor communications skills, tend to be self-absorbed, and tend to lack the ability to empathically relate to their partner's feelings and pain (Coleman, 2003)

DIRECTIONS FOR FUTURE RESEARCH, ADVOCACY AND TRAINING

The Deep South was once the battleground for the civil rights movement that advanced social justice for African Americans and is now the territory where the struggle for equality for the LGBT community is taking shape. The irony is that with all the civil rights gains for African Americans over the past fifty years, and the recent leaps in advances across the country of the rights of same-sex couples to marry and gain benefits for their partners, there are still major barriers for LGBT members in southern states. Mississippi is the most southern of the Southern states and is still passing legislation that will guarantee open discrimination, and deny redress of basic civil and human rights to citizens that fall outside of the mainstream.

CONCLUSION

This chapter exposes the continuing need for research within the LGBT community as too little is known about the stressors and challenges within the community. As such, outing discrimination, access to emergency shelter, the availability of culturally competent doctors, nurses, social workers, police offices and other social service front line workers, and equal protection under the law are all areas in need of exploration in urban and rural communities across the South. It cannot be assumed that LGBT individuals are knowledgeable about and able to access needed social services. Research on how to improve communication within their community and provide the needed outreach for LGBT youth and vulnerable adults will be critical over the coming years. The false notion that protecting and accepting members of the LGBT community into the fabric of American Southern society would be an assault on the religious freedoms of the mainstream population is an argument that could be used to discriminate against any group deemed an outcast. This is why there is a critical need for more research to inform the advocacy efforts that are developing in Mississippi and other Southern states. The need for this research can also be used to inform best practices with LGBT youth, adults and racial and ethnic group members. Continuing research would help the evolution of LGBTQ affirmative practice and competency-based training for social service providers working with members of the LGBT community.

Finally, as compelling as Sophia's story is to our understanding of the violence associated with IPV in LGBT relationships, in order to gain a broader understanding of IPV and the abuse one woman can subject onto another, case studies and research is also needed with women like Deborah. For studies on her need to subdue and dominate, not just in her relationship with Sophia, but in other same sex relationships, would provide invaluable insight into her need to express herself through violence and terrorism in her relationships with others.

REFERENCES

Alexander, C. J. (2002). Violence in gay and lesbian relationships. *Journal of Gay and Lesbian Social Services*, *14*, 95-98.

Anderson, K. L. (2002). Perpetrator or victim? Relationship between intimate partner violence and well-being. *Journal of Marriage & Family*, *64*, 851-863.

Ard, K. L. & Makadon, H. J. (2011). Addressing intimate partner violence in lesbian, gay, bisexual, and transgender patients. *Journal of General Internal Medicine*, *26*(8), 930–933.

Bornstein, D. R., Fawcett, J., Sullivan, M., Senturia, K. D. & Shiu-Thornton, S. (2006). Understanding the experiences of lesbian, bisexual and trans survivors of domestic violence. *Journal of Homosexuality*, *51*(1), 159-81.

Botelho, G. (2014, May, 21). State-by-state: A frenzied few months on the same-sex marriage front. CNN Justice. http://www.cnn.com/2014/05/21/justice/same-sex-marriage-state-breakdown/

Brown, L. S. & Pantalone, D. (2011). Lesbian, gay, bisexual, and transgender issues in trauma psychology. *Traumatology*, *17*(2), 1-3.

Burke, T. W. & Owen, S. S. (2006). Same-sex domestic violence: Is anyone listening? *The Gay & Lesbian Review*, *8*(1), 6-7.

Center for American Progress: Domestic Violence in the LGBT Community (2014, June 14). Retrieved from http://www. americanprogress. org/issues/lgbt/news/2011/06/14/9850/domestic-violence-in-the-lgbt-community/

Centers for Disease Control (2013). NISVS: An Overview of 2010 Findings on Victimization by Sexual Orientation. Cdc:Gov.

Coker, A. L., Smith, P. H. & and Fadden, M. K. (2005). Intimate Partner Violence and Disabilities among Women Attending Family Practice Clinics. *Journal of Women's Health*, *14*(9), 829-838.

Coker, A. L., Davis, K. E., Arias, I., Desai, S., Sanderson, M., Brandt, H. M. & Smith, P. H. (2002). Physical and mental health effects of intimate partner violence for men and women. *American Journal of Preventive Medicine*, *23* (4). 260 – 268. Available: http://www. ajpmonline. org/article/S0749-3797(02)00514-7/fulltext

Coleman, V. E. (2003). Treating the lesbian batterer: Theoretical and clinical considerations *Journal of Aggression, Maltreatment & Trauma. 7*, 159-205.

Craft, S. M. & Serovich, J. M. (2005). Family-of-origin factors and partner violence in the intimate relationships of gay men who are HIV positive. *Journal of Interpersonal Violence, 20*, 771-791.

Cruz, J. M. & Peralta, R. L. (2001). Family violence and substance use: The perceived effects of substance use within gay male relationships. *Violence and Victims, 16*, 161-172.

Department of Justice (2014). Violence against Women Act.

Domestic Abuse Intervention Programs (DIAM). (2011). The Duluth Model. Available: http://www.theduluthmodel. org/training/wheels. html

Fortunata, B. & Kohn, C. S. (2003). Demographic, psychosocial, and personality characteristics of lesbian batters. *Violence and Victims, 18*, 557-568.

Friedman, S. H. & Loue, S. (2007). Incidence and prevalence of intimate partner violence by and against women with severe mental illness. *Journal of Women's Health, 16*(4), 471-480.

Gay Rights in the U. S. State by State (2012). The Guardian. Available: http://www. theguardian.com/world/interactive/2012/may/08/gay-rights-united-states

Golding, J. M. (1999). Intimate partner violence as a risk factor for mental disorders: A meta-analysis. *Journal of Family Violence, 14* (2), 99-132.

Harvard Law Review (2005). Constitutional-standing-Tenth Circuit denies standing to man seeking invalidation of Utah's consensual Sodom law-D. L. S. v. Utah, 374 F. 3d 971 (10th Cir. 2004). *Harvard Law Review, 118, 11070-1077*. Lexis Nexis.

Haugen, A. F. (2012). When it rains, it pours: The Violence against Women Act's failure to provide shelter for the storm of domestic violence. *The Scholar: St. Mary's Law Review on Minority Issues, 14*, 1035 Lexis Nexis.

Hill, N., Woodson, K., Ferguson, A. & Parks, C. (2012). Intimate partner abuse among African American lesbians: Prevalence, risk Factors, theory and resilience. *Journal of Family Violence 27*, 401-413.

Letellier, P. (1994). Gay and bisexul male domestic violence victimization: Challenges to feminist theory and responses to violence. *Violence and Victims, 9*, 95-105.

Lilith, R. (2001). Reconsidering the abuse that dare not speak its name: A Criticism of recent legal scholarship regarding same-gender domestic violence, *Michigan Journal of Gender & Law, 7*, 181, 190-191.

Lundy, S. E. (1993). Abuse that dare not speak its name: Assisting victims of lesbian and gay domestic violence in Massachusetts. New England Law Review, 28, 273. Retrieved from Lexis Nexis.

McDonald, C. (2012). The social context of woman-to-woman intimate partner abuse (WWIPV). *Journal of Family Violence. 27*, 635-646.

Mereish, E. H., O'Cleirigh, C. & Bradford, J. B. (2014). Interrelationships between LGBT-based victimization, suicide, and substance use problems in a diverse sample of sexual and gender minorities. *Psychology, Health & Medicine, 19*(1), pp. 1-13.

Merrill, G. S. & Wolfe, V. A. (2000). Battered gay men: An exploration of abuse, help seeking, and why they stay. *Journal of Homosexuality, 39*(2), 1-30.

Mississippi Religious Freedom Restoration Act (2014). SB 2681.

Murray, C. E., Mobley, K. A., Buford, A. P. & Seaman-DeJohn, M. M. (2006/2007). Same-sex intimate partner violence: Dynamics, social context, and counseling implications. *The Journal of LGBT Issues in Counseling*, *1*(4), 7-30.

National Coalition of Anti-Violence Programs. (2013). Media Release: 2012 Report on Intimate Partner Violence in Lesbian, Gay, Bi-sexual, Transgendered, Queer and HIV – Affected Communities in the U. S. National Coalition of Anti-Violence Programs (AVP). Available: http://www.avp.org/storage/documents/ncavp_2012_ipvreportmediarelease.pdf

National Network to End Domestic Violence (2014). 2014 Budget restores & increases resources for victims. Retrieved from NNEDV website http://nnedv. org/news/4183-2014-budget-restores-increases-resources-for-victims. html

Murray, C. E., Mobley, K. A., Buford, A. P. & Seaman-DeJohn, M. M. (2006/2007). Same-sex intimate partner violence: Dynamics, social context, and counseling implications. *The Journal of LGBT Issues in Counseling*, *1*(4), 7-30.

Office of Violence against Women (2014). FY 2014 Performance Budget. Available: www.justice.gov/jmd/2015justification/pdf/ovw-justification.pdf

Peterman, L. M. & Dixon, C. G. (2003). Domestic violence between same-sex partners: Implications for counseling. *Journal of Counseling and Development*, *81*, 40-47.

Potoczniak, M. J. & Mourot, J. E., Crosbie-Burnette, M. & Potoczniak, D. J. (2003). Legal and psychological perspectives on same-sex domestic violence. *Journal of Family Psychology*, *17*, 252-59.

Ristock, J. L. (2003). Exploring dynamics of abusive lesbian relationships: Preliminary analysis of a multisite, qualitative study. *American Journal of Community Psychology*, *31*, 329-41.

Rohrbaugh, J. B. (2006). Domestic violence in same-gender relationships. *Family Court Review*, *44*, 287-299.

Russell, G. M., Bohan, J. S., McCarroll, M. C. & Smith, N. G. (2011). Trauma, recovery, and community: Perspectives on the long-term impact of anti-LGBT politics. *Traumatology*, *17*(2), 14-23.

Serra, N. E. (2013) Queering International Human Rights: LGBT Access to Domestic Violence Remedies. *American University Journal of Gender, Social Policy & the Law*, *21*, 583. Lexus-Nexus.

Shwayder, M. (2013). A Same-Sex Domestic Violence Epidemic Is Silent: *The Atlantic*. Available: http://www.theatlantic.com/health/archive/2013/11/a-same-sex-domestic-violence-epidemic-is-silent/281131/

Stevens, S., Korchmaros, J. D. & Miller, D. (2010). A Comparison of victimization and perpetration of intimate partner violence among drug abusing heterosexual and lesbian women. *Journal of Family Violence*, *25*(7), 639-649.

Szymanski, D. M. & Balsam, K. F. (2011). Insidious trauma: Examining the relationship between heterosexism and lesbians' PTSD symptoms. *Traumatology*, *17*(2), 4-13.

Talicska, J. D. (2012). Out of one closet and into another: Why abused homosexual males refrain from reporting their abuse and what to do about it. *American University Modern American*, *8*, 21. Lexus Nexus.

Tucker, K. (2009). Beyond the wheel: Bullet points. Available: http://www.nwnetwork.org

Turell, S., Herrmann, M., Hollander, G. & Galletly, C. (2012). Lesbian, gay, bisexual, and transgender communities' readiness for intimate partner violence prevention. *Journal of Gay & Lesbian Social Services*, *24*, 289-310.

Turell, S. C. (2000). A descriptive analysis of same-sex relationship violence for a diverse sample. *Journal of Family Violence*, *15*(3), 281-293.

Wuest, J., Ford-Gilboe, M., Merritt-Gray, M., Varcoe, C., Lent, B., Wilk, P. & Campbell, J. (2009). Abuse-related injury and symptoms of posttraumatic stress disorder as mechanisms of chronic pain in survivors of intimate partner violence. *Pain Medicine*, *10(*4), 739-747.

Wuest, J., Merritt-Gray, M., Ford-Gilboe, M., Lent, B., Varcoe, C. & Campbell, J. C. (2008). Chronic pain in women survivors of intimate partner violence. *The Journal of Pain*, *9*(11), 1049-1057.

Younglove, J. A., Kerr, M. G. & Vitello, C. J. (2002). Law enforcement officers' perceptions of same-sex domestic violence: *Journal of Interpersonal Violence*, *17*, 760-72.

Zaligson, J. (2007). LGBTQ Survivors in domestic violence shelters: Discussions with providers about clients, homophobia, and outreach. *Conference Papers -- American Sociological Association*, 1. Retrieved from EBSCO: http://citation.allacademic.com/ meta/p_mla_apa_research_citation/1/8/4/6/3/pages184637/p184637-9.php

In: Overcoming Domestic Violence
Editors: Myra F. Taylor, Julie Ann Pooley et al.

ISBN: 978-1-63321-956-4
© 2015 Nova Science Publishers, Inc.

Chapter 12

THE PUBLIC HEALTH APPROACH TO DOMESTIC VIOLENCE PREVENTION

Damien J. Williams[1]*, Anna J. Gavine[1] and John Carnochan[1,2]
[1]University of St Andrews, Scotland, UK
[2]Scottish Violence Reduction Unit, Scotland, UK

ABSTRACT

Domestic violence (DV) including intimate partner violence (IPV) and child maltreatment (CM) poses a considerable public health problem. It is evident that DV is associated with a host of health and behavioural consequences, and maltreated children face a significant lifelong burden. Furthermore, the cycle of violence hypothesis, while dismissed by some, suggests that young children exposed to DV are at an increased risk of being victims or perpetrators of such violence in the future. The public health approach to DV focuses on preventing violence from occurring in the first place. Evidence from primary and secondary research suggests that family-based interventions particularly during the child's early years have the greatest potential in addressing IPV and CM, and subsequently breaking the cycle of DV. However, adopting a life-course perspective identifies additional stages of vulnerability, during which appropriate intervention should occur in order to address DV. While it has been difficult to place DV on the policy agenda, and more needs to be done in this regard, this should not impede, immediate action in terms of implementing evidence-based interventions to support families with young children (e.g., through home visitation programmes) and offering support at each transition in the life-stage (e.g., school enrichment and dating violence intervention programmes) in order to tackle this important public health issue. Ensuring safe and nurturing families offers an important means by which to break the cycle of DV and ensure the health and well-being of future generations.

Keywords: Public Health, Prevention, Intimate Partner Violence, Child Maltreatment, Cycle of Violence

---

* Corresponding author: Dr. Damien J. Williams, Lecturer in Public Health Sciences, School of Medicine, University of St Andrews, North Haugh, St Andrews, Scotland, KY16 9TF, Tel: +44 (0)1334 463481, Email: djw11@st-andrews.ac.uk.

INTRODUCTION

Domestic violence (DV) has an adverse effect on recipients, and places a significant social and financial burden on society (McFeely et al., 2013). The term "domestic violence" is often used interchangeably with "intimate partner violence", "spousal abuse", "domestic abuse", and "family violence", and mainly focuses on the perpetration of DV by males on their female partners. For the purposes of the current chapter, we adopt the definition of DV as "A general term for violence directed against children in a family, i.e., child abuse; against a spouse or partner; against a dependent older person, i.e., elder abuse; or against some other household member" (Last, 2007, p. 97). While elder abuse and violence against other household members are important emerging public health problems (see Krug, Dahlberg, Mercy, Zwi, & Lozano, 2002) the current chapter will focus on violence against a spouse/partner (hereafter referred to as intimate partner violence or IPV) or a child/offspring (hereafter referred to as child maltreatment or CM) as two intricately connected forms of DV (Alhusen, Ho, Smith, & Campbell, 2014).

The chapter will consecutively explore the issues of IPV and CM, highlighting the prevalence and impact of these acts, and then identifying their interconnection through a consideration of the "cycle of violence" as a causal mechanism that leads from CM to IPV. This is followed by a description of the public health approach to violence prevention, with a discussion of how to break the cycle of violence, as a means to address the intergenerational transmission of DV.

INTIMATE PARTNER VIOLENCE

While IPV can occur against males by their female partners (e.g. Drijber, Reijnders, & Ceelen, 2013) and in same sex relationships (e.g. Finneran & Stephenson, 2013) the "overwhelming burden of partner violence is borne by women at the hands of men" (Heise & Garcia-Moreno, 2002, p. 89). The United Nations (1993) Declaration on the Elimination of Violence Against Women, Article 1, states that gender-based violence (e.g., IPV) includes "any acts that results in, or is likely to result in, physical, sexual or psychological harm or suffering to women, including threats of such acts, coercion or arbitrary deprivation of liberty, whether occurring in public or in private life" (p. 3). Whilst IPV is a widespread problem the prevalence of physical and/or sexual partner violence varies between countries, with a multi-country study reporting lifetime prevalence rates of between 15% and 71% across ten countries (Garcia-Moreno, Jansen, Ellsberg, Heise, & Watts, 2006). Moreover, a considerable number of the study's respondents (21%-90%) experienced one or more acts of controlling behaviour, which was associated with physical and sexual violence. Garcia-Moreno et al. (2006) also reported that physical IPV was associated with self-reported poor health. Indeed, the severity of IPV in 15-49 year old females has been equated to cancer (World Bank, 1993) and acknowledged as "one of the most pervasive human rights violations across the globe" (Finley, 2010, p. 7).

From his work as a forensic social worker Stark (2007) notes that IPV is an ongoing problem and "the physical abuse is often interweaved with tactics of intimidation, isolation, and control". Stark argues that *coercive control* is the defining characteristic of IPV and concludes that "[w]hat is done to them is less important than what their partners have prevented them from doing for themselves by appropriating resources; undermining their social support; subverting their rights to privacy, self-respect, and autonomy; and depriving them of substantive equality" (p. 13).

IPV imposes a considerable cost on the health and well-being of individuals and incurs a significant social and economic cost to society (Heise & Garcia-Moreno, 2002). However, it has been argued that the most noteworthy "cost" of IPV is that "paid" by the children who witness (and often experience) such treatment (Kelly, 2003). Groves, Zuckerman, Marans, and Cohen (1993) refers to those children who witness the abusive behaviour between adults on whom they depend as the "silent victims" of IPV as it can potentially result in severe emotional and developmental problems. In recognition of this impact, IPV has itself been identified as a type of CM (Gilbert et al., 2009). What is more, through such exposure a child *may* learn to view DV as normative (Kelly, 2003) and increase the risk of future perpetration and victimisation (World Health Organization [WHO], 2007).

CHILD MALTREATMENT

CM often occurs in settings that conventional wisdom would suggest are places of safety (i.e. the home; Korbin, 2003) as the abuser tends to be a relative or someone known to the child (Lutenbacher, Cohen, & Conner, 2004). Young children are particularly vulnerable to maltreatment as they are reliant on others for their basic needs and do not have the capabilities to flee, report, or protect themselves (Smyke, Wajda-Johnston, & Zeanah, 2004). The WHO states that:

> "Child abuse or maltreatment refers to all forms of physical and/or emotional ill-treatment, sexual abuse, neglect or negligent treatment of commercial or other exploitation, resulting in actual or potential harm to the child's health, survival, development or dignity in the context of a relationship of responsibility, trust or power." (WHO, 1999)

The longer a child is exposed to maltreatment, the more likely they will be affected by it; however, it is possible for even a single incident to have a detrimental effect (Felitti et al., 1998). Moreover, exposure to one type of maltreatment increases a child's risk of experiencing another form (May-Chahal & Cawson, 2005).

ADVERSE CHILDHOOD EXPERIENCES

The impact of a range of childhood trauma (e.g., exposure to IPV, parental separation, mental illness in household, criminal household member) on health and behavioural outcomes, has been investigated by the Adverse Childhood Experiences (ACE) study, which is a retrospective cohort study of 17,337 United States (U.S.) adults (54% female) across two waves (see Anda et al., 2009 for details of specific questions and response categories):

Wave 1 (Felitti et al., 1998) and Wave 2 (Dong et al., 2004) data demonstrated the pervasiveness of ACEs and the interconnectedness of the different categories of ACE. For instance, Felitti et al. found that for respondents who reported at least one ACE, the probability of exposure to any additional category ranged from 65%–93% and the probability of at least two additional exposures ranged from 40%–74%. Likewise, Dong et al. found that of the two-thirds of respondents reporting at least one ACE, 81%–98% of respondents experienced at least one additional ACE with 11%-25% reporting having experienced all seven categories of ACE.

A wealth of publications over the years has linked ACE's to a range of health and behavioural outcomes (Felitti & Anda, 2010) including: chronic conditions, such as liver disease, ischemic heart disease, chronic obstructive pulmonary disease; health risk behaviours such as alcohol abuse, illicit drug abuse, obesity, sexual risk behaviour, smoking; mental health such as autobiographical memory disturbances, depression/depressed affect, hallucinations, suicidality, work absenteeism; reproductive health/sexual behaviour such as foetal death, promiscuity, sexual risk behaviours in women, sexually transmitted diseases, teen pregnancy, unintended pregnancy; victimisation and perpetration such as *intimate partner violence* (see http://acestudy.org/ for a full inventory of supporting literature).

While the vast body of work is based on a specific U.S. cohort, ACE studies have recently been conducted in other developed (e.g. United Kingdom, see Bellis, Lowey, Leckenby, Hughes, & Harrison, 2014) and developing countries (e.g. Philippines, see Ramiro, Madrid, & Brown, 2010) confirming the link between ACEs and a variety of adverse health and behavioural outcomes, and a particular link with IPV (see Mair, Cunradi, & Todd, 2012; Pournaghash-Tehrani & Feizabadi, 2009; Whitfield, Anda, Dube, & Felitti, 2003). Moreover, the findings of the ACE studies are supported by a substantial body of wider literature (e.g. Gilbert et al., 2009; Wright, Crawford, & Del Castillo, 2009) that demonstrates the detrimental effect of CM on health and behavioural outcomes.

CHILD MALTREATMENT AND DAMAGE TO THE DEVELOPING BRAIN

The findings of the ACE study are consistent with data from studies of the organisation of the central nervous system as a function of experience (Anda et al., 2006). An appropriately stimulating environment invokes activity in specific brain regions leading to growth of the brain; however, the lack of stimulation and nurturing that typically accompanies maltreatment may impair development (Society for Neuroscience, 2002). The first five years are particularly important for brain development and acquisition of skills, and any adverse experiences in that period of life can negatively impact these processes. This can predispose individuals to an increased risk of mental and physical health problems, and emotional, behavioural, social, and educational problems (Irwin, Arjumand, & Hertzman, 2007) although there is evidence that early intervention can redress these consequences (O'Connor, Rutter, Beckett, Keaveney, & Kreppner, 2000). However, prolonged exposure to severe, or unpredictable stress (known as "toxic stress") such as that associated with childhood maltreatment can affect normal physiological mechanisms (Shonkoff et al., 2012). For instance, it can result in variations in cortisol (stress hormone) levels by the hypothalamic pituitary adrenal (HPA) axis (Gunnar & Donzella, 2002). This can alter the development of the brain by sensitising neural pathways and overdeveloping regions involved in responses to anxiety and fear, while under-developing other neural pathways and regions of the brain leading to emotional, learning, and behavioural problems that persist over the life-course (McCollum, 2006; Perry, 1997).

CHILD MALTREATMENT AND EPIGENETICS

The prenatal and postnatal environment is important for the expression of genes, known as epigenetic changes (Uher & Weaver, 2014). Epigenetics refers to the stable and heritable change in gene expression (or phenotype) without changing the underlying genotype (Waddington, 1942). Such changes are part of normal development, but "disruptions in epigenetic modification disturb normal developmental programs" (Feinberg, 2008, p. 1348). Epigenetic changes accumulate across the lifespan (Fraga et al., 2005) and are particularly susceptible during early development (Masterpasqua, 2009). Thus, adverse environments during the formative years can influence the expression of genes and future health and behaviour (Masterpasqua, 2009). While much of the research has been conducted with rodents, initial human studies have identified the epigenetic changes associated with CM. For instance, McGowan et al. (2009) undertook post-mortem examinations of the hippocampi of victims of suicide who had experienced CM and identified a greater degree of epigenetic changes (including decreased levels of glucocorticoid receptor expression, as well as increased levels of methylation specific to the gene known to regulate glucocorticoid expression) compared to victims of suicide-only and a non-suicide control group. More recently, Perroud et al. (2014) found a robust association between the degree of methylation in the human glucocorticoid receptor gene in blood samples of adult patients with bipolar disorder and the number of retrospective self-reported experiences of CM. Thus, epigenetics provides an indication of how CM can become "engraved in the circuitry of the developing brain" (Uher & Weaver, 2014, p. 3).

CHILD MALTREATMENT AND MONOAMINE OXIDASE A GENE

An area of particular interest in the development of violence is the role of the monoamine oxidase A (MAOA) gene. This gene encodes for the MAOA enzyme, which metabolizes the neurotransmitters noradrenaline, serotonin and dopamine, high levels of which are associated with aggression (Caspi et al., 2002). Caspi et al. reported that males who had suffered childhood maltreatment and had a low MAOA genotype were more likely to be convicted of a violent crime than maltreated males with a high MAOA genotype. Additionally, maltreated males with a low MAOA activity were also more likely to be convicted of a violent crime compared to non-maltreated males with low MAOA activity. Similarly, Foley et al. (2004) reported that low MAOA activity has been found to increase risk of conduct disorder in the presence of an ACE in boys aged 8-17 years. The maltreated males with low MAOA genotype were also more likely to be convicted of a violent crime compared to the non-maltreated males with a low MAOA genotype. This evidence is suggestive of a polymorphism in the MAOA gene which moderates the impact of childhood maltreatment (Caspi et al., 2002).

CM could disrupt experience-dependent neurochemical signals during "critical periods" of development leading to major abnormalities or deficits in neurodevelopment thereby impeding progress toward appropriate developmental milestones (McCollum, 2006). This can result in profound and lasting neurobehavioral consequences with a myriad of health, emotional, and behavioural outcomes, and can serve to perpetuate the "cycle of violence" (Perry, 1997).

CYCLE OF VIOLENCE

"[T]he idea that violence begets violence has become firmly established in the minds of professionals and the general public alike" (Widom, 1989b, p. 251). The seminal work of Cathy Widom was instrumental in the development of the concept of the "cycle of violence" following the observation that young men and women exposed to violence (witnessing or experiencing) during childhood and adolescence were at *greater risk* of perpetrating violence in the future (Widom, 1989a).

The relationship between CM and later use of violence has been supported in a number of studies (e.g. Dodge, Bates, & Pettit, 1990; Wright & Fagan, 2013). Kalmuss (1984) illustrates the association between martial aggression and exposure to violence or abuse in a representative sample of 2,143 U.S. adults:

- 1% to 2% among those who experienced no violence/abuse
- 3% to 4% among those who experienced child violence/abuse
- 6% to 8% among those who witnessed DV/abuse
- 12% to 17% among those who experienced and witnessed violence/abuse

In addition, a body of evidence supports "a persistent cycle of violence perpetrated against women that begins in childhood … reemerges later in adolescence and early adulthood … and ultimately places the next generation at considerable risk for victimisation" (Noll, 2005, p. 455). One of the most influential studies was by Coid et al. (2001) who found that females living in a socio-economically deprived area who had been severely beaten during childhood (16 years and under) had an odds ratio of 3.58 of suffering domestic abuse as an adult. This effect has also been found in less socio-economically deprived populations with Moeller et al. (1993) reporting that the likelihood of abuse as an adult was exponentially related to the number of abusive episodes suffered as a child.

The association between early exposure to violence and later perpetration or victimization was acknowledged in *Breaking the cycles of violence* (WHO, 2007). This report explored the intergenerational transmission of violence as a means to prevent CM and other forms of violence. In particular, the report identified four ways in which victimisation during childhood is associated with perpetration *and* victimisation in adulthood (WHO, 2007, p. 8): victim of violence in the home or community; child abuser in the home; perpetrator of violence against an intimate partner in the home; and perpetrator of violence in the community.

The intergenerational transmission of violence can be supported by Social Learning Theory (Bandura, 1978) which proposes that observational learning through family role models, may serve to reinforce the appropriateness of violent behaviour as a method of conflict resolution or as coping method, which is re-enacted through adolescence into adulthood (Black, Sussman, & Unger, 2010). Evidence indicates that individuals who lived in violent families and witnessed and/or experienced violent behaviours during their childhood, were significantly more likely to commit violent behaviours toward their spouse than those who lived in non-violent families (e.g. Alhusen et al., 2014; Black et al., 2010; Mair et al., 2012; Pournaghash-Tehrani & Feizabadi, 2009). One must also be cognizant of the ideological values of hegemonic masculinity that pervade our largely patriarchal society and serve to perpetuate the culture of DV.

However, Heyman and Smith Slep (2002) emphasise that "it is important to note that the cycle of violence is hardly a sealed fate" (p. 870). The majority of children exposed to violence do not follow the cycle of violence and go on to become violent in later life, demonstrating resilience in the face of adversity (Durant, Pendergrast, & Cadenhead, 1994; Widom, 1989a). Indeed, a number of factors have been linked to the perpetration and victimisation of IPV, beyond simply exposure to CM (see Capaldi, Knoble, Shortt, & Kim, 2012).

Nonetheless, if there is variation in incidence/prevalence then there are factors that underpin such variation that can increase risk of or protect against DV. Moreover, identification of risk factors and protective factors (although the latter is a slowly emerging field of research) can be targeted to prevent DV.

PREVENTION AND PUBLIC HEALTH

The WHO argue that "violence, like a range of other environment- and behaviour-related health problems—including HIV/AIDS, cardiovascular diseases, and diabetes— can largely be predicted and prevented" (Brundtland, 2002, p. 1580). The public health approach, therefore, offers a viable means by which to prevent violence "by employing scientific theory and data collection, problem identification, surveillance, program development and implementation research, and program effectiveness research.... inter- and intra-agency collaboration and dissemination of prevention research and programs" (Ketterlinus, 2008, p. 2).

PUBLIC HEALTH AND VIOLENCE

Violence has traditionally been the purview of the criminal justice system. Akers, Potter, and Hill (2012) note that traditionally the criminal justice system has adopted deterrence approaches to crime, whereas public health utilises behavioural, biomedical and environmental interventions to health problems. Whilst prison as a sanction is a legitimate intervention, it is only partially successful in preventing violence; for it only has capacity to work when the offender is in prison, and not always even then. However, prison deterrence is not sufficient to prevent all crime, including violence. If it were true one would expect the

U.S., with the highest prison population rates in the world (Walmsley, 2014) to have the lowest rates of crime and violence. This is not the case. While criminal justice deterrence should be an option of last resort, it has become the response of first resort (and at times the only response) to violence.

In recognition that criminal justice has not solved the problem of violence, it is believed that a public health approach is warranted (Prothrow-Stith & Davis, 2010). Although criminal justice and public health acknowledge the presence of risk factors or "root causes" and aim to prevent violence from occurring in the first instance, they differ in their approaches (Akers et al., 2012). It is argued that public health can and should work with the criminal justice system, as well as education and social services to prevent violence (Prothrow-Stith & Davis, 2010).

THE PUBLIC HEALTH APPROACH TO VIOLENCE PREVENTION

Violence was declared "a major and growing public health concern around the world" at the 49th World Health Assembly in 1996. The public health approach to violence prevention was then formalised in the WHO *World report on violence and health* (see Krug et al., 2002).

VIOLENCE PREVENTION

Public health distinguishes between three levels of prevention: primary, secondary and tertiary (Orbell, 2000). Whilst prevention has traditionally focused on victims (i.e. preventing and reducing the impact of violent injury) it is also now acknowledged in the prevention of violence perpetration (Dahlberg & Krug, 2002). Prothrow-Stith and Davis (2010) conceptualise the three levels of violence prevention as: primary ("upfront") prevention focuses on taking action before the risk factors for violence emerge, and for which every member of a community can benefit; secondary ("in the thick") prevention involves reacting to the presence of risk factors for violence, which then determines the action to be taken tertiary ("aftermath") prevention involves reducing the likelihood of the re-occurrence of violence.

The focus of public health is on primary prevention (Cohen, Chavez, & Chehimi, 2010) however, resources have often been directed toward secondary and tertiary prevention. While secondary and tertiary prevention has its place in violence prevention, it is widely acknowledged that the best chance of addressing violence is to deal with the root causes and prevent violence from happening in the first instance (see Instutute of Medicine & National Research Council , 2014; Prothrow-Stith & Davis, 2010).

THE 4-STEP MODEL

In order to prevent violence from occurring in the first instance, the WHO propose a 4-step model (Violence Prevention Alliance, 2014):

1. *Understand the scale of the problem.* As violence is under-reported to the police, systematic collection of data from different sources (e.g., police, health, self-reported, social work, education) on the scale, type and outcomes of violence is necessary.
2. *Identify risk and protective factors.* Identify the causes and correlates of violence and the associated risk and protective factors.
3. *Develop and evaluate interventions.* Using information gathered in steps one and two, intervention can be developed and evaluated.
4. *Scale up those programmes and interventions that have been proven to work.* Promising programmes can then be scaled up and measured in terms of impact and cost-effectiveness.

SOCIO-ECOLOGICAL MODEL

A large body of research from a wide range of disciplines has identified the myriad risk, and to a lesser extent protective factors for violence (e.g. Krug et al., 2002). In applying Bronfenbrenner's (1989) original idea of the ecological system which conceptualised how the various aspects of an individual's "environment" interact to influence child development, Dahlberg and Krug (2002) developed the socio-ecological model comprising four nested levels:

1. *Individual level:* This includes biological and personal history factors, which increase an individual's risk of engaging in violence (e.g., impulsivity, low academic achievement, substance abuse, lack of conflict management skills, aggressive behaviour).
2. *Relationship level*: This includes relationships with peers, family mmbers and intimate partners (i.e. CM and exposure to IPV increases risk of future perpetration or victimisation of violence).
3. *Community level*: This includes settings where social interactions take place, namely schools, workplaces and neighbourhoods. Certain characteristics of these settings can increase risk of violence (e.g., high residential mobility, high population density, high levels of unemployment and social isolation) and lead to a general acceptance of violence as part of everyday life.
4. *Societal level*: This involves larger societal factors, which may support or reject violence directly (e.g., social norms that support use of violence) or indirectly (e.g., patriarchal societies, priority to parental rights over child welfare).

Not only does the model serve to illustrate the complex inter-relation of the various factors that can lead to violence, it also offers direction as to the development of preventive interventions (see Dahlberg & Krug, 2002). Indeed, the most effective prevention interventions will be those that address issues at more than one level to account not only for the individual but also their environment.

BREAKING THE CYCLE OF VIOLENCE

The typical response to incidents of DV, when intervention does occur, is "crisis-oriented" involving the often temporary removal from the home of the victim or perpetrator (Lutenbacher et al., 2004). In light of the overlap and intersection of IPV and CM and the negative consequences on child development (Alhusen et al., 2014) it is necessary to develop appropriate prevention programmes, which can play a role in breaking the cycle of violence (WHO, 2007).

LIFE-COURSE PERSPECTIVE TO BREAK THE CYCLE OF DOMESTIC VIOLENCE

In order to effectively prevent DV it is deemed important to adopt a life-course perspective (Spivak et al., 2014; Tremblay, 2006; WHO, 2007). The WHO (2007) provide a revised version of the cycle of violence that highlights the different influences at key life stages in the developmental progression from CM to antisocial and violent behaviour, including DV (see Figure 1).

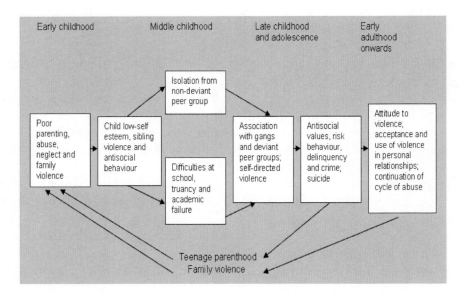

Figure 1. The developmental progression from childhood maltreatment to antisocial and violent behaviour. (Taken from WHO, 2007, p. 9, with permission).

Interventions delivered in early childhood often take the form of parenting programmes (e.g. Early Start: Fergusson, Grant, Horwood, & Ridder, 2005; Positive Parenting Programme: Prinz, Sanders, Shapiro, Whitaker, & Lutzker, 2009) which aim to strengthen parent-child relationships and can be delivered as home visits or classes (WHO, 2009b). In a systematic review Daro, Edleson, and Pinderhughes (2004) reported that family-based interventions (i.e. early family visitation, family support) were the most effective means of achieving measurable reductions on direct indicators of CM. Moreover, in a systematic review of reviews Mikton and Butchart (2009) concluded that parenting programmes appear effective in reducing risk factors for CM and show promise in being able to prevent CM. However, it is important to note that not all such programmes are effective and evaluation is often limited (WHO, 2009b).

Interventions in early childhood can also include support for children with pre-school behavioural problems (e.g., low self-esteem, antisocial behaviour; WHO, 2007). This can take the form of pre-school enrichment programmes, which aim to help develop children's social, emotional and cognitive skills, and prepare children for school (Sethi, Hughes, Bellis, Mitis, & Racioppi, 2010). For instance, the Chicago Child-Parent Centres (Reynolds, Ou, & Topitzes, 2004) demonstrated a significant decrease in juvenile violent offences, and the Early Head Start programme (Love et al., 2005) demonstrated improvements in aggressive behaviour by children and reduced corporal punishment by parents. However, the (WHO, 2009a) caution that the evidence is less robust for programmes delivered universally, compared with that for selectively delivered programmes.

Whilst there is a clear need for early intervention in breaking the cycle of violence, there is also a need for intervention during middle and late childhood to prevent progression to violent behaviour. In particular, children exposed to DV are at risk of difficulties in school and being isolated from non-deviant peers. Academic enrichment programmes have demonstrated some success with educational outcomes (e.g., numeracy, literacy, academic performance, and school engagement) but the impact on violence is limited, with some programmes even reporting negative outcomes (WHO, 2009a). For instance, a randomized controlled field trial of the 21st Community Learning Centres Programme (James-Burdumy et al., 2005), which offers homework sessions and academic activities, reported no improvement in academic achievement and higher levels of suspensions and other disciplinary actions.

The link between CM and IPV is believed to be mediated by problematic development (i.e. antisocial behaviour and substance use problems; Capaldi et al., 2012). To address these issues the WHO (2007) indicate that selected interventions are necessary during adolescence and beyond. Multisystemic therapy has been identified as one way of identifying risk factors contributing to anti-social behaviours (e.g., family, school, alcohol abuse) and developing protective factors against violence by working with the young person *and* their family (Sethi et al., 2010). Although, it has shown some success in reducing violent re-offending in juvenile offenders (Schaeffer & Borduin, 2005) a systematic review of such interventions delivered to young people who had either been abused or neglected, or young people who were at risk of incarceration, reported that multisystemic therapy was no more effective than usual treatment at improving social, behavioural and emotional outcomes (Littell, Popa, & Forsythe, 2005).

What is more, education programmes on positive relationships, sexual health, and pregnancy during adolescence and early adulthood are believed to be important in breaking the cycle of violence (WHO, 2007). Indeed, Spivak et al. (2014) highlight the importance of helping teens learn to establish healthy, nonviolent relationships. In a systematic review of a variety of interventions to prevent IPV (e.g., screening, victim advocacy, couples counselling, media campaigns, mandatory arrests, coordinated community response) not only was it found that most were forms of secondary prevention, but the only recommended intervention was dating violence prevention programs, which were identified as primary prevention (Whitaker, Baker, & Arias, 2007). Thus, while there is a growing number of programmes that aim to develop healthy relationships by developing skills such as empathy and conflict resolution (Sethi et al., 2010) these have demonstrated limited long-term effectiveness in reducing such violence (e.g., Foshee et al., 2000) or do not to specifically focus on prevention of IPV (Heise & Garcia-Moreno, 2002).

While there is mixed evidence of the effectiveness of some of these interventions one must not fall for the common evidence-based practice fallacy: lack of evidence proves lack of effect (Williams & Donnelly, in press). It may simply be that the appropriate evaluation has not yet been undertaken (Williams, Gavine, Ward, & Donnelly, in press) and further research and rigorous evaluation is required (Alhusen et al., 2014; Capaldi et al., 2012). Moreover, the focus on the inner two layers of the socio-ecological model (individual and relationship) must be complemented by attending to the outer layers (community and societal) (Spivak et al., 2014). This needs to consider interventions across health, education, employment, and criminal justice to address the social determinants that serve to perpetuate the cycle of DV.

CONCLUSION

The impact of DV can have long-term consequences for health and well-being, and poses a considerable public health problem. We have a moral imperative to protect the integrity and human rights of children; however, children cannot be fully protected unless we also protect vulnerable parents and guardians. The overlap and intersection between CM and IPV offers an opportunity to break the cycle of DV (Alhusen et al., 2014) but this will require a concerted effort by the whole of society. The public health approach with its focus on preventing violence from occurring in the first place, offers a way of setting about this; however, there have been difficulties in placing DV on the policy/public health agenda (Vine, Elliott, & Keller-Olaman, 2010).

The Director-General of the WHO emphasises the need to raise awareness of DV and further our understanding of the problem (see Garcia-Moreno, Heise, Jansen, Ellsberg, & Watts, 2005). While there is a specific need for advocacy work, and further research and robust evaluation to understand the dynamics of the cycle of violence in order to develop appropriate interventions (Alhusen et al., 2014) this must not impede the implementation of existing evidence-based programmes. Indeed, there is considerable support for focusing prevention efforts before birth and during early childhood (e.g., Irwin et al., 2007; Tremblay, 2006) and by making family processes the focus for primary prevention (e.g., Alhusen et al., 2014; Whitaker et al., 2007) for which effective programmes are available incorporating home visitation and education/support delivered by community nurses. Ensuring safe and nurturing families offers an important means by which to break the cycle of DV and ensure the health and well-being of future generations.

REFERENCES

Akers, T. A., Potter, R. H. & Hill, C. V. (2012). *Epidemiological Criminology: A Public Health Approach to Crime and Violence*. San Francisco: John Wiley & Sons.

Alhusen, J., Ho, G. K., Smith, K. & Campbell, J. (2014). Addressing intimate partner violence and child maltreatment: Challenges and opportunities. In J. E. Korbin & R. D. Krugman (Eds.), *Handbook of Child Maltreatment* (vol. 2, pp. 187-201): Springer Netherlands.

Anda, R. F., Dong, M. X., Brown, D. W., Felitti, V. J., Giles, W. H., Perry, G. S., et al. (2009). The relationship of adverse childhood experiences to a history of premature death of family members. *BMC Public Health, 9*.

Anda, R. F., Felitti, V. J., Bremner, J. D., Walker, J. D., Whitfield, C. H., Perry, B. D., et al. (2006). The enduring effects of abuse and related adverse experiences in childhood. *European Archives of Psychiatry and Clinical Neuroscience, 256*(3), 174-186.

Bandura, A. (1978). Social learning theory of aggression. *Journal of Communication, 29*(3), 12-29.

Bank., W. (1993). *World Development Report 1993: Investing in Health*. New York, NY: Oxford University Press.

Bellis, M. A., Lowey, H., Leckenby, N., Hughes, K. & Harrison, D. (2014). Adverse childhood experiences: Retrospective study to determine their impact on adult health behaviours and health outcomes in a UK population. *Journal of Public Health, 36*(1), 81-91.

Black, D. S., Sussman, S. & Unger, J. B. (2010). A further look at the intergenerational transmission of violence: Witnessing interparental violence in emerging adulthood. *Journal of Interpersonal Violence, 25*(6), 1022-1042.

Bronfenbrenner, U. (1989). Ecological systems theory. *Annals of Child Development, 6*, 187-249.

Capaldi, D. M., Knoble, N. B., Shortt, J. W. & Kim, H. K. (2012). A systematic review of risk factors for intimate partner violence. *Partner Abuse, 3*(2), 231-280.

Caspi, A., McClay, J., Moffitt, T. E., Mill, J., Martin, J., Craig, I. W., et al. (2002). Role of genotype in the cycle of violence in maltreated children. *Science, 297*(5582), 851-854.

Cohen, L., Chavez, V., & Chehimi, S. (Eds.) (2010). *Prevention is Primary: Strategies for Community Well-being* (2nd ed.). San Francisco, CA: Jossey-Bass.

Coid, J., Petruckevitch, A., Feder, G., Chung, W.-S., Richardson, J. & Moorey, S. (2001). Relation between childhood sexual and physical abuse and risk of revictimisation in women: a cross-sectional survey. *The Lancet, 358*(9280), 450-454.

Dahlberg, L. & Krug, E. G. (2002). Violence: A global public health problem. In E. G. Krug, L. Dahlberg, J. A. Mercy, A. B. Zwi & R. Lozano (Eds.), *The world report on violence and health*. Geneva: WHO.

Daro, D., Edleson, J. L. & Pinderhughes, H. (2004). Finding common ground in the study of child maltreatment, youth violence, and adult domestic violence. *Journal of Interpersonal Violence, 19*(3), 282-298.

Dodge, K. A., Bates, J. E. & Pettit, G. S. (1990). Mechanisms in the Cycle of Violence. *Science, 250*(4988), 1678-1683.

Dong, M., Anda, R. F., Felitti, V. J., Dube, S. R., Williamson, D. F., Thompson, T. J., et al. (2004). The interrelatedness of multiple forms of childhood abuse, neglect, and household dysfunction. *Child Abuse & Neglect, 28*(7), 771-784.

Drijber, B. C., Reijnders, U. L. & Ceelen, M. (2013). Male victims of domestic violence. *Journal of Family Violence, 28*(2), 173-178.

Durant, R. H., Pendergrast, R. A. & Cadenhead, C. (1994). Exposure to Violence and Victimization and Fighting Behavior by Urban Black-Adolescents. *Journal of Adolescent Health*, *15*(4), 311-318.

Feinberg, A. P. (2008). Epigenetics at the epicentre of modern medicine. *JAMA*, *299*(11), 1345-1350.

Felitti, V. J. & Anda, R. F. (2010). The relationship of adverse childhood experiences to adult medical disease, psychiatric disorders and sexual behavior: implications for healthcare. . In R. A. Lanius, E. Vermetten & C. Pain (Eds.), *The impact of early life trauma on health and disease: The hidden epidemic* (pp. 77-87). Cambridge, UK: Cambridge University Press.

Felitti, V. J., Anda, R. F., Nordenberg, D., Williamson, D. F., Spitz, A. M., Edwards, V., et al. (1998). Relationship of childhood abuse and household dysfunction to many of the leading causes of death in adults - The adverse childhood experiences (ACE) study. *American Journal of Preventive Medicine*, *14*(4), 245-258.

Fergusson, D. M., Grant, H., Horwood, L. J. & Ridder, E. M. (2005). Randomized trial of the Early Start program of home visitation. *Pediatrics*, *116*(6), e803-e809.

Finley, L. L. (2010). Examining domestic violence as a state crime: Nonkilling implications. In J. E. Pim (Ed.), *Global nonkilling working papers*. Honolulu, Hawaii: Center for Global Nonkilling.

Finneran, C. & Stephenson, R. (2013). Intimate partner violence among men who have sex with men: A systematic review. *Trauma, Violence, & Abuse*, *14*(2), 168-185.

Foley, D. L., Eaves, L. J., Wormley, B., Silberg, J. L., Maes, H. H., Kuhn, J., et al. (2004). Childhood adversity, monoamine oxidase A genotype, and risk for conduct disorder. *Archives of General Psychiatry*, *61*(7), 738-744.

Foshee, V. A., Bauman, K. E., Greene, W. F., Koch, G. G., Linder, G. F. & MacDougall, J. E. (2000). The Safe Dates program: 1-year follow-up results. *American Journal of Public Health*, *90*(10), 1619.

Fraga, M. F., Ballestar, E., Paz, M. F., Ropero, S., Setien, F., Ballestar, M. L., et al. (2005). Epigenetic differences arise during the lifetime of monozygotic twins. *Proceedings of the National Academy of Sciences of the United States of America*, *102*(3), 10604.

Garcia-Moreno, C., Heise, L., Jansen, H. A. F. M., Ellsberg, M. & Watts, C. (2005). Violence against women. *Science*, *310*(5752), 1282-1283.

Garcia-Moreno, C., Jansen, H. A. F. M., Ellsberg, M., Heise, L. & Watts, C. H. (2006). Prevalence of intimate partner violence: Findings from the WHO multi-country study on women's health and domestic violence. *The Lancet*, *368*(9543), 1260-1269.

Gilbert, R., Widom, C. S., Browne, K., Fergusson, D., Webb, E. & Janson, S. (2009). Burden and consequences of child maltreatment in high-income countries. *The Lancet*, *373*(9657), 68-81.

Groves, B., Zuckerman, B., Marans, S. & Cohen, D. J. (1993). Silent victims children who witness violence. *JAMA*, *269*(2), 262-264.

Gunnar, M. R. & Donzella, B. (2002). Social regulation of the cortisol levels in early human development. *Psychoneuroendocrinology*, *27*(1-2), 199-220.

Heise, L. & Garcia-Moreno, C. (2002). Violence by intimate partners. In E. G. Krug, L. Dahlberg, J. Mercy, A. B. Zwi & F. J. Lozano (Eds.), *World report on violence and health* (pp. 87-122). Geneva: WHO.

Heyman, R. E. & Smith Slep, A. M. (2002). Do child abuse and interparental violence lead to adulthood family violence? *Journal of Marriage and Family, 64*(4), 864-870.

Instutute of Medicine & National Research Council. (2014). *The Evidence for Violence Prevention Across the Lifespan and Around the World: Workshop Summary*. Washington, DC.

Irwin, L. G., Arjumand, S. & Hertzman, C. (2007). *Early Child Development: A Powerful Equalizer*. Vancouver, BC: Human Early Learning Partnership.

James-Burdumy, S., Dynarski, M., Moore, M., Deke, J., Mansfield, W., Pistorino, C., et al. (2005). *When Schools Stay Open Late: The National Evaluation of the 21st Century Community Learning Centers Program. Final Report*. US Department of Education.

Kalmuss, D. (1984). The intergenerational transmission of marital aggression. *Journal of Marriage and Family, 46*(1), 11-19.

Kelly, K. A. (2003). *Domestic Violence and the Politics of Privacy*. Ithaca, NY: Cornell University Press.

Ketterlinus, R. D. (2008). Introduction. In R. D. Ketterlinus (Ed.), *Youth violence: Interventions for health care providers* (pp. 1-6). Washington, DC: APHA Press.

Korbin, J. E. (2003). Children, childhoods, and violence. *Annual Review of Anthropology, 32*, 431-446.

Krug, E. G., Dahlberg, L. L., Mercy, J. A., Zwi, A. B. & Lozano, R. (Eds.). (2002). *World Report on Violence and Health*. Geneva: WHO.

Last, J. M. (2007). *A Dictionary of Public Health*. Oxford, UK: Oxford University Press.

Littell, J., Popa, M. & Forsythe, B. (2005). Multisystemic therapy for social, emotional, and behavioral problems in youth aged 10-17. *Cochrane Dsatabase of Systematic Reviews, 4*, CD004797.

Love, J. M., Kisker, E. E., Ross, C., Raikes, H., Constantine, J., Boller, K., et al. (2005). The effectiveness of early head start for 3-year-old children and their parents: lessons for policy and programs. *Developmental Psychology, 41*(6), 885.

Lutenbacher, M., Cohen, A. & Conner, N. M. (2004). Breaking the cycle of family violence: understanding the perceptions of battered women. *Journal of Pediatric Health Care, 18*(5), 236-243.

Mair, C., Cunradi, C. B. & Todd, M. (2012). Adverse childhood experiences and intimate partner violence: testing psychosocial mediational pathways among couples. *Annals of Epidemiology, 22*(12), 832-839.

Masterpasqua, F. (2009). Psychology and epigenetics. *Review of General Psychology, 13*(3), 194-201.

May-Chahal, C. & Cawson, P. (2005). Measuring child maltreatment in the United Kingdom: A study of the prevalence of child abuse and neglect. *Child Abuse & Neglect, 29*(9), 969-984.

McCollum, D. (2006). Child maltreatment and brain development. *Minnesota Medicine, 89*(3), 48-50.

McFeely, C., Whiting, N., Lombard, N., Brooks, O., Burman, M. & McGowan, M. (2013). Domestic abuse and gender inequality: An overview of the current debate. Retrieved 13th March 2014 from: http://hdl.handle.net/1842/8769

McGowan, P. O., Sasaki, A., D'Alessio, A. C., Dymov, S., Labonte, B., Szyf, M., et al. (2009). Epigenetic regulation of the glucocorticoid receptor in human brain associates with childhood abuse. *Nature Neuroscience, 12*(3), 342-348.

Mikton, C. & Butchart, A. (2009). Child maltreatment prevention: A systematic review of reviews. *Bulletin of the World Health Organization*, *87*(5), 353-361.

Moeller, T. P., Bachmann, G. A. & Moeller, J. R. (1993). The combined effects of physical, sexual, and emotional abuse during childhood: Long-term health consequences for women. *Child Abuse & Neglect*, *17*(5), 623-640.

Noll, J. G. (2005). Does childhood sexual abuse set in motion a cycle of violence against women?: What we know and what we need to learn. *Journal of Interpersonal Violence*, *20*(4), 455-462.

O'Connor, T. G., Rutter, M., Beckett, C., Keaveney, L. & Kreppner, J. M. (2000). The Effects of Global Severe Privation on Cognitive Competence: Extension and Longitudinal Follow-up. *Child Development*, *71*(2), 376-390.

Orbell, S. (2000). What is prevention? In M. Porter, D. Alder & C. Abraham (Eds.), *Psychology and sociology applied to medicine: An illustrated text* (pp. 64-65). Edinburgh: Churchill Livingstone.

Perroud, N., Dayer, A., Piguet, C., Nallet, A., Favre, S., Malafosse, A., et al. (2014). Childhood maltreatment and methylation of the glucocorticoid receptor gene NR3C1 in bipolar disorder. *The British Journal of Psychiatry*, *204*(1), 30-35.

Perry, B. D. (1997). Incubated in terror: Neurodevelopmental factros in the "cycle of violence". In J. D. Osofsky (Ed.), *Children in a violent society*, (pp. 124-149). New York, NY: The Guilford Press.

Pournaghash-Tehrani, S. & Feizabadi, Z. (2009). Predictability of physical and psychological violence by early adverse childhood experiences. *Journal of Family Violence*, *24*(6), 417-422.

Prinz, R. J., Sanders, M. R., Shapiro, C. J., Whitaker, D. J. & Lutzker, J. R. (2009). Population-based prevention of child maltreatment: The US Triple P system population trial. *Prevention Science*, *10*(1), 1-12.

Prothrow-Stith, D. & Davis, R. A. (2010). A public health approach to preventing violence. In L. Cohen, V. Chavez & S. Chehimi (Eds.), *Prevention is primary: Strategies for community well-being* (2nd ed., pp. 323-350). San Francisco, CA: Jossey-Bass.

Ramiro, L. S., Madrid, B. J. & Brown, D. W. (2010). Adverse childhood experiences (ACE) and health-risk behaviors among adults in a developing country setting. *Child Abuse & Neglect*, *34*(11), 842-855.

Reynolds, A. J., Ou, S.-R. & Topitzes, J. W. (2004). Paths of effects of early childhood intervention on educational attainment and delinquency: A confirmatory analysis of the Chicago Child-Parent Centers. *Child Development*, *75*(5), 1299-1328.

Schaeffer, C. M. & Borduin, C. M. (2005). Long-term follow-up to a randomized clinical trial of multisystemic therapy with serious and violent juvenile offenders. *Journal of consulting and clinical psychology*, *73*(3), 445.

Sethi, D., Hughes, K., Bellis, M., Mitis, F. & Racioppi, F. (Eds.). (2010). *European Report on Preventing Violence and Knife Crime Among Young People*. Copenhagen: WHO Regional Office for Europe.

Shonkoff, J. P., Garner, A. S., Siegel, B. S., Dobbins, M. I., Earls, M. F., Garner, A. S., et al. (2012). The lifelong effects of early childhood adversity and toxic stress. *Pediatrics*, *129*(1), e232-e246.

Smyke, A. T., Wajda-Johnston, V. & Zeanah, C. H. (2004). Working with traumatized infants and toddlers in the child welfare system. In J. D. Osofsky (Ed.), *Young children and trauma: Intervention and treatment* (pp. 260-284). New York, NY: Guilford Press.

Spivak, H. R., Jenkins, E. L., van Audenhove, K., Lee, D., Kelly, M. & Iskander, J. (2014). CDC grand rounds: A public health approach to prevention of intimate partner vioelnce. *Morbidity and Mortality Weekly Report, 63*(2), 38-41.

Stark, E. (2007). *Coercive Control: How Men Entrap Women in Personal Life*. Oxford, UK: Oxford University Press.

Tremblay, R. E. (2006). Prevention of youth violence: Why not start at the beginning? *Journal of Abnormal Child Psychology, 34*(4), 481-487.

Uher, R. & Weaver, I. C. G. (2014). Epigenetic traces of childhood maltreatment in peripheral blood: a new strategy to explore gene-environment interactions. *The British Journal of Psychiatry, 204*(1), 3-5.

Vine, M. M., Elliott, S. J. & Keller-Olaman, S. (2010). To disrupt and displace: placing domestic violence on the public health agenda. *Critical Public Health, 20*(3), 339-355.

Violence Prevention Alliance . (2014). *The Public Health Approach*. Retrieved 17th April 2014 from: http://www.who.int/violenceprevention/approach/public_health/en/

Waddington, C. H. (1942). Canalization of development and the inheritance of acquired characters. *Nature, 150*(3811), 563-565.

Walmsley, R. (2014). *World Prison Population List* (10th ed.). London: International Centre for Prison Studies.

Whitaker, D., Baker, C. & Arias, I. (2007). Interventions to prevent intimate partner violence. In L. Doll, S. Bonzo, D. Sleet & J. Mercy (Eds.), *Handbook of injury and violence prevention* (pp. 203-221): Springer US.

Whitfield, C. L., Anda, R. F., Dube, S. R. & Felitti, V. J. (2003). Violent childhood experiences and the risk of intimate partner violence in adults: Assessment in a large health maintenance organization. *Journal of Interpersonal Violence, 18*(2), 166-185.

WHO. (1999). *Report of the Consultation on Child Abuse Prevention*. Geneva: World Health Organization.

WHO. (2007). *The Cycles of Violence: The Relationship Between Childhood Maltreatment and the Risk of Later Becoming a Victim or Perpetrator of Violence. Key Facts*. Copenhagen: World Health Organization Regional Office for Europe.

WHO. (2009a). *Violence Prevention the Evidence: Preventing Violence by Developing Life Skills in Children and Adolescents*. Geneva.

WHO. (2009b). *Violence Prevention the Evidence: Preventing Violence Through the Development of Safe, Stable and Nurturing Relationships Between Children and their Parents and Caregivers*. Geneva.

Widom, C. S. (1989a). The cycle of violence. *Science, 244*(4901), 160-166.

Widom, C. S. (1989b). Does violence beget violence? A critical examination of the literature. *Psychological Bulletin, 106*, 3-28.

Williams, D. J. & Donnelly, P. D. (in press). Is violence a disease? Situating violence prevention in public health policy and practice. *Public Health*.

Williams, D. J., Gavine, A. J., Ward, C. L. & Donnelly, P. D. (in press). What is evidence in violence prevention? In P. D. Donnelly & C. L. Ward (Eds.), *Violence: A global health priority* (pp. 125-131). Oxford, UK: Oxford University Press.

Wright, E. M. & Fagan, A. A. (2013). The cycle of violence in context: Exploring the moderating roles of neighborhood disadvantage and cultural norms. *Criminology*, *51*(2), 217-249.

Wright, M. O., Crawford, E. & Del Castillo, D. (2009). Childhood emotional maltreatment and later psychological distress among college students: The mediating role of maladaptive schemas. *Child Abuse & Neglect*, *33*(1), 59-68.

In: Overcoming Domestic Violence   ISBN: 978-1-63321-956-4
Editors: Myra F. Taylor, Julie Ann Pooley et al.   © 2015 Nova Science Publishers, Inc.

Chapter 13

DOMESTIC VIOLENCE AGAINST WOMEN IN WAR AND ARMED CONFLICTS

Jinan Usta[1] and Neil Singh[2]*

[1]American University of Beirut, Lebanon
[2]University of Cambridge NHS Trust, Cambridge, England, UK

ABSTRACT

During wars and displacement, there is a collapse in the social and moral order: bonds within communities and families may get destabilized; violence becomes more acceptable, with resources barely available for survivors and priority is given for food and shelter. Most research and interventions addressing sexual and gender based violence during war focus on violence perpetrated by armed troops, while violence perpetrated by family members is often overlooked. This chapter focuses on domestic violence against women in the specific context of armed conflicts or war. It provides a brief overview of the reported data on domestic violence in various conflict-zones. The existing literature suggests that domestic violence is a highly prevalent 'silent epidemic' in times of war, flaring up when there is loss of social structure and order. To give an understanding of the link between conflicts and domestic violence, the factors contributing to domestic violence in war-time are analyzed based on the four levels of the Heise 'ecological model', : environment, community, relationship, and individual. The chapter will conclude by suggesting proactive actions—at each of the four levels stated in the ecological model—to be implemented by governmental, nongovernmental and UN agencies, in order to effectively prevent, recognize and address domestic violence in times of crisis and conflicts.

Keywords: Domestic violence, gender-based violence, intimate-partner violence, war, refugee

---

* Corresponding author: Dr. Jinan Usta, Clinical Associate Professor, Department of Family Medicine, American University of Beirut Medical Center, PO Box: 11-0236, Riad El Solh, Beirut 1107 2020, Lebanon. Tel: 00961-3-344939; 00961-1-753783, Email: ju00@aub.edu.lb.

INTRODUCTION

"Everything that happens in global society is reflected in the family." (Smith, 1989)

War poses a major global health problem and has a catastrophic effect on the well-being of societies and nations (Murthy, 2006; Dewachi, 2014). Women have traditionally been less likely to orchestrate and perpetrate war, and yet they bear a significant fraction of the psychological, physical and social harms of war. (Depoortere et al., 2004; Hynes et al., 2004; UNFPA, 2001; UNFPA 2006; Van Herp et al., 2003).

To date, most research attention has focused on the systematic targeting of women by opposing troops (Coomaraswamy, 2002; Leaning et al., 2009). However, recent data suggest that women at war face just as much danger inside as outside their own homes (El Jack, 2003; Haider, 2009), and war may bring the silent epidemic of domestic violence (DV) (Usta et al., 2008; Stark & Ager, 2011). In the 19th century, in his essay "The Subjection of Women", John Stuart Mill recognized the relationship between what he called 'wife torture' and international violence. He wrote that the tyranny at home is the model for tyranny abroad, and that the Englishman's habit of household tyranny established the pattern of his foreign policy (Jones, 2013). Indeed, violence against women follows the rates of societal violence, and countries with high violence rates in the general population typically experience high femicide rates (Geneva Declaration, 2011a; Geneva Declaration, 2011b). Yet, in spite of this suggested link between collective violence and DV (Catani et al., 2008; Gupta et al., 2009), DV during conflict has not been adequately studied.

This chapter aims, therefore, to examine the inter-relationship between two forms of violence: one occurring between clans or countries in the public arena, and the other happening silently between familiar individuals in the private sphere. The information presented is based on several researches done in various war-zones that related war and at least one form of DV. Accordingly, a theoretical explanation of this association is offered. Finally, interventions used to address DV in conflict situations are summarised with suggestions of possible avenues for future research and activism.

In this chapter, 'Domestic violence' will be used to denote violence against women occurring within the domestic sphere, including cases where the perpetrator is an intimate partner, spouse or other direct family member. Recognizing that both males and females can be subject to violence, most of the available literature concerns men perpetrating DV against women. The best meta-analysis done on the topic cites that 65% of DV victims in peace-time are female (Archer, 2000), although a minority of studies report that men in some refugee camps have higher lifetime rates of violence than women (Khawaja & Barazi, 2005). Moreover, we will use the terms conflict and war interchangeably, meaning: '*actual, intentional* and *widespread* armed conflict between political communities" (Orend, 2005**)**. Recognizing that "war" comes in many forms—civil, colonial and guerilla to name but a few— that vary drastically in duration and impact (Krug et al., 2002), we will disregard these differences for the sake of simplicity and because of the scarcity of information available on each.

PREVALENCE

For several reasons, it may be difficult to provide solid information on the association between DV and armed conflict. Firstly, DV may be deemed a relatively unimportant research topic compared to other issues related to war, such as poverty and malnutrition (Kishor & Johnson, 2004). Secondly, available figures are most likely to be approximate underestimates; in a stressful environment where violence becomes normalised, survivors are less likely to report and tend to suffer in silence, not risking shame and possible stigmatisation. In Lebanon, women easily answered questions on political violence, but remained reluctant to discuss sexual violence and domestic abuse (Wilkens et al., 2010). Further, women subject to rape or sexual violence may be reluctant to disclose the abuse for fear of shame or stigmatization (Onyango et al., 2003). Thirdly, the knock-on effects of war—overwhelming instability, violence, shattered social trust, splintering of families and communities and the breakdown of law and order—make it even more difficult for survivors to report violence through formal mechanisms (World Health Organisation, 2007; Byrne, 1996). In addition, the infrastructure needed to monitor DV is impaired in times of warfare (Farnsworth et al., 2012). Moreover, research examining DV during or after conflict is often difficult to contextualise due to lack of baseline data from peace-time; different research methodologies employed; different types of DV measured; or different forms, and severity, of conflict. Most studies restricted their focus to physical and sexual partner abuse, leaving other forms of DV (psychological and economic, for example) greatly overlooked (Usta et al., 2008). They also rely on subjective reporting by survivors, although this has been shown, in some settings, to be an unreliable source of data. In East Timor, for instance, women reported that rates of DV had decreased since the conflict ended, but this was not reflected in the quantitative data collected from the same population (Hynes et al., 2004). Bearing all this in mind, we will summarize the available data in order to inform our theorizing in the next section of this chapter.

There is some evidence to suggest that DV might increase during, or in the aftermath of, war (Ward, 2002; Zimmerman, 1995). However, in the absence of systematic surveys that document the frequency of domestic violence in conflict or post conflict countries, most of the information available on the matter rely to a great extent on the sporadic findings published by several organizations and agencies working in refugee camps. Their findings suggest that war violence translates into increased peri- and post-conflict domestic violence, as evidenced by high levels of spousal beatings in refugee and resettlement communities (Pittaway, 2004). Human Rights Watch reports increased levels of domestic violence during the second Intifada in the West Bank and Gaza (Human Rights Watch, 2006); extensive domestic violence against refugee women in Tanzania (Human Rights Watch, 2000), and in Nepal (Human Rights Watch, 2003). The conflicts in Sri Lanka have also been linked to increases or high levels of domestic violence either in general (Paudel, 2007) or in the specific setting of refugee camps (Rajasingham-Senanayake, 2004). The level of domestic violence caused by the war in South-Sudan has been described as 'appalling' (Jok, 1999). Overall, rates of domestic violence in war are higher than most of the rates of wartime rape and sexual violence perpetrated by individuals outside of the home: 4%–22% of women experience sexual violence in conflict (Stark & Ager, 2011).

Although the conclusion of war is welcomed and thought of as a time of renewal, it is also often precisely the moment when domestic violence may really begin in earnest and "violence moves home". For many women this may simply herald a transition from one form of violence to another. The prevalence of DV in countries recovering from war regularly exceeds 50% (Garcia-Moreno, 2005), DV victimization rates as high as 76.6% (Coker & Richter, 1998), 75.9% (Avdibegovic & Sinanovic, 2006) and 61% (Khawaja, 2004) have been reported in post-war settings. In Lebanon, a helpline for violence survivors normally receives around 15 calls per week, noted only three calls during the month of Israel-Hizbollah war in 2006, while 52 calls came in during the first week after the conflict ended. (Kvinna till Kvinna 2010). After war in Peru, the incidence of DV differed from 47.3% in peaceful districts to 53.4% in the war torn areas (Gallegos, JV 2011). Higher levels of rape and domestic violence have been reported in many post-conflict situations (Bastick, et al., 2007).

THEORY

It is said that *"War magnifies the everyday injustices that many women live with in peacetime. During periods of armed conflict, all forms of violence increase, particularly violence against women and girls"* (UNHCR, 2006). This implies that violence against women is an existing phenomenon in the society, and that conflict increases it possibly by potentiating its predisposing factors.

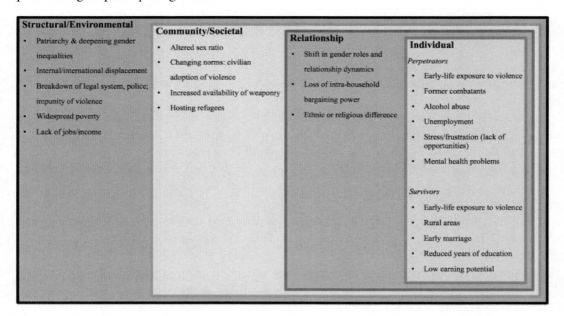

Figure 1. Ecological framework depiting factors affecting Domestic Violence Against Women during war and armed conflict.

From the several theories advocated to explain DV (Loue, 2001), the 'ecological model' (Heise, 1998) will be used in this chapter to illustrate this theory. This model has been proposed to explain violence against women by relating several factors operating at four different levels: structural; community; relationship; and individual. Since war has a drastic effect on all of these levels, this ecological model is best suited to explain how changes created by armed conflicts operate to sustain or exacerbate DV, and to show the 'cumulative risk' that makes DV far more likely to happen in conflicts (Pittaway & Rees, 2006). These factors are summarised in figure 1 (see Figure 1) and explained further thereafter.

FACTORS OPERATING AT THE STRUCTURAL LEVEL

Patriarchy and Deepening of Gender Inequalities

DV against women in times of war is best viewed, not as something completely new, but rather as an extension of power asymmetry, underlying gender inequalities that were pre-existing in society (Nikolic-Ristanovic, 2000; Stark & Wessels, 2012). In the absence of an effective state, an anachronistic view of gender-roles may prevail, where the 'man of the house' takes the role of protector. As quoted by a non-governmental organisation in Lebanon, *"for women to remain secure, they have to accept the rules of the game. When they cease to submit, they may encounter violence"* (Wilkens et al., 2010). This can be further potentiated, in the occasional situation where the conflict is perceived to be against American hegemony, by perception of feminism and women's rights as another part of Western cultural imperialism and hence ignored or even actively rejected (Cotter, 2002). It is to be noted that most of the related studies and observations took place in patriarchal developing countries where most of the wars have recently occurred. A question remains how war would affect power symmetry in countries where gender equality is better established.

Internal/International Displacement

Displacement dislocates people from their familiar support networks and places them in an unfamiliar environment where they have to struggle to secure shelter, food and income for them and their children. Displacement conditions (such as overcrowding, lack of basic services and public transport, absence of entertainment opportunities, lack of jobs and the burden of a large dependent family) produce frustrations that may unleash violent behaviour. For instance, displacement was found to increase the rate of DV in Uganda, where 52% of women living in internally displaced camps experienced physical partner abuse in the previous year (Stark et al., 2010).

Broken Safety Net: Breakdown of Legal System, Loss of Police, Impunity of Violence

During armed conflicts, a culture of violence and lack of respect for human rights as well as general lawlessness and a climate of impunity prevail. There is a breakdown of the legal system, the justice and police institutions are weakened, increasing the risk of victimization of vulnerable groups such as women and children. In the Occupied Palestinian Territories, "security vacuum" is forwarded to explain why domestic violence increased during conflict

(Ulltveit-Moe, 2004). In Yogoslavia, the police did not respond, or intervened ineffectively, to the calls of women reporting abuse and justified the violent behaviour as a consequence of war trauma (Nikolic-Ristanovic, 2000). Impunity for acts of violence perpetrated during the conflict as well as weak ruling of law in post-conflict settings were found to result in legacy of tolerance of abuse against women and girls and increased trafficking. A DV perpetrator may only be asked to pay a small fine, or the survivor herself may be advised to be more obedient by community elders (Ward & Vann, 2002).

Widespread Poverty/Lack of Jobs

During armed conflicts there are decreased resources, jobs, source of incomes as well as an increase in losses and destruction of properties. Refugees may additionally face the burden of a higher cost of living in the host country (Usta & Masterson, 2012). A survey among Iraqi refugees in Syria indicates a potential relationship between DV and household financial distress (Tappis et al., 2012), possibly because of an increase in the level of frustration which is often taken out on the weak (Skjelsbaek, 2001). Under the weight of such economic hardship, women may feel pressured to drop out of school, marry young, accept low-paid jobs, or take on risky income generating work such as prostitution. Limited resources were also found to be a contributing factor to DV perpetrated by in-laws and co-wives against women returned from captivity (Annan & Brier, 2010).

FACTORS OPERATING AT THE COMMUNITY OR SOCIETAL LEVEL

Altered Sex Ratio

Wars lopsidedly affect the demographic tree by changing the sex ratio, as more men than women are usually killed during wars. A one standard deviation decrease in the sex ratio (men: women) was shown to increase a woman's lifetime-risk of being a victim of DV by 65% (La Mattina, 2013). After the genocide in Rwanda, women who got married in provinces that had more decrease in the sex ratio were more likely to become victims of intimate partner violence, less likely to have economic decision-making powers, less likely to use contraception methods, and married less educated husbands. The effect was more detrimental on literate women, who had to lower their reservation values as a consequence of the reduction in the number and 'quality' of potential husbands caused by genocide (La Mattina, 2013).

Changing Norms: Civilian Adoption of Violence

The sustained witnessing of violent acts during war is associated with elevated risks of both physical and sexual violence in the family (Koenig et al., 2006) and alters community-level norms concerning wife beating (Waldmann, 2007). Repeatedly viewing violence can lead to widespread tacit tolerance and acceptance of the use of physical violence to solve private and social problems; "emotional blunting" in perpetrators, victims and witnesses alike; and ultimately to an ever-present culture of violence. For example, after the 2006 Israel-Lebanon conflict, it was observed that the Lebanese children changed the way they played—deliberately trying to hurt each other and challenging each other as to how many beatings they could take before starting to cry (Wilkens et al., 2010). A link between rape perpetrated as an instrument of warfare and a following increase in the prevalence of rape in the domestic context was observed in the Democratic Republic of Congo (Bartels et al., 2010). Such "civilian adoption of rape" is likely due to altered norms in the post-conflict setting, leading to citizens changing how they exert personal power, adopting techniques used by soldiers in recent wars (Adelman, 2003).

Increased Availability of Weaponry

It is thought that spikes in DV during and after conflict are partly due to the availability and proliferation of weaponry (Dakkad, 2007; Rehn & Johnson-Sirleaf, 2002) that may continue after war ceases. In Bosnia and Croatia (Nikolic-Ristanovic, 2000) some men who returned from war regularly used weapons (e.g., pistols, bombs) for threatening their partners.

Hosting Refugees

War may affect other countries not directly involved in the conflict. For instance, hosting refugees places major strains on societies and families. Serbian women who have had both refugees and violent husbands in their homes reported that their husbands became more violent. The imbalance in the family created by newcomers is used by men as a reason for violence against women (Nikolic-Ristanovic, 2000).

FACTORS OPERATING AT THE RELATIONSHIP LEVEL

Shift in Gender Roles and Relationship Dynamics

War can shift relationship dynamics, and thus predispose couples to DV, in three key ways: loss of the male-breadwinner status; newfound female financial independence; and mismatch between realities and expectations.

Wars are periods where hegemonic masculinity—expressed through power, status in the family and economic independence—is both venerated and threatened. Traditionally, men are expected to be providers and defenders of freedom, honour and of their women and homeland. Nowadays, when armed conflicts consist mostly of shelling and bombing, in addition to loss of earnings, men find it difficult to fulfil this role, and so may feel emasculated.

At the same time, women may be obliged during war to take on non-traditional tasks that would ordinarily fall to their partners. Women who previously performed unpaid domestic duties are pressured to take on paid work. They are also the focus of attention of most relief and protection programs put in place during conflict by UN agencies and international organizations. This can be a cause for great angst for many men, as it can undermine their role as 'provider', making them feel useless (Haider, 2009). After the conflict is over, women are expected to relinquish these newfound rights, roles and freedoms. Some women may find it hard to be relegated again to traditional domestic duties, whilst men may not want to give up their traditional role (Fisher, 2013).

This tension leaves many men feeling humiliated, guilty and angry, sometimes sparking DV to silence such dissent (El Jack, 2003). DV can constitute a means for men to reaffirm their power over women; in other words, men who fail to live up to masculine ideals may compensate by dominating their partners through violence (Munn, 2008). This was the observation in the Occupied Palestinian Territories (Ulltveit-Moe, 2004) and in Yugoslavia (Nikolic-Ristanovic, 2000). Thus, women face a double bind, on the one hand being economically forced to work, whilst on the other hand being abused for challenging male authority.

Loss of Intra-Household Bargaining Power

Wars deprive women of their 'social safety-net' (e.g., communal resources, safe spaces, social support networks, state welfare) and thus weaken their intra-relationship bargaining power, leaving them less able to stop or escape DV (Agarwal, 1997). When asked about the violence they were subject to, Syrian refugee women admitted to an increase in violence perpetrated by their husbands, but they were not considering acting upon it, in order not to lose the security of their settlement. One admitted: 'he threatens to take me back to Syria if I open my mouth' (Usta & Masterson, 2012).

Ethnic or Religious Difference

Ethnic or religious differences, which may be unimportant in peace-time, can exacerbate DV during war if each member of the marital couple belongs to one of the opposing groups: "the abstract hatred against other nationalities was smoothly transformed into hatred against very close persons such as wives; they are seen as concrete symbols of enemies" (Nikolic-Ristanovic, 2000).

FACTORS OPERATING AT THE LEVEL OF THE INDIVIDUAL

For many reasons, armed conflicts place significant stress on individuals: Experiences of trauma (direct or indirect), feeling of insecurity and instability, scarce resources, displacement, loss of income, uncertainty about the future, death or disability of a close friend or family member place major toll on the coping mechanisms of people. In patriarchal societies, men's responses to stress are often violent; they view violence against women and spouses as their only option to release frustrations and emotions and gain some power and control over their lives. Women, on the other hand, commonly respond non-violently to trauma, persecution and commensurate experiences of loss and change (Pittaway & Rees, 2006) allowing the cycle of violence to perpetuate.

In addition to being raised in a patriarchal society, sporadic research hints to individual characteristics predisposing an individual to become a perpetrator or survivor of domestic violence during or after war. These are:

Perpetrators

Factors that have been linked to DV perpetration in conflict were alcohol abuse (Annan & Brier, 2010); unemployment; and stress (Catani et al., 2008). In addition, individuals are more likely to perpetrate IPV if they were exposed to conflict early in life (Clark et al., 2010, Gupta et al., 2009). This exposure has been associated with ill mental health. A study including random samples from selected districts exposed to violence revealed that post-traumatic stress disorder was present in 37.4% in Algeria, 28.4% in Cambodia, 15.8% in Ethiopia, and 17.8% in Gaza (Jong et al., 2001). Perpetrators of IPV were found to suffer from mental health problems as much as, or even more than, victims (Verduin et al., 2013). Other studies indicate that war related post-traumatic stress last for several years (Mollica et al., 2001), possibly explaining why DV persists after the war ends.

Involvement in armed conflict, whether current or former combatant, seems to increase the risk of DV perpetration, as reflected by several studies on: male veterans seeking mental health treatment (Teten et al., 2009), military couples (Rentz et al., 2006), military personnel in active duty (Marshall et al., 2005), navy personnel (Fonseca et al., 2006), and reserve soldiers (Schmaling et al., 2011).

However, these findings are not consistent as the study by Tetan et al. revealed that men veterans were more likely also to experience physical and psychological aggression from their female intimate partners (Teten 2009). Moreover, women former combatants had similar rates of experiencing DV to female former non- combatant (Clark 2010) reflecting that engaging in armed conflict is not by itself a determining factor to perpetrate violence.

Survivors

Growing up in a violent environment makes some women more accepting of DV. This is called the 'tolerance effect'. In Peru, exposure to civil war violence, especially during a woman's early life increased the probability that she would later be a victim of DV, made it more likely that she would find men beating women justifiable, and reduced the average time after marriage or union that DV starts occurring. Presumably, this is secondary to war creating alterations in the psychology of young girls, which persists into adulthood (Gallegos & Gutierrez, 2011).

A study in Kosovo found factors associated with DV: living in rural areas; being poor, unemployed or on benefits; and having less than a secondary school education (Farnsworth & Qosaj-Mustafa, 2008). In addition, increased decision-making power within the household for single, never-married Palestinian women is strongly associated with a lower risk of being a survivor of DV (Palestinian Central Bureau of Statistics, 2006). Similar results were not obtained for increased education levels and labour force participation (Assaf & Chaban, 2013).

INTERVENTIONS AND RECOMMENDATIONS

Most interventions that combat the violence to which women are subjected to in times of war address sexual violence or gender based violence perpetrated by armed individuals or non-family members. A meta-analytic review of these interventions with an evaluation of their outcome (Spangaro et al., 2013) revealed that the apparent increases to risk of sexual violence resulted from lack of protection, stigma, and retaliation associated with interventions. Positive outcomes were more related to multiple-component interventions and to sensitive community engagement. Obstacles preventing women from seeking help following sexual violence included lack of anonymity, risking divorce or loss of marriage prospects. The programs that were most successful were the ones that did not rely on the women reporting to be activated.

Based on the above, it becomes clear that addressing DV in times of conflict is difficult. Obstacles include loss of infrastructure and referral guidelines (if ever present during peacetime) that may provide services for violence survivors, and militarization of services which prevent survivors from reporting violence (Dewachi et al., 2014). Additional obstacles could include: language barriers, particularly when the available interpreters are frequently family members; risk of deportation by the abusive partner; lack of familiarity with existing services; or being afraid to be treated with insensitivity, hostility, and/or discrimination. This fear was deemed justified as some mainstream organizations may lack socio-cultural understanding and/or may have discriminatory or insensitive attitudes toward refugees (Runner et al., 2009). Considering the context of a displaced community struggling to survive in what could be a hostile and discriminatory environment, acknowledging IPV as a problem is viewed as detrimental to the collective survival of the community. Therefore, "there is strong pressure to maintain a positive image of their community and remain silent about the problem of IPV" (Runner et al., 2009).

Trials assessing interventions that address DV in conflict are scarce. They mainly focus on empowering women through 'gender dialogue groups' (Gupta et al., 2013) and 'group-based psychosocial counselling' (Manneschmidt & Griese, 2009), but some suggest that there is also value in targeting men for education sessions (Hossain, 2013). However, a comprehensive approach to DV is needed, spanning from working on the risk factors (primary prevention) to assisting survivors (tertiary prevention).

Based on the Ecological Framework, relevant actors—governments, United Nation agencies and non-governmental organisations—can plan strategies that combat DV in wartime using a holistic and multi-pronged approach. In the same way that riverbanks are better built before floods, the suggested measures are better implemented during peacetime to promote the resilience of the population, and help prevent DV (Enarson, 1997).

At the Structural/Environmental Level

- *Promoting a non-violence culture* is essential: This entails advocating for human rights and educating and training on conflict resolution skills, non-discrimination and addressing the needs of minority, vulnerable and refugee populations in a culturally sensitive manner (Levesque, 2001).
- *Involving women in the reconstruction of society post-conflict and in the peace building process* is imperative: The UN Security Council Resolutions 1325 and 2122 aim to strengthen women's roles in conflict prevention and resolution, stating that women need to be protected from gender-based violence and involved in peace making. Gender equality can help prevent not only DV, but also war; gender inequality increases the likelihood that a state will experience internal conflict (Caprioli, 2003).
- *Preventing violence and protecting women is vital.* This is made possible by providing pedestrian and vehicular patrols to vulnerable areas; establishing a system for responding to DV survivors with standard operational procedures to be activated at time of crisis; enacting safety protocols (e.g., firewood patrols or distribution) to reduce vulnerability.
- *Preparing personnel* through the use of codes of conduct, culture sensitive training on attitudes/protocols/responses with military/peacekeepers/police/aid workers; policies to reduce opportunity by personnel for sexual exploitation and abuse; and increased recruitment of female personnel.
- *Building infrastructure* such as water/sanitation facilities; availability of DV shelters and schools for children.
- *Strengthening judicial processes* is crucial. After first recognizing DV as a legal crime, we must act to create mechanisms to ensure that violence doesn't move home when the nation transitions from war to peace, or from revolution to government (Scanlon & Mudell, 2009).

At the Community Level

- *Mobilizing the community* was found to be an effective strategy to combat sexual violence in armed conflict (Spangaro et al., 2013). The protocol for a community mobilization intervention in Uganda to prevent VAW and reduce HIV/AIDS was published (Abramsky et al., 2012), but the results are still pending.
- *Promoting reporting* through establishing referral pathways for survivors; and making these pathways known and accessible.
- *Addressing risk factors* of DV like alcohol and drug abuse
- *Decreasing social isolation* possibly by encouraging the development of support groups within the refugee population. Syrian displaced women recognised that supporting each other was helpful to go through the hardship of displacement (Usta & Masterson, 2012)

At the Relationship Level

- *Educating* both men and women seems to be one of the most potent interventions as reflected from the study done by Hossain (Hossain, 2013). This needs to include education on human rights, literacy programs, gender equality and changing gender roles, and establishing a culture of tolerance and respect for differences as well.

At the Individual Level

- *Responding to survivors* through provision of medical and/or psycho-social care, forensic assessment of survivors and advocacy, a list of interpreters available who can speak the language of potential survivors, and of shelters
- *Promoting livelihood strategies:* Provision of training and/or support (e.g., micro-finance, social skills) to women to increase their economic independence and reduce their vulnerability to violence
- *Initiating combatant-focused initiatives* such as disarmament, demobilisation and reintegration (DDR) programs that aim at reducing sexual violence and rehabilitation of survivors assaulted during capture by combatants; promotion of the engagement with combat leaders
- *Rehabilitating perpetrators* through conflict resolution training programs, anger management, and challenging gender roles/masculinity.

CONCLUSION

Domestic violence is an under recognised problem from which women suffer tremendously during wars. Factors operating during peacetime are magnified during wartime, pushing domestic violence to higher levels. This chapter, we hope, serves as a reminder that although women and children are hit by stray bullets and targeted by opposing troops, they are often hurt by those closest to them, in their own homes. It seems that combating violence in general and advocating for gender equality are logical preventive measures to decrease domestic violence against women. It may be necessary to include domestic violence within the various forms of gender based violence that women suffer from in wars, and incorporate a plan to address it within the GBV response that is usually deployed by the various UN and international agencies active during humanitarian crisis.

ACKNOWLEDGMENT

The authors wish to acknowledge the insightful comments provided by Dr. Nathalia Linos in the writing of this chapter.

REFERENCES

Abramsky, T., Devries, K., Kiss, L., Francisco, L., Nakuti, J., Musuya, T., Kyegombe, N., Starmann, E., Kaye, D., Michau, L. & Watts, C. (2012). A community mobilisation intervention to prevent violence against women and reduce HIV/AIDS risk in Kampala, Uganda (the SASA! Study): study protocol for a cluster randomised controlled trial. *Trials. 13*, 96.

Adelman, M. (2003). The military, militarism, and the militarization of domestic violence. *Violence Against Women. 9*(9), 1118–1152.

Agarwal, B. (1997). 'Bargaining' and gender relations: within and beyond the household. *Feminist Economics. 3*(1), 1-5.

Al-Krenawi, A., Graham, J. R. & Sehwail, M. A. (2007). Tomorrow's players under occupation: an analysis of the association of political violence with psychological functioning and domestic violence, among palestinian youth. *Am J Orthopsychiatry., 77*, 427–433.

Annan, J. & Brier, M. (2010). The risk of return: intimate partner violence in Northern Uganda's armed conflict. *Social Science and Medicine. 70*, 152-159.

Archer, J. (2000). Sex differences in aggression between heterosexual partners: A meta-analytic review. *Psychological Bulletin. 126*, 651-680.

Assaf, S. & Chaban, S. (2013). Domestic violence against single, never-married women in the Occupied Palestinian Territory. *Violence against Women, 19*, 422-441.

Avdibegovic, E. & Sinanovic, O. (2006). Consequences of domestic violence on women's mental health in Bosnia and Herzegovina. *Croatian Medical Journal., 47*, 730-741.

Bartels, S., Van Rooyen, M., Leaning, J., Scott, J. & Kelly, J. (2010). Now, the world is without me: an investigation of sexual violence in Eastern Democratic Republic of Congo. *Harvard Humanitarian Initiative Report, with support from Oxfam America.*

Bastick, M., Grimm, K. & Kunz, R. (2007). Sexual violence in armed conflict: global overview and implications for the security sector. *Geneva Centre for the Democratic Control of Armed Forces.*

Byrne, B. (1996). Towards a gendered understanding of conflict. *IDS Bull*, 27-31.

Caprioli, M. (2003). *Gender equality and civil wars.* Available from: http://siteresources. worldbank.org/INTCPR/214578-1111996036679/20482367/ WP8trxtsep3.pdf World Bank Conflict Prevention and Reconstruction Unit, Working Paper No. 8. World Bank, Washington.

Catani, C., Jacob, N., Schauer, E., Kohila, M. & Neuner, F. (2008). Family violence, war, and natural disasters: A study of the effect of extreme stress on children's mental health in Sri Lanka. *BMC Psychiatry, 8*(1), 33.Catani, C., Schauer, E., Elbert, T., Missmahl, I., Bette. J. P. & Neuner, F. (2009). War trauma, child labor, and family violence: life adversities and PTSD in a sample of school children in Kabul. *Journal of Trauma Stress, 22*, 163–71.

Clark, C. J., Everson-Rose, S. A., Suglia, S. F., Btoush, R., Alonso, A. & Haj-Yahia, M. M. (2010). Association between exposure to political violence and intimate-partner violence in the occupied Palestinian territory: a cross-sectional study. *Lancet, 375*, 310–16.

Coker, A. L. & Richter, D. L. (1998). Violence against women in Sierra Leone: frequency and correlates of intimate partner violence and forced sexual intercourse. *African Journal of Reproductive Health, 2,* 61-72.

Coomaraswamy, R. (2002). Commission on Human Rights, Special Rapporteur on Violence against Women, Integration of the Human Rights of Women and the Gender Perspective, 57. *U.N. Economic & Social Council. Doc. E/CN.4/2001/73*

Cotter, J. (2002). War and domestic violence. www.redcritique.org/SeptOct02/printversions/ waranddomesticviolenceprint.htm. Red Critique.

Dakkad, H. (2007). Tackling sexual violence, abuse and exploitation. *Forced Migration Review, Special issue.* 39-40.

Depoortere, E., Checci, F., Broillet, F., Gerstl, S., Minetti, A., Gayraud, O., Briet, V., Pahl, J., Defourny, I., Tatay, M. & Brown, V. (2004). Violence and mortality in West Darfur, Sudan (2003-2004): Epidemological evidence from four surveys. *Lancet, 364,* 1315-1320.

Dewachi, O., Skelton, M., Nguyen, V. K., Fouad, F., Sbu Setaa, G., Maasri, Z. & Giacaman, R. (2014) Changing therapeutic geographies of the Iraqi and Syrian wars. Health in the Arab world: a view from within. *Lancet. 383,* 449–57.

El Jack, A. (2003) Gender and armed conflict. Bridge. *Brighton, England: University of Sussex.*

Enarson, E. (1997). Responding to domestic violence and disaster: Guidelines for Women's Services and Disaster Practitioners. *BC Institute against Family Violence.*

Farnsworth, N. & Qosaj-Mustafa, A. (2008). Security begins at home: research to inform the first national strategy and action plan against domestic violence in Kosovo. *Prishtina, Kosovo, the Kosova Women's Network.*

Farnsworth, N., Qosaj-Mustafa, A., Ekonomi, M., Shima, A. & Dauti-Kadriu. D. for the Kosova Women's Network. (2012). *At what cost? Budgeting for the implementation of the legal framework against domestic violence in Kosovo.* United Nations Development Programme.

Fisher, C. (2013). Changed and changing gender and family roles and domestic violence in African refugee background communities post-settlement in Perth, Australia. *Violence against Women., 19,* 833-847.

Fonseca, C. A., Schmaling, K. B., Stoever, C., Gutierrez, C., Blume, A. W. & Russell, M. L. (2006). Variables associated with intimate partner violence in a deploying military sample. *Military Medicine., 171,* 627–631.

Gallegos, J. V. & Gutierrez I. A. (2011). The effect of civil conflict on domestic violence: the case of Peru. *SSRN Working Paper Series,* 1-29.

Garcia-Moreno, C., Jansen, H. A. F. M., Watts, C., Ellsberg, M. C. & Heise, L. (2005). *WHO multi-country study on women's health and domestic violence against women: Initial results on prevalence, health outcomes and women's responses.* World Health Organisation.

Geneva Declaration. (2011a). Chapter 3: *Armed violence after war: categories, causes, and consequences.* Global Burden of Armed Violence.

Geneva Declaration. (2011b). Chapter 4: *When the victim is a woman.* Global Burden of Armed Violence.

Gupta, J., Acevedo-Garcia, D., Hemenway, D., Decker, M. R., Raj, A. & Silverman, J. G. (2009). Premigration exposure to political violence and perpetration of intimate partner violence among immigrant men in Boston. *American Journal of Public Health*, *99*(3), 462.

Gupta, J., Falb, K. L., Lehmann, H., Kpebo, D., Xuan, Z., Hossain M., Zimmerman, C., Watts, C. & Annan, J. (2013). Gender norms and economic empowerment intervention to reduce intimate partner violence against women in rural Côte d'Ivoire: a randomized controlled pilot study. *BMC International Health and Human Rights*, *13*, 46.

Haider, H. (2009). Helpdesk Research Report: Conflict and sexual and domestic violence against women. Governance and Social Development Resource Centre.

Heise, L. (1998). Violence against women: An integrated, ecological framework. *Violence against Women. 4*(3), 262-290.

Hossain, M. (2013). *Working with men to prevent violence against women in a conflict-affected setting: A cluster RCT of a male-focused IPV prevention intervention in rural Cote d'Ivoire.* SVRI Forum.

Human Rights Watch. (2000). *Seeking protection: Addressing sexual and domestic violence in Tanzania's refugee camps.* New York: Human Rights Watch.

Human Rights Watch. (2003). Trapped by inequality: Bhutanese refugee women in Nepal. *New York: Human Rights Watch.*

Human Rights Watch. (2006). A question of security: violence against Palestinian women and girls. *New York: Human Rights Watch.*

Hynes, M., Robertson, K., Ward, J. & Crouse, C. (2004). A determination of the prevalence of gender-based violence among conflict-affected populations in East Timor. *Disasters*, *28*, 294-321.

Jok, J. M. (1999). Militarization and gender violence in South Sudan. *Journal of Asian and African Studies*, *34*(4), 427–442.

Jones, A. (2013). *War against women at home and abroad.* http://www.thenation.com/article/173463/war-against-women-home-and-abroad. The Nation.

Jong, J. T., Komproe, I. H., Van Ommeren, M., El Masri, M., Araya, M., Khaled, N., van de Put, W. & Somasundarum, D. (2001). Lifetime events and posttraumatic stress disorder in four postconflict settings. *Journal of the American Medical Association*, *286*(5), 555–562.

Khawaja, M. (2004). Domestic violence in refugee camps in Jordan. *International Journal of Gynaecology & Obstetrics*, *86*, 67-69.

Khawaja, M. & Barazi, R. (2005). Prevalence of wife beating in Jordanian refugee camps: Reports by men and women. *Journal of Epidemiology & Community Health*, *59*, 840-841.

Kishor, S. & Johnson, K. (2004). Profiling domestic violence: A multi-country study. *Calverton, Maryland: ORC Macro.*

Koenig, M. A., Stephenson, R., Ahmed, S., Jejeebhoy, S. J. & Campbell, J. (2006). Individual and contextual determinants of domestic violence in North India. *American Journal of Public Health*, *96*(1), 132-138.

Krug, E. G., Mercy, J. A., Dahlberg, L. L. & Zwi, A. B. (2002). The world report on violence and health. *Lancet*, *360*, 1083–88.

La Mattina, G. (2013). *Armed conflict and domestic violence: evidence from Rwanda.* Working Paper.

Leaning, J., Bartels, S. & Mowafi, H. (2009). Sexual violence during war and forced migration. In M. S. Forbes & J. Tirman, *Women, migration and conflict: breaking a deadly cycle*. Washington DC: Springer, 173-199.

Levesque, R. J. R. (2001). Culture and family violence: Fostering change through human rights law. *Law and public policy*. Washington D.C., US: American Psychological Association.

Loue, S. (2001) Intimate partner violence: societal, medical, legal and individual responses. New York: Kluwer Academic/Plenium Publishers.

Manneschmidt, S. & Griese, K. (2009). Evaluating psychosocial group counselling with Afghan women: is this a useful intervention? *Torture*, *19*(1), 41-50.

Marshall, A. D., Panuzio, J. & Taft, C. T. (2005). Intimate partner violence among military veterans and active duty servicemen. *Clinical Psychology Review*, *25*, 862–876.

Mollica, R. F., Sarajlic, N., Chernoff, M., Lavelle, J., Vukovic, I. S. & Massagli, M. P. (2001). Longitudinal study of psychiatric symptoms, disability, mortality, and emigration among Bosnian refugees. *Journal of the American Medical Association*, *286*(5), 546–554.

Munn, J. (2008). The hegemonic male and Kosovar nationalism, 2000-2005. *Men and Masculinities*. *10*, 4.

Murthy R.S. & Lakshminarayana R. (2006). Mental health consequences of war: a brief review of research findings. *World Psychiatry*, *5*(1), 25–30.

Nikolic-Ristanovic, R. (2000). Domestic violence against women in the conditions of war and economic crisis. *In 'Women, violence and war: wartime victimzation of refugees in the Balkans'*.

Onyango, G., Atyam, A., Arwi, C., Acan, G. (2005). Girl mothers of Northern Uganda. Paper presented at the conference on 'Girl mothers in fighting forces and their post-war reintegration in Southern and Western Africa. *Bellagio, Italy*.

Orend, B. (2005). War. *Stanford Encyclopedia of Philosophy*. plato.stanford.edu/entries/war.

Palestinian Central Bureau of Statistics. (2006). Violence against women in Palestinian society: Domestic violence survey 2005/2006. *Palestinian National Authority*, *3*, 5.

Paudel, G. S. (2007). Domestic violence against women in Nepal. *Gender Technology and Development*. *11*(2), 199–233.

Pittaway, E. (2004). *The ultimate betrayal: An examination of the experiences of domestic and family violence in refugee communities*. Occasional Paper Center for Refugee Research, University of New South Wales, Australia.

Pittaway, E. & Rees, S. (2006). Multiple jeopardy: domestic violence and the notion of cumulative risk for women in refugee camps. *Women against Violence*, *18*, 18-25.

Rajasingham-Senanayake, D. (2004). Between reality and representation: women's agency in war and post-conflict Sri Lanka. *Cultural Dynamics*. *16*, 141–168

Rehn, E. & Johnson-Sirleaf, E. (2002). Chapter 1: violence against women, in 'women, war and peace: the independent expert's assessment on the impact of armed conflict on women and women's role in peace building', *UNIFEM* p. 14

Rentz, E., Martin, S., Gibbs, D., Clinton-Sherrod, M., Hardison, J. & Marshall, S. (2006). Family violence in the military: A review of the literature. *Trauma, Violence & Abuse.*, *7*, 93-108.

Runner, M., Yoshihama, M. & Novick, S. (2009). Intimate partner violence in immigrants and refugees communities: challenges, promising practices and recommendations. *Family Violence Prevention Fund. Robert Wood Johnson Foundation*.

Scanlon, H. & Muddell, K. (2009). Gender and transitional justice in Africa: Progress and prospects. *International Center for Transitional Justice.*

Schmaling, K. B., Blume, A. W. & Russell, M. L. (2011). Intimate partner violence and relationship dissolution among reserve soldiers. *Military Psychology.*, *23*, 685-699.

Skjelsbaek, I. (2001). Sexual violence in times of war: a new challenge for peace operations?, in 'Women and International Peacekeeping, Olsson, L. and Tryggestad, T.L. eds. *Routledge*, 69-84

Smith, L. (1989). Domestic violence: an overview of the literature. *Home Office Research and Planning Unit, London*

Spangaro, J., Adogu, C., Ranmuthugala, G., Powell-Davies, G., Steinacker, L. & Zwi, A. (2013) What evidence exists for initiatives to reduce risk and incidence of sexual violence in armed conflict and other humanitarian crises? A systematic review. *PLoS ONE 8*(5), e62600.

Stark, L., Roberts, L., Wheaton, W., Acham, A., Boothby, N. & Ager, A. (2010). Measuring violence against women amidst war and displacement in northern Uganda using the 'neighborhood method'. *J Epidemiol Community Health.*, *64*(12), 1056–1061.

Stark, L. & Ager, A. (2011). A systematic review of prevalence studies of gender based violence in complex emergencies. *Trauma, Violence & Abuse.*, *12*, 127–134.

Stark, L. & Wessels, M. (2012). Sexual violence as a weapon of war. *Journal of the American Medical Association.*, *308*(7), 677-8

Tappis, H., Biermann, E., Glass, N. & Doocy, S. (2012). Domestic violence among Iraqi refugees in Syria. *Health Care for Women International. 33*, 285-297.

Teten, A. L., Schumacher, J. A., Taft, C. T., Stanley, M. A., Kent, T. A., Bailey, S. D. & White, D. L. (2009). Intimate partner aggression perpetrated and sustained by male Afghanistan, Iraq, and Vietnam veterans with and without posttraumatic stress disorder. *Journal of Interpersonal Violence. 9*, 1612-163

Ulltveit-Moe, T. (2004). Lives blown apart: crimes against women in times of conflict: stop violence against women. *Amnesty International, London.*

UNFPA. (2001). The Impact of Conflict on Women and Girls: A UNFPA Strategy for Gender Mainstreaming in Areas of Conflict and Reconstruction.

UNFPA. (2006). Women are the Fabric, Reproductive Health for Communities in crisis-Addressing Sexual Violence.

Usta, J., Farver, J. A. & Zein, L. (2008). Women, war, and violence: surviving the experience. *J Women's Health. 17*, 793-804.

Usta, J. & Masterson, A. R. (2012). Assessment of reproductive health and gender based violence among displaced Syrian women in Lebanon. *UNFPA.* [http://data.unhcr.org/syrianrefugees/download. php?id=980]

Van Herp M., Parque, V., Rackley, E. & Ford, N. (2003). Mortality, violence, and lack of access to health care in the Democratic Republic of Congo. *Disasters.*, *27*(2), 141-153.

Verduin, F., Engelhard, E. A. N., Rutayisire, T., Stronks, K, & Scholte, W. F. (2013). Intimate partner violence in Rwanda: the mental health of victims and perpetrators. *J Interpers Violence.*, *28*, 1839-1858.

Waldmann, P. (2007). Is there a culture of violence in Colombia? *International Journal of Conflict and Violence. 1*(1), 61–75.

Ward, J. (2002). If not now, when? Addressing gender-based violence in refugee, internally displaced, and post-conflict settings: a global overview. *New York: the Reproductive Health for Refugees Consortium.*

Ward, J. & Vann, B. (2002). Gender-based violence in refugee settings. *Lancet. 360*, s13-14.

Wilkens, A., Strand, L., Shoukeh, N. & Fathallah, S. K. (2010). Links between domestic violence and armed conflict: Report from a Field Trip in Lebanon March 7-17. *Kvinna till Kvinna, Lebanon.*

World Health Organization. (2007). Ethical and Safety Recommendations for researching, documenting and monitoring sexual violence in emergencies. http://www.who.int/gender/ documents/EthicsSafety_web.pdf. *Geneva: World Health Organisation.*

Zimmerman, K. (1995). Plates in a basket will rattle: domestic violence in Cambodia: a summary. *Phnom Penh, Project Against Domestic Violence.*

In: Overcoming Domestic Violence   ISBN: 978-1-63321-956-4
Editors: Myra F. Taylor, Julie Ann Pooley et al.   © 2015 Nova Science Publishers, Inc.

Chapter 14

VIOLENCE AGAINST WOMEN IN SCENARIOS OF SERIOUS ECONOMIC CRISIS

Victoria A. Ferrer-Perez[*] *and Esperanza Bosch-Fiol*
University of Balearic Islands, Spain

ABSTRACT

Violence against women (VAW) and particularly intimate partner violence against women (IPVAW) are health problems of epidemic and global proportions. An in-depth study conducted by the United Nations in 2006 revealed that the violence that was perpetrated on victims of VAW and IPVAW are grounded within a human rights framework a historical unequal expression of power relations between women and men: "*Women's economic inequalities and discrimination against women in areas such as employment, income, access to other economic resources and lack of economic independence reduce women's capacity to act and take decisions, and increase their vulnerability to violence*" and "*policies such as structural adjustment, deregulation of economies and privatization of the public sector have tended to reinforce women's economic and social inequality, especially within marginalized communities*". Using data from Spain, this chapter reflects on and identifies indicators that help to establish the impact that economic crisis scenarios have on IPVAW, both epidemiologically (in terms of possible changes in the incidence and prevalence of violence) and at an individual level (in terms of the effects on the health and quality of life of women).

Keywords: Violence against women, intimate partner violence against women, economic crisis effects.

Violence against women (VAW) and particularly intimate partner violence against women (IPVAW) are health problems of epidemic and global proportions (FRA, 2014; García-Moreno, Jansen, Ellsberg, Heise, & Watts, 2006; Hagemann-White, 2001; Heise &

---
[*] Corresponding author: Dr. Victoria A. Ferrer-Pérez, University lecturer, Faculty of Psychology, University of Balearic Islands, Spain – 07122. Tel. 00 34 971 17 34 80. Email: victoria.ferrer@uib.es.

García-Moreno, 2002; Krahé, Bieneck, & Möller, 2005; Kury, Obergfell-Fuchs, & Woessner, 2004; UN, 2006; WHO, 2013). However, documenting the magnitude of VAW and IPVAW and producing reliable comparative data to guide policy and monitor process has been difficult (DeVries et al., 2013a). For instance, the multi-country study conducted by the World Health Organization (García-Moreno et al., 2006) concluded that between 15%-75% of women experience physical and/or sexual violence at the hands of an intimate partner at some time during their lives. In Europe VAW and IPVAW violence affects close to 25% of women at some time in their lives (Hagemann-White, 2001; Kury et al., 2004). In a recent report, the WHO (2013) estimated that between 19.3% (in Western Europe) and 27.9% (in Central Europe) of ever partnered women report lifetime intimate partner violence experience in European countries. In this regard, an even more recent report (FRA, 2014), based on interviews with 42,000 women across 28 member states of the European Union (EU), reveals that of all women who have a (current or previous) partner 22% have experienced physical and/or sexual partner violence since the age of 15 (8% by a current partner, 26% by a previous partner).

As far as Spain is concerned, different surveys (see Medina-Ariza & Barberet, 2003; Ministry of Health, Social Affairs, and Equality, 2012; National Health Survey, 2006) show considerable variability (Ferrer, Bosch, & Riera, 2006) demonstrate that between 11%-25% of Spanish women have experienced IPVAW at some time in their lives, and between 3%-15% have experienced IPVAW in the last year. These findings resemble those of a recent EU report (FRA, 2014) which showed that in Spain of all women who have a (current or previous) partner, 13% have experienced physical and/or sexual partner violence by a partner since the age of 15 (4% by a current partner, 18% by a previous partner).

Additionally, data is available on formal complaints filed and the number of women killed as a result of IPVAW. In this sense, Spanish police have compiled data on formal complaints filed since 1984 and these data have begun to be systematically analysed up to 1992 (Acale, 1999). Initially the body in charge of systematizing this information was the Women's Institute, but in 2006 the State Observatory on Violence against Women took over this task and drew up new indicators for compiling information (Women's Institute, 2008).

Data analysis revealed that the number of formal complaints filed over the intervening years has risen substantially, going from 11,516 reports in 1983 to 128,543 in 2012 (GCJ, 2012a; GDGV, 2013; Women's Institute, 2008). Aside from a possible rise in the number of cases, the reasons for this variability has not only to do with the diversity of criteria and procedures for compiling information (Ferrer et al., 2006), but also to legislative changes, changes in Spanish attitudes towards IPVAW and changes in the Spanish demographic profile.

Another important indicator in determining the magnitude of IPVAW is the number of women killed at the hands of their intimate partners. On this matter too there has been data variability and major controversy as to the most appropriate criteria and methodology for their collection (Ferrer et al., 2006; Stockl et al., 2013). The global systematic review carried out by the WHO (Stockl et al., 2013; WHO, 2013) included available data from 66 countries. Across these countries, 13.5% of all homicides were committed by an intimate partner and 38.6% of female homicides were perpetrated by an intimate partner. In Spain, the work carried out by the State Observatory on Violence against Women (GDGV, 2013; Women's Institute, 2008) has produced data dating back to 1999. This Spanish homicide data reveals that between 1999 and 2013, 931 women died at the hands of their intimate partners or ex–

partners (62 women are killed annually [with female homicides ranging from 50 in 2001 to 76 in 2008]).

In summary, the findings from the different national surveys and other sources demonstrate that in Spain the levels of IPVAW are similar to the levels documented in other countries for women from a similar cultural and economic background. Hence, IPVAW is considered a serious social problem (Medina-Ariza & Barberet, 2003; WHO, 2013).

CAUSES OF VIOLENCE: THE ROLE OF ECONOMIC INEQUALITIES

In the analysis of VAW and, particularly, of IPVAW, different explanatory models have been put forward. Initially, unicausal models were used. These models sought to determine the origin of VAW and IPVAW violence by examining the individual characteristics of the persons who committed it and/or experienced the violence in its many forms (such as personality, socio-economic situation or stress). Subsequently, broader explanations were used, including sociological (e.g., the perspective of violence, family conflict, the feminist perspective) or psychological theories (e.g., theory of social learning, of exchange, of stress) (Bosch & Ferrer, 2002).

Currently, there is a broad consensus that the analysis of VAW/IPVAW violence must be approached using multicausal models. These models consider VAW to be a complex phenomenon that can only be explained by the intervention of a set of specific factors in the general context of power inequalities between men and women on an individual, group, national and world scale (Rodríguez-Menés & Safranoff, 2012; UN, 2006). Some of these models would be, for instance, those formulated by Stith and Farley (1993), O'Neil and Harway (1999), or Heise (1998).

Based on a feminist interpretive framework (De Miguel, 2005), and along the lines of developing multivariate models round patriarchy, the present research proposes the pyramidal model which is applicable to both VAW in general and IPVAW in heterosexual partners (Bosch & Ferrer, 2013; Bosch, Ferrer, Ferreiro, & Navarro, 2013). This model includes some elements present in the aforementioned multicausal models and, also, provides additional key explanations. To be precise, it proposes that VAW would occur after and aggressor's violence would escalate across five stages (patriarchal background, differential socialization, expectations of control, trigger events, and the violence itself). Also, it proposes that a filtering process would explain what happens with men who have experienced the same patriarchal background and have been exposed to the same keys of socialization, yet who do not exercise this violence. On the other hand, the pyramid model proposes that men who fully adopt patriarchal power relations and are convinced of the privileges afforded by their gender would only need a spark (or trigger event) in order to resort to violence.

Some of these trigger events, particularly those of a personal nature (e.g., mental illness, life events, abuse of drugs or alcohol), have in turn been considered to be in themselves causes of gender-based violence (i.e., as unicausal psychiatric models) (Blázquez, Moreno, & García-Baamonde, 2010). However, currently available evidence (Foran & O'Leary, 2008; WHO, 2006) points towards these personal factors not representing causal factors of VAW, but rather they are enablers or dis-inhibitors of VAW (Gil, Vives-Cases, Alvárez-Dardet, & Latour, 2006).

Within the context of the pyramidal model, it is suggested that IPVAW trigger events activate the aggressor's fear of losing control over their partner (Chant, 2001) and/or legitimises their violent behaviour towards the victim. Hence, in certain situations triggers act as *excuses* for the abuser to start using control strategies (and violence) that they consider legitimate to use. Thus, the list of these possible events is very long and includes various types of events:

- Personal events: such as abuse of alcohol or other drugs; mental illness; circumstances that increase stress or generate frustration, like marriage, separation, birth of a son/daughter, labour difficulties, economic conflicts in the household, or demands for greater independence by the woman; unpredictable situations, such as changes in life events, illnesses, etc.
- Social events: such as legislative modifications; economic crises; changes in social model; etc.
- Political-religious events: such as religious fundamentalism; coming to power of ultra-conservative governments; etc.

THE CRISIS AND ITS REPERCUSSIONS ON GENDER EQUALITY IN SPAIN

The world economic crisis that began in late 2007 has had serious repercussions on a large part of the world, particularly southern Europe including Spain. Initially, the consequences of the crisis were essentially macroeconomic (mainly as a result of a reduction in employment and increase in the number of unemployed people). However, the bursting of the real estate bubble and adjustments by Spanish governments since 2010 demanded by the European Commission, the Central European Bank and the International Monetary Fund have led to the restructuring of economic policy, social cover, public services, the tax system and the labour market (Beteta, 2013). All this has gradually resulted in the dismantling of the welfare state. (For a detailed analysis of what these adjustments have involved and their effects, see Economists deal with the crisis, 2012; Spanish Economic and Social Council, 2012).

The effects of the crisis and ensuing adjustments have had a particular impact on women and equality (Beteta, 2013; Castro, 2013). In short, there has been a reduction in or the elimination of what were regarded to have been well-established employment and social rights, and this is resulting in a growth in poverty, social exclusion and inequality in Spain (Brunel, 2013). Evidently, this scenario of crisis and cuts affects the whole of the Spanish population, but the impact is higher for women, given that they started out from a weaker social and economic position (Beteta, 2013). This initial weak position and also the first effects of the crisis and ensuing cuts are reflected by different indexes, such as the *Gender Equality Index* (EIGE, 2013) or the *Global Gender Gap Index* (WEF, 2013).These indexes show that, as occurs in the rest of the world's countries, although formal equality can be a reality in legislation, genuine or effective equality in Spanish society has far from been achieved as yet. These indexes also suggests that austerity policies and cuts in public spending in Spain that were supposedly applied to counteract the economic crisis are a threat to equal opportunities between men and women since, in general terms, they have increased the gender gap.

THE IMPACT OF ECONOMIC FACTORS ON THE IPVAW

As the *In-depth study on all forms of violence against women* (UN, 2006) points out, the central premise of an analysis of this violence within a human rights framework is grounded in the fact that such violence is an expression of historically unequal power relations between women and men but:

> "women's economic inequalities and discrimination against women in areas such as employment, income, access to other economic resources and lack of economic independence reduce women's capacity to act and take decisions, and increase their vulnerability to violence… Women's lack of economic empowerment, also reflected in lack of access to and control over economic resources in the form of land, personal property, wages and credit, can place them at increased risk of violence" (…) "While economic independence does not shield women from violence, access to economic resources can enhance women's capacity to make meaningful choices, including escaping violent situations and accessing mechanisms for protection and redress" (…) and "policies such as structural adjustment, deregulation of economies and privatization of the public sector have tended to reinforce women's economic and social inequality, especially within marginalized communities" (p. 32).

In this regard, it is important to note that inequality in the access to resources (denying access to money, preventing access to education/training or to a job) may be considered, in itself, a form of violence (economic) against women (Council of Europe, 2011).

What is more, this inequality may also increase women's susceptibility to violence and abuse, and perpetuate the situation of violence by curbing women's initiative to put an end to it (Beteta, 2013). In the specific case of IPVAW, among the diverse reasons as to why women do not break off their relationship with a partner who assaults them and/or do not report the violence they are experiencing would be fear of the aggressor, lack of trust in the legal system, shame, social tolerance towards abuse, and difficulty in seeing themselves as victims; but also their economic dependence on the aggressor (Amor & Echeburúa, 2010; Ferrer et al., 2006; Menéndez, Pérez, & Lorence, 2013; Watts & Zimmerman, 2002), either due to want of a job or their own economic resources, or because of a lack of housing, or other circumstances. By way of example, in a study conducted among 600 women victims of IPVAW who had resorted in Spain to a temporary employment agency in search of employment, 64% stated that the crisis had curbed their desire to report the violence they were experiencing in the fear of finding themselves without employment or resources (ADECCO, 2012).

That is to say, the greater vulnerability of the victims brought about by the economic crisis could result in a decrease in the number of complaints filed and/or increase in the refusal to go ahead with the legal process involved in withdrawing the complaint (GCJ, 2012b). Both elements would contribute to increasing the hidden pocket of abuse, and to the invisibilisation of this serious social problem. Along these lines, it is important to take into account the fact that, although the approach to VAW within the framework of human rights ought to be comprehensive, governments rarely include socio-economic factors in their legislative and policy responses to this violence (Ertürk, 2009).

In Spain, on the other hand, one of the instruments in the fight against IPVAW provided for in Organic Act 1/2004 on Integral Protection Measures against Gender Violence were precisely a battery of measures of economic support in order to provide women victims of this violence with minimum subsistence resources that would enable them to become economically independent of their abuser and manage to break the economic control this person could be exercising over them (measures such as the possibility of obtaining an unemployment subsidy even if they had given up their job voluntarily, the justification of possible non-attendance due to the abuse, ease of geographical mobility, or specific labour insertion programmes) (Llop, 2013).

However, the implementation of these measures reached a very small number of women. For instance, between 2007 and 2011 only 110,022 female victims of IPVAW were able to benefit from measures such as Active Insertion Income (106,761 women), subsidised contracts (1,958 women) or the aid specified in article 27 of Organic Act 1/2004 (1,303 women) (GDGV, 2013). Although the data are not strictly comparable, some insight into the coverage afforded by these measures can be gained if we take into account the fact that they reached only 16.6% of the women who reported IPVAW during this period.

Subsequently there have been cutbacks in equality policies and in those specifically aimed at VAW and IPVAW (Beteta, 2013), including: reduction of actions for socio-labour reinsertion of women victims of violence; closure of offices providing information and care for victims; elimination of support programmes; or reduction or elimination of sensitisation, prevention and intervention programmes. For instance, the budget for the initiative, *Actions for the comprehensive prevention of gender-based violence* received a 28% cutback in the Spanish Budget between 2011 and 2013 (from 30.4 to 21.9 million euros).

Nevertheless, not only are economic cutbacks important, but so can ideological reversals (such as questioning whether IPVAW is, in fact, gender-based violence and, therefore, the social inequalities that are the result of a patriarchal society) come to have devastating effects, including decreased social sensitisation, reduced willingness of women to report, or reversals in terms of prevention. A thorough analysis of this issue goes beyond the purposes of this study, but a review of newspaper archives gives a good account of this.

Faced with this situation, different voices in Spain and, most especially, feminist organisations and the Observatory against Domestic and Gender Violence of the General Council of the Judiciary (GCJ) have warned of the possible effects of the cutbacks on VAW and IPVAW arising from austerity policies.

In this context, this section reflects on and seeks to identify indicators that can help us to establish the impact that economic crisis scenarios have on IPVAW, both epidemiologically (in terms of possible changes in the incidence and prevalence of this violence) and at an individual level (in terms of the effects on the health and quality of life of women who suffer from it).

With this aim in mind we use by way of example the data available for the period 2007-2013 regarding some indicators of VAW and of the response of the states proposed by the UN (Ertürk, 2008), by gathering the most up-to-date information available in each case and always bearing in mind the fact that IPVAW is a hidden crime - that is, an *iceberg* phenomenon which is proportionately barely visible in relation to its occurrence - wherefore the real figures concerning its incidence are difficult to know (Ferrer et al., 2006; Gracia, 2009; Menéndez et al., 2013).

SURVEYS CONCERNING IPVAW

Finding out the proportion of the female population who have ever experienced violence in their life and in the last 12 months is one of the basic indicators in order to assess the magnitude of VAW and IPVAW, and the best way to obtain these data is through population surveys (Ertürk, 2008).

In this regard, and as mentioned above, in Spain different surveys have been conducted (Medina-Ariza & Barberet, 2003; National Health Survey, 2006) but, out of all of these, the ones that are particularly interesting for the purposes of this chapter are the macro surveys (Ministry of Health, Social Affairs, and Equality, 2012), since by offering data corresponding to four different times, they enable us to carry out a comparative analysis and also to observe certain possible reflections of the economic crisis in the labour situation of the women interviewed.

Hence, on the one hand, these surveys show that among the women who claim to have experienced this violence, the proportion of these who were in paid employment (35.9% in 1999, 43.2% in 2002, 53.4% in 2006 and 46.0% in 2011) was greater than all the women surveyed in all cases. Another interesting fact is the presence of unemployed women, who out of all the women surveyed amounted to 7.7% in 2006 and 17.2% in 2011; yet among those who had experienced abuse at some time in their life, this amounted to 11.6% in 2006 and 25.8% in 2011. Finally, the macro survey conducted in 2011 reveals that by analysing abused women according to their labour situation, the greatest proportion of abused women are among the unemployed (16.3%) and the least among students (4.6%); meanwhile, the greatest proportion of women who had left abuse was among pensioners and those who found paid employment (80.0% and 75.2%, respectively) and the least was among those who were engaged in domestic or unpaid work (55.0%).

In short, these data could suggest either that occupational activity involves a new awareness of IPVAW, or that suffering this violence stimulates or necessitates the women that suffer it to find a job so that they are not dependent financially on their aggressors (Ministry of Health, Social Affairs, and Equality, 2012).

FORMAL COMPLAINTS DUE TO IPVAW

During the period between 2007 and 2012, 800,608 formal complaints for IPVAW were filed in Spain (that is, an average of 133,435 complaints per year or 366 complaints per day) (GCJ, 2012a; GDGV, 2013). Figure 1 presents the annual distribution of these formal complaints and the rate per million women over 15 years of age that they represent.

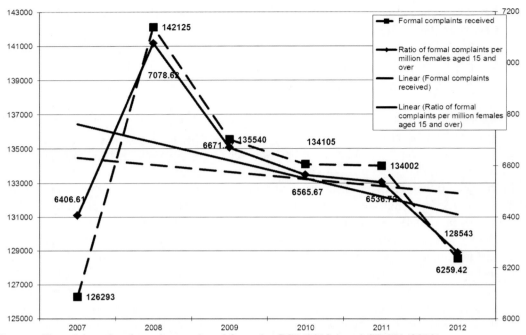

Source: Own elaboration from data retrieved from the GCJ (2012a) and GDGV (2013).

Figure 1. Formal complaints of IPVAW by year.

A retrospective analysis reveals that the number and rate of formal complaints made due to IPVAW has increased considerably in Spain in recent decades. Hence, for the period 1997-2000, one in 200 Spanish women over 17 years of age filed a complaint for this reason (Vives-Cases, Álvarez-Dardet, & Caballero, 2003). According to other estimates (Ferrer et al., 2006) at the beginning of the 1990s there was in Spain a rate of 854 complaints filed per year for IPVAW per million women, which rose to 1,160 complaints filed per million at the beginning of the 2000s, and reached 2,868 complaints filed per million in 2005; that is, this rate trebled in Spain over 15 years. Furthermore, as can be observed in Figure 1, this rate doubled once again (reaching around 6,500 complaints per million) during the first decade of the 21st century. In relation to these data, it is worth remembering that a higher rate of complaints can be interpreted as a sign of women's greater trust in the state to combat the violence, greater exercise of the right to redress, or less tolerance towards this violence; although it may also be a fruit of improvements in procedures for filing or collecting complaints (Ertürk, 2008).

Nevertheless, and despite this upward trend, if we limit ourselves to the period between 2007 and 2013, we observe how both indicators (especially the rate of formal complaints filed) tend to decrease. Particularly notable is the fact that between 2007 and 2008 a rise of 12.5% occurred in the number of complaints filed due to IPVAW, however, since this point of inflection, this number has continually decreased (4.6% in 2009, 1.1% in 2010, 0.1% in 2011 and 4.1% in 2012). In fact, if the numbers of complaints for the first quarter of 2013 are maintained (60,981), a new drop will occur (5.1%). Although the period of time analysed is short, it would have been expected that, should the previous conditions have been maintained (of social awareness, support to victims, etc.) the number of complaints filed due to IPVAW would have continued to rise progressively. Instead, the reduction in the number of complaints filed may be an indication that cutbacks in social protection are dissuading women from filing a complaint, because of the fear of not receiving economic aid or physical protection from IPVAW (Beteta, 2013).

A basic indicator of process in this field is the number of women who abandon or withdraw their complaint (Ertürk, 2008). Figure 2 presents this data along with the percentage they represent relative to the total complaints filed.

As can be observed, throughout the period analysed, abandonments have steadily increased, both in absolute numbers (with a rise of 22.7% between 2007 and 2012), and in relation to the total number of complaints filed (in 2007 abandonments amounted to 10.1% of the total complaints filed and in 2012 they amounted to 12.0%). It is important to clarify that the GCJ (2012c) considers an abandonment the manifestation of the IPVAW victim's will for the legal proceeding initiated against their abuser not to go ahead (which is known in non-legal fields as a withdrawal of the complaint). Although the withdrawal, by itself, need not necessarily affect the legal proceeding, in a significant proportion of cases when the victim abandons proceedings or the proceedings are stopped or finalised with no punishment for the aggressor, however, in accordance with current legislation, in many cases, a woman victim who does not go ahead with the complaint process cannot gain access to the (little) aid available.

Another issue of interest concerns restraining orders that are initiated and adopted (Figure 3). A restraining order is a legal ruling when there is well-founded evidence of IPVAW and an objective situation of risk to the victim; it establishes a statute of comprehensive protection of victims and orders their protection through the adoption, by the same court, of criminal and civil injunctions, whilst also activating other social welfare measures.

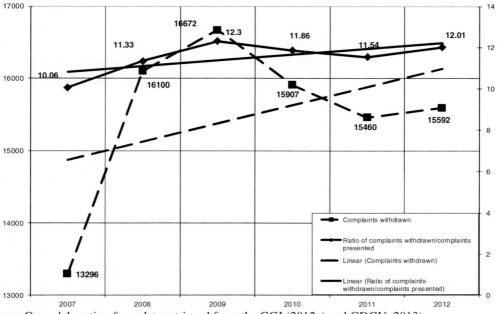

Source: Own elaboration from data retrieved from the GCJ (2012a) and GDGV, 2013).

Figure 2. Complaints withdrawn.

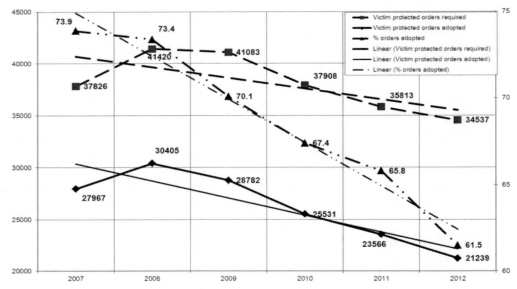

Source: Own elaboration from data retrieved from the GCJ (2012a).

Figure 3. IPVAW victims with protective orders.

As can be observed in Figure 3, both the number of restraining orders initiated and the number finally adopted decreased between 2007 and 2012. However, the greatest drop is in the percentage of restraining orders adopted in relation to the ones initiated. In some settings these data have been interpreted as the result of the resistance of certain judiciaries to comply with the precepts laid down in Organic Act 1/2004, resistance which, as these figures reveal, could have gained weight over time. Another possible reason for this drop could be the result of the courts being provided with insufficient grounds to grant the protective orders. Evidently, an attempt to analyse this question in depth is beyond the scope of this work, but it is interesting to put these data on record as they have or may have repercussions on the safety of the women who decide to go ahead with their process of breaking up with their aggressor.

WOMEN KILLED BECAUSE OF IPVAW

As has been repeatedly acknowledged by the WHO, IPVAW has fatal consequences on health, including homicides, suicides, maternal mortality and deaths related to HIV/AIDS (Campbell, 2002; Heise & García-Moreno, 2002; Plichta, 2004; WHO, 2004).

As regards intimate partner feminicides (in accordance with the terminology used by Special Rapporteur on VAW, Manjoo, 2012), according to the data provided by the GDGV (2013), 443 women were murdered between 2007 and 2013 by their partner or ex-intimate partner in Spain (that is, an average of 63 women per year). Figure 4 presents the annual distribution of the number of women murdered along with the rate per million women over 15 years of age that these represent (calculated, according to the indications of Vives-Cases, Alvárez-Dardet, Torrubiano and Gil (2008), as the proportion between the number of women murdered by their partner or ex-partner in one year and the number of women over 15 years of age registered in the municipal register on 1 January of the same year).

As can be seen, both indicators (especially the number of women murdered) tend to decrease over the period of time analysed. In fact, government sources (GDGV, 2013) point out that this is a stable trend and that the annual mean of women murdered has decreased consistently since the implementation of Organic Act 1/2004 (from 72 in 2003-2005 to 66 in 2006-2011).

In principle, any decrease in the number of deaths is positive. However, it is important to incorporate some qualifying points that can help measure the sense of these figures better. Thus, for instance, if we relate the number of women murdered not to the population of women over 15 years of age, but rather to the number of complaints due to IPVAW, we can confirm that, although a decrease is likewise produced (from 5.62 women murdered for every 10,000 complaints filed in 2007 to 4.05 in 2012), the fact is that it is neither as uniform nor as pronounced as the aforementioned rate could imply.

Another issue to point out is related to the legal protection of the women murdered. Hence, the information available (GDGV, 2013, 2014) reveals that only 25.1% of the women murdered in Spain between 2007 and 2013 had reported the violence they experienced (and, of these, 10.8% had given up going ahead with the legal proceedings); only 20.3% had requested a restraining order; and 14.2% had restraining orders in force at the time of their murder. That is, most of the women murdered because of IPVAW in Spain during this period had not resorted to the legal system. On the other hand, in a detailed analysis concerning the characteristics of the women murdered by their partners or ex-partners in 2011, the GCJ (2012b) informs that, of those who had made a formal complaint (16), 62.5% (10) were in paid work and 12.5% (2) were receiving a pension, that is, three-quarters of those who took steps to report the violence they were suffering were earning their own livelihood. This fact can be considered an indication that economic independence encourages women who suffer IPVAW to report it.

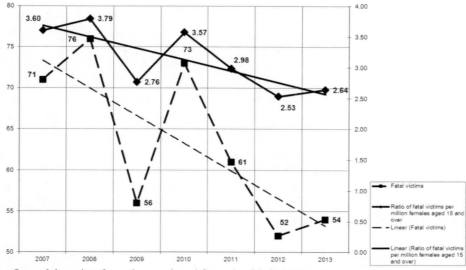

Source: Own elaboration from data retrieved from the GDGV (2013, 2014).

Figure 4. Fatal victims of IPVAW.

Determining the amount of maternal deaths due to either HIV/AIDS or suicides that can be attributed to IPVAW is more complicated (Ertürk, 2008). In relation to HIV/AIDS, women who have experienced violence have a risk of HIV infection that is increased by up to three times, a risk that could be increased directly through sexual violence, or indirectly through increased risky behaviour or inability to negotiate barrier contraceptive use (WHO, 2004). With regards to suicides, Devries et al. (2013b) conducted a meta-analytical study to find out the incidence of depression and suicides among people who had experienced situations of violence with their partner, but only found three studies that met their necessary requirements to be able to be included in this study. From an analysis therein, they concluded that, among women, IPVAW was associated to suicide attempts. Along these lines, a study carried out in Spain on a sample of women victims of IPVAW (Lorente, Sánchez de Lara, & Naredo, 2007) showed that 63.2% of these had made an attempt at suicide and 80% were considering suicide as a possible way out of the situation.

Meanwhile, after a review of studies on this issue, Lorente et al. (2007) concluded that between 20% and 40% of the women who commit suicide every year would have experienced situations of IPVAW. If we take these figures as a point of reference, and taking into account the fact that, according to the National Institute of Statistics (2014), in Spain there were between 2007 and 2012 a total of 4,585 cases of suicide by women (oscillating between 690 in 2010 and 815 in 2012, the highest figure in the period analysed, with an increase of 9.40% over the previous year), it could be thought that between 917 and 1,834 of these were victims of IPVAW. However, a lack of more detailed information on this issue prevents us, for the time being, from progressing in the analysis of a possible relationship between both aspects.

CONCLUSION

Many experts agree coincide that there is no single profile either of aggressors or women victim of IPVAW; that IPVAW does not affect one particular, specific or differentiated group; and that there are no socio-demographic, individual, family or social indicators that are present in most IPVAW cases or which, by themselves, allow the problem to be explained in a causal way (Bosch & Ferrer, 2002; Menéndez et al., 2013). Quite the contrary, the data available make it possible to declare that this is a problem that can be characterised as transversal and universal.

Nevertheless, despite the fact that it is not a phenomenon exclusive to any socio-economic class, more disadvantaged social contexts are more vulnerable and at greater risk of suffering violence (Menéndez et al., 2013; UN, 2006). Thus, this type of contexts can become facilitating or trigger factors for the abuser, while situations of economic dependence are one more pressure factor that victims could find themselves subjected to (GCJ, 2013b). On the other hand, economic independence of the women who experience IPVAW can favour their way out of the situation of violence in which they find themselves (ADECCO, 2012; Brunel, 2013; Devries, 2013a).

This relationship between IPVAW and factors of a socio-economic type (widely developed in reports such as the one presented by Ertürk, 2009) points towards the predicted impact an economic crisis such as the one that began in 2007 can have on this violence. Throughout this chapter we have presented a short analysis of the evolution of some important indicators of IPVAW that offer an initial approximation in this regard. However, the most significant conclusion we can reach is that the main effects of the economic crisis and of the austerity policies put into practice to (supposedly) overcome it are not as yet fully visible at the time of writing. In fact, some purely ideological measures are contributing to the invisibilisation of the problem and its evolution.

In this sense, an initial problem is the reduction in data available and the decrease in sources offering data. Thus, for instance: the National Health Survey, which in its 2006 edition included a section on IPVAW, eliminated this section from its 2011 edition. Certain government institutions (such as the State Observatory on Violence against Women or the Observatory on Women's Health) and non-government ones (such as the Queen Sofía Centre for the Study of Violence) which used to be responsible for compiling information on VAW, have either been eliminated or have ceased to be operational. Furthermore, the Women's Institute, Spain's government-funded autonomous organisation for equality, which, amongst other things, used to promote, support and fund awareness campaigns, studies, research and reports on VAW, has seen both its budget allocation and its capacity for action reduced.

In relation to prevention, not only have social sensitisation campaigns been reduced, as commented above, but also cutbacks in healthcare have, as one of their consequences, brought about a decrease in actions for early detection of IPVAW, including the stagnation of training programmes for healthcare professionals or screening programmes for the early detection of violence during medical visits. What is more, the exclusion of certain segments of the population from the Spanish public healthcare system (such as illegal immigrants or the long-term unemployed who are not entitled to benefits) makes any preventive action aimed at them impossible.

Yet another relevant issue is that, as part of the measures to address the crisis, the Spanish government levied a charge for accessing the legal system in 2013 which does not affect criminal proceedings but does affect civil ones. This, in practice, means that a woman who is a victim of IPVAW (unless she can prove she has no economic resources) must pay a fee in order to be able to divorce her abuser (and an even higher fee if she does not agree with a part of the divorce decree and wishes to appeal). Although at the time of writing these conclusions it is, as yet, difficult to trace its effect, there is a definite fear that these fees may hinder or delay the decision of women experiencing situations of IPVAW to put an end to their relationship with their abusers.

In short, the available evidence reveals not only the relationship between IPVAW and socio-economic situation, but also the possible effects the economic crisis can have on this violence since, as we have pointed out, the less social protection there is, the greater the precariousness, the greater the risk of suffering violence and also the greater the difficulties to get away from it. Throughout this chapter we have presented some data and reviewed some indicators that provide information in this regard. Nevertheless, it is necessary to continue delving further and investigating more profoundly in order to achieve a series of indicators that is as complete and comprehensive as possible so as to know these effects in detail and to articulate the tools that will enable us to revert them.

ACKNOWLEDGMENTS

This work has been carried out in the framework of Competitive Research Groups financed by the Department of Education, Culture and Universities of the Balearic Government, the European Union and the European Regional Development Fund (ERDF).

REFERENCES

Acale, M. (1999). *El delito de malos tratos físicos y psíquicos en el ámbito familiar* [The crime of physical and psychological abuse in the family]. Valencia, Spain: Tirant Lo Blanch.

ADECCO (2012). *I Informe mujeres víctimas de la violencia de género y empleo* [I report women victims of domestic violence and employment]. Madrid, Spain: Author. Retrieved from: http://www.fundacionadecco.es/_data/SalaPrensa/SalaPrensa/Pdf/472.pdf

Amor, P. J. & Echeburúa, E. (2010). Claves psicosociales para la permanencia de la víctima en una relación de maltrato [Psychosocial keys to the permanence of the victim in an abusive relationship] *Clínica Contemporánea, 12*(2), 97-104.

Beteta, Y. (2013). La feminización de la crisis financiera global. La regresión del estado del bienestar en España y su impacto en las políticas de igualdad y de erradicación de la violencia contra las mujeres. Nuevos retos [The feminisation of the global financial crisis. The regression of the wlefare state in Spain and its impact on th equal opportunities policies and the compaigns to erradicate the violence against women. New challenges]. *Asparkía, 24*, 36-53.

Blázquez, M., Moreno, J. M. & García-Baamonde, E. (2010). Revisión teórica del maltrato psicológico en la violencia conyugal. *Psicología y Salud, 20*(1), 65-75.

Bosch, E. & Ferrer, V. A. (2002). *La voz de las invisibles. Las víctimas de un mal amor que mata* [The voice of the invisible. The victims of an evil love that kills] Madrid, Spain: Editorial Cátedra. Colección Feminismos.

Bosch, E. & Ferrer, V. A. (2013). Nuevo modelo explicativo para la violencia contra las mujeres en la pareja: el modelo piramidal y el proceso de filtraje [New explicanatory model for violence against women in couples: the pyramidal model and the filtering process]. *Asparkía, 24*, 54-67.

Bosch, E., Ferrer, V. A., Ferreiro, V. & Navarro, C. (2013). *La violencia contra las mujeres: el amor como coartada* [Violence against women: love as alibi]. Barcelona, Spain: Antrophos.

Brunel, S. (2013). *Las políticas de recortes y su impacto en las políticas de igualdad y prevención de la violencia* [The policies of cuts and their impact on equality policies and violence prevention]. *Revista Estudios y Cultura, 56*, 58. Retrieved from: http://www.1mayo.ccoo.es/nova/files/1018/Revista56.pdf

Campbell, J. C. (2002). Health consequences of intimate partner violence. *Lancet, 359*, 1331–36.

Castro, C. (2013). ¿Cómo afecta la crisis y las políticas de austeridad a los derechos de las mujeres y a la igualdad? [How the crisis and the austerity policies on the rights of women and equality affects?]. In L. Vicent, C. Castro, A Agenjo, & Y. Herrero (Eds.), *El desigualdad impacto de la crisis sobre las mujeres* [The unequal impact of the crisis on women] (pp. 13-21). Madrid, Spain: FUHEM.

Chant, S. (2001). Men in crisis? reflections on masculinities, work and family in northwest Costa Rica. In C. Jackson (Ed.), *Men at work: labour, masculinities, development* (pp. 199-218). London, UK:. Frank Cass

Council of Europe (2011). *Council of Europe Convention on preventing and combating violence against women and domestic violence.* Retrieved from: http://www.coe.int/ t/dghl/standardsetting/convention-violence/about_en.asp

De Miguel, A. (2005). La construcción de un marco feminista de interpretación: la violencia de género [Building a feminist framework of interpretation: gender violence]. *Cuadernos de Trabajo Social, 18*, 231-248.

Devries, K. M., Mak, J. Y. T., García-Moreno, C., Petzold, M., Child, J. C., Felder, G., Lim, S., Bacchus, L. J., Engell, R. E., Rosenfeld, L., Pallito, C., Vos, T., Abrahams, N. & Watts, C. H. (2013a). The global prevalence of intimate partner violence against women. *Science, 340*, 1527-1528.

Devries, K. M., Mark, J. Y., Bacchus, L. J., Child, J. C., Falder, G., Petzold, M., Astbury, J. & Watts, C. H. (2013b). Intimate partner violence and incident depressive symptoms and suicide attempts: a systematic review of longitudinal studies. *PLOSMedicine, 10*(5), e1001439.

Economists deal with the crisis. (2012). No es economía, es ideología [Not economics is ideology]. Bilbao, Spain: Deusto S. A. Ediciones. Retrieved from: http://www. economistasfrentealacrisis.com/

EIGE (European Institute for Gender Equility) (2013). *Gender Equality Index Report.* Italy: Author. doi: 10.2839/99105 Retrieved from: http://eige.europa.eu/content/document/ gender-equality-index-report

Ertürk, Y. (2008). *Indicators on violence against women and State response.* A/HRC/7/6. United Nations. General Assembly. Retrieved from: http://www2.ohchr.org/english/ bodies/ hrcouncil/docs/7session/A-HRC-7-6.doc

Ertürk, Y. (2009). *Political economy of women's human rights.* A/HRC/11/6. United Nations. General Assembly. Retrieved from: http://www2.ohchr.org/english/bodies/hrcouncil/ docs/11session/A.HRC.11.6.pdf

Ferrer, V. A., Bosch, E. & Riera, T. (2006). Las dificultades en la cuantificación de la violencia contra las mujeres en la pareja: análisis psicosocial [The difficulties in the quantification of the violence against women in the couple: psychosocial analysis]. *Psychosocial Intervention, 15*, 181-202.

Foran, H. M. & O'Leary, K. D. (2008). Alcohol and intimate partner violence: A meta – analytic review. *Clinical Psychology Review, 28*, 1222-1234.

FRA (European Union Agency for Fundamental Rights). (2014). Violence against women: an EU-wide Surrey. Main results. Luxembourg: Publications Office of the European Union. Retreived from: http://fra.europa.eu/sites/default/files/fra-2014-vaw-survey-main-results_en.pdf

García-Moreno, C., Jansen, H. A., Ellsberg, M., Heise, L. & Watts, C. H. (2006). Prevalence of intimate partner violence: findings from the WHO multi-country study on women's health and domestic violence. *Lancet, 368*, 1260-1269.

GCJ (General Council of the Judiciary). (2012a). *La violencia sobre la mujer en la estadística judicial: datos anuales de 2012* [Violence on women in the judicial statistics: 2012 annual data]. Retrieved from: http://www.poderjudicial.es/cgpj/es/Temas/Violencia _domestica_y_de_genero/Actividad_del_Observatorio/Datos_estadisticos/La_violencia_s obre_la_mujer_en_la_estadistica_judicial__Datos_anuales_de_2012

GCJ (General Council of the Judiciary). (2012b). *Informe sobre víctimas mortales de la violencia de género y de la violencia doméstica en el ámbito de la pareja o ex pareja 2011* [Report on fatal victims of domestic violence and domestic violence in the area of partner or former partner 2011]. Retrieved from: http://www.poderjudicial.es/cgpj/es/ Poder_Judicial/En_Portada/Informe_sobre_victimas_mortales_de_la_violencia_de_gener o_y_de_la_violencia_domestica_en_el_ambito_de_la_pareja_o_ex_pareja_en_2011

GCJ (General Council of the Judiciary). (2012c). *Datos estadísticas judiciales en aplicación de la LO 1/2004. Resumen de los 7 años (Datos desde julio 2005 a julio 2012)* [Judicial statistics under the 1/2004 data. Summary of 7 years (data from July 2005 to July 2012)]. Retrieved from: http://www.poderjudicial.es/cgpj/es/Temas/Violencia_domestica_y_de_ genero/Actividad_del_Observatorio/Datos_estadisticos/Balance_de_siete_anos_de_la_cr eacion_de_los_Juzgados_de_Violencia_sobre_la_Mujer__2005_2012_

GDGV (Government Delegation for Gender Violence). (2013). *Fifth Annual Report of the National Observatory on Violence against Women*. Madrid, Spain: Ministry of Health, Social Affairs, and Equality. Retrieved from: http://msssi.gob.es/ssi/violenciaGenero/ publicaciones/colecciones/PDFS_COLECCION/Informe_Ejecutivo_V_Ingles.pdf

GDGV (Government Delegation for Gender Violence). (2014). *Ficha estadística de víctima mortales por violencia de género (2012, 2013)* [Statistical record of fatal victim of gender violence (2012, 2013)]. Madrid, Spain: Ministry of Health, Social Affairs, and Equality. Retrieved from: https://www.msssi.gob.es/ssi/violenciaGenero/portalEstadistico/ home.htm

Gil, D. Vives-Cases, C., Alvárez-Dardet, C. & Latour, J. (2006). Alcohol and intimate partner violence: do we have enough information to act? *European Journal of Public Health*, *16*(3), 279-285.

Gracia, E. (2009). The context of domestic violence: social and contextual factors associated with partner violence against women. In K. S. Perlman (Ed.), *Marriage: roles, stability and conflict* (95-109). New York: Nova Science Publishers.

Hagemann-White, C. (2001). European research on the prevalence of violence against women. *Violence against Women*, *7*, 732-759.

Heise, L. L. & García-Moreno, C. (2002). Violence by intimate partners. In E.G. Krug, L. L. Dahlberg, K. A. Mercy, A. B. Zwi, & R. Lozano (Eds.), *World Report on Violence and Health* (87-122). Geneva, Switzerland: World Health Organization.

Heise, L. L. (1998). Violence against women: an integrated ecological framework. *Violence Against Women*, *4*, 262-290.

Krahé, B., Bieneck, S. & Möller, I. (2005). Understanding gender and intimate partner violence from an international perspective. *Sex Roles*, *52*, 807-827.

Kury, H., Obergfell-Fuchs, J. & Woessner, G. (2004). The extent of family violence in Europe: a comparison of Nacional Surverys. *Violence against Women*, *10*, 749-769.

Llop, P. (2013). Aspectos destacados en el último informe sobre víctimas mortales del observatorio contra la violencia doméstica y de género [Highlights of the latest report on fatalities observatory against domestic violence and gender]. *Revista de Estudios, Análisis, Reflexión y Debate*, *49*, 24-26.

Lorente, M., Sánchez de Lara, C. & Naredo, C. (2007). *Suicidio y violencia de género* [Suicide and gender violence]. Madrid, Spain: Ministerio de Sanidad y Consumo – Federación de Mujeres Progresistas.

Manjoo, R. (2012). *Report of the Special Rapporteur on violence against women, its causes and consequences.* A/HRC/20/16. United Nations. General Assembly. Retrieved from: *http://www.ohchr.org/Documents/Issues/Women/A.HRC.20.16_En.pdf*

Medina-Ariza, J. & Barberet, R. (2003). Intimate partner violence in Spain: findings from a National Survey. *Violence Against Women, 9,* 302-322.

Menéndez, S., Pérez, J. & Lorence, B. (2013). La violencia de pareja contra la mujer en España: Cuantificación y caracterización del problema, las víctimas, los agresores y el contexto social y profesional [Partner violence against women in Spain: Quantification and characterization of the problem, victims, aggressors, and the social and professional context]. *Psychosocial Intervention 22,* 41-53.

Ministry of Health, Social Affairs and Equality. (2012). *Macroencuesta sobre violencia de género 2011. Principales resultados* [Macro–survey on gender violence 2011. Main results]. Retrieved from: http://www.observatorioviolencia.org/documentos.php?id=299

National Health Survey. (2006). *State of health. Absolute figures. Type of aggressor, by sex. Population aged 16 years old and over that has suffered aggression or mistreatment.* Retrieved from: http://www.ine.es/jaxi/tabla.do?path=/t15/p419/a2006/p01/l1/&file=01068.px&type=pcaxis&L=1

National Institute of Statistics. (2014). *Defunciones según causa de muerte.* Retrieved from: http://www.ine.es/jaxi/menu.do?type=pcaxis&path=/t15/p417/&file=inebase

O'Neil, J. M. & Harway, M. (1999). Preliminary multivariate model explaining the causes of men's violence against women. In M. Harway, & J. O'Neil (Eds.), *What causes men's violence against women?* (12-18). Thousand Oaks, CA: Sage Publications.

Organic Act 1/2004 on Integral Protection Measures against Gender Violence. *Boletín Oficial del Estado núm. 313,* 42166-42197.

Plichta, S. B. (2004). Intimate partner violence and physical health consequences: policy and practice implications. *Journal of Interpersonal Violence, 19,* 1296–1323.

Rodríguez-Menés, J. & Safranoff, A. (2012). Violence against women in intimate relations: A contrast of five theories. *European Journal of Criminology, 9*(6), 584-602.

Spanish Economic and Social Council. (2012). *Memoria sobre la situación socioeconómica y laboral de España 2012* [Report on socio-economic and employment situation in Spain 2012]. Madrid, Spain: Author. Retrieved from: http://www.ces.es/en/memorias

Stith, S. M. & Farley, S. C. (1993). A predictive model of male spousal violence. *Journal of Family Violence 8*(2), 183-201.

Stockl, H., Devries, K., Rotstein, A., Abrahams, N., Campbell, J., Watts, C. & García-Moreno, C. (2013). The global prevalence of intimate partner homicide: a systematic review. *The Lancet, 382,* 859-865.

UN (United Nations). (2006). *In-depth study on all forms of violence against women. Report of the Secretary-General* (A/61/122/Add.1). Retrieved from: http://daccess-dds-ny.un.org/doc/UNDOC/GEN/N06/419/74/PDF/N0641974.pdf?OpenElement

Vives-Cases, C., Alvarez-Dardet, C., Torrubiano, J. & Gil, D. (2008). Mortalidad por violencia del compañero íntimo en mujeres residentes en España (1999-2006) [Mortality intimate partner violence in women living in Spain (1999-2006)]. *Gaceta Sanitaria, 22*(3), 232-235.

Vives-Cases, C., Alvárez-Dardet, C. & Caballero, P. (2003). Violencia del compañero íntimo en España [Intimate partner violence in Spain]. *Gaceta Sanitaria, 17*(4), 268-274.

Watts, C. & Zimmerman, C. (2002). Violence against women: global scope magnitude. *The Lancet, 359*, 1232-1237.

WEF (World Economic Forum). (2013). *The Global Gender Gap Report 2013.* Geneva, Switzerland: Author. Retrieved from: http://www3.weforum.org/docs/WEF_GenderGap_ Report_2013.pdf

WHO (World Health Organization). (2004). Violence Against Women and HIV/AIDS: Critical Intersections. Intimate Partner Violence and HIV/AIDS. *Information Bulletin Series, 1*. Retrieved from: http://www.who.int/hac/techguidance/pht/ InfoBulletinIntimate PartnerViolenceFinal.pdf

WHO (World Health Organization). (2006). *Interpersonal violence and alcohol.* Retrieved from: http://www.who.int/violence_injury_prevention/violence/world_report/factsheets/ pb_violencealcohol.pdf

WHO (World Health Organization). (2013). *Global and regional estimates of violence against women: prevalence and health effects of intimate partner violence and non-partner sexual violence.* Geneva, Switzerland: Author. Retrieved from: http://www.who. int/reproductivehealth/publications/violence/9789241564625/en/index.html

Women's Institute. (2008). *La mujer en cifras (1983-2008)* [Women in Numbers (1983-2008)] Madrid, Spain: Author.

In: Overcoming Domestic Violence
Editors: Myra F. Taylor, Julie Ann Pooley et al.

ISBN: 978-1-63321-956-4
© 2015 Nova Science Publishers, Inc.

Chapter 15

SPORT-RELATED DOMESTIC VIOLENCE: EXPLORING THE COMPLEX RELATIONSHIP BETWEEN SPORTING EVENTS AND DOMESTIC VIOLENCE

Damien J. Williams and Fergus G. Neville*
University of St Andrews, Scotland, UK

ABSTRACT

The link between sport and violence is widely acknowledged. While the focus has been on "player violence" and "crowd violence" it is recognised that a variety of other incidents of sports-related violence exist, including domestic violence. Empirical and anecdotal evidence point toward increased rates of domestic violence among male athletes. Moreover, there is evidence that domestic violence also increases around sporting events in wider society; however, the evidence is at times contradictory. It is not argued that sport causes domestic violence, but that it can provide the conditions that enable forms of domestic violence. It is acknowledged that the evidence is at most correlational, and that further work is needed to understand this complex association. In particular, the "holy trinity" of sports, alcohol, and hegemonic masculinity is offered to explain this association. The wide appeal of sport can, however, be exploited to engage with males and support them in confronting the issues that underpin domestic violence, in conjunction with female empowerment and the pursuit of gender equality.

Keywords: Sport, domestic violence, hegemony, alcohol

* Corresponding author: Dr Damien J. Williams, Lecturer in Public Health Sciences School of Medicine, University of St Andrews North Haugh St Andrews Scotland, KY16 9TF, Tel: +44 (0)1334 463481, Email: djw11@st-andrews.ac.uk.

INTRODUCTION

Sport plays a paradoxical role within society. On the one hand, it is associated with many direct and indirect benefits to individuals, communities, and societies. On the other hand, it is associated with a powerful set of ideological values that can serve to perpetuate some of society's problems, including domestic violence. The chapter begins by exploring this paradoxical relationship, followed by a review of the literature concerning the link between sport and domestic violence; looking first at the link between athletes and domestic violence before considering the research linking sporting events and domestic violence in wider society. These findings are then contextualised through a consideration of the "holy trinity" of sport, hegemonic masculinity, and alcohol, and the limitations are discussed. The chapter concludes by identifying directions for future research, and highlighting ways in which the popularity of athletes and sports in general can be utilised as one strategy in addressing domestic violence.

SOCIETAL BENEFITS OF SPORT

It is well-known that sport participation confers many health benefits (e.g., DeBeliso et al., 2014; Ommundsen, Løndal, & Loland, 2014) as well as a number of social and economic benefits of sport spectatorship. Furthermore, the supporting of a sports team can be a valuable source of identity and community in a modern deindustrialised, secular society (Edge, 1997). Such identification with a social group can itself convey health benefits through the provision of structure and meaning, and the preconditions for positive social interactions (Sani, Herrera, Wakefield, Boroch, & Gulyas, 2012).

The act of collectively watching a sporting event with strangers can shift social relations from mistrust and uncertainty towards intimacy and comradeship, through a sharing of team or national identity (Neville & Reicher, 2011). This is because co-present people come to be seen as fellow members of one's social group, rather than as 'other'. As London Mayor Boris Johnson noted at the post-Olympics parade in 2012, "For the first time in living memory you [the athletes] caused tube train passengers to break into spontaneous conversation with their neighbours" (BBC, 2012).

Recognition of shared group membership can be accompanied by a shared understanding of the social norms associated with the group. This means that strangers can comfortably act and interact within the confines of a group's normative parameters without fear of behaving in an inappropriate manner. In this way, collective behaviour at sporting events is determined by commonly understood societal rules of how to act. However, while society shapes audience behaviour, sport spectatorship can in turn shape and challenge societal rules, and as Dunning (1999, p. 221) notes: "Sport is one of the most successful means of collective mobilization humans have so far devised". Indeed, sports crowds can be a vehicle for collective action, such as the use of Barcelona's Nou Camp as a site for resistance against Franco's dictatorship (Shobe, 2008), or the Hillsborough Family Support Group's campaign for police accountability following the Hillsborough disaster (see http://hfsg.co.uk/).

The hosting of major sporting events can also facilitate debate and re-construction of the meaning of national identities towards inclusive definitions (e.g., Germany during the 2006

World Cup; Kersting, 2007), and can be used to 'sell' countries to an international audience resulting in national social and economic benefits. Sport spectatorship can also deliver significant economic benefits at local levels. Paid attendance to sporting events can help fund community sporting assets, sustain employment, and supporters can provide a valuable income source to bars, restaurants, and hotels near sporting arenas.

In addition to the positive aspects of sport participation and spectatorship, the remnants of the historical roots of the often violent, "celebrations of class and patriarchal power" (Kidd, 2013, p. 554) that excluded females or made them play by male rules (Christesen & Kyle, 2014) highlights the fundamental role sport played, and still does play in society. Indeed, Jackson (1993) states that sport provides "an important site for examining important social problems", including "a critical look at violence" (p. 9).

THE CULTURE OF SPORT

A reinvigoration of the importance of sport emerged during the late 19th and early 20th century in the British Empire (Mangan, 1986) and spread across the globe (Kidd, 2013). This was largely attributed to fears that changes in working conditions and emerging social structures would result in the feminization of the middle and upper-middle classes (Wenner & Jackson, 2009) referred to as the "crisis of masculinity" (Messner, 1995). Thus, existing sports were adopted and shaped in such a way that the structure, rules, values, and meanings socialized young males in a particular kind of masculinity (Mangan, 1986) what Burgess, Edwards, and Skinner (2003) referred to as "controlled masculinity". These sports involved displays of strength, power and/or endurance (usually involving physical violence) thereby reinforcing notions of male physical prowess (Dunning, 1999).

Sport-related violence is not restricted to males, but to understand such violence requires an understanding of gender identity (Coakley & Pike, 2009). It is stated that modern sport has evolved into a male institution for the performance of ideological values and power relations that characterise masculinity (see Kidd, 2013). Such behaviour is most evident in team sports (i.e., soccer, American football, rugby, and ice hockey). For example, Weinstein, Smith, and Wiesenthal (1995) noted that in ice hockey, fighting and intimidation are essential elements of the tradition and culture of the game, and found that teammates and coaches viewed violence (especially fights) as indicating greater competence than playing or skating skill. Moreover, Burgess et al. (2003) noted that even in sports where there is limited opportunity for overt displays of violence (e.g., baseball, cricket, etc.) participants can signify their masculinity through movement (i.e., "strutting") talking (i.e., swearing) and actions (i.e., spitting) combined with off-field performances to reinforce their masculinity.

Sport serves to construct and prioritise a range of masculine selves whereby toughness and aggression (either manifest or implied) are rendered normative (Burgess et al., 2003). Females who participate in "violent sports" serve to disrupt "existing gender norms, causing social instability" (Gill, 2007, p. 416). Gill argues that by engaging in a violent and masculine sport female players compromise their femininity, and in so doing are able to assert an alternate form of femininity - "resistant femininity" - which does not assume the role of women as victims and men as aggressors.

SPORT IN THE CIVILISING PROCESS

Sport is not the only way in which to exhibit traditional masculine qualities (i.e., power, strength, and violence) and overtly reject traditional feminine values (i.e., expression and beauty) (Burgess et al., 2003), but it does offer the primary means of masculinity-validating experience, and has become part of the civilising process (Elias & Dunning, 1986). Moreover, given the extent to which young males vigorously pursue the formation of a masculine identity (Weinstein et al., 1995) the important function of sport for younger males must not be overlooked as they may not be able to demonstrate masculinity in other ways (i.e., "wage-earning, heterosexual relationships, or fatherhood"; Burgess et al., 2003, p. 202).

DEVELOPING MASCULINITY

The widespread availability of televised sport can sanction masculine behaviours within its rules. This can promote violence and danger as normative, desirable, and rewarding, and can be easily accessed, learned, and reinforced (Cowan, 2001). For instance, a large proportion of young children and adolescents reported regularly witnessing violence in televised sport, and perceived such acts as rewarding and exciting (Messner et al., 1999). Indeed, Leonard (1993) stated:

> Would you recognise (let alone enjoy) boxing without punching; football without tackling; full-contact karate without kicking? Modern sport ... is the controlled, rule-bound, limited violence called 'aggro.'(p. 158)

Power, symbolic violence, and status are embedded in many aspects of sport (Dunning, 1999) from team names and emblems, to the language used to describe games, and the nature of the performance. Thus, violence in sport can become normalised (Weinstein et al., 1995) thereby entrenching the "gender order" (Cowan, 2001). However, Burgess et al. (2003) argue that while immersion within sport makes an "oppressive presentation of self .... a realisable and accessible option" (p. 199) involvement in sport does not inevitably lead to the presentation of a tough and aggressive self. The concern is that the lessons learned through sport (participation or spectatorship) may be realised in other aspects of life, such as domestic settings (Wenner & Jackson, 2009) in the form of domestic violence.

SPORTS-RELATED VIOLENCE

There is acknowledgement of the link between sport and violence (e.g., Jamieson, 2009; Young, 2012) but this differs considerably in type and extent according to the type of sport (Guilbert, 2004). Each sport adopts a formal set of rules to ensure the safety of participants, and transgression of those rules often carries severe penalties (e.g., a period of suspension from the game/event for athletes; see McFee, 2004). Moreover, some sports have evolved to outlaw the most violent/dangerous practices (e.g., "butt-blocking", "face tackling", and "spearing" in American football; see National Federation of State High School [NFSH],

2013). While the majority of players refrain from violent acts, there can be an expectation of aggression within the rules of the sporting code, which can at times result in tragic outcomes (e.g., Baxter, 2005).

In addition to violence among athletes on or off "the field of play" Young (2012) notes that the focus has been on violence involving fans traditionally referring to collective forms of violence against persons and property. Moreover, Jamieson (2009) identifies a host of "problems" in which a violent event is related to the sporting activity, venue, or "spill-over" associated with, amongst others, various sport participants, including: players, their coaches and family; supporters and officials. However, Young (2000, p. 391) asserts that a variety of other sports-related violence "cannot easily be separated from the sports process and that only begin to make sense when the socially, culturally and historically embedded character of sport is closely scrutinized". He further indicates that this is most apparent in the case of domestic violence. While much of the literature on sport and domestic violence has focused on partner abuse by male athletes (Young, 2012) there is also evidence of a link between professional competitive sport and increased levels of domestic violence in wider society (e.g., Williams, Neville, House, & Donnelly, 2013).

DOMESTIC VIOLENCE AND MALE ATHLETES

It is claimed that violence against women, and domestic violence more specifically, is an "integral and accepted part of competitive sports" and that sport "has become a "breeding ground for domestic violence and sexual assault scandals" (Moser, 2004, p. 70). Indeed, Crosset (1999) notes that violence against women by male athletes represents an important social issue in sport, which has received more media attention than any other. Critical analysis has tended to focus on the major US college and professional sports (i.e., football, baseball, hockey, and basketball; see Benedict, 1999). Such incidents are often referred to as "high profile" due to the considerable media coverage they garner. However, Enck-Wanzer (2009) argues that the way in which the media covers incidents of domestic violence by professional athletes can in fact serve to perpetuate the problem. In particular, she is critical of the decontextualized way in which the media portray black athletes, which serves to scrutinize black masculinity and "pathologize black men as naturally aggressive" (p. 1) while downplaying hegemonic white masculinity.

The question of whether male athletes are more inclined to perpetrate domestic violence has often been discussed from a US perspective, but concerns have also been raised in Australia and the UK. For instance, Flood and Dyson (2007, p. 44) highlight a spate of incidents of "violent, coercive, and harassing behaviour" against women (including domestic violence) perpetrated by Rugby League and Australian Football League players during 2004 and 2005. In the UK, Radford and Hudson (2005) discuss the handling of the signing of domestic violence perpetrator, Paul "Gazza" Gascoigne, to Middlesbrough Football Club and the inadequate public relations campaign including an invitation for him to sign the Zero Tolerance pledge, which was never taken-up.

Webb (2012) points to a number of anecdotal sources (i.e., domestic violence experts, sports sociologists, and former athletes) that support the idea that athletes may be more likely to commit acts of domestic violence than non-athletes, but notes that there is inconclusive evidence to support such assertions. However, the impact of such behaviour can extend into wider society, wherein amateur participants or spectators *may* emulate the behaviour of professional athletes.

SPORTS EVENTS AND DOMESTIC VIOLENCE IN SOCIETY

There has been concern over the association between sporting events and domestic violence. Brimicombe and Cafe (2012) note that on days leading up to the biggest sporting events, considerable attention is given to the potential rise in domestic violence. The concern and interest in the link between sporting events and domestic violence were raised largely following a controversial press release in 1993 in which domestic violence was reported to be greatest on Super Bowl Sunday compared to any other time in the year.

National Football League. The first empirical study of the association between National Football League (NFL) games (involving the Washington Redskins) and traumatic injuries in females (operationalised as the frequency of admissions to hospital emergency rooms) occurred in northern Virginia (see White, Katz, & Scarborough, 1992). Controlling for day of the week, month, year and special holidays during the 1988-1989 season, time series analysis indicated that the frequency of admissions (including assaults, falls, gun shots, lacerations, stabbings, and being hit by objects) increased when the Redskins won but not at any other time. However, rather than having data specifically related to domestic violence, the authors could only speculate that a number of the admissions resulted from domestic violence.

Sachs and Chu (2000) explored Los Angeles Sheriff Department (at the time home to the Los Angeles Raiders and Los Angeles Rams) domestic violence dispatches between January 1993 and December 1995 (including two full NFL seasons). They examined differences in dispatches from Wednesday (when football is not played) to Sunday (when football games are played) for the non-football season, football season, playoff weeks, and Super Bowl week. The study found no statistically significant increases in domestic violence during NFL games across the study period. Moreover, they found that Super Bowl Sunday did not represent the biggest day for domestic violence dispatches.

However, Gantz, Bradley, and Wang (2006) analysed domestic violence police dispatches by day in 15 NFL cities, and found a small but significant increase in domestic violence dispatches on or after Super Bowl Sunday. They also noted a large rise in dispatches around major holidays (e.g., Christmas). However, Grohol (2010) cautions against the study findings on the grounds that the publication was not published in a peer-reviewed journal, and presumably did not receive a rigorous review process.

Using a different dataset relating to crisis line calls and safe house admission, Oths and Robertson (2007) found no evidence of an increase on what they refer to as "drinking events/holidays" including Super Bowl (also Labour Day, Halloween, Memorial Day, Fourth of July, and New Years Eve) relative to non-drinking holiday and major non-drinking events (i.e., Easter, Thanksgiving, and Christmas). They concluded that the patterning of calls and admissions contradicted that based on hospital and police data.

One of the major limitations of previous studies exploring the association between American football and domestic violence is that they were largely based on small data sets.

To remedy this, Card and Dahl (2011) recently examined police reports of family violence for 8664 regular season Sunday fixtures across 12 full years (1995-2006) involving: Carolina Panthers, Denver Broncos, Detriot Lions, Kansas City Chiefs, New England Patriots, and Tennessee Titans. The authors accounted for match outcomes emotional valence of outcome (i.e., unexpected/expected win, loss, or draw) in their analysis. Contrary to previous findings, Card and Dahl found that only unexpected losses led to an increase in domestic violence reports (by 10%); games where losses were expected had small, insignificant effects.

Thus, evidence regarding a link between NFL and domestic violence is rather contradictory; however, the largest, most methodologically sound study by Card and Dahl (2011) provides the most reliable finding that confirms that match outcome is important.

Soccer World Cup. The soccer World Cup is one of the biggest globally televised sporting events, and has also been the target of research exploring links with domestic violence. Brimicombe and Cafe (2012) studied the association between domestic violence and England fixtures during the 2010 World Cup in South Africa using aggregate English police force data. It was found that when the England national team either won or lost there was a significant increase in reports. What is more, this held when compared to two matched comparator conditions, including: 2010 non-match days, or the 2009 non-tournament year. However, when England drew there was no difference in reporting rates. The authors highlight the importance of match outcome in terms of the resulting levels of domestic violence reports. They also acknowledge the limitation of using aggregated data in terms of making causal claims, but temper this by stating: "We can think of no other event occurring on the Wednesday of England's win and the Sunday of England's exit from the World Cup that would explain these significant increases in the rate of reported domestic violence" (p. 35).

Kirby, Francis, and O'Flaherty (in press) examined the influence of viewing England World Cup fixtures across three tournaments 2002 (Korea/Japan) 2006 (Germany) and 2010 (South Africa). Reported incidents of domestic abuse to Lancashire Constabulary, UK rose each time England played in the tournaments. What is more, it was found that incidents increased by 26% when England won or drew, and by 38% when they lost, with an 11% increase the day after England played. The authors acknowledge the limitations inherent in their study, namely its limited size, use of police data, and difficulties of defining "domestic violence".

Scottish Old Firm derby. The "Old Firm" fixture between Glasgow Rangers and Celtic has been blighted by incidents of collective violence and sectarianism (Carnochan & McCluskey, 2011). Moreover, in response to media reports based on police data, there has been concern about the fixture's influence on violence against women (see Scottish Parliament, 2011). However, there are a number of limitations in the "analyses" described in these media reports (see Williams et al., 2013). Two independent studies were completed concurrently exploring the association between Old Firm derbies and domestic violence, in the form of domestic incidents reported to the police.

First, Williams et al. (2013) sought to mitigate some of the issues raised in the media reports in two ways: initially, by making comparisons between a greater number of comparable time periods (e.g., the same day of the week and time of day) over four years; and subsequently, by comparing Old Firm matches with Scotland International matches played at

Hampden Park in Glasgow to account for the role of high-profile football in the city (and underlying variables that could account for increased levels of domestic abuse; e.g., alcohol misuse).The authors found that reported domestic incidents for the 24-hours from kick-off were significantly greater for Old Firm derbies than all other comparators.

Secondly, Dickson, Jennings, and Koop (2013) adopted a similar approach to Card and Dahl (2011) and found that only Old Firm matches were associated with large increases in reports of domestic incidents largely irrespective of the timing or outcome of the match. However, they found support for Card and Dahl's idea that unexpected loses (and not other outcomes) result in increased incidents of domestic violence but only when the game is important (i.e., when the title is still undecided).

One critique of studies exploring associations between sporting events and domestic violence is that "domestic violence is a complex on-going event and not simply a one-off incident attributable to sport or alcohol" (see Brimicombe & Cafe, 2012, p. 32). However, understanding the conditions that lead to incidents being reported can play a role in identifying appropriate ways to intervene. We agree with Brimicombe and Café's analysis:

> "It is not that [sporting events] cause the violence, but rather that the excitement, disappointment and flow of adrenalin resulting from watching a ... team play may exacerbate existing tensions within a relationship and result in lost tempers and violence or abuse. Such behaviour may be made worse or more likely when alcohol has been consumed" (p. 33)

The importance of time. Much of the research exploring the association between sporting events and reported domestic violence has not taken account of *time*, including seasonality, time of day and day of week, which can give rise to a host of other confounding factors. While Dickson et al. (2013) found no monthly effect on reported domestic violence when controlling for the Christmas period a number of studies have demonstrated that summer months and higher temperatures correlate with increases in reports of domestic violence (e.g., Anderson, 2001) and violence-related injury hospital admissions (e.g., Bellis et al., 2012). It is important to note that such a link may not relate to temperature *per se*, but with additional factors such as increased alcohol consumption during periods of warm weather (and decreased consumption during January in the UK; Sheen & Tettenborn, 2011) and increased family contact during holiday periods (Braaf & Gilbert, 2007). In addition to seasonal effects, further studies have identified time patterns associated with domestic violence, such that reported violence increases significantly during evenings (e.g., Cohn, 1993) and weekends (e.g., Shepherd, 1990) specifically Friday and Saturday evenings (Bellis et al., 2012). It is, therefore, imperative that any investigation of the relationship between specific sporting events and reported domestic violence control for season and time effects and account for associated confounders.

HOLY TRINITY: ALCOHOL, SPORT, AND HEGEMONIC MASCULINITY

It has been suggested that domestic violence operates at the nexus of a social constellation comprising alcohol, sport, and hegemonic masculinity (Palmer, 2011) - the "holy trinity" (Wenner, 1998). Having explored the link between sport and domestic violence, we will now briefly discuss the links with alcohol and hegemonic masculinity.

ALCOHOL, SPORT, AND, DOMESTIC VIOLENCE

"[I]t remains difficult to have any involvement in sport – as a participant or a fan – without being exposed to a strong message that alcohol and sport are inextricably linked" (Jones, Phillipson, & Lynch, 2006, para. 1). Indeed, in a systematic review by Kwan, Bobko, Faulkner, Donnelly, and Cairney (2014), adolescent sport participation was positively associated with alcohol use in 14 out of 17 studies.

This relationship between sport participation and alcohol resonates with the former footballer Richard Gough's assertion that "The team that drinks together, wins together" (in Campbell, 2007). While alcohol may play a part in some forms of sport participation, it is also a common feature of the spectator experience, with alcohol regularly consumed before and after major sporting events, if not actually served within arenas (Enock & Jacobs, 2008). Outside of stadia, spectators may only have access to televised sporting events in bars and other licensed premises, thereby ensuring that the presence of alcohol is a part of their spectator experience (Wenner, 1998).

The association between alcohol and domestic violence pervades the research literature and popular understandings of the problem. Alcohol use is a consistent risk factor for intimate partner violence across different social contexts (Capaldi, Knoble, Shortt, & Kim, 2012). In a meta-analysis of North American studies, Black, Schumacher, Smith, and Heyman (1999, cited in Heise & Garcia-Moreno, 2002) reported that every study which considered alcohol use as a risk factor for domestic violence uncovered a significant relationship.

Male alcohol consumption may also increase the severity of intimate partner violence (Finney, 2004) and consequently the extent of physical injuries suffered. This may then increase the likelihood of police and medical service involvement (Brecklin, 2002) which may partly explain the relationship between partner alcohol use and *reported* domestic violence.

Any relationship between alcohol use and violence is likely to be mediated by social variables. For example, there is evidence to suggest that if people believe alcohol is related to violence, then they behave more violently having consumed alcohol (Collins & Messerschmidt, 1993).

In South Africa some men also report using alcohol to provide courage to administer domestic violence which they feel is socially expected of them (see Heise & Garcia-Moreno, 2002). Alcohol use can also form the basis of arguments (e.g., over drunken behaviour, spending time and money in bars instead of at home) and can escalate existing conflict (Quigley & Leonard, 2000). However, while approximately one third of intimate partner violence in the UK, for example, is committed under the influence of alcohol, two thirds is therefore committed without (Humphreys, Regan, & Thiara, 2005). This suggests that although alcohol should be considered a risk factor for domestic violence, it should not be regarded as the underlying cause.

HEGEMONIC MASCULINITY, SPORT, AND DOMESTIC VIOLENCE

It has been argued that modern sport was socially constructed to instil an idealised form of masculinity, which has become hegemonic through its "acceptance" within society (Connell, 1990). Hegemonic forms of masculinity serve to reinforce the dominance of men in most aspects of life, referred to as patriarchy. Hearn (2004) suggests that "[h]egemony involves both the consent of some men, and, in a very different way, the consent of some women to maintain patriarchal relations of power" (p. 52). The "consent" by females is not a willing approval, but rather a reluctant acceptance of patriarchy. Nonetheless, Burgess et al. (2003) boldly states that "[s]port is now indelibly connected to 'hegemonic masculinity'" (p. 200).

Connell and Messerschmidt (2005) outline the formulation of the concept of hegemonic masculinity:

> "[T]he pattern of practice (i.e., things done, not just a set of role expectations or an identity) that allowed men's dominance over women to continue .... [W]as distinguished from other masculinities, especially subordinated masculinities .... Certainly normative .... [E]mbodied the currently most honored way of being a man ... [I]t ideologically legitimated the global subordination of women to men" (p. 832)

Radford and Stanko (1996) consider men's use of violence against women fundamental in securing and maintaining "male dominance and female subordination" (p. 65). Moreover, they highlight the family as "a central institution in patriarchal society" wherein the "private struggles around patriarchal power relations frequently features as a form of control of the powerless by the powerful" (p. 78). Thus, domestic violence could be seen as central to the expression of hegemonic masculinity and the maintenance of patriarchy. Nonetheless, Connell and Messerschmidt (2005) emphasise that hegemony can be expressed in numerous ways, including positive practices (e.g., "bringing home a wage, sustaining a sexual relationship, and being a father" p. 840) but acknowledge that it can also include "toxic practices" (particularly violence) that serve to stabilize gender power hierarchies.

FUTURE DIRECTIONS

Further research is needed to unpick the complex relationship between sport and domestic violence, and implement evidence-based strategies to break this relationship. To date, much of the research has been largely observational, but if sport does not "cause" domestic violence then potential mediating factors must be examined. Future studies could include the cross-referencing of alcohol sales during major sporting events with domestic violence reports, and qualitative work looking at how particular hegemonic expressions of masculinity relate to sport and violence. Qualitative research with survivors of domestic violence who were assaulted during sporting events might also shed light on the relationship.

In order to conduct such research, however, there needs to be greater consistency in the definition of domestic violence, and the pursuit of research methods that reflect this definition. Domestic violence incorporates the relentless pattern of physical violence *and* non-violent tactics to control the domestic relationship (Johnson, 2008) referred to as *coercive* control (Stark, 2007). The nature and extent of the behaviours that underpin domestic violence, have been likened to those of political terrorists and hostage-takers (Stark, 2007). Yet, research usually takes a myopic focus on physical violence (through the use of health and police data) in relation to sport. An examination of the prevalence of all forms of domestic violence and their associations with sporting events would provide a fuller account of the dynamics of the relationship (Braaf & Gilbert, 2007).

However, obtaining an accurate measure of prevalence is further hindered by chronic underreporting. Small scale in-depth studies frequently uncover larger estimates than national surveys due to the greater detail covered and the sensitive nature of the topic (Heise & Garcia-Moreno, 2002), but this form of research is not conducive to linking patterns of abuse to sporting events. Police reports of domestic incidents provide one form of "objective" measure (see Williams et al., 2013), although this method is potentially confounded by survivor non-reporting, and different police practices around incident recording, categorising, and levels of activity in any given area (Bellis et al., 2012). An alternative method is to examine health data, including presentation to emergency departments, which cover violent incidents which have not been reported to the police (Bellis et al., 2012); however, this clearly has a bias toward physical injury.

Moreover, although the research literature demonstrates statistical relationships between some sporting events and domestic violence, this is not true for all sports, and some events may even provide protective factors (Bellis et al., 2012). Further research is required to elucidate the factors behind these relationships, including the normative use of alcohol and alternative expressions of masculinity, which can then be used to design strategies that effectively tackle the association found between certain sporting events and domestic violence.

It is also worth noting that while the vast majority of the literature concerning sport-related domestic violence considers male-on-female violence, this does not mean that female-on-male or same-sex sport-related domestic violence does not occur. Indeed, some of the studies reviewed in this chapter refer to anonymised police data for which the gender of the victim and perpetrator are unknown (e.g., Williams et al., 2013). An indication of the alternative forms of sport-related domestic violence is alluded to in a study by Carlyle, Scarduzio, and Slater (in press) who found that in a sample of media reports detailing female perpetrators of domestic violence, there was a greater than expected likelihood of the victims being a sports figure. However, this finding is complicated by the likelihood of greater media coverage for incidents involving sport personalities. The sparse literature regarding female-on-male or same-sex sport-related domestic violence is a clear avenue for future research, particularly given exposure to some similar, potential risk factors (e.g., attendance at sporting events and sport-related alcohol consumption).

Finally, it is apparent that much of the research on sport-related domestic violence originates from Western cultures. Given the worldwide popularity of sport participation and spectatorship, and relevant cultural differences (e.g., the role of sports in society, the nature of masculinity, and norms around alcohol consumption) it is important that this research field extends to diverse contexts.

SPORT AS A MEANS OF ADDRESSING VIOLENCE

While this chapter has outlined the theoretical background and evidence base for sport-related domestic violence, we wish to conclude more optimistically by stressing the positive role that sport can play in helping to address domestic violence. Recent research has suggested that social norm misperceptions contribute to gender violence (e.g., Neighbors et al., 2010). Sport participation and spectatorship can, therefore, function as an opportunity to correct these misperceptions and change behaviour. The creation of occasions for men (both athletes and spectators) to publically express their opposition to gender violence can send a powerful message about a group's social norm. For example, the White Ribbon Campaign (see www.whiteribboncampaign.org) is a global project that encourages high profile athletes and spectators to wear white ribbons to specified sporting events. The meaning of the campaign is then explained to spectators (i.e., to stand against gender violence) who are encouraged to show their support with a round of applause.

Furthermore, some initiatives have used the social status of university and professional athletes to combat gender violence. The Mentors in Violence Prevention campaign encourages prominent sports personalities to speak out against gender violence, and provides training for bystander intervention (Katz, 1995). Norm misperceptions in support of gender violence are therefore not only corrected by high profile group members, but men are given an active role in non-violent intervention in situations of gender violence.

Other initiatives use sport with females as a means of tackling gender violence. Women Win (see www.womenwin.org) is an international organisation that encourages sport as a means of providing females with a safe space in which to speak about experiences and problems, learn about legal rights, and gain empowerment. Similarly, the United Nations High Commissioner for Refugees (see http://www.unhcr.org/pages/4a0d90946.html) run sport projects which provide education on gender and sexual violence to vulnerable children who often lack alternative educational opportunities. It is worth noting that these strategies move beyond a traditional "cathartic" hypothesis which states that participation or spectatorship of violent sports prevents violent behaviour in non-sporting spheres. Despite perseverance in public consciousness, this hypothesis has received little empirical support (Wann et al., 1999). Indeed, Dunning (1999) notes that modern sport aims to create tension as opposed to relieving/discharging it.

CONCLUSION

To begin the chapter we discussed the paradoxical role of sport in society, and to end we focused on the paradoxical relationship in the sport-domestic violence nexus. On the one hand, there is an emerging evidence base that points toward a high incidence of domestic violence among professional and amateur male athletes, suggesting an increase in reports of domestic violence around certain sporting events. This has been associated with the prevailing ideological values of hegemonic masculinity that pervade the male-dominated socially constructed institution of sport. Although there is relatively consistent evidence for the link between specific sporting events (e.g., Old Firm soccer fixture) and reported domestic violence, one cannot generalise this association to all sporting events, athletes and spectators.

This is due to reported null associations and contradictory results in different spheres of sport, coupled with a relative scarcity of robust analysis of the association including roles for potential mediating variables (e.g., alcohol consumption, conceptions of masculinity, expectation of result). It is also acknowledged that not all males (athletes, spectators, or neither) express masculinity through violent means, and not all sport-related domestic violence is likely to be perpetrated by males on females. Thus, future research is needed to explore the contexts in which sport-related violence may occur, confirm the risk factors for such violence, and delineate protective factors to combat these risks. Furthermore, sport may have a role to play in domestic violence prevention through engaging males and supporting them in confronting and tackling the toxic practices that are often associated with hegemonic masculinity, in conjunction with female empowerment and the pursuit of gender equality.

REFERENCES

Anderson, C. A. (2001). Heat and violence. *Current Directions in Psychological Science*, *10*(1), 33-38.

Baxter, A. (2005). Hockey violence: The Canadian criminal code and professional hockey. *The Manitoba Law Journal*, *31*(2), 281.

BBC. (2012). London 2012: Olympians and Paralympians cheered by crowds. Retrieved 13th March 2014 from: http://www. bbc.co.uk/news/uk-19540587

Bellis, M. A., Leckenby, N., Hughes, K., Luke, C., Wyke, S. & Quigg, Z. (2012). Nighttime assaults: Using a national emergency department monitoring system to predict occurrence, target prevention and plan services. *BMC Public Health*, *12*(1), 746.

Benedict, J. (1999). *Public Heroes, Private Felons: Athletes and Crimes Against Women*. Boston, MA: Northeastern University Press.

Braaf, R. & Gilbert, R. (2007). Domestic violence incident peaks: Seasonal factors, calendar events and sporting matches. Australian Domestic and Family Violence Clearinghouse website. Retrieved 29th January 2013 from:

http://www.adfvc.unsw.edu.au/PDF%20files/Stakeholder% 20paper_%202.pdf.

Brecklin, L. R. (2002). The role of perpetrator alcohol use in the injury outcomes of intimate assaults. *Journal of Family Violence*, *17*(3), 185-197.

Brimicombe, A. & Cafe, R. (2012). Beware, win or lose: Domestic violence and the World Cup. *Significance*, *9*(5), 32-35.

Burgess, I., Edwards, A. & Skinner, J. (2003). Football culture in an Australian school setting: The construction of masculine identity. *Sport, Education and Society*, *8*(2), 199-212.

Campbell, N. (2007). How football's intimate details become drowned in drink. *The Guardian*. Retrieved 16th March 2014 from:

http://www.theguardian.com/football/2007/feb/08/sport.comment

Capaldi, D. M., Knoble, N. B., Shortt, J. W. & Kim, H. K. (2012). A systematic review of risk factors for intimate partner violence. *Partner Abuse*, *3*(2), 231-280.

Card, D. & Dahl, G. B. (2011). Family violence and football: The effect of unexpected emotional cues on violent behavior. *The Quarterly Journal of Economics*, *126*(1), 103-143.

Carlyle, K. E., Scarduzio, J. A. & Slater, M. D. (in press). Media portrayals of female perpetrators of intimate partner violence. *Journal of Interpersonal Violence*.

Carnochan, J. & McCluskey, K. (2011). Violence, culture and policing in Scotland. In D. Donnelly & K. Scott (Eds.), *Policing Scotland* (2 ed., pp. 399-424). Abingdon, UK: Routledge.

Christesen, P. & Kyle, D. G. (Eds.). (2014). *A Companion to Sport and Spectacle in Greek and Roman Antiquity*. Oxford, UK: John-Wiley & Sons.

Coakley, J. & Pike, E. (2009). *Sports in society: Issues and controversies*. Maidenhead, UK: McGraw-Hill Higher Education.

Cohn, E. G. (1993). The prediction of police calls for service: The influence of weather and temporal variables on rape and domestic violence. *Journal of Environmental Psychology*, *13*(1), 71-83.

Collins, J. J. & Messerschmidt, P. M. (1993). Epidemiology of alcohol-related violence. *Alcohol Health and Research World*, *17*(2), 93-99.

Connell, R. W. (1990). An iron man: The body and some contradictions of hegemonic masculinity. In M. A. Messner & D. F. Sabo (Eds.), *Sport men, and the gender order: Critical feminist perspectives* (pp. 83–95). Champaign, IL: Human Kinetics.

Connell, R. W. & Messerschmidt, J. W. (2005). Hegemonic masculinity: Rethinking the concept. *Gender & Society*, *19*(6), 829-859.

Cowan, A. (2001). Boys, masculinity and television violence: What is the difference between superheroes and football heroes? Paper presented at the TASA 2001 Conference, The University of Sydney.

Crosset, T. (1999). Male athletes' violence against women: A critical assessment of the athletic affiliation, violence against women debate. *Quest*, *51*(3), 244-257.

DeBeliso, M., Walsh, J., Climstein, M., Heazlewood, I. T., Kettunen, J., Sevene, T., et al. (2014). World Masters Games: North American participant medical and health history survey. *The Sport Journal*. Retrieved 4th April 2014 from: http://thesportjournal.org/article/world-masters-games-north-american-participant-medical-and-health-history-survey/

Dickson, A., Jennings, C. & Koop, G. (2013). *Domestic Violence and Football in Glasgow: Are Reference Points Relevant?* Retrieved 18th October 2013 from http://repo.sire.ac.uk/bitstream/ 10943/439/1/SIRE-DP-2013-33.pdf

Dunning, E. (1999). *Sport Matters: Sociological Studies of Sport, Violence and Civilization*. London: Routledge.

Edge, A. (1997). *Faith of our Fathers: Football as a Religion*. Edinburgh, UK: Mainstream.

Elias, N. & Dunning, E. (1986). *Quest for Excitement. Sport and Leisure in the Civilizing Process*. Oxford, UK: Basil Blackwell.

Enck-Wanzer, S. M. (2009). All's fair in love and sport: Black masculinity and domestic violence in the news. *Communication and Critical/Cultural Studies*, *6*(1), 1-18.

Enock, K. E. & Jacobs, J. (2008). The Olympic and Paralympic Games 2012: Literature review of the logistical planning and operational challenges for public health. *Public Health*, *122*(11), 1229-1238.

Finney, A. (2004). Alcohol and intimate partner violence: Key findings from the research. *Home Office Findings 216*. London: Home Office.

Flood, M. & Dyson, S. (2007). Sport, athletes, and violence against women. *No To Violence Journal*, *4*(3), 37-46.

Gantz, W., Bradley, S. D. & Wang, Z. (2006). Televised NFL games, the family, and domestic violence. In A. A. Raney & J. Bryant (Eds.), *Handbook of sports and Media* (pp. 365-381). Mahwah, NJ.: Lawrence Erlbaum Asscoaites Publishers.

Gill, F. (2007). 'Violent' femininity: Women rugby players and gender negotiation. *Women's Studies International Forum, 30*(5), 416-426.

Grohol, J. (2010). Super Bowl Sunday, domestic violence & your health. Retrieved 22nd January 2014 from: http://psychcentral.com/blog/archives/2010/02/04/super-bowl-sunday-domestic-violence-your-health/

Guilbert, S. (2004). Sport and violence: A typological analysis. *International Review for the Sociology of Sport, 39*(1), 45-55.

Hearn, J. (2004). From hegemonic masculinity to the hegemony of men. *Feminist Theory, 5*(1), 49-72.

Heise, L. & Garcia-Moreno, C. (2002). Violence by intimate partners. In E. G. Krug, L. Dahlberg, J. Mercy, A. B. Zwi & F. J. Lozano (Eds.), *World report on violence and health* (pp. 87-122). Geneva: WHO.

Humphreys, C., Regan, L. & Thiara, R. K. (2005). Domestic violence and substance use: Overlapping issues in separate services? London: Home Office and Greater London Authority.

Jackson, S. J. (1993). Beauty and the beast: A critical look at sports violence. *New Zealand Journal of Health, Physical Education & Recreation, 26*(4), 9-13.

Jamieson, L. (2009). *Sport and Violence: A Critical Examination of Sport.* Oxford, UK: Butterworth-Heineman.

Johnson, M. P. (2008). *A Typology of Domestic Violence: Intimate Terrorism, Violence Resistance, and Situational Couple Violence.* Lebanon, NH: Northeastern University Press.

Jones, S. C., Phillipson, L. & Lynch, M. (2006). Alcohol and sport: Can we have one without the other? Paper presented at the Australian and New Zealand Marketing Academy (ANZMAC) Conference, Queensland University of Technology. http://ro.uow.edu.au/hbspapers/75/

Katz, J. (1995). Reconstructing masculinity in the locker room: The Mentors in Violence Prevention Project. *Harvard Educational Review, 65*(2), 163-175.

Kersting, N. (2007). Sport and national identity: A comparison of the 2006 and 2010 FIFA World Cups. *Politikon: South African Journal of Political Studies, 34*(3), 277-293.

Kidd, B. (2013). Sports and masculinity. *Sport in Society, 16*(4), 553-564.

Kirby, S., Francis, B. & O'Flaherty, R. (in press). Can the FIFA World Cup football (Soccer) tournament be associated with an increase in domestic abuse? *Journal of Research in Crime and Delinquency.*

Kwan, M., Bobko, S., Faulkner, G., Donnelly, P. & Cairney, J. (2014). Sport participation and alcohol and illicit drug use in adolescents and young adults: A systematic review of longitudinal studies. *Addictive Behaviors, 39*(3), 497-506.

Leonard, W. M. (1993). *A Sociological Perspective of Sport* (4 ed.). New York, NY: Macmillan.

Mangan, J. A. (1986). *The Games Ethic and Imperialism: Aspects of the Diffusion of an Ideal.* New York, NY: Viking Penguin.

McFee, G. (2004). *Sport, Rules and Values.* London: Routledge.

Messner, M. A. (1995). *Power at Play: Sports and the Problem of Masculinity*. Boston, MA: Beacon Press.

Messner, M. A., Hunt, D., Dunbar, M., Chen, P., Lapp, J. & Miller, P. (1999). *Boys to Men: Sports Media Messages about Masculinity: A National Poll of Children, Focus Groups, and Content Analysis of Sports Programs and Commercials*. Oakland, CA: Children Now. Retrieved 19th March 2014 from: http://eric.ed.gov/?id=ED440775.

Moser, C. A. (2004). Penalties, fouls, and errors: Professional athletes and violence against women. *Sports Lawyers Journal, 69*, 69-87.

Neighbors, C., Walker, D. D., Mbilinyi, L. F., O'Rourke, A., Edleson, J. L., Zegree, J., & Roffman, R. A. (2010). Normative misperceptions of abuse among perpetrators of intimate partner violence. *Violence Against Women, 16*(4), 370-386.

Neville, F. G. & Reicher, S. D. (2011). The experience of collective participation: Shared identity, relatedness and emotionality. *Contemporary Social Science, 6*(3), 377-369.

NFHS. (2013). *National Federation of State High School Associations 2013 football rules changes* Retrieved 30th March 2014 from:
http://theconcussionblog.com/tag/butt-blocking/

Ommundsen, Y., Løndal, K. & Loland, S. (2014). Sport, children, and well-being. In A. Ben-Arieh, F. Casas, I. Frønes, & J. E. Korbin (Eds.), *Handbook of child well-being: Theories, methods and policies in global perspective* (vol. 2, pp. 911-940). London: Springer.

Oths, K. & Robertson, T. (2007). Give me shelter: Temporal patterns of women fleeing domestic abuse. *Human Organization, 66*(3), 249-260.

Palmer, C. (2011). *Violence Against Women and Sport: A Literature Review*. Rerieved 20th January 2013 from: http://www. endviolenceagainstwomen.org.uk/resources/22/violence-against-women-and-sport-a-literature-review-by-dr-catherine-palmer

Quigley, B. M. & Leonard, K. E. (2000). Alcohol and the continuation of early martial aggression. *Alcoholism: Clinical and Experimental Research, 24*(7), 1003-1010.

Radford, J. & Hudson, E. (2005). Balls and permissions: Theorising the link between football and domestic violence. In T. Skinner, M. Hester & E. Malos (Eds.), *Researching gender violence: Feminist methodology in action* (pp. 190-209). Devon, UK: Willan Publishing.

Radford, J. & Stanko, E. A. (1996). Violence against women and children: The contradiction of crime control under patriarchy. In M. Hester, L. Kelly & J. Radford (Eds.), *Women, violence and male power: Feminist activism, research and practice* (pp. 65-80). Buckingham, UK: Open University Press.

Sachs, C. J. & Chu, L. D. (2000). The association between professional football games and domestic violence in Los Angeles County. *Journal of Interpersonal Violence, 15*(11), 1192-1201.

Sani, F., Herrera, M., Wakefield, J. R. H., Boroch, O. & Gulyas, C. (2012). Comparing social contact and group identification as predictors of mental health. *British Journal of Social Psychology, 51*(4), 781-790.

Scottish Parliament. (2011). First Minister's question time: Secretary of State for Scotland (meetings). From http://scottish.parliament.uk/parliamentarybusiness/28862.aspx?r=6228

Sheen, D. & Tettenborn, M. (2011). *British beer and pub association handbook 2010*. London: British Beer & Pub Association.

Shepherd, J. (1990). Violent crime in Bristol: An accident and emergency department perspective. *British Journal of Criminology, 30*(3), 289-305.

Shobe, H. (2008). Place, identity, and football: Catalonia, Catalonisme, and Football Club Barcelona, 1899–1975. *National Identities*, *10*(3), 329-343.

Stark, E. (2007). *Coercive control: How men entrap women in personal life*. Oxford, UK: Oxford University Press.

Wann, D. L., Carlson, J., Holland, L., Jacob, B., Owens, D. & Wells, D. D. (1999). Beliefs in symbolic catharsis: The importance of involvement with aggressive sports. *Social Behavior adn Personality*, *27*(2), 155-164.

Webb, B. (2012). Unsportsmanlike conduct: Curbing the trend of domestic violence in the National Football League and Major League Baseball. *Journal of Gender, Social Policy & the Law*, *20*(3), 741-761.

Weinstein, M. D., Smith, M. D. & Wiesenthal, D. L. (1995). Masculinity and hockey violence. *Sex Roles*, *33*(11-12), 831-847.

Wenner, L. A. (1998). In search of the sports bar: Masculinity, alcohol, sports and mediation of public space. In G. Rail (Ed.), *Sport and postmodern times* (pp. 301-332). Albany, NY: State University of New York.

Wenner, L. A. & Jackson, S. J. (2009). Sport, beer, and gender in promotional culture: On the dynamics of a holy trinity. In L. A. Wenner & S. J. Jackson (Eds.), *Sport, beer, and gender: Promotional culture and contemporary social life* (pp. 1-34). New York, NY: Peter Lang Publishing, Inc.

White, G. F., Katz, J. & Scarborough, K. E. (1992). The impact of professional football games upon violent assaults on women. *Violence and Victims*, *7*(2), 157-171.

Williams, D. J., Neville, F. G., House, K. & Donnelly, P. D. (2013). Association between Old Firm football matches and reported domestic (violence) incidents in Strathclyde, Scotland. *SAGE Open*, *3*(3).

Young, K. (2000). Sport and violence. In J. Coakley & E. Dunning (Eds.), *Handbook of sports studies* (pp. 382-407). Thousand Oaks, CA: Sage.

Young, K. (2012). *Sport, Violence and Society*. Abingdon, UK: Routledge.

SECTION FOUR

In: Overcoming Domestic Violence
Editors: Myra F. Taylor, Julie Ann Pooley et al.

ISBN: 978-1-63321-956-4
© 2015 Nova Science Publishers, Inc.

Chapter 16

CHILD MALTREATMENT: A PHENOMENOLOGICAL STUDY OF ADULT MALES' RECOLLECTED CHILDHOOD MEMORIES OF EXPERIENCING ABUSE AND WITNESSING DOMESTIC VIOLENCE IN THE FAMILY HOME

Myra F. Taylor[*], *Teresa Goddard and Julie Ann Pooley*
Edith Cowan University, Joondalup, Western Australia, Australia

ABSTRACT

The series of studies reported in this book so far have presented an unequivocal account of domestic violence and the devastating impact it can have on the lives of females, and individuals involved in LGBT relationships. Nonetheless, what is missing from the discourse so far is an understanding of the male experience. To help fill this void the results of three exemplar studies detailed in the next three chapters are based on a phenomenological research study conducted at Edith Cowan University (ECU) in Western Australia. The project examined what impact child maltreatment had on eight male participants' childhood lives as well as their adult relationships.

This first chapter opens with a brief synopsis of the growing recognition that domestic violence (including witnessing violence) is a form of maltreatment and closes with a detailed account of the qualitative methodology employed in the study. The second chapter details the male participants' recollected memories of their childhood experiences of maltreatment. The third chapter reveals the psychosocial damage that the popular belief that an abused child will grow up to become an abusive adult had on the lives of the participants. The fourth and final chapter in this series details how the participants tried to move on from their damaged lives by engaging in various resilience building intervention programs. The chapter closes with a discussion of the implications that child maltreatment experiences can have not only on the lives of males affected by child abuse, but also on the wider adult male populace.

---

[*] Corresponding author: Myra F. Taylor Edith, Cowan University, 270 Joondalup Drive Joondalup, WA 6007 Australia.

INTRODUCTION

Child maltreatment is the umbrella term given to instances of child abuse and neglect, and more recently, to the childhood witnessing of acts of interparental domestic violence (WHO, 2014). In order to develop an understanding of the implications that child maltreatment can have on the lives of men this chapter opens with both a definition of child abuse and neglect and, also, of child witnessing. These definitional understandings are followed by prevalence estimates of both child abuse and child witnessing. Next a brief outline is provided of the risk factors for child maltreatment. The chapter closes with an account of the present study's methodology. The findings emanating out of the study are presented in the three chapters immediately following this introductory chapter.

Child Abuse and Neglect

A precise definition of child abuse is difficult to formulate given its many different variations, however, the term 'child abuse' is generally considered to be synonymous with any conceptualization of child maltreatment (Euser et al., 2013). Characteristically, child abuse is defined as a targeted or exploitative act that is directed towards a child and is committed (or permitted to be committed) on the child by the child's parent or caregiver and, which places the child at-risk of serious (i.e., more than transitory) *physical abuse* (e.g., hitting, shaking, throwing, burning, bitting, poisoning, choking, slapping, spanking); *emotional abuse* (e.g., rejection, teasing, bullying, impairment of child's sense of self); *sexual abuse* (e.g., inappropriate touching, sexual kissing, sexual stimulation, penetration, rape, sodomy, prostituting, witnessing of sexual acts), or results in the *neglect* (e.g., abandonment; failure to provide) of a child's basic need for food, housing, healthcare, hygienic living conditions, supervision, and medical treatment (Behura, 2011; Child Welfare Information Gateway, 2013; Department of Child Protection, 2010; Paavilainen, & Tarkka, 2003; Queensland Government, 2013; Stoltenborgh, Bakermans-Kranenburg, Van Ijzendoorn, & Alink, 2013). Acts of child abuse can also constitute any form of communication (e.g., verbal, written, visual) that continually humiliates shames or frightens a child, or fails to adequately nurture their development to such an extent that the child manifests sustained signs of developmentally inappropriate function or behaviour (Behura, 2011).

Witnessing Domestic Violence

There is growing recognition that the witnessing of interparental domestic violence by a child within the family home is tantamount to child abuse as the witnessing act has a profound impact on the child's development. Consequently, child witnessing is increasingly classified as a non-specified form of child maltreatment (Euser et al., 2013). For, the act of witnessing domestic violence is recognised as being particularly disturbing to children as it typically involves the very people (parents/caregivers) with whom the child is most emotionally attached (UNCF, 2012). Hence, the generally accepted clinical definition of child witnessing is an act that results in the traumatized watching by a child of a fight between his/her parents in which one parent is the perpetrator of the act and the other is the victim and, which commonly involves elements of both physical and verbal abuse (Kantor & Little, 2003; O'Brien et al., 2013).

There is also an increasing realization that the current definition of child witnessing is not sufficient for it fails to capture the totality of the child witnessing experience. Namely, the horror and shame that accompanies the experience of hearing parental violence; seeing parental violence, being forced to spy on a parent, being coerced into participating in an act of violence, intervening to stop an act of violence, or being used as a weapon or hostage by one or both parents (Gonzales, Chronister, Linville, & Knoble, 2012; Knickerbocker et al., 2007; O'Brien et al., 2013). Consequently, repeated calls have been made for the development of a broader witnessing definition, one that captures the childhood experience of 'living with violence', 'being exposed to violence' and 'being affected by violence' (Bedi & Goddard, 2007; Gewirtz & Medhanie, 2008; Humphreys, 2010; Kantor & Little, 2003; O'Brien et al., 2013; Powell & Murray, 2008; Richards, 2011).

PREVALENCE

Considerable variation exists between different countries' internal prevalence rate estimates of child maltreatment (Radford, Corral, Bradley, & Fisher, 2013; Stoltenborgh, van Ijendoorn, Euser, & Bakermans-Kranenburg, 2011). Given that prevalence rates are difficult to estimate it is widely accepted that the actual numbers of child protection cases recorded internally and globally are likely to be a gross under-recording of the actual numbers of child maltreatment cases occurring within families in countries across the world (Radford, Corral, Bradley, & Fisher, 2013). For, it is posited that many incidents go unreported due to the age of the victim and the inter-family culture of silence that surrounds instances of child abuse, neglect and domestic violence (Finkelhor, Turner, Ormrod, & Hamby, 2010; Gilbert et al., 2012). A further problem with current child maltreatment prevalence estimates is that they are frequently based on only the most severe cases that are referred to child welfare authorities for investigation or intervention. However, this approach fails to capture the large number of hidden cases of maltreatment that occur in families where the non-abusing parent fails to report the abuse (see Bolen & Lamb, 2004; Gibson & Morgan, 2013).

Child Abuse and Neglect Rates

Despite the likely underestimation of the size of the child maltreatment problem the number of child protection cases recorded in a country do provide some insights into the amount of children who are being monitored and/or receiving help. For instance, in Australia, between 2010 and 2011 a total of 237,273 notifications of child maltreatment reports were recorded. Upon investigation, 40,466 of the reports were substantiated (i.e., a reasonable cause was found to exist to substantiate the belief that the reported child had, or was likely to have been abused, harmed or neglected) (Australian Institute of Health and Welfare, 2012). Such rates of child maltreatment are not unique though to Australia as the U.S. Department of Health and Human Services Administration for Children and Families (2012) reports that in

2012 3.4 million American children were the subject of a child maltreatment report (i.e., for child abuse and/or neglect). Of these, approximately 3 million cases were referred for further investigation. Furthermore, child maltreatment figures emanating out of the United Kingdom indicate that 1 in 11 children each year experience physical abuse and, also, as a cohort, maltreated children account for 1% of all child injury-induced visits to emergency departments (Woodman, Pitt, Wentz, Hodes, & Gilbert, 2008). Global child maltreatment estimates suggest that approximately 155,000 child deaths occur each year as a direct consequence of parental abuse or neglect (Louwers et al., 2011). Moreover, the World Health Organization (WHO, 2014) estimates that 20% of women and between 5-10% of men are sexually abused as a child and that nearly a quarter of all people (23%) worldwide are physically abused as children. Interestingly, there seems to be some inter-country variations in terms of the types of maltreatment being reported. For instance, in the developed and developing regions of the world frequency reports suggests that the physical abuse of children occurs at rates of between 2-23% of the child population, however, in some areas (e.g., Africa) the physical abuse occurrence rate is as high as 37-60% (Akmatov, 2011, WHO, 2013).

Child Witnessing Rates

The rates of children witnessing interparental domestic violence are not too dissimilar from the child abuse rates. Australian police records reveal that 6-9% of all Australian households are involved in one or more domestic violence incidents each year (People, 2005), with the highest rates occurring within Indigenous households (Indermaur, 2001). In America, the US Department of Justice figures reveal that in 21-38% of all recorded domestic violence cases children were present in the home (Catalano, Smith, Snyder, & Rand, 2009; Gonzales, Chronister, Linville, & Noble, 2012). Moreover, globally it is estimated that each year between 133-275 million children witness acts of domestic violence within the family home (Gil-Gonzalez, Vives-Cases, Ruiz, Carrasco-Portino, & Alvarez-Dardet, 2007; Pinheiro, 2006). Again, it is widely acknowledged that the available estimates of child witnessing under-report the size of the problem and, as such are only the tip of the child witnessing iceberg (Euser et al., 2013; O'Brien, Cohen, Pooley, & Taylor, 2013). It is widely suggested that the under-reporting of child witnessing incidents occurs largely because of police suboptimal reporting procedures as when adult incidents of domestic violence are recorded police do not routinely record whether the violence was witnessed by the dyad's children (O'Brien et al., 2013; Louwers et al., 2011; Richards, 2011).

RISK FACTORS ASSOCIATED WITH CHILD MALTREATMENT

A number of risk factors exist for child maltreatment many of which relate to the parents' experience of trying to raise children in communities where they only have limited psychosocial and economic support resources (Euser, Van Ijzendoorn, Prinzie & Bakermans-Kranenburg, 2011; Stoltenborgh, Bakermans-Kranenburg, Van Ijzendoorn, & Alink, 2013). For example, child maltreatment occurs more frequently in families where there is a combination of a) low levels of parental education attainment, unemployment or underemployment of one or both parents, substance abuse, interparental hostilities, marital breakdown, circumstantial poverty, repeated housing relocations or where single or immigrant parents are under-supported, and b) where children experience insecure parental bonding, repeated moves to new schools, low levels of school attainment, peer acceptance problems, gender non-conformity issues, reside in a large family environment, and grow up in a community where there is a cultural acceptance of child abuse and domestic violence (Akmatov, 2011; Gewirtz & Edleson, 2007; Euser et al., 2013; Gomez, 2011; Holt, Buckley, Whelan, 2008; Mullender et al., 2002; Neugebauer, 2000; Roberts, Rosario, Corliss, & Koenen, 2012; Sebre et al., 2004; Vittrup, Holden, & Buck, 2006; Zink et al., 2005). Moreover, children who experience child maltreatment and/or exposure to domestic violence in the family home are known to be at a heightened risk for negative *internalizing* (e.g., withdrawal, somatic complaints, anxiety, depression) and *externalizing* (e.g., delinquency, aggression) behavioural outcomes, particularly during adolescence (Moylan et al., 2010). Furthermore, children who experience the 'double maltreatment whammy' of child abuse and child witnessing have been determined to be more likely to manifest negative life outcomes than are children who solely experience child abuse or solely witness domestic violence (Bourassa, 2007; Ellonen, Piispa, Peltonen, & Lica, 2013; Herrenkohl, Sousa, Tajima, Herrenkohl, & Moylan, 2008 O'Brien, Cohen, Pooley, & Taylor, 2013, Yexley, Borrowsky, & Ireland, 2002).

GENDER DIFFERENCES

Stoltenborgh and colleagues (2013) in their meta-analysis of 9,698,801 participants concluded no overall gender difference exists in children's experiences of maltreatment. However, a number of studies have recorded some specific gender abuse differences in terms of type and location. For instance, it has been found that in some regions of the world boys are at a higher risk for physical abuse than girls, and girls are at a greater risk for sexual abuse than boys (see Akmatov, 2011; Miles & Thomas, 2007; UNCF, 2012). Also, while Chinese parents typically use less severe forms of corporal punishment on their female children than they do on their male children, in the Philippines and Thailand the parents' gendered use of corporal punishment is reversed (UNCF, 2012). Similarly, whereas UNCF found sexual abuse to be significantly more common in girls than in boys in most countries in Asia, Miles and Thomas (2007) report that in Cambodia boys are three times more likely to be raped than are girls. One gender difference that is of particular note in relation to the present study, was reported by Shen (2009) who noted that boys who experience both forms of child maltreatment (i.e., child abuse and childhood witnessing) have lower levels of self-esteem than do girls exposed to both forms of maltreatment.

Given the prevalence rates of maltreatment in boys have historically been particularly difficult to correlate due to low rates of disclosure (Payne et al., 2014; Schraufnagel, Davis, George, & Norris, 2010), when it comes to determining whether girls or boys are at a higher risk of negative outcomes following maltreatment experiences, the existing studies to date have yielded inconclusive results. For example, girls have been found to be at a greater risk than boys for developing internalizing behaviours (e.g., depression, anxiety, fearfulness, low self-esteem, helplessness) following experiences of child maltreatment, while boys have been found to be at greater risk than girls for developing externalizing behaviours (e.g., aggression, hyperactivity) (Ellonen, Piispa, Peltonen, & Lica., 2013; Evans, Davis, & DiLillo, 2008; Hartman, Turner, Daigle, Exum, & Cullen, 2009; Sternberg et al., 1993).

What is somewhat surprising though is that although widespread agreement exists as to the vulnerability of girls to child maltreatment, in comparison, far less understanding exists of the male child maltreatment experience. Therefore, to provide the reader with a male perspective the next three chapters detail the life course experiences of Australian adult males who have as a child experienced abuse and also have witnessed domestic violence. The methodology employed is detailed below.

METHOD

Research Design

Unlike some other qualitative studies that aim to generate theory that is transferable to other populations, the sole objective of exemplar studies, such as the one presented here, is to develop an understanding of a hitherto poorly understood phenomenon within a defined context. In this study a phenomenological methodology was adopted to explore the childhood maltreatment experiences of men as well as the effects their child maltreatment experiences subsequently had on their adult lives.

A key attribute of exemplar studies of this nature is that they allow data from within, and across one or more datasets to be intensely interrogated and rigorously contrasted (Cresswell, 1998; Miles & Huberman, 1994; Stake, 1995). The benefit of using an exemplar methodology is that the findings become an archetype for other research studies. Indeed, Flyvbjerg (2006) maintains that exemplar studies are critically important as 'a scientific discipline without a large number of thoroughly executed case studies is a discipline without a systematic production of exemplars, and a discipline without exemplars is an ineffective one' (p. 219). The value of multiple exemplar studies to a discipline is that by weight of their combined numbers they generate findings that produce insights into an investigated phenomenon which are reflective of the lived experience of the wider population (Punch, 2005; Stake, 1995).

This phenomenological exemplar study was designed within the symbolic interactionist tradition within Social Theory. Its social constructionist epistemology assumes that people construct and mediate their understanding of self through interactions with others (Charmaz, 2006). Interpretative phenomenology draws upon the theoretical framework of symbolic interactionism which emphasises the subjective meanings that individuals learn and assign to the social objects, activities, and environments that surround their everyday lives (Biggerstaff & Thompson, 2008; Brocki & Wearden, 2006; Given, 2008; Reid, Flowers, & Larkin, 2005; Smith & Osborn, 2003). Thus, the adoption of an interpretative phenomenological research approach was considered pertinent to developing an in-depth understanding of adult males' childhood experiences of living in a family home where abuse and domestic violence were an ongoing part of family life. For, this approach allows participants to view, and make sense of, their childhood experiences while at the same time allowing researchers to listen and reflect on the participants' lived experiences without being unduly influenced by their prior knowledge or preconceptions on the subject (Daly, 2007; Hanson, Morales, Clark Plano & Creswell, 2007; Lopez & Willis, 2004; Lowes & Prowse, 2001). Furthermore, phenomenological research is considered to be an archetypal method of qualitative research as it recognises that participants are the primary experts on the issue under investigation for they have lived the experience (Alexander & Clare, 2004).

The Research Question

The central research question upon which this study was framed was: *In what ways are men's adult lives shaped by their childhood maltreatment experiences*? This central question informed its three guiding questions: *What recollections do adult males have of their childhood experiences of abuse and their handling of that abuse? What impact do recollected memories of childhood maltreatment have on the daily functioning and social interactions of adult males? Do childhood experiences of maltreatment effect the ability of adult males to cope with future adversities?*

According to Blumer (1969) psychosocial questions of this nature can be addressed through the process of applying Social Theory's three basic precepts to such an investigation. The first precept being human beings respond to and act upon their different life experiences based on the meanings they attach to each new experience. Second, the meaning that individuals attach to these experiences are derived from their social encounters with other human beings, and third, such meanings are modified through the interpretative thought processes that individuals use following their social encounters so as to make sense and deal with their experiences (Houghton, Carroll, O'Donoghue, & Taylor, 2006). Utilizing these three basic precepts as a guide this study explored the male experience of child maltreatment within the family home; the male reaction to child maltreatment during their pre-adolescent and adolescent lives; the adult male legacy of childhood experiences of abuse and domestic violence; and the understanding of adult males as to how their childhood maltreatment experiences influenced their ability to lead fulfilled adult lives. In this way, Social Theory's three basic precepts were used to inform the construction of the study's interview schedule displayed in Table 1.

Semi-structured interviews were selected as being an appropriate means of data collection as this technique facilitates the conversational flow of information within a flexible format (Englander, 2012). Specifically, semi-structured interviews allow the interviewer to guide the flow of the conversation through employing a mix of predetermined open-ended and closed questions (Daly, 2007). This non-prescriptive questioning technique is considered to be effective as it provides participants with a relaxed atmosphere in which to recount their experiences and at the same time provides the interviewer with the ability to deviate from the interview schedule and introduce further *prompting* (e.g., 'How did that make you feel?'), *probing* (e.g. 'What was that like for you?'), and *follow-up* questions (e.g. 'Could you tell me more about that') in order to clarify and extend the participants' narratives (Liamputtong, 2009; Low, 2007; Kvale, 1996). The combination of open and closed questions is considered particularly efficacious as it allows participants to respond at whichever depth they consider appropriate (Vinten, 1995).

Table 1. Interview schedule

#	Questions
1	What do you remember about your childhood? • *What type(s) of abuse did you experience as a child? Can you give me an example?* • *What was your relationship with the abuser?* • *How long did the abuse continue for?* • *Did you tell anyone about the abuse?* • *How did the abuse stop?*
2	How have your childhood experiences impacted on your adult life? How have they impacted: • *On your emotions and the way you express them?* • *On the way you interact with others socially?* • *On the nature of your intimate relationships?* • *On the way you behave in general?* • *On the way you think?*
3	As an adult, how have you coped with issues relating to your childhood abuse? • *What does the term 'coping' mean to you?* • *What strategies have you used to cope?* • *Can you tell me about a time in your adult life when you've felt you weren't coping, as a result of your childhood abuse experiences*?
4	What does the term 'resilience' mean to you? • *Do you give up easily or do you persevere with things/relationships?* • *Do you have a positive or negative view on life? Why is that?* • *Do you feel that your childhood abuse experiences have made you stronger in any way? Please explain.*
5	When you look back at your past, how do you view your childhood?

Participants

While there is no established 'right size' for qualitative research studies, it is commonly accepted that small sample sizes allow for greater contextualisation of the study's research data (Brocki & Wearden, 2006; Reid, Flowers, & Larkin, 2005; Smith & Osborn, 2003). For, the difficulty with large samples is that subtle inflections of meaning can be lost during the interpretation process (Collins & Nicolson, 2002). Therefore, a sample size of eight adult males was deemed appropriate as this number is sufficient to a) secure the validity of the findings; b) to facilitate open and confiding relationships between the interviewer and the participants; c) to enable in-depth examinations of the sample's convergent and divergent viewpoints; and d) to provide illuminative insights into the participants' lives (McKenzie & Crouch, 2006; Smith & Osborn, 2003).

The study's inclusion criteria were: i) participants needed to be male and over the age of 20 years; ii) participants had to have experienced child maltreatment; and c) participants had to be willing to openly discuss how their childhood maltreatment experiences had impacted on their ability to function as an adult. No restriction was placed on the type of maltreatment so participants were able to narrate both personal incidents of child abuse as well as experiences of witnessing other family members being abused.

As can be seen in Table 2 three (37.5%) participants identified themselves as being Australian, three (37.5%) as being from an Asian background, and two (25%) from a European background. Of the eight participants, six (75%) had experienced physical abuse as a child, four (50%) sexual abuse, two (25%) verbal abuse, four (50%) psychological abuse, and one (12.5%) spiritual abuse. Five participants (62.5%) had witnessed the abuse of another family member (e.g., parent, grandparent, sibling, cousin), seven (87.5%) had experience two or more types of abuse, and five (62.5%) had been abused by more than one person. One (12.5%) participant was retired, one (12.5%) was a tertiary graduate employed in university study, one (12.5%) was employed in a field corresponding to his TAFE (vocational) qualifications, one (12.5%) was a self-employed tradesman, one (12.5%) was a self-employed business owner, and the remaining three (37.5%) participants were employed in jobs requiring information technology (I.T.) skills.

PROCEDURE

Ethics approval was sought and obtained from the administrating university's Human Research Ethics Committee. Upon obtaining approval, an online search of all the organizations (e.g., Men's Sheds, men's support services) that have contact with male survivors of child maltreatment was conducted. Once a list of relevant service providers had been complied, each organization was contacted by telephone and the aims of the research explained to the organization's gatekeepers (i.e., individual(s) within the organization who have direct contact with the organization's male clientele). Upon an organization expressing interest in the project, they were then provided with a supply of recruitment flyers, information letters, and consent forms to distribute to prospective participants. Where appropriate the organizations placed this information on their websites or displayed the information in their reception areas. In addition, the flyers, information letters and consent forms were placed on social media sites, such as Facebook and chat forums for survivors of childhood abuse (for example, The Wounded Warrior: Male Survivors) as well as on the administrating university's notice boards. As a result, five participants were recruited through the auspices of The Mankind Project (MKP), a network of self-directed men's groups, communities and training centers situated in various locations across Australia. The remaining three participants were recruited by participants recruiting other participants. Upon making contact with the research team prospective participants were informed of both their participatory rights and their participation requirements (i.e., take part in an interview). Any questions raised at this time were addressed. On gaining a prospective participant's participation agreement, a mutually agreeable time and public place (e.g., library, café) for the face-to-face interview was arranged.

Table 2. Information on participants experiences of child abuse and domestic violence within their childhood family home

Background:	Participant #							
	1	2	3	4	5	6	7	8
Cultural background								
Position in family	European 1 of 2	Asian 1 of 5	European 5 of 5	Australian 1 of 1	Asian 1 of 2	Asian 1 of 2	Australian 1 of 2	Australian 1 of 3
Generational history of abuse	Yes			Yes	Yes	Yes		Yes
Generational history of alcohol abuse				Yes	Yes	Yes		Yes
Abuse type:								
Physical	Yes	Yes	Yes		Yes	Yes		Yes
Sexual	Yes	Yes	Yes				Yes	
Verbal	Yes			Yes				Yes
Psychological	Yes	Yes			Yes	Yes		
Religious							Yes	
Witnessed abuse	Yes	Yes		Yes	Yes	Yes		
Duration of abuse	Until late teens	Until age13	Until teens		Until late teens	Until late teens		Until late teens
Relationship of abuser to participant:								
Mother		Yes	Yes	Yes				
Father		Yes				Yes		Yes
Sister	Yes		Yes		Yes			
Grandfather	Yes					Yes		
Other Caregiver	Yes			Yes			Yes	

Prior to the commencement of the interview permission was sought from each participant to audio record the interview. In addition, they were informed that the study was not concerned with the 'rightness' or 'wrongness' of their responses, but rather the emphasis was on their own personal experiences and their interpretation of those experiences. No time limit was set for each interview, and as such interviews ranged between approximately 26-140 minutes. At the completion of the interview participants were informed that they would be forwarded a copy of their interview transcript which they could then edit prior to the start of the analysis. Participants were also informed that on completion of the analysis and before publication they would be provided with an opportunity to review and comment on the study's findings. Finally, participants were provided with a list of counselling options.

DATA ANALYSIS

Data analysis occurred concurrently with data collection in so far as each interview was transcribed as soon as feasibly possible after completion. Next, all of the participants' responses to each question were entered into an Excel spreadsheet. The dual phenomenological concepts of 'bracketing' ('keeping a distance from one's own subjectivity' while engaging in inspection) and 'epoche' (synthesising) were employed (Bednall, 2006; Crist & Tanner, 2003; Lowes & Prowse, 2001; Pascal, 2010) in what Smith and Osborn (2003) refer to as the step-by-step approach to data analysis. To facilitate the rigor, holistic balance, and objective interpretation of the study's *'corpus'* (its eight individual interview transcription datasets) the interpretive analytic skills of two coders were employed (Clarke, 2009).

During the initial inspection phase, the coders independently familiarized themselves with the transcripts by reading them several times (Braun & Clarke, 2006; Liamputtong, 2009). During the course of their continual rereading of the transcripts, the coders independently identified and bracketed any prejudgements, personal biases or assumptions which arose in relation to the maltreatment issues of child abuse and witnessing domestic violence (Carpenter & Suto, 2008; Hayes, 2000). The dependability (i.e., the assessment of the quality of the data collection and the analysis) was ensured through the process of creating an Excel spreadsheet audit trail (see Baxter & Eyles, 1997; Carlson, 2010; Lincoln & Guba, 1985). In this regard, all of the quotes identified during the course of the reading as being pertinent to the study were listed in the first column of the spreadsheet and any unfocused memo notes relating to each quote were entered into the adjacent column.

During the second synthesising stage of the analytic process, inter-relational connections between the identified category codes were highlighted in different colours in the spreadsheet so as to identify their common conceptual link (Baxter & Jack, 2008; Bryman, 2008; Saldañda, 2011). These codes and patterns were continually resorted, regrouped and recombined until potential subthemes (i.e., units of meaning) emerged (Bazeley, 2009; Cresswell, 1998; Willig, 2008). In turn, these subthemes were repeatedly refined until a number of encompassing theme names were developed (Braun & Clarke, 2006; Groenewald, 2004). The two coding authors compared their spreadsheets and in instances where thematic disagreement occurred, a third researcher adopted the role of adjudicator coder. Thematic saturation was achieved at the point when no new themes or subthemes emerged Brocki &

Wearden, 2006). Illustrative quotes were then extracted from the transcripts to provide evidential support to the themes and subthemes (Biggerstaff & Thompson, 2008). Confirmability (i.e., the extent to which the characteristics of the findings can be confirmed by other readers) was determined by an adjudicating author checking the internal coherence of the findings (Bradley, 1993). Finally, a thematic map of the analysis was generated (see Figure 1) and its credibility was validated through engaging in a process of member-checking (i.e., sending the analysis to the study's participants to ask for their comment on its accuracy).

ANALYSIS RIGOUR

To ensure the study's research rigour the issue of data reliability was assured by a non-transcribing researcher checking the accuracy of 10% of the transcriptions (see Creswell, 2007); Rourke, Anderson, Garrison, & Archer, 2001) and by each participant reviewing their own transcripts, and also checking the researchers' findings to ensure their accuracy and integrity (Leech & Onwueghuzie, 2007; Liamputtong, 2009). In the present study member checking was considered an integral part of the research process because in provided a checking mechanism to both clarify and ground the research in the recounted stories of child maltreatment (Carpenter & Suto, 2008; Collins & Nicholson, 2002).

DIFFICULTIES ASSOCIATED WITH RESEARCH THAT IS RELIANT ON PARTICIPANTS' RECOLLECTED MEMORIES

A widely recognised complication associated with research studies such as this which ask participants to recall sensitive information is that their recalled experiences may be distorted or impaired and, thus, produce a more or a less 'disturbing' version of what really happened (Johnson, Raye, Mitchell, & Ankudowich, 2012; Payne et al., 2014). Characteristically, these distorted versions generally occur in individuals who have adopted avoidant coping strategies to deal with their traumatic childhood maltreatment experiences and who have not progressed beyond this destructive form of coping (Goodman, Quas, & Ogle, 2009). For, in such avoidant individuals, there exists a variety of 'forgetting' and 'selective memory repression mechanisms' (e.g., poor encoding, memory consolidation, reactivation, or rehearsal failure) (Graham-Bermann & Edleson, 2001; Roth, 2004; Russell, Springer, & Greenfield, 2010; Varia & Abidin, 1999). Although these techniques exist a number of studies have demonstrated that while non-traumatic retrospective memories are malleable and sometimes inaccurate, however, memories that are associated with traumatic experiences are processed and stored in a way which is dissimilar to non-traumatic memories (Chu, Frey, Ganzel, & Matthews, 1999; Mannuzza, Klein, Klein, Bessler, & Shrout, 2002). For instance, in their investigation of 90 females admitted into a treatment unit specializing in trauma-related disorders Chu and colleagues found that the participants' recovered memories were not what could be termed 'pseudo-memories' constructed in collusion with a psychotherapist/

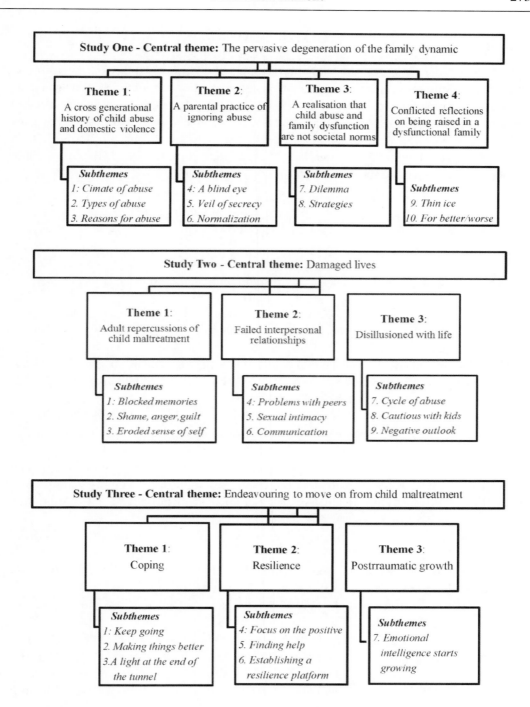

Figure 1. Thematic map of the study's central themes and component subthemes hypnotist, but rather were memories that had been first remembered at home alone, or in the company of friends and then later independently corroborated. Hence, traumatic memories tend to be what could be termed as 'entrenched memories', so the potential for partially recovered or suppressed memories to be inaccurately remembered, according to Hardt and Rutter (2004) is rare.

CONCLUSION

Even though certain prevalence and child maltreatment type variations exist, most child maltreatment studies (e.g., those based and not-based on recollected memories) conclude that a) children are vulnerable to maltreatment because of their dependency on adults; b) child maltreatment is a global phenomenon; and c) child maltreatment in all its forms contravenes the United Nation's Convention on the Rights of the child (Kitzmann, Gaylord, Holt, & Kenny, 2003; Moylan et al., 2010; Sternberg, Baradaran, Abbot, Lamb, & Guterman, 2006; Stoltenborgh, Bakermans-Kranenburg, Van Ijzendoorn & Alink, 2013).

REFERENCES

Akmatov, M. K. (2011). Child abuse in 28 developing and transitional countries: Results from the Multiple Indicator Cluster Surveys. *International Journal of Epidemiology, 40*, 219-227.

Alexander, N. & Clare, L. (2004). You still feel different: The experience of meaning of women's self-injury in the context of a lesbian or bisexual identity. *Journal of Community and Applied Psychology, 14*, 70-84.

Australian Institute of Health and Welfare. (2012). *Child protection Australia 2010–11.* Canberra: AIHW. Retrieved from 12 March 2014: http://www.aihw.gov.au/WorkArea/DownloadAsset.aspx?id=10737421014

Baxter, J. & Eyles, J. (1997). Evaluating qualitative research in social geography: Establishing rigour in interview analysis. *Transactions of the Institute of British Geographers, 22*, 505=525.

Baxter, P. & Jack, S. (2008). Qualitative case study methodology: Study design and implementation for novice researchers. *The Qualitative Report, 13*, 544-559.

Bazeley, P. (2009). Analysing qualitative data: More than identifying themes. *Malaysian Journal of Qualitative Research, 2*, 6-22.

Bedi, G. & Goddard, C. (2007). Intimate partner violence: What are the impacts on children? *Australian Psychologist, 42*, 66-77.

Bednall, J. (2006). Epoche and bracketing within the phenomenological paradigm. *Issues in Educational Research, 16*, 123-138.

Behura, S. (2011). A psychosocial approach to the study of child abuse. *Social Science International, 27*, 301-311.

Biggerstaff, D. & Thompson, A. R. (2008). Interpretive phenomenological analysis (IPA): A qualitative methodology of choice in healthcare research. *Research in Psychology, 5*, 214-224.

Blumer, H. (1969). *Symbolic interactionism: Perspective and method.* Englewood Cliffs, NJ: Prentice Hall.

Bolen R. M. & Lamb, L. (2004). Ambivalence of non-offending guardians after child sexual abuse disclosure. *Journal of Interpersonal Violence, 19*, 185-211.

Bourassa, C. (2007). Co-occurrence of interparental violence and child physical abuse and its effect on adolescents' behaviour. *Journal of Family Violence, 22*, 691-701.

Braun, V. & Clarke, V. (2006). Using thematic analysis in psychology. *Qualitative Research in Psychology*, *3*, 77 – 101.

Brocki, J. M. & Wearden, A. (2006). A critical evaluation of the use of interpretive phenomenological analysis (APA) in health psychology. *Psychology & Health*, *21*, 87-108.

Bryman, A. (2008). *Social research methods*. New York: Oxford University Press.

Carlson, J. A. (2010). Avoiding Traps in Member Checking. *Qualitative Report*, *15*, 1102-1113.

Carpenter, C. & Suto, M. (2008). *Qualitative Research for Occupational and Physical Therapists*. Oxford: Blackwell Publishing.

Catalano, S., Smith, E., Snyder, H. & Rand, M. (2009). Female victims of violence. US Bureau of Justice Statistics. Retrieved from 22 Aril 2014: http://www.bjs.gov/ content/ pub/pdf/fvv.pdf

Charmaz, K. (2006). *Constructing grounded theory*. London: Sage.

Child Welfare Information Gateway. (2013). *What is child abuse and neglect?* Washington, DC: U.S. Department of Health and Human Services, Children's Bureau. Retrieved from 12 March 2014: https://www.childwelfare.gov/pubs/factsheets/whatiscan.pdf

Chu, J. A., Frey, L. M., Ganzel, B. L., & Matthews, J. A. (1999). Memories of childhood abuse: dissociation, amnesia, and corroboration. *American Journal of Psychiatry*, *156*, 749-755.

Clarke, P. (2009). Understanding the experience of stroke. *The Gerontologist*, *49*, 293-302.

Collins, K. & Nicolson, P. (2002). The meaning of 'satisfaction' for people with dermatological problems. *Journal of Health Psychology*, *7*, 615-629.

Cresswell, J. (1998). *Research design: Qualitative, quantitative and mixed methods approaches.* (2nd ed.). Thousand Oaks, CA: Sage.

Creswell, J. (2007). *Qualitative Inquiry and Research Design*. Thousand Oaks, CA: Sage Publications.

Crist, J. D. & Tanner, C. A. (2003). Interpretation analysis methods in hermeneutic interpretive phenomenology. *Nursing Research*, *52*, 202-205.

Daly, K. J. (2007). *Qualitative Methods for Family Studies and Human Development*. Thousand Oaks, CA: Sage.

Department of Child Protection, Government of Western Australia. (2010). *How do I recognise when a child is at risk of abuse or neglect?* Retrieved from 30 January 2014: http://www.dcp.wa.gov.au/ChildProtection/Documents/HowDoIRecogniseWhenAChildI sAtRiskOfAbuseOrNeglect.pdf

Ellonen, N., Piispa, M., Peltonen, K. & Lica, M. O. (2013). Exposure to parental violence and outcomes of child psychosocial adjustment. *Violence and Victims*, *28*, 3-15.

Englander, M. (2012). The interview: data collection in descriptive phenomenological human scientific research. *Journal of Phenomenological Psychology*, *43*, 13-35.

Euser, S., Alink, L., Pannebakker, F., Vogels, T., Bakermans-Kranenburg, M. & Van Ijzendoorn, M. (2013). The prevalence of child maltreatment in the Netherlands across a 5 year period. Child *Abuse & Neglect*, *37*, 841-851.

Evans, S. E., Davies, C. & DiLillo, D. (2008). Exposure to domestic violence: A meta-analysis of child and adolescent outcomes. *Aggression and Violent Behavior*, *13*, 131-140.

Finkelhor, H, Turner, H., Ormrod, R., & Hamby, S. (2010). Trends in childhood violence and abuse exposure: Evidence from two national surveys. *Archives in Pediatrics and Adolescent Medicine*, *164*, 238-242.

Flyvbjerg, B. (2006). Five misunderstandings about case-study research. *Qualitative Inquiry*, *12*, 219-245.

Gewirtz, A. & Edleson, J. L. (2007). Young children's exposure to intimate partner violence. *Journal of Family Violence*, *22*, 151-163.

Gewirtz, A. & Medhanie A. (2008). Proximity and risk in children's witnessing of intimate partner violence. *Journal of Emotional Abuse*, *8*, 67–82.

Gibson, K. & Morgan, M. (2013). Growing up with child sexual abuse in an experimental commune. *Journal of Community and Applied Social Psychology*, *23*, 300-313.

Gil-Gonzalez, D., Vives-Cases, C., Ruiz, M. T., Carrasco-Portino, M. & Alvarez-Dardet, C. (2007). Childhood experiences of violence in perpetrators as a risk factor of intimate partner violence. *Journal of Public Health 10*, 1–9.

Gilbert, R., Fluke, J., O'Donnell, M., Gonzalez-Izquierdo, A., Bronwell, M., Gulliver, P., Janson, S. & Sidebotham, P. (2012). Child maltreatment: Variations in trends and policies in developed countries. *Lancet*, *379*, 758-772.

Given, L. M. (2008). *Qualitative Research Methods.* London: Sage.

Goddard, T. (2013). *A male perspective regarding the impact of childhood abuse on resilience and coping in adulthood.* Unpublished thesis: Edith Cowan University, Western Australia.

Gomez, A. M. (2011). Testing the cycle of violence hypothesis. *Youth & Society*, *43*, 171-192.

Gonzales, G., Chronister, K. M., Linville, D. & Knoble, N. B. (2012). Experiencing parental violence: A qualitative examination of adult men's resilience. *Psychology of Violence*, *2*, 90-103.

Goodman, G. S., Quas, J. A. & Ogle, C. M. (2009). Child maltreatment and memory. *Annual Review of Psychology*, *61*, 325-351.

Graham-Bermann, S. A. & Edelson, J. L. (2001). Introduction in S.A. Grahamm-Bermann & J.L. Edelson (Eds.), *Domestic violence in the lives of children* (1-12). Washington, DC: American Psychology Association.

Groenewald, T. (2004). A phenomenological research design illustrated. *International Journal of Qualitative Method*, *3*, 1-26.

Hanson, W. E., Morales, A., Clark Plano, V. L. & Creswell, J. W. (2007). Qualitative research designs: selection and implementation. *The Counselling Psychologist*, *35*, 236-264.

Hardt, J. & Rutter, S. (2004). Validity of adult retrospective reports of domestic violence childhood experiences: Review of the evidence. *Journal of Child Psychology and Psychiatry*, *45*, 260-273.

Hayes, N. (2000). *Doing psychological research: Gathering and analysing data.* Buckingham, Philadelphia: Open University Press.

Hartman, J. L., Turner, M.G., Daigle, L., Exum, M. L. & Cullen, F. T. (2009). Exploring the gender differences in protective factors. *Journal of Offender Rehabilitation*, *46*, 81-111.

Herrenkohl, T., Sousa, C., Tajima, E., Herrenkohl, R. & Moylan, C. (2008). Intersection of child-abuse and children's exposure to domestic violence. *Trauma, Violence & Abuse, 9*, 84-99.

Holt, S., Buckley, H. & Whelan, S. (2008). The impact of exposure to domestic violence on children and young people. *Child Abuse and Neglect, 32*, 797-810.

Houghton, S., Carroll, A. M., O'Donoghue, T. & Taylor, M. F. (2006). *From traditional to ecological.* New York: Nova Science Publishers, Inc.

Humphreys, C. (2010). Problems in the system of mandatory reporting of children living with domestic violence. *Journal of Family Studies, 14*, 228-239.

Indermaur, D. (2001). *Young Australians and domestic violence.* Trends & Issues in Crime and Criminal Justice #195, Canberra: Australian Institute of Criminology.

Johnson, M. K., Raye, C. L., Mitchell, K. J. & Ankudowich, E. (2012). The cognitive neuroscience of true and false memories. In R.F. Belli, *True and False Recovered Memories* (15-52). New York: Springer.

Kantor, G. K. & Little, L. (2003). Defining the boundaries of child neglect. *Journal of Interpersonal Violence, 18*, 338-355.

Kitzmann, K.M., Gaylord, N.K., Holtm A. R. & Kenny, E. D. (2003). Child witnesses to domestic violence: A meta-analytic review. *Journal of Consulting and Clinical Psychology, 71*, 339-352.

Knickerbocker, L., Heyman, R. E., Smith-Slep, A. M., Jouriles, E. N. & McDonald, R. (2007). Co-occurrence of child and partner maltreatment. *European Psychologist, 12*, 36-44.

Kvale, S. (1996). *Interviews: an introduction to qualitative research interviewing.* Thousand Oaks, CA: Sage.

Leech, N. L. & Onwuegbuzie, A. J. (2007). An array of qualitative data analysis tools: A call for data analysis triangulation. *School Psychology Quarterly, 22*, 557-584.

Liamputtong, P. (2009). *Qualitative research methods.* South Melbourne, Victoria: Oxford University Press.

Lincoln, Y. & Guba, E. G. (1985). *Naturalistic inquiry.* Beverley Hills, CA: Sage.

Lopez, K. A. & Willis, D. G. (2004). Descriptive versus interpretive phenomenology: their contributions to nursing knowledge. *Qualitative Health Research, 14*, 726 - 735.

Louwers, E. C., Korfage, I. J., Affourtit, M. J., Scheewe, D. J., van de Merwe, M. H., Vooijs-Moulaert, F. A., Woltering, C. M., Jongejan, M. H., Ruige, M., Moll, H. A. & De Koning, H. J. (2012). Effects of systematic screening and detection of child abuse in emergency departments. *Pediatrics, 130*, 457-464.

Low, J. (2007). Unstructured Interviews and Health Research. In Saks, M., & J. Allsop (Eds.), *Health Research: Qualitative, Quantitative and Mixed Methods.* London: Sage.

Lowes, L. & Prowse, M. A. (2001). Standing outside the interview process? The illusion of objectivity in phenomenological data generation. *International Journal of Nursing Studies, 38*, 471-480.

Mannuzza, S., Klein, R. G., Klein, D. F., Bessler, A. & Shrout, P. (2002). Accuracy of adult recall on childhood attention deficit hyperactivity disorder. *The American Journal of Psychiatry, 159*, 1882-89.

McKenzie, H. & Crouch, M. (2006). The logic of small samples in interview based qualitative research. *Social Science Information, 45*, 483-499.

Miles, M. B. & Huberman, A. M. (1994). *Qualitative data analysis* (2nd ed.). Thousand Oakes, CA: Sage.

Miles, G. & Thomas, N. (2007). Don't grind an egg against a stone: Children's rights and violence in Cambodian history and culture. *Child Abuse Review, 16*, 383-400.

Moylan, C. A., Herrenkohl, T. I., Sousa, C., Tajima, E. A., Herrenkohl, R. C. & Russo, M. J. (2010). The effects of child abuser and exposure to domestic violence on adolescent internalizing and externalizing behavior problems. *Journal of Family Violence*, *25*, 53-63.

Mullender, A., Hague, G., Imam, U., Kelly, L., Malos, E. & Regan, L. (2002). *Children's perspectives on domestic violence.* London: Sage Publications Ltd.

Neugebauer, R. (2000). Research on intergenerational transmission of violence: The next generation. *Lancet*, *355*, 1116-1117.

O'Brien, K. L., Cohen, L., Pooley, J. A. & Taylor, M. F. (2013). Lifting the domestic violence cloak of silence: Resilient Australian women's reflected memories of their childhood experiences of witnessing domestic violence. *Journal of Family Violence*, *28*, 95-108.

Pascal, J. (2010). Phenomenology as a research method for social work contexts. *New Scholarship in the Human Services*, *9*, 1-22.

Paavilainen, E. & Tarkka, M. T. (2003). Definition and identification of child abuse by Finnish public health nurses. *Public Health Nursing*, *20*, 49-55.

Payne, J. S., Galvan, F. H., Williams, J. K., Prusinski, M., Zhang, M., Wyatt, G. E. & Myers, H. F. (2014). Impact of childhood sexual abuse on the emotions and behaviours of adult men from three ethnic groups in the USA. *Culture, health & sexuality*, (Efirst), 1-15.

People, J. (2005). *Trends and patterns in domestic violence assaults.* Crime and Justice Bulletin, 89. Sydney, Australia: NSW Bureau of Crime Statistics and Research.

Pinheiro, P. (2006). *World report on violence against children.* New York: UNICEFF. Retrieved from 22 January 2014: http://www.crin.org/docs/UNVAC_World_Report_ on_Violence_against_Children.pdf

Powell, A. & Murray, S. (2008). Children and domestic violence: Constructing a policy problem in Australia and New Zealand. *Social and Legal Studies*, *17*, 453-473.

Punch, K. F. (2005). *Introduction to Social Research.* London: Sage.

Queensland Government (2013). *What is child abuse?* Brisbane, Australia: Department of Communities, Child Safety and Disability Services. Retrieved from 3 March 2014: http://www.communities.qld.gov.au/childsafety/protecting-children/what-is-child-abuse

Radford, L., Corral, S., Bradley, C. & Fisher, H. L. (2013). The prevalence and impact of child maltreatment and other types of victimization in the UK. *Child Abuse & Neglect*, *37*, 801-813.

Reid, K., Flowers, P. & Larkin, M. (2005). Interpretive phenomenological analysis: An overview and methodological review. *The Psychologist*, *16*, 24-27.

Richards, K. (2011). *Children's exposure to domestic violence in Australia.* Trends & Issues in Crime and Criminal Justice No. 419: Canberra: Australian Institute of Criminology.

Roberts, A. L., Rosario, M., Corliss, H. L. & Koenen, K. C. (2012). Childhood gender nonconformity: A risk indicator for childhood abuse and posttraumatic stress in youth. *Pediatrics*, *129*, 410-417.

Roth, D. H. (2004). *Adult reflections on childhood verbal abuse.* University of Saskatchewan, Canada: Unpublished Master thesis.

Rourke, L., Anderson, T., Garrison, D. R. & Archer, W. (2001). Methodological issues in the content analysis of computer conference transcripts. *International Journal of Artificial Intelligence in Education*, *12*, 8-22.

Russell, D., Springer, K. W. & Greenfield, E. A. (2010). Witnessing domestic abuse in childhood as an independent risk factor for depressive symptoms in young adulthood. *Child Abuse & Neglect, 34*, 448-453.

Saldañda, J. (2011). *Fundamentals of qualitative research: Understanding qualitative research.* New York: Oxford University Press.

Schraufnagel, T. J., Davis, K. C., George, W. H. & Norris, J. (2010). Childhood sexual abuse in males and subsequent risky sexual behavior. *Child Abuse and Neglect, 34*, 369-378.

Sebre, S., Sprugevica, I., Novotni, A., Bonevski, D., Pakalniskiene, V., Popescu, D., Turchina, T., Friedrich, W. & Lewis, O. (2004). Cross-cultural comparisons of child-reported emotional and physical abuse: Rates, risk factors and psychosocial symptoms. *Child Abuse and Neglect, 28*, 113-27.

Shen, A. (2009). Long-term effects of interpersonal violence on child physical maltreatment on PTSD and behaviour problems. *Child Abuse & Neglect, 33*, 148-160.

Smith, J. A. & Osborn, M. (2003). Interpretative phenomenological analysis. In J.A. Smith (Ed.) Qualitative psychology: *A practical guide to methods*. London: Sage.

Stake, R. E. (1995). *The art of case study research.* Thousand Oaks, CA: Sage.

Sternberg, K. J., Lamb, M. E., Greenbaum, C., Cicchetti, D., Dawud, S., Cortes, R. M., et al. (1993). Effects of domestic violence on children's behavior problems and depression. *Developmental Psychology, 29*, 44-52.

Sternberg, K. J., Baradaran, L. P., Abbott C. B., Lamb, M. E. & Guteman, E. (2006). Type of violence, age, and gender differences in the effects of family violence on children's behavior problems: *A mega-analysis. Developmental Review, 26*, 89-112.

Stoltenborgh, M., Bakermans-Kranenburg, M., van Ijzendoorn, M. & Alink, L. (2013). Cultural-geographical differences in the occurrence of physical abuse? A meta-analysis of global prevalence. *International Journal of Psychology, 48*, 81-94.

Stoltenborgh, M., van Ijzendoorn, M., Euser, E. & Bakermans-Kranenburg, M. (2011). A global perspective on child sexual abuse: Meta-analysis of prevalence around the world. *Child Maltreatment, 16*, 79-101.

United Nations Children's Fund (UNCF). (2012). *Measuring and Monitoring child protection systems.* Bangkok, Thailand: UNICEF East Asia Pacific Regional Office.

U.S. Department of Health and Human Services, Administration for Children and Families, Children's Bureau. (2012). *Child maltreatment 2012.* Retrieved from 6 March, 2014: http://www.acf.hhs.gov/programs/cb/research-data-technology/statistics-research/child-maltreatment

Varia, R. & Abidin, R. R. (1999). The minimizing style: Perceptions of psychological abuse and quality of past and current relationships. *Child Abuse and Neglect, 23*, 1041-1055.

Vinten, G. (1995). Open versus closed questions: An open issue? *Management Decision, 33*, 27-31.

Vittrup, B., Holden, G. W. & Buck, J. (2006). Attitudes predict the use of physical punishment. *Pediatrics, 117*, 2055-2064.

Willig, C. (2008). *Introducing qualitative research in psychology: Adventures in theory and method.* Buckingham: Open University Press.

Woodman, J., Pitt, M., Wentz, R., Hodes, D. & Gilbert, R. E. (2008). Performance on screening tests for child physical abuse in accident and emergency departments. *Health Technology Assessment, 12*, 1-95.

World Health Organization (WHO). (2013). European report on preventing child maltreatment. Copenhagen, Denmark: WHO Regional Office for Europe. Retrieved from 26 February 2014: http://www.euro.who.int/en/publications/abstracts/european-report-on-preventing-child-maltreatment

World Health Organization (WHO). (2014). *Child maltreatment: Fact sheet #150.* Retrieved from 20 February 2014: http://www.who.int/mediacentre/factsheets/fs150/en/index.html

Yexley, M., Borrowsky, I. & Ireland, M. (2002). Correlation between different experiences of intra-familial physical violence and violent adolescent. *Journal of Interpersonal Violence, 17*, 707-720.

Zink, T., Kamine, D., Musk, L., Sill, M., Field, V. & Putman, F. (2005). What are providers' reporting requirements for children who witness domestic violence? *Clinical Pediatrics, 43*, 449-460.

Chapter 17

'WALKING ON THIN ICE': THE PERVASIVE DEGENERATION OF THE FAMILY DYNAMIC IN HOMES WHERE DOMESTIC VIOLENCE IS A LIVED REALITY AND WHERE CHILDREN UNDER THE AGE OF 18 EXPERIENCE ABUSE

Myra F. Taylor[*], *Teresa Goddard and Julie Ann Pooley*
Edith Cowan University, Joondalup, Western Australia, Australia

This chapter documents the participants' narratives of their childhood experiences of maltreatment. Its core theme: *'The pervasive degeneration of the family dynamic in homes where domestic violence is a lived reality and where children under the age of 18 experience abuse',* encapsulates the four themes and ten subthemes (see Table 1) that emerged from the analysis of the participants' accounts of the abuse they had witnessed and experienced as a child. Collectively, these sub/themes provide a much needed insight into the lives of boys growing up in a dysfunctional and abusive family environment. The first theme: *An intergenerational history of child maltreatment* captures participants' reflections on the types of maltreatment they experienced as a child. The second theme: *Reasons for abuse* reveals how participants considered their child maltreatment experiences to be a consequence of their parents' inappropriate parenting practices, unrealistically high expectations, excessive consumption of alcohol, and mental illness. Moreover, in order to hide the existence of domestic violence and child abuse within the family home, participants' reported that their non-abusing parent either denied the maltreatment, ignored the maltreatment, or cloaked it in a veil of secrecy in their attempt to maintain a 'happy family façade'. As a result, participants stated their childhood experiences of maltreatment became normalised. The third theme: *A realization that child abuse and family dysfunction are not societal norms* reveals that as participants entered their mid-to-late adolescent years they began to take more proactive steps towards preventing or stopping the maltreatment. In the fourth and final theme the

---

[*] Corresponding author: Myra F. Taylor, Edith Cowan University, 270 Joondalup Drive Joondalup, WA 6007 Australia.

participants' *Conflicted memories of being raised in a dysfunctional family* are described. Each of these four themes is explained in greater depth below.

Table 1. Component parts of the study's core theme relating to adult memories of childhood maltreatment: *A pervasive degeneration of the family dynamic in homes where domestic violence is a lived reality and where children under the age of 18 experience abuse*

Theme	Subtheme
One: A cross-generational family history of domestic violence and alcohol abuse	1. *Intergenerational climate of abuse* 2. *Types of abuse* 3. *Reasons for abuse*
Two: Parental practice of ignoring abuse	4. *Looking away* 5. *A veil of secrecy* 6. *Normalisation of abuse*
Three: A realisation that child abuse and family dysfunction are not societal norms	7. *Pre-adolescent dilemma* 8. *Adolescent strategies*
Four: Conflicted reflections on being raised in a dysfunctional family	9. *'Walking on thin ice'* 10. *'Could've been better could've been worse'*

THEME ONE: AN INTERGENERATIONAL HISTORY OF CHILD MALTREATMENT

Subtheme 1: Intergenerational Climate of Abuse: *'My Mind Boggles at the Thinking of the People in My Life Who Were Meant to Protect Me'*

Participants spoke of their awareness of an intergenerational history of maltreatment within their extended families. As such, they commented that even as a child they were aware that the abuse they were experiencing and the domestic violence they were witnessing were not experiences exclusive unto them. For, even as a young child they realized that the unpleasant occurrences happening to them were also happening to other family members (i.e., grandparents, siblings, aunts, uncles, cousins). Typical comments included:

> *On my mother's side there's been sexual abuse... Mum she was pretty mean... very um dominant... she always had to have things her own way... but I suppose you have to look at that in context. I mean she had a troubled childhood herself. (Participant #1)*

> *Other members (cousins) of the family have obviously had it (sexual abuse) happened to them as well. (Participant #3)*

As children, participants revealed that the one thing they had learnt from their maltreatment experiences was that there was 'more than one way to be hurt and more than one way to hurt others'.

Subtheme 2: Types of Abuse: *'It Wasn't a Positive Environment for Development'*

Participants commonly remembered experiencing and witnessing four different types of maltreatment as child, namely, verbal abuse, psychological abuse, physical abuse, and sexual abuse. In terms of the participants recollection of the first type of abuse, *verbal abuse,* they recalled this was not just something they continually witnessed occurring between their parents, but it was also something that was often directed at them by one or both of their parents or another close family member (e.g., grandparent or sibling). Participants indicated that over time their experiences of verbal abuse lowered their self-esteem and caused them to emotionally withdraw into themselves. Particularly, during instances when they wanted to escape the hurtful words that were being bandied about between their parents as well as the hurtful words that were directed towards them or a sibling. One participant explained:

> With the verbal abuse mum was the main one... I'd often be criticized by my mother on the way I behaved around other people.... And it gave me low self-esteem... I guess it continued for some time because I became very withdrawn. (Participant #1)

Although the physical process of withdrawal from the source of the verbal abuse (e.g., retreating to their bedroom or hiding under their bedcovers) helped block out the audible elements of the abuse it was the second type of maltreatment, *psychological abuse*, that participants considered was responsible for fragmenting their sense of self-worth.

It is evident from the participants' recounted narratives that their experiences of psychological abuse occurred both at an emotional and a cognitive level. In terms of explaining the impact that such experiences had on their emotional sense of wellbeing, participants stated that over time, as they became more cognitively aware of the abuse and domestic violence occurring within the family home, they first began to experience feelings of humiliation, shame, and fear. One participant explained:

> My granddad used to always put me down and you know say little comments to put me down and make me feel bad and make me feel dumb and stupid. It was the humiliation... it was like psychological abuse... like mind f*cked for want of a better word... You were just made to feel like you were a failure even if you did deliver... It wasn't a positive environment for development... because even if you did deliver you were never commended and, it was just like make sure you do it again. (Participant # 6)

Participants explained that the third type of maltreatment, *emotional abuse,* that was leveled at them during their childhood years was deleterious because it left them feeling they were somehow responsible for the domestic violence occurring within the family home. Indeed, participants revealed that as a child they developed an inner belief that they must have done something bad to initiate the abuse that they witnessed occurring between their parents and, also, the abuse that was directed at them. In internalizing the belief that they were somehow at fault, participants stated they grew up believing they were worthless and, if only they did better, then the abuse would abate. Consequently, participants blamed themselves for their family's dysfunction. In addition, being in a heightened state of alert for the next instance of abuse, participants stated they had found it particularly difficult to concentrate on their school work. They asserted their school grades were 'never as good as they could have been' and, as a result, they often attracted the ire of their abusive parent.

Participants' experiences of the fourth type of maltreatment, *physical abuse* were varied. Participants recalled times when they were 'grabbed', 'pushed', 'whipped with a stick', 'belted with a ruler', 'hit with a belt', or 'beaten up pretty badly' by a parent, grandparent, or sibling. It was commonplace for these physical acts of abuse to continue for a protracted period of time before the physical signs of their maltreatment came to the attention of an adult outside of the family domain (e.g., teacher, school nurse, or doctor). For example, the following comment details the catalogue of physical abuse that was inflicted on one participant by his mother and which continued for several years before it was documented and acted upon by a school nurse:

> The real physical abuse wasn't discovered until I was about six... and I was hospitalized... I had three broken fractures... Originally, it was all about tough love... but the tough love was scolding hot water, burning hot plates, broken bats, cigarette burns and oh... one time a chopping knife. When I was close to seven... the disability services stepped in... they finally found her beating the shit out of me... and because I kept on running away... they removed me for a period of time... right up to the age of 10... Then, I went back for three years... and when she took me back home she beat the crap out of my toes with a hammer... Also, at that time she thought I was masturbating... so she got really angry and almost tore my penis off... By 13 I'd basically given up all hope of being able to get out of the house. At that time I was a bit smelly... grubby, and the school nurse used to let me have a bite to eat and have a shower, and sometimes, if needed, a sleep... The nurse recorded every bruise, every broken bone, every dislocated knee... and she also was monitoring me psychologically. It was she who organized for me to get out of that place (family home). (Participant #2)

Other participants who had been physically abused also recounted multiple experiences of abuse. Though, they explained, as young children they had been unaware that the things that they were experiencing actually constituted abuse. For, at such a young age, participants stated they believed that the *'harsh discipline'* their parent(s) were using on them was just what all parents used to discipline 'bad children'.

Similarly, participants stated they had considered at that early pre-adolescent stage that their experiences of sexual abuse were just something parents (or grandparents) did to their children. Especially, when after informing their non-abusing parent/grandparent about what was happening to them, their tales of abuse were either dismissed or ignored. One participant recounted his experiences as follows:

> We had to go and stay with the grandparents you know on school holidays so a lot of it (sexual abuse) happened around them... He (grandfather) would have all sorts of games and stuff which you know always had a sinister side to them... like he had tractors and we'd always have to sit between his legs on the tractor... and because they

(grandparents) owned most of the houses we lived in... they'd always be coming over and somehow he'd always mange to have 'alone time' with us. My aunty and uncle ended up pressing charges against him (as the grandfather also molested the participant's three female cousins)... but he didn't end up going to jail... Basically he had to go through a therapy sort of thing... He was at our house at this point so while he was having therapy he was still doing it to me. My mum and grandmother would leave me there with him.. They essentially left me in the care of the person that had been found guilty of abuse. (Participant #3)

In two such cases, participants' sexual abuse experiences were compounded by also being sexually abused by a trusted person external to the family (e.g., babysitter, family friend, teacher).

Feelings of being traumatized by the abuse and being left unprotected in the care of the people committing the abuse were common to all four types of child maltreatment.

Subtheme 3: Reasons for Abuse: *'The Problem Wasn't Me'*

The first reason participants gave for the existence of child abuse and interparental violence was that a degree of intergenerational maltreatment transference occurred within the family home. They accredited the proliferation of this transference to the reality that their own parents had experienced or witnessed abuse in their childhood home. Consequently, when the participants' parents grew up and had children of their own they had no appropriate parenting model upon which to draw and so they replicated their parents' (i.e., the participants' grandparents) destructive parenting practices. One participant explained:

My dad... when his dad was drunk... was witness to my grandfather being violent with my grandmother... and that's how my dad was with me and my sister... his form of discipline... was just to go to the extreme like his dad did... not really realizing what it does to a child. He didn't really know how to be a dad. (Participant #6)

The second reason that participants gave for their parents' intergenerational transference of an inappropriate parenting style was that their parents had also grown up in families where they had been subjected to *unrealistically high achievement expectations*. Hence, when their parents had children they transferred their parents' (i.e. the grandparents) expectations onto their children (i.e., the participants). Specifically, participants spoke of their parents' high scholastic expectations and, when they as children failed to meet these achievement expectations, they were subjected to verbal abuse and physical punishment. One participant described his experiences as follows:

Because my grandmother's brother helped out like with fees for school and stuff (for the participant's father)... he (grandfather) took a shot at my old man when he didn't succeed or didn't get high enough results for what he thought he should be getting ... and so my Dad he pretty much transferred that (expectation) onto us. My dad's attitude was that if I'm paying for something, then I expect it to be how I want it to be. (Participant #6)

The third reason participants gave for their parents' intergenerational transference of inappropriate parenting practices was *their parents' excessive alcohol consumption*. In this regard, participants recalled multiple incidents when alcohol-fuelled violence occurred between their parents, between their parents and their grandparents, and between their grandparents during their childhood years. For example:

> *My father has had his own issues with an abusive alcoholic father ... and on my mother's side well her father was an alcoholic... He was a happy drunk... but there were times when the happiness would turn to not-so-happy drunk...Yeah like a few times a week there'd be a massive fight in our house where punches were thrown and everyone was getting involved trying to break up her and dad teeing off on each other. (Participant #4)*

Participants indicated that alcohol abuse was prevalent amongst their extended families. Also, that at the time of their own experiences of child maltreatment their abusing parent had often been inebriated.

The fourth reason participants gave for their parents' intergenerational transference of child maltreatment was that one of their parents had a *mental illness*. For instance one participant recalled:

> *My mother had lots of health issues... I think that was due to the death of two boys... I had two brothers, but they deceased really young... and she (mother) was in and out of a psychiatric hospital... She was on Vallium for all of her life, and I know she had shock treatment... Mum used to tell me her sickness was caused by me... The problem wasn't me though the problem was she couldn't cope. (Participant #4)*

Participants commonly indicated there had been an intergenerational history of mental illness and/or alcoholism within their extended families, which had compounded the family's underlying dysfunction. One participant explained:

> *My father has his own issues with an abusive alcoholic father and a mother with mental issues so there was already a lot of dysfunction. (Participant #7)*

Indeed, participants concluded that the underlying level of dysfunction occurring within their extended family created the perfect climate for an intergenerational transference of child maltreatment to occur.

THEME 2: PARENTAL PRACTICE OF IGNORING ABUSE

Subtheme 4: Looking Away: *'I've Still Got Issues with the Way the Family Dealt with It'*

While suffering their abusing parent/grandparent's maltreatment participants could not understand why their non-abusing parent/grandparent (and other extended family members) ignored the abuse they saw was being perpetuated on them as a child. For instance, one participant explained that he could not as a child comprehend why his father had not interceded on his behalf when his mother had on multiple occasions severely physically abused him:

> As I got older like a teenager I just got used to seeing you know dad's drinking...and I sort of drank too... and mum...she just acted like nothing was really happening... she just never really questioned it. I can also remember... I got caught smoking marijuana and when I got home ...she (mother) belted me, you know hit me on the ground and kicked me ... yelling at me and dad saw it (but) he just acted like nothing really happened. (Participant #8)

Participants also revealed that as teenagers they had found it unfathomable how their witnessing (i.e., non-abusing) parent/grandparent who was morally tasked by society with their care could knowingly turn a 'blind eye' to the abuse that was being inflicted on them. One participant related:

> I've still got issues with the way that the family dealt with it (grandfather sexual abuse). My grandmother, she never did anything... and my mum basically did squat about it too... and so nothing ever happened. (Participant #3)

Participants also revealed that rather than acting to protect them from the abuse and prevent it from reoccurring, their non-abusing parent either denied the abuse was occurring, or had advised them to 'just get over it' and to 'just accept' that 'that is how things are'.

Subtheme 5: A Veil of Secrecy: *'Mum, She Was Just Like Playing Happy Families'*

Participants interpreted their non-abusing parent's inaction to be a deliberate choice on their behalf to ignore the abuse. Participants reasoned that by ignoring the existence of abuse their parents were able to maintain the social facade of being a 'happy family'. Maintaining a functional family image was particularly important to the participants' mothers. One participant explained:

> So it all came to light in the family and... you'd think that would be the end of it, but no... my mum basically did squat about it. She ignored it... Mum she was just like playing happy families... and when confronted about it she said: 'You know that he didn't do it'. (Participant #6)

Participants revealed that as a child they had found their witnessing parent's denial of the abuse they were experiencing both confusing and difficult to reconcile with their lived reality.

Subtheme 6: Normalisation of Abuse: *'You Just End Up Thinking That's Just How Things Are'*

Participants indicated that their parents' denials of their maltreatment and, the commonplace frequency of their abuse and witnessing experiences, led them in their pre-adolescence years (a time when they had limited social contacts outside of the family) to believe that such experiences were in some way normal. For, at this juncture in their lives participants believed that other children living in other families were experiencing the same things they were experiencing. Thus, their maltreatment experiences was rationalized in their childhood minds as just being an ongoing part of their existence. Four participants stated:

> At this point (early childhood)... I just didn't really know any different... it was just something that had always been happening in my life so I just didn't know differently... it never struck me... how bad it (abuse) was. (Participant #1)

> It was a really... weird environment, but it became the norm... You just end up thinking yes that's just how things are... You just consider it (maltreatment) as normal family function. (Participant #7)

> You just think that the environment you're in... well that's the norm. (Participant #5)

> I didn't really know any different...you don't really know any better when that's all that has ever happened to you. (Participant #3)

The normalization of abuse continued until the participants' childhood social circle expanded to encompass other families outside of their nuclear and extended family networks.

THEME 3: A REALISATION THAT CHILD ABUSE AND FAMILY DYSFUNCTION ARE NOT SOCIETAL NORMS

Subtheme 7: The Pre-Adolescent Dilemma: *'One Part of Me Really Wanting Desperately to Share and Another Part of Me Was Absolutely Gripped With Fear'*

As participants entered into their early adolescent years their social horizons expanded and, thus, when they visited other people's homes they came to realize that maltreatment was not a social norm and what was happening to them was wrong. However, the problem they faced was in deciding what to do about the maltreatment and who to tell. For, at this stage they realized that if they did tell someone, then the act of telling would shatter their mother's carefully crafted happy family image. One participant described this dilemma in the following terms:

> You become more aware that you're standing out from the crowd... that for me was around the age of 11... I became aware in Year 5 or Year 6 of the tension that was within

me... this absolute intense tension that arose inside of me. Like one part of me really wanting desperately to share and another part of me was absolutely gripped with fear... it felt like it was tearing me apart. ... I felt like I was about to explode, that's probably the best way I can describe it you know... like internal combustion. (Participant # 7)

Once they had witnessed non-abusive parenting in action in the families of their school friends participants revealed they had become embarrassed and self-conscious about the maltreatment that was occurring within their own home.

Powerless to do anything to alter the situation during their pre-adolescent years participants revealed that the strategy they adopted to deal with their 'tell-or-not-to-tell-anyone-else' dilemma was to internalize (i.e., not disclose) their experiences and to socially withdraw into themselves. Participants stated that they had learnt that if they made themselves a less visible target they could then pass under the radar of both adult and peer scrutiny. One participant explained thus:

I wasn't very happy... I sort of found it very difficult to interact with other people... communicate and socialise with them. I became very withdrawn... I didn't fit in very well... I just wanted people to leave me alone... I wasn't meaning to draw attention, but I obviously was... I guess I was being viewed (by peers) as a bit of an outcast. (Participant #1)

Another participant disclosed that as a child he had taken his withdrawal to such an extreme that he engaged in a form of selective mutism:

I think one of the main ways it affected me was it pushed me into my own isolated inner world... I just didn't really connect verbally... I used to rely on other kinds of ways to communicate. Yeah, I seem to remember developing a certain kind of miming, using my body language... or a sign language... to express myself rather than opening my mouth and talk. (Participant #7)

The main disadvantage as a child in adopting a withdrawal approach participants revealed was that it reduced the chance that they would receive the help they needed to stop their maltreatment. A third participant explained:

Because my grades weren't good enough... I mean I passed and all that sort of stuff, but you know I think if anyone had of looked hard enough they would have noticed... but coz I was so quiet... you just sit at a point where no one really takes any attention of you. (Participant #3)

Hence, a state of pre-adolescent limbo ensued where participants neither attracted, nor received the attention they required and, thus, their maltreatment continued on into their early to mid-adolescent years.

Subtheme 8: Adolescent Strategies: *'I Rebelled' – 'I Tried to Commit Suicide'*

As the participants moved into their adolescent years they revealed they became better able to employ a range of strategies to limit or prevent further instances of maltreatment. For example, they engaged in acts of *physical rebellion*, or *spending increasing amounts of time hanging out with friends* outside of the family home and, in some instances, *running away* from home. Indeed, participants recalled their overarching plan to end their experiences of maltreatment was to *leave home* as soon as they could.

Of the three commonly employed adolescent strategies, physical rebellion was the strategy participants stated was the most effective in stopping a female family member from continuing to perpetrate abuse on their person. For, participants explained, there came a time in their physical development when they grew either stronger or bigger than their female abuser and, thus, were able to physically fight back. One participant commented:

> *I guess the physical and verbal abuse mainly came from my mother... until I was probably around 12 or 13. It was sort of at that time I sort of like got strong enough to... fight her back... I rebelled against her and you know sort of demonstrated to her that I wasn't gonna be hurt by the physical abuse anymore. (Participant #1)*

While, this strategy was effective for some normally developing participants, it did not work for late-developing or deeply withdrawn participants. Nor, did it work in instances when the abusing parent was a physically strong dominant male (or female). One participant who had withdrawn into himself during his pre-adolescent years remembered that in the depths of his adolescent despair over his inability to stop the maltreatment he had attempted suicide. He recalled:

> *I tried to kill myself when I was 14... I took an overdose of pills... Um at that stage I felt very depressed ... not only did I feel depressed, but I felt I was useless... you know because of my low self-esteem and because of the childhood (abuse) experiences that I had... I didn't really have much of a place in the world and that's why I decided I should end it. (Participant #1)*

Whether participants chose the rebellious or withdrawal coping strategy their common desire was to leave the family home.

THEME 4: CONFLICTED REFLECTIONS ON BEING RAISED IN A DYSFUNCTIONAL FAMILY

Subtheme 9: An Unpredictable Family Environment: *'Walking on Thin Ice'*

Participants indicated that their childhood memories of growing up in a dysfunctional family home where experience of intermittent abuse on their person and, the intermittent witnessing of interparental incidences of domestic violence was their norm, was punctuated somewhat incongruously by good times. While these good times were welcome, the maltreatment times were so intense that participants recollected there were numerous occasions in their childhood when they experienced considerable emotional turmoil. For instance, one participant recalled his experience of surges of anger raging through his body following each maltreatment episode:

> *There was an occasion when I was 10 where I copped 'a belting' from dad and I was standing on the stairs biting my lip and just raging to the point where I had drawn blood. (Participant #6)*

Other participants described their childhood home as being 'a very tender environment', partly because of the volatile nature of the family environment, partly because of the self-belief that they were a 'burden' on their parents, and partly because they considered themselves to be a scapegoat for their parents' conflict. Participants indicated that as a result of the pervasive and recurrent nature of the maltreatment which occurred within their family home, the family dynamic degenerated to a point where their enduring childhood memory was one of *'walking on thin ice'*.

Subtheme 10: Family Life: *'It Could Have Been Better and It Could Have Been Worse'*

In summarizing their childhood experience of growing up in dysfunctional and abusive family environment participants commented that although their upbringing had been harsh and considerably different from that of their peers, they appreciated the efforts their parents made during the good times to try to make up for the bad times. For example:

> *Now, how do I view my childhood? Um there's a part of me saying my mum and dad and other people in my life did the best they could, even though they were dysfunctional. (Participant #4)*

> *Yeah... I've got a funny view of it I guess. Um you know I certainly had a loving mother, but when it came to the biggest thing in my life that she needed to deal with she failed... and that's like tough to deal with when you look back, or when you look at other families... I've thought sometimes I really disliked the childhood I had, even though it was in a loving family at times... I don't have a particularly fond view of my childhood. Um yeah, it could have been better and it could have been worse as well. (Participant #1)*

Participants stated that they had learnt over the course of their childhood that the best option for dealing with their maltreatment experiences was to *'just focus just on the good times and pretty much act as if the bad times never happened'*.

DISCUSSION

Undoubtedly, child maltreatment is a major public health problem, as such, any experience increases the risk of adverse physical, cognitive and emotional developmental outcomes occurring in the maltreated child (Denholm, Power, Thomas, & Li, 2013).

Moreover, recent research has suggested that the negative developmental impact of multiple experiences of maltreatment can be cumulative in terms of their severity (Chartier, Walker, & Naimark, 2010; Denholm et al., 2013). In other words, children (regardless of gender) who experience serious and sustained maltreatment tend to manifest more severe life-course persistent negative outcomes than do children who experience less severe abuse or no abuse at all (Ellonen, Piispa, Peltonen, & Lica, 2013).

Maltreated children (regardless of gender) manifest a wide range of atypical behaviours which frequently occur in combinational presentations, the make-up of which is dependent on the age of the child and the type of maltreatment they experience. Typically, they include but are not restricted to, head-banging/rocking, insecure attachment, bedwetting, hypervigilance, disturbed sleep patterns, nightmares, shrinking from contact, over-compliance/passivity, unexplained crying, school concentration difficulties, poor peer interaction skills, stealing food or money, unhealthy weight trajectories, abuse of animals, unexplainable marks on body or broken bones, frequent absenteeism from school, anxiety, social/school withdrawal, aggression, moodiness, irritability, excessive risk-taking, running away from home, feelings of fear, terror, shame, angst, confusion, self-blame, insecurity, powerlessness, hopelessness, and loneliness (Browne & Winkleman, 2007; Child Welfare Information Gateway, 2013; Heim, Shugart, Craighead, & Nemeroff, 2010; Holt, Buckley, & Whelan, 2008; Huth-Bocks, Levendosky, & Semel, 2001; Jun et al., 2012; Lundy & Grossman, 2005; Martin, 2002; McIntosh, 2002; Mullender et al., 2002; Reynolds, Wallace, Hill, Weist, & Nabors, 2001; Zink et al., 2005).

While male participants in this chapter recalled experiencing many of these atypical child development behaviours, it is somewhat concerning that in only one instance of severe and protracted maltreatment did an adult outside of the family domain (i.e., a school nurse) recognise the tell-tale signs of child abuse and intercede on the child's behalf. In light of this and, the study's overarching theme: *The pervasive degeneration of the family dynamic in homes where domestic violence is a lived reality and where children under the age of 18 experience abuse,* it would appear self-evident that a greater emphasis needs to be placed on educating adults (i.e., teachers, school nurses, school counsellors, general practitioners, social workers, family support agency staff and police) who interface with children manifesting signs of maltreatment.

Some divergence exists within the literature as to what age-group of child is most at risk for atypical development. Some experts maintain that the earlier the experience of maltreatment, the more damaging the effect (Barker-Collo & Read, 2003; Ogloff, Cutajar, & Mullen, 2012), while others argue that young-age is a protective factor due to the brain's under-developed cognitive inability to fully comprehend child maltreatment experiences (Finkelor, 1995; Ogloff, Cutajar, & Mullen, 2012). However, as the child enters the school system and becomes more cognitively aware, it is evident that a need arises for teachers and paraprofessionals working within schools to be alert for the signs of maltreatment and to intercede on behalf of the child.

This imperative is strengthened by recent research which suggests child maltreatment may be a causal factor for the development of hypervigilance (WHO, 2014). For, it has been reasoned that children who are constantly alert for imminent threats of danger are more likely than non-abused children to develop impulse control difficulties (Perry, 2006). Additionally, instances of malnutrition resulting from parental neglect have been demonstrated to slow the passage of electrical messages within the child's brain (Shonkoff & Phillips, 2000) to the point where impairments can occur in the maltreated child's nervous, immune, and language production systems (Child Welfare Information Gateway, 2009; WHO, 2014). The potential cognitive consequences of child maltreatment are posited to be declines in verbal retrieval skills, a reduced capacity to problem solve and future plan, declines in short-term verbal memory recall, impaired attentional focus, and difficulties with abstract reasoning, which collectively can lower the child's self-esteem (Navalta, Polcari, Webster, Boghossian, & Teicher, 2006; Ritchie et al., 2011). Therefore, teachers with a student who is falling below his/her expected level of achievement need to be alert to the possibility that child maltreatment may be an underlying reason for the child's scholastic under-performance.

In terms of social workers and family support agency workers there is also a need for a greater awareness of the impact that parental alcohol and substance abuse has on the lives of children. Especially, given Dube, Anda, Felitti, Croft, Edwards, and Giles (2001) have demonstrated a strong association exists between parental alcohol abuse and the co-occurrence of child abuse. More specifically, their findings reveal that the presence of an alcoholic parent in a family doubles the likelihood that the family's children, regardless of their gender, will experience maltreatment. Furthermore, that a within family co-occurrence of alcohol misuse and domestic violence generates the strongest associative likelihood of child maltreatment (Dube, et al., 2001). These findings are particularly pertinent given this study's revelation that both the abusing and the observing parent can be adept at masking the presence of domestic violence and child abuse through creating a plausible happy family façade.

A further implication of not recognising a false family façade can be years of maltreatment and an increased likelihood that the maltreated child will become orientated towards non-compliant antisocial and/or criminal behaviours. Indeed, research has demonstrated that male maltreated children are 1.43 times more likely than their non-maltreated peers and 2.2 times more likely than female maltreated children to come in contact with police for a criminal offence during their prepubescent and adolescent years (Ogloff, Cutajar, & Mullen, 2012). Consequently, child maltreatment is recognised as posing a significant financial burden to the policing, judicial and social welfare services (Cecil, Viding, Barker, Guirney, & McCrory, 2014). Hence, as police tend to be the first authority to interact with antisocial youth outside of the home environment an imperative exists for police to improve and standardize their recordkeeping of juvenile apprehensions, especially, given that the link between childhood maltreatment and acts of youth antisociality/criminality is robust. In this regard, a mandatory reporting procedure could be put in place to compel police when attending domestic violence incidents to record how many children live in the family home, how many children witnessed the domestic violence incident, and the age and gender of each witnessing child. Moreover, when entering such incident reports police could be required to ascribe each witnessing child with a specific identifying code (e.g., a domestic violence witnessing number). By mandating this recording procedure a child maltreatment victim register would be developed. Such information would provide crime/social researchers with an accurate means of quantifying the prevalence of child witnessing, which in turn, could lead to the better development and targeting of intervention programs.

The benefit for police in engaging in this reporting procedure is that they would be able to check their child maltreatment register when a young person was apprehended for the first time and, make an evidenced-based determination as to whether the apprehended juvenile was an 'at-risk' individual. In cases where police determine that a juvenile was on the maltreatment register they would then have the option of diverting the juvenile through to a child health agency where a psychological assessment could be carried out. In doing so, this approach would provide at-risk juveniles with an opportunity to obtain the specialized help they need to avoid progressing along a criminal offending trajectory. In addition, by diverting at-risk children the police would reduce the pressures that maltreatment-related recidivist offending places on both the Police and the Judiciary's systems. Recognition of the potentiality for recidivist adolescent offending among maltreated children comes from Forsman and Långström's (2012) study of over 18,000 twins, for their results revealed that neglected, physically abused and sexually abused children have a moderately increased risk of being convicted of a violent offence as an adult. However, Forsman and Långström caution that further research is needed to determine the extent of the links between child maltreatment and the kinds of violence victims of child maltreatment commit as an adult.

The need for a proactive approach to dealing with childhood manifestations of atypical physical, sexual, emotional and psychosocial behaviours is particularly critical given that research has demonstrated victimized children are at an increased risk for morbidity and pain (Forsman & Långström, 2012; Paras et al., 2009; Wegman & Stetler, 2009). Indeed, the trauma associated with child maltreatment is widely considered to be a determinant for adolescent delinquency, adult violence perpetration and victimization (Gomez, 2011). This supposition is based on the intergenerational cycle of violence hypothesis which proposes that individuals who experience abuse as a child are more prone than non-maltreated children to becoming violent offenders, or perpetrators/victims of abuse as they progress through their adolescent and adult life-cycles (Gomez, 2011; Heyman & Slep, 2002).

However, some concerns have been raised about the robustness of the cycle of violence hypothesis as clearly not all children who are maltreated grow up to victimize their own offspring and, nor, do all perpetrators of child abuse and domestic violence originate out of homes where domestic violence was a family norm. In an effort, to determine the strength of the association between child maltreatment and future adult violent offending Reckdenwald, Mancini, and Beauregard (2013) investigated the case histories of 624 inmates incarcerated for a sex offence. Their rationale for conducting the research being the widespread belief that much of adult perpetrated violence is learnt childhood behaviour (see Bandura's 1997 Social Learning Theory hypothesis as well as Ormrod's 1999 explanation). This belief is formulated around an assumption that children learn their future ways of behaving from observing how adults interact with each other and with them. Thus, it was reasoned that if children witness domestic violence and experience abuse in the family home they will emulate such behaviours as they grow. However, while the Reckdenwald, Mancini, and Beauregard results did provide some support for the cycle of violence hypothesis, the researchers concluded that the link between child maltreatment and later perpetrated violence is largely dependent on the type of maltreatment that the child experiences. In this regard, the Reckdenwald and colleagues revealed that there is some evidence that the negative impacts of both physical and sexual child abuse do adhere to the logic behind the cycle of violence hypothesis, however, this evidence is not definitive in other common forms of abuse, psychological and verbal abuse. In terms of the present study this finding is especially noteworthy as half of the participants had reported that they had been subjected as a child to psychological abuse. A second important finding emanating out of the Reckdenwald, Maccini, and Beauregard study is that the detrimental effects of childhood maltreatment also extends to adults who witness domestic violence as a child.

Finally, it is interesting to note that in the present study the male participants described their everyday experiences of growing up in a family where they witnessed and experienced abuse as being analogous to *'walking on ice'*, given an earlier study detailing adult female's recollected memories of growing up witnessing and experiencing abuse, similarly described their childhood lives as one of *'walking on eggshells'* (O'Brien, Cohen, Pooley, & Taylor, 2013). Clearly growing up in a dysfunctional and abusive family environment has a negative impact on children. Therefore, when faced with the dilemma of trying to navigate a way through their maltreatment experiences children often adopt a variety of adaptive and maladaptive coping strategies. For instance, some abused children mimic their non-abusing parent's avoidance strategy of 'ignoring the bad times and focusing on the good times'. Indeed, Cecil, Viding, Barker and McCrory (2014) suggest that the coping strategies maltreated children learn in their childhood years often become their modus operandi in adult life. Therefore, it would be prudent for schools to teach all students appropriate coping strategies for dealing with life's adversities.

CONCLUSION

Child maltreatment is an insidious and pervasive aspect of the human condition. A lack of understanding of the prevalence of child abuse and the childhood witnessing of domestic violence has unwittingly contributed to the current situation where an intergenerational climate of abuse allows young children to grow up believing that such behaviour is 'normal'. While, pre/adolescents on learning through their socialization with peers that child maltreatment is not a societal norm attempt to take steps to reduce the likelihood of further maltreatment, however, the damage it would appear has already been done to their inner psyche. The extent of this damage is evidenced in the next chapter.

REFERENCES

Bandura, A. (1977). *Social learning theory.* Englewood Cliffs, NJ: Prentice Hall.

Barker-Collo, S. & Read, J. (2003). Models of response to childhood sexual abuse. *Trauma, Violence, and Abuse, 4,* 95-111.

Browne, C. & Winkelman, C. (2007). The effect of childhood trauma on later psychological adjustment. *Journal of Interpersonal Violence, 22,* 684-697.

Cecil, C. A., Viding, E., Barker, E. D., Guiney, J. & McCrory, E. J. (2014). Double disadvantage: The influence of childhood maltreatment and community violence exposure on adolescent mental health. *Journal of Child Psychology and Psychiatry, Efirst.* Retrieved 11 March 2014: http://onlinelibrary.wiley.com/doi/10.1111 /jcpp.12213/pdf

Chartier, M. J., Walker, J. R. & Naimark, B. (2010). Separate and cumulative effects of adverse childhood experiences in predicting adult health and health care utilization. *Child Abuse & Neglect, 34,* 454-464.

Child Welfare Information Gateway. (2009). *Understanding the effects of maltreatment on brain development.* Washington, DC: U.S. Department of Health and Human Services, Children's Bureau.

Child Welfare Information Gateway. (2013). *What is child abuse and neglect?* Washington, DC: U.S. Department of Health and Human Services, Children's Bureau.

Denholm, R., Power, C., Thomas, C. & Li, L. (2013). Child maltreatment and household dysfunction in a British birth cohort. *Child Abuse Review*, *22*, 340-353.

Dube, S. R., Anda, R. F., Felitti, V. J., Croft, J. B., Edwards, V. J. & Giles, W. H. (2001). Growing up with parental alcohol abuse: exposure to childhood abuse, neglect, and household dysfunction. *Child Abuse and Neglect*, *25*, 1627-1640.

Elliott, G. C., Cunningham, S. M., Linder, M., Colangelo, M. & Gross, M. (2005). Child physical abuse and self-perceived social isolation among adolescents. *Journal of Interpersonal Violence*, *20*, 1663-1684.

Ellonen, N., Piispa, M., Peltonen, K., & Lica, M. O. (2013). Exposure to parental violence and outcomes of child psychosocial adjustment. *Violence and Victims*, *28*, 3-15.

Finkelhor, D. (1995). The victimisation of children. *American Journal of Orthopsychiatry*, *65*, 177-193.

Forsman,M., & Långström, N. (2012). Child maltreatment and adult violent offending: Population-based twin study addressing the 'cycle of violence' hypothesis. *Psychological Medicine*, *42*, 1977-1983.

Gibson, K. & Morgan, M. (2013). Growing up with child sexual abuse in an experimental commune. *Journal of Community and Applied Social Psychology*, *23*, 300-313.

Gomez, A. M. (2011). Testing the cycle of violence hypothesis. *Youth & Society*, *43*, 171-192.

Heim, C., Shugart, M., Craighead, W. E., & Nemeroff, C. B. (2010). Neurobiological and psychiatric consequences of child abuse and neglect. *Developmental Psychobiology*, *52*, 671-690.

Heyman, R. E. & Slep, A. M. (2002). Do child abuse and interparental violence lead to adulthood family violence? *Journal of Marriage and Family*, *64*, 864-870.

Holt, S., Buckley, H. & Whelan, S. (2008). The impact of exposure to domestic violence on children and young people. *Child Abuse and Neglect*, *32*, 797-810.

Huth-Bocks, A. C., Levendosky, A. A. & Semel, M. A. (2001). The direct and indirect effects of domestic violence on young children's intellectual functioning. *Journal of Family Violence*, *16*, 269-290.

Jun, H. J., Corliss, H., Boynton-Jarrett, R., Spiegelman, D., Austin, S. B. & Wright, R. J. (2012). Growing up in a domestic violence environment. *Journal of Epidemiology and Community Health*, *66*, 629-635.

Lundy, M. & Grossman, S. F. (2005). Elder abuse: Spouse/intimate partner abuse and family violence among elders. *Journal of Elder Abuse & Neglect*, 16, 85-102.

Martin, S. G. (2002). Children exposed to domestic violence: Psychological considerations for health care practitioners. *Holistic Nursing Practice*, *16*, 7-15.

McIntosh, J. E. (2002). Thought in the face of violence: A child's need. *Child Abuse & Neglect*, *26*, 229-241.

Mullender, A., Hague, G., Imam, U., Kelly, L., Malos, E. & Regan, L. (2002). *Children's perspectives on domestic violence.* London: Sage Publications Ltd.

Navalta, C. P., Polcari, A., Webster, D. M., Boghossian, A. & Teicher, M. H. (2006). Effects of childhood sexual abuse on neuropsychological and cognitive function in college women. *The Journal of Neuropsychiatry and Clinical Neurosciences*, *18*, 45-53.

O'Brien, K. L., Cohen, L., Pooley, J. A. & Taylor, M. F. (2013). Lifting the domestic violence cloak of silence: Resilient Australian women's reflected memories of their childhood experiences of witnessing domestic violence. *Journal of Family Violence*, *28*, 95-108.

Ogloff, J. R., Cutajar, M. C., Mann, E., Mullen, P., Wei, F., Hassan, H. & Yih, T. (2012). *Child sexual abuse and subsequent offending and victimisation: A 45 year follow-up study. Trends and issues in crime and criminal justice*, *(440)*, 1. Retrieved 23 March 2014 from: http://www.med.monash.edu.au/psych/research/centres/cfbs/csa.html

Ormrod, J. E. (1999). *Human learning (3rd ed.)*. Upper Saddle River, NJ: Prentice-Hall.

Paras, M. L., Murad, M. H., Chen, L. P., Goranson, E. N., Sattler, A. L., Colbenson, K. M., Elamin, M. B., Seime, R. J., Prokop, L. J. & Zirakzadeh, A. (2009). Association between self-reported childhood sexual abuse and adverse psychosocial outcomes. *Archives of General Psychiatry*, *59*, 139-145.

Peltonen, K., Ellonen, N., Larsen, H. & Helweg-Larsen, K. (2010). Parental violence and adolescent mental health. *European Child and Adolescent Psychiatry*, *19*, 813-822.

Perry, B. D. (2006). Applying principles of neurodevelopment to clinical work with maltreated and traumatized children. In N.B. Webb (Ed.), *Working with traumatized youth in child welfare*. (27-52). New York: The Guilford Press.

Reckdenwald, A., Mancini, C. & Beauregard, E. (2013). The cycle of violence: Examining the impact of maltreatment early in life on adult offending. *Violence and Victims*, *28*, 466-482.

Reynolds, M. W., Wallace, J., Hill, T. F., Weist, M. D. & Nabors, L. A. (2001). The relationship between gender, depression, and self-esteem in children who have witnessed domestic violence. *Child Abuse & Neglect*, *25*, 1201-1206.

Ritchie, K., Jaussent, I., Stewart, R., Dupuy, A. M., Courtet, P. & Malafosse, A. (2011). Adverse childhood environment and late-life cognitive functioning. *International Journal of Geriatric Psychiatry*, *26*, 503-510.

Shonkoff, J. P. & Phillips, D. A. (2000). *From neurons to neighbourhoods: The science of early child development*. Washington, DC: National Academy Press.

Wegman, H. L. & Stetler, C. (2009). A meta-analytic review of the effects of childhood abuse on medical outcomes in adulthood. *Psychosomatic Medicine*, *71*, 805-812.

World Health Organization (WHO). (2014). *Child maltreatment: Fact sheet #150*. Retrieved from 11 February 2014: http://www.who.int/mediacentre/factsheets/fs150/en/index.html

Young, S. (1997). The use of normalization as a strategy in the sexual exploitation of children by adult offenders. *Canadian Journal of Human Sexuality, 6 (4)*, 1 - 18. Retrieved from 16 April 2014: http://www.taasa.org/library/pdfs/TAASALibrary178.pdf

Zink, T., Kamine, D., Musk, L., Sill, M., Field, V. & Putman, F. (2005). What are providers' reporting requirements for children who witness domestic violence? *Clinical Pediatrics*, *43*, 449-460.

In: Overcoming Domestic Violence
Editors: Myra F. Taylor, Julie Ann Pooley et al.

ISBN: 978-1-63321-956-4
© 2015 Nova Science Publishers, Inc.

Chapter 18

'FEELING LIKE YOU'RE DAMAGED AND LIKE YOUR LIFE IS OUT OF YOUR CONTROL': THE MALE PERSPECTIVE ON LIVING WITH THE ADULT AFTERMATH OF CHILD MALTREATMENT

*Myra F. Taylor, Teresa Goddard and Julie Ann Pooley**
Edith Cowan University, Joondalup, Western Australia, Australia

This chapter documents eight male participants' narratives on the repercussions that their childhood experiences of maltreatment have had on their adult lives. Its core theme: *'Damaged lives'* is comprised of three themes and nine subthemes. Collectively, these sub/themes provide insights into the male adult experience of trying to function in the adult world through an internal lens of having experienced maltreatment as a child. Each of these three themes is displayed in Table 1. The first theme: *Adult repercussions of child maltreatment* reveals that even though some participants' more horrific memories of their maltreatment experiences were suppressed, certain triggers (some predictable and some unpredictable) caused elements of these supressed memories to resurface. Once triggered the anguish associated with the maltreatment memory lessened their adult internal sense of control. In this regard, participants indicated that their adult feelings of being out of cognitive control allowed their former childhood emotions of shame, guilt and anger to reduce their adult sense of self-worth. The second theme: *Failed interpersonal relationships,* reveals that as a result of being scarred by their maltreatment adult males experienced significant sexual intimacy and communication difficulties. The third theme: *Disillusionment with life* details how males are conflicted by the 'cycle of violence hypothesis'. Specifically, because the common belief that an *abused child will become an adult abuser* resides ever present in the minds of adult males. Furthermore, it governs their actions to such an extent that some participants described their reluctance to have (or avoidance of) contact with young children. The chapter closes with a discussion of the

---

* Corresponding author: Myra F. Taylor Edith Cowan University, 270 Joondalup Drive Joondalup, WA 6007 Australia.

harm that society's widely held *abused-child-adult-abuser hypothesis* has on the adult lives of male victims of child maltreatment.

Table 1. Component parts of the study's core theme relating to adult experiences of childhood maltreatment: *Damaged lives*

Theme	Subtheme
One: Adult repercussions of child maltreatment	*1 Vague, blocked and reoccurring memories* *2. Feelings of shame, guilt and anger* *3. Eroded sense of self*
Two: Failed interpersonal relationships	*4. Peer relationship problems* *5. Sexual intimacy difficulties* *6. Communication difficulties*
Three: Disillusionment with life	*7. Cycle of abuse public perception* *8. Cautious around children* *9. Negative outlook*

THEME ONE: ADULT REPERCUSSIONS OF CHILD MALTREATMENT

Subtheme 1: Vague, Blocked, and Reoccurring Memories: '*My Memory Can Be Just Awful*'

While all eight males were able to recall their child maltreatment experiences in general terms (e.g., 'mum kicked me'; 'dad hit me'; 'granddad sexually abused me') they did not elaborate on the specific details surrounding their maltreatment. On the contrary, participants spoke about a disconnect that existed between their mind and body when it came to recalling their maltreatment experiences. Indeed, participants maintained that their brain had over the intervening years learnt to repress (avoid recalling) some of the more horrific day-to-day aspects of their maltreatment and, as a result they had reoccurring vague or snippet memories of the abuse they had experienced or witnessed as a child. For instance one participant stated:

> *I'm aware... of a lot of the ways in which it (memory) feeds back to me that something happened even though I don't have specific memories.* (Participant #5)

Another participant contended that his specific maltreatment memories were lodged in the 'deeper more pre-cognitive level' of his brain. He explained:

> *The pain has been horrendous... The biggest issue is... I cannot say well this happened to me. It's my block... but it's like my DNA knows.* (Participant #3)

This contention was supported by other participants who similarly maintained that their brain's ability to repress some of the most horrific aspects of their maltreatment experiences was a cognitive self-protection mechanism that allowed them to operate on a daily basis with their less painful generalised maltreatment memories rather than their painful explicit ones. One participant explained:

I can only talk about my childhood and how it crosses over with being exposed to abuse from the point of view of talking about effects as opposed to memories or recollections of any kind of incident. Although you know there're... vague sorts of memories. (Participant #7)

However, the memory blocking mechanism was not total, as some triggers enabled aspects of their repressed child maltreatment memories to resurface either in their dreams or in their thoughts. Once resurfaced, participants revealed it was difficult to stop their brain from replaying the remembered memory snippet over and over again. For example two participants stated:

I get some bad dreams like... some pretty nasty dreams... because I sort of keep my guard up so much that sometimes sleep is the only way my body can sort of get rid of my emotions. (Participant #1)

There's been times when I've sort of like repeated the issues over and over in my mind... basically random thoughts that you know really shouldn't be there... and they're like from nearly 10 years ago... they're the sort of things that I can never seem to get over... and they just keep repeating over and over ... when they should be dead and buried. (Participant #4)

Participants revealed that they had come to realise they could interrupt their reoccurring maltreatment memories if they deliberately went to a different place in their mind. One participant explained:

If I don't really focus (on the intrusive memory) then I can go elsewhere. (Participant #1)

While recognising the relief to be had from consciously (or subconsciously) repressing certain aspects of their maltreatment memories one participant voiced concern that his adult memory retention and recall abilities had been impaired during the repression process. Another participant commented:

I've got a real shocking memory, (because of the abuse) I can't remember anything, like even if it's from a week ago, or something, a lot of the times if it's not something really important to me I've got no chance of remembering it. (Participant #2)

A poor memory was not the only cognitive difficulty that participants linked to their maltreatment experiences. Some participants perceived their present adult difficulties with maintaining focus was linked to their childhood inability to concentrate. They recalled that as a child instead of paying attention to what was going on around them at school their mind was constantly focussing on their last maltreatment experience and contemplating the next. This childhood ability to ignore their surrounds and hyper-focus they revealed was still active in their adult life. One participant explained:

I essentially switch off... and go elsewhere... I can just go off into my own little a world and it can happen while I'm driving or you know just sitting at work or something... and so focus definitely has been a big issue for me. (Participant #1)

Participants also attributed their current poor decision making skills to their child maltreatment experiences. They claimed that the oscillating indecision they experienced as a child with regards to whether to 'tell' or 'not-tell' someone about their maltreatment had resulted (both then and now) in them feeling 'stuck' in an indecisive loop whenever they are faced with a difficult decision. Other participants recalled how they reacted instinctively as a child (i.e., subconciously employing a 'fight or fright response') to their maltreatment and indicated that even as adults they still tended to react impulsively when faced with a difficult situation. Indeed, participants consistently recalled many adult instances where they had made a spur-of-the-moment decision that they later regretted, given that it generally resulted in a negative outcome for either themselves or another family member. For example:

A few years ago also I was in trouble with the law for driving without a license... so I got my licence suspended... this really caused problems you know back then for me coz I was self-employed and had to drive around. I lost my license for like nine months... I had to get others to drive me around until I could get my E-class license, back. (Participant #2)

Participants stated it was difficult to alter this impulsive decision making pattern as there was sometimes an element of self-sabotage involved:

I feel in a certain sense that I'm out of control. And I don't mean out of control in behavioural ways or in in my expressions, I just mean like there's a part of me that feels like I'm plotting a course for myself...that's against my best intentions. There's this part of me that's playing out a scenario where I undermine all of what I'm hoping for. (Participant #6)

Participants concluded that their experience of not always being in cognitive control of their actions undoubtedly had a detrimental effect on their adult cognitive and psychosocial functioning. (Further quotes supporting this subtheme and the next eight subthemes are provided in Table 2).

Table 2. Supplementary examples of the negative impacts that childhood maltreatment experiences had on adult male participants lives

Impact	Experience
Blocked memories	*'It's here still my memory, my body knows... it's here in my physical body'*
Recurring memories	*'Memories of the abuse came up... it was almost like a movie, it came straight in and it just played out'*

Impact	Experience
Poor working memory	*'My memory can be just awful sometimes'* *I can't remember anything, like even if it's from a week ago I just feel like I can't remember'* *'I can be having a conversation with my partner and I'm just not even listening..... Like I've gone elsewhere'*
Poor decision making	*'If you feel stuck or something like that it can be really hard to make decisions'* *'I get very easily confused um... with judgement'*
Sense of shame	*'I was in a place of feeling ashamed to be alive'* *'There was like... a lot of shame around um the fact that I was...part of that environment'*
Unpredictable anger	*'I lose control really easily... I don't hit my wife or anything like that, but.... I do have problems controlling my anger'* *'If someone's annoys me... I just, I can't stop thinking about it... I'm so angry'*
Eroded self-esteem	*'I wasn't ok um, with my vulnerability and weakness'* *'In every situation it's always the negatives I see'*
Social interaction difficulties	*'Not getting close to people and not allowing people to get close to me'* *'I'm a fairly, I'm a lonely person... I find it difficult to make friends ...I mean I do have have a number of friends, but really I only call them acquaintances... loneliness is a big part of my life'*
Sexual intimacy difficulties	*'I was not kind of authentically present enough, if that makes sense... It ties into that thing of leaving my body or just not being available'* *'I hurt the people who I was in relationship with... through um just really um not being integrated enough in myself'*
Communication difficulties	*I've always struggled with communication and you know articulating my feelings; or even knowing what my feelings were (laughs)'*
Reluctance to procreate	*'I worry that if I ever do have kids one day, you know they...they wanna sleep in beds and stuff like that'* *'I just don't want someone else to have to go through that (abuse)... I don't want them to have the same life I did'*
Reoccurring thoughts of abuse	*'It's just basically these random thoughts that you know really shouldn't be there'* *'It happens inside me. It's something that has happened and I'm certainly not proud of it'*

Table 2. (Continued)

Impact	Experience
Contributes to mental illnesses	'*I think it set the grounds for anxiety to sort of be there pretty regularly*' "*It created anxiousness over thinking things worrying about the future*' '*I was on antidepressants for a short time, but I didn't really think they helped me at all*'

Subtheme 2: Feelings of Shame, Guilt, and Anger: *'When I Get Angry I Just Can't Stop'*

On realising as adolescents that their maltreatment experiences were not consistent with societal norms of acceptable behaviour participants stated they first began to experience feelings of personal shame. This shame arose from being part of a dysfunctional family that engaged in acts of child abuse and domestic violence. Participants stated that as a result they continued to internalize and reprocess their childhood shame as adults. One participant explained that this reprocessing had had the dual outcomes of lowering his adult sense of self-worth, and negatively impacting on his physical and mental health. He stated:

> *I've struggled with my health, and a lot of that was impacted directly from my interactions and experiences... you know all that shame... that inner tension and the fear around that... I mean I'm processing it and it's like my body's constantly being compromised... it's affected my digestion...and there's contempt within myself.* (Participant #6)

Emotional turmoil was a common adult experience, for at the back of the participants' minds there lingered feelings of childhood guilt that they had been in some way responsible for the maltreatment they had experienced at that time (e.g., *'if only I'd been more perfect then it wouldn't have happened'*). One consequence of this childhood notion of being responsible for the maltreatment they had experienced was that as adults they set themselves very high (and sometimes impossible) achievement standards. Moreover, when they failed to reach these standards they revealed that their latent childhood sense of guilt was reinforced. One participant explained:

> *You can have this profound sort of guilt when you have something like that (child abuse)... you can really dwell on things and beat yourself up if you do one thing that you are not quite happy with....whereas normal people will seem to just move on from things... (but) I can really get caught in just guilt.* (Participant #1)

In addition, participants asserted that their low sense of self-worth would often cause them to withdraw and isolate themselves from others. One participant described his self-isolating periods as being 'detached from reality' and in a 'mind space' where he was so 'stuck' there was 'no forward movement' in his thinking.

While participants revealed certain triggers could induce self-isolating responses, they were aware that other triggers could provoke a polar opposite angry response. They stated their anger usually manifested itself as uncontrolled rage during which they were prone to losing their temper and being verbally and physically aggressive. Furthermore, they revealed their angry outbursts could last for an extended period of time. One participant described his explosive anger in the following terms:

I'm definitely more of a reserved sort of person... but, if something irritates or frustrates me I get angry... definitely my first reaction a lot of the time won't be to talk about it ... it will just be boom... like it's really hard to manage my emotions because a lot of it is internal. (Participant #5)

Moreover, participants contended that their mood swings which ranged from 'reserved withdrawal' to 'explosive anger' could occur quite suddenly and, at such moments, they usually lost control of their ability to think rationally. For example:

I've had lots of occasions where I've... lost my shit... like getting bad service and then I've thrown plates of food against walls in restaurants and threatened to pull waiters over the counters... like gone off my face in public swearing my head off... and when I was doing it I was just raging, I was just angry. (Participant #3)

I've sort of expressed anger instead of like being you know...a little bit more passive... I've been a little more verbal than I should've been. There's been situations like I've lost my temper at work... probably sort of started arguments with people I probably shouldn't of. There's been situations where I could've handled it better... and ended up losing my job as a result. (Participant #3)

*I actually flipped... I actually said to one man: 'One more step and I'll f***ing kill you!'... two things will happen, either I'll f***ing kill you or you'll kill me. (Participant #7)*

Participants maintained that such bouts of uncontrollable rage stemmed from their childhood experiences of anger over their inability to stop the maltreatment that was happening within the family home. One participant explained:

It's given me a bit of a violent streak... I think always being a witness and not being big enough or old enough to sort of defend my sister, or myself you know... all of those occasions have sort of carried through...to the point where I (now) lose control really easily. (Participant #8)

Another participant suggested that his inability to control his anger was intergenerational in its origin. He surmised:

I've always had a feeling that I'm carrying all this shit and all the anger, the rage, the pain of all my generations. (Participant #3)

Participants surmised that one consequence of living with periodic uncontrollable explosions of rage was that when the anger subsided they remonstrated with themselves. A common rebuke they belaboured themselves with being: 'You're a damaged weak b*stard'.

Subtheme 3: Eroded Sense of Self: *'It Takes Away Your Confidence Little Bit By Little Bit'*

Participants confided that they often felt 'a bit clueless' as to how to deal with the aftermath of their angry mood swings. For, their ineffectual attempts at reconnecting with the people at the receiving end of their anger often ended with the recipient recoiling and distancing themselves from the participant. Consequently, participants concluded their already low self-confidence and sense of self-worth was further eroded 'bit by little bit'. For instance, one participant troubled by self-doubt confided:

> *You know it has had a kind of snowball effect... You know I just always feel a little bit clueless... just a bit lost... in my own self-reflection... in my own state of my mind... It's a very private thing... only I know where I go in my head and yeah only I know how disturbing my thoughts can be.* (Participant #6)

Another participant revealed that his low sense of self-worth had affected every facet of his adult life:

> *Your self-confidence it like affects you in different areas...it effects everything; it effects your self-confidence in sitting exams, going into competitions, your relationships; your working life... you sort of just expect a lot more from people that you work with... and from your normal relationships.* (Participant #7)

Being in a state of frequent internal conflict participants confided had meant that their vulnerabilities and weaknesses were exposed which, in turn, became problematic when they first endeavoured to establish and sustain an intimate adult relationship.

THEME TWO: FAILED INTERPERSONAL AND INTIMATE RELATIONSHIPS

Subtheme 4: Peer Relationship Problems: *'It Has Made Me Very Mistrustful'*

As participants entered into adult friendship and dating relationships they claimed their formative maltreatment experiences influenced their ability to interact and socialize with others. In this regard, participants revealed that when they were children they had learnt over time not to trust other people. Hence, as adults, taking people at face value was something participants found particularly hard to do. Moreover, this distrust of others was often gender specific. For example, if a participant had been abused by a male as a child then they tended to have difficulty in trusting males and, similarly, if they had been abused by a female then they recounted problems in trusting females. Two participants recalled:

> *Social interaction is a tricky one... its quite difficult obviously for me to trust anyone... I have a lot of trouble... with male relationships.* (Participant #1)

> *I'm not able to form close relationships, that's been an issue with me in dealing with women... don't get me wrong I'm attracted to women, I'm not gay... and I'm not being a misogynistic ...but yeah I find\in the case of women, I think because my mother was the abuser... it's made me very mistrustful.* (Participant #4)

Consequently, during their dating years participants stated that one of their relationship avoidance tactics was to not place themselves in situations where their maltreatment memories would likely be triggered. For instance, participants revealed they would purposely avoid individual liaisons and instead endeavour to always socialize with others in a group setting. Even in instances, where a group friendship progressed into an intimate dating relationship their underlying distrust of adults, as well as their triggered maltreatment memories frequently combined to become a barrier to formalizing the relationship. One participant who had been abused by his mother explained:

> *Because I sort of need to fit in and I don't need anyone looking at me or asking questions or anything like that I've a lot of female friends, but then it's difficult to do things with them socially... something about it just doesn't make sense or doesn't click... There's just something about the way they speak and act and stuff... that doesn't fit with me... a lot of the time it can be a very sexual sort of conversation. I've never been that comfortable with that and a wall closes off... I've had a lot of trouble with this because they (female friends) always think you're in love with them ...and in my case that wasn't always true. And so they'd treat you quite abruptly because all of a sudden they thought you were into them... and all I just wanted was to be friends. Then I'm like: 'I never asked you out or anything'... and then they're like: 'Yeah, but you know I think you do (love me)', and then I'm like: 'Well you're wrong!' 'When something like that happens I can be incredibly quick to just cut off. Like all together.* (Participant #8)

While, participants indicated that with the passage of time they became 'more comfortable' around adults of the same gender as their abuser and as a result their social anxiety lessened. However, their underlying distrust still made it hard for them to form lasting relationships.

Subtheme 5: Sexual Intimacy Difficulties: *'I Learnt a Long Time Ago to Turn That Off'*

Although loneliness was a facet of some un-partnered participants' lives other participants who had married (or formed a defacto relationship) indicated their childhood sexual abuse experiences had resulted in significant sexual intimacy difficulties. One participant explained:

Intimate relationships, yeah that's certainly a tricky one; I mean partly because I've always had a lot of trouble in that area. It starts out as a good thing, but... you'll be in that sort of state and you'll get flashbacks or whatever of things and that can be quite the mood killer... So in terms in terms of physical intimacy... and this is particularly difficult with my partner who's like a long term partner. While everything functions, if you will, I can be gone... and she knows, she notices... and that's quite difficult and that's caused us a lot of problems. She knows I'm not there. You can have this incredible auto pilot mode that you go into... that's when I can't stop what I'm doing, but I don't really want to be here or doing this anymore, and that's when the eyes glaze over. I just don't feel anything basically... I learnt a long time ago to turn that off. Unfortunately I haven't figured out how to reverse that thing that the younger me sort of put in place. When you you've been used or abused or whatever ...you learn to not enjoy any of it. (Participant #1)

Intimacy problems that were not addressed in the initial stages of participants' partnered relationships generally worsened as the relationship progressed. Moreover, as the relationship deteriorated there were periods when it stabilized, plateaued or improved for a period of time before deteriorating further. These 'on and off again' periods in the participants' minds mirrored their good-time-bad-time child maltreatment experiences. As a result, the participants' belief that this was the way that all relationships progressed was reinforced. One participant reflected:

Over the course of 10 years I guess, there was this deterioration... not just in our relationship which deteriorated fairly early on... but it was lots of very tumultuous on again off again reinforcement of I suppose of my own (childhood) trauma ... (and) the ways in which it has impacted on me. (Participant #6)

In summarizing the impact that their child maltreatment experiences had on their adult intimate relationships participants indicated their intimacy problems were partly related to their inability to fully trust their partner and partly to the unrealisable 'expectations' they had for their partner, in so far as always wanting partner 'perfection'. Their inability to articulate why they wanted perfection was according to participants an underlying issue in the relationship breakdown.

Subtheme 6: Communication Difficulties: *'I've Always Struggled with Articulating My Feelings'*

The most consistently voiced communication problem participants faced was their inability to adequately express their inner feelings. Two participants explained:

I find it hard, I don't always really express much emotion... guys don't really do that, or talk about things... it's you know weak to do that. I find it pretty hard to even think of putting into words what I'm feeling a lot of the time. I find it hard to say what I feel, so... showing it just comes more naturally. I lose my temper and yell and scream... and the other thing I do is I sulk when I don't get my way, instead of talking about the problem. (Participant #2)

I can't sit there and have a standard conversation, I act like how I was as a child... because that how I was told... or how I was taught to deal with conflict... so I struggle to maintain relationships because... I haven't been taught how to successfully maintain relationships... how relationships should be, or how families should be, or how a marriage should be. (Participant #8)

Participants maintained that their communication difficulties were directly related to their former child maltreatment experiences. For these experiences had taught them to listen to what people say through an interpretive lens (i.e., not to take people's words at face value and to always look for hidden meanings). In addition, when a maltreatment trigger provoked them to respond angrily towards their partner, it was difficult for participants to control their anger even though they knew their rage was distressing their partner. Furthermore, participants explained they could not at such times empathise with their partner's distress as for them rage and abuse were a normalized part of their life experience. One participant explained:

When I have disagreements in relationships... I don't deal with them in the way that most people would. I just don't. I just have arguments where I just terrorise the house pretty much.... because I just think that's normal... I've no issue with arguing on to you know the early hours of the morning, because that's what the norm was for us (childhood family)... but normal people don't see that (Participant #3)

A common consequence of their intimate and non-intimate relationship failures participants stated was that they contributed to their adult disillusionment with life.

THEME THREE: DISILLUSIONMENT WITH LIFE

Subtheme 7: Cycle of Abuse Perception: *'If You Were Abused You'll Become an Abuser'*

One of the things that participants stated caused them considerable distress and contributed to their disillusionment with life was the widespread belief that a person who was abused (or witnessed abuse) as a child will grow up to be an abuser (or domestic violence perpetrator). While participants rationalised there were numerous cases where people who had been maltreated as children had grown up to be 'normal' adults who were involved in loving family relationships, however, the problem they faced as an adult victims of child maltreatment was society's failure to comprehend that the abused-abuser cycle does not always apply. One participant explained:

The one thing I've a massive issue with, which seems to be in society, is this statement... 'if you were abused you'll become an abuser'... I've heard someone say that before... and I really had to hold my tongue... I thought how can you say that? Like is everyone that's mugged going to become a mugger? There's this perception that if you're abused as a kid you're gonna become one of them... I thought oh shit... I don't want to become one....and you go through this really difficult stage where it impacts on your adult life… and that's a really hard thing to deal with. To basically be told well you were abused, ergo you're going to be one (an abuser). (Participant #1)

While the majority of participants unequivocally stated that they were not going to abuse their own children, one participant who had fathered children, to his chagrin, explained that although he had not intended to he was guilty of perpetuating the circle of violence as he had abused his own children. He explained that during a fit of anger one time he had made a conscious decision to 'break' his children:

I took a lot of my anger and rage out on my kids… And I'll be quite honest with you, I made a conscious decision, and this is what really shits me off… to break them… you know… to make them cry and to break them. The consequence of that is my kids… see those actions as normal. So I've got two boys, my grown up kids… who've got huge anger problems. (Participant #4)

This participant deeply regretted his actions and lived in fear that his sons would in time repeat their abuse on his grandchildren.

Subtheme 8: Cautious Around Children: *'I Definitely Live in Fear of Doing It'*

Participants stated that just being aware of the societal belief that if you were abused as a child then as an adult you will become an abuser as an adult was a very hard thing for them to deal with. Some participants revealed this abused-abuser cycle belief had become so ingrained in their psyche they had become extremely cautious around other people's children. This caution extended to the point where participants avoided not only holding their friends' children, but also being alone with children. One participant described his avoidant behaviour as follows:

Um, 'impacts on adult life'… well I'm always been very, very cautious about how I am around children. I've been a little bit too harsh sometimes… because I didn't want to come across like I was doing anything wrong….I don't have any particular 'beef' with them (children)… but I'll go out of my way to show a disinterest…(Participant #5)

In addition, as the next quote reveals, the fear of becoming an abuser led some participants to decide not to have children for they reasoned by not procreating they could end their family's cycle of abuse:

Yeah, it (childhood family) wasn't a nice environment, like I don't look back on it fondly at all. I don't want to create that again for somebody else, and coz I haven't experienced what it's like to have a good childhood I don't know how to offer that to someone else. (Participant #6)

Another participant conceded that although he knew he should not heed the thought, but because if the abused-abuser cycle belief was so entrenched in his mind, it never left him. He provided the example of coming home and hugging his daughter and then discovering in the course of their conversation she had been learning about incest at school that day. He recalled that instantly the abused-abuser idiom sprang to mind and so he immediately stopped interacting with her. He confided:

> *I get quite uncomfortable talking about it because I hate thinking of myself doing things like that.* (Participant #1)

The thought of being destined to become an abuser participants claimed was insidious as it lurked ever present in their mind. One participant explained that although he was not a paedophile and found paedophilia abhorrent he could understand why some men living with the constant thought that they were destined to become an abuser would eventually become orientated towards paedophilia. He explained:

> *You know the ways in which that shadow self plays out... is that at different times and in different ways, I can see for myself that I could very easily fall into behaving in certain ways that would have me be an abuser... I can see there's such a fine line because you know of experiences of being violated... and, there have been very clear thoughts or feelings that have arisen for me at certain times. Um where you know that line is just razor thin... and you feel like you're being pulled into potentially a pattern of... playing out that role. All I have to depend on is my own self-reflection and my... filtering it through my own sense of integrity I guess, and a desire to rise above... a desire to be conscious... and, I think when that's like showing up in your internal landscape well that's a hugely confronting thing because it's just you and this demon, and your battling it out. So you know in some sense I feel like I can have immense compassion for the abuser...I can see the process within myself and I don't think that to a large extent our culture has that kind of way of looking at it. I mean I think the current focus on paedophilia is akin to a witch hunt really. I understand, I mean of course I'm not dismissing the seriousness of it, but I think it's an inability to understand the psychological unravelling (factors that lead to paedophilia)... and to view them as a wound of the psyche.* (Participant #6)

Participants revealed that their diminished sense of self-worth left them not only believing there was a possibility they could replicate the abuse they had experienced as a child on their own children (or someone else's children), but also that society viewed them as potential abusers. Living with this stigmatizing and demoralizing label participants claimed underpinned their disillusionment with life.

Subtheme 9: Negative Outlook: *'It's Always The Negatives I See, It's Never The Positives'*

As a result of the various impacts that their childhood experiences of maltreatment have had on their adult lives participants concluded they had developed a 'very negative way of looking at life'. Moreover, this negative way of thinking had reduced their quality of life, and, in some instances, contributed to their diagnosis of a mental illness (e.g., mood disorder, anxiety disorder, panic attacks, depression). Three participants elaborated:

> *It takes away a bit of quality of life because everything just becomes a panic... and I think once you've got that... once your brains wired like that, it goes through into a lot of other things as well... just in your standard interactions with people your anxiety is like quite high. I mean when you're waiting on something or you've got an expectation of something and then your anxiety's sort of like goes... into overdrive.* (Participant #8)

> *The issue for me has mainly been depression. I mean anxiety has been a constant issue for me, and it still is. I guess with mood swings I've noticed recently I occasionally go into very deep you know states of depression.* (Participant #4)

> *A big thing I've I got... is an addictive personality... and problems with impulse control... like once I get something in my head, or latch onto something, I do it continuously... until it's out of my head. I just have to keep thinking about it, doing it... and as I've gotten older... it's gotten worse. It's caused a lot of problems for me, with the gambling addiction I've had... with my life, with my wife, my work, and with losing my business.* (Participant #2)

Participants consistently expressed a general cynicism towards, and disillusionment with, the people around them, and with society as a whole. In particular, participants talked about having a negative view on life as a result of their ongoing experiences of being judged and not being accepted by others because of their child maltreatment experiences. Society's indifference to the plight of male victims of maltreatment participants claimed reduced their ability to empathise with the woes of others. For, the thought: '*I've had to go through a lot more than that*!' was ever present in their mind. Ultimately, participants concluded there was nothing they could do to alter other people's perceptions of them or other people's belief in the male abused-abuser cycle. As one participant summated: '*Well the way people perceive you... well, that's just the way the world is!*'

DISCUSSION

Recent research suggests that the more frequent and severe an adult's exposure to maltreatment as a child was then the greater the risk they have for experiencing poor adult physical, psychological, behavioural and social outcomes (Bensley, Van Eenwyk, & Wynkoop-Simmons, 2003; Ellonen, Piispa, Peltonen, & Lica, 2013; Meltzer, Doos, Vostanis, Ford, & Goodman, 2009; Peltonen, Ellonen, Larson, & Helweg-Larsen, 2010). It has been suggested that suboptimal adult maltreatment outcomes (e.g., inappropriate ways of relating, resolving conflict and communicating) and ways of coping (e.g., social withdrawal, aggression) need to be viewed within the context that these outcomes were modelled and learned (Diamond & Muller, 2004; Zimet & Jacob, 2001). Therefore, a greater societal understanding of the developmental effects of child maltreatment is necessary given that this research has demonstrated that severe childhood maltreatment experiences can result in dissociative adult behaviours. Moreover, these dissociative behaviours can manifest as repressed/amnesic memories, cognitive control difficulties, interpersonal communication difficulties, emotion regulation difficulties and social alienation (Graham-Bermann & Edleson, 2001; Roth, 2004; Meyer & Carver, 2000; O'Brien, Cohen, Pooley, & Taylor, 2013; Tomoda, Polcari, Anderson, & Teicher, 2012; Varia & Abidin, 1999).

A growing number of studies suggest that the cognitive functioning difficulties adult survivors of childhood maltreatment typical experience may be related to structural and functional changes (e.g., poor access to short term and working memory store of visual, spatial, and verbal information) that can occur in a child's developing brain at the time that they experienced the maltreatment (Gould, Clarke, Heim, Harvey, Majer, & Nemeroff, 2012; Romero-Marinez, Figueiredo, & Moyo-Albiol, 2013; Schluter, Tautolo, & Paterson, 2011). Additionally, a childhood failure to acquire adequate cognitive emotion regulation has been posited to increase the likelihood that survivors of child maltreatment as adults will rely on anger and aggression as their primary means of expressing their negative emotions (Allen, 2011).

The long-term effect of multiple exposures to child maltreatment have also been linked to poor adult mental health outcomes (Cecil, Viding, Barker, Guirney, & McCrory, 2014; Dube, Anda, Felitti, Chapman, Williamson & Giles, 2001; Murthi, Servaty-Seib, & Elliott, 2006; Russell, Springer, & Greenfield, 2010). These negative outcomes include, but are not limited to depression, smoking, obesity, substance abuse, high-risk sexual behaviours, phobias, memory impairments and suicide ideation/attempt, as well as the diagnosis of comorbid conditions (e.g., schizophrenia, attachment disorder, eating disorder, panic disorder, anxiety disorder, posttraumatic stress disorder, personality disorder) (Child Welfare Information Gateway, 2009; Dube et al., 2001; Heim, Shugart, Craighead, & Nemeroff, 2010; Kulkarni, Graham-Bermann, Rauch, & Seng, 2011). Consistent with this, this study's participants related their mental ill-health (i.e., depression, anxiety and suicide ideation) to their childhood low sense of self-worth.

It has been suggested that an abused-abuser link exists between child maltreatment and adult intimate partner violence (Kernsmith, 2006). For instance, Bevan and Higgins (2002) determined that men who experience neglect as a child are more likely to be physically abusive towards their intimate partner and, also that men who witness interparental violence as a child are more likely to be psychological abusive towards their intimate partner (see Kerley, Xu, Sirisunyaluck, & Alley, 2009). In addition, Whitfield, Anda, Dube, and Felitti (2003) found children who have been abused by their mother (as was the case in two participants in the present study) were four times as likely as non-maltreated children to perpetrate adult acts of family violence. Research findings of this nature are consistent with the widely publicised Cycle of Violence Hypothesis which suggests abused children are likely to grow up to become adult abusers (Caykoylu, Ibiloglu, Taner, Potas, & Taner, 2011; Gomez, 2011; Heyman & Slep, 2002; Romero-Marinez, Figueiredo, & Moyo-Albiol, 2013).

Consistent with this abused-abuser Cycle of Violence Hypothesis, other contemporary research has posited that child maltreatment experiences result in dysfunctional attachment styles, comprehension deficits, social incompetence, and intimacy regulation difficulties (Drapeau & Perry, 2004). In other words, maltreated children are likely as adults to misinterpret the behaviours of others, be less skilled in forming friendships, and be inept at initiating and maintaining intimate relationships (Elliott, Cunningham, Linder, Colangelo, & Gross, 2005). One explanation for child maltreatment related adult relationship problems comes from Psychodynamic Theory, which hypothesizes that early childhood trauma damages the unconscious child sense of self and, in turn, distorts the victim's adult ways of relating (Goldenberg & Goldenberg, 2008; Jacobs, 2006).

While no evaluation of the Cycle of Violence Hypothesis has demonstrated an unequivocal and definitive association between child maltreatment and adult perpetuation of abuse, what is clear in the literature (and from the current study) is that a small number of men who experienced maltreatment in their childhood replicate their learnt inappropriate and violent parenting practices they witnessed as a child (Kerley, Xu, Sirisunyaluck, & Alley, 2009). However, it is important for society to understand that being maltreated as a child and having an inappropriate maltreatment parenting model is not an iron-cast determinant for later-life abuse perpetration. All maltreated boys do not become abusive, violent men. Indeed, what is clear from the present research is that the adult cognitive burden of living with an 'abused-child-adult-abuser' label is an onerous one for males to carry. For, one implication of having a 'future abuser' label (as demonstrated in the present study) ascribed to your person is that it seeps into every aspect of the abused child's adult relationships, particularly, adult intimate partner relationships. Indeed, so widespread is the perpetuation of the 'abused-child-adult-abuser' label that in adulthood when male survivors of child maltreatment are ending a failed domestic relationship (with or without children) they are often automatically characterised as being the aggressor and their partner female as the victim (Mercadante, Taylor, & Pooley, 2014). One problem with adopting this rigid male-abuser-female-victim perspective is that it can create a bias against males when they apply for (or defend against) a domestic violence restraining order application within the courts, or when a child custody application is being considered. Hence, there is a need for extreme caution to be applied to the ascription of genderized blanket labels and most particularly ones which characterize and normalize the belief that all males are inherently violent.

More problematic still, as demonstrated within this study, is the ability of an abused-child-adult-abuser label to distort the adult relationships of male victims of child sexual abuse not only with their own children, but also with the children of other people as well. Of concern, is that the adult male self-doubt around their parenting and social interaction with children abililies is being normalized by the prevailing societal belief that males who were sexually abused as children will become society's next cohort of sexual abusers, predators, and paedophiles, despite the lack of a substantive body of empirical evidence to support such a belief. Indeed, Glasser and colleagues (2001) in their retrospective evaluation of a *clinical* sample of 135 male victims of childhood sexual abuse found that while 59% of this high-risk cohort of abused males went on to perpetrate sexual abuse, there was little to no evidence of an intergenerational cycle of sexual abuse existing within the general cohort of sexually maltreated children. Hence, as a society, greater awareness needs to be generated of the potential harm and far-reaching consequences that any unqualified ascription of an 'abused-child-adult-abuser' label can have on the adult lives of males who were abused as children.

REFERENCES

Allen, B. (2011). Childhood psychological abuse and adult aggression. *Journal of Interpersonal Violence, 26*, 2093 - 2110.

Bensley, L., Van Eenwyk, J. & Wynkoop Simmons, K. (2003). Childhood family violence and women's risk for intimate partner violence and poor health. *American Journal of Preventive Medicine*, *25*, 38-44.

Caykoylu, A., İbiloglu, A. O., Taner, Y., Potas, N. & Taner, E. (2011). The correlation of childhood physical abuse history and later abuse in a group of Turkish population. *Journal of Interpersonal Violence*, *26*, 3455-3475.

Cecil, C. A., Viding, E., Barker, E. D., Guiney, J. & McCrory, E. J. (2014). Double disadvantage: The influence of childhood maltreatment and community violence exposure on adolescent mental health. *Journal of Child Psychology and Psychiatry*, Efirst. Retrieved 11 March 2014: http://onlinelibrary.wiley.com/doi/ 10.1111/ jcpp.12213/pdf

Child Welfare Information Gateway. (2009). *Understanding the effects of maltreatment on brain development.* Washington, DC: U.S. Department of Health and Human Services, Children's Bureau.

Diamond, R. & Muller, R. T. (2004). The relationship between witnessing parental conflict during childhood and later psychological adjustment among university students. *Canadian Journal of Behavioural Science*, *36*, 295-309.

Drapeau, M. & Perry, J. C. (2004). Childhood trauma and adult interpersonal functioning. *Child Abuse and Neglect*, *28*, 1049-1066.

Dube, S. R., Anda, R. F., Felitti, V. J., Croft, J. B., Edwards, V. J. & Giles, W. H. (2001). Growing up with parental alcohol abuse. *Child Abuse and Neglect*, *25*, 1627-1640.

Elliott, G. C., Cunningham, S. M., Linder, M., Colangelo, M. & Gross, M. (2005). Child physical abuse and self-perceived social isolation among adolescents. *Journal of Interpersonal Violence*, *20*, 1663-1684.

Ellonen, N., Piispa, M., Peltonen, K. & Lica, M. O. (2013). Exposure to parental violence and outcomes of child psychosocial adjustment. *Violence and Victims*, *28*, 3-15.

Glasser, M., Kolvin, I., Campbell, D., Glasser, A., Leitch, I. & Farrelly, S. (2001). Cycle of child sexual abuse: Links between being a victim and becoming a perpetrator. *British Journal of Psychiatry*, *179*, 482-494.

Goldenberg, H. & Goldenberg, I. (2008). *Family therapy: An overview* (7th ed.). Belmont, CA: Thomson Brooks/Cole.

Gomez, A. M. (2011). Testing the cycle of violence hypothesis. *Youth & Society*, *43*, 171-192.

Gould, F., Clarke, J., Heim, C., Harvey, Philip D., Majer, M. & Nemeroff, C. B. (2012). The effects of child abuse and neglect on cognitive functioning in adulthood. *Journal of Psychiatric Research*, *46*, 500-506.

Graham-Bermann, S. A. & Edelson, J. L. (2001). Introduction in S.A. Grahamm-Bermann & J.L. Edelson (Eds.), *Domestic violence in the lives of children* (1-12). Washington, DC: American Psychology Association.

Heim, C., Shugart, M., Craighead, W. E. & Nemeroff, C. B. (2010). Neurobiological and psychiatric consequences of child abuse and neglect. *Developmental Psychobiology*, *52*, 671-690.

Heyman, R. E. & Slep, A. M. (2002). Do child abuse and interparental violence lead to adulthood family violence? *Journal of Marriage and Family*, *64*, 864-870.

Jacobs, M. (2006). *The presenting past: The core of psychodynamic counselling and therapy.* Maidenhead, England: Open University Press.

Kerley, K. R., Xu, X., Sirisunyaluck, B. & Alley, J. M. (2010). Exposure to family violence in childhood and intimate partner perpetration or victimization in adulthood. *Journal of Family Violence*, *25*, 337-347.

Kernsmith, P. (2006). Gender differences in the impact of family of origin violence on perpetrators of domestic violence. *Journal of Family Violence*, *21*, 163-171.

Kulkarni, M. R., Graham-Bermann, S., Rauch, S. A. & Seng, J. (2011). Witnessing versus experiencing direct violence in childhood as correlates of adulthood PTSD. *Journal of Interpersonal Violence*, *26*, 1264-1281.

Meltzer, H., Doos, L., Vostanis, P., Ford, T. & Goodman, R. (2009). The mental health of children who witness IPV. *Child and Family Social Work*, *14*, 491-501.

Mercandante, C., Taylor, M. F. & Pooley, J. A. (2014). "I wouldn't wish it on my worst enemy": Western Australian Fathers' perspectives on their marital separation experiences. *Marriage and Family Review*, *50*, 318-341.

Meyer, B. & Carver, C. S. (2000). Negative childhood accounts, sensitivity, and pessimism: a study of avoidant personality disorder features in college students. *Journal of Personality Disorders*, *14*, 233-248.

Murthi, M., Servaty-Seib, H. L. & Elliott, A. N. (2006). Childhood sexual abuse and multiple dimensions of self-concept. *Journal of Interpersonal Violence*, *21*, 982-999.

O'Brien, K. L., Cohen, L., Pooley, J. A. & Taylor, M. F. (2013). Lifting the domestic violence cloak of silence: Resilient Australian women's reflected memories of their childhood experiences of witnessing domestic violence. *Journal of Family Violence*, *28*, 95-108.

Peltonen, K., Ellonen, N., Larsen, H. & Helweg-Larsen, K. (2010). Parental violence and adolescent mental health. *European Child and Adolescent Psychiatry*, *19*, 813-822.

Romero-Martínez, A., Figueiredo, B. & Moya-Albiol, L. (2013). Childhood history of abuse and child abuse potential.*Child Abuse & Neglect*, efirst 0145-2134.

Roth, D. H. (2004). *Adult reflections on childhood verbal abuse*. University of Saskatchewan, Canada: Unpublished Master thesis.

Russell, D., Springer, K. W. & Greenfield, E. A. (2010). Witnessing domestic abuse in childhood as an independent risk factor for depressive symptoms in young adulthood. *Child Abuse & Neglect*, *34*, 448-453.

Schluter, P. J., Tautolo, E. & Paterson, J. (2011). Experience of physical abuse in childhood and perpetration of physical punishment and violence in adulthood amongst fathers. *Pacific Health Dialogue*, *17*, 148-162.

Tomoda, A., Polcari, A., Anderson, C. M. & Teicher, M. H. (2012). Reduced visual cortex gray matter volume and thickness in young adults who witnessed domestic violence during childhood. *PloS One*, *7*, e52528.

Varia, R. & Abidin, R. R. (1999). The minimizing style: Perceptions of psychological abuse and quality of past and current relationships. *Child Abuse and Neglect*, *23*, 1041-1055.

Whitfield, C. L., Anda, R. F., Dube, S. R. & Felitti, V. J. (2003). Violent childhood experiences and the risk of intimate partner violence in adults. *Journal of Interpersonal Violence*, *18*, 166-185.

Zimet, D. M. & Jacob, T. (2001). Influences of marital conflict on child adjustment: Review of theory and research. *Clinical Child and Family Psychology Review*, *4*, 319-335.

In: Overcoming Domestic Violence
Editors: Myra F. Taylor, Julie Ann Pooley et al.

ISBN: 978-1-63321-956-4
© 2015 Nova Science Publishers, Inc.

Chapter 19

ENDEAVOURING TO MOVE FORWARD FROM CHILD MALTREATMENT BY ENGAGING IN THE THERAPEUTIC PROCESS OF PSYCHE REPAIR: THE ADULT MALE'S ATTEMPT AT ESTABLISHING A MORE FULFILLED ADULT LIFE

Teresa Goddard, Myra F. Taylor and Julie Ann Pooley*
Edith Cowan University, Joondalup, Western Australia, Australia

This chapter describes the pathway that the eight Australian males whose lives had been severely damaged by their experience of child maltreatment took towards establishing a more fulfilled adult life. This pathway is encapsulated in the chapter's core theme: *'Endeavouring to move forward from child maltreatment through engaging in the therapeutic process of psyche repair'*, which in turn is comprised of three themes and seven subthemes (See Table 1). The first theme, *Theme One: Coping*, details how at the start of the long journey towards psychic repair the men existed in a state of emotional and cognitive confusion. Moreover, their first step out of that confusion was to create practical external strategies for dealing with the triggers that unleashed their inappropriate behavioural responses to adverse interpersonal events. Indeed, it was only through a process of establishing practical coping strategies that these former victims of child maltreatment were able to configure a pathway forward. This pathway as reported in *Theme Two: Resilience,* involved seeking professional help for their underlying problems and building a resilience platform as a foundation on which they could repair their damaged sense of self. The final theme, *Theme Three: Posttraumatic growth* reveals that once this resilience platform was in place, the adult male victims of child maltreatment subsequently experienced a noticeable growth in their emotional intelligence. The chapter closes with a discussion on the need for therapeutic services for males and an increased societal understanding of the factors that precipitate

---

* Corresponding author: Myra F. Taylor, Edith Cowan University, 270 Joondalup Drive Joondalup, WA 6007 Australia.

incidents of domestic violence in both males and females who have, and have not, been victims of child maltreatment.

Table 1. Component parts of the study's core theme relating to adult victims' experiences of trying to build a more fulfilled life: *Endeavouring to move forward from child maltreatment through engaging in the therapeutic process of psyche repair'*

Themes			Subthemes
Theme One:	**Coping**	Subtheme 1:	*'Getting through and just being able to deal with things and just keep going'*
		Subtheme 2:	*'Learning from your mistakes and finding a way to make things better'*
		Subtheme 3:	*'Thinking there's a light at the end of the tunnel'*
Theme Two:	**Resilience**	Subtheme 4:	*'Just focusing on being positive and you know the good things'*
		Subtheme 5:	*'Finding help when I needed it and getting stuff off my chest'*
		Subtheme 6:	*'Resilience is like a permanent foundation from which to move forward'*
Theme Three:	**Posttraumatic growth**	Subtheme 7:	*'All of a sudden my emotional intelligence actually started growing'*

THEME ONE: COPING

Subtheme 1. 'Getting through and Just being Able to Deal with Things and Just Keep Going'

Participants spoke of their desire to find a means of not only coping with the adult emotional aftermath of their child maltreatment experiences, but also with their daily struggle to find a way forward in their damaged lives. In this regard, participants described that prior to reaching the starting point in their journey towards recovery they existed in a state of flux and indecision. During which time they drifted from one adverse situation to the next, reacting instinctively to each critical incident in their daily lives. At this stage of their life participants revealed they were devoid of any cohesive ability to make plans or to set goals for their future. Three participants explained:

> (At that stage)... just to manage and cope with it (life)... that was a lot to deal with and for a long time I kept on telling myself: "I can't do this, I can't figure this out". (Participant #2)

(At that stage)... in many ways I didn't really have a grip on how to be in the world and I think that's been a theme that I've grappled with. You know I'm just always feeling a little bit clueless... and feeling like I was just a bit lost... just drifting. (Participant #7)

(At that stage)... I didn't really plan, or think too much... I just dealt with it (life) as it came. That's probably why I reckon a lot of things didn't work out for me. I just couldn't make any plans or concentrate on things (Participant #8)

The first attempt which most participants made to alter their disordered and dysfunctional lives was their adoption of a range of avoidant coping strategies. These negative behavioural and cognitive strategies included (but were not limited to) excessive alcohol consumption, blocking abuse memories as soon as they appeared, shunning likely trigger situations, and keeping so busy that they were both physically and mentally distracted from the emotional pain that dominated their lives. Additionally, when describing the ways in which their abuse experiences had impacted upon their adult ability to cope effectively with adverse events participants related that at times during their early adult years when their emotional pain morphed into despair they had ideated about (or attempted) suicide. Two participants recalled:

Your emotions cripple you... I can understand why people want to commit suicide... coz when I did ... was I actually contacted the shadow part of me... I'd never dreamed of committing suicide, but I absolutely got there. (Participant #3)

The suicide attempt occurred you know because of the childhood experiences that I had and... because of you know my low self-esteem. (Participant #5)

Another common avoidant coping strategy that participants utilized to deflect the pain and inner turmoil arising out of their child maltreatment experiences was to excessively use drugs, alcohol and sex as a numbing agent. One participant recalled:

A lot of people say that you drink alcohol to ease the pain of you know an unpleasant issue... and based on my life experiences... you can also use ... external substance like drugs, alcohol, or sex to cope... I mean I guess in the past you know I used to drink a lot... I'd say I was a binge drinker... heavy into alcohol consumption... you know it was just sort of basically an escape mechanism. (Participant #8)

At this dysfunctional stage in their adult lives participants revealed that all they basically were doing was existing from day to day and trying to cope with each new adverse event they encountered. Moreover, because they were devoid of any positive coping strategies they often vented their inner pain through hurting the people closest to them (i.e., friends, family members, work mates). They described this dysfunctional stage as a time of 'futile attempts' to change their life and to 'move on' from their former child maltreatment experiences. Four participants described this stage as follows:

Coping kind of meant for me getting through just getting through... and, yeah, coping with the situation that was at hand... Yeah, getting through as best as I could with the knowledge that I had. (Participant #2)

I wasn't accepted with the (maltreatment) experiences I'd already gone through and so it gave me the idea that society couldn't cope with someone with so much problems... that the world hated people with problems... and so my coping mechanism was to grin and bear it. Also to trust no one... and to put a few hurdles out there. (Participant #6)

My coping was just being able to stay alive... to hang in there when faced with anything... and I suppose and just trying to find a way round it all. (Participant #5)

Coping just meant to me moving on, not letting things affect you too much, just keep going and not thinking about things too much... just keep moving forward. Just not letting things affect you too much... Yeah, just keep going and don't think about things too much. (Participant #4)

Subtheme 2: 'Learning from Your Mistakes and Finding a Way to Make Things Better'

Eventually, participants stated there came a realization that if they were ever going to progress beyond this existence stage of living, then they needed begin to take some responsibility for repairing their damaged lives. For some participants this meant that instead of sabotaging their attempts to improve their lives by adopting negative avoidant coping strategies, they needed instead to put in place a raft of new positive coping strategies. For instance, one participant described his positive coping strategies in terms of purposefully developing a 'thicker skin'. He reasoned that by developing a thicker skin he would be better able to consider each new adverse life event on its own merits and not instantly construe it to be another direct assault on his person. He explained:

Well I guess it's about how thin your skin is I suppose... how strong you are... and how to keep going through whatever you know is in your way. (Participant #1)

For another participant positive coping meant trying to find ways that did not involve harming himself or others regardless of what kind of adverse situation he was dealing with at the time. He described his quest for a better way forward in his life in the following terms:

When you're faced with anything (it's about) just trying to find a way around it... I think; yeah finding a way around things kind of makes you have a better... natural ability to deal with shit. (Participant #6)

Subtheme 3: 'Thinking There's a Light at the End of the Tunnel'

The participants revealed that the first advancement in their attempts to find a better way forward in their lives came about when they reached the realization that not only was there a better way of doing things, but that there was also a light at the end of the maltreatment tunnel. For, indeed, it was possible to repair some aspects of their damaged lives. Importantly, participants came to the conclusion that what they needed to achieve this better life was to turn their destructive thought patterns into constructive ones. For, they asserted, it was only through reframing their child maltreatment experiences that they would be able to stop being the victim of their past. Typically they reflected:

> I suppose coping... is sort of letting your mind go and just making up a different life in your head… you know looking at each situation on its own merits, and sort of deciding what I'm gonna do in this moment is just keep moving forward and dealing with things as they come. (Participant #6)

THEME TWO: RESILIENCE

Subtheme 4: Just Focusing on being Positive and You Know the Good Things

While, participants considered 'coping' to largely be the external doing component of trying to repair their damaged lives, 'resilience' in contrast was seen to be the attitudinal change that occurred within the person. In this regard, participants spoke of needing to accept the things they could not change (i.e., their maltreatment, their failed relationships) and work on changing the things that were within their remit to change. One way of achieving this attitudinal change they stated was to focus their energies on trying to think positively and set themselves achievable goals. A second change participants stated they needed to make was to recognise that they would encounter many setbacks in their drive to achieve these goals. Finally, participants viewed resilience as being the ability to reach the goals they set and in the process make positive incremental changes to their present state of mind. They iterated:

> Resilience… it's more than just being aware… I think it comes down to understanding why things were the way they were. (Participant #5)

> Resilience is… having the ability for things to just slide along you without buckling you know too much. (Participant #6)

> Resilience is yeah being thick skinned, when you have shit thrown at you and it means that if something happens it doesn't have to affect me… I can deal with it. (Participant #4)

> I think part of resilience is also some having safe guards when things might not go as well as planned. (Participant #2)

> To me what resilience means is developing my own willingness to … I think the term I like is 'show up'… just really showing up to whatever… you know even when you're 'quaking in your shoes'. (Participant #7)

> Resilience, I guess is constantly striving to improve yourself… or you know constantly trying to attain a goal that you wanna achieve without any negativity getting in your way. (Participant #1)

Subtheme 5: Finding Help When I Needed It and Getting Stuff off My Chest

While there was no consistent step-by-step program for achieving a resilient state of mind, there were a number of common pathways that participants followed. One of which was to better inform themselves of the life time affect that child maltreatment has on the adult psyche. As such participants initially borrowed or bought psychoanalytic books or researched the topic online. For example, one participant recounted:

Reading general psycho analytical books…reading up on the dynamics of child raising and the effects on later life really, really helped… reading and understanding the dynamics was probably the biggest healer that I've sort of had… because then you can understand it from all sides of the picture not just from your own internal view point. (Participant #6)

Once participants had developed an understanding that the emotional distress they were experiencing in their life was not unique to them, but was also common to other men who had experienced child maltreatment, then they typically began to reach out for help. While some reached out to family and friends to begin with, however, they all eventually sought the services of a variety of mental health professionals (e.g., counsellors, psychologists, NGO workers, mental health groups, men's groups). Moreover, once the participants had made contact with a mental health professional, they participated in one-on-one therapeutic work. From, this initial counselling experience the men subsequently sourced and attended a variety of group therapy programs. For instance they recalled:

I had sessions with a therapist on anger… just writing down what I was feeling… and how I survived. I remember the affirmations. What I did was I just stood in front of the mirror and actually said all these positive things about myself… and I've just recently done this year some constellation work (spiritual/energy therapy)… and also with the MKP there was an amount of healing that occurred there too. (Participant #4)

I thought in my brain that there had to be something… so I started looking for men's groups… men's help stuff… I started doing the Mankind Project (MKP) and a few others, for example, the Men's Gathering… that was really good… and another workshop called… UPPED, which stands for Power, Diversity and Privilege… and it might be Unification, I can't remember… that worked really well. That was more of a mixed group… I did the Vappassina course, … a 10 day silent retreat which was physically, mentally and emotionally hard… and I also did The Grail, which is another kind of workshop run by women; which was a challenge for me… and shocked me, to say the least. (Participant #2)

Participants differentiated between the personal benefits of attending one-on-one sessions with a therapist from those of attending group mental health programs. For example, in terms of one-on-one benefits participants typically related:

It stopped all the noise that was going through my head. All the questions I like had… they were all pebbles in a pond, so to speak… and it showed me that there was another way…a much more peaceful way… to deal with all this stuff. (Participant # 4)

> Going to therapy was kinda good in just being able to speak about things and have someone explain how things form the past effect why I'm thinking the way I do now, or why I'm behaving the way I do now. Just to have someone there when you just don't really want to be alone with your thoughts, and you just want to spurt it out. (Participant #6)

In terms of group work participants revealed that they found a sense of acceptance being in a session with other men who had similarly experienced child maltreatment. For the group created a safe environment in which they could disclose their past and present experiences 'without feeling bad' as well as feeling safe in the knowledge that the group would provide them with the non-judgemental support they needed. Two participants described their experiences of group work as follows:

> Speaking with them it sort of opened up the past and made me realise that it was quite a deeper issue... and through it all I just surrendered to the process... and learnt not to be impatient for some sort of immediate relief or resolution. (Participant #7)

> I had to go through the pain of acknowledging the good parts of me... and liking myself for of all the things I've accomplished... and also for being human, and for screwing up... and making mistakes. (Participant #3)

Participants reflected that although the professional one-on-one therapy sessions programs contributed to their resilience building efforts, however, what they had found worked the best was to engage in both individual and group therapy sessions. For, this mix enabled them to establish a variety of ways of learning how to cope and learning how to become resilient.

Subtheme 6: 'Resilience Is Like a Permanent Foundation from Which to Move Forward'

There was a general consensus among the participants that one of the main benefits of attending therapy sessions was that it provided them with the requisite emotional and cognitive skills to build an internal resilience platform upon which they could stabilize their emotions and develop a much needed sense of self-worth. Moreover, participants revealed that they were under no illusion that therapy was a 'magic cure all' that would bring them instant rewards. They credited the slowness of the process to the reality that therapy for male victims of child maltreatment is an initiative that is still very much in its infancy. One participant explained:

> I'm not saying that all of these services work really well.....because some of them are still in their infancy ....and they (mental health professionals) are still learning to cope with what's really happening with us guys. (Participant #2)

Despite the shortcomings in the current therapeutic help available to male survivors of child maltreatment, the participants believed that their involvement in the range of therapies and interventions currently available to them enabled them to reach the conclusion that resilience is an ability to reach a stage in their adult life where they feel if not completely emotionally strong, but 'fairly strong'. This strength they asserted came from their post therapy ability to 'let go' of some aspects of their past. In doing so, participants stated that they came to realise they possessed the capacity to build on the resilience platform they had established within their therapy sessions and, importantly, to use this platform to improve themselves and their future life. Two participants explained:

> I actually finally find I'm now able to begin to really let go. I feel resilient enough to be able to… to actually say it's gonna be okay. I certainly feel a lot more at ease and feel blessed that I've had the opportunity to turn some of these things around. And, that I've had the opportunity to find some healing. (Participant #8)

> I've made small changes over time you know to I guess try to create myself a better life for myself… it's been difficult you know… so I'm probably only half way there. I still feel that I've got sort of a fair distance to go, but I guess I know that the only way forward is to be resilient… and to work on it constantly. (Participant #5)

Participants commonly reached the conclusion that the state of being resilient meant recognising that they could strive towards the light at the end of the maltreatment tunnel.

THEME 3: POSTTRAUMATIC GROWTH

Subtheme 7: 'All Of A Sudden My Emotional Intelligence Actually Started Growing'

One of the measures that participants referred to as being indicative of the personal growth that had occurred in their lives once they developed a resilience platform was their new found awareness and empathy for other people's feelings. They described this empathetic ability in terms of being able to 'walk in someone else's shoes' and, in terms of it being a major advancement in their emotional intelligence. For, they stated, it allowed them for the first time to see both sides of an event. Moreover, they maintained that once they had attained this state of empathetic understanding they were then able to treat people quite differently, more compassionately. One participant reflected:

> I'm not so narrow-minded or pig-headed now to believe that I'm always right… for now I know to treat people with you know more respect… Yeah, and to treat a person you know like an individual… and not to try to make them something that they're not… and not to convert them into somebody you know they may not want to be. (Participant #5)

Another facet of their lives that participants noticed had changed since they had experienced growth in their emotional intelligence was their ability to make informed decisions, rather than relying like they had formerly on their reactive responses. As such, participants saw the ongoing growth in their interpersonal cognitions and their emotional intelligence to be indicative that they had not only developed a resilience platform, but that this platform was continuing to grow and develop. Two participants summarized their posttraumatic growth experiences in the following terms:

> It's been a lot of hard work to get to the point...where my decision making is a bit safer or wiser... I guess it's my determination... you know the will to survive. Although I would much prefer that I didn't have to go through any of that stuff...but I think a lot of it has given me a very strong personality now. (Participant #4)

> I'm at a level where I don't feel my experiences hinder, or devalue, or diminish me... if anything my experiences have probably made me more resilient because if I want something I just keep going now until I get it... Would I have changed anything? Maybe some things, but I certainly feel a lot more at ease and feel blessed that I've had the opportunity to turn some of these things around. And, I've had the opportunity to find some healing, some personal growth, some grounding, and some people that actually care and give a damn about me... a lot of good friends, new friends... and yeah a lot of laughter along the way. (Participant #2)

None of the participants considered that their posttraumatic growth was complete. All acknowledged that they had been scarred by their child maltreatment experiences and realized that the damage done to their psyche would take a long time (if not a life time) to repair. Having accepted that their journey towards psyche repair was still ongoing, participants were pleased that their efforts to date had resulted in manifest improvements in their lives. In this regard, the following two participants encapsulated the thoughts of the other participants when they concluded:

> I'm starting to you know to get a sense that I'm entering the world as opposed to being trapped in my own inner state of permanent conflict and pain and limitation... I now have a kind of foundation that is grounded. (Participant #7)

> I can't say that I've completed all my work coz I'm sure that there's more work to be done... but I'm absolutely glad now that it's over... that I'm no longer that abused child. I've been able to I suppose reassure my inner child. (Participant #2)

DISCUSSION

It is important to note that the perspectives detailed in this chapter (and the two preceding chapters) are those of eight resilient male survivors of child maltreatment, who through their efforts managed to attain a relatively stable and healthy level of functioning. Therefore, it should be understood that their posttraumatic growth achievements are not reflective of other male survivors of child maltreatment who are still trapped in a dysfunctional space and, because of this, are unable to maintain employment or to volunteer to participate in research projects such as the one described in the this and the previous two chapters. Indeed, this chapter is arguably presenting the best case scenario of what can be achieved in the lives of males who pursue an extensive program of psyche repair.

It should also be noted that there is a general consensus within the abuse literature that child maltreatment can result in long-term difficulties for adult male survivors and that these difficulties are similar in some regards to the difficulties noted in the more substantial body of female abuse survivor literature (Banyard, Williams, & Siegel, 2004; Sagy & Dotan, 2001; Young, Harford, Kinder, & Savell, 2007). Although, the long-term consequences of male childhood abuse remains relatively under researched (O'Leary, 2009), an increasing amount of research suggests that in spite of the risk for poor long term mental health outcomes some adults (as evidenced in this chapter) do overcome the adverse consequences of child maltreatment (see McGloin & Widom, 2001). More specifically, such adult survivors of child maltreatment demonstrate an ability to establish relatively stable levels of adult functioning and, consequently can present as being resilient (Bonanno, Galea, Bucciarelli, & Vlahov, 2007).

Clearly, it could be argued that the ideal would be to be put in place therapeutic intervention programs as close as possible to the time when the maltreatment occurred, because then the damage that maltreatment causes to an abused child's psyche can be prevented from extending into the child's adult life. However, the reality is that male maltreatment often goes undetected in childhood, thus, it is somewhat inevitable that many maltreated children will enter adulthood unsupported, unrecognised as victims of abuse and, also carrying a considerable, but invisible emotional and cognitive burden. The most common manifestations of this burden are feelings of fear, guilt and humiliation as well as feelings of shame around a compromised masculine identity. Characteristically, this burden is expressed as bouts of anger and self-sabotaging behaviour (Dhaliwal, Gauzas, Antonowicz, & Ross, 1996; Spataro, Moss, & Wells, 2001). So entrenched can these behaviours become that it is commonplace (as demonstrated in this chapter) for unsupported adult males to initially manifest a range of destructive avoidant coping strategies. For instance, in some cases engaging in substance abuse (i.e., alcohol, illicit drugs) so as to dull the pain emanating out of their conflicted emotions, or in other cases focusing the bulk of their energies on some non-emotive aspect of their damaged lives (e.g., work) (Dhaliwal, Gauzas, Antonowicz, & Ross, 1996; Spataro, Moss, & Wells, 2001; Walsh, Fortier, & DiLillo, 2010). It is not surprising then that these destructive avoidant coping strategies tend to seriously impair the ability of male survivors of child maltreatment to form and sustain interpersonal relationships, both in their public and private lives.

To date, the resiliency of the adult cohort of child maltreatment survivors has largely been focused on the experiences of female survivors (Sagy & Dotan, 2001). Despite this gender imbalance, a limited body of literature relating to the adult male post-maltreatment experience is beginning to emerge and to provide some understanding as to why it is that some male survivors of child abuse fare better than others (O'Leary & Gould, 2008). For example, research by Gonzales, Chronister, Linville, and Knoble (2012) investigated the various factors contributing to resilience in adult males who had been exposed to interparental violence and violence against their person in childhood. Their findings reveal six factors that were consistently regarded by the study's 12 male participants as being pivotal to their development of resilience. These included forming safe relationships with caring adults, developing a non-violent personal identity, making meaning of their former abuse experiences, developing positive coping strategies, engaging in social activities, and attaining personal or professional achievements.

Therefore, the psyche repair pathway that the men in this chapter took towards achieving resilience and a functional (post-maltreatment) adult life are by no means unique to them, for this pathway seems to be germane to other male and female survivors of a wide range of traumas. For example, research by Sesar, Simic, and Barisic, (2010) suggests that is it commonplace for individuals dealing with traumatic experiences to develop an extensive repertoire of coping strategies. However, these strategies are characteristically in the first place self-destructive, involve considerable risk taking, have with little recourse to self-care, and are generally self-sabotaging (Liem, James, O'Toole, & Boudewyn, 1997).

It is also noteworthy that the repertoire of avoidant coping strategies that the adult male suvivors of child maltreatment in this chapter stated they had adopted were largely external and practical in nature. This revelation is consistent not only with the Sesar et al. (2010) study, but also with the current definition of coping as being the intentional behaviours that individuals use to draw upon and manage the external demands they find immediately distressful (see Affleck & Tennen, 1996; Aldwin, Sutton, & Lachman, 1996; Folkman & Moskowitz, 2004). What also is interesting is that in this chapter the adult male victims of child maltreatment detailed were only able to gain an element of control over their external lives once they had engaged in the cognitively-focused strategy of reframing the narrative of their life (see Morano, 2010; Sesar, Simic, & Barisic, 2010; Walsh, Fortier, & DiLillo, 2010). This assertion is consistent with the findings of Cohen, Ferguson, Harms, Pooley and Tomlinson (2011) who posited that when human individuals are faced with adversity they have an inherent capacity to move away from their negative modes of thinking by constructing a more future-focused and optimistic outlook on life.

Finally, it is noteworthy that the decision that men in this chapter to seek out professional help in order to develop a resilient future is again not peculiar to male survivors, as it appears to be a well-trodden pathway that people from all genders and walks of life tend to follow when attempting to overcome abuse. For example, Popescu, Drumm, Dewan, and Rusu (2010) in their examination of the coping behaviours of 1,756 adults who had been primary (child abuse and neglect) and secondary (witnessing parental violence) victims of child maltreatment similarly found that following their instigation of the negative coping strategies (e.g., alcohol, drugs, seeking, and/or attempting suicide) their participants subsequently engaged in an extensive process of professional help-seeking (e.g., sourcing self-help books and attending counselling, support groups) in order to rebound from their abuse experiences.

According to Cohen and colleagues (2011) the desire to recover from a traumatic experience is the very essence of the human resilience 'bounce-back' quality. Resilience being defined as the stress-resistant thriving human quality that provides humans with the ability to exhibit in the face of adversity both a level of internal resourcefulness and hope (Pooley & Cohen, 2010). Indeed, it is these very resilient qualities that people characteristically use to 'navigate' their way to 'healing' through establishing (just like the men described in this chapter did) a set of short and long-term goals (Ahern, Ark, & Byers, 2008; Anderson & Bang, 2012; Luthar, Chiccetti, & Becker, 2000; Masten, 1994; 2001; O'Brien, Cohen, Pooley, & Taylor, 2013; Schilling, 2008). One of the few studies that have researched the issue of male resilience, the Kia-Keating, Grossman, Sorsoli, and Epstein's (2005) study, examined the post-abuse development of a masculine identity in 16 male survivors of childhood sexual abuse. They found that although resilient males struggled with the expectations of conventional masculinity, they were able in collaboration with a therapist to renegotiate their masculine identity and establish a role for themselves within society (Kia-Keating, Grossman, Sorsoli, & Epstein, 2005).

Cohen et al. (2011) and Unger (2008) suggest that this ability to develop internal resilience is reliant on the quality of the protective resources that are available to the person seeking help. What should be of great concern to all people wanting to eliminate domestic violence is that the quality of the therapeutic support resources available to men are generally substandard to those available to female survivors of child maltreatment and domestic violence. This lack of male-orientated therapeutic support resources occurs partly because there is only a very limited societal understanding of the problems that men face and, partly, due to the demonization of men as abusers and the widespread presentation of women as victims in abuse cases. This lack of understanding of the male experience is somewhat surprising given that an earlier study by McGloin and Widom (2001) which interviewed 676 participants who were formerly abused in childhood and 520 non-abused participants and found that not only did fewer abused individuals meet the criteria for resilience, but those abused individuals who met the criteria for resilience were mostly females.

Without a doubt, the lower level of resilience in male survivors of child maltreatment is a serious issue that needs to be further researched and addressed. The feminist lobby to their credit has been extremely effective in procuring the necessary support resources to help female child and adult victims of abuse and domestic violence to rebound from adversity. Therefore, it is possible that lessons learnt from such feminists' endeavours now can be applied to bettering the support resources available to males. In this regard, a successful outcome of the findings of the research detailed in this and the previous two chapters would be the development and implementation of male gender specific interventional programs to assist boys and men to understand and move beyond the trauma and internal conflict arising from their childhood experiences of maltreatment. A second successful outcome would be an expanded awareness in society that male violence is sometimes, but not always, predicated on past experiences of abuse. Thus, a task for future research is to extend the research presented in this chapter by establishing the precipitating triggers in all genders (i.e., males, females, and unspecified) of individuals who commit acts of violence upon their intimate partners, regardless of whether they were, or were not, the victims of child maltreatment.

Another task for future research is to expand the current understanding of DV beyond its male perpetrator characterization. For, as this research clearly reveals, DV is not a scourge that can be relegated into the hegemonic male domain basket. Indeed, the DV issue is undoubtedly broader than this. Thus, any resolution of the DV issue undoubtedly needs to be extended beyond its current simplistic male-abuser-female-victim conceptualization. Especially, given the demonstrated harm that the blanket ascription of the male abuser label can have on the male psyche.

Finally, the need to research the precipitating factors for DV is becoming critical since recent research has shown that females today are committing as many if not more acts of physical violence during dating relationships than are their male counterparts (Close, 2005; Mulford, & Giordano, 2008; Rivera-Rivera, L., Allen-Leigh, Rodrìguez-Ortega, Chávez-Ayala, & Lazcano-Poncel, 2007). Thus, it is logical to hypothesize that in the not too distant future the numbers of females committing acts of violence within a domestic relationship will escalate. Thus, the authors posit that *the central issue area of concern* and research endeavour *needs to be the DV act and not the gender of the perpetrator.*

REFERENCES

Affleck, G. & Tennen, H. (1996). Constructing benefits from adversity: Additional significance and dispositional underpinnings. *Journal of Personality, 64*, 899-922.

Aldwin, C., Sutton, K. J. & Lachman, M. (1996). The development of coping resources in adulthood. *Journal of Personality, 64*, 837-872.

Ahern, N. R., Ark, P. & Byers, J. (2008). Resilience and coping strategies in adolescents–additional content. *Paediatric Care, 20*, S1-S8.

Anderson, K. M. & Bang, E. J. (2012). Assessing PTSD and resilience for females who during childhood were exposed to domestic violence. *Child & Family Social Work, 17*, 55-65.

Banyard, V. L., Williams, L. M. & Siegel, J. A. (2004). Childhood sexual abuse: a gender perspective on context and consequences. *Child Maltreatment, 9*, 223-238.

Bonanno, G. A., Westphal, M. & Mancini, A. D. (2012). Loss, trauma, and resilience in adulthood. *Annual Review of Gerontology & Geriatrics, 32*, 189-210.

Close, S. M. (2005). Dating violence prevention in middle school and high school youth. *Journal of Child and Adolescent Psychiatric Nursing, 18*, 2-9.

Cohen, L., Ferguson, C., Harms, C., Pooley, J. A. & Tomlinson, S. (2011). Family systems and mental health issues: A resilience approach. *Journal of Social Work Practice, 25*, 109-125.

Dhaliwal, G. K., Gauzas, L., Antonowicz, D. H. & Ross, R. R. (1996). Adult male survivors of childhood sexual abuse: Prevalence, sexual abuse characteristics, and long-term effects. *Clinical Psychology Review, 16*, 619-639.

Folkman, S. & Moskowitz, J. T. (2004). Coping: Pitfalls and promise. *Annual Review of Psychology, 55*, 745-774.

Gonzales, G., Chronister, K. M., Linville, D. & Knoble, N. B. (2012). Experiencing parental violence: A qualitative examination of adult men's resilience. *Psychology of Violence, 2*, 90-103.

Kia-Keating, M., Grossman, F. K., Sorsoli, L. & Epstein, M. (2005). Containing and resisting masculinity: Narratives of renegotiation among resilient male survivors of childhood sexual abuse. *Psychology of Men & Masculinity, 6*, 169 - 185.

Liem, J. H., James, J. B., O'Toole, J. G. & Boudewyn, A. C. (1997). Assessing resilience in adults with histories of childhood sexual abuse. *The American Journal of Orthopsychiatry, 67*, 594-606.

Luthar, S. S., Cicchetti, D. & Becker, B. (2000). The construct of resilience: A critical evaluation and guidelines for future work. *Child development, 71*, 543-562.

Masten, A. (1994) Resilience in individual development: successful adaptation despite risk and adversity. In M. C. Wang and E. W. Gordon (Ed.), *Educational resilience in inner city America: Challenge and prospects* (pp. 3–25). Hillsdale, NJ: Erlbaum.

Masten, A. S. (2001). Ordinary magic: Resilience processes in development. *American Psychologist, 56*, 227.

McGloin, J. & Widom, C. S. (2001). Resilience among abused and neglected children grown up. *Development and Psychopathology, 13*, 1021-1038.

Morano, C. (2010). Resilience and coping with trauma: Does gender make a difference? *Journal of Human Behavior in the Social Environment, 20*, 553-568.

Mulford, C. & Giordano, P. C. (2008). Teen dating violence: A closer look at adolescent romantic relationships. *National Institute of Justice Journal, 261,* 34-40.

O'Brien, K. L., Cohen, L., Pooley, J. A. & Taylor, M. F. (2013). Lifting the domestic violence cloak of silence: Resilient Australian women's reflected memories of their childhood experiences of witnessing domestic violence. *Journal of Family Violence, 28,* 95-108.

O'Leary, P. J. (2009). Men who were sexually abused in childhood: Coping strategies and comparisons in psychological functioning. *Child Abuse & Neglect, 33,* 471-479.

O'Leary, P. J. & Gould, N. (2008). Men who were sexually abused in childhood and subsequent suicidal ideation: Community comparison, explanations and practice implications. *British Journal of Social Work, 39,* 950-968.

Pooley, J. A. & Cohen, L. (2010). Resilience: A definition in context. *Australian Community Psychologist, 22,* 30-37.

Popescu, M., Drumm, R., Dewan, S. & Rusu, C. (2010). Childhood victimization and its impact on coping behaviors for victims of intimate partner violence. *Journal of Family Violence, 25,* 575 - 585.

Rivera-Rivera, L., Allen-Leigh, B., Rodrìguez-Ortega, G., Chávez-Ayala, R. & Lazcano-Poncel, E. (2007). Prevalence and correlates of adolescent dating violence: A baseline study of a cohort of 7,960 male and female Mexican public school students. *Preventive Medicine, 44,* 477-484.

Sagy, S. & Dotan, N. (2001). Coping resources of maltreated children in the family: A salutogenic approach. *Child Abuse & Neglect, 25,* 1463-1480.

Schilling, T. A. (2008). An examination of resilience processes in context: The case of Tasha. *The Urban Review, 40,* 296-316.

Sesar, K., Simic, N. & Barisic, M. (2010). Multi-type childhood abuse, strategies of coping, and psychological adaptations in young adults. *Croatian Medical Journal, 51,* 406-416.

Spataro, J., Moss, S. A. &Wells, D. L. (2001). Child sexual abuse: A reality for both sexes. *Australian Psychologist, 26,* 177-183.

Unger, M. (2008). Resilience across cultures. *The British Journal of Social Work, 38,* 218-235.

Walsh, K., Fortier, M. A. & DiLillo, D. (2010). Adult coping with childhood sexual abuse: A theoretical and empirical review. *Aggression and Violent Behavior, 15,* 1-13.

Young, M. S., Harford, K. L., Kinder, B. & Savell, J. K. (2007). The relationship between childhood sexual abuse and adult mental health among undergraduates: Victim gender doesn't matter. *Journal of Interpersonal Violence, 22,* 1315-1331.

In: Overcoming Domestic Violence
Editors: Myra F. Taylor, Julie Ann Pooley et al.

ISBN: 978-1-63321-956-4
© 2015 Nova Science Publishers, Inc.

Chapter 20

OVERCOMING THE GENDER DYAD: ENGAGING MEN AND BOYS IN DOMESTIC VIOLENCE PREVENTION

Lana Wells[*], Alina Turner and Merrill Cooper
University of Calgary, Calgary, Canada

ABSTRACT

The entrenched gender dyad of female victim and male perpetrator in domestic violence discourse influences the underlying philosophy and assumptions that guide the design of government policies, programs and community activities and limits long-term, systematic dismantling of socio-cultural conditions that enable violence to exist. The promotion of positive fatherhood is offered as one useful strategy to begin to engage boys and men in domestic violence prevention efforts and to shift broader domestic violence narratives beyond the current gendered conception of vulnerability to domestic violence.

Keywords: Domestic violence, primary prevention, men and boys, fatherhood, gender dyad

INTRODUCTION

As I look back on what I've learned about shame, gender, and worthiness, the greatest lesson is this: If we're going to find our way out of shame and back to each other, vulnerability is the path and courage is the light. To set down those lists of what *we're supposed to be* is brave. To love ourselves and support each other in the process of becoming real is perhaps the greatest single act of daring greatly (Brown, 2012, p. 109).

International declarations calling for the meaningful involvement of men and boys in promoting gender equality and preventing and ending domestic violence have emerged over the past two decades (United Nations, 1994, 1995, 2008; United Nations Division for the

---

[*] Corresponding author: Lana Wells Brenda Strafford Chair in the Prevention of Domestic Violence and Associate Professor, Faculty of Social Work, University of Calgary, Calgary, Alberta, Canada, T2N 1N4 Tel: +1 (403) 220-6484, Email: lmwells@ucalgary.ca.

Advancement of Women, 2004). Research confirms that ending domestic violence requires the engagement of boys and men as allies, advocates, role models, partners, change agents, leaders, bystanders and violence disrupters (Crooks, Goodall, Hughes, Jaffe, & Baker, 2007; DeKeseredy, 1988; DeKeseredy & Kelly, 1995; DeKeseredy, Schwartz, & Alvi, 2000; Flood, 2011; Groth, 2001; Katz, 1995; Kaufman, 2001).

To date, efforts to engage men and boys in domestic violence reduction and prevention[12] initiatives have been limited in three primary ways: First, country- and state-wide plans led by governments around the world rarely address the current and potential roles of men and boys in prevention efforts. A recent review of national, provincial and state domestic violence and violence against women (VAW) frameworks, strategies and plans completed between 2003 and 2014 (Wells, Pickup, & Esina, 2014)[13] found that, of the 77 plans, only 31 identified men and boys as part of the solution in violence prevention and merely 16 of those included an explicit strategy and/or action.

Second, a comprehensive international review of current programs, policies and community activities from around the world found that efforts to engage men and boys in violence prevention are few, under-evaluated and diffuse (Wells et al., 2013). These initiatives are often small-scale and not connected to or integrated within broader gender equality or violence prevention strategies at national, provincial or regional levels, thereby limiting their potential to effect systemic change (Flood, 2010, 2011; Minerson et al., 2011; Wells et al., 2013).

Third, most violence prevention plans, strategies and initiatives are grounded on the assumption that females are more vulnerable to domestic violence than men are. It is clear that domestic violence remains a gender asymmetrical phenomenon, with a disproportionate impact on women. Worldwide, the prevalence rate of violence against women ranges from 15% to 71% and on average, 30% of women who have been in a relationship report that they have experienced some form of physical or sexual violence by their partner (World Health Organization (WHO), 2005). Further, we know that "women experience more serious, injurious, and repeated violence than men" (Nixon & Tutty, 2010, p. 67). However, recent research indicates that, at least in North America, girls and women now appear to perpetrate domestic violence as often as or more often than men do (Cutbush et al., 2010; Foshee, 1996; Langhinrichsen-Rohling, Selwyn, & Rohling, 2011; Swahn, Simon, Arias, & Bossarte, 2008).

Authors argue that the entrenched gender dyad of female victim and male perpetrator influences the underlying philosophy and assumptions that guide the design of country/state/provincial plans, policies, programs and community activities and limits long-term, systematic dismantling of socio-cultural conditions that enable violence to exist. The chapter begins with a discussion of the ways in which the feminist discourse has shaped government and community responses to domestic violence, followed by a review of recent evidence challenging the male abuser/female victim dyad and current view about women's heightened vulnerability to abuse. Drawing on research about female-perpetrated domestic

---

[12] In this context, we are specifically targeting *primary* prevention defined as reducing the number of new instances of domestic violence by intervening before any violence has occurred. Primary prevention "relies on identification of the underlying, or 'upstream', risk and protective factors for [domestic violence], and acts to address those factors" (Harvey, Garcia-Moreno, & Butchart, 2007, p.5).

[13] Countries included in the study were: Canada, United States, United Kingdom, European Union, Australia and New Zealand. State-wide plans were from Canada, United States and Australia. For full report please go to www.preventdomesticviolence.ca

violence, an alternate view of boys and men as victims and perpetrators is presented. The chapter then presents an analysis of worldwide action plans and initiatives that have attempted to engage boys and men and their key limitations related to the dominant domestic violence discourse and how they are limited by conventional feminist assumptions about domestic violence. The promotion of positive fatherhood is offered as a useful strategy to begin to engage boys and men and shift broader domestic violence narratives beyond the current gendered conception of vulnerability.

DOMINANT FEMINIST DISCOURSE AND ITS IMPACT ON DOMESTIC VIOLENCE RESPONSES

Feminist theory provides an essential critique of gender inequality and patriarchy (Gardiner, 2005; hooks, 2000; Judith, 2012). Hegemonic masculinity (Connell, 1987) is a concept used to describe men's dominant social position in relation to women and other, "less desirable," forms of masculinity. As a dominant discourse defining what it means to "be a man," hegemonic masculinity incorporates violence among a number of other social behaviours considered to be masculine (Bowker, 1998; Hatty, 2000; Kaufman, 1999; Kimmel, 2000, Seidler, 1996). Thus, masculinities "can be expressed or embodied through violence" (Peralta, Callanan, Steele, & Wiley, 2011, p. 117). Hegemonic masculinity incorporates both aggressive and violent practices, which, in turn, reaffirm gender inequality through the ongoing construction of a hierarchy of masculinities built on the notion of inferior femininity (Peralta, Tuttle, & Steele, 2010). The feminist critique of hegemonic masculinity challenges patriarchal structures and deconstructs gender as a culturally and historically power-laden practice. This destabilization of masculinity has proven to be an essential tool to identifying and challenging oppressive gender-based policies and practices and remains foundational to feminist efforts since the second-wave of feminism (Gardiner, 2005). This approach has significantly shaped and influenced the violence against women/domestic violence prevention discourse that has and continues to inform research, government and community-based responses around the world.

The critique of patriarchy and gender hierarchy has grounded feminist efforts to redress gender imbalance in the 1960s and 1970s, and dominates discourse about the nature, scope and prevalence of domestic violence worldwide. Policies and programs intended to protect victims of abuse or punish and rehabilitate abusers are common responses to the pervasiveness of domestic violence internationally. These efforts are usually based in the gender dyad, consisting of the masculine aggressor and his vulnerable female counterpart (Bowker, 1998; Parrott & Zeichner, 2003; Seidler, 1996). The victim is to be protected, sequestered and supported; the abuser is to be punished, rehabilitated and monitored. The proliferation of batterer intervention programs and domestic violence shelters for women around the world exemplifies this response. Wells et al.' (2014) review of 77 national and state-wide plans reveal that the majority of government investments, legislation, policies and programs has been directed towards a "response" to domestic violence (after the violence has occurred) within the context of heterosexual relationships and within a broader social construct influenced by a gender dyad paradigm.

Though such programmatic and policy interventions are an essential part of the social infrastructure necessary to respond to domestic violence, by failing to critically reflect on the underlying discourse shaping these measures, the opportunity to truly challenge the conditions that promote the permeation of violence in everyday life may be missed. The critique of hegemonic masculinity inherently assumes gender asymmetry, yet this foundation is being challenged by a number of new developments.

THE FEMALE PERPETRATOR

A growing body of research indicates that, at least in North America, girls and women now perpetrate partner violence as often as, or more often than, boys and men (Cutbush et al., 2010; Foshee, 1996; Langhinrichsen-Rohling et al., 2012; Zweig et al., 2013) and bidirectional violence is the most common pattern of violence in abusive heterosexual dating relationships (Johnson, 2011). As one example, a recent review of 50 American studies of various types (large population samples, smaller community samples, university samples, treatment seeking samples, and criminal justice-related samples) found that in heterosexual and gay/lesbian/bisexual couples experiencing domestic violence, the violence was bidirectional about half the time, and unidirectional female-to-male violence was as common as or more common than unidirectional male-to-female counterparts (Langhinrichsen-Rohling et al., 2012).

The most common form of teen dating violence is psychological aggression: Adolescent girls now perpetrate physical violence as often as or more often than boys do, even though girls suffer more serious physical harm than boys as a result (Swahn et al., 2008). A seminal study by Foshee et al. (1996) found that almost twice as many adolescent girls perpetrated dating violence compared to boys (28% versus 15%), although girls were more likely than boys to report using physical violence in self-defence (15% versus 5%). A large American study recently found that girls were more likely than boys to report perpetrating physical violence (30% versus 19%) and psychological violence (40% versus 28%), but boys were significantly more likely to physically injure their dates (Swahn et al., 2008). Although girls are far more likely than boys to be victims of sexual cyber dating abuse, cyber dating abuse overall appears to be perpetrated roughly equally by boys and girls (Cutbush et al., 2010; Zweig et al., 2013). Some research indicates that teen dating violence is often a precursor to violence in adult intimate relationships (Pepler, 2014; Sinha, 2012).

It appears that males continue to perpetrate the most common and severe forms of domestic violence (Black et al., 2011; Dutton & Nicholls, 2005; Holtzworth-Munroe et al., 2000; Johnson, 2008; Johnson, 2011; Sugarman & Frankel, 1996; Statistics Canada, 2011), but research has yet to provide a clear picture of the severity of the violence perpetrated by girls and women. In addition, it is difficult to pin down precise female perpetration rates because they vary depending on the type of study, methodology, definition of violence, sample size, and characteristics of the study population (Cooper & Wells, 2013).

These findings challenge the prevailing paradigm guiding research, government and community responses to domestic violence, which implicitly and explicitly assume girls and women to be the primary victims of violence perpetrated by males (Sinah, 2012; Statistics Canada, 2011; VicHealth, 2007) leading many researchers to question the gender dyad informed by feminist discourse. Though it would be imprudent to conclude that male violence against women is no longer relevant to the discussion, the research indicates that new approaches to prevention are required. Further, our understanding of vulnerability to violence requires careful reflection and study. As both genders engage in domestic violence, identifying risk factors that are distinct and common can render a more nuanced understanding of domestic violence perpetration and victimization (Capaldi et al., 2012; Renner & Whitney, 2012) which can help to hone and improve prevention efforts. A number of studies conducted over the past two decades suggest that physical acts of domestic violence are often predictable for both girls and boys based on common risk factors and developmental trajectories (Chiodo et al., 2012; Lussier, Farrington, & Moffitt, 2009; Raiford, Wingood, & DiClemente, 2007; Wolfe, Crooks, Chiodo, & Jaffe, 2009). On the other hand, research shows that these risk factors and their mechanisms of influence may be highly nuanced according to gender, thus the ways in which they may be malleable to intervention may be different (Cornelius & Resseguie, 2007; Shorey, Meltzer, & Cornelius, 2010). Regardless of whether prevention approaches should be universal or targeted (Centers for Disease Control, 2008), the research certainly suggests that prevention programs specifically geared to dating relationships are unlikely to be effective if they generally portray boys as perpetrators and girls as victims (Archer, 2000; Capaldi, Kim, & Shortt, 2007; Ehrensaft, 2008; Whitaker et al., 2006).

Unfortunately, considerable research gaps limit our understanding of gender-based developmental trajectories toward violence victimization and perpetration. This is in part a result of the paradigm of female vulnerability, which shapes research approaches resulting in a predominant preoccupation with female victimhood at the expense of probing domestic violence comprehensively. Few studies have followed large samples of girls over a sufficient period of time to "better understand the association between individual, relationship, and contextual factors that contribute to female-perpetrated interpersonal violence across the lifespan" (Williams, Ghandour, & Kub, 2008, p. 245). Challenging the notion of the vulnerable female victim as the norm allows for consideration of alternative solutions at the programmatic, policy and societal levels that reach beyond the gender dyad.

MALES, VICTIMIZATION, AND THE CONSTRUCTION OF MASCULINITY

Boys and men are themselves vulnerable to violent victimization and gender and social constructs, both of which can increase their risk of becoming perpetrators. This reconsideration of vulnerability can significantly strengthen our understanding of domestic violence and shape our responses accordingly.

First, it is well established that both direct maltreatment and indirect maltreatment through exposure to violence in the home are predictors of emotional problems, as well as a range of aggressive and delinquent behaviours, for both male and female children and adolescents (Coohey, Renner, & Sabri, 2013; Evans, Davies, & DiLillo, 2008; Kitzman et al., 2003; Moylan et al., 2010; Wolfe et al, 2003). Many studies have found that boys who have been maltreated are more likely to develop externalizing behaviours, such as aggression, whereas girls are more likely to develop internalizing problems, such as depression (Arata et al., 2007; Wolfe & Scott, 2001), although some studies have concluded that maltreated children of both genders can develop aggressive and anti-social behaviours and attitudes (Calvete & Orue, 2013; Maas, Herrenkohl, & Sousa, 2008). A meta-study found that any childhood sexual abuse increased male perpetration of sexual violence towards women more than threefold (WHO, 2010), with other studies showing that even experiencing lesser forms of abuse (such as spanking) and hostile family relations increases risk of violent behaviour (Wolfe et al., 2001; Russell, 2008). Experiencing or witnessing abuse and violence can lead to the inability to regulate emotions (Cummings et al., 2009; Harding et al., 2012; Katz, Hessler, & Annest, 2007), and teaches young people that abuse is appropriate, justifiable, and deserved, and that aggressive behaviour can be a useful way of achieving certain goals (Calvete, 2007, 2008; Calvete & Orue, 2013; Henry et al., 2000). Research also shows that these problems can continue into adulthood (Ansara & Hindin, 2011; Herrenkohl et al., 2013; Smith, Ireland, & Thomberry, 2005; Wall & Barth, 2005).

Second, some societal factors can increase the propensity of boys and men to perpetrate domestic violence. These include traditional gender and social norms supportive of violence, societal norms that support male superiority and sexual entitlement, weak legal sanctions against domestic violence, and a high tolerance for crime and other violence (VicHealth, 2007; WHO, 2010). Men are more likely than women to hold attitudes that support or are linked to the perpetration of violence, and social constructions of masculinity play a role in some men's perpetration of sexual assault (Kimmel, 2000; Pease, 2008; Texas Council on Family Violence, 2012; VicHealth, 2007). In many cultures, societal norms uphold the belief that physical strength and sexual dominance are intrinsic male qualities (WHO, 2010). Hypermasculinity predisposes men to engage in behaviours that assert physical dominance and power in interpersonal interactions, particularly those interactions with women (Parrott & Zeichner, 2003). This display of sexual dominance, power and aggression "serves to 'uphold' the macho personality" (Parrott & Zeichner, 2003, p. 70).

CHALLENGES TO ENGAGING BOYS AND MEN IN VIOLENCE PREVENTION

Wells et al.' (2014) review of 77 national and provincial/state domestic violence/violence against women plans published between 2003 and 2014, along with an international scoping review of evidence based policies and practices, suggest a dearth of policies, investments, strategies and programs specifically geared to engaging men and boys as allies, partners, change agents, leaders, bystanders and violence disrupters, or potentially vulnerable to violence. Thirty-one of the government plans identified the engagement of men and boys in violence prevention as an approach to prevent or reduce domestic violence, however, only 16 plans were explicit with strategies, actions and investment. Of those that did take this approach, examples include working with the White Ribbon Campaign on engaging men and boys in building awareness and working with men as allies (Greece, Council of Australia, Tasmania, Portugal), targeting men in education campaigns (PEI, Texas) especially athletes (New Hampshire, New York), providing a men's resource centre (Norway), better supporting fathers (Alberta, Australia), and a national workplace strategy (Australia) to engage men and boys in violence prevention.

Wells et al.' (2013) review of 67 international promising policies and practices that focus on engaging men and boys in domestic violence prevention confirmed that much of the work to engage men and boys in preventing violence is diffuse, small scale, and poorly funded. Promising practices are emerging (Baobaid & Hamed, 2010; Communities and Families Clearinghouse Australia, 2010; Dogruöz & Rogow, 2009; Fraser, 2010; Goodman & Lwin, 2008; Guedes, 2012; Men Against Violence, 2012; I am a Kind Man. 2011; Men Stopping Violence, 2012; Sheehy & Allan, 2005; Supporting Father Involvement Program, 2011; Trevethan, Moore, & Allegri, 2005; United Nations Division for the Advancement of Women, 2004) but most efforts have not been subjected to rigorous evaluation and which approaches are most effective has yet to be determined (Flood, 2010). The majority of initiatives consist of programmatic efforts, rather than systematic responses at regional or national levels. Again, the predominant view of the vulnerable female victim and her male abuser may be limiting the adoption of comprehensive approaches to engaging boys and men in violence prevention. Without a new discourse that moves beyond the gender dyad that includes a strong policy base, institutional support, and long-term funding, programs and initiatives to engage men and boys will continue to remain localized, small in scope, short-term in duration, and under-evaluated and steeped in the paradigm that only views men as perpetrators (Wells et al., 2013).

Interestingly, the fundamental challenges associated with engaging men and boys in violence prevention arise from the dominant feminist paradigm permeating domestic violence advocacy and response. The critique of fully embracing prevention work with boys and men includes the fear that it may divert resources and attention away from women's campaigns and services; that the feminist orientation to this complex social issue may be excluded in strategy development; and that men could potentially "co-opt" the anti-violence movement and gain a disproportionate amount of media attention, underscoring their position of privilege (Pease, 2008; Texas Council on Family Violence, 2012). Notably, the underlying gender dyad paradigm is evident in these arguments whereby women are the oppressed and vulnerable, requiring protection, while men are violent aggressors who must be curbed from doing harm. It is strongly agreed that being mindful of these challenges is warranted, however, including men as partners, allies, change makers, leaders, bystanders, and violence disrupters, as well as potential victims in prevention work, is a critical step to building long-lasting solutions to domestic violence.

BEGINNING WITH FATHERS

Wells et al.' (2013) recent paper, *Engaging Men and Boys in Domestic Violence Prevention: Opportunities and Promising Approaches*, identified a number of "entry points"[14]

---

[14] *Engaging Men and Boys in Domestic Violence Prevention: Opportunities and Promising Approaches* was developed in partnership with White Ribbon Canada and consists of a scoping study of the relevant international literature in the area of violence prevention work with men and boys. In this report, we identify seven entry points as critical areas of focus for violence prevention. These are: 1) Build and promote positive fatherhood; 2) Support men's health and mental wellbeing; 3) Leverage sports and recreation settings to influence norms and behaviours; 4) Engage men in the workplace to build parenting and healthy relationship skills; 5) Support healthy male peer relationships and networks; 6) Engage men as allies in violence prevention; and 7) Support Aboriginal healing. If interested in the report, please go to www.preventdomesticviolence.ca

to engage boys and men in domestic violence prevention that emerged from the review. Fatherhood is proposed as an essential first area of focus from a research, policy and programmatic perspective to move prevention efforts beyond the traditional view of vulnerability.

The engagement of fathers as key participants in family strengthening and support can improve the lives of men, women, and children (Shapiro, Krysik, & Pennar, 2011; Barker & Verani, 2008; Pruett, 2000). By normalizing the role of caring for children, the restrictions of traditional definitions of masculinity are replaced with a broader vision of men's capacity in family life and society (MenCare, 2011). Caring for children and being engaged in the lives of young people can increase men's emotional well-being and capacity to express emotions and experience empathy (Horn, Blankenhorn, & Pearlstein, 1999; Allen & Daly, 2007). This can lower levels of family conflict and violence and increase opportunities for children to grow up in emotionally and physically safe environments (Shapiro et al., 2011; Barker & Verani, 2008).

Until recently, the vast majority of the parenting research and interventions focused on mother-child relationships. Research pertaining to fathers as parents has largely been limited to the ways in which fathers' economic and other contributions foster family stability and support mothers' ability to parent well (Coley & Schindler, 2008; Greene & Moore, 2000; Kalil, Ziol-Guest, & Coley, 2005; Tamis-LeMonda et al., 2004). Research is now confirming and clarifying the vital and distinct role that fathers play in child development (Coley & Schindler, 2008). New studies indicate that, for better and for worse, fathers influence their children independently from mothers and as strongly as mothers (Zanoni et al., 2013). In addition, fathers are increasingly involved in childrearing in two-parent families, particularly in North American contexts, and there has been a clear trend toward shared custody and shared parenting in families in which the parents are separated or divorced (Beaupré, Dryburgh, & Wendt, 2010).

Supporting fathers to become more positively engaged in the lives of their children is a promising strategy to prevent violence in the next generation among both girls and boys. Fathers who are positively engaged take an active role in caring for their child's social, emotional, cognitive and physical health, and they promote their child's well-being and security. Positive father involvement also means taking on nurturing and caretaking roles, and modeling behaviours that promote gender equity and peaceful ways of resolving conflicts. There are two primary components of healthy or positive fathering: being positively involved in the child's life and having an authoritative parenting style (Asmussen & Weizel, 2010). Family conditions that help fathers to parent well include having a respectful, equitable relationship with the child's mother (or co-parent), even if the parents no longer live together. Positive father involvement means interacting with children in loving and consistent ways, and taking an active role in looking after them to ensure that they are safe and their emotional, social, cognitive, and physical needs are addressed (Lamb et al., 1985; Pleck, 2010).

A systematic focus on positive fatherhood can be a significant leverage point in reducing vulnerability to domestic violence for both girls and boys, thereby challenging the notion of exclusive female vulnerability. Comprehensive fatherhood initiatives require a reconsideration of the gender dyad as they address boys as both the potential victims of abuse but also at risk for becoming perpetrators. Such measures can further decrease the risk for girls to become victims and abusers in adulthood. Examples of supporting positive father involvement include governments and organizations offering progressive parental leave policies for men, replicating evidence-based fatherhood programs, creating father friendly organizations within both the private and social sector, social media campaigns to change norms and behaviours, and educational and networking programs to help fathers enhance their roles in the family. The Fatherhood Institute in the UK submits that shared parenting results in a greater overall satisfaction reported by both parents, an increased likelihood of family stability, and generally favourable developmental and social outcomes for children (2011).

CONCLUSION

This critique of the normative gender dyad permeating domestic violence discourse aims to broaden the work of feminist advocates rather than diminish it. An exclusive focus on women as victims and men as perpetrators of domestic violence serves to exclude boys and men as potential partners in domestic violence prevention efforts. Our understanding of vulnerability to violence and violence prevention must be broadened, all the while paying heed to the global reality of persistent and pervasive gender-based violence (DeKeseredy and Schwartz, 2011) and the disproportionate harm suffered by girls and women who are victims of domestic violence. The intersection of individuals' experiences of domestic violence as it relates to class, race, gender and sexual orientation, age, and ability must be a further critical consideration (Collins Hill, 2012; hooks, 2000; Misra, 2012). Initiatives developed to prevent and address violence need to acknowledge the socio-cultural and historical context of men and women's experiences in their communities (Casey et al., 2013), particularly in light of the impacts of racism, homophobia, and other forms of oppression (Mitchell, 2013; Ruxton & van der Gaag, 2013).

In addition, domestic violence cannot be solely conceptualized as a family or interpersonal problem; the structural inequities that reproduce this violence are intimately interconnected and both underpin and reinforce other forms of violence. Strategically tackling domestic violence from this perspective requires a multi-level systemic approach tailored for population groups across the lifecycle, with a simultaneous focus at varying social levels. While paying heed to gender effects, such approaches must include boys and men in domestic violence prevention efforts to create a society where domestic violence is no longer viewed as inevitable.

REFERENCES

Allen, S. & Daly, K. (2007). *The effects of father involvement an updated research summary of the evidence*. Retrieved from: http://www.fira.ca/cms/documents/29/ Effects_of_Father_Involvement.pdf

Ansara, D. L. & Hindin, M. J. (2011). Psychosocial consequences of intimate partner violence for women and men in Canada. *Journal of Interpersonal Violence*, 26(8), 1628-1645.

Arata, C. M., Langhinrichsen-Rohling, J., Bowers, D., & O'Brien, N. (2007). Differential correlates of multi-type maltreatment among urban youth. *Child Abuse & Neglect*, 31(4), 393-415.

Archer, J. (2000). Sex differences in aggression between heterosexual partners: A meta-analytic review. *Psychological Bulletin, 126*(5), 651-680.

Asmussen, K. & Weizel, K. (2010). *Evaluating the evidence: Fathers, families and children.* London, EN: National Academy for Parenting Research, King's College London.

Baobaid, M. & Hamed, G. (2010). Addressing domestic violence in Canadian Muslim communities: A training manual for Muslim communities and Ontario service providers. Retrieved from http://www.lfcc.on.ca/MFSP_Manual_2010.pdf

Barker, G. (2001). *Peace Boys in a War Zone: Identifying and coping among adolescent men in a Favela in Rio de Janeiro, Brazil* (Doctoral dissertation). Retrieved from ProQuest Dissertations and Theses database. (3015499)

Barker, G. & Verani, F. (2008). Men's participation as fathers in the Latin American and Caribbean region: A critical literature review with policy considerations. Retrieved from http://www.promundo.org.br/wp-content/uploads/2010/03/Mens%20Participation% 20as%20Fathers%20in%20the%20Latin%20American(2008)-ING.pdf

Beaupré, P., Dryburgh, H. & Wendt, M. (2010). Making fathers 'count.' *Canadian Social Trends* [Online serial], 90.

Black, M. C., Basile, K. C., Breiding, M. J., Smith, S. G., Walters, M. L., Merrick, M. T., & Stevens, M. R. (2011). *The national intimate partner and sexual violence survey (NISVS): 2010 summary report.* Atlanta, GA: National Center for Injury Prevention and Control, Centers for Disease Control and Prevention.

Bowker, L. H. (1998). *Masculinities and violence.* Thousand Oaks, CA: SAGE Publications.

Brown, B. (2012). *Daring greatly: How the courage to be vulnerable transforms the way we live, love, parent, and lead.* New York, NY: Gotham Books.

Calvete, E. (2007). Justification of violence beliefs and social problem-solving as mediators between maltreatment and behavior problems in adolescents. *The Spanish Journal of Psychology, 10*(1), 131-140.

Calvete, E. (2008). Justification of violence and grandiosity schemas as predictors of antisocial behavior in adolescents. *Journal of Abnormal Child Psychology, 36*(7), 1083-1095.

Calvete, E. & Orue, I. (2013). Cognitive mechanisms of the transmission of violence: Exploring gender differences among adolescents exposed to family violence. *Journal of Family Violence, 28*, 73-84.

Capaldi, D. M., Kim, H. K. & Shortt, J. W. (2007). Observed initiation and reciprocity of physical aggression in young, at-risk couples. *Journal of Family Violence, 22*(2), 101–111.

Capaldi, D. M., Knoble, N. B., Shortt, J. W. & Kim, H. K. (2012). A systematic review of risk factors for intimate partner violence. *Partner Abuse, 3*(2), 231-280.

Casey, E. A., Carlson, J., Fraguela-Rios, C., Kimball, E., Neugut, T. B., Tolman, R. M. & Edelson, J. L. (2013). Context, challenges, and tensions in global efforts to engage men in the prevention of violence against women: An ecological analysis. *Men and Masculinities, 16*(2), 228-251.

Centers for Disease Control. (2008). *Strategic direction for intimate partner violence prevention: Promoting respectful, nonviolent intimate partner relationships through individual, community, and societal change.* Retrieved from http://www.cdc.gov/ violenceprevention/pdf/IPV_Strategic_Direction_Full-Doc-a.pdf.

Chiodo, D., Crooks, C. V., Wolfe, D. A., McIsaac, C., Hughes, R. & Jaffe, P. G. (2012). Longitudinal prediction and concurrent functioning of adolescent girls demonstrating various profiles of dating violence and victimization. *Prevention Science*, *13*(4), 350-359.

Coley, R. L. & Schindler, H. S. (2008). Biological fathers' contributions ot maternal and family functioning. *Parenting: Science and Practice*, *8*(4), 294-318.

Collins Hill, P. (2012). Looking back, moving ahead: Scholarship in service to social justice. *Gender and Society*, *26*, 14-22.

Communities and Families Clearinghouse Australia (2010). *Promising practice profiles: Aboriginal dads program*. Retrieved from http://www.aifs.gov.au/cafca/ppp/profiles/pppdocs/cfc_aboriginal_dads.pdf

Connell, R. (1987). *Gender and power: Society, the person, and sexual politics.* Redwood City, CA: Stanford University Press.

Coohey, C., Renner, L. M. & Sabri, B. (2013). Victimization, parenting, and externalizing behavior among Latino and White adolescents. *Journal of Family Violence*, *28*, 359-368.

Cooper, M. & Wells, L. (2013). *Is a new approach to violence prevention needed? Discussing the implications of emerging research for intimate partner violence prevention among adolescent girls.* Calgary, AB: The University of Calgary, Shift: The Project to End Domestic Violence.

Cornelius, T. L. & Resseguie, N. (2007). Primary and secondary prevention programs for dating violence: A review of the literature. *Aggression and Violent Behavior*, *12*(3), 364-375.

Crooks, C. V., Goodall, G. R., Hughes, R., Jaffe, P. G. & Baker, L. (2007). Engaging men and boys in preventing violence against women: Applying a cognitive-behaviour model. *Violence Against Women*, *13*(3), 217-239.

Cummings, E. M., El-Sheikh, M., Kouros, C. D. & Buckhalt, J. A. (2009). Children and violence: The role of children's regulation in the marital aggression-child adjustment link. *Clinical Child and Family Psychology Review*, *12*, 3-15.

Cutbush, S., Ashley, O. S., Kan, M. L., Hampton, J. & Hall D. M. (2010). *Electronic aggression among adolescent dating partners: Demographic correlates and associations with other types of violence.* Retrieved from http://www.rti.org/pubs/apha10_cutbush_poster.pdf.

de Keijzer, F. B. (2004). Masculinities: Resistance and change. In S. Ruxton (Ed.), *Gender equality and men: Learning from practice* (pp. 28-49). United Kingdom: Oxfam.

DeKeseredy, W. S. (1988). Premarital woman abuse: The multidimensional influence of male peer support. *Sociological Viewpoints*, *4*(2), 44-60.

DeKeseredy, W. S. & Kelly, K. (1995). Sexual abuse in Canadian university and college dating relationships: The contribution of male peer support. *Journal of Family Violence*, *10*(1), 41-53.

DeKeseredy, W. S., Schwartz, M. D. & Alvi, S. (2000). The role of profeminist men in dealing with woman abuse on the Canadian college campus. *Violence Against Women*, *6*(9), 918-935.

DeKeseredy, W. S. & Schwartz, M. D. (2011). Theoretical and definitional issues in violence against women. In C. M. Renzetti, J. L. Edleson, & R. K. Bergen (Eds.), *Sourcebook on violence against women, 2nd ed.* (3-20). Thousand Oaks, CA: Sage.

Dogruöz, D. & Rogow, D. (2009). And how will you remember me, my child? Redefining fatherhood in Turkey. *Quality/Calidad/Qualité* [Online serial], *19*.

Dutton, D. G. & Nicholls, T. L. (2005). The gender paradigm in domestic violence theory: Part 1 – The conflict of theory. *Aggression and Violent Behavior*, *10*(6), 680-713.

Ehrensaft, M. K. (2008). Intimate partner violence: Persistence of myths and implications for intervention. *Children and Youth Services Review*, *30*(3), 276-286.

Esplen, E. (2006). *Engaging men in gender equality: Positive strategies and approaches.* Retrieved from http://www.ids.ac.uk/idspublication/engaging-men-in-gender-equality-positive-strategies-and-approaches-overview-and-annotated-bibliography.

Evans, S. E., Davies, C. & DiLillo, D. (2008). Exposure to domestic violence: A meta-analysis of child and adolescent outcomes. *Aggression and Violent Behavior*, *13*, 131-140.

Fatherhood Institute. (2011). *The fatherhood report: The fairness in families index.* Retrieved from http://www.cite.gov.pt/pt/destaques/complementosDestqs/FI-FiFI-Report-2010_FINAL.pdf

Finkelhor, D., Moore, D., Hamby, S. L. & Straus, M. A. (1997). Sexually abused children in a national survey of parents: Methodological issues. *Child Abuse and Neglect*, *21*(1), 1-9.

Flood, M. (2010). Where men stand: Men's roles in ending violence against women. Retrieved from http://www.whiteribbon.org.au/uploads/media/WR-PR-Series-Flood-Report-No-2-Nov 2010 full-report-final.pdf

Flood, M. (2011). Involving men in efforts to end violence against women. *Men and Masculinities*, *14*(3), 358-377.

Foshee, V. (1996). Gender differences in adolescent dating abuse prevalence, types, and injuries. *Health Education Research, 11*(13), 275-286.

Foumbi, J. & Lovich, R. (1997). *Role of men in the lives of children: A study of how improving knowledge about men in families helps strengthen programming for children and women.* Retrieved from http://www.xyonline.net/sites/default/files/UNICEF,%20Role%20of%20Men%20in%20the%20Lives%20of%20Children%201997.pdf

Fraser, C. (2010). *Supporting the transition to fatherhood: An evaluation of 'hit the ground crawling' in Staffordshire.* Retrieved from http://www.fatherhoodinstitute.org/wp-content/uploads/2010/07/Supporting-the-transition-to-fatherhood-Hit-the-Ground-Crawling-in-Staffordshire.pdf

Gardiner, J. K. (2005). Men, masculinities, and feminist theory. In M. S. Kimmel, J. Hearn, & R. W. Connell (Eds.), *Handbook of studies on men & masculinities* (35-50). Thousand Oaks, CA: Sage Publications.

Gaudin, J. M. & Dubowitz, H. (1997). Family functioning in neglectful families: Recent research. In J. Berrick & N. Bartk (Eds.), *Child welfare research review*, Vol. *2* (28-62). New York, NY: Columbia University Press.

Gender Secretariat. (2008). *Action plan for Sida's work against gender-based violence 2008-2010.* Retrieved from http://www.chs.ubc.ca/archives/files/Action%20Plan%20for%20Sida%27s%20Work%20against%20Gender-Based%20Violence%202008-2009.pdf

Goodman, D. & Lwin, K. (2008). *Evaluation of the pilot: Fatherhood group.* Retrieved from http://www.childwelfareinstitute.torontocas.ca/wp-content/uploads/07-08-fathering-group-evaluation-k-lwin-jul-08.pdf

Greene, A. D. & Moore, K. A. (2000). Non-resident father involvement and child well-being among young children in families on welfare. *Marriage & Family Review*, *29*(2-3), 159-180.

Groth, B. (2001). Lessons from the spiritual lives of men who work in the movement to end violence against women and children. *Journal of Religion & Abuse, 2*(1), 5-31.

Guedes, A. (2012). *Men and boys knowledge module.* Retrieved from http://www. endvawnow.org/uploads/modules/pdf/1328564467.pdf

Harding, H. G., Morelen, D., Thomassin, K., Bradbury, L. & Shaffer, A. (2012). Exposure to maternal- and paternal-perpetrated partner violence, emotion regulation, and child outcomes. *Journal of Family Violence, 28,* 63-72.

Hatty, S. E. (2000). *Masculinities, violence, and culture.* Thousand Oaks, CA: SAGE Publications.

Henry, D., Guerra, N., Huesmann, R., Tolan, P., VanAcker, R. & Eron, L. (2000). Normative influences on aggression in urban elementary school classrooms. *American Journal of Community Psychology, 28*(1), 59-81.

Harvey, A., Garcia-Moreno, C. & Butchart, A. (2007). *Primary pprevention of intimate-partner violence and sexual violence: Background paper for WHO expert meeting May 2-3, 2007.* Geneva, Switzerland: World Health Organization.

Herrenkohl, T. L., Hong, S., Klika, J. B., Herrenkohl, R. C. & Russo, M. J. (2013). Developmental impacts of child abuse and neglect related to adult mental health, substance use, and physical health. *Journal of Family Violence, 28*(2), 191-199.

Holtzworth-Munroe, A., Meehan, J. C., Herron, K., Rehman, U. & Stuart, G. L. (2000). Testing the Holtzworth-Munroe and Stuart (1994) batterer typology. *Journal of Consulting and Clinical Psychology, 68*(6), 1000–1019.

Hooks, b. (2000). *Feminist theory: From margin to center (2nd ed.).* Cambridge, MA: South End Press.

Horn, W. F., Blankenhorn, D. & Pearlstein, M. B. (1999). *The fatherhood movement: A call to action.* Lanham, MD: Lexington Books.

I am a Kind Man. (2011). Retrieved from http://www.iamakindman.ca

Johnson, M. P. (2008). *A typology of domestic violence: Intimate terrorism, violent resistance, and situational couple violence.* Boston, MA: Northeastern University Press.

Johnson, M. P. (2011). Gender and types of intimate partner violence: A response to an anti-feminist literature review. *Aggression and Violent Behavior, 16*(4), 289-296.

Judith, L. (2012). *Gender inequality: Feminist theories and politics.* New York: Oxford University Press.

Kalil, A., Ziol-Guest, K. M. & Coley, R. L. (2005). Patterns of father involvement in teenage-mother families: Predictors and links to mothers' psychological adjustment. *Family Relations, 54*(2), 197-211.

Katz, J. (1995). Reconstructing masculinity in the locker room: The mentors in violence prevention project. *Harvard Educational Review, 65*(2), 163-174.

Katz, L. F., Hessler, D. M., & Annest, A. (2007). Domestic violence, emotional competence, and child adjustment. *Social Development, 16,* 513-538.

Kaufman, M. (1999). *The seven p's of men's violence.* Retrieved from http://www.michaelkaufman.com/

Kaufman, M. (2001). Building a movement of men working to end violence against women. *Development, 44*(3), 9-14.

Kimmel, M. S. (2000). *The gendered society.* New York, NY: Oxford University Press.

Kitzman, K. M., Gaylord, N. K., Holt, A. R. & Kenny, E. D. (2003). Child witness to domestic violence: A meta-analytic review. *Journal of Consulting and Clinical Psychology, 71*, 339–352.

Lamb, M. E., Pleck, J. H., Charnov, E. L. & Levine, J. A. (1985). Paternal behaviour in humans. *American Zoologist, 25*, 883-894.

Langhinrichsen-Rohling, J., Selwyn, C., & Rohling, M. L. (2012). Rates of bi-directional versus uni-directional intimate partner violence across samples, sexual orientations, and race/ethnicities: A comprehensive review. *Partner Abuse, 3*(2), 199-230.

Lee, D. S., Guy, L., Perry, B., Sniffen, C. K. & Mixon, S. A. (2007). Sexual violence prevention. *The Prevention Researcher, 14*(2), 15-20.

Lussier, P. Farrington, D. P., & Moffitt, T. E. (2009). Is the antisocial child father of the abusive man? A 40-year prospective longitudinal study on the developmental antecedents of intimate partner violence. *Criminology, 47*(3), 471-780.

Maas, C., Herrenkohl, T. I. & Sousa, C. (2008). Review of research on child maltreatment and violence in youth. *Trauma, Violence & Abuse, 9*(1), 56-67.

Men Against Violence. (2012). *About.* Retrieved from http://www.mavinc.org/about.html

Men Stopping Violence. (2012). *Programs.* Retrieved from http://www.menstoppingviolence.org/page/1010/Programs

MenCare. (2011). A Global *Fatherhood campaign.* Retrieved from http://www.mencare.org/sites/menengage/files/themes/files/menengage_web/Men%20Care%20%20Prospectus%20-%20with%20references.pdf

Minerson, T., Carolo, H., Dinner, T. & Jones, C. (2011). *Issue brief: Engaging men and boys to reduce and prevent gender-based violence.* Retrieved from http://whiteribbon.ca/wp-content/uploads/2012/12//wrc_swc_issuebrief.pdf

Misra, J. (2012). Introduction: Well, how did I get here? *Gender and Society, 26*, 5-13.

Mitchell, R. (2013). Domestic violence prevention through the constructing violence-free masculinities programme: An experience from Peru. *Gender and Development, 21*(1), 97-109.

Moylan, C. A., Herrenkohl, T. I., Sousa, C., Tajima, E. A., Herrenkohl, R. C. & Russo, M. J. (2010). The effects of child abuse and exposure to domestic violence on adolescent internalizing and externalizing behavior problems. *Journal of Family Violence, 25*, 53-63.

Nixon, K. & Tutty, L (2010). "Where have all the women gone?" Woman abuse and Canadian social policy. *Canadian Review of Social Policy, 63/64*, 63-82.

Parrott, D. J. & Zeichner, A. (2003). Effects of hypermasculinity on physical aggression against women. *Psychology of Men & Masculinity, 4*(1), 70-78.

Pepler, D. *It takes a network to raise a child! How PREVNet is working together to promote safe and healthy relationships for children and youth.* Presented at the Banff XLVI: Preventing through Promoting Healthy relationships Conference, March 16-19, 2014, Banff, Alberta, Canada.

Pease, B. (2008). *Engaging men in men's violence prevention: Exploring the tensions, dilemmas and possibilities.* Retrieved from http://www.adfvc.unsw.edu.au/PDF%20files/Issues%20Paper_17.pdf

Peralta, R. L., Callanan, V. J., Steele, J. L. & Wiley, L. C. (2011). The effects of gender identity and heavy episodic drinking on alcohol-related violence. *Gender Issues, 28*, 111-133.

Peralta, R. L., Tuttle, L. A. & Steele, J. L. (2010). At the intersection of interpersonal violence, masculinity, and alcohol use: The experiences of heterosexual male perpetrators of intimate partner violence. *Violence Against Women*, *16*(4), 387-409.

Pleck, J. H. (2010). Paternal involvement: Revised conceptualization and theoretical linkages with child outcomes. In M. E. Lamb (Ed.), *The role of the father in child development* (5th ed., pp. 58-93). Hoboken, NJ: Wiley.

Pruett, K. (2000). *Father-need*. New York, NY: Broadway Books.

Osofsky, J. D. (2000). Infants and violence: Prevention, intervention, and treatment. In J. D. Osofsky, & H. E. Fitzgerald (Eds.), *WAIMH handbook of infant mental health*, *Volume 4* (pp. 164-196). New York, NY: Wiley Publishers.

Raiford, J. L., Wingood, G. M. & DiClemente, R. J. (2007). Prevalence, incidence, and predictors of dating violence: A longitudinal study of African American female adolescents. *Journal of Women's Health*, *16*(6), 822-832.

Renner, L. M. & Whitney, S. D. (2012). Risk factors for unidirectional and bidirectional intimate partner violence among young adults. *Child Abuse & Neglect*, *36*(1), 40-52.

Russell, N. (2008). *What works in sexual violence prevention and education*. Retrieved from http://www.justice.govt.nz/policy/supporting-victims/taskforce-for-action-on-sexual-violence/documents/What%20Works%20in%20Prevention.pdf

Ruxton, S. & van der Gaag, N. (2013). Men's involvement in gender equality: European perspectives. *Gender and Development*, *21*(1), 161-175.

Seidler, V. (1996). Masculinity and violence. In L. May, R. Strikwerda, & P. D. Hopkins (Eds.), *Rethinking masculinity: Philosophical explorations in light of feminism* (2nd ed, pp. 63-78). Lanham, MD: Rowman & Littlefield Publishers.

Shapiro, A. F., Krysik, J. & Pennar, A. L. (2011). Who are the fathers in healthy families Arizona? An examination of father data in at-risk families. *American Journal of Orthopsychiatry*, *81*(3), 327-336.

Sheehy, S., & Allan, J. (2005). *Fatherhood support program: Group-work course manual*. Retrieved from http://www.wch.sa.gov.au/services/az/other/nwcfip/fatherhood/pdfs/grp_course_manual.pdf

Shorey, R. C., Meltzer, C. & Cornelius, T. L. (2010). Motivations for self-defensive aggression in dating relationships. *Violence and Victims*, *25*(5), 662–676.

Sinha, M. (2012). *Family Violence in Canada: A Statistical Profile*, *2010*. Retrieved from http://www.statcan.gc.ca/pub/85-002-x/2012001/article/11643-eng.htm.

Smith, C. A. & Farrington, D. P. (2004). Continuities in antisocial behavior and parenting across three generations. *Journal of Child Psychology and Psychiatry*, *45*(2), 230–247.

Smith, C. A., Ireland, T. O. & Thornberry, T. P. (2005). Adolescent maltreatment and its impact on young adult antisocial behavior. *Child Abuse & Neglect*, *29*(10), 1099–1119.

Statistics Canada. (2011). *Family violence in Canada: A statistical profile* (Catalogue no. 85-224-X). Ottawa, ON: Minister of Industry.

Sugarman, D. B. & Frankel, S. L. (1996). Patriarchal ideology and wife-assault: A meta-analytic review. *Journal of Family Violence*, *11*(1), 13-40.

Supporting Father Involvement (SFI) Program. (2011). *Evidence-based practice*. Retrieved from http://www.supportingfatherinvolvement.org/research.html

Swahn, M. H., Simon, T. R., Arias, I. & Bossarte, R. M. (2008). Measuring sex differences in violence victimization and perpetration within date and same-sex peer relationships. *Journal of Interpersonal Violence*, *23*(8), 1120-1138.

Tamis-LeMonda, C. S., Shannon, J. D., Cabrera, N. J. & Lamb, M. E. (2004). Fathers' and mothers' play with their 2- and 3-year-olds: Contributions to language and cognitive development. *Child Development*, *75*(6), 1806-1820.

Texas Council on Family Violence. (2012). *Men's non-violence project: Standing together for justice – guide to engaging men and boys in preventing violence against women and girls.* Retrieved from http://www.tcfv.org/pdf/mensguide/EngagingMenandBoys.pdf

Trevethan, S., Moore, J. & Allegri, N. (2005). *The "in search of your warrior" program for Aboriginal offenders: A preliminary evaluation.* Retrieved from http://publications.gc.ca/collections/collection_2010/scc-csc/PS83-3-172-eng.pdf

United Nations. (1994). Report of the international conference on p*opulation and development.* Retrieved from http://www.un.org/popin/icpd/conference/offeng/poa.html

United Nations (1995). *Report of the fourth world conference on women.* Retrieved from http://www.un.org/womenwatch/daw/beijing/pdf/Beijing%20full%20report%20E.pdf

United Nations. (2008). *Women 2000 and beyond: The role of men and boys in achieving gender equality.* Retrieved from http://www.un.org/

United Nations Division for the Advancement of Women. (2004). *The role of men and boys in achieving gender equality: Report of the expert group meeting Brasilia, Brazil, 21 to 24 October, 2003.* Retrieved from http://www.un.org/womenwatch/daw/egm/men-boys2003/reports/Finalreport.PDF

VicHealth. (2007). *Preventing violence before it occurs: A framework and background paper to guide the primary prevention of violence against women in Victoria.* Carlton, South Victoria: Author.

Wall, A. E. & Barth, R. P. (2005). Aggressive and delinquent behavior of maltreated adolescents: risk factors and gender differences. *Stress, Trauma and Crisis: An International Journal*, *8*(1), 1-24.

Wells, L., Lorenzetti, L., Carolo, H., Dinner, T., Jones, C., Minerson, T. & Esina, E. (2013). *Engaging men and boys in domestic violence prevention: Opportunities and promising approaches.* Calgary, AB: The University of Calgary, Shift: The Project to End Domestic Violence.

Wells, L., Pickup, T. & Esina, E. (2014). *A review of government domestic violence/violence against women frameworks, plans and strategies 2003 – 2014* (Unpublished manuscript). Calgary, AB: University of Calgary, Shift: The Project to End Domestic Violence.

Whitaker, D. J., Morrison, S., Lindquist, C., Hawkins, S. R., O'Neil, J. A., Nesius, A. M. & Reese, L. (2006). A critical review of interventions for the primary prevention of perpetration of partner violence. *Aggression and Violent Behavior*, *11*(2), 151-166.

Williams, J. R., Ghandour, R. M. & Kub, J. E. (2008). Female perpetration of violence in heterosexual intimate relationships: Adolescence through adulthood. *Trauma, Violence, & Abuse*, *9*(4), 227-249.

Wolfe, D. A., Crooks, C. C., Chiodo, D. & Jaffe, P. (2009). Child maltreatment, bullying, gender-based harassment, and adolescent dating violence: Making the connections. *Psychology of Women Quarterly*, *33*(1), 21-24.

Wolfe, D. A., Crooks, C. V., Lee, V., McIntyre-Smith, A. & Jaffe P. G. (2003). The effects of children's exposure to domestic violence: A meta-analysis and critique. *Clinical Child and Family Psychology Review*, *6*, 171-187.

Wolfe, D. A. & Scott, K. (2001). Child maltreatment: risk of adjustment problems and dating violence in adolescence. *Journal of the American Academy of Child and Adolescent Psychiatry, 40*(3), 282–289.

Wolfe, D. A., Scott, K., Wekerle, C. & Pittman, A. L. (2001). Child maltreatment: Risk of adjustment problems and dating violence in adolescence. *Journal of the American Academy of Child and Adolescent Psychiatry, 40*(3), 282-289.

World Health Organization. (2005). *WHO multi-country study on women's health and domestic violence against women: Summary report of initial results on prevalence, health outcomes and women's responses.* Geneva, Switzerland: Author.

World Health Organization and London School of Hygiene and Tropical Medicine. (2010). *Preventing intimate partner and sexual violence against Women: Taking action and generating evidence.* Geneva, Switzerland: Author.

Zanoni, L., Warburton, W., Bussey, K. & McMaugh, A. (2013). Fathers as 'core business' in child welfare practice and research: An interdisciplinary review. *Children and Youth Services Review, 36*(7), 1055-1070.

Zweig, J. M., Dank, M., Yahner, J. & Lachman, P. (2013). The rate of cyber dating abuse among teens and how it relates to other forms of teen dating violence. *Journal of Youth and Adolescence, 42*(7), 1063-1077.

SECTION FIVE: CONCLUDING CHAPTER

In: Overcoming Domestic Violence
Editors: Myra F. Taylor, Julie Ann Pooley et al.

ISBN: 978-1-63321-956-4
© 2015 Nova Science Publishers, Inc.

Chapter 21

CONCLUDING THOUGHTS: DOMESTIC VIOLENCE AND POSSIBLE PATHWAYS FORWARD

*Myra F. Taylor** and Julie Ann Pooley*
Edith Cowan University, Joondalup, Western Australia, Australia

The Editors of this book have provided a wide range of research evidence in their attempt to broaden the current understanding and debate about the nature of domestic violence (DV) in both localized and global settings. The complexity of addressing the DV issue can be understood when trying to determine a DV definition, accurate DV prevalence rates, factors which contribute to an individual being a victim, witness or perpetrator of DV, implementable ameliorating DV polices/interventions, identifying structural/cultural DV barriers and the list goes on. Moreover, the book's diverse chapters clearly reveal that DV is a loaded topic with many varied and sometimes conflicting viewpoints, thus, it is undoubtedly a perplexing societal issue for authorities to address.

While, historically evidence reveals the existence of DV in past human civilizations, it is somewhat ironic that in the 21st century we are still trying to define, determine prevalence rates, identify vulnerability factors and devise interventions. However, one positive for society is that as a global community we are willing to embrace new understandings of the DV problem, as well as, initiatives which can be put in place to reduce its occurrence. With this in mind it is important that we as scholars, collectively, unequivocally, and upfront state that we do not agree with any form of domestic violence for it is destructive to all involved (primary and secondary victims, perpetrators, and witnesses).

SO WHAT HAVE WE LEARNED FROM THE CHAPTERS IN THIS BOOK?

First, the definition as presented by Allan and Allan in Chapter 2 provides a broad view of the types or forms of DV. Inherent in the definition are the personal characteristics and factors that may predispose a person to become a victim or perpetrator of domestic violence.

* Corresponding author: Myra F. Taylor, Edith Cowan University, 270 Joondalup Drive Joondalup, WA 6007 Australia.

Second, research abounds on women's experiences of DV. For example, the chapters by McInnes (Chapter 10) and Williams, Gavine and Carnochan (Chapter 12) exemplify the strong role feminists have played in bringing DV to the forefront of the political agenda and in seeking recognition of the plight of women and children living with DV. In keeping with the feminist appraisal of DV, Usta and Singh (Chapter 13) report on a highly situational form of DV, namely, violence against women (VAW) during times of war and armed conflict, Williams and Neville (Chapter 15) highlight the relationship between sporting events and VAW and Ferrer-Perez and Bosch-Fiol (Chapter 14) have identified the impact that economic crisis scenarios have on IPVAW. In doing so, these latter three chapters contrast the situational from the contextual the role of societal influences with regard to VAW.

Third, the work of Carter Snell (Chapter 4) in identifying the vulnerability of teenagers and young adults to dating violence provides a more contemporary view of DV. Blais, Hébert, Gervais and Bergeron (Chapter 5) further extend our understanding of dating DV by providing evidence of the prevalence of dating violence among sexual minority youth. The area of sexual minority violence is also explored at a very personal level through the work of Schroeder Orsby & Bruns (Chapter 11) where violence between same-sex couples is articulated via a case study of lesbian violence in the Deep South of America. The description and discussion of DV in minority sexual groups is not a new concept, but it has taken time to appear in the literature. Collectively, these chapters through their exposure of DV in the non-heterosexual world undoubtedly further extend the DV debate.

Fourth, in terms of looking at a more global approach to DV this book provides a number of chapters looking at the plight of women in different cultures. For example Schineanu and Earnest (Chapter 9) reveal how spirituality and social supports within the Indian culture can assist Indian women to cope with DV. Further to this, Sabri (Chapter 7) utilises Bronfenbrenners' ecological model to detail ways in which interventions can assist South Asian women subjected to violence. Whilst, Mahapatra and Schatz (Chapter 8) look at the prevalence rates of DV in South Asian migrant women living in the United States of America, Henderson Thurston and Roy (Chapter 6) reveal the inherent difficulties women who have escaped DV in their country of origin, subsequently experience within the structural inequalities embedded within their host country.

Fifth, in exploring DV barriers many of the authors are able to highlight examples of specific language, culture, economics and systemic structural barriers that need to be addressed. However in the chapter by Ellis and McCarry (Chapter 3) it is argued that there is a culture of preventionism, which essentially implies that 'all social problems/issues can be prevented rather than resolved'. This is an interesting perspective as it places the onus on individuals, groups, and systems to come up with strategies to prevent undesirable outcomes rather than looking at ways to resolve the issue in the first place. A debate on resolution is a much wider debate as it calls into question a broader understanding of the DV issue.

Sixth, while there is a broader understanding of the groups that are affected by DV, there is a relative dearth of DV literature that reports on males as victims rather than perpetrators. Hence, four of the book's chapters (Chapters 16-19) explore the male experience of child maltreatment and the subsequent impact this has not only on their ability to form healthy adult relations, but also how their sense of self-worth is further eroded by the prevailing Cycle of Violence's intergenerational abused-child-adult abuser prophesy. Finally, the chapter by Wells, Turner and Cooper (Chapter 20) while paying heed to gender effects, recognizes the need to include boys and men in domestic violence reduction efforts if a society is to be created where domestic violence is no longer viewed as being inevitable.

So What Can be Done to Reduce the Occurrence of Domestic Violence?

As can be seen from Table 1 there is no one simple solution to the DV problem, but rather multiple interlinked pathways towards its reduction. While these pathways are the ideal that our collective research suggests should be followed, these suggestions are tempered by the recognition that governments, authorities and agencies all have finite budgets to deal with the pervasive DV social issue. Therefore, the list presented in Table 1 should be construed as a DV reduction aspirational goal which needs to be worked towards and implemented as resources allow. However, it should be noted that any failure to implement these initiatives is a false economy as the cost to society of the damage caused by DV to child and adult lives is staggering to comprehend. Thus, while the cost of implementation to the public purse in the short-term might appear high, failure to implement will undoubtedly incur a much higher longer-term financial and social cost.

Table 1. Contributors' suggested pathways for reducing the occurrence of domestic violence

Suggested pathways forward	Chapters	Advocating authors
Further research into different forms of gendered DV, the design and evaluation of the effectiveness of current DV interventi-on programs and DV reduction initiatives, the impacts of social stigma, prejudice on accessing support, revision of the Cycle of Violence hypothesis and mechanisms for improving the resilience and posttraumatic growth of survivors & perpetrators of DV.	2, 4, 5, 11, 12, 14, 19	Allan & Allan; Carter-Snell; Blais, Hébert, Gervais, & Bergeron; Schroeder, Osby, & Bruns; Williams, Gavine, & Carnochan; Williams & Neville, Goddard, Taylor & Pooley
Improved protective assistance at the individual, community, societal and relational levels for survivors of abuse.	2, 10, 12, 13	Allan & Allan; Williams, Gavine, & Carnochan; McInnes;Usta & Singh
Recognising and addressing gendered structural inequalities and disadvantage.	3, 10	Ellis and McCarry; McInnes
Improved integration of service agencies.	4, 6, 10	Henderson, Thurston, & Roy; Carter-Snell; McInness
Development of infrastructure and intervention programs that are adaptable to meet the diverse accommodation, education, employment, financial, health, and criminal justice needs of survivors.	6, 12, 13, 14	Henderson, Thurston, & Roy; Williams, Gavine, & Carnochan; Usta & Singh; Ferrer-Perez & Bosch-Fiol
Improving public, health, police and judicial avenues for recognizing, disclosing, recording, and documenting violence.	5, 10, 12, 13	Blais, Hébert, Gervais, & Bergeron; McInnes; Williams, Gavine, & Carnochan; Usta & Singh; Taylor, Goddard, & Pooley

Table 1. (Continued)

Suggested pathways forward	Chapters	Advocating authors
Targeting protective and risk factors.	5, 13	Blais, Hébert, Gervais, & Bergeron; Usta & Singh
Increasing availability of DV resources and services, incorporating home visitation and education/support delivered by community nurses.	5, 12	Blais, Hébert, Gervais, & Bergeron; Williams, Gavine, & Carnochan
Improving the knowledge, sensitivity and training of domestic violence workers and administrating personnel particularly in relation to the debilitating trauma caused by DV.	5, 10, 13, 17	Blais, Hébert, Gervais, & Bergeron; Mc Innes; Usta & Singh; Taylor, Goddard, & Pooley
Removal of stigmatizing labels, and service access and program attendance barriers.	6, 18	Henderson, Thurston, & Roy; Taylor, Goddard, & Pooley
Public education campaigns about DV, creating awareness of and addressing the socio-cultural beliefs affecting victims lives and, then linking them to culturally appropriate services.	7, 8, 18	Sabri; Mahapatra & Schatz; Taylor, Goddard, & Pooley
Social advocacy: Empowering survivors of violence programs by providing them with the education, housing and employment opportunities they need in order to break free from an abusive relationship.	7, 10, 12	Sabri; McInnes Williams, Gavine, & Carnochan;
Acknowledge survivors of DV as harbingers of change and utilize them to inspire other survivors within specific community groups.	8	Mahapatra & Schatz
Introduction of community education strategies that engage perpetrators in the process of changing attitudes on domestic violence and towards protecting victims.	9, 13	Schineanu & Earnest; Usta & Singh
Introduction of initiatives and therapeutic support services that enable DV survivors to develop the resilience and coping strategies they need to deal with the trauma they have sustained.	9, 13, 19	Schineanu & Earnest; Usta & Singh; Goddard, Taylor, & Pooley
Educating children, parents and teachers about DV.	12, 17, 20	Williams, Gavine, & Carnochan; Taylor, Goddard, & Pooley; Wells, Turner & Cooper
Rehabilitating perpetrators through conflict resolution training programs, anger management, and fatherhood training programs.	13	Usta & Singh; Wells, Turner, & Cooper
Normalizing and improving the caring role of fathers.	18, 20	Taylor, Goddard, & Pooley; Wells, Turner, & Cooper

So What Can be Done to Help Current Victims of Domestic Violence?

Globally, the available prevalence counts of domestic violence clearly indicate that women are disproportionately affected by DV and that women endure more serious injuries as a result. This is somewhat explained by the patriarchal family structures that exist in many developing countries that cast women into the role of the primary caregiver and men in the role of the primary wage-earner. This division of labour creates an imbalance of power, which in turn, creates a climate where DV can prevail.

While, DV is a universal social problem that affects all social classes both in the developing and developed world, however, within the developed world the rigidity of the conceptual male-abuser-female-victim dynamic is altering. This change is hypothesized to be occurring partly because of the more equal division of parenting responsibilities within families as many families in the developed world are comprised of two wage-earning parents who share the daily care of their children and who often supplement their care with external informal/formal care arrangement. Partly, because of a rise is in the number of young women committing acts of dating and relational violence and, partly, because of the growing recognition within some population cohorts of the changing gender composition of families given the growth in the number of same-sex family relationships. Hence, there is an increasing imperative to revisit the gendered male-abuser-female-victim stereotype and, concentrate efforts on eliminating entrenched tolerances of interpersonal and interparental violence when dealing with the aftermath of DV. Specifically, there is a need to empower all individuals effected by DV to become resilient individuals capable of building constructive non-violent future lives.

Empowerment

Empowerment is a strength-based process which allows disempowered individuals to gain a sense of mastery and control over their lives and, in doing so, develop the necessary skills they need to become independent problem solvers and decision makers (Rappaport, 1981; 1984; Zimmerman, 1995). To achieve such a level of empowerment, disempowered individuals need to be aware of the choices open to them and to develop the belief that they have the capacity to set their own goals, the personal conviction to bring their desired outcomes to fruition, and the ability to advocate for them self, for it is then that they can directly influence their situational circumstances (Bourne & Russo, 1998; Kieffer, 1979; Zimmerman, 1995).

Given that the act of empowerment is contextually bound by the setting in which the act takes place, it is important that all education, health, accommodation, financial, spiritual, and emotional support actions put in place to empower survivors of DV be delivered in a culturally appropriate manner (Becker et al., 2008; Dalal, 2011; Howell et al., 2014). Thus, it is contended that in order to achieve DV survivor empowerment some specific changes needs to occur in the way in which many authorities, organisations and communities deal with survivors. Specifically, instead of operating from the historical mindset wherein 'experts' and administrators create inventories of problems to be fixed and where clients receive passive help, it is recommended that frontline workers be better trained not only in their use of empowerment-oriented language in their dealings with survivors, but also importantly on how to collaboratively construct, facilitate and inform wellness survivor groups. For, in doing so workers and survivors jointly establish a structure wherein survivors provide each other with an ongoing emotional support network. An advantage of this type of cost-effective self-help empowerment outcome is that it enables the healing process to continue within the networks in the absence of a frontline facilitator (Cowen, 1991; Rappaport, 1985; Swift & Levine, 1897; Zimmerman, 1995).

Resilience and Posttraumatic Growth in the Aftermath of Domestic Violence

Psychological resilience is the stress-resistant personal quality that allows individuals to adapt, thrive and guard against the development of psychiatric disturbances despite experiencing a serious threat or adverse life experience (Ahern, Ark, & Beyers, 2008). Resiliency is the buffering 'bounce-back' process of struggling to respond to a stressful event, grieving for a return to a pre-stress happy state, and enduring and coping with the present adversity. While, posttraumatic growth is the post-stress adjustment which progresses beyond achieving a state of resilience to creating a state of personal growth, wherein the resilient individual accepts their changed post-stress reality, learns from their prior adversity experiences and then apply that knowledge to embrace new life events (Bonanno, Galea, Bucciarelli, & Vlahov, 2007; Pooley, Cohen, O'Connor, & Taylor, 2012). Additionally, it is hypothesized that posttraumatic growth qualities could be passed on to the individual's offspring and, in doing so, act as a protective factor for future generations (Wathan et al. 2012).

Finally, the research in this book reveals that DV is an intimately entwined and interconnected social problem which requires a multi-level systemic approach. While the immediate requirement is for accommodation, education, employment, financial, health and judicial assistance, there is also a pressing need for survivors, witnesses, and perpetrators of DV to receive blame-free help, in order that they can create longer-term resilient posttraumatic growth pathways towards a healthy and productive life. Importantly, this help needs to be extended to all affected by DV if a meaningful reduction in DV is to occur.

REFERENCES

Ahern, N. R., Ark, P., & Byers, J. (2008). Resilience and coping strategies in adolescents. *Paediatric Nursing, 20,* 32-36.
Becker, K. D., Mathis, G., Mueller, C. W., Issari, K., & Atta, S. S. (2008). Community-based treatment outcomes for parents and children exposed to domestic violence. *Journal of Emotional Abuse, 8,* 187-204.
Bonanno, G. A., Galea, S., Bucciarelli, A., & Vlahov, D. (2007). What predicts psychological resilience after disaster? *Journal of Consulting and Clinical Psychology, 75,* 671-682.
Cowen, E. L. (1991). In pursuit of wellness. *American Psychologist, 46,* 404-408.

Dalal, K (2011). Does economic empowerment protect women from intimate partner violence? *Inj Violence Research, 3,* 35–44.

Howell, K. H., Miller, L. E., Lilly, M., Burlaka, V., Grogan-Kaylor, A. C, and Graham-Bermann S. A. (2014, online). Strengthening positive parenting through intervention: Evaluating the Moms' Empowerment Program for women experiencing intimate partner violence. *Journal of Interpersonal Violence.* DOI: 10.1177/0886260514533155

Kieffer, C. H. (1979). Citizen empowerment: A developmental perspective.

Pooley, J. A., Cohen, L., O'Connor, M., & Taylor, M. F. (2012). Posttraumatic stress and posttraumatic growth and their relationship to coping and self-efficacy in Northwest Australian cyclone communities. *Psychological Trauma, Theory, Research, Practice and Policy, 5,* 392-399.

Rappaport, J. (1981). In praise of paradox: A social policy of empowerment over prevention. *American Journal of Community Psychology, 9,* 1-25.

Rappaport, J. (1984). Studies in empowerment: Introduction to the issue. *Prevention in human services, 3,* 1-7.

Rappaport, J. (1985). The power of empowerment language. *Social Policy, 16,* 15-21.

Swift, C. & Levine, G. (1897). Empowerment an emerging mental health technology. Journal of Primary Prevention, 8, 71-94.

Wathen, C. N., MacGregor, J., Hammerton, J., Coben, J. H., Herrman, H., Stewart, D. E., & MacMillan, H. (2012). PreVAiL Research Network Priorities for research in child maltreatment, intimate partner violence and resilience to violence exposures: results of an international Delphi consensus development process. *BMC Public Health, 12,* 684

Zimmerman, M. A. (1995). Empowerment theory: Issues and illustrations. *American Journal of Community Psychology, 23,* 581-600.

SECTION SIX: ACKNOWLEDGMENTS

In: Overcoming Domestic Violence
Editors: Myra F. Taylor, Julie Ann Pooley et al.

ISBN: 978-1-63321-956-4
© 2015 Nova Science Publishers, Inc.

Chapter 22

ABOUT THE EDITORS AND CONTRIBUTORS

Dr. Myra F. Taylor, PhD is a highly experienced and internationally recognised researcher working within Edith Cowan University's Lifespan Resilience Research Group located within the Faculty of Engineering, Health and Science at Edith Cowan its School. Her research focus is on youth pathways into crime, youth subcultures, violent behaviours in young people and the effect that such violence has on the resilience of families and societal policy making. This research builds on Myra's expertise in the area of childhood and adolescent emotional and behavioural disorders. Myra is a widely published author with numerous books, book chapters and journal articles in these and other related fields. E-mail: myra.taylor@ecu.edu.au

Dr. Julie Ann Pooley, PhD is currently the Associate Dean of Teaching and Learning for the Faculty of Engineering, Health and Science and an Associate Professor within the School of Psychology at Edith Cowan University. Julie Ann has been involved in teaching in both the undergraduate and postgraduate psychology programs and has been a recipient of a National Teaching Award and Citation by the Australian University Teaching Committee (2003, 2011). Her research focuses on resilience at the individual and community levels. Julie Ann has been involved in and directed many community based research consultancies, projects and workshops and has been involved in the generation of many different community oriented reports for various cities and districts. E-mail: j.pooley@ecu.edu.au

Dr. Robert S. Taylor, PhD is a retired geoscientist with degrees from both the prestigious Imperial College, University of London and the University of Durham. Robert is held in high international standing in his field and is regularly sourced for advice in the earth science areas as well as for his extensive knowledge and interest in issues pertaining to world politics and social history.

CONTRIBUTORS

Chapter 1: Broadening the domestic violence debate

Dr. Myra F. Taylor see Editor biography
Dr. Julie Ann Pooley see Editor biography

Chapter 2: The definition and nature of domestic violence

Dr. Alfred Allan PhD is qualified in law and psychology and is endorsed both as a clinical and forensic psychologist in Australia. The current focus of his practice, teaching and research is on mental health and professional law, ethics, policy and practice; remedial behaviour and violent offending. He is currently Professor of Psychology and acting Director of the Social Justice Research Centre at Edith Cowan University in Perth, Western Australia.

Dr. Maria Allan, PhD is qualified in psychology and lectures at Edith Cowan University in Perth, Western Australia.   The current focus of her teaching and research is on psychometric assessment; remedial behaviour; and violent offending.

Chapter 3: Dating and intimate partner violence in young people

Dr. Jane Ellis is Senior Research Fellow at the University of Central Lancashire where she is involved in the PEACH Project, a scoping review of evidence on preventive interventions in domestic abuse for children and young people in the general population. Previously she has conducted research and consultancy on prevention work in schools for voluntary organizations and government, and was a member of the DCSF/DfE Advisory Group on Violence against Women and Girls. She has a number of publications on violence prevention. Before undertaking her PhD she worked with children, young people and their families in formal and non-formal educational settings, as a teacher and community education worker.

Dr. Melanie McCarry is a Senior Guild Research Fellow in the Connect Centre for International Research on Interpersonal Violence and Harm, University of Central Lancashire, UK. Melanie is advancing theoretical frameworks on abuse and violence in young people's relationships and developing ethical models for working with children and young people. She recently conducted the first UK national study on violence and exploitation in young people's relationships, which made a significant impact in critical understanding and government policy. Recent research includes children affected by domestic violence; violence against women in rural areas; forced marriage and domestic violence in same sex relationships.

Chapter 4: Youth dating violence: A silent epidemic

Dr. Catherine Carter-Snell RN PhD is an Associate Professor and resident "Nursing Education Scholar" in the School of Nursing and Midwifery at Mount Royal University in Calgary, Alberta Canada. She is also coordinates the Forensic Studies program. Both the online forensic courses and the research network are focused on promoting interdisciplinary understanding of the consequences of violence and to promote violence prevention. Catherine is certified nationally as an Emergency nurse (ENC-C) and internationally as a sexual assault examiner for adolescents and adults (SANE-A). She is actively involved in clinical practice, working on call as a nurse examiner with sexual assault and domestic violence patients in Emergency departments locally. She has been recognized in both the Court of Queen's Bench and Provincial Court as an expert in the area of sexual assault examination.

Chapter 5: Dating violence among sexual-minority youth (SMY) in the Western world

Dr. Martin Blais is associate professor at the Sexology Department of the Université du Québec à Montréal and a researcher at the Interdisciplinary Research Centre on Intimate Relationship Problems and Sexual Abuse. His areas of research interest are sexual minorities, sexual health, intimate relationships, and sociology of sexuality and intimacy.

Dr. Martine Hébert is a professor at the Sexology Department of the Université du Québec à Montréal, co-chair of the Marie-Vincent Inter-University Chair in Child Sexual Abuse, and researcher at the Interdisciplinary Research Centre on Intimate Relationship Problems and Sexual Abuse. Her areas of research interest are child sexual abuse, dating violence, trajectories of resilience in children and youth victims of interpersonal violence, and evaluation of prevention and intervention programs.

Jesse Gervais is a master's candidate in the Culture, Society, Gender and Sexuality program of the Sexology Department at the Université du Québec à Montréal. His areas of research interest are child maltreatment, dating violence perpetration and victimization, and sexual minorities.

Félix-Antoine Bergeron is a BA candidate in sexology in the Sexology Department, Université du Québec à Montréal, and research assistant with the CIHR Team on Interpersonal Traumas. His areas of research are sexual minorities and dating violence.

Chapter 6: Systemic violence and immigrant women having escaped domestic abuse: Meaningfully reducing structural barriers to leaving intimate partner and familial violence

Dr. Rita Isabel Henderson, PhD, is a post-doctoral fellow in the Department of Community Health Sciences at the University of Calgary. Her research focuses on forms of structural violence experienced by youth from diverse ethno-cultural communities. In addition to recent work with Aboriginal and refugee youth, she carried out extended fieldwork following the migration paths of a family of six adult sisters from Tanzania who settled and resettled around the world. She has carried out more than two years of investigation into intergenerational trauma among settler and indigenous Mapuche communities in southern Chile. With a background in Anthropology, she is particularly committed to synthesizing the depth and breadth of ethnographic knowledge to affect policy decisions. She is expanding her research into Teaching and Learning among vulnerable communities, most recently in the form of facilitating youth-powered documentaries with urban Aboriginal youth.

Dr. Wilfreda Thurston, PhD, is Professor at the University of Calgary's Department of Community Health Sciences and Department of Ecosystem and Public Health and Adjunct Professor in the Faculty of Nursing. Prior to joining academia in 1991, she worked in family and children's services, addictions, and was director of a shelter for women escaping abusive relationships. Her program of research and training includes development and evaluation of health promotion programs and health services that address social inequities, including immigrant and refugee populations, and especially Aboriginal peoples. Particular foci include the interplay of gender, culture and socioeconomics as determinants of health; prevention through the health sector of gender-based interpersonal violence; and, public participation as a key tenet of population health promotion. Community-based participatory methods are prominent in her program of research.

Amrita Roy, MSc, is presently a MD-PhD Candidate in the University of Calgary's Faculty of Medicine. Her PhD studies are in the Population and Public Health program of the Department of Community Health Sciences. She is particularly interested in the health of marginalized groups, and has been involved in numerous academic and community projects related to Aboriginal populations, immigrant and refugee populations, women, youth, and global health. Her PhD dissertation is taking a mixed-methods approach to examining the determinants of depression in pregnant Aboriginal women, with a special focus on understanding the influence of structural and systemic factors such as race, gender, social exclusion and intergenerational trauma. In the future, she hopes to continue to work in collaboration with communities, both as a population health researcher and a physician.

Chapter 7: Domestic violence among South Asian women: An ecological perspective

Dr. Bushra Sabri is a Research Associate at Johns Hopkins University School of Nursing. Dr. Sabri has a background in social work, with extensive cross-cultural and cross-national experiences in research, health care and social service settings. She has been involved in several quantitative and qualitative research projects focusing on interpersonal violence, risk factors and health outcomes of interpersonal violence, and intimate partner homicides. Her focus has been on minority and immigrant women. This research builds on her expertise in the area of domestic violence among Asian populations.

Chapter 8: Domestic Violence: Prevalence among South Asian migrant women

Dr. Neely Mahapatra is an Assistant Professor in the Division of Social Work at University of Wyoming, Laramie. Her research focus includes violence against minority women including immigrant South Asian women, refugees and other immigrant populations, human trafficking, international social work, social and public policy, and social justice. Her overall vision is to invest time in collaboration and development of best practices with immigrant women experiencing domestic violence and facilitate multidisciplinary research in the field of violence and victimization.

Dr. Mona C. Struhsaker Schatz, Professor at the University of Wyoming, Division of Social Work. She served as Director of the Division from 2006 to 2010. She served on the Council of Social Work Education's Commission on Professional Development (2004-2010) and completed her elected term on the Board of Directors of the National Association of Deans and Directors of Schools of Social Work (2007-2010). Her research areas include social work practice, generalist social work education, family and child welfare practice, international social work practice, foster care, child welfare, and aging.

Chapter 9: Coping with domestic violence in India: The role of spirituality and social support

Dr. Andreia Schineanu is a researcher who for the past 15 years has worked in the broad field of public health, particularly domestic violence, alcohol and other drugs, mental health, Australian Aboriginal health and community development. Currently she is undertaking academic research in the area of abuse of older people in rural Australia.

Dr. Jaya Earnest is an educator, researcher and sociologist who has worked for over 26 years in India, Kenya, Uganda, Rwanda, Timor-Leste and Australia. She is currently the Director of Graduate Studies in the Faculty of Health Sciences, Associate Professor of International Health and Postgraduate Research Co-ordinator in the International Health Program, at Curtin University in Western Australia. Jaya teaches postgraduate courses in international health, and supervises doctoral global health research projects. An accomplished researcher, Jaya is undertaking research in Uganda, India and Australia focussed on women and youth.

Chapter 10: A feminist perspective: System responses to Australian mothers exiting an abusive relationship

Dr. Elspeth McInnes AM is a sociologist and senior lecturer in the School of Education of the University of South Australia. Her research interests include social policy, gendered violence, parental separation and child protection. Dr McInnes also has extensive community sector experience through leadership and policy roles with the National Council of Single Mothers and their Children (NCSMC), the Australian Council of Social Services (ACOSS) and Women Everywhere Advocating Violence Elimination (WEAVE).

Chapter 11: Mississippi still burning: The LGBT struggle for intimate partner violence protection under the law – a case study in the Deep South

Dr. Julie Schroeder, PHD is a professor in the School of Social Work, Jackson State University. Dr. Schroeder has an extensive record of research and publications primarily involving the nexus of the criminal justice system and social justice. She served as Co-PI on a Department of Justice domestic violence prevention grant, "Not On Our Campus", a prevention program for intimate partner violence, sexual assault, and stalking on JSU's campus. Dr. Schroder also provides expert testimony in capital murder trials through the MS Office of Capital Defence. She has authored several articles on capital mitigation. Dr. Schroeder also sits on the Board of Directors for the MS ACLU.

Dr. Olga Osby earned her Master of Social Work (MSW) and Doctor of Social Work (DSW) degrees from Howard University in Washington, D.C. Currently she is an Associate Professor at Jackson State University in the College of Public Service, School of Social Work. Dr. Osby is also the 2013-2014 recipient of the Delta Sigma Theta, Sorority, Inc., Distinguished Professor Endowed Chair to further her research on the role and perception of grandfathers in rearing their grandchildren. Dr. Osby is actively engaged in the community, serving on the Board of the American Civil Liberties Union of Mississippi (ACLU-MS), and was elected to serve as the Mississippi representative to the National Board of the ACLU. She is currently serving her second term on the Commission on Conferences and Faculty Development (CCFD), for the Council on Social Work Education.

Dr. Diana L. Bruns is the Chairperson of the Criminal Justice and Sociology Department and Professor at Southeast Missouri State University in Cape Girardeau, MO. Her research interests include issues in policing, assessment and leadership in higher education and family violence. She has published in areas of criminal justice, sociology, business, management and higher education. Dr. Bruns teaches in the areas of research methods, statistics, criminology, and drugs and behavior. She currently is serving at the NGO liaison for the International Police Executive Police Symposium in New York City, New York, Geneva, Switzerland and Vienna, Austria.

Chapter 12: The public health approach to domestic violence prevention

Dr Damien J. Williams is a Lecturer in Public Health Sciences in the School of Medicine at the University of St Andrews. His research interests include violence and aggression, violence prevention, health promotion, and health inequalities. He was the co-recipient of the inaugural 2011 Elizabeth Russell Award from the Faculty of Public Health for his work on gang violence prevention. More recently, he has worked on gender violence and domestic violence intervention strategies, and was lead author of a paper exploring the association between specific sporting events and domestic violence, which received considerable media coverage.

Dr. Anna J. Gavine is a Research Fellow in Population and Behavioural Health Sciences at the University of St. Andrews. Her main research interests are in the mixed-methods evaluations of programmes for the primary prevention of youth violence and in conducting systematic reviews examining the effectiveness of violence prevention programmes.

Mr. John Carnochan is a knowledge exchange consultant at the University of St Andrews and Scottish Violence Reduction Unit (VRU). He is a former Detective Chief Superintendent with Police Scotland, and co-founder and former co-director of the VRU. His interests are in violence prevention, with a particular focus on the early years and violence against women. John was awarded the Queens Police Medal in 2007 for distinguished police service; made a Fellow by Distinction of the UK Faculty of Public Health in 2010 for his work on violence prevention; and was made an Officer of the Order of the British Empire (OBE) in the 2013 Queen's Birthday Honours for services to community safety.

Chapter 13: Domestic violence against women in war and armed conflicts

Dr. Jinan Usta is an Associate Professor in the Department of Family Medicine at the American University of Beirut Medial Center. She has special interest in the field of reproductive health and family violence and has several publications on published widely on women's health, domestic violence, child abuse and refugee health.

Dr. Neil Singh is a Research Fellow at the American University of Beirut. He studied medicine at Cambridge University and has collaborated with Jinan Usta in developing a manual to help physicians deal with domestic violence survivors.

Chapter 14: Violence against women in scenarios of serious economic crisis

Dr. Victoria A. Ferrer-Pérez is university lecturer and member of the Gender Studies Research group at the University of Balearic Island in Spain. Her area of research interest is violence against women and, particularly, the analysis of its causes from a psychosocial point of view.

Dr. Esperanza Bosch-Fiol is university lecturer and director of the Gender Studies Research group at the University of Balearic Island in Spain. Her particular area of research interest is violence against women.

Chapter 15: Sport-related domestic violence: Exploring the complex relationship between sporting events and domestic violence

Dr. Damien J. Williams is a Lecturer in Public Health Sciences in the School of Medicine at the University of St Andrews. His research interests include violence and aggression, violence prevention, health promotion, and health inequalities. He was the co-recipient of the inaugural 2011 Elizabeth Russell Award from the Faculty of Public Health for his work on gang violence prevention. More recently, he has worked on gender violence and domestic violence intervention strategies, and was lead author of a paper exploring the association between specific sporting events and domestic violence, which received considerable media coverage.

Dr. Fergus G. Neville is a Research Fellow in Public Health at the University of St Andrews. He is interested in the roles that social identities and norms play in shaping human behaviour, including violence. He was awarded his PhD in 2012 for his research on the social psychology of crowd experience and behaviour. His recent work has included research on domestic violence intervention strategies, and an exploration of the association between specific sporting events and domestic violence.

Chapter 16: Child maltreatment: A phenomenological study of adult male's recollected childhood memories of experiencing abuse and witnessing domestic violence in the family home

Dr. Myra F. Taylor, PhD is a highly experienced and internationally recognised researcher working within Edith Cowan University's Lifespan Resilience Research Group located within the Faculty of Engineering, Health and Science at Edith Cowan its School. Her research focus is on youth pathways into crime, youth subcultures, violent behaviours in young people and the effect that such violence has on the resilience of families and societal policy making. This research builds on Myra's expertise in the area of childhood and adolescent emotional and behavioural disorders. Myra is a widely published author with numerous books, book chapters and journal articles in these and other related fields.

Teresa Goddard, is a postgraduate student currently completing her Master of Psychology (Clinical). She has obtained a Bachelor of Arts (Psychology) Honours, and has extensively volunteered as a telephone crisis counsellor. Teresa is interested in the field of forensic psychology, as well as further research into male specific interventions, support programs, and treatments.

Chapter 17: *'Walking on thin ice'*: **The pervasive degeneration of the family dynamic in homes where domestic violence is a lived reality and where children under the age of 18 experience abuse**

Dr. Myra F. Taylor, PhD is a highly experienced and internationally recognised researcher working within Edith Cowan University's Lifespan Resilience Research Group located within the Faculty of Engineering, Health and Science at Edith Cowan its School. Her research focus is on youth pathways into crime, youth subcultures, violent behaviours in young people and and the effect that such violence has on the resilience of families and societal policy making. This research builds on Myra's expertise in the area of childhood and adolescent emotional and behavioural disorders. Myra is a widely published author with numerous books, book chapters and journal articles in these and other related fields.

Teresa Goddard, is a postgraduate student currently completing her Master of Psychology (Clinical). She has obtained a Bachelor of Arts (Psychology) Honours, and has extensively volunteered as a telephone crisis counsellor. Teresa is interested in the field of forensic psychology, as well as further research into male specific interventions, support programs, and treatments.

Dr. Julie Ann Pooley, PhD is currently the Associate Dean of Teaching and Learning for the Faculty of Engineering, Health and Science and an Associate Professor within the School of Psychology at Edith Cowan University. Julie Ann has been involved in teaching in both the undergraduate and postgraduate psychology programs and has been a recipient of a National Teaching Award and Citation by the Australian University Teaching Committee (2003, 2011). Her research focuses on resilience at the individual and community levels. Julie Ann has been involved in and directed many community based research consultancies, projects and workshops and has been involved in the generation of many different community oriented reports for various cities and districts.

Chapter 18: 'Feeling like you're damaged and like your life is out of your control': The male perspective on living with the adult aftermath of child maltreatment

Dr Myra Taylor, PhD is a highly experienced and internationally recognised researcher working within Edith Cowan University's Lifespan Resilience Research Group located within the Faculty of Engineering, Health and Science at Edith Cowan its School. Her research focus is on youth pathways into crime, youth subcultures, violent behaviours in young people and and the effect that such violence has on the resilience of families and societal policy making. This research builds on Myra's expertise in the area of childhood and adolescent emotional and behavioural disorders. Myra is a widely published author with numerous books, book chapters and journal articles in these and other related fields.

Teresa Goddard, is a postgraduate student currently completing her Master of Psychology (Clinical). She has obtained a Bachelor of Arts (Psychology) Honours, and has extensively volunteered as a telephone crisis counsellor. Teresa is interested in the field of forensic psychology, as well as further research into male specific interventions, support programs, and treatments.

Dr. Julie Ann Pooley, PhD is currently the Associate Dean of Teaching and Learning for the Faculty of Engineering, Health and Science and an Associate Professor within the School of Psychology at Edith Cowan University. Julie Ann has been involved in teaching in both the undergraduate and postgraduate psychology programs and has been a recipient of a National Teaching Award and Citation by the Australian University Teaching Committee (2003, 2011). Her research focuses on resilience at the individual and community levels. Julie Ann has been involved in and directed many community based research consultancies, projects and workshops and has been involved in the generation of many different community oriented reports for various cities and districts.

Chapter 19: Endeavouring to move forward by engaging in the therapeutic process of psyche repair

Dr. Myra F. Taylor, PhD is a highly experienced and internationally recognised researcher working within Edith Cowan University's Lifespan Resilience Research Group located within the Faculty of Engineering, Health and Science at Edith Cowan its School. Her research focus is on youth pathways into crime, youth subcultures, violent behaviours in young people and and the effect that such violence has on the resilience of families and societal policy making. This research builds on Myra's expertise in the area of childhood and adolescent emotional and behavioural disorders. Myra is a widely published author with numerous books, book chapters and journal articles in these and other related fields.

Teresa Goddard, is a postgraduate student currently completing her Master of Psychology (Clinical). She has obtained a Bachelor of Arts (Psychology) Honours, and has extensively volunteered as a telephone crisis counsellor. Teresa is interested in the field of forensic psychology, as well as further research into male specific interventions, support programs, and treatments.

Dr. Julie Ann Pooley, PhD is currently the Associate Dean of Teaching and Learning for the Faculty of Engineering, Health and Science and an Associate Professor within the School of Psychology at Edith Cowan University. Julie Ann has been involved in teaching in both the undergraduate and postgraduate psychology programs and has been a recipient of a National Teaching Award and Citation by the Australian University Teaching Committee (2003, 2011). Her research focuses on resilience at the individual and community levels. Julie Ann has been involved in and directed many community based research consultancies, projects and workshops and has been involved in the generation of many different community oriented reports for various cities and districts.

Chapter 20: Overcoming the Gender Dyad: Engaging Men and Boys in Domestic Violence Prevention

Lana Wells is the Brenda Strafford Chair in the Prevention of Domestic Violence at the University of Calgary's Faculty of Social Work. She is also a Fellow at the School of Public Policy, University of Calgary. Lana is currently leading Shift: The Project to End Domestic Violence. Shift's mandate is to develop and support the implementation of research-based primary prevention strategies in partnership with government, academics, community, public, private, non-profit organization and citizens.

Dr. Alina Turner founded Turner Research & Strategy Inc. in 2013, a consulting company that provides research and strategy development support to advance social change. Her areas of expertise include homelessness, affordable housing, immigration and gender issues. Her current practice focuses on system planning and integration, policy and program development.

Merrill Cooper is the managing partner at Guyn Cooper Research Associates Ltd., a Calgary-based consulting firm specializing in social sciences research, qualitative and quantitative evaluation, policy analysis and development, and not-for-profit and governmental program and sector planning.

Chapter 21:

Dr. Myra F. Taylor, PhD is a highly experienced and internationally recognised researcher working within Edith Cowan University's Lifespan Resilience Research Group located within the Faculty of Engineering, Health and Science at Edith Cowan its School. Her research focus is on youth pathways into crime, youth subcultures, violent behaviours in young people and the effect that such violence has on the resilience of families and societal policy making. This research builds on Myra's expertise in the area of childhood and adolescent emotional and behavioural disorders. Myra is a widely published author with numerous books, book chapters and journal articles in these and other related fields.

Dr. Julie Ann Pooley, PhD is currently the Associate Dean of Teaching and Learning for the Faculty of Engineering, Health and Science and an Associate Professor within the School of Psychology at Edith Cowan University. Julie Ann has been involved in teaching in both the undergraduate and postgraduate psychology programs and has been a recipient of a National Teaching Award and Citation by the Australian University Teaching Committee (2003, 2011). Her research focuses on resilience at the individual and community levels. Julie Ann has been involved in and directed many community based research consultancies, projects and workshops and has been involved in the generation of many different community oriented reports for various cities and districts.

In: Overcoming Domestic Violence   ISBN: 978-1-63321-956-4
Editors: Myra F. Taylor, Julie Ann Pooley et al.   © 2015 Nova Science Publishers, Inc.

Chapter 23

ABOUT THE SCHOOL OF PSYCHOLOGY AND SOCIAL SCIENCE, EDITH COWAN UNIVERSITY, AUSTRALIA

Edith Dircksey Cowan was born in 1861 at Glengarry near Geraldton. She believed that education was fundamental to tackling the social issues of the day and further, that it was the key to growth, change and improvement. She fought tirelessly to improve conditions for women, children, families, the poor, the under-educated and the elderly. She promoted sex education in schools, migrant welfare and the formation of infant health centres.

In 1894, Edith Cowan was one of the founders of the Karrakatta Club, which became the centre of a movement for reform, making Edith Cowan the best known woman in Australia during the first 30 years of this century.

Among her many achievements, Edith Cowan was instrumental in obtaining votes for women in Western Australia. She was Vice-President of the Women Justices' Association and the Western Australian League of Nations Union. She helped found the Children's Protection Society which was the precursor of the Children's Court and helped create the Western Australian National Council for Women, of which she was President from 1913 to 1921.

The Guidance of Infants Act (1922) which allowed women to apply to the courts if their husbands left them without adequate maintenance was amended by the efforts of Edith Cowan and she also argued that a woman should be legally entitled to a share of her husband's income. In 1923 she was appointed to the Anglican Synod, which was predominately male, and the press commended the church for moving with the times.

Her contribution to the war effort was vast; she worked on many committees and on the formation of the WA League of Nations Union. Awarded an OBE in 1920 for her work during the war, she was elected as an endorsed Nationalist, defeating the previous Attorney General. In 1921, at the age of 60 years, she became the first woman elected to an Australian Parliament. Her most important feat as a parliamentarian was her contribution to the passing of the Women's Legal Status Bill, which became an Act in 1923. The Bill opened legal and other professions to Western Australian women for the first time.

Edith Cowan contributed significantly to the development of education, particularly in government schools. She worked tirelessly to raise funds for students to attend universities in other states, prior to a university being built in Western Australia, obtaining government support for her scheme. Her work in this area was acknowledged by naming Western Australia's oldest education institution and newest university after her, as well as her image being added to the Australian $50 note.

Edith Cowan died on 9 June 1932 aged 71. A memorial to her in the form of a clock tower was unveiled in Kings Park on 9 June 1934.

SCHOOL OF PSYCHOLOGY AND SOCIAL SCIENCE

The School of Psychology and Social Science represents four main discipline areas: Psychology, social science, counselling and speech pathology. The School offers courses in all levels, from bachelors to doctoral degrees, and provides service teaching within degrees in other schools at ECU. There are well developed collaborations in teaching and research across disciplines and with staff from other schools. Staff are engaged in research collaborations with external government and non-government agencies as well as commercial institutions.

The disciplines within the school are all highly focused on measurement and analysis; we are proud of our research culture that is embedded in all of our courses and expressed in the staff research enterprise. We are committed to providing students with knowledge of how humans think, function and behave in a multitude of settings, and the various factors that can impact on normal function.

Our undergraduate programs in psychology are designed to train people to think like a psychologist, and our postgraduate programs in psychology train graduates to become psychologists. The Bachelor of Social Sciences offers grounding in community work and the ability to choose from a range of specialisations. You will learn about the world you live in, how to work in that world and change things for the better. You can choose from Children and Family Studies, Community Studies, Counselling, or Youth Work. The School of Psychology and Social Science also has close links with the profession of psychology, and the professions of welfare and community work. The School also has excellent links with community and government agencies.

Students can also study to become practicing speech pathologists working with children and adults who have communication and/or swallowing disorders. The Bachelor of Speech Pathology course involves topics such as linguistics, psychology, and speech science, applying these to both the science and the social impact of communication and swallowing disorders. Conditions such as stuttering, delayed language development, communication problems after stroke and developmental disability are covered within the course and students learn about the most recent evidence-based practice in the treatment of these. In order to ensure clinical competency, students are assured of a wide variety of clinical practicum placements in hospital and community settings in both metropolitan and rural areas. Academic staff on this course are internationally recognised leaders in their fields of research as well as having extensive clinical experience.

Our approach to teaching, and the curricula of our courses are guided by the Australian Psychological Society, the Australian Psychology Accreditation Council, the Australian Institute of Welfare and Community Works Inc. and students who complete a Major in Children and Family Studies receive Accreditation under the Community Services (Child Care) legislation to work as trained staff in Child Care.

Some of the school's postgraduate programs involve industry practica, including one practicum in our own clinic (the ECU Psychological Services Centre) for psychology postgraduates.

Website: http://www.ecu.edu.au/schools/psychology-and-social-science/overview

SECTION SEVEN: INDEX

INDEX

B

C

D

E

I

T

U